DATE DUE FOR RETURN

This book may be recalled before the above date

Global Warming

THE GREENPEACE REPORT

Edited by Jeremy Leggett

Oxford · New York

OXFORD UNIVERSITY PRESS

1990

Oxford University Press, Walton Street, Oxford OX2 6DP
Oxford New York Toronto
Delhi Bombay Calcutta Madras Karachi
Petaling Jaya Singapore Hong Kong Tokyo
Nairobi Dar es Salaam Cape Town
Melbourne Auckland
and associated companies in
Berlin Ibadan

Oxford is a trade mark of Oxford University Press

First published 1990 as an Oxford University Press paperback
and simultaneously in a hardback edition

British Library Cataloguing in Publication Data
Leggett, Jeremy
Global warming: the Greenpeace report.
1. Environment. Effects of carbon dioxide
I. Title   II. Greenpeace
363.7384
ISBN 0–19–217781–8
ISBN 0–19–286119–0 pbk

Library of Congress Cataloging in Publication Data
Global warming: the Greenpeace report/edited by Jeremy Leggett.
p. cm. Includes index.
1. Global warming. 2. Global warming—Government policy.
I. Leggett, Jeremy K. II. Greenpeace UK.
363.73'87—dc20 QC981.8.G56G583 1990 90–40115
ISBN 0–19–217781–8
ISBN 0–19–286119–0 (pbk.)

Text processing by the Oxford Text System
Printed in Great Britain by
Clays Ltd.
Bungay, Suffolk

60 03687578

Contents

Biographies

The Editor

Dr Jeremy Leggett is Director of Science at Greenpeace UK. Before joining Greenpeace in 1989, he spent eleven years on the faculty of the Department of Geology at Imperial College of Science, Technology, and Medicine. He has written over fifty scientific papers, has won two major awards for his research, and was appointed a Reader at the age of 33. His numerous articles on environmental issues and science policy have appeared in publications which include *New Scientist*, the *Guardian*, the *Independent*, *The Times*, the *Sunday Times*, and the *Observer*. He has sat on several advisory committees for the UK Natural Environment Research Council.

In the order the papers appear:

Dr Stephen H. Schneider, a leading climatologist and environmental-policy analyst, is head of the Interdisciplinary Climate Systems at the US National Center for Atmospheric Research. He is editor of the interdisciplinary journal *Climate Change*, author of a popular best-seller, *Global Warming*, which received the American Meteorological Society's Louis Battan Award, and has contributed to over 150 scientific publications on climate theory, modelling, model validation, and the implications of climate-change.

Professor David Schimel is an Associate Professor at the Department of Forest and Wood Sciences at Colorado State University. He received his BA in Biology and Applied Mathematics in 1977, and worked at the Ecosystems Center of the Marine Biological Laboratory until 1979. He received his Ph.D. from Colorado State

University in 1982 and was a research scientist in CSU's Natural Resource Ecology Laboratory from 1982 to 1988. His research examines trace-gas biochemistry in terrestrial ecosystems.

Dr Mick Kelly is a Senior Research Associate at the Climatic Research Unit in the School of Environmental Sciences at the University of East Anglia. He has been researching the greenhouse effect since the 1970s, and has written more than fifty scientific papers on this and other aspects of climate. He has contributed to recent studies on the greenhouse effect for the US Department of Energy and the Scientific Committee on Problems of the Environment (SCOPE).

Dr George M Woodwell is President and Director of the Woods Hole Research Center in Massachusetts. He has studied the biotic interactions associated with global warming for many years, and has published more than 300 papers on ecology. He has held appointments on the faculty of the university of Maine and at Yale University. He was for fourteen years a staff member at the Brookhaven National Laboratory, and for ten years was with the Marine Biological Laboratory in Woods Hole. He was President of the Ecological Society of America from 1977 to 1978, is a Fellow of the American Academy of Arts and Sciences, and a member of the National Academy of Sciences.

Dr Brian Huntley, a botanist, has been a lecturer in plant ecology at the University of Durham since 1981, researching responses of plants to past climate change. He has written more than twenty-five scientific papers and has edited an important volume synthesizing the history of vegetation over the last 2 million years. His advice has been sought by the IPCC on the role of palaeoenvironmental data in forecasting future climate-change.

Professor Andrew Haines is Professor of Primary Health Care at University College and Middlesex School of Medicine, London. His research interests are in the fields of prevention and epidemiology, and he has published a large number of papers. He is Honorary Director of 'Action in International Medicine', a recently formed organization which promotes collaboration between colleges and academies of medicine and allied health professions around the world, particularly on projects to improve the infrastructure of health care in developing countries.

Professor Jose Goldemberg is Secretary of State for Science and Technology in the Brazilian Government. He obtained his Ph.D. in Physical Sciences in 1954, and became a full professor at the University of São Paulo. His past appointments have included President of the Brazilian Association for the Advancement of Science, President of the Energy Company of the State of São Paulo, and Rector of the University of São Paulo. He is author of many technical papers and books on nuclear physics and energy, and was a co-author of the international best-seller *Energy for a Sustainable World*.

Dr Amory Lovins is Director of Research at Rocky Mountain Institute, a public charity which fosters resource efficiency and whose research is used by more than 160 energy utilities and related organizations in thirty countries. Dr Lovins has published a dozen books and hundreds of papers on energy issues. A former Oxford don, he has held various academic chairs, served on the US Department of Energy's senior advisory board, holds five honorary doctorates, and has been the recipient of the Onassis Prize and the 'Alternative Nobel Prize'.

Carlo LaPorta, President of Analysis, Review and Critique Division of R&C Enterprises in Washington, DC, is a consultant to industry and government on renewable-energy policy and market development. His past posts include European Affairs Analyst at the Library of Congress, Director of Research at the Solar Energy Industries Association, and Director of Programs at the Renewable Energy Institute. He holds a Master's degree in international relations from the Johns Hopkins University School of Advanced International Studies.

Michael Walsh managed significant US Government programmes in motor-vehicle pollution. He headed the Environment Protection Agency's programme at the time when the most stringent auto-emissions standards in the world were introduced. Since leaving the EPA he has been a technical consultant to organizations which include the Senate Committee on Environment and Public Works, the Office of Technology Assessment, the United Nations, the World Bank, the OECD, and numerous governments in both developed and developing countries.

Dr Bill Keepin, an energy and environment consultant living in Berkeley, California, has held research positions at the International Institute for Applied Systems Analysis, Princeton University, the Beijer Institute of the Royal Swedish Academy of Sciences, and Rocky Mountain Institute. Dr Keepin has lectured and published widely, testified on energy issues, and advised senior management of major oil companies.

Dr Birgit Bodlund was a Program Manager for Government Energy Supply Research and Development before joining Vattenfall (the Swedish State Power Board) as Head of Energy Systems Section in the Development and Environment Division. She now directs Vattenfall's new initiative for biomass-based power production. She serves on the Board of Directors of the Swedish Building Research Council.

Evan Mills is a Visiting Research Scientist in the Department of Environmental and Energy Systems Studies at the University of Lund, Sweden. He worked for eight years with the US Department of Energy's Lawrence Berkeley Laboratory analysing energy-efficiency technologies, policies, and planning issues. Author of forty-five publications in the field of energy and environment, he is currently working with Swedish national policy-and-planning agencies on long-term electricity-environment issues.

Tomas Karlsson has been Marketing Manager at Orebro Energi AB, a Swedish energy company, since 1989. Prior to that, he served on the Policy and Planning Staff of Vattenfall, the Swedish State Power Board.

Professor Thomas Johansson is Professor of Energy Systems Analysis in the Department of Environmental and Energy Systems Studies, University of Lund, Sweden. He has written many articles on energy, and co-authored eleven books, including the influential *Energy for a Sustainable World* with Professor Goldemberg. He served on the Board of Directors of the Swedish Nuclear Power Inspectorate between 1977 and 1988, and has been a member of the Board of Directors of Vattenfall since 1988.

Professor Norman Myers has worked on tropical forests since 1970, and especially during his twenty-four years of residence in the tropics. Author of more than 250 research papers, he was Senior

Advisor on tropical forests to the Brundtland Commission, and contributed to the World Bank's Task Force on Tropical Forests. He is author of the best-selling book *The Primary Source: the tropical forests and our future*. His numerous professional appointments and honours include a Regents Professorship and Albright Lecturership at the University of California, and a place on the United Nations Environment Program (UNEP) Global 500 Roll of Honour for Environmental Achievement.

Dr Anne Ehrlich is Senior Research Associate in biology and Associate Director of the Center for Conservation Biology at Stanford University, USA. Her numerous publications cover population biology and a range of related policy issues. She has served as a consultant to the White House Council on Environmental Quality's 'Global 2000' Report, published in 1980. In 1988 she was elected an Honorary Fellow of the California Academy of Sciences, and in 1989 was selected for the UNEP Global 500 Roll of Honour.

Dr Kilaparti Ramakrishna obtained his Ph.D. in International Environmental Law from Jawaharlal Nehru University, New Delhi, and was Assistant Professor at the Indian Academy of International Law and Diplomacy prior to attending Harvard Law School in 1985 as a Fulbright Visiting Scholar. An Indian national, he has focused his research on global warming and climatic-change issues from the perspective of developing countries for the last two years at the Woods Hole Research Center, USA, where he is Senior Associate for International Environmental Law.

Dr Susan George, an American who lives in France, is a Fellow and Associate Director of the Transnational Institute (Amsterdam) whose brief is 'to address the fundamental disparities between the rich and poor peoples and nations of the world, investigate their causes and develop alternatives for their remedy'. She was educated at Smith College, the Sorbonne, and the École des Hautes Études en Sciences Sociales in Paris. Her books are *How the Other Half Dies: the Real Reasons for World Hunger*, *Feeding the Few: Corporate Control of Food*, 'Les Stratèges de la Faim' (doctoral dissertation), *Food for Beginners, A Fate Worse than Debt*, and *Ill Fares the Land*. She is a member of the International Board of Greenpeace.

Introduction

" ...the United Nations Intergovernmental Panel on Climate Change – its scientists excepted – has failed in its responsibilities in what has been the most important international consultation process in history. The policy-makers have consistently refused to listen to the dire and virtually unanimous warnings from the world's climate scientists: they continue to recommend the distribution of a few bandages in the face of an effective plague warning... This is what makes the *Greenpeace Report* so important ... it says what the IPCC should have said about how we must respond to the greenhouse threat... "

Global climate change has emerged as a major scientific and political issue within a few short years. Politicians the world over are shuffling for position in the wake of opinion polls showing steady escalation of public concern. Scientific journals are crammed with comment and analysis. Forty-nine Nobel-prizewinning scientists have appealed to President Bush to curb greenhouse-gas emissions, professing that 'global warming has emerged as the most serious environmental threat of the 21st century ... only by taking action now can we insure that future generations will not be put at risk'.[1] Even nuclear-weapons laboratories host conferences on the greenhouse effect these days.[2]

The message is clear: humankind is heading for deep trouble unless we drastically cut our emissions of greenhouse gases into the atmosphere. In May 1990 the world's climate scientists formalized the message – clear as it already was from the pages of the science journals – in a report for the Intergovernmental Panel on Climate Change (IPCC), a body set up in 1988 by the UN General Assembly to advise world leaders on the seriousness of global climate change. 'We are certain', said the 300-plus scientists from more than twenty countries, that 'emissions resulting from human activities are substantially increasing the atmospheric concentrations of the greenhouse gases … These increases will enhance the greenhouse effect, resulting on average in an additional warming of the Earth's surface.' The scientists went on to make the prediction, based on their computer simulations of climate, that if greenhouse-gas emissions continue at their present rates the world average temperature will rise by a full degree Celsius (nearly 2° Fahrenheit) or thereabouts within just thirty years. A full degree may not sound like much, but it is a global average, and the record of past climate shows that global average temperatures have never risen so fast before. Within less than half a century – if we carry on with 'business as usual' – we will be experiencing average temperatures never before felt while humans have walked on the planet.[3]

Furthermore, the IPCC scientists say that their assessment is likely to be an underestimate: the uncertainties involved in predicting climate change are legion, but the aspects of the climate system omitted from the computerized climate-simulations on which their predictions are based are such that the warming is most likely to be amplified by natural processes.[4] One of several ways this is likely to happen is as a result of warming oceans being unable to take as much carbon dioxide out of the atmosphere as they do at present. Carbon dioxide, which comes largely from the burning of coal, oil, and gas, is the main greenhouse gas. The other principal greenhouse gases are chlorofluorocarbons (CFCs), methane, and nitrous oxide.

In a world rapidly becoming inured to sweeping change on the political stage, we have witnessed the emergence of an environmental threat which cuts to the heart of how humans choose to operate society – a problem which is truly global in both consequence and cause. Greenhouse gases are produced in their current superabundance as a result of the ways we humans produce and use energy, by the use of certain industrial chemicals (CFCs and related gases), and by intensive agriculture and tropical deforestation. In a world in which the greenhouse effect is allowed to continue its buildup, we would all – at some stage – be losers, and we would all – to varying degrees – be responsible.

No quantum leap in scientific understanding explains this situation. What we have been caught unawares by – scientists, industrialists, farmers, policy-makers, environmentalists, and ordinary people alike – is quite possibly a coincidence. The 1980s saw the emergence of computer models which, in all the world's climate-modelling centres, began predicting unprecedented global warming in the decades to come. They also saw the five hottest years in recorded history. Media-worthy manifestations of the warm '80s – droughts, floods, freak storms – whether themselves the product of greenhouse warming or of natural climatic fluctuations – conspired to fix the public spotlight on global warming.[5]

The issue came into focus in 1988. An international conference hosted by the Canadian government in Toronto produced a consensus statement which spoke of effects 'second only to global nuclear war' if humankind did not mobilize effectively and cut greenhouse-gas emissions appreciably.[6] The concern of the United Nations was awakened. Thus was the Intergovernmental Panel on Climate Change born.

Most governments have delayed their policy decisions until the IPCC reports in August 1990 – many in undisguised trepidation. The implications of concerted action to cut global emissions of greenhouse gases are not for the politically faint-of-heart. Simple ameliorating measures such as investment in renewable forms of energy-production, and wholesale energy efficiency, are perceived by five-year-cycle politicians and the industrial interests which lobby them so effectively as being too far outside the present frame of reference to be workable. And this is not to mention any attempt at a rethink of the economics which each year requires tens of billions of dollars to be transferred from the developing countries to the industrialized countries – positive transfers from South to North due to debt service alone having been in excess of $300 billion since 1982 – or any committed effort to cut weapons-spending by more than a few token per cent. Already, environmentalists talk of the NIMTOO syndrome: Not In My Term Of Office.

Yet the first whiffs of panic are in the air. The Dutch deputy prime minister, for example, told the president of Brazil in 1989 that if deforestation in the Amazon was continued to its completion, emitting as it does such vast quantities of carbon dioxide, Holland would cease to exist as a country, flooded by rising seas as global temperatures rose.[7]

Also taken by surprise, the relevant vested interests have now begun inevitable spoiling tactics. The world spends up to a trillion dollars a year on its coal, oil, and gas,[8] and a further trillion dollars on its weapons.[9] The multinational infrastructure spawned by these juggernauts over the years cannot look with relish on a world in which fossil-fuel burning must be cut to the bone, and concepts of national security trampolined from the military to the environmental.

'Crisis? What crisis?' Readers of an editorial in the *Wall Street Journal* on 6 February 1990 could be forgiven this age-old response. They read of the grave dangers of 'scientific faddism' and the unreliability of the 'global warming models of various agency bureaucrats'. The editorial was a response to environmentalists' criticism of a speech President Bush had given to the third plenary of the IPCC in Washington a few days before. In it, Bush had spelt out that 'we all recognise that the atmosphere is changing in unexpected and unprecedented ways', and 'we know the future of the Earth must not be compromised'. Fine sentiments, but – to the exasperation of many present – the president made no specific commitments to buy insurance against such eventualities. 'The politics and opinion', the president informed us, 'have outpaced the science.' Sitting in the audience, I struggled to assimilate this Orwellian reversal of what I see each week in the scientific journals. The *Wall Street Journal*'s editorial writer spoke for corporate America a few days later: 'We hope the President hangs tough on this one.'[10]

The first serious political heat from global warming began to be felt during April of 1990. An attempt by the Bush Administration to recruit other governments to its 'business-as-usual' approach to the greenhouse effect collapsed in Washington, because most European countries – excepting the UK – want action to abate it. At a White House-hosted seminar on global warming, the West German environment minister, Mr Töpfer, caused a stir by announcing that he would be suggesting to the German government that Germany's emissions of carbon dioxide should be cut by at least 25 per cent – unilaterally – by the year 2005. Holland was among those who accused the Bush administration of an unseemly attempt to delay an effective international policy response to the greenhouse effect in order to protect US industry. A group of twelve European governments want international negotiations for an agreement to protect global climate – a Climate Convention – to begin even ahead of the World Climate Conference in October 1990.

The IPCC climate scientists are only one of three working-groups in the IPCC process. Their conclusions will be combined with those of two others: one studying the impacts of climate change (Working Group 2: Potential Impacts), and the other the policy responses (Working Group 3: Response Strategies). It is the integrated results of the three working-groups, combined as an overall IPCC Report, which are due to be released in August 1990. By June, it was already clear that the dire warnings the scientists issued when their report was completed in May had been ignored by the policy-makers of the third IPCC working-group. Their report did not even refer to 'global warming' – merely to 'potential climate change'.[11] This despite the scientists' agreement that they are 'certain' of global warming unless significant efforts are made to cut greenhouse-gas emissions.

The Response Strategies Working Group did not even come down on the side of a freeze in greenhouse-gas emissions, much less the deep cuts the scientists clearly indicate will be necessary if any attempt is to be made to slow or arrest the greenhouse effect. The IPCC scientists calculate 'with confidence' that, to stabilize the carbon dioxide composition of the atmosphere at its present level, cuts in global emissions of that particular greenhouse gas would need to exceed 60 per cent. They are not alone in such calculations. Similar conclusions have been drawn by the US Environmental Protection Agency, in a report long stalled in the Washington bureaucracy,[12] and in a recent study Greenpeace commissioned from a leading climate scientist at the University of East Anglia's Climate Research Unit,[13] summarized in Chapter 4 of this book.

The atmosphere already contains 25 per cent more carbon dioxide than it has done for at least 160,000 years. And the gas is building up steadily at 0.5 per cent per year.[14] In view of this, many experts advocate cuts in global carbon dioxide emissions of 20 per cent in the next decade. Even this, however, would only be a start if the goal is to stabilize the greenhouse-gas content of the atmosphere. If that is not the goal, then the clear implication of the IPCC scientists' report is that the corollary of a decision to continue with business-as-usual – or anything approaching it – is a willingness to mortgage tomorrow's environmental security in the interests of today's corporate profit, and a reluctance to take on the challenge of change.

The stakes are high with global warming, as even President Bush has noted. In his February address to the IPCC, speaking of the need not to jeopardize the future of the planet, he observed: 'We bear a sacred trust in our tenancy here – and a covenant with those most precious to us: our children and theirs.' Mrs Thatcher has spoken, in similar vein, of 'the prospect of irretrievable damage to the atmosphere, to the oceans and to the Earth itself'.[15] Now that the world's climate scientists have taken away any possible excuse for further procrastination, it is only a matter of time before the full extent to which Bush and Thatcher have compromised themselves becomes clear. While ostensibly waiting for the opinion of the IPCC, their interim policy-making hardly engenders confidence that they are taking the greenhouse threat seriously. In the US, for example, the Department of Energy projects a 22-per-cent increase in carbon dioxide emissions by 2010, and President Bush opposed a provision in the Clean Air Act that would require car manufacturers to increase vehicle efficiency to 40 miles per gallon as a means of cutting carbon dioxide emissions from oil. In the UK, among many such examples, the Department of Transport is planning for an 80–140-per-cent increase in the number of cars on the roads, and the Department of Energy has been busy inflating its energy projections to minimize the impact of any decision to cut emissions.[16]

Meanwhile, concern grows apace among the public. In the UK, an opinion poll showed that almost everyone has now heard of the greenhouse effect, 76 per cent are worried by it (28 per cent 'very worried'), and almost 80 per cent think the government is doing too little about it (41 per cent 'far too little').[17] In the USA, 60 per cent of the public believe that global warming is a worrying issue, and 72 per cent want the US government to take the lead in acting on it.[18] All this was before the publication of the IPCC scientists' report. Those commentators who have predicted that the greenhouse effect will be the policy issue of the 1990s are so far very much on course.

A host of expert studies, summarized in several chapters of the *Greenpeace Report*, have shown that carbon dioxide emissions can be cut substantially over the next decade, and at negative cost. Given the right legislative framework, it is generally far cheaper to save energy than to find extra capacity for generating it. And with prices-per-kilowatt-hour plummeting for a number of renewable means of energy production, there are now many means of generating new future-energy requirements in greenhouse-friendly ways which do not involve the burning of fossil fuels. But all this requires a collective willingness to countenance change, and the right approach to state intervention and investments. The UK government leads the cast of those impaled on its own prejudices. Research and development expenditure for energy efficiency in 1989–90 was just £8.9 million ($15.5 million), for all renewables just £18 million ($31.4 million). The government regularly spends these kinds of sums on its own advertising. Elsewhere the picture is the same. In the USA, funding for energy efficiency and renewables has been cut hugely in the 1980s. In the European Community, research-and-development budgets for nuclear are still much higher than for renewables and energy efficiency combined.

Global Warming: the Greenpeace Report was born of our certainty in Greenpeace that the scientists in IPCC would fairly reflect the unprecedented scientific consensus which exists in the world today, and our equal certainty that most governments would choose to ignore them insofar as they possibly could. Thus it is that the United Nations Intergovernmental Panel on Climate Change – its scientists excepted – has failed in its responsibilities in what has been the most important international consultation process in history. The policy-makers have consistently refused to listen to the dire and virtually unanimous warnings of the climate scientists: they continue to recommend the distribution of a few bandages in the face of an effective plague warning.

Yet policy responses by governments are due to be formulated based on the IPCC report, and a common approach to negotiations on a Climate Convention are due to be decided in ministerial negotiations at the World Climate Conference at the end of October, also based on what the IPCC report says. If the IPCC scientists' Working Group is to be believed – and who else do we have to go to for an opinion on the future greenhouse threat than the world's most eminent climate scientists? – a viable future for humankind could be at stake, to say nothing of the ecological traumas which unmitigated global warming would impose on the natural environment and its hapless denizens. Yet this kind of urgency finds no place in the approach of the IPCC policy-makers.

This is what makes the *Greenpeace Report* such an important book. In Section 1, on the science, it summarizes clearly the double-edged nature of the risks arising from our poor understanding of climate change. In Section 2, on impacts, it summarizes the dreadful consequences of global warming – even at the levels predicted by the IPCC scientists (much less at the amplified levels which the IPCC scientists believe positive feedbacks are 'likely' to engender).[19] Most important of all, in Section 3, it shows the full variety of means for abating – and even halting – global warming.

The *Greenpeace Report* is written by leading scientists and energy analysts from the US, the UK, Sweden, Brazil, and India. Each person writes his or her chapter as an individual – this is not a committee report. But the report's central messages are clear, and shared by all authors, whether they agree with the full Greenpeace agenda on global warming – as spelt out in the final chapter – or not. These messages are: that humankind is in potentially serious trouble as a result of the greenhouse threat; that the risks of doing nothing far outweigh any possible risks associated with responding; and that the means of responding – primarily, substituting energy efficiency and renewables for the use of fossil fuels, eliminating use of CFCs and related greenhouse-gas chemicals, ending deforestation, and changing methods of agriculture – are available and ready for implementation if humankind can but find the collective will to square up to change. *This, then, is the book which says what the Intergovernmental Panel on Climate Change – in order to be consonant with the warnings of its own scientists' Working Group – should have said about how we must respond to the greenhouse threat.*

Those who understand the global-warming crisis might be forgiven for wondering whether humankind is indeed capable of fashioning itself an escape route, given the glacial progress to date. Rhetoric has often been impressive, progress always minimal. We hear talk from world leaders of the need for stewardship, and we see cuts in budgets for energy efficiency. We see leaders queuing up to host international seminars, yet not committing themselves even to freeze – much less cut – carbon dioxide emissions. All today's decision-makers will be dead and gone when the worst impacts of global warming, as predicted by the current climate models, arrive. They may not even be around to rue their missed opportunities if the very worst case analysis comes to pass: a coincidence of positive feedbacks which causes a runaway greenhouse effect, setting us on course for an atmosphere of the kind found on planets devoid of life.

Yet progressive oases have formed. The West German and Dutch governments, and the state governments of Vermont (USA) and Victoria (Australia), are aiming for carbon dioxide cuts by the end of the century. So is the city of Toronto. And we live in a world where paradigms are shifting, walls collapsing, week by week. In the few months I have spent editing this book, I have seen the Berlin Wall come down, the Central Committee of the Soviet Communist Party vote for a multi-party state, a Warsaw Pact summit convene with more non-communist than communist heads of state, and Nelson Mandela walk to freedom.

Yet I have also heard a senior EC official – a man responsible for advising European governments on their energy policy – use the following words: 'If the IPCC scientists are right, then we are on the *Titanic*, and the only question that remains is whether we go first class or steerage. I prefer first class.' As we will show in this book, he is sadly misguided and irresponsible in this view. But his is the view which those of us who want to honour our 'covenant with our children and theirs' must overcome. The picture of a different kind of future which we present in this book shows us the only practical way by which we can be sure of honouring that covenant.

Our grandfathers and grandmothers succeeded – against all expectations at the time – in abolishing slavery. So too can we – against the cynical adherence to the status quo of people like the EC official – avoid mortgaging our children's future by continuing our great global game of roulette with greenhouse gases.

Jeremy Leggett
London, 6 July 1990

1

Science

" ...we have an authoritative early warning system:
an agreed assessment of some three hundred of the
world's leading scientists of what is happening to the
world's climate ... a report of historic significance
...what it predicts will affect our daily lives. "

*UK Prime Minister Margaret Thatcher, on the morning of the
completion of the United Nations Intergovernmental Panel on
Climate Change scientists' (Working Group 1) report, 15 May 1990*

Summary

In 1988, the United Nations General Assembly asked the world's climate scientists to prepare a report to world leaders on the seriousness of the greenhouse threat. The scientists unveiled their report at a packed press conference in rural England in May 1990.

'We are certain', they said, that 'emissions resulting from human activities are substantially increasing the atmospheric concentrations of the greenhouse gases ... These increases will enhance the greenhouse effect, resulting on average in an additional warming of the Earth's surface.'

The next morning, almost every UK newspaper had the greenhouse effect radiating from its front pages. 'Race to save our world', announced the *Daily Express* in banner headlines. It is rare indeed that a scholarly report receives so much prominence in the media.

By how much will the Earth warm? The IPCC scientists' computer simulations – models – of climate predict increases in average global surface temperature of around 1°C (1.8°F) by 2030 and 3°C (5.4°F) before the end of the next century if deep cuts are not made in greenhouse-gas emissions. The first chapter of the *Greenpeace Report* shows just how unprecedented this temperature rise would be.

But – as all climate scientists will tell you – there are many uncertainties involved in making climate models and so predicting climate change. So why worry? Why not wait and see if further scientific research cannot narrow down the uncertainties? In the second chapter, Dr Stephen Schneider of the US National Center for Atmospheric Research argues that we cannot afford to wait. The likelihood of the world's climate scientists being right is sufficiently high – notwithstanding the possibility that their current predictions are in fact underestimates of next century's reality – that there is no choice but to stem human emissions of greenhouse gases immediately.

'The complexity of the [climate] system means that we cannot rule out surprises', say the IPCC scientists in their report. This is prudent humility. The scientific consensus before the Antarctic ozone hole was discovered was that CFCs would not harm the atmosphere. In the science of global warming, potential surprises lurk in the 'feedbacks' to the climate system – natural phenomena which can be awakened in a warming world to amplify warming ('positive' feedbacks) or dampen it ('negative' feedbacks). Because of their many uncertainties, many of these feedbacks are left out of even the world's best climate models. But the IPCC scientists concluded as follows: 'It appears likely that, as climate warms, the feedbacks will lead to an overall increase, rather than decrease in natural greenhouse gas abundances. For this reason, climate change is likely to be greater than the estimates we have given...'

This portentous conclusion should have been made more explicit in the IPCC scientists' report. It is one of the most significant conclusions drawn by the scientists, swinging as it does the debate over uncertainties firmly in the direction of adopting the 'precautionary principle'. In the first section of the *Greenpeace Report*, Dr Jeremy Leggett, Greenpeace UK's Scientific Director, and Professor David Schimel, of the Department of Forest and Wood Sciences at the University of Colorado, describe what these feedbacks might entail in terms of potential 'surprises'.

The IPCC scientists showed clearly that simply to freeze emissions of carbon dioxide at present-day levels will merely allow atmospheric concentrations of this, the principal greenhouse gas, to continue their ascent into levels never before experienced while humans have been on the planet – with all the risks for future generations which that involves. Yet, as the IPCC scientists conclude, 'the long-lived greenhouse gases (like carbon dioxide) would require immediate reductions in emissions from human activities of over 60 per cent to stabilise their concentrations at today's levels.'

This – unless the world can be persuaded to more than halve its use of coal, oil, and gas overnight – is an impossible goal. What can we do to stabilize greenhouse-gas concentrations over more realistic time-frames? This is the vital question which Dr Mick Kelly, of the University of East Anglia's Climate Research Unit, addresses in the fourth chapter.

Chapter 1
The Nature of the Greenhouse Threat

Jeremy Leggett

" ...in a 'business-as-usual' world in which greenhouse gas emissions continue at today's rates, we are
heading for rates of temperature-rise unprecedented
in human history; the geological record screams a
warning to us of just how unprecedented... And this
conclusion pertains only to existing model
predictions, not the natural amplifications [positive
feedbacks] of global warming which the world's
climate scientists profess are 'likely'... "

Greenhouse gases are gases which cause infra-red radiation to be
retained in the atmosphere, so warming the Earth's surface and the
lower part of the atmosphere (Fig. 1.1). They have been present in
trace quantities in the atmosphere for the great majority of Earth's history. Water vapour, because of its abundance, is by far the most important natural greenhouse gas. Carbon dioxide (CO_2), the second most
important greenhouse gas, is added to the atmosphere both naturally
and unnaturally. It has been added naturally by volcanoes throughout the Earth's history, and cycled though the many natural pathways
carbon follows in nature. Without the presence of CO_2, the temperature at the Earth's surface would be some 33°C lower than it is today
– inimical to life.[1] But CO_2 is also added unnaturally as a result of current human activities – principally by the burning of fossil fuels and

the destruction (today) of the rain forests (clearing of temperate forests contibuted significantly in the past). Hence, it is necessary to distinguish between the natural greenhouse effect, and the human-made (or anthropogenic) *enhanced* greenhouse effect. In this book, the authors use the terms 'greenhouse effect' and 'global warming' interchangeably to describe the enhanced greenhouse effect.

The greenhouse gases will by now be well known to everyone who follows world news regularly. They are listed, along with their common sources, the rates by which they are increasing in the atmosphere, and their current contributions to global warming,[2] in Table 1.1.

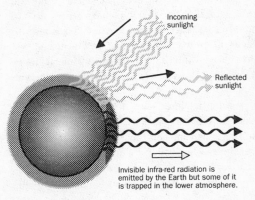

Incoming sunlight

Reflected sunlight

Invisible infra-red radiation is emitted by the Earth but some of it is trapped in the lower atmosphere.

Fig. 1.1. How the greenhouse effect works. Energy from incoming solar radiation reaches the Earth. Some is reflected. Most readily penetrates the atmosphere and warms the Earth's surface. Invisible infra-red radiation is emitted by the Earth and cools it down. But some of this infra-red is trapped by greenhouse gases in the atmosphere, which acts as a blanket, keeping the heat in. (Source: UK Department of the Environment, Global Climate Change, May 1990).

Earth's climate involves much more than the atmosphere. A climate is produced by complex interactions between the atmosphere, oceans, ice-caps, living things, and even rocks and sediments. Scientists speak of the 'climate system', meaning all the categories of the natural environment which interact in producing climate. The climate system has essentially five components: the atmosphere, ocean, cryosphere,[3] biosphere,[4] and geosphere.[5]

When the climate system is in equilibrium, as it was before the Industrial Revolution and the subsequent greatly expanded emissions of anthropogenic greenhouse gases, absorbed solar radiation is exactly balanced by radiation emitted to space by the Earth and atmosphere. Any factor which can alter this balance, and so change climate, is known as a radiative forcing agent.[6] These agents include the radiatively active gases we call greenhouse gases, but also solar radiation, aerosols,[7] and albedo.[8]

The physical process by which greenhouse gases can elevate air temperatures has been known since the end of the last century.[9] However, many scientists have until recently found little of concern in the amounts of greenhouse gases emitted by humans. This is in part due to the known natural variability of climate over the last few million years. Recent analyses of cores of undisturbed sediment from the ocean floor and of ice from Antarctica have supported earlier ideas that the world alternated between ice ages and interglacial periods, with a rhythm controlled by the way the Earth orbits the Sun.[10] Because past interglacials (periods between ice ages) seem to have lasted around 10,000 years, and because we have been around 10,000 years in the present interglacial, many scientists assumed that Earth was due for another ice age, and that human emissions of greenhouse gases would not alter this natural course – would perhaps even slow it.

In the 1980s, however, scientists modelling future climate change based on emission rates of greenhouse gases in the present and recent past have converged on the view that – in the absence of an effort to cut greenhouse-gas emissions – Earth is heading for an increase in global average temperatures unprecedented in human history. This consensus – which has actually existed for about a decade in the minds of all but a tiny minority of climate modellers[11] – has recently crystallized in the form of the Intergovernmental Panel on Climate Change (IPCC) Working Group 1 Report, a long report completed in May 1990 by more than 300 of the world's leading climate scientists.[12]

This chapter is an introduction to the main findings of the IPCC scientists' report, to the uncertainties in the science which underlies predictions of global warming, and to feedbacks in the climate system. Feedbacks are central to the way we appraise the risks associated with global warming. They are physical phenomena which can be set in motion by the warming atmosphere and ocean, working in a way which which can dampen the warming (negative, or 'cooling' feedbacks) or enhance it (positive or 'warming' feedbacks).

Table 1.1: The common greenhouse gases, their origins, rates of buildup in the atmosphere, and their contributions to global warming in the 1980s

Gas*	Principal sources	Current rate of annual increase and concentration†	Contibution to global warming (%)†
Carbon dioxide (CO_2)	Fossil fuel burning (*c.*77 %) Deforestation (*c.*23 %)Δ	0.5% (353 ppmv)¶	55
Chlorofluorocarbons (CFCs) and related gases (HFCs and HCFCs) §	Various industrial uses: refrigerants foam blowing solvents	4% (280 pptv CFC-11 484 pptv CFC-12)	24
Methane (CH_4)	Rice paddies Enteric fermentation Gas leakage	0.9% (1.72 ppmv)	15
Nitrous oxide (N_2O)	Biomass burning Fertilizer use Fossil-fuel combustion	0.8 % (310 ppbv)	6

Sources and notes: *The contribution from tropospheric ozone is also significant, but is very difficult to quantify. Ozone forms in the troposphere as a result of chemical interactions between uncombusted hydrocarbons and nitrogen oxides, produced by fossil-fuel burning, in the presence of sunlight.

†IPCC, *Working Group 1 Report*, Policymakers' Summary, p. 6.

‡ibid., estimates for the decade of the 1980s.

Δ ibid., Section 1, p. 12, rounded (see original table for error margins).

§Note that production of CFCs began only a few years before the Second World War. Now that these gases are known to deplete ozone, the chemical industry is preparing replacements – hydrochlorofluorocarbons (HCFCs) and hydrofluorocarbons (HFCs). Though they do not deplete ozone so badly (and are yet to be produced in commercial quantities), they are potent greenhouse gases.

¶ppmv = parts per million volume;ppbv = parts per billion volume; pptv = parts per trillion volume.

1.1 Predicting future climate change

There are less than ten major climatology centres where large-scale computer-models of future climate are run.[13] Such models, known as Global Circulation Models or GCMs, use enormous computing power in an attempt to take account of the many interrelating aspects of nature which fashion future climate. Stephen Schneider explains how these models work in Chapter 2.

Currently, the GCMs predict a rise of global average temperature of between 1.5 and 4.5°C for an effective doubling of carbon dioxide over its pre-industrial levels.[14] 'Effective doubling' means a doubling of the overall greenhouse effect of pre-industrial levels of carbon dioxide, that is, an increase in carbon dioxide which, when added to the effect of the increase in other greenhouse gases, is equivalent to a doubling of pre-industrial carbon dioxide levels alone. This effective doubling will happen by around 2030 if we keep on emitting greenhouse gases at the rates we are today.[15]

Because of the thermal inertia of the oceans (the slowness with which they warm up), climatologists distinguish 'realized' warming from 'equilibrium' warming.[16] The realized warming predicted by the IPCC scientists is around 1°C above present levels by 2025 and 3°C before the end of the next century. The equilibrium warming is that achieved after the additional committed warming has come about. Today, for example, world average temperatures are about 0.3 to 0.6°C warmer than they were in pre-industrial times.[17] This may or may not be attributable to greenhouse warming, because of the inate variability of climate. But the committed warming of greenhouse-gas emissions – the warming which would take us to an equilibrium state with respect to the greenhouse-gas emissions between 1880 and 1989 – will involve an additional rise of between 0.5°C and 1.5°C at some time in the future.[18] The IPCC scientists conclude from their best climate models that if radiative forcing increases steadily, the realized temperature at any time is about 60 to 80 per cent of the committed temperature. They are not able to say whether the slow rise to equilibrium which would occur in the (unlikely) event that forcing were simply held constant would take decades or centuries.[19] For simplicity, then, it is best to refer to warming in terms of realized temperatures. The IPCC scientists' predictions of realized temperature rise in the next century are shown in Fig. 1.2. In the *Greenpeace Report*, authors talk about realized temperature unless otherwise specified.

1.2 Lessons from past climate change

To understand the implications for the natural environment of the temperature changes predicted by the IPCC, knowledge of the climate record of the geological past is helpful. In recent years, scientists have much refined our appreciation of ancient climate change using studies of cores from ice and sediments. In ice, measurements of oxygen and hydrogen isotopes allow measurement of the air temperature at the time the ice formed.[20] A continuous record of ice up to 160,000 years old has been drilled in Antarctica. In ocean and lake sediments, the shells of tiny planktonic organisms also yield such isotopic information. In this case, oxygen isotopes give a measure of the temperature of the water in which the shell formed. Using ice and sediments of different ages, temperature-trends can be built up. Many such studies have been completed in recent years,[21] allowing scientists to draw up increasingly detailed reconstructions of climate and ocean currents, stretching (in the case of ocean-sediment studies) tens of millions of years into the past.

A great advantage of ice-core studies such as these is that the carbon dioxide content of the air at different times can be measured by analysing minute bubbles of air trapped at different levels in the ice. When this was done, scientists saw that the carbon dioxide content of the air follows the temperature almost in step. In interglacial periods it is high, averaging around 280 parts per million (ppm), and in glacial times it is low, averaging 210 ppm, and falling as low as 180 ppm.[22] (The concentration today is fully 353 ppm – a level which has never been approached before while humans have lived on the planet.) Why do we find such a pattern? In recent years, a strong consensus has grown among scientists that it is changes in the way the Earth orbits the sun that switches the planet from a glacial world to an interglacial one, and vice versa.[23] However, left alone such changes in orbital parameters would not be strong enough to explain the rapidity and magnitude of the switches seen in ice- and sediment-cores. The changes must be amplified by feedbacks of various kinds, and among these greenhouse gases undoubtedly played a role. Stephen Schneider discusses this important evidence further in Chapter 2.

Figure 1.2 depicts the trend in global average surface temperatures associated with the most recent glacial-to-interglacial transition, and shows the temperature-rise predicted by the IPCC as a result of the man-made greenhouse effect. The upper illustration is a generalization of global average temperatures, based on the overall data from studies of ice-cores, microfossil shells, and other indicators of ancient climate such as the fossil remains of pollen and other fragments of plant species which, by analogy with their descendants, were temperature sensitive.[24] Relatively rapid warming occurred over a few millenia, carrying the world into the modern interglacial phase, during which time civilization evolved.

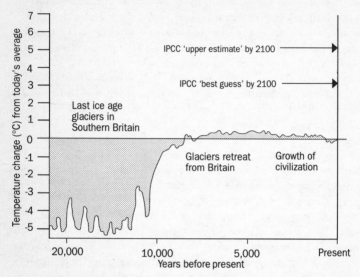

Fig. 1.2: Generalized global average temperatures during and immediately before the history of human civilization. (a) The past 20,000 years. (b) (Overleaf) The past 1,000 years. The averages depict a range of analyses from sediment- and ice-cores. Note how temperatures last rose quickly around 12,000 years ago as the world emerged from the last ice age. Global average temperatures rose some 5°C over several millenia at that time. The average temperature rise predicted beyond 1990 by the IPCC scientists is many times faster. In (a) the temperature-rise would be lost in the thickness of the line which forms the right-hand margin of the figure. In (b) the grey peak is the 'best guess' of the IPCC scientists. The black peak is the upper range of the estimates from the IPCC models. As the IPCC scientists observe, however, the likelihood of positive feedbacks – many of them unaccounted for in climate models – means that the real temperature rise in the next century is 'likely' to be even higher than that predicted.
(After International Geosphere Biosphere Program Report no. 6, Global Changes of the Past, July 1988, and UK Department of the Environment, Global Climate Change, May 1990, modified to include the IPCC scientists' results).

During the present interglacial, mean global temperatures do not seem to have varied much either side of the present global average of 15°C. At times, such as the 'Little Ice Age' of the sixteenth to eighteenth centuries, temperatures were on average lower. At other times, such as the medieval warm period when the Vikings colonized Greenland – possibly naming it after its verdancy – temperatures were on average higher. Never did the average seem to be more than

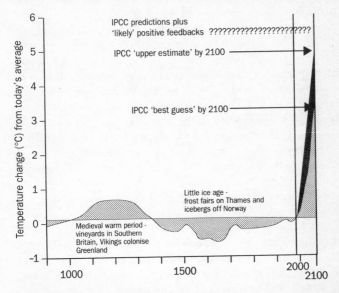

about one degree Celsius higher than the present, yet there were remarkable differences in climate during these times. For example, during 1816 – 'the year without a summer', though the average global temperature was less than 1°C below today's, there were frosts in June as far south as New England, and disastrous crop failures.[25]

The speed of the global average temperature rise predicted by the IPCC scientists is clear from Fig. 1.2. The figure shows the 'best guess' track of temperature rise – assuming that greenhouse-gas emissions continue to grow as they are today – of 1°C above today's average surface temperature by 2030, and around 3°C before the end of the next century. They also show the upper estimate of realized temperatures predicted by the models (more than 5°C above today's by 2100). What they do not show is any representation of the temperature track which would be followed if – as the IPCC scientists conclude is 'likely'[26] – positive feedbacks currently not represented in the climate models come into play.

Limiting ourselves to the next century, and concentrating on rates of change, rather than absolute temperatures, it is instructive to compare events in the glacial-interglacial transition around 10,000 years ago, with the GCM-based predictions for the twenty-first century and beyond. Averaging the post-glacial 5°C temperature-rise out, the global average temperature changed at a rate of around 1°C every 500 years or so (though there is evidence from Greenland that temperatures may have changed much faster than this for periods of several decades at a time).[27] Even taking the 'best guess' IPCC, the realized temperature-rise will be around 3°C by around 2100,[28] a rate of change of about 1°C every 30 years or so, or 0.3°C per decade. Given the range of current GCM estimates, Stephen Schneider calculates that the rate of global average temperature rise will be around 10 to 100 times faster than occurred in the glacial–interglacial transition around 10,000 years ago.[29] Brian Huntley examines the implications of such unprecedentedly rapid changes in temperature in Chapter 6 of this book.

The main point is clear from Fig. 1.2 and the foregoing discussion: positive feedbacks or no positive feedbacks, if the great majority of the world's climate scientists are correct, in a 'business-as-usual' world in which greenhouse-gas emissions continue at today's rates, we are heading for rates of temperature-rise unprecedented in human history; the geological record screams a warning to us of just how unprecedented, and of how stressed the natural environment will become if that happens. And this conclusion pertains only to existing model-predictions, not the natural amplifications of global warming which the world's scientists profess are 'likely' if greenhouse gas concentrations are allowed to continue building up in the atmosphere (as explained in Section 1.5).

It is important to appreciate an additional point. The temperature-increase as a result of excessive anthropogenic greenhouse-gas emissions is in principle open-ended. Scientists present their computer predictions in terms of the next fifty, or at most 100, years, only because here the uncertainties are less daunting. Absolute temperatures on Earth were once much higher. Geologists estimate that global average temperatures were some 10–15°C higher than today during the age of the dinosaurs around 100 million years ago. From reconstructions of climate carried out by palaeontologists, this seems to have been the warmest the Earth's atmosphere has ever been in the c.600-million-year history of higher animal life.[30] If greenhouse gases continue to be emitted at current rates, the consequent global warming will eventually generate temperatures which outstrip those experienced by any animal which has ever lived on the planet.

1.3 Are the first manifestations of the anthropogenic greenhouse effect already evident?

When one of NASA's foremost scientists testified in Congress during the 1988 drought that 'with a high degree of confidence we can associate the warming [of around 0.5°C in mean global temperature this century] with the greenhouse effect',[31] he unleashed a storm of criticism.[32] Some other scientists have since agreed with him that the physical manifestations of the anthropogenic greenhouse effect are already evident. Richard Houghton and George Woodwell have said: 'The heat and drought that have afflicted North America and other regions of the Earth in recent years are consistent with the predictions of a global warming trend. There are other indications of an accelerated warming.' They cite reports of increasing depth to permafrost in the Alaskan and Canadian Arctic, increase in the average temperature of Canadian lakes, decline in the annual maximum extent of sea-ice surrounding Antarctica and the Arctic, and the decline of glaciers in Europe and elsewhere.[33] Unusual climatic events in recent years — Hurricane Hugo, floods in Africa and India, windstorms in Europe — have generated speculation that the 'signal' of the enhanced greenhouse effect has 'arrived'.

In September 1989, the Arctic ice was reported to be thinning dramatically. The UK Scott Polar Institute released a report based on sonar measurements made by British nuclear submarines, showing that the ice in an area north of Greenland had thinned from an average of 6.7 m in 1976 to 4.5 m in 1987.[34] Unusual loss of ice was also reported at a British Antarctic Survey base, consequent on an increase in mean air temperature of 1.1°C between 1982 and 1986.[35]

All this can still be described as circumstantial or even 'anecdotal' evidence, given the known natural variability of climate. The IPCC scientists conclude that the size of twentieth-century warming 'is broadly consistent with predictions of climate models, but is also of the same magnitude of natural climate variability ... the unequivocal detection of the enhanced greenhouse effect from observations is not likely for a decade or more'.[36] However, as Wallace Broecker has pointed out, 'the fact that we cannot prove that the warming during the last century was caused by man-induced greenhouse gases is not the major issue. Rather the issue is that, by adding infrared-absorbing gases to the atmosphere, we are effectively playing Russian roulette with our climate.'[37]

1.4 The carbon cycle

Before we go on to look at the methods of simulating climate in the next chapter, we need to consider the atmosphere in the context of its relationship with other components of the climate system. A variety of natural processes govern the way in which carbon is exchanged between the atmosphere and the main carbon reservoirs of the planet; the biota, the soil, and the oceans. Figure 1.3 is a simplified portrayal of these processes. The quantities of carbon are in billions (1000 millions) of tonnes (gigatonnes, or Gt).

The terrestrial biota – all life on land (dominated, in terms of volume, by plant life) – absorbs around 102 Gt of carbon per year in the CO_2 which is drawn down during photosynthesis – the production of organic molecules from carbon dioxide and water in the presence of sunlight.[38] This is about 14 per cent of the total atmospheric content of CO_2. Respiration from the biota – production of carbon dioxide as a result of the utilization of organic molecules – puts c.50 Gt of carbon back into the atmosphere each year. Bacterial decomposition of dead plant matter in soils, mostly from surface litter, adds a further c.50 Gt of carbon in the CO_2 given up to the atmosphere. Hence there is an approximate balance in the carbon accountancy between the terrestrial biota and the atmosphere, with perhaps 2 Gt of carbon being retained in the terrestrial biota each year.

In the oceanic domain, CO_2 is also drawn down from the atmosphere. This is a result of both chemical and biological processes. Carbon dioxide is taken into solution as bicarbonate ions, and single-celled plants (phytoplankton) are a sink for carbon dioxide as a result of their photosynthesis. A total of about 92 Gt of carbon per year is drawn from the atmosphere in this way. From the surface waters, around 90 Gt of carbon is returned to the atmosphere each year. Both physical and biological processes are again responsible: release of

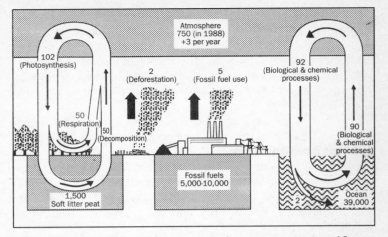

Fig. 1.3. Generalized portrayal of the carbon cycle, showing main reservoirs and fluxes. Quantities of carbon are in Gt (reservoirs) and Gt per annum (fluxes). Estimates are from IPCC, Scientific Assessment of Climate Change, *fig. 1.1, and references therein. The figure is based on Stephen Schneider's drawing in* Scientific American, *Dec. 1989.*

carbon dioxide directly from seawater by diffusion, and as a result of respiration by phytoplankton. The net result is that about 2 (plus or minus 0.5) Gt of carbon is sequestered each year in the oceans.[39]

In the absence of human influences, the carbon accountancy of the terrestrial biota, oceans, and atmosphere would be in equilibrium, with the net draw-down of carbon dioxide into the terrestrial biota and oceans being crudely balanced over time by additions to the atmosphere of carbon dioxide from volcanic activity.[40] However, as we have seen, humans have had an increasing influence on the carbon cycle since the dawn of industrial society.

Fossil fuels – coal, oil, and gas – are made of carbon derived from pre-existing life. Coal is made primarily of compacted plant remains. Oil is derived chiefly from the thermal maturation (chemical change resulting from burial) of organic matter, chiefly in marine sediments, derived principally from ancient phytoplankton. Gas is derived primarily from the thermal maturation of organic matter, in a variety of sediments, derived principally from plant remains. All this carbon – in the absence of mining and burning by humans – is effectively cut off from the natural carbon cycle. But humans are burning fossil fuels at a rate which currently adds 5.7 (plus or minus 0.5) Gt of carbon to the atmosphere each year. To this must be added the c.2 Gt of carbon derived from burning and clearing forests.[41] Hence, when this is added to the 2 Gt or so sequestered in the oceans and the 2 Gt or so retained in the terrestrial biota, there is a net increase of about 3 Gt of carbon in the atmosphere each year. This net increase of CO_2 in the atmosphere as a fraction of the total anthropogenic input is known as the airborne fraction.

How much has the arithmetic of the carbon cycle been changed since fossil-fuel burning began, and since the 1950s, when concerted tropical deforestation began?[42] Table 1.2 summarizes the salient statistics. We know from the ice-core data that about 280 ppm of carbon dioxide is the quantity found in a stable atmosphere during inter-glacial times. This equates to about 575 Gt of carbon. For comparison, this is around the same quantity of carbon as is present in all living plants.[43]

Table 1.2: Some quantities of carbon in the climate system in billion tonnes (Gt of carbon)

CO_2 in the atmosphere today	750
CO_2 in the pre-industrial atmosphere	575
Present annual release from fossil-fuel burning	more than 5
Present annual release from deforestation	c.2
Amount of carbon in phytomass (all plants)	560
Carbon in recoverable coal and oil	4,000
Carbon in potentially recoverable fossil fuels	5,000–10,000

The current carbon dioxide content of the atmosphere, as directly measured at places like Hawaii, is 353 ppm (Fig. 1.4). This equates to 750 Gt of carbon. In other words, since 1860, humans have added around 175 Gt of carbon to the atmosphere. Most of this has clearly come since the Second World War. Figure 1.5 shows a major reason why this has been the case: burning of fossil fuels. Since the Second World War we have experienced a growth in fossil-fuel demand which has averaged in excess of 5 per cent annually.[44]

By how much more do humans have it in their power to unbalance the carbon cycle? If we continue to increase the rate at which we burn fossil fuels, within some 200 years of having commenced such burning in a concerted way at the beginning of the industrial age humans could have added more carbon to the atmosphere than is present in the entire mass of living things on the planet (since, in terms of carbon, all living animals are only a small fraction of the mass of carbon

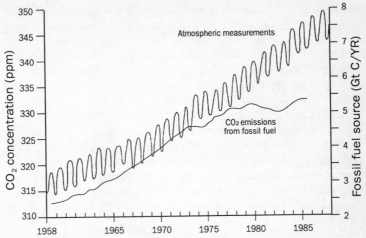

Fig. 1.4. Atmospheric CO_2 concentrations (as measured at Mauna Loa, Hawaii, since 1958). They have increased more or less linearly. Note how the CO_2 emissions from fossil fuels increased less rapidly after the oil-price hike in the early 1970s, yet the concentration of CO_2 in the atmosphere has continued its steep rise. This could be due to an escalation of tropical deforestation, or release of carbon dioxide from soils warmed by the removal of forest cover, or possibly a decreasing ability of the oceans to draw down CO_2 from the atmosphere, or a combination of factors. Note also the annual expression in the data of seasonal changes in photosynthesis and respiration.
Source: *D. A. Lashof and D. A. Tirpak (eds.),* Policy Options for Stabilizing Global Climate *(US Environmental Protection Agency, 1989).*

in living plants). But that, in principle, is not necessarily the end of our ability to impact the carbon cycle. Fossil-fuel reserves contain between 5000 and 10,000 Gt of carbon.[45] Proven coal and oil reserves contain 4,000 Gt, 730 of them in China alone.[46] There is nothing to stop humans exploiting these – indeed, current energy plans in almost all countries envisage an increased rate of burning.[47] China, for example, intends to burn enough coal to put 3 Gt of carbon into the atmosphere – more than half the current global total – by 2025.[48]

Assuming the same ratio of airborne fraction to carbon sequestered in biota or oceans, the burning of all 4,000 Gt of known coal and oil reserves would increase the CO_2 content of the atmosphere by almost 2,000 Gt of carbon, more than trebling that of today's atmosphere. By exactly how much this would elevate the surface temperatures on Earth is impossible to say, because of uncertainties in climate response which I summarize in the next section of this chapter. As

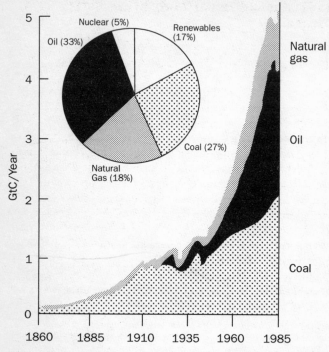

Fig. 1.5. Growth in fossil-fuel consumption since the Industrial Revolution, and current world energy consumption. (Note that the proportion of renewables increases in some estimates depending on how biomass is counted in less developed countries.)
(Source: British Petroleum, Worldwatch)

has been noted, temperatures during the age of the dinosaurs (in the Cretaceous period, 140 to 66 million years ago) were up to 10–15°C higher than today. Geochemists have calculated that these involved an atmospheric CO_2 content four to eight times higher than that observed today.[49]

Are fossil-fuel reserves the only means by which the carbon cycle could be destabilized? The answer is no. This is where the feedbacks to the climate system come in.

1.5 Feedbacks and uncertainty in predicting climate change

I have already referred to the many interactions between the physics, chemistry, and dynamics of the atmosphere, and between the biosphere and the rest of the climate system. 'No current model accounts for these interactions', wrote a group of American climate modellers in the May 1989 issue of *Physics Today*, 'and we are perhaps decades away from developing one that does. In the meantime, we face the unenviable task of judging the seriousness of the anthropogenic effect with a very limited comprehension of the climate system. The question, however, is not: Is the problem serious? but, At what concentration levels will the trace gases trigger an unprecedented climate change?'[50] This is a forthright articulation of the concerns which lay behind a number of the statements made by the IPCC scientists in their report. 'The complexity of the system means that we cannot rule out surprises', they wrote in the Executive Summary.[51] This was a reference to the feedbacks in the climate system. They concluded that, 'although many of these feedback processes are poorly understood, it seems likely that, overall, they will act to increase, rather then decrease, greenhouse gas concentrations in a warmer world.'[52] Another reference to these uncertainties behind the 'best guess' predictions they make of climate change in the next century reads: 'because natural sources and sinks of greenhouse gases are sensitive to a change in climate, they may substantially modify future concentrations. ...For this reason, climate change is likely to be greater than the estimates we have given.'[53]

This is a crucial aspect of the debate over the scientific uncertainties about global warming. In the remainder of this chapter I briefly summarize each of the feedbacks described by the IPCC scientists in their report. Stephen Schneider, David Schimel, and George Woodwell also discuss aspects of the feedbacks in later chapters. The feedbacks are summarized in Table 1.3.

1.5.1 Water vapour

A warmer atmosphere will contain more water vapour, as a result of increasing rates of evaporation. Water vapour is itself a potent greenhouse gas. Hence, this is a positive feedback, and has recently been demonstrated as such using satellite-based measurements from the Earth Radiation Budget Experiment (ERBE) to show that on the

Table 1.3: Principal feedbacks in the greenhouse effect
(Source: *IPCC Scientific Assessment of Climate Change with additional information from Lashof, in* Climatic Change *(1989), vol. 14, and references therein.)*

	Sign: (+ve or –ve)	Included in GCMs?	Comments (for references and further details see text)
Water vapour	+ve	yes	Empirically demonstrated from space
Ice and snow	+ve	yes	Moderately well understood
Clouds	Unknown	yes	Net –ve forcing in modern world; potentially biggest feedback in a warming world*
Tropospheric chemistry	Unknown	no	Potential +ve, escalating drain on hydroxyl (OH)
Aerosol particles	Unknown	no	DMS from phytoplankton
Ocean temperature	+ve	yes	Major uncertainties in scale
Ocean circulation	+ve	latest	Potentially large and very rapid
Oceanic gas-exchange rates	Unknown	yes	Probably minor
Oceanic biogeochemical cycling	Unknown	no	Possibly +ve
Carbon dioxide fertilization	Unknown	no	Probably -ve in short term
Eutrophication/toxification	-ve	no†	Some propose this as a technical fix
Temperature and plant respiration	+ve	latest	Potentially large
Soil moisture	Both	yes	Depends on precipitation and latitude
Vegetation distribution	Unknown	no	Potentially +ve
Vegetation albedo	+ve	latest	Probably significant at the end of ice age‡
Ultraviolet radiation (UV-B) and phytoplankton	+ve	no	Major uncertainties, possibly large
UV-B and terrestrial biota	+ve	no	Importance increases with size of terrestrial carbon sink
Rice fields	+ve	no	Soil moisture a critical unknown§
Natural wetlands	+ve	no	Probably minor§
Methane in permafrost	+ve	no	Future level of water tables an unknown§
Organic matter in permafrost	+ve	no	Magnitude depends on temperature in soils
Methane hydrates in permafrost	+ve	no	Probably slow, but large in long term
Offshore methane hydrates	+ve	no	Scale uncertain – possibly huge; possibly short-term

Column 2 shows whether the feedback is likely to add to the greenhouse effect (+ve) or dampen it (–ve). Column 3 shows whether the feedbacks are included in climate models. Note that there is a great difference between GCMs (large-scale models run on super-computers) and smaller-scale experimental climate models. The column refers to GCMs.

*A number of parameters of clouds can change in a warming world – the IPCC Report stresses quantity, altitude, and water content – but these are probably too interdependent to be regarded as individual feedbacks.

†Included in latest research models (smaller-scale models than GCMs).

‡The information in this line of the table is based on Lashof and references therein.

§The IPCC Report reserves judgement on the sign of these feedbacks. Positive character based on Lashof and references therein.

modern planet the amount of infra-red radiation trapped in the atmosphere increases significantly with sea surface temperature. Climate modellers simulate this feedback in GCMs, and the empirical data obtained by Raval and Ramanathan proved consistent with the magnitude of feedback predicted by GCMs before the ERBE data were obtained.[54]

1.5.2 Ice and snow

In a warming world, ice and snow in mountain glaciers and parts of the polar regions will melt. This means that, with less bright ice cover than the modern world, the surface of the warming world is able to reflect less incoming solar radiation back to space. The 'darker' surface absorbs more radiation: a positive feedback. Climate modellers factor this into their GCMs. Though this is a well-understood process in modelling climate, the IPCC scientists conclude that the real situation 'is probably more complex' and 'there is a need to more fully diagnose the interactive nature of the feedback mechanism'.[55]

1.5.3 Clouds

Clouds occupy only about a tenth of the volume of the troposphere,[56] and of the cloud volume only about a millionth is occupied by condensed water. Yet changes in cloud cover and their radiative consequences are probably the biggest uncertainty in predicting the magnitude of global warming.[57] Clouds, through changes in such characters as their amount, altitude, and water content, can act as both positive and negative feedbacks to global warming. The Earth Radiation Budget Experiment shows that in the modern world, the overall effect of clouds is to cool the Earth. But such a situation will not necessarily be maintained in a warming world. For example, if more clouds form at higher (and colder) altitudes than in the modern world, as some GCMs predict, they will emit less radiation and thus act as a positive feedback to the greenhouse effect.[58] Similar uncertainties pertain to predicting the sign of feedbacks produced by changing either the amount of clouds and/or their water content.[59]

Climate modellers attempt to simulate such cloud feedbacks in GCMs. Indeed, it is largely the slight changes in parameterizations of clouds that cause model predictions to rise and fall within the range of doubling temperatures published to date by the major climate-modelling centres. For example, a recent run of the UK Meteorological Office model resulted in the predicted doubling temperature falling from about 5.5 to 1.9°C as a result of changes in the way clouds are portrayed ('parameterized') in the models. As the authors observed, however, 'although the revised cloud scheme is more detailed, it is not necessarily more accurate than the less sophisticated scheme'.[60] While this GCM prediction of global average temperature upon doubling of carbon dioxide has gone down, others have gone up.[61] Stephen Schneider discusses this aspect of climate modelling further in his chapter.

1.5.4 Tropospheric chemistry

The chemistry of the troposphere involves a complex web of chemical feedbacks, but those of greatest concern are the reactions affecting the hydroxyl radical, OH. Hydroxyl is the 'cleansing agent' of the atmosphere. It is a chemical scavenger which oxidizes gases as diverse as methane, carbon monoxide, nitrogen oxides, non-methane hydrocarbons (NMHCs), HCFCs and HFCs. A warmer Earth will have higher absolute humidity, and therefore will allow more OH to form in its atmosphere. But at the same time, there will be a strong drain on hydroxyl as a result of the escalating emissions (in a business-as-usual world) of the gases it oxidizes. Which factor will win? Scientists vary in their opinions, and climate modellers do not attempt the sum in their models. Hameed and Cess, for example, argue that the result will be a small negative feedback.[62] Ramanathan *et al.* and Lashof, on the other hand, have argued for a positive feedback.[63]

The uncertainties here are huge, and the stakes are very high. The natural quantity of hydroxyl in the atmosphere is minute,[64] and an atmosphere in which hydroxyl is severely depleted is an atmosphere in which the lifetime (and hence Global Warming Potential) of critical greenhouse gases – methane, HCFCs, and HFCs – is increasing. It is also an atmosphere in which carbon monoxide, nitrogen oxides, and NMHCs are being allowed to build up by default, less OH being available to oxidize them. These gases – through chemical reactions in the presence of sunlight – lead to the production of yet another greenhouse gas, tropospheric ozone.[65]

1.5.5 Aerosol particles

Human-made sulphur emissions, which have increased over the Northern Hemisphere during the last century as a result of burning of fossil fuels, form aerosols which influence the radiative properties of clouds in such a way as to cool the Earth. Hence, this is a human-made negative forcing. Though it is difficult to be sure of the magnitude of the forcing, it is conceivable that it is comparable to the greenhouse forcing so far this century (though of opposite 'sign').[66] In other words, were it not for sulphur emissions, the observed rise in global average temperature this century of 0.3 to 0.6°C[67] might have been twice as large.

Natural feedbacks might arise from aerosols in the future. This is because phytoplankton (microscopic algae in the surface waters of the ocean) generate DMS (dimethyl sulphide), a gas which leads to the formation of cloud condensation nuclei. Increased phytoplankton concentrations might be expected to generate more DMS, and hence more clouds, as David Schimel describes in Chapter 3. But there is no evidence of either the sign or the magnitude of the feedback which might be expected in a warming world.

Negative forcing of climate from human-made sulphur emissons should be viewed not as a potential contribution to abating global warming, but as part of the problem. This is because the sulphur-dioxide emissions which engender the cloud-condensation nuclei which give rise to the feedback also promote acidification in the atmosphere. Given the importance of the terrestrial biota as a sink for carbon dioxide – a point considered in more detail later – damage to forest ecosystems as a result of acidification actually imperils an important natural reservoir in the carbon cycle in a way which could add to the carbon dioxide content of the atmosphere by default. David Schimel elaborates on this point in his chapter.

1.5.6 Ocean temperature

The overall flux of carbon dioxide between the atmosphere and the ocean-surface waters is driven by the differences in partial pressure of CO_2 across the sea surface.[68] As the temperature of sea-water rises, so the solubility of CO_2 decreases and the partial pressure of CO_2 in the surface waters of the ocean increases. This has the effect of decreasing the overall uptake of CO_2 by the oceans: a positive feedback.[69] A common estimate is that of the total anthropogenic emissions of CO_2 in the modern world, around a quarter seems to be sequestered in the terrestrial biota (by photosynthesis) and a quarter seems to be drawn into the ocean – by both chemical processes (diffusion) and biological processes (photosynthesis by phytoplankton).[70] Hence, an important sink for the main greenhouse gas will be depleted as sea-surface temperatures go up.

By how much will the future atmospheric CO_2 increase be amplified? Lashof estimates 5 per cent,[71] but the uncertainties are large. The UK Natural Environmental Research Council has allocated considerable resources to investigating this problem, and the effects of temperature on biological productivity in the oceans, as part of its

Biogeochemical Ocean Flux Study (BOFS).[72] The stakes associated with these uncertainties are high: the oceans are a huge reservoir for CO_2 – they contain fifty times more than the atmosphere and twenty times more than the biosphere, and, as Taro Takahashi has put it, 'the unique feature of the oceans is that a large body of deep water highly supersaturated with CO_2 [that is, unable to absorb any more than it already has] is capped with a thin layer of warm and less dense water that prevents the rapid transfer of carbon dioxide from the deep water reservoir to the atmosphere.'[73]

1.5.7 Ocean circulation

Apart from temperature and the ready ability of CO_2 to dissolve in sea-water, two other major factors govern the ocean's capacity to hold CO_2. The first is the presence of a 'biological pump', whereby CO_2 is carried from the surface waters to deeper waters in a rain of organic detritus, comprising dead micro-organisms, faecal material, and so on. I return to this process later. The second is the rate and pattern of ocean-water circulation.[74]

Circulation of water masses in the oceans is complex, and driven by the climate system. Hence, as climate changes, ocean circulation is likely to follow suit. As sea-surface temperatures rise, the thermocline (the layer of the ocean immediately below the permanently-mixed surface layer) may become more stable and resistant to the vertical mixing of water. Uptake of CO_2 depends on this mixing: phytoplankton productivity is limited by the the supply of nutrient-rich deeper water. The net effect, as the IPCC scientists conclude, is that the uptake of anthropogenic CO_2 is likely to be slowed down.[75] This potential feedback is popularly known as the 'plankton multiplier'.

Such changes are difficult, to the point of impossibility, to quantify in modelling studies, but the geological record offers a warning that they can be abrupt, and severe. Studies of air trapped in ice cores from Greenland show that during the transition from the last ice age to the present interglacial, more than 10,000 years ago, very significant changes in atmospheric CO_2 concentration – of the order of 50 ppmv or 20 per cent of the total content of CO_2 in the air – seem to have occurred within less than a century, in parallel with regional temperature changes on the order of 5°C.[76] The IPCC scientists and others argue that these were probably caused by changes of large-scale currents in the North Atlantic region.[77]

1.5.8 Wind patterns and oceanic gas-exchange rates

The magnitude of gas transfer between the sea surface and the atmosphere, or vice versa, depends on the turbulence of the surface layer of the ocean, and hence on the wind-speed above it.[78] In a warming world, changing climatic patterns will involve changing wind patterns. The higher the wind-speed, the higher the transfer velocity of carbon dioxide. The IPCC scientists judge that vertical mixing is more important than gas-exchange in determining the net carbon dioxide uptake of the global ocean, and conclude that this feedback is likely to be minor.[79]

1.5.9 Modification of oceanic biogeochemical cycling

The IPCC scientists voice fears that the present balance of the 'biological pump' in the modern oceans may be unbalanced in a warming ocean. Today, the rain of organic detritus (and hence nutrients) from surface waters is balanced by an upward transport of dissolved carbon and nutrients in areas of up-welling water. Such areas include the polar regions and areas along the eastern margins of the major ocean basins. According to the IPCC WG1 Report, 'the balance could become disturbed consequent on variations in ocean dynamics so as to influence atmospheric carbon dioxide'. However, 'it is not possible at present to predict the direction and magnitude of such effects'.[80]

1.5.10 Carbon dioxide fertilization

A well-known and much-quoted facet of increasing CO_2 in the atmosphere is that short-term experiments under controlled conditions in glasshouses promote increased rates of photosynthesis and growth in most plants. Were this to translate to natural ecosystems, as CO_2 levels rose in the future atmosphere, the result would be a significant negative feedback on global warming. Forests would be of particular importance if they were to expand their biomass, because about two-thirds of all photosynthesis is carried out by forests.[81] But the real world is different from a glasshouse. Lashof calculates that doubling carbon dioxide would lead to an increase of global biomass of more than 15 per cent, but the IPCC scientists conclude that 'it is not clear whether the increases in photosynthesis and growth will persist for more than a few growing seasons, whether they will occur at all in natural ecosystems, and to what degree they will result in an increased storage of carbon in terrestrial ecosystems'.[82]

These uncertainties become all the more troubling if recent work by Takahashi, Tans, and others proves correct. There is a measured net accumulation in the modern-day atmosphere of about 3 Gt of carbon from all CO_2 (fossil fuels and deforestation), as we have seen.[83] Fossil-fuel burning causes the emission of 5.7 (plus or minus 0.5) Gt of carbon.[84] Takahashi and his colleagues calculate that as much as 2 to 3 Gt of carbon per year may be being sequestered in the biota of the northern hemisphere.[85] In other words, if they are right, a sizeable proportion of the sum of carbon dioxide emissions from fossil-fuel burning and deforestation is today being taken into northern hemisphere forests. Takahashi calculates that only about 1.6 Gt of carbon per year finds its way into the oceanic reservoirs.[86] These forests, then, might perhaps already have responded to carbon fertilization from emissions of carbon dioxide since the Industrial Revolution. The future well-being of the forests is, therefore, all the more vital. Given the escalating acidification of the modern world and the additional stresses from other air pollutants and unpredictable soil-water changes associated with global warming, this future well-being of forests cannot be relied on.

1.5.11 Eutrophication and toxification

The application of nitrogenous fertilizers in agriculture causes the emission of the greenhouse gas nitrous oxide, but also contributes to a negative feedback to the greenhouse effect.[87] Nitrates from the application of fertilizer to soils find their way into rivers, lakes, and seas, where they promote eutrophication – stagnation of water following runaway growth of algae. There has been considerable recent concern over this issue on environmental grounds, with a number of unusual algal phenomena in lakes and at sea coming under the scrutiny of scientists.[88] According to one scientist quoted in the IPCC Report, eutrophication in the oceans and on land could be generating a quantity of new biomass as large as 1 Gt of carbon per year.[89]

Tentative proposals have been advanced in some quarters for the artificial stimulation of phytoplankton in the open ocean, by provision of missing nutrients so as to promote photosynthesis as a means of artificially boosting the oceanic sink for carbon dioxide. But such a technical fix would risk the genesis of the kinds of toxic algal blooms seen in greater-than-natural quantities in the North Sea, for example, in recent years, and would in any case raise a whole host of legal and ethical issues.

1.5.12 Temperature and respiration by land vegetation

As temperature increases, so rates of photosynthesis and respiration in plants and microbes also increase. But respiration increases at a faster rate than photosynthesis. This will be an important positive feedback in a warming world,[90] because today the processes are in approximate balance: photosynthesis is estimated to draw around 102 Gt of carbon into the terrestrial biota each year, while the biota respire around 50 Gt and decomposition of organic matter in soils accounts for around 50 Gt.[91] Some have calculated that the additional flux of carbon to the atmosphere may be great from this feedback. Woodwell has estimated as much as perhaps 3 to 10 Gt of carbon each year consequent on a 4°C doubling temperature.[92] Lashof criticizes such an estimate for not distinguishing labile (easily decomposed) from refractory (resistant to decomposition) soil-carbon components, but still himself calculates a flux of 0.5 Gt of carbon per year:[93] nearly 10 per cent of the annual flux from fossil-fuel burning.

1.5.13 Soil moisture

Changes in soil-water content will clearly affect carbon fixation and storage by the terrestrial biota. Increased moisture results in increased storage of carbon in peat and stimulated plant growth in previously dry areas. However, the reverse is true as well, and since the GCMs vary greatly in their predictions of soil-moisture changes, the IPCC scientists conclude that 'it is not possible to predict reliably either the geographical distribution of changes in soil water or the net effect of these changes on carbon fluxes and storage in different ecosystems'.[94]

1.5.14 Vegetation distribution

1.5.14.1 Carbon dioxide sinks The health of forests, a vital sink for carbon dioxide, will depend very much on the rate of temperature-change. If they can migrate and adapt, there may be no net change in the sink. If the rates are too fast for successful migration, and/or if urban and cultivated barriers prove insuperable, the forests will suffer and net sink will diminish. The IPCC Report reserves judgement on this,[95] but Brian Huntley and other authors have argued on the basis of the way vegetation responded to a 5°C temperature-rise at the end of the ice age, that even for the 'best guess' rates of change, forests will suffer (see Chapter 6). Overpeck *et al.* have also argued that global warming will promote increased rates of forest disturbance (fires, storms, and coastal flooding) capable of significantly altering the total biomass, and the compositional response of forests to warming, hence depleting the carbon sink.[96]

1.5.14.2 Albedo Changes in the terrestrial biota will also affect the overall albedo of the planet. Lashof believes this to be 'probably the most significant feedback produced by the terrestrial biosphere'.[97] The most important process is decreased albedo – a positive feedback – as a result of a pole-ward shift in the tundra-boreal forest boundary. Such a change may have significantly amplified the temperature change at the end of the last ice age.[98]

1.5.15 UV-B radiation

1.5.15.1 Effects on phytoplankton An increase in the intensity of UV-B radiation at the Earth's surface is known to be a result of depletion of stratospheric ozone. The IPCC scientists conclude that 'this might have negative effects on the marine biota due to a decrease of marine productivity and thus on the biological carbon pump'.[99] This would have the effect of increasing carbon dioxide concentrations in surface waters, and hence in the atmosphere. Other studies have drawn attention to this problem – not just a positive feedback but a potentially grave threat to world food security.[100]

1.5.15.2 Effects on terrestrial biota The same comments apply to the increased exposure to UV-B of the terrestrial biota. Empirical studies show that many crops are adversely affected by such exposure, and the IPCC scientists conclude that the problem might affect the strength of the biospheric carbon dioxide sink over land. It should be pointed out that the Montreal Protocol – designed to limit the CFCs and halons which cause the majority of ozone depletion in the stratosphere – will not significantly alleviate this problem for decades. This is because of the long atmospheric lifetime of the main ozone depleters and the fact that the Protocol, in its revised form, allows the production of these substances for a further ten years, and of 'substitutes' (HCFCs) which also deplete stratospheric ozone.

1.5.16 Tropical methane sources

1.5.16.1 Rice fields Rice paddies produce around 110 million tonnes of methane per year, about 20 per cent of the total anthropogenic emissions of methane.[101] Methane has a global-warming potential of 63 over a twenty-year time-frame: that is, 1 kg of methane in that period will produce 63 times the global warming of 1 kg of carbon dioxide.[102] Given that methane production from rice paddies is heavily dependent on temperature and soil moisture – increases generate larger fluxes – this is a non-trivial problem. It is compounded by a surprising paucity of *in situ* measurements from the rice paddies of the world, and great variation in the data that is available.[103] The IPCC scientists offer no opinion on whether net fluxes will increase or decrease in a warming world,[104] but Lashof[105] estimates on the basis of available data that methane emissions from rice fields will increase by more than 30 million tonnes per year.

1.5.16.2 Natural wetlands: The world's wetlands emit around 115 million tonnes of methane per year. The IPCC scientists favour recent estimates that reverse the relative importance of tropical and high-latitude sources: they cite 55 million tonnes from tropical wetlands and 39 million tonnes from high-latitude wetlands. They offer no view of which way changes in soil moisture might drive the feedback from tropical wetlands.[106] In Lashof's analysis, low-latitude wetlands are less of a potential feedback for methane emissions than rice paddies, because they tend to be carbon-limited.[107]

1.5.17 High latitude methane sources

1.5.17.1 Methane in permafrost In the flat tundra, the level of the water table is vital in controlling methanogenesis in soil. A change in just a few centimetres can be significant, as the IPCC scientists point out, because flooded soils can produce a factor of 100 more methane than dry soils.[108] Warmer, wetter soils would, therefore, result in increased methane emissions. However, warmer, dryer soils might produce decreased methane emissions. The IPCC authors reserve judgement on the sign of the feedback.[109] Lashof reasons that the amount of emissions can be expected to increase at high latitudes as a result of melting tundra, because the 'emissions season' will be longer from ground which is frozen for less time each year.[110] Nisbett, in a wide-ranging review of methane production from northern sources, also argues cogently for a positive feedback from wetlands.[111]

1.5.17.2 Organic matter in permafrost Another dynamic favouring positive feedback from methane at high latitudes is the fact that there is an abundance of decomposable organic matter frozen in the permafrost. At these latitudes, as the IPCC scientists observe, 'emissions of methane are significantly larger at warmer temperatures, due to accelerated microbiological decomposition of organic material'.[112] It should be borne in mind that even the doubling temperatures predicted by the GCMs will involve increases of air temperature in the Arctic of up to 15°C.[113] If any of the other positive feedbacks considered in this paper come into play, without compensating negative feedbacks, the temperature-rise will be more profound still.

1.5.17.3 Methane hydrates in permafrost Methane hydrates, ice-like solids comprising a network of water crystals and methane gas trapped under pressure within it,[114] occur below the permafrost and in the offshore areas of the Arctic. The reservoir of methane in hydrates is vast, and very poorly quantified. At the lower end of a range of published estimates, a commonly quoted value is around 10,000 Gt, of which 400 Gt may be beneath the permafrost.[115] This reservoir is itself more than an order of magnitude larger than all the carbon in atmospheric carbon dioxide – 750 Gt – and in all life on Earth – around 760 Gt according to one estimate.[116] But published estimates for the size of the global methane-hydrate reservoir vary upwards from 10,000 Gt by fully three orders of magnitude.[117]

Opinions vary among the few scientists who have studied this potentially enormous feedback to the greenhouse effect. Because the surface of the hydrate layer is more than 100 metres beneath the surface of the permafrost, it is probable that there will be no appreciable release for many decades, because the temperature wave from the warmed Arctic ground surface would penetrate the ground only slowly. Keith Kvenvolden – cited by the IPCC scientists in a non-committal paragraph of the report – adopts a sanguine view, calculating that the flux of methane from hydrate decomposition would within a century not exceed 100 million tonnes per year. However, in the longer term – given continuing greenhouse-gas emissions from anthropogenic sources and/or natural sources awakened by positive feedbacks – there is no theoretical limit to the destabilization of these deposits. Gordon MacDonald[118] and Ewan Nisbett[119] have both argued that wholesale destabilization of methane hydrates dominated the mechanism which ended the ice ages. Nisbett argues that, in the warming world to come, assuming a business-as-usual approach to greenhouse-gas emissions, 'the danger from a thermal runaway caused by methane release from permafrost is minor, but real ... even if there is only a 1 per cent chance that such events will occur, the social implications are profound'.[120] His fear centres on the possibility that surface temperature-rise will not reach the hydrates by simple – and slow – conduction, but by a faster process of convective transfer of heat into the ground via fractures. This would result in episodic belches of methane.[121] Such methane eruptions have already been observed in the offshore Soviet Arctic.[122]

1.5.17.4 Offshore methane hydrates Hydrates occur world-wide in submarine settings deeper than 200 to 500 metres, and, because the pressure of water helps to keep the water in the hydrate in its crystalline phase, they occur closer to the surface of the sediment than they do below the permafrost. At these depths in the cold Arctic ocean, hydrate is stable at or near the sea-floor. As Nisbett observes, 'any slight warming of the Arctic water will release hydrate from the sea floor almost immediately. A temperature change of a few degrees will liberate methane from the uppermost sea-floor sediment at this depth within a few years .'[123]

The quantity of hydrate at risk from such destabilization is unknown. Though only a small fraction of the total global methane-hydrate reservoir, it is none the less undoubtedly a huge quantity. The extent to which Arctic waters at the depths of concern will warm is also unknown. The uncertainties here are enormous and the stakes probably higher than with any other potential feedback.

1.6 The effects of cutting greenhouse-gas emissions

The IPCC scientists consider several scenarios for mixes and quantities of greenhouse-gas emissions into the atmosphere in the decades to come. Two important conclusions emerge. The first involves the fact that atmospheric concentrations of CO_2, nitrous oxide, and CFCs adjust only slowly to changes in emissions. This is because these gases have relatively long atmospheric lifetimes. Because of this slow adjustment in atmospheric concentrations, continuing to emit these

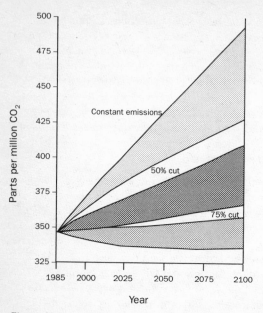

Fig. 1.6. *Impact on atmospheric CO_2 concentrations of cutting global carbon dioxide emissions by 50% and 75%, compared to continuing with constant emissions (at 1985 levels of 5.9 billion tons of carbon per year). The spread of values is because two different models of oceanic CO_2 uptake have been assumed.*
Source: *D. A. Lashof and D. A. Tirpak,* Policy options for stabilizing global climate *(US Environmental Protection Agency, 1989).*

gases at anything like present levels will commit the atmosphere to increasing concentrations for decades to centuries, with all that this involves in elevated radiative forcing and consequent global warming. A corollary is, as the IPCC scientists point out, 'the longer emissions continue to increase [at present-day rates], the greater would reductions have to be to stabilise [concentrations] at a given level. If there are critical concentration levels that should not be exceeded, then the earlier emission reductions are made, the more effective they are.'[124] The IPCC scientists, and other scientists who collaborated on a recent study for the US Environmental Protection Agency,[125] have calculated what would be required to stabilize the concentrations of the long-lived greenhouse gases at present atmospheric levels. The result in the case of CO_2 is an immediate cut in excess of 60 per cent (Table 1.4, Fig. 6). In Chapter 4, Mick Kelly works through some model calculations of what emissions reductions would have to be implemented over the next few decades in order to halt global warming.

Table 1.4: Cuts in emissions needed for stabilization of greenhouse gases at present atmospheric levels

Greenhouse gas	IPCC estimated cut (%)	EPA estimated cut (%)
CO_2	>60	50–80
CH_4	15–20	10–20
N_2O	70–80	80–85
CFC-11	70–75	75–100
CFC-12	75–85	75–100
HCFC-22	40–50	n/a

Chapter 2
The Science of Climate-Modelling and a Perspective on the Global-Warming Debate

Stephen H. Schneider

"...Many critiques somehow understress the fact that the sword of uncertainty has two blades: that is, uncertainties in physical or biological processes which make it possible for the present generation of models to have overestimated future warming effects, are just as likely to have caused the models to have underestimated change...**"**

The Earth's climate changes. It is vastly different now from what it was 100 million years ago when dinosaurs dominated the planet and tropical plants thrived at high latitudes; it is different from what it was even 18,000 years ago, when ice-sheets covered much more of the northern hemisphere. In the future it will surely continue to evolve. In part the evolution will be driven by natural causes, such as slow changes in the Earth's orbit over many thousands of years. But future climatic change, unlike that of the past, will probably have another comparably important source as well: human activities. We may already be feeling the climatic effects of having polluted the atmosphere with gases such as carbon dioxide.

Not all knowledgeable scientists agree on the likelihood that current climatic trends are human-induced. Some, but not many, even dispute that potentially unprecedented climatic changes are being built into the twenty-first century by human activities. This debate has spilled over on to the editorial pages and covers of magazines and newspapers, with often bitter and confusing charges and counter-charges being hurled back and forth. The primary victim of this noisy, sometimes polemical, set of exchanges is public confidence that there is a scientific consensus on the significant chance for unprecedented climatic changes from human activities in the decades ahead. There-fore, the restatement of that consensus in the Intergovernmental Panel on Climate Change (IPCC) Working Group report[1] should go a long way toward rebuilding that public confidence upon which policy actions to slow the buildup of greenhouse gases depend.

However, the public rarely reads 300-page assessments written in a dozen styles by scores of scientists from dozens of countries. Fur-thermore, such assessments as IPCC rarely attempt to refute specific critics, even if those critics have been leading effective public cam-paigns that are, in my view, confusing rather than enlightening public understanding of a complex problem such as climate change. There-fore, I offer this view of the scientific debate over the causes and implications of global warming as a supplement to the IPCC report. It is my intention to make the global-warming issues more accessible to a wider audience and to put some perspective on the highly visible, often acrimonious media debate that has caused such confusion in 1989 and 1990. I begin with an overview of the principal tool used to project future climate: climatic models[2] (from which much of this discussion is derived).

2.1 Why build a model?

To predict the result of some event in nature it is common to build and perform an experiment. But what if the issues are very complex or the scale of the experiment unmanageably large? To forecast the effect of human pollution on climate poses just such a dilemma, for this uncontrolled experiment is now being performed on Laboratory Earth. How then can we be anticipatory, if no meaningful physical experiment can be performed? While nothing can provide certain answers, we can turn to a surrogate lab, not a room with test-tubes and Bunsen burners, but a small box with transistors and microchips. We can build mathematical models of the Earth and perform our 'experiments' in computers.

Mathematical models translate conceptual ideas into quantitative statements. There are a range of models, from those that simply treat one or two processes in detail to large-scale, multi-process simulation models. Such models are not faithful simulators of the full complexity of reality, of course, but they can tell us the logical consequences of explicit sets of plausible assumptions. To me, that certainly is a big step beyond pure conception – or to put it more crudely, modelling is a major advance over 'hand-waving' forecasts of global changes.

The kinds of problems that can be studied by climate models include the downstream atmospheric effects of unusual ocean-surface temperature patterns (for example, so-called 'El Nino' events), climatic effects of volcanic explosions, ice age–interglacial sequences, ancient climates, the climatic effects of human pollutants such as carbon dioxide (CO_2) and even the climatic after-effects of nuclear war. We will consider a few examples of these later on.

2.2 Basic elements of models

To simulate the climate, a modeller needs to decide which components of the climatic system to include and which variables to involve. For example, if we choose to simulate the long-term sequence of ice ages (glacials) and warm periods (interglacials), our model needs to include as explicitly as possible the effects of all the important interacting components of the climatic system operating over the past million years or so. Besides the atmosphere, these include the ice masses, upper and deep oceans, and the up-and-down motions of the Earth's crust. Even life influences the climate, and thus must be included too; plants, for example, can affect the chemical composition of the air and seas as well as the reflectivity (that is, albedo) or water-cycling character of the land. These mutually inter-acting subsystems form part of the internal components of the model. On the other hand, if we are only interested in modelling very short-term weather events – say, over a single week – then our model can ignore any changes in the glaciers, deep oceans, land shapes, and forests, since these variables obviously change little over one week's time. For short-term weather, only the atmosphere itself needs to be part of the model's internal climatic system.

The slowly varying factors such as oceans or glaciers are said to be external to the internal part of the climatic system being modelled. Modellers also refer to external factors as boundary conditions, since they form boundaries for the internal model components. These boundaries are not always physical ones, such as the oceans, which are at the bottom of the atmosphere, but can also be mass or momentum or energy fluxes across physical boundaries. An example is the solar radiation impinging on the Earth. Solar radiation is often referred to by climatic modellers as a boundary-forcing function of the model for two reasons: the energy output from the sun is not an interactive, internal component of the climatic system of the model; and the energy from the sun forces the climate toward a certain temperature distribution.

We could restrict a model to predict only a globally averaged temperature that never changes its value over time (that is, which is in equilibrium). This very simple model would consist of an internal part that, when averaged over all of the atmosphere, oceans, biosphere, and glaciers, would describe two characteristics: the average reflectivity of the Earth and its average greenhouse properties. The boundary condition for such a model would be merely the incoming solar energy. Such a model is called zero-dimensional, since it collapses the east–west, north–south, and up–down space dimensions of the actual world into one point that represents some global average of all Earth-atmosphere system temperatures in all places. It also collapses all three-dimensional processes into a global average, which may in some cases, such as heat transport by winds, completely neglect that process. If our zero-dimensional model were expanded to resolve temperature or winds at different latitudes and longitudes and heights, then it would be three-dimensional. The *resolution* of a model refers to the number of dimensions included and to the amount of spatial detail with which each dimension is explicitly treated.

Modellers speak of a hierarchy of models that ranges from simple earth-averaged, time-independent, temperature models up to high-resolution, three-dimensional, time-dependent models known as general circulation models (GCMs). While three-dimensional, time-dependent models are usually more dynamically accurate, they are very computer-intensive. Thus, it is sometimes necessary to run physically, chemically, and (somewhat) biologically comprehensive models at lower resolution. Choosing the optimum combination of factors is an intuitive art that trades off completeness and (the modellers hope) accuracy for tractability and economy. Moreover, the theoretical feasibility of long-range simulation must also be evaluated; in other words, some problems are inherently unpredictable. For those problems where predictability is not ruled out in principle, such a trade-off between accuracy and economy is not 'scientific' *per se*, but rather is a value judgement, based on the weighing of many factors. Making this judgement depends strongly on the problem the model is being designed to address.

2.3 The problems of parameterizations and climatic feedback mechanisms

Clouds, being very bright, reflect a large fraction of sunlight back to space, thereby helping control the Earth's temperature. Thus, predicting the changing amount of cloudiness over time is essential to reliable climate simulation. But most individual clouds are smaller than even the smallest area represented by the smallest resolved element ('grid box') of a global-climate or weather-prediction model. A single thunderstorm is typically a few kilometres in size, not a few hundred – the size of many 'high-resolution' global-model grids. Therefore, no global-climate model available now (or likely to be available in the next few decades) can explicitly resolve every individual cloud. These important climatic elements are therefore called sub-grid-scale phenomena. Yet, even though we cannot explicitly treat all individual clouds, we can deal with their collective effects on the grid-scale climate. The method for doing so is known as parameterization, a contraction for 'parametric representation'.

Instead of solving for sub-grid-scale details, which is impractical, we search for a relationship between climatic variables we do resolve (for example, those whose variations occur over larger areas than the grid size) and those we do not resolve. For instance, climatic modellers have examined years of data on the humidity of the atmosphere averaged over large areas, and have related these values to cloudiness averaged over that area. It is typical to choose an area the size of a numerical model's grid – a few hundred kilometres on a side. While it is not possible to find a perfect correspondence between these averaged variables, reasonable relationships have been found in a wide variety of circumstances. These relationships typically require a few factors, or parameters, some of which are derived empirically from observed data, not computed from first principles. The parameterization method applies to almost all simulation models, whether dealing with physical, biological, or even social systems. The most important parameterizations affect processes called feedback mechanisms. This concept is well known outside of computer-modelling circles. The word 'feedback' is vernacular. As the term implies, information can be 'fed back' to you that will possibly alter your behaviour.

So it is in the climate system. Processes interact to modify the overall climatic state. Suppose, for example, a cold snap brings on a high albedo snow cover which tends to reduce the amount of solar heat absorbed, subsequently intensifying the cold. This interactive process is known to climatologists as the snow-and-ice/albedo/temperature feedback mechanism. Its destabilizing, positive-feedback effect is becoming well understood and has been incorporated into the parameterizations of most climatic models. Unfortunately, other potentially important feedback mechanisms are not usually as well understood. One of the most difficult ones is so-called cloud feedback, which could be either a positive or negative feedback process, depending on circumstances. Another is the extent to which changes in soil temperature or soil moisture from climate change could alter the microbial decomposition of dead organic matter into heat-trapping gases such as carbon dioxide or methane.[3] David Schimel examines these uncertainties in the next paper.

2.4 Model verification

Given the uncertainties associated with model parameterizations and feedbacks, then, can we have confidence in model predictions? At least several methods can be used, and none by itself is sufficient. First, we must check overall model-simulation skill against the real climate for today's conditions to see if the control experiment is reliable. The seasonal cycle is one good test. Fig. 2.1, from the work of Syukuro Manabe and R. J. Stouffer at the Geophysical Fluid Dynamics Laboratory at Princeton, NJ, shows how remarkably well a three-dimensional global-circulation model can simulate the regional distribution of the seasonal cycle of surface air-temperature – a well-understood climate change that is, when averaged over the Earth, larger than ice age–interglacial changes! The seasonal-cycle

Fig. 2.1. A three-dimensional climate model has been used to compute the winter-to-summer temperature differences all over the globe. The model's performance can be verified against the observed data shown below. This verification exercise shows that the model quite impressively reproduces many of the features of the seasonal cycle. These seasonal temperature extremes are mostly larger than those occurring between ice ages and interglacials or for any plausible future carbon-dioxide change.
(Source: S. Manabe and R. J. Stouffer, 'Sensitivity of a global climate model to an increase of CO_2 concentration in the atmosphere', Journal of Geophysical Research (1980), vol. 85, pp. 5529–54.)

simulation is a necessary test of what can be called 'fast physics', like cloud formations, but it doesn't tell us how well the model simulates slow changes in ice cover or soil organic matter or deep-ocean temperatures, since these variables do not change much over a seasonal cycle, though they do influence long-term trends.

A second method of verification is to test in isolation individual physical sub-components of the model (such as its parameterizations) directly against real data and/or more highly resolved process models. This still is no guarantee that the net effect of all interacting physical subcomponents has been properly treated, but it is an important test. For example, the upward infra-red radiation emitted from the planet to space can be measured from satellites or calculated in a climate model. If this quantity is subtracted from the emitted upward infra-red radiation at the Earth's surface, then the difference between these quantities, G, can be identified as the 'Greenhouse Effect', as on Fig. 2.2 from Raval and Ramanathan.[4] Although radiative processes may not be the only ones operative in nature or in the general circulation model (GCM) results, the close agreement among the satellite results (thick line labelled ERBE on Fig. 2.2), a GCM (thick dashed line labelled GCM), and line-by-line radiative transfer calculations (thin dashed line) all give strong evidence that this physical sub-component is well modelled at grid scale. Another validation test is to compare model-generated and observed statistics of grid-point daily variability.[5] Some variables, (for example, temperature) are well modelled whereas others (such as relative humidity) yield poorer simulations of observed variability.

Thirdly, some researchers express more confidence a priori in a model whose internal make-up includes more spatial resolution or physical detail, believing that 'more is better'. In some cases and for some problems this is true, but by no means for all. The 'optimal' level of complexity depends upon the problem we are trying to solve and the resources available to the task.

All three methods must constantly be used and reused as models evolve if we are to improve the credibility of their predictions. And to these we can add a fourth method: the model's ability to simulate the very different climates of the ancient Earth or even those of other planets.

Perhaps the most perplexing question, though, is whether we should ever consider our confidence in models' forecasts sufficient reason to alter our present social policies – on CO_2-producing activities, for example. Viewed from this angle, the seemingly academic field of mathematical climate modelling could become a fundamental tool for assessing public policy.

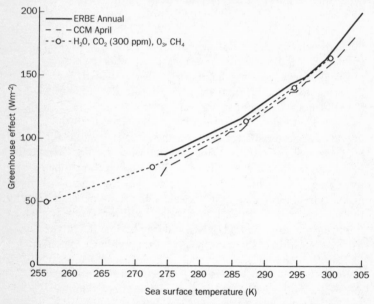

Fig. 2.2. Comparison of greenhouse-effect heat-trapping parameter G and ocean surface temperature, retrieved from three sources: bold line, ERBE annual values, obtained by averaging April, July, and October 1985 and January 1986; thick dashed line, three-dimensional climate-model simulations for a perpetual April simulation (National Center for Atmospheric Research, Community Climate Model); thin dashed line, line-by-line radiation-model calculations by Dr. A. Arking using CO_2, O_3, and CH_4. The line-by-line and climate model results come close to ERBE observed values.

2.5 Sensitivity and scenario analysis

Although the ultimate goal of any forecasting simulation may be to produce a single, accurate, time-series projection of some evolving variable, a lesser goal may still be quite useful and certainly is more realizable: to specify plausible scenarios of various uncertain or unpredictable variables, and then to evaluate the sensitivity of some predicted variable to either different scenarios or different model assumptions.

For example, in order to predict the societal impact of climatic changes from increasing concentrations of certain trace gases like CO_2, it is first necessary to invoke behavioural assumptions about future population, economic, and technological trends. (Such factors are external to the climatic-forecast model, of course, but must be forecast none the less.) Although these may be impossible to forecast with confidence, a set of plausible scenarios can be derived. The differential consequences for the climatic forecast of each of these scenarios can then be evaluated.

Another sort of sensitivity analysis involves building a model which incorporates important, but highly uncertain, variables into its internal structure. Key internal factors, such as the cloud feedback or vertical oceanic mixing parameters, can be varied over a plausible range of values in order to help determine which internal processes have the most importance for the sensitivity of the climate to, say, CO_2 buildup. Even though one cannot be certain which of the simulations is most realistic, sensitivity analyses can: (a) help set up a priority list for further work on uncertain internal model elements, and (b) help to estimate the plausible range of climatic futures to which society may have to adapt over the next several decades. Given these plausible futures, some of us might choose to avoid a low-to-moderate-probability, high-consequence outcome associated with some specific scenario. Indeed, public policy often seeks to avoid plausible, high-cost scenarios. So, too, do people who purchase insurance. On the other hand, more risk-prone people might prefer extra scientific certainty before asking society to invest present resources to hedge against uncertain, even if plausible, climatic futures. At a minimum, cross-sensitivity analysis, in which the response of some forecast variables to multiple variations in uncertain internal and/or external parameters, allows us to examine quantitatively the differential consequences of explicit sets of plausible assumptions.

In any case, even if we cannot produce a reliable single forecast of some future variables, we might be able to provide much more credible sensitivity analyses, which can have practical applications in helping us to investigate a range of probabilities and consequences of plausible scenarios. Such predictions may simply be the best 'forecasts' that honest natural or social scientists can provide to inform society on a plausible range of alternative futures of complex systems.[6] How to react to such information, of course, is in the realm of values and politics.

Let us proceed, then, to several examples of this process.

2.6 Climatic model results

2.6.1 Ancient climates

To investigate future climatic changes, let us first turn, not to the present, but to ancient times. If the same basic models that we use to estimate effects of greenhouse-gas increases into the next century can be applied to the ancient climatic changes (palaeoclimates) and a reasonable simulation is obtained, then both scientific explanation of the palaeoclimate and some verification of the model's ability to reproduce radically different future climatic periods can be obtained.

Three-dimensional atmospheric-circulation-model studies which explicitly resolve land and sea and also explicitly calculate atmospheric motions have been applied to the sequence of climatic changes from the past ice age 18,000 years ago up to the present. One of the most successful palaeoclimatic simulations to date was performed by John Kutzbach and several colleagues at the University of Wisconsin in Madison.[7] Kutzbach attempted to explain the warmest period in recent climatic history, the so-called 'climatic optimum' that occurred between about 5,000 and 9,000 years ago. It was a time when summer-time northern continental temperatures were probably several degrees warmer than at present and monsoon rainfall was more intense throughout Africa and Asia. Kutzbach found that the optimum could be explained simply by the fact that the tilt of the Earth's axis (its obliquity) was slightly greater then than now. Also, the orbit was such that the Earth was closest to the sun (that is, had its perihelion) in June rather than in January as now. These variations, slight perturbations in the Earth's orbit, do not make substantial changes in the annual amount of solar radiation received on the Earth, but do change substantially the difference between winter and summer heating periods. About 5 per cent more solar heat over much of the northern hemisphere in summer, and a comparable amount less in winter, occurred 9,000 years ago compared to the present. This change was sufficient in Kutzbach's simulations to substantially alter mid-continental warming in the summer months, which led to enhanced Asian and African monsoonal rainfall and river run-off in the models.

His results matched quite well with considerable amounts of palaeoclimatic evidence gathered by an international team of scientists,[8] and are helping to explain one of the important mysteries in the palaeoclimatic record. Brian Huntley gives more details of this important work in a later paper in this volume.

2.6.2 Forecasting global warming into the twenty-first century

The most important question surrounding the greenhouse-gas controversy is simply: What will be the regional distribution of climatic changes associated with significant increases in CO_2 and other trace greenhouse gases? (Other trace gases such as chlorofluorocarbons, methane, nitrogen oxides, or ozone can, all taken together, have a comparable greenhouse effect to CO_2 over the next century.)[9] To investigate such possibilities one needs a model with regional resolution. It needs to include processes such as the hydrologic cycle and the storage of moisture in the soils – since these factors are so critical to both climatic change and its impacts on agriculture and water supplies. To investigate plausible climatic scenarios, modellers have typically run 'equilibrium simulations' in which instantaneously increased values of carbon dioxide are imposed at an initial time and held fixed while the model is allowed to approach a new equilibrium.

Syukuro Manabe and R. T. Wetherald, for example, in one of the most widely quoted results (shown in Fig. 2.3), find a summer 'dry zone' in the middle of North America, as well as increased moistness in some of the monsoon belts. All of this was from a doubling of CO_2 held fixed over time. The model was allowed to run several decades of simulated time in order to reach equilibrium. But Manabe's team used an artificially constructed ocean that consisted of a uniform mixed-layer depth of 70 metres with no heat flow to or from the deep ocean below. While this shallow 'sea' allows the seasonal cycle to be satisfactorily simulated (see Fig. 2.1), a purely mixed-layer ocean does not include the important processes whereby water is transported horizontally from the tropics toward the poles or vertically between the mixed layer and the abyssal depths. The latter processes slow the approach toward thermal equilibrium of the surface waters, and certainly would affect the transient evolution of the surface-temperature changes in the ocean due to the actual time-evolving increase of trace greenhouse gases.

Thus, during the transient phase of warming, the surface-temperature increases from latitude to latitude and land to sea could have a different pattern than at equilibrium. This, in turn, could cause significantly different climatic anomalies during the transient phase than would be inferred from equilibrium-sensitivity tests to fixed increases in trace gases.

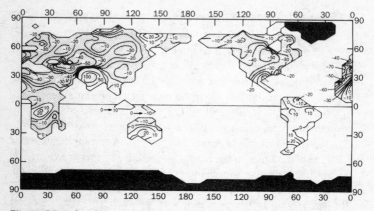

Fig. 2.3. CO_2-induced change in soil moisture expressed as a percentage of soil moisture obtained from a computer model with doubled CO_2 compared to a control run with normal CO_2 amounts. Note the non-uniform response of this ecologically important variable to the uniform change in CO_2.
(Source: S. Manabe and R. Wetherald, 'Reduction in Summer Soil Wetness Induced by an Increase in Atmospheric Carbon Dioxide', Science (1986), vol. 232, p. 626.)

To answer this transient response question more reliably, it has been proposed that three-dimensional atmospheric models be coupled to fairly realistic three-dimensional oceanic models. To date, only a handful of such model experiments have been run,[10] but none over the century-or-two time scale needed to adequately address this important issue. One reason for detailing the CO_2 transient/regional climate-anomaly example here is to exemplify the need for various sensitivity experiments across a hierarchy of models. Such methods are especially essential during the development phase of modelling. In 1980, Starley Thompson and I ran quasi-one-dimensional models to examine the potential importance of this transient issue.[11] However, these models could not provide reliable simulations because of their physical simplicity. But the one-dimensional models were economically efficient enough to be able to be run over the century time-span needed to explore the CO_2 transient issue. Our findings suggested that it is imperative to run high-resolution, coupled atmospheric, oceanic, cryospheric, and land-surface sub-model models if regional, time-evolving scenarios of climatic changes are to have any hope of credibility. On the other hand, the more complex three-dimensional general-circulation models are not yet at an adequate phase of development to have trustworthy coupled atmosphere/ocean models that are both well verified and economical enough to be run over the hundred years needed for greenhouse-gas-transient simulations. Thus, the simple model helps to identify and bound potentially important problems, provide some quantitative sensitivity studies, and help set priorities for three-dimensional coupled model research or needed observational programs over the next few decades. Since the agricultural and other environmental impacts of increasing greenhouse gases depend on the specific regional and seasonal distribution of climatic change, resolution of the transient-climate-response debate, among others, is critical for climatic-impact assessment and ultimate adaptive responses to the advent or prospect of increasing greenhouse gases.

How long might it take to make major progress in such coupled modelling research? Some advocates of delaying a preventive-policy response to the prospect of global warming have suggested that significant progress can be made in only three to five years, given a $100 million boost in research funding.[12] While I agree that enhanced research effort is likely to accelerate progress, it is absurd to talk of reliable regional climate projections in less than decadal time scales. It will take three to five years of expanded research effort just to get the computer power and coupled atmosphere/ocean/ land/ice models running routinely over fifty- to one-hundred-year simulated time frames. Satellite programs to provide data to validate the models are now in the planning stage, but a decade will pass before the needed data will become widely available. Then, some ten to fifteen years from now, if we are lucky and no major scientific or technical obstacles are encountered, scientific consensus may be reached on regional projections. More likely, another five to ten years will be needed to deal with such obstacles that we cannot now foresee. Chapter 11 of IPCC also suggests ten to twenty years as a hopeful time frame for major research progress.[13] Preventive policy can't wait that long, in my opinion.

2.7 The current global-warming debate

However, before discussing any potential management responses to such projections, let me first point out that not all knowledgeable scientists are in agreement as to the probability that such changes will occur. In fact, if one has followed the very noisy, often polemical, debate in the media recently, one might get the (I believe false) impression that there are but two radically opposed schools of thought about global warming: (1) that climatic changes will be so severe, so sudden, and so certain that major species-extinction events will intensify, sea-level rise will create tens of millions of environmental refugees, millions to perhaps billions of people will starve, and devastated ecosystems will be a virtual certainty; or alternatively (2) there is nothing but uncertainty about global warming, no evidence that the twentieth century has done what the modellers have predicted, and the people arguing for change are just 'environmental extremists' – thus, there is no need for any management response to an event that is improbable, and in no case should any such response interfere with the 'free market' and the problems of bankrupt nations.[14] Unfortunately, while such a highly charged and polarized debate makes entertaining opinion-page reading or viewing for the ratings-dominated media, it provides a very poor description of the reality of the actual scientific debate or the broad consensus on basic issues within the scientific community. In my opinion, the 'end of the world' or 'nothing to worry about' are the two least-likely cases, with almost any scenario in between having a higher probability of occurrence.

Fig. 2.4 shows a projection of global-warming possibilities into the twenty-first century drawn by an international group of scientists that was convened in the mid-1980s by the International Council of Scientific Unions. This assessment is very similar to that in the IPCC report. Fig. 2.4 shows warming from a very moderate additional half-degree Celsius up to a catastrophic 5°C or greater warming before the end of the next century. I do not hesitate to call the latter extreme catastrophic, because that is the magnitude of warming that occurred between about 15,000 years ago and 5,000 years ago, the end of the last ice age to our present interglacial epoch. It took nature some 5,000 to 10,000 years to fully accomplish that warming, and it was accompanied by a 100-metre-or-so rise in sea level, thousands-of-kilometres migration of forest species, radically altered habitats, species extinctions, species evolution, and other major environmental changes. Indeed, the ice age-to-interglacial transition revamped the ecological face of the planet.

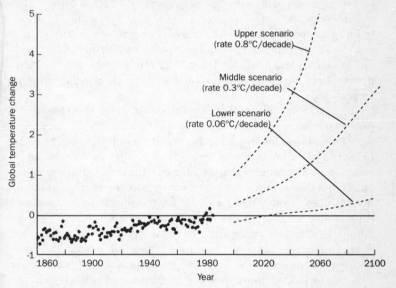

Fig. 2.4. Three scenarios for global temperature change to the year 2100 derived from combining uncertainties in future trace-greenhouse-gas projections with uncertainties of modelling the climatic response to those projections. Sustained global temperature changes beyond 2°C (3.6°F) would be unprecedented during the era of human civilization. The middle-to-upper range represent climatic change at a pace ten to one-hundred times faster than typical long-term natural average rates of global change. (Source: J. Jaeger, Developing Policies for Responding to Climatic Change: a summary of the discussions and recommendations of the workshops held in Villach, 28 September to 2 October 1987.)

If the mid-to-upper part of the scenarios occurred as rapidly as they are projected on Fig. 2.4, then indeed they would justify the substantial concern that many scientists have over the prospect of global warming. On the other hand, the many unknown factors which make most scientists, myself included, hesitant to make anything other than qualitative or intuitive probabilistic kinds of forecasts could well suggest a twenty-first-century climate in which global temperature would change by only a degree or so. While even that seemingly small change might be serious for certain life forms (for example, some plant or animal species living near the tops of mountains, which would be driven to extinction with even a small warming), by and large, changes of less than a degree or so taking place over a century or more would clearly add less stress to natural (and certainly to human) systems than would changes of several degrees taking place in fifty years or less. Indeed, the rate of change may be a most critically important factor to the adaptive capacity of both human and natural systems, particularly the latter, since ecosystems don't have the option of planting new seeds to match the new climate the way our farmers do.[15]

Critics of immediate policy responses to global warming are quick to point out the many uncertainties that could reduce the average projections made by climate models (such as the middle line on Fig. 2.4). Indeed, most climate modellers include similar caveats in their papers, and many of us do resent somewhat the implications of some critics that they are the ones who are responsibly pointing out these uncertainties to the public, whereas the modellers are deliberately suppressing uncertainties in order to overstate the issue.[16] Many critiques[17] somehow understress the fact that the sword of uncertainty has two blades: that is, uncertainties in physical or biological processes which make it possible for the present generation of models to have overestimated future warming effects, are just as likely to have caused the models to have underestimated change.

Other critics[18] have argued that sub-grid-scale processes (namely tropical cumulus convection) could be such strong negative feedbacks as to cut currently assessed global-warming estimates (typically 2–4°C for doubled CO_2) by a factor of four or more. They offered no global-model calculations to back up their assertions. But, if there were a gross error (for example, of a factor of 5) in estimating how cloudiness change, for example, could amplify or damp the models' projections to hypothetical scenarios of increased CO_2, the models would simply be incapable of capturing the seasonal cycle of surface temperature to anywhere near the degree of precision they appear to. Fig. 2.1 showed that, indeed, the seasonal cycle is typically well simulated. Cloudiness changes occur very rapidly. They unfold on a time frame much faster than a season. But effects of the deep-ocean changes take decades or more. Therefore, the seasonal-cycle test is not a direct validation of all potentially important global-warming processes. It is not a test of the reliability of a model forecast of the regional change in storm tracks, for example, which is so critical to land management. On the other hand, the seasonal test does give us, say, a factor of 2 to 3 confidence that the magnitude of global surface-temperature change projected in Fig. 2.4 has a good chance of being correct – indeed, that is why I often refer to the prospect for global warming in the twenty-first century as 'coin-flipping odds of unprecedented change', since a sustained global change of more than 2°C would be unprecedented during the past 10,000-year era of human civilization's development.

Earlier, we noted that A. Raval and V. Ramanathan at the University of Chicago used satellite observations to study the very important water vapour–greenhouse feedback mechanism, a process that is central to most models' estimates of some 3°C (plus or minus 1.5°C) long-term warming from doubling CO_2. They conclude that 'the greenhouse effect is found to increase significantly with sea surface temperature. The rate of increase gives compelling evidence for the positive feedback between surface temperature, water vapour and the greenhouse effect; the magnitude of the feedback is consistent with that predicted by climate models.'[19] In other words, the heat-trapping capacity of the atmosphere is well measured on Earth, and much of the, sometimes polemical, debate in the media over the greenhouse effect has little reality. This empirical confirmation of the natural greenhouse effect and that of climate models stands in stark contrast to the theoretical postulates of the critics, that somehow stabilizing water-vapour feedback processes in parts of the tropics will reduce present model estimates of global warming by a factor of 4 or so.

It is well known that the 25-per-cent increase in carbon dioxide that is documented since the Industrial Revolution, the 100-per-cent increase in methane since the Industrial Revolution, and the introduction of man-made chemicals such as chlorofluorocarbons (also responsible for stratospheric ozone depletion) since the 1950s, should have trapped about two extra watts of radiant energy over every square metre of the Earth. That part is well accepted by most climatological specialists. However, what is less well accepted is how to translate that two watts of heating into 'x' degrees of temperature change, since this involves assumptions about how that heating will be distributed among surface-temperature rises, evaporation increases, cloudiness changes, ice changes, and so forth. The factor of 2 to 3 uncertainty in global temperature-rise projections as cited in typical

US National Academy of Sciences reports or the IPCC reflects a legitimate estimate of uncertainty held by most in the scientific community. Indeed, recent attempts by a British group to mimic the effects of cloud droplets halved their model's sensitivity to doubled CO_2 – but the end result is still well within the often cited 1.5–4.5°C range. However, the authors of the study at the British Meteorological Office wisely pointed out that 'although the revised cloud scheme is more detailed, it is not necessarily more accurate than the less sophisticated scheme'.[20] I have never seen this forthright and important caveat quoted by any of the global-warming critics, who almost always cite the British work as a reason to lower our concern by a factor of 2 or so.

Finally, as stated earlier, prediction of the detailed regional distribution of climatic anomalies, that is, where and when it will be wetter and drier, how many floods might occur in the spring in California or forest fires in Siberia in August, is simply highly speculative, although some plausible scenarios can be given, as is done in the IPCC report[21] or in an earlier assessment (Table 2.1) from a 1987 US National Academy of Sciences committee on possible climate changes following a doubling of CO_2.[22]

Another criticism of global-warming projections has been the non-perfect match between the warming of the Earth and the smooth increase in greenhouse gases over the past hundred years (see Fig. 2.5, bottom portion). It has been alleged that since much of the warming in the twentieth century took place between 1915 and the 1940s followed by a cooling at the very time the global greenhouse gases were building up, the temperature trends in the twentieth century cannot be attributed to greenhouse-gas buildup.

There are actually several flaws in that argument. First, nature fluctuates. Trends of several tenths of a degree Celsius warmings and coolings over decades are part of the natural record, and indeed are normal. Scientists call this 'climatic noise'. These are not predictable as far as anyone can tell, since they appear to be caused by the internal redistribution of energy and chemicals among the principal reservoirs: the atmosphere, oceans, ice, land surfaces, and life. Therefore, natural fluctuations could be a partial explanation of the sharp warming to the 1930s, the cooling to 1975, and possibly even the spectacularly rapid rewarming of the late 1970s into the 1980s – the warmest decade of the instrumental record. Secondly, we do not know precisely what other potential 'forcings' (that is, processes that could force the climate to change) were doing over the past 100 years. These include energy output from the sun, atmospheric particles from volcanic eruptions, or particles generated by human activities.

Table 2.1: Possible climate changes from doubling of CO_2
Source: US National Academy of Sciences

Large Stratospheric Cooling (virtually certain). Reduced ozone concentrations in the upper stratosphere will lead to reduced absorption of solar ultraviolet radiation and therefore less heating. Increases in the stratospheric concentration of carbon dioxide and other radiatively active trace gases will increase the radiation of heat from the stratosphere. The combination of decreased heating and increased cooling will lead to a major lowering of temperatures in the upper stratosphere.

Global-Mean Surface Warming (very probable). For a doubling of atmospheric carbon dioxide (or its radiative equivalent from all the greenhouse gases), the long-term global-mean surface warming is expected to be in the range of 1.5 to 4.5°C. The most significant uncertainty arises from the effects of clouds. Of course, the actual rate of warming over the next century will be governed by the growth rate of greenhouse gases, natural fluctuations in the climate system, and the detailed response of the slowly responding parts of the climate system, i.e., oceans and glacial ice.

Global-Mean Precipitation Increase (very probable). Increased heating of the surface will lead to increased evaporation and, therefore, to greater global-mean precipitation. Despite this increase in global-average precipitation, some individual regions might well experience decreases in rainfall.

Reduction of Sea Ice (very probable). As the climate warms, total sea ice is expected to be reduced.

Polar Winter Surface Warming (very probable). As the sea-ice boundary is shifted poleward, the models predict a dramatically enhanced surface warming in winter polar regions. The greater fraction of open water and thinner sea ice will probably lead to warming of the polar surface air by as much as three times the global-mean warming.

Summer Continental Dryness/Warming (likely in the long term). Several studies have predicted a marked long-term drying of the soil moisture over some mid-latitude interior continental regions during summer. This dryness is mainly caused by an earlier termination of snowmelt and rainy periods, and an earlier onset of the spring-to-summer reduction of soil wetness. Of course, these simulations of long-term equilibrium conditions may not offer a reliable guide to trends over the next few decades of changing atmospheric composition and changing climate.

High-Latitude Precipitation Increase (probable). As the climate warms, the increased poleward penetration of warm, moist air should increase the average annual precipitation in high latitudes.

Rise in Global-Mean Sea Level (probable). A rise in mean sea level is generally expected due to thermal expansion of sea water in the warmer future climate. Far less certain is the contribution due to melting or calving of land ice.

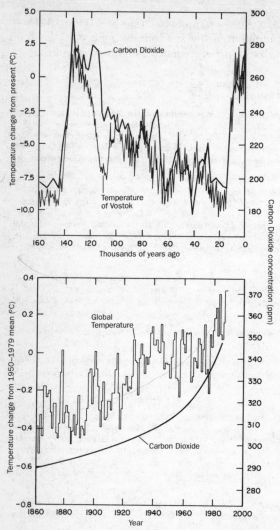

Fig. 2.5. Carbon dioxide and temperature are very closely correlated over the past 160,000 years (top) and, to a lesser extent, over the past 100 years (bottom). The long-term record, based on evidence from Antarctica, shows how the local temperature and atmospheric CO_2 rose nearly in step as an ice age ended about 130,000 years ago, fell almost in synchrony at the onset of a new glacial period, and rose again as the ice retreated about 10,000 years ago. The recent temperature record shows a slight global warming as traced by workers at the Climatic Research Unit of the University of East Anglia. Whether the accompanying buildup of CO_2 in the atmosphere caused the half-degree warming is hotly debated.

This problem of cause and effect, metaphorically, is akin to a criminal investigation in which the whereabouts of only one principal suspect is known, but the whereabouts of other possible, secondary suspects were not carefully observed. In this case, of course, the 'crime' is the 0.5°C (plus or minus 0.2°C) warming trend of the twentieth century, and the known principal 'suspect' is the greenhouse-gas increase, as seen on the bottom of Fig. 2.5. Unfortunately, since we do not have quantitatively accurate ways of measuring precisely what the other potential climatic forcings were (that is, the unwatched other 'suspects'), we can't rule out some possible role for them. Such other forcings include energy output of the sun, sulphur-oxides pollution, land-use changes, and volcanic eruptions.

Furthermore, although some critics have suggested that a century-long heating-up of the sun of a few tenths of a percent could account for the twentieth-century warming of the Earth,[23] these critics often forget to mention that it is equally likely, since it was unmeasured to the required accuracy, that the sun could have cooled down by that amount, thereby having damped some of the greenhouse effect that otherwise would have been in the record, thus fooling us into thinking that the global warming from pollution to date is less than it actually was. Quite simply, the critics can't have it both ways. What we don't know could increase or decrease our estimates.

Some studies[24] have tried to estimate what greenhouse gases, volcanic or solar forcings may have contributed to twentieth-century temperature trends. Indeed, adding all three forcings in such estimates does improve the match of our computer model simulations to observed temperature trends. However, as all these scientists readily admit, without more quantitatively reliable information on what the forcings actually were, these exercises can do nothing more than sketch out plausible, rather than definitive, results. The Intergovernmental Panel on Climate Change[25] also emphasized this difficulty. Nevertheless, the IPCC concluded, once again, that a 1.5 to 4.5°C warming is quite likely to cover what the actual long-term temperature response to CO_2 doubling will be. But most still agree that without ten to twenty more years of thermometer, solar, pollution, and volcanic observations, it will be difficult to pin down anything to 99-per-cent certainty.

Arguing that climate models have been unable to predict a detailed sequence of decade-by-decade temperature fluctuations has,

I have noted, been a favourite tactic of some global-warming critics. But this criticism is akin to arguing that, because we are not able to predict the individual rolls of a pair of dice, we therefore cannot predict the long-term odds of getting any two faces. All gamblers know better! Though we know the statistics for rolling any particular number, we certainly would not be expected to know what sequence of numbers would be obtained on independent rolls.

In the spring of 1990 two NASA scientists[26] made headlines by claiming that their experimental satellite temperature soundings found no global-warming trend in the 1980s. However, no one decade could ever be expected to show a global-warming trend unambiguously greater than climatic noise; a point which they underemphasized, and which was also neglected in most media coverage of their work. Moreover, the Spencer and Christy satellite results actually confirmed, rather than denied, the already published thermometer global surface-temperature-trend analyses in which the early and late 1980s were record warm years, and the mid-1980s were a few tenths of a degree cooler.[27] (Incidentally, these cooler years roughly coincided with a stratospheric aerosol cloud created in 1983 by the major eruption of the El Chicon volcano.)

In short, those arguing that an absence of exact match on a decade-by-decade basis between observed temperature fluctuations and greenhouse gas buildups somehow demonstrates that greenhouse-gas sensitivity of models is wrong, are simply off in their logic since such agreement should not be possible in detail as long as a large degree of climatic noise continues to make up much of the decade-by-decade temperature records. Fortunately, we are now measuring energy output of the sun, eruptions of volcanoes, and other pollution-generated activities, and can thus account better for their effects. Finally, we are watching the other 'suspects'. Thus, as greenhouse gases continue to build up in the future, if greenhouse warming does not take place at roughly the predicted rate during the 1990s and into the 2000s, then indeed it will be possible to argue on the basis of some direct evidence that the effect predicted by current models is off base.

Modellers will continue to develop and refine new models by turning to larger computers to run them and more observations to improve and verify them. We must ask the indulgence of society to recognize that immediate, definitive answers are not likely, as coupling of higher-resolution atmosphere, ocean, ice, land surface, and chemistry submodels will take a decade or more to develop. In essence, what climate models and their applications typify is a growing class of problems not unique to climate but also familiar in other disciplines: nuclear-waste disposal, safety of food additives or drugs, efficacy of strategic defence, and so forth. These are problems for which guaranteed 'scientific' answers cannot be obtained – except by performing the experiment on ourselves. To deal with these complex socio-technical problems requires a new understanding of the central role of (somewhat bounded) uncertainty and the willingness to deal with probabilistic estimation; it also calls for more modelling – provided the context of that modelling is understood and parallel observational programs for validation are concurrently pursued. Efficient functioning of society will depend upon our understanding of both the utility and limitations of models. However, in some senses, more than economic efficiency is at stake, as the very survival of some – particularly in low-lying coastal areas – will depend on present decisions we make to deal with plausible climatic futures.

If the public is totally ignorant of the nature, use, or validity of climatic (or many other kinds of) models, then public policy-making based on model results will be haphazard at best. In this case, the decision-making process tends to be dominated by special interests or a technically trained élite.

Chapter 3
Biogeochemical Feedbacks in the Earth System

David Schimel

" ...Feedbacks between atmosphere and biosphere are non-linear, sensitive to initial conditions, and capable of enormous amplifications. Complex feedbacks in the Earth System can produce unexpected and potent responses ... Without crying wolf, it is worthy of our concern as a society that biogeochemical and ecological feedbacks may result in more rapid environmental change than is predicted by purely physical models... **"**

Many of the greenhouse gases are produced or consumed by life processes. The discipline which studies the production, consumption and circulation of chemicals in the environment by and through the biota is known as biogeochemistry. Biogeochemistry and physical climate can interact to produce feedbacks, if, for example, a change in climate causes an increase or decrease in a greenhouse gas which causes a further change in climate.

Some major uncertainties in predicting the response of global climate to greenhouse forcing result from inadequate understanding of the feedbacks between biogeochemical and physical processes in the Earth System.[1] Some of these feedbacks are geophysical, such as the response of clouds and the hydrological cycle, or the coupling of atmospheric and oceanic heat budgets.[2] Other interactions are biogeochemical; for example, the controls over the oceanic and terrestrial uptake or release of CO_2. The palaeorecord (Earth history read from fossils and rocks) shows unambiguously that changes in biochemistry accompany changes in climate: as shown by the large changes in CO_2 and methane that occur during the onset and retreat of ice ages.[3] While it is difficult to infer and impossible to prove causal relationships between changes in biogeochemistry and in climate from palaeodata, they document a strong relationship between the two.

Greenhouse forcing can be thought of in two parts; the radiative forcing that greenhouse gases exert on the physical climate, and the dynamic forcing to the Earth System that occurs as the effect of the continuously changing greenhouse-gas concentrations. While much attention has been paid to estimating the forcing from a changed but constant CO_2 on climate through radiation, clouds, and the oceanic heat budget, it is the rate of change in forcing that will determine how fast climate will change, and hence much of the impact on humanity. The rate of greenhouse forcing should be one of the better-known aspects of the global-change problem, CO_2 and CFC (chlorofluorocarbon) emissions being relatively predictable or known from industrial statistics.[4] However, greenhouse forcing is determined by the atmospheric burden of gases, which is not the same as the amount emitted. In this chapter, I show that the atmospheric burden of the full suite of biogenic trace gases cannot be well predicted as a function of the industrial input of greenhouse gases to the atmosphere. The atmospheric concentrations of CO_2, methane, nitrous oxide, and other gas species are influenced by a large number of biological processes which will themselves be changing as greenhouse forcing changes. These biological feedbacks should, as best we know, cause acceleration of the greenhouse effect, with one major exception.

3.1 Biogeochemical feedbacks and atmospheric CO_2

The major greenhouse species under direct human influence is, of course, carbon dioxide. CO_2 is produced from fossil-fuel consumption and by organic-matter decomposition, and is consumed by photosynthesis. Exchange with the carbonate cycle in rock and water significantly modulates the cycle, with oceanic uptake of CO_2 being a major sink over years to centuries, and the rock cycle dominating over geological time. Considerable uncertainty exists over the sinks for industrial CO_2, as well as over biological sources, that is, deforestation, land conversion to agriculture, and effects of climatic change. Considerable uncertainty also exists as to how the global carbon cycle will function in the future if atmospheric CO_2 concentration and climate vary from the present.

The changing global environment will change the way in which the terrestrial carbon cycle functions. Enhanced CO_2 will lead to increased photosynthesis – an effect called CO_2 fertilization – under certain conditions. Three factors may limit the significance of this increase. First, it may be transient, as some evidence shows that plants may acclimatize to increased CO_2 and show a gradually decreasing response. This acclimatization should be larger in perennial than annual plants.[5]

Secondly, the effects of CO_2 may be attenuated by constraints from other limiting factors. Nutrients or water may limit CO_2 uptake at levels only slightly greater than under current CO_2 concentrations. The interaction of CO_2 fertilization with other limiting factors requires far more study in a range of ecosystems with varying limiting factors. CO_2 fertilization has the potential to alter nitrogen-use efficiencies by allowing increased enzyme efficiency (photosynthetic enzymes contain large amounts of nitrogen). It can also increase water-use efficiency. Under most circumstances, these changes in water- or nitrogen-use efficiencies will result in the production of plant tissue with reduced content of N and other nutrients. This is because CO_2 fertilization does not enhance nutrient availability through any known mechanism, and with increased efficiency more biomass must be produced on the same amount of nutrients. The production of plant tissue with higher carbon-to-element ratios will increase microbial uptake of nutrients when that tissue is decomposed, competing with plants and reducing nutrient availability.[6] This feedback will tend to reduce the effects of CO_2 fertilization on primary production, homeostatically. We have evaluated the consequences of increasing CO_2 on carbon storage in a grassland model (Fig. 3.1) and found the behaviour described above to apply; that is, feedback through plant-microbial competition for nutrients limited the effects of CO_2-induced increases in resource-use efficiencies.

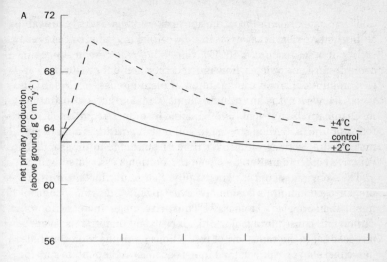

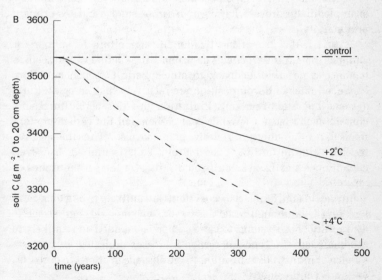

Fig 3.1. We used the Century model[7] to simulate the effects of climate-change on two grassland sites. Mean annual temperatures were increased linearly over fifty years, with changes varying seasonally as described in Schimel et al.[8] (a) Annual above-ground net primary productivity increased in both sites as excess nitrogen was liberated during the decomposition of soil organic matter. As the excess nitrogen was lost, production declined to or below the previous steady state. (b) Soil organic carbon was monotonically lost as a result of increased temperatures.[9]

Third, an extrapolation of the above effect suggests that the availability of terrestrial ecosystems to store carbon is limited by the availability of other resources. If CO_2 were to increase carbon storage in some or most ecosystems, how much carbon could they store? A certain amount of carbon can be stored in plant biomass, especially in wood. However, the maximum biomass of forests is constrained mechanically, by nutrients and light and by human requirements for forest products. Carbon storage in soil organic matter is a more permanent sink, having a turnover time of hundreds to thousands of years. All organic matter, however, has nutrients associated with it, and soil organic matter is usually quite rich in nutrients. For example, nitrogen in humus is generally five to twenty times more concentrated than in plant biomass.[10] Thus, any major increase in soil carbon will constitute a major sink for N and other nutrients, eventually leading to the same sort of restrictions on primary productivity described above. In effect, the humus becomes a competitive sink for nutrients with the plants, and production must decline. Bogs and other wetland areas where peat accumulates are the contemporary examples of this process, having high carbon storage and low primary productivity.

A priori, the use of fertilization in agriculture to support or enhance the direct CO_2 effects on primary production would seem to enhance a negative feedback to atmospheric CO_2 concentration. However, rates of decomposition are relatively high in agricultural systems and rates of carbon stabilization low. Most agricultural soils contain at the most a few per cent carbon and the carbon content tends to decline slowly or stabilize at low levels.[11] Thus the negative feedback due to fertilizing agricultural soils is limited. However, carbon once stabilized in cultivated soils may last for thousands of years.[12]

In conclusion, terrestrial ecosystems are unlikely to be a long-term sink for CO_2, although certain areas for some intervals may so serve. The ability of ecosystems to store carbon is bounded and unlikely to accommodate the types of carbon increases projected as a consequence of industrial civilization in the absence of efforts to curb CO_2 emissions appreciably.

If greenhouse-gas emissions lead to increased temperatures, this will also affect the carbon cycle. Increased temperatures, other factors being equal, will accelerate decomposition and cause loss of stored carbon, increasing the atmospheric inputs of CO_2.[13] In general, decomposition is quite sensitive to temperature.[14] In the recent simulation exercise referred to earlier, we showed that across a range of grasslands, increased temperature resulted in carbon losses despite enhanced production due to CO_2 enrichment (Fig. 3.1). While this result is only for one ecosystem type, other models exhibit similar behaviour for other ecosystems,[15] suggesting it may be a fairly general result. If this is true, then CO_2 fertilization responses (which are problematical, as argued above) may not keep pace with respiration losses resulting from increases in temperature. The positive response of decomposition to temperature constitutes a direct and possibly strong positive feedback from biogeochemistry to physical climate. George Woodwell elaborates further on this possibility in Chapter 5.

3.2 Methane

Methane is a significant greenhouse gas produced during anaerobic decomposition. Principal sources of methane include paddy rice cultivation, wetlands, wild and domestic livestock, termites, natural gas, and other anaerobic environments.[16] Methane is increasing in the atmosphere at a rate of about 1 per cent per year. The causes of this increase are poorly known. Some of it may be due to expanding livestock herds, increasing rice cultivation, and increases in anthropogenic sources such as natural-gas leaks or landfills. Methane is relatively short-lived in the atmosphere, with a lifetime of less than ten years as a result of consumption in the atmosphere and to a small degree in soils.[17] Because consumption is a significant term in the global budget, changes in consumption-rate could also account for part of the increase in atmospheric concentration; that is, either increasing sources, or decreasing sinks, or some combination could be resulting in the observed increase in atmospheric concentrations.

Rice cultivation is currently responsible for 60–140 teragrams per year (Tg/y) of methane emissions out of global total emissions of 400–640 Tg/y.[18] As populations increase in Asia, so too will the area and intensity of rice cultivation; significant increases in rice cultivation are projected in order to feed growing Asian populations.[19] Methane production from rice is related to rice production, details of management, and organic amendments. Schutz showed that methane emissions from rice are the result of very dynamic and inter-active processes, including turnover of the precursor compounds (acetate and CO_2), reoxidation of the methane before emission and transport into the atmosphere.[20] Considerable research is still required before methane emissions from rice can be predicted accurately and management systems to reduce emissions developed. Organic amendments of rice paddy soils are essential to sustaining or increasing yields, and appear to be increasing.[21] Thus, rice will likely remain a strong and increasing source of methane for some time to come. In addition, increasing temperature and moisture should increase methane output from rice paddies, adding a biological positive feedback to the anthropogenic one.

The theme of this chapter is feedbacks between biogeochemistry and radiative forcing: what potential feedbacks exist in the biogeochemistry of methane? Three feedbacks are currently receiving particular scrutiny. First, massive quantities of methane exist in the form of clathrates (or hydrates) – methane trapped in permafrost onshore and offshore in polar regions. Significant warming in the high latitudes could conceivably release these, greatly increasing the methane burden in the atmosphere.[22] The likelihood of this is unknown, though controversial, and some monitoring is required.

Secondly, huge amounts of carbon are stored in soils of northern ecosystems such as tundra and boreal forest. If significant climate warming occurred in these regions, would methane emissions increase, leading to a stronger greenhouse effect and thus positive feedback? At first glance, this should occur, as decomposition rates are temperature-sensitive[23] and increase with temperature. Indeed, significant field data shows that methane fluxes may increase with temperature. However, climate-change in the north could lead to drying out of wetlands, as evaporation and plant transpiration increase. This would lead, probably, to enhanced decomposition and CO_2 release, but could stabilize or reduce methane emissions. This is because methane production requires wet, anaerobic conditions. While warming in the north is almost certain to result in positive feedback via CO_2 release, the role of northern soils in methane generation is unclear and requires better predictions of regional climate-change.[24]

While the controls over methane production in wetlands are understood in a general sense, recent research on the seasonal cycle of methane emissions[25] indicates that emissions of methane are subject to complex control. While temperature is a factor, small-scale environmental controls are also important, and in particular methane fluxes are related to timing of growth, reproduction, and death in marsh vegetation. This dependence on the state of the vegetation, also found in rice culture, suggests that global-change effects on marsh vegetation will affect methane emissions.

Thirdly, the role of soils in methane consumption is undergoing some re-examination. While the global sink strength for methane in soils is low relative to sources and consumption in the atmosphere, it could be significant relative to the increasing trend. Recently, Melillo and colleagues showed that chronic additions of nitrogen to forest ecosystems, as occurs in acid-precipitation-affected areas, can affect trace-gas exchange.[26] In particular, increasing nitrogen availability may competitively inhibit methane oxidation in soils. Thus, as the area of ecosystems impacted by acid precipitation increases, the role of these areas in methane consumption should decrease. This may also occur in areas converted to agriculture and fertilized. This process, the nitrogen inhibition of methane uptake, is not significant to the atmospheric concentration of methane, but may influence the rate of increase in the atmosphere. Since the lifetime, and hence the global-warming potential, of methane is strongly influenced by them, any change in the sinks for methane should be viewed with concern. The N-fertilization methane-consumption connection is a sobering example of how interconnected biogeochemical cycles of the elements are, and how large is the potential for surprise.

3.3 Nitrous oxide

Nitrous oxide is produced in soils; about 90 per cent of global N_2O emissions are thought to be from soils. Its potential contribution to global warming is large because it is an effective absorber of infrared radiation and very long-lived in the atmosphere; a recent conference assigned it a potential for thermal absorption of 150 relative to 1 for CO_2.[27] It is currently thought to contribute about 5 per cent to radiative forcing. However, although the biology of N_2O is relatively well known, '... the budget for the N_2O-exchange between terrestrial ecosystems and the atmosphere is largely unknown'.[28] That is, the geographic distribution and magnitude of sources are poorly known. This ignorance, coupled with N_2O's long atmospheric lifetime and hence effect on greenhouse forcing, makes it a priority for additional research.

As noted above, our understanding of the N_2O budget is very limited but data indicate that increases in the rate of nitrogen cycling, as could be expected in a warmer, wetter world, could lead to increases in emissions.[29] Mankind has already increased global nitrogen cycling through fertilization, and enhanced decomposition and industrial emissions by a substantial fraction, 50 per cent in some estimates. It is surprising the N trace-gas emissions have increased as little as they have; the potential for large changes in N_2O emissions is real. Disturbance and land conversion in the tropics may also lead to enhanced emissions of N_2O, linking this gas to the more general problems of deforestation and land conversion. N_2O is an area for priority research and monitoring, especially in areas undergoing rapid environmental change.

3.4 The chemistry–cloudiness interaction

Recently, Charlson *et al.*[30] suggested that emissions of di-methyl-sulphide (DMS) from marine plankton could act as a global thermostat. The basic mechanism proposed is as follows: (1) Marine emissions of DMS are a major source of sulphate to the marine atmosphere, and sulphate aerosols are the major source of cloud-condensation nuclei in the marine atmosphere;[31] (2) Increasing sulphate aerosols will lead to increasing cloudiness, and resultant cooler ocean-surface temperatures; (3) This will eventually lead to reduced plankton activity, hence reduced DMS emissions, closing the loop (Fig. 3.2).

To expand on the above, DMS is produced by marine phytoplankton (algae) as a by-product of their metabolism. DMS is the predominant marine volatile sulphur compound in the oceans and its exchange is a significant factor in the global sulphur cycle. Its current distribution in the global ocean is fairly well understood, but how it could change in distribution or amount is not well quantified.[32] DMS is thought to be produced as a by-product of the osmoregulation of planktonic cells, or their adjustment to salt. DMS is thus produced as a by-product of one of the fundamental processes in marine plankton,

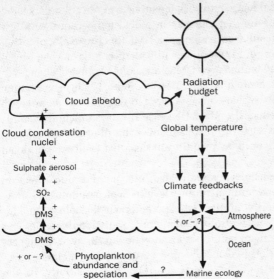

Fig. 3.2.
A schematic diagram of the Di-methyl-sulphide-mediated cloud–climate feedback.[32] Note the dependence of the cycle on the response of marine ecology and phyto-plankton speciation.

but certain groups predominate, chiefly the coccolithforids. Because of the dependence on species of plankton, the feedback via DMS involves the population dynamics of marine organisms. Andreae has also proposed that DMS emissions are related to marine nitrogen levels.[33]

After its emission to the atmosphere, DMS undergoes a complex series of chemical reactions with various oxidizing chemicals in the atmosphere. In general, however, DMS is oxidized to methane-sulphonic acid and SO_2. SO_2 is rapidly converted to sulphate in the marine atmosphere. These two chemicals form aerosols; that is, they form tiny droplets of water containing the sulphur compound. Sulphur-containing aerosols form the majority of cloud-condensation nuclei over the oceans. Cloud-condensation nuclei are the particles (aerosols in this case) around which droplets of water condense to form cloud-water droplets. These cloud-water droplets scatter solar radiation, resulting in a net reflection of solar energy back to space. Increasing emissions of DMS should lead to more condensation nuclei, cloudiness should increase with the abundance of condensation nuclei, and this should result in cooling because of the high reflectivity of marine clouds. The global radiation balance, and hence mean global temperature, is sensitive to marine clouds. Model calculations indicate that changes in global temperature of a few degrees should result from a change in DMS flux by a factor of 2.[34]

Several factors could complicate this picture; for example, warming might not lead to increased DMS emissions because of changes in plankton species away from high DMS emitters. Changes in oceanic nutrients due to global-change-altered ocean-current circulation patterns could reduce the effect. Decreased evaporation under clouds might counteract the DMS enhancement of cloudiness. None the less, this mechanism could be a significant negative feedback on global warming.

This negative feedback should lead to a 'thermostatic' effect on mean global temperature, damping the effects of greenhouse forcing. While many factors complicate this potential feedback loop, including interactions with hydrology, plankton population dynamics and the physics of aerosol cloudiness interactions, this type of biogeophysical interaction is plausible, and may represent a class of processes whose composite effect controls the sensitivity of the physical-climate system to biogeochemical perturbation. It is worth noting that while increases in cloudiness may stabilize mean global temperature, they will also reduce the average solar irradiance at the sea surface and increase the variance of incoming radiation; both of these outcomes would likely reduce marine primary productivity.

This is one of the few postulated stabilizing feedbacks in the biogeochemistry physical-climate system. Note that present-day anthropogenic sulphate emissions act as a negative forcing to global warming, as the IPCC scientists describe.[35]

3.5 Non-linear atmosphere–biosphere feedbacks

Feedbacks between atmosphere and biosphere are non-linear, sensitive to initial conditions, and capable of enormous amplifications. Complex feedbacks in the Earth System can produce unexpected and potent responses. Several responses have been observed that may be signs of early warnings of such phenomena: Antarctic ozone depletion, the increasing amplitude of the CO_2 seasonal cycle, or the unexplained sources of nitrous oxide. A few generalizations emerge concerning interactions between the biota and the physical environment.

First, with respect to a single variable, organism response is often described by a 'subsidy-stress curve', where increasing the value of the variable (for example temperature or nitrogen) increases activity up to some level at which point stress is induced. Neither temperature, water, nor nutrients have linear effects on organisms over the range of variation found in nature.

Secondly, controls over biological activity are interactive. For example, increasing temperature may increase photosynthetic enzyme activity but induce water stress in plants at some soil-moisture levels but not at others. Thus, the effect of temperature on CO_2 exchange is a function of water availability. Complex interactions occur with respect to trace-gas evolution generally. As an example, consider the controls over nitrous oxide emission. Increasing temperature increases both inorganic nitrogen production and nitrous oxide emission. However, a sustained temperature increase can lead to depletion of organic substrate; and the effect of temperature on gas production over time is a function of initial substrate amount and turnover. Interactions also occur with increasing water; as water increases denitrification increases. Nitrous oxide production peaks, however, at intermediate water contents because under saturating conditions most of the nitrous oxide is consumed and further reduced to nitrogen.

A third type of non-linear interaction occurs as a result of changes in biological species composition. Changing environmental conditions can cause replacement of one species or group of species by another, with effects on atmosphere–biosphere exchange. For example, DMS is predominantly produced by one group of phytoplankton, the coccolithoforids. DMS production can change radically when sea-water geochemistry or biology changes to favour or inhibit these organisms. In terrestrial systems, the amount and nature of secondary compounds emitted, such as the various non-methane hydrocarbons, is specific to certain taxa of plants. Replacement of one group of plants by another can lead to complete change in regional hydrocarbon emissions. Changes due to species interactions can be binary, and may cause trace-gas exchange to respond in the opposite direction to that predicted from the sign of the change in the forcing function.

3.6 Conclusions

Feedbacks in the Earth System occur over a range of time-scales. Processes within the atmosphere have the shortest response times. The response of the cloud system to increased heat storage can be thought of as virtually instantaneous in the context of decadal changes in forcing. The coupling of atmospheric heating to marine heat transport is not well understood, but probably operates on annual to decadal time-scales.[36] Time-scales of change in biogeochemical cycles vary from near-annual responses in photosynthesis and microbial processes to rates of change associated with terrestrial carbon storage, which will change over decadal to millennial times.

These rates of change must be considered when evaluating uncertainty associated with global change. Current attention is focused on feedbacks in the physical climate and hydrological-cycle subsystems of the Earth System.[37] These uncertainties must be resolved for General Circulation Models of the atmosphere-ocean to be quantitatively useful. In the longer term, uncertainty associated with biogeochemical cycles must also be addressed. There are two reasons for this. First, the 'airborne fraction' of CO_2 – that portion of industrial release retained in the atmosphere – is very sensitive to changes in marine and terrestrial uptake by the biota. Thus, the carbon cycle must be modelled to make predictions of the atmospheric-heating term in the climate-change equation when simulating decadal changes. Simulation of changes in the carbon cycle over ten to fifty years will be a major challenge to the biological community, but one which must be met.

Secondly, most of the atmosphere–biosphere feedbacks now under study result in positive feedback, or worsening of global warming. The strength of many of these feedbacks is not known, and study of the coupled systems is in its infancy. Without crying wolf, it is worthy of our concern as a society that biogeochemical and ecological feedbacks may result in more rapid environmental change than is predicted by purely physical models.

We are not now able to manage the impacts of biogeochemical feedbacks very well, as many of them are the result of processes distributed over large areas, resulting from broad climate-change, agriculture, or regional-scale atmospheric pollution.[38] We need both better understanding of processes as they are expressed in large spatial scales, and the political-economic structures for implementing changes that affect large areas and 'non-point source' impacts on the environment. Management must begin to take into account the great degree of coupling that occurs between spatially separated parts of the global system.[39]

3.7 Recommendations

Presenting the arguments for a strong role of biogeochemical feedbacks in climate change is often frustrating because on the one hand, one must present complex and often counter-intuitive arguments as to how the interactions occur, whilst on the other hand, the palaeo-record presents us with clear evidence that biogeochemistry and climate are strongly coupled together. What is needed to clarify the issues in this area? Below I list a few ideas:

1. We need some large-scale experiments designed to 'preview ' the effects of changing CO_2 and climate, sustained over a decade or so. The US National Science Foundation's Long Term Ecological Research Program has proposed that experiments be initiated in a range of ecosystems to test the direct effects of sustained CO_2 increase on plant and soil processes. This same group has proposed that long-term soil-warming experiments be done to test the soil carbon-nutrient-productivity ideas described above. Large-scale experiments have been central to the debate on acid deposition (whole lake studies in Sweden, the US and Canada) and are needed in the global-change area. Experiments such as these, conducted in different areas to establish general relationships, would be powerful in analysing the sensitivity of ecosystems and would provide graphic examples for presentation to policy-makers and the public.

2. We need to do a better job of representing, at least schematically, feedbacks in models of the climate and the Earth System. Stephen Schneider writes in this volume of the role of sensitivity analysis and scenarios with respect to climate models. Such sensitivity analyses could be performed using representations of biogeochemical feedbacks to evaluate their significance in controlling the rate of climate-change. Development of models capable of conducting such analyses should be accelerated and used for guidance in research and policy.

3. Biogeochemistry directly links global change with commodities of concern to people. Changes in terrestrial productivity and carbon budgets translate directly into production of food and fibre, with the largest changes likely in those societies least able to use technological remedies. Decreases in soil carbon storage affect the global CO_2 budget but also translate into reduced fertility, increased erosion, and deteriorating water quality. The term 'biogeochemistry' does not convey much meaning to many citizens and policy-makers, but who should be concerned about biogeochemical interactions? Farmers, foresters, and users of forest products, those concerned with water quality and the cleanliness of the air, all have direct interests in the biogeochemical consequences of global change, yet these concerns have not been clearly articulated to policy-makers and the public. This communication must be improved, and the consequences of changing biogeochemistry (that is, soil fertility, water quality, greenhouse feedbacks) included in policy debates.

4. The global nitrogen cycle should receive more attention. Human-induced changes to the global nitrogen budget are as large or larger proportionately than in the carbon cycle. Nitrous oxide has an effect on global warming variously estimated as 150[40] to 300[41] times that of CO_2. The budget of nitrous oxide is virtually unknown, except for the rate of increase in the atmosphere. Nonlinearities in nitrogen-cycling could greatly increase nitrous-oxide emissions, given the human acceleration of the global nitrogen cycle. In addition to nitrous oxide, biogenic emissions of nitric oxide are significant, although very poorly quantified. Nitric oxide is a major control over tropospheric ozone, and changes in nitric-oxide emissions could have significant impacts on tropospheric chemistry with implications for many important trace-gas species. The state of knowledge of the global nitrogen cycle is such that we cannot reliably predict changes to nitrogen cycling. This deficiency must be remedied; the global nitrogen cycle should receive attention in the near future comparable to that of the carbon cycle.

Chapter 4
Halting Global Warming

Mick Kelly

" ...The combined effect of the elimination of chlorofluorocarbon production [and all related substitute chemicals] by the year 1995, a halt to deforestation by the year 2000, and a 50-per-cent reduction in fossil-fuel emissions by the year 2030 would be to reduce the future rate of warming by more than a third compared to the business-as-usual projection. But the effective carbon dioxide content of the atmosphere continues to rise. In order to reach the goal of stabilization, further measures are needed... "

The purpose of the study described in this chapter is to identify a set of reductions in greenhouse-gas emissions which could halt global warming, thereby providing a necessary bench-mark against which targets influenced by political pragmatism can be judged. On the basis of environmental need, a stable climate subject only to natural variability must be the goal if the security of life on Earth is to be ensured.

Basing policy targets on a tolerable rate of warming, if that can be defined, can only be acceptable in the short term. As long as warming continues, adaptation will have to occur whatever the rate of change.

Can stable ecosystems develop when the environment is constantly changing? What set of climatic conditions will humanity plan for? Once critical thresholds are passed, adaptation may no longer be possible. The aim must be to keep the rate and duration of adaptation as short as possible, thereby minimizing adverse impacts.

If a stable climate is to be achieved, the first requirement must be to halt the rise in the greenhouse-gas content of the atmosphere so that no further enhancement of the greenhouse effect occurs. The precise aim of this study, then, is to define what is needed to halt the rise in the 'effective carbon dioxide concentration' of the atmosphere. The effective carbon dioxide concentration takes into account the contribution of all the major greenhouse gases, each individual contribution being specified in terms of the concentration of carbon dioxide that would enhance the greenhouse effect to the same extent. Once the effective carbon dioxide content has been stabilized, climate should eventually reach a stable state. It is important to note that this will not occur immediately, as the climate system responds slowly to changes in the composition of the atmosphere.

The level at which global temperature does ultimately stabilize will be significantly higher than the level prevailing in the pre-industrial period prior to the nineteenth century, when there was little human influence on climate. It may be that processes are initiated which result in further climatic change even though no additional enhancement of the greenhouse effect occurs. The issue then will be whether or not further measures should be taken to decrease the strength of the greenhouse effect and stabilize climate at a level closer to the pre-industrial norm. The immediate goal, though, must be to halt the current rise in the strength of the greenhouse effect.

In order to demonstrate what could be achieved if immediate action were to be taken, progressive measures are specified over the period to 2020 which will ensure that the effective carbon dioxide content of the atmosphere stabilizes by the mid-twenty-first century. This time-frame, although ambitious, is consistent with the implementation of large technological projects and the time-scale of change in socio-economic structures. The issue of feasibility is considered in later chapters in this volume.

The analysis takes as its starting point an emission-reduction scenario which is based on measures which should be adopted as they are eminently justifiable on grounds that are already established.

Additional measures are then incorporated, until a single strategy – the 'stabilizing' scenario – is developed which would halt the rise in the effective carbon dioxide content of the atmosphere. A series of computer models developed in the Climatic Research Unit at the University of East Anglia is used to assess the effect of the emission-reduction scenarios on the composition of the atmosphere and on global temperature.

■ Initially, the 'first-step' scenario considers the effects of eliminating the production of chlorofluorocarbons and related chemicals, and halting deforestation.

■ Secondly, the '50-per-cent' scenario adds control of energy-related carbon dioxide emissions, along the lines broadly suggested by the 1988 Toronto Conference, *The Changing Atmosphere*.

■ Finally, the 'stabilizing' scenario strengthens the carbon dioxide targets and adds control targets for methane and nitrous oxide to achieve the goal of stabilizing the effective carbon dioxide concentration of the atmosphere.

A 'business-as-usual' scenario is developed as a baseline against which to compare the effectiveness of these scenarios.

In assessing the consequences of these scenarios, the analysis is based on the latest consensus science, including allowance for key uncertainties, as documented in a series of reports during the mid-1980s,[1] the EPA report, *Policy Options for Stabilizing Global Climate*, published in 1989,[2] and additional references cited where relevant.

Various parameters and estimates have been revised as part of the work of the Intergovernmental Panel of Climate Change.[3] Relevant to this study are revisions being made to the historical record of greenhouse-gas concentrations and to the radiative forcing associated with concentration changes. Consideration of the interim results of this process indicates that it is unlikely that any of these changes will alter significantly the general conclusions of the present report. Further details are in a technical appendix to this study, which is available in expanded form as a Special Report from Greenpeace International.[4]

4.1 Modelling the changing atmosphere

4.1.1 Atmospheric composition

Reducing emissions of carbon dioxide, methane, nitrous oxide, and the chlorofluorocarbons (notably, CFC-11 and CFC-12) must be the focus of any attempt to curb global warming. These gases account for around 90 per cent of the enhancement of the greenhouse effect that has already occurred (Fig. 4.1). In order to determine what is necessary to stabilize the effective carbon dioxide concentration of the atmosphere and thereby halt global warming, a series of decade-by-decade reduction targets for these gases are specified and the effects on the composition of the atmosphere and global surface air-temperature are modelled.

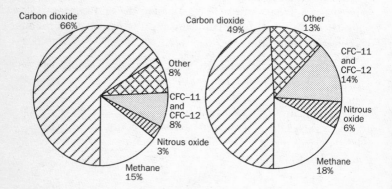

Fig. 4.1. Percentage contribution of the different greenhouse gases to global warming: a. 1880–1980; b. 1980s. 'Other' includes tropospheric ozone, halons, and stratospheric water vapour.
(Source: *D. A. Lashof and D. A. Tirpak (eds.),* Policy Options for Stabilizing Global Climate *[Environmental Protection Agency, Washington, DC, 1989].)*

Predicting the manner in which greenhouse-gas emissions will affect the atmospheric composition is not a simple matter. Emission rates, whether from human or natural sources, are uncertain. The physical, chemical, and biological processes that remove greenhouse gases from the atmosphere are poorly understood. The record of past variations, crucial if theoretical models are to be tested, is short.

Moreover, the manner in which the production and removal of the gases may be affected by future changes in the composition of the atmosphere and in climate is uncertain. To what extent will other pollutants affect the removal of methane from the atmosphere by hydroxyl radicals? Will the oceans become more, or less, effective as a sink for carbon dioxide? Will rising temperature trigger additional releases of methane from now-frozen ground in polar regions?

Even the most sophisticated models of the effects of emissions on atmospheric concentrations have deficiencies. They are research tools, used primarily to improve understanding of the relevant processes rather than as a means of firm prediction.[5]

The models used in this study – as in most other studies of this nature – are based on the most essential processes alone, in order to reduce the influence of additional sources of uncertainty resulting from the inclusion of poorly understood mechanisms. They are, however, sufficiently accurate to determine the broad consequences of emission reductions. Their simplicity means that they do not require lengthy computer time and can be run many times in 'sensitivity studies' in order to test the influence of key assumptions.

In the case of carbon dioxide and the chlorofluorocarbons, the models explicitly relate emissions and production, respectively, to atmospheric concentration.

The carbon dioxide model is based on the assumption of a fixed 'airborne fraction' of 50 per cent.[6] This means that half the carbon emitted as a result of human activity remains in the atmosphere, consistent with the historical record. A sensitivity study is undertaken to examine the implications of a varying airborne fraction. The proportion of carbon remaining in the atmosphere may drop below 50 per cent if emissions are reduced substantially.

The chlorofluorocarbon model, developed in the Climatic Research Unit by Wigley,[7] simulates the consequences of the variable production of CFC-11 and CFC-12. Other chlorofluorocarbons and related chemicals are accounted for by increasing the enhancement of the greenhouse effect caused by CFC-11 and CFC-12 by a fixed percentage. The accuracy of this model may be affected if substantial reductions in CFC-11 and CFC-12 production occur. While a reasonable approximation as far as the present-day situation is concerned, the model will underestimate the overall contribution of the chlorofluorocarbons in the event that substitutes for CFC-11 and

CFC-12 which are themselves greenhouse gases are deployed. For the sake of convenience, the term 'chlorofluorocarbons' is used in this chapter to denote CFC-11, CFC-12, and all related ozone-depleting chemicals.

As far as methane and nitrous oxide are concerned, theoretical models of the relationship between emissions and atmospheric composition are severely limited and estimates tend to be based on empirical relationships derived from past evidence.[8] The formulations used in this study are based on the extrapolation of past trends in atmospheric concentration. Reduction scenarios are specified in terms of a proportionate decrease in the annual rise in concentration that would have occurred had recent trends continued.

Following the methodology developed in the Climatic Research Unit by Warwick and Wilkinson,[9] emissions are specified for fixed ten-year planning periods (to 2000, 2010, 2020, and so on) in the case of carbon dioxide, methane, and nitrous oxide. Targets for the end of each planning period are implemented linearly over the preceding ten years. (While exponential trends may be considered more realistic, the precise formulation makes little difference to the overall results.) In the case of the chlorofluorocarbons, the date by which a percentage reduction target is achieved is specified to allow for the possibility of rapid cuts prior to the end of the present century. All emission-reduction targets are global in nature.

The output of this suite of models is a year-by-year projection of the atmospheric concentration of the major greenhouse gases over the period 1991 to 2050. The rise in the concentration of each gas is then converted into the radiative forcing it would generate – the enhancement of the greenhouse effect – and the increase in forcing, totalled for all the greenhouse gases, is expressed in terms of the effective carbon dioxide concentration. This is the amount of carbon dioxide that would have the same effect. It is important to note that it is this parameter that is to be stabilized, not necessarily the concentrations of the individual greenhouse gases.

No account is taken of the contribution of ozone, stratospheric water vapour, and other minor greenhouse gases. While this means that the results of this analysis may underestimate the effective carbon dioxide concentration, the effect is not substantial and is comparable to the many other sources of uncertainty in the projections.

4.1.2 Global climate

In order to assess how the change in atmospheric composition will affect global temperature, use is made of a model of the basic elements of the climate system developed in the Climatic Research Unit by Wigley and Raper.[10] The model incorporates a simplified ocean which enables it to simulate the role of the oceans in delaying the response of surface air-temperature to any change in atmospheric composition. This is known as a 'transient response' simulation.

The transient response is important because the enhancement of the greenhouse effect warms both the atmosphere and the upper layers of the ocean. The oceans heat up more slowly than the atmosphere, due to their higher thermal inertia, and this delays, or damps, the atmospheric response. Energy that would otherwise have been available to heat the air is taken up by the oceans. As a result, the full effect of any change in atmospheric composition as far as surface air-temperature is concerned may not be seen until many decades have passed and a balance, or equilibrium, between the oceans and the atmosphere is reached.

This means that only a proportion of the atmospheric warming that will eventually be generated by the current greenhouse-gas content of the atmosphere will have been realized at any point in time. The effect on climate of a particular greenhouse-gas content of the atmosphere can, therefore, be expressed in two ways: in terms of the realized warming – the transient response – or in terms of the equilibrium temperature once the point of balance has been reached.

Two aspects of a model of this nature are critical in determining the simulated response of the climate system to enhancement of the greenhouse effect: the climate sensitivity and the absorption of heat by the oceans.[11]

The climate sensitivity is a measure of the degree to which 'feedback' will amplify or reduce the basic radiative effect of the greenhouse gases, and is subject to considerable uncertainty, as is described in Chapters 1 and 2 of this book. For example, cloud cover may alter in character as temperatures rise. This may result in positive feedback as certain cloud types increase the insulation of the surface of the planet, trapping more heat, or negative feedback as other types of cloud reflect more solar energy away from the surface. The net effect is difficult to establish, although it is believed to be positive. The range of plausible estimates of the climate sensitivity, varying by a factor of 3, is the major source of uncertainty in this series of models.

As noted above, the absorption of heat by the oceans affects the delay in the atmospheric response. In the model used in this study, it is particularly affected by the diffusion rate, upwelling velocity, and the temperature of the water sinking during bottom-water formation.

In order to illustrate the range of uncertainty in the climate projections, results are presented for three cases – 'upper', 'central', and 'lower', defined in Table 4.1 – spanning the plausible range of estimates in the climate sensitivity and the diffusion rate.[12] These are not the only sources of uncertainty in the climate model but serve to demonstrate the point that there is a considerable range of possibilities as far as the rate of future warming is concerned.

Table 4.1: Key parameters in the global temperature simulations

Case	Doubling temperature (°C)	Diffusivity (cm²s⁻¹)
Lower	1.5	2.0
Central	3.0	1.0
Upper	4.5	0.5

Note: The climate sensitivity is specified in terms of the 'doubling temperature' – the equilibrium-temperature rise associated with a doubling of carbon dioxide concentrations. A higher ocean diffusivity means a slower atmospheric response.

cm^2s^{-1} = square centimetre per second

The climate model takes as its input estimates of the effective carbon dioxide concentration, converts these estimates into radiative forcing,[13] and calculates the global surface air-temperature likely to prevail in each year. This is the realized warming or transient response. It also calculates year-by-year the temperature that would prevail once the climate system reached equilibrium with the atmospheric composition in that year. This is referred to here as the equilibrium temperature. The model simulation covers the period 1765 to 2050, using historical concentrations for the period to 1990[14] and projections for the period 1991 to 2050. All temperature estimates are expressed as a departure from the pre-industrial level, defined as the temperature prevailing in 1765.

It is important to bear in mind that the projections made using these models cannot be considered definite forecasts. There are too many uncertainties involved in modelling the climatic response to greenhouse-gas emissions. The fact that estimates are, at times, quoted to a precision of one or two decimal places is simply to facilitate the comparison of results and should not be taken as an expression of accuracy. The projections are, however, of sufficient accuracy to indicate the relative effectiveness of the various control strategies under discussion. The implications of key uncertainties are documented where relevant, and further details of the models can be found in the full report of this study.[15]

4.2 Business as usual

Before identifying a strategy that will stabilize the greenhouse effect, the likely outcome if current emission trends were to continue without action to curb releases of the major greenhouse gases is considered. This is the 'business-as-usual' projection. It provides a point of reference for the reduction scenarios.

In developing the business-as-usual projection, it is assumed that:

■ Carbon dioxide emissions resulting from fossil-fuel combustion will grow at a rate of 1 per cent a year over the period to 2050;[16]

■ The annual contribution of the biosphere through land-use modification and related factors (essentially the balance between deforestation and reforestation) will increase linearly from 0.8 petagrams (800 million metric tons) of carbon in 1990 to 2.05 Pg in 2040 before declining to 1.8 Pg of carbon in 2050, following the 'Slowly Changing World' projection developed by the US Environmental Protection Agency;[17]

■ Methane concentrations will rise at a constant 16 parts per billion volume (ppbv) a year and nitrous oxide concentrations at a constant 0.8 ppbv a year, in line with recent experience;

■ In the case of the chlorofluorocarbons, there will be full compliance with the Montreal Protocol of 1987 on the part of all producer nations,[18] and the use of substitutes that are greenhouse gases will be avoided.

This is not an extreme set of assumptions. For example, no account is taken of the possibility that there may be an acceleration of recent trends if the world follows a high-energy pathway.[19] It represents the middle ground. There are, however, two aspects of the projection which warrant further discussion. These concern uncertainties in the biospheric contribution and its future history, and the consequences of the phase-out of CFC-11 and CFC-12 production.

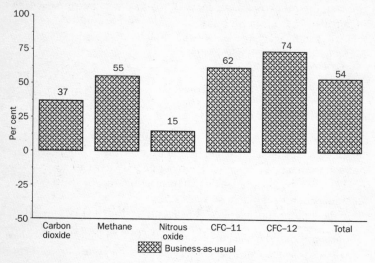

Fig. 4.2. Business-as-usual projection of the percentage change in greenhouse-gas concentrations over the period 1990–2050. 'Total' is the effective carbon dioxide concentration. The concentrations in the year 2050 are: carbon dioxide, 486 ppmv; methane, 2,694 ppbv; nitrous oxide, 364 ppbv; CFC-11, 461 pptv; CFC-12, 849 pptv; and effective carbon dioxide, 634 ppmv.

(Note: ppmv = parts per million volume, ppbv = parts per billion volume, pptv = parts per trillion volume).

The assumption of a present-day release of 0.8 Pg (800 million metric tons) of carbon a year from the biosphere is consistent with the airborne fraction and pre-industrial atmospheric concentration of carbon dioxide assumed in this study.[20] While there is evidence to suggest that the current release is higher – perhaps approaching 2 Pg of carbon a year[21] – the atmospheric concentration in 2050 is unlikely to be too different if this were the case. Deforestation levels would decline, rather than rise, over the period to 2050, as remaining forested areas were exhausted more rapidly. Moreover, a lower airborne fraction would have to be assumed to ensure consistency with the past record of emissions and atmospheric concentration.

In projecting chlorofluorocarbon concentrations, it is assumed that all producer nations – including those currently classed as low producers or users – will adhere to the current terms of the 1987 Montreal Protocol as they apply to high-producer nations. In effect, this anticipates some strengthening of the current provisions of the agreement.

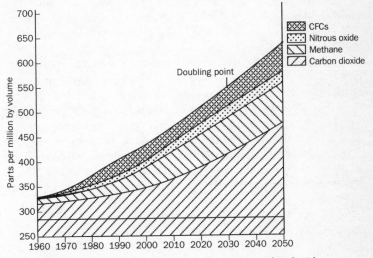

Fig. 4.3. Business-as-usual projection of the trend in effective carbon dioxide concentration. The relative contribution of the different gases is shown. The pre-industrial baseline is indicated by the horizontal bar.

It is also assumed that there will be no use of substitutes that are themselves greenhouse gases as the major chlorofluorocarbons are phased out. In an extreme case in which HCFC-22, for example, is deployed to compensate totally for reduced use of CFC-11 and CFC-12, the radiative forcing – the enhancement of the greenhouse effect – due to HCFC-22 could significantly offset the reduction in forcing projected in the business-as-usual scenario as production of CFC-11 and CFC-12 is eliminated.[22] For the purposes of this scenario it is assumed that this outcome will be avoided. In later scenarios, avoidance of substitutes that are greenhouse gases (HCFCs, HFCs) becomes an explicit policy target.

Fig. 4.2 shows the change in the atmospheric concentrations of the major greenhouse gases resulting from the business-as-usual scenario. By 2050, the carbon dioxide concentration increases by 37 per cent of the present value; methane by 55 per cent; nitrous oxide by 15 per cent; CFC-11 by 62 per cent; and CFC-12 by 74 per cent. The effective carbon dioxide concentration reaches double the pre-industrial baseline during the early 2030s, as illustrated in Fig. 4.3, and rises to 634 ppmv by the year 2050, 54 per cent above the 1990 value. The most striking feature of the relative contribution of each gas is that the chlorofluorocarbons continue to make a substantial contribution, despite the reduction in production due to the Montreal Protocol.

At present, the effective carbon dioxide concentration is rising at a rate of 3 to 4 per cent every five years. This is well above the rate of change characteristic of earlier decades, reflecting the rapid increase in emissions since 1950. As far as atmospheric pollution is concerned, the developments of the past forty years mark as important a stage as the industrial revolution. In terms of radiative forcing, the current rate of change means that the greenhouse effect is being enhanced at the rate of 8 per cent every five years, clearly illustrating the penalty associated with any delay in action to curb global warming.

The concentration projections resulting from the business-as-usual scenario are, for the most part, consistent with those associated with the 'Slowly Changing World' scenario developed by the US Environmental Protection Agency (EPA).[23] The 'Slowly Changing World' scenario assumes a continuation of the recent experience of modest economic growth with no concerted action in response to global warming. The chlorofluorocarbon projections are considerably lower than those of the EPA study, which are based on more pessimistic assumptions concerning the effectiveness of the Montreal Protocol.

The effect on global surface air-temperature is shown in Fig. 4.4. This is the realized warming, taking into account the delaying effect of the oceans. As described in the previous section, a range of values is given for any point in time to illustrate the range of uncertainty in the climate projections. In the following discussion, the temperature projection based on the 'central' values of the climate sensitivity and ocean diffusivity is given first, followed by the margin of uncertainty defined by the 'lower' and 'upper' values. All temperature estimates are expressed as deviations from the pre-industrial level.

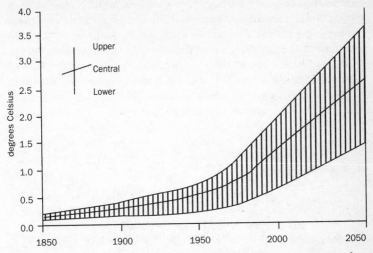

Fig. 4.4. *Business-as-usual projection of the trend in global surface air-temperature for the upper (doubling temperature, 4.5°C; ocean diffusivity, 0.5 cm²s⁻¹), and central (3.0°C; 1.0 cm²s⁻¹), and lower (1.5°C; 2.0 cm²s⁻¹) cases. The global temperature is expressed as a deviation from the pre-industrial norm.*

According to this simulation, a rise in global temperature of 1.1±0.5°C above the pre-industrial level should have occurred by 1990 as a result of past greenhouse-gas emissions. Taking account of future emissions, global temperature may rise 2.6±1.1°C above the pre-industrial level by the year 2050. Over the period 1990 to 2050, the average warming rate – based on the difference between the *model estimate* of the realized warming in 1990 and 2050 [24] – is 0.26±0.12°C a decade. This is three to seven times greater than experienced over the past one hundred years. By the year 2050, the equilibrium warming – the warming that will have occurred once the oceans and atmosphere reach balance – stands at 3.6±1.8°C above the pre-industrial level.

The potential impact of this change in climate is clear when it is placed in historical context. Even towards the lower end of the range of uncertainty, a rise in global temperature of 2°C above the pre-industrial level represents a shift to a climatic state not seen before during human civilization. As the IPCC scientists point out, global surface temperatures have probably fluctuated by little more than 1°C in the 10,000 years since the end of the last glaciation.[25] Global temperature has not risen more than 3°C above the level prevailing in the nineteenth century since at least the end of the Eem-Sangamon period, around 125,000 years ago. To find an analogue for a world more than 5°C warmer than recent experience, it may be necessary to go back at least three million years to the Pliocene period. Global warming represents a disruption of the environment that is without parallel in human experience.[26]

This, then, is the future that is to be avoided.

4.3 A first step

With four major greenhouse gases and a diverse range of sources, there are many ways in which one might set about identifying a strategy which will achieve the goal of halting the rise in effective carbon-dioxide concentration. Two basic criteria are used to establish a starting point around which further components of the strategy can be built:

■ Priority is given to measures which are justifiable because they will result in benefits in other environmental areas;

■ Priority is given to measures in areas that minimize the adverse societal impacts of the strategy.

Underlying these criteria is the principle that the stabilizing strategy should aim to reduce – and certainly should not aggravate – other environmental and social problems, including the present lack of equity between North and South.

Two policy targets are identified on the basis of these criteria, providing a framework within which further targets can be identified.

First, it is assumed that the production of the chlorofluorocarbons and all related ozone-depleting chemicals will be eliminated during the 1990s. Furthermore, there will be no deployment of substitutes that are themselves greenhouse gases as the use of these chemicals ends. Both the impact of the chlorofluorocarbons on the stratospheric ozone layer and the fact that their use cannot be considered essential in comparison to the activities giving rise to the other greenhouse gases justifies this priority target.

Second, it is assumed that deforestation, the main source of land-use related carbon dioxide, will be halted by the year 2000. Deforestation is the cause of many environmental, economic, and social problems and represents the loss of an invaluable resource.[27]

The 'first-step' scenario is, therefore, based on two measures:

■ The elimination of the production of chlorofluorocarbons and all related ozone-depleting chemicals by 1995, and the avoidance of substitutes that are greenhouse gases;

■ A halt to deforestation (more precisely, net emissions from the biosphere) by the year 2000.

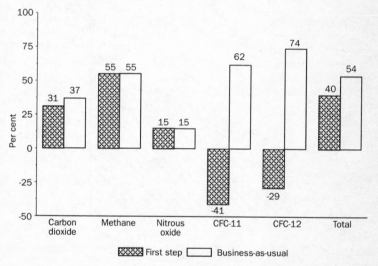

Fig. 4.5. First-step projection of the percentage change in greenhouse-gas concentra-tions over the period 1990–2050. 'Total' is the effective carbon dioxide concentration. The concentrations in the year 2050 are: carbon dioxide, 465 ppmv; methane, 2,694 ppbv; nitrous oxide, 364 ppbv; CFC-11, 167 pptv; CFC-12, 345 pptv; and effective carbon dioxide, 578 ppmv.

Methane and nitrous oxide emissions and energy-related emissions of carbon dioxide follow the business-as-usual projection.

Because of the elimination of chlorofluorocarbon production, CFC-11 and CFC-12 concentrations fall by 41 per cent and 29 per cent respectively of their present-day value by the mid-twenty-first century. In the business-as-usual projection, they rose by 62 per cent and 74 per cent respectively. Halting deforestation reduces the rise in carbon dioxide concentration from 37 per cent to 31 per cent above the current level.

As a result of these two measures, the date at which the effective carbon dioxide concentration reaches twice the pre-industrial level is delayed by about ten years. Compared to the business-as-usual projection, the effective carbon dioxide concentration in the year 2050 drops from 634 to 578 ppmv, 40 per cent above the present-day value. Both measures contribute equally to the reduction in forcing.

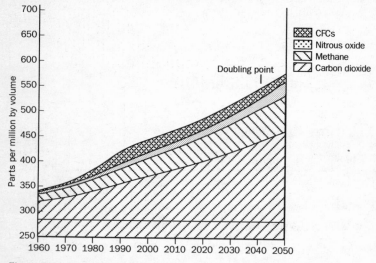

Fig. 4.6. First-step projection of the trend in effective carbon dioxide concentration. The relative contribution of the different gases is shown. The pre-industrial baseline is indicated by the horizontal bar.

The warming realized by the year 2050 under the first-step scenario stands at 2.4±1.0°C above the pre-industrial level, a reduction of 0.2±0.1°C below the business-as-usual projection. The warming rate between 1990 and 2050 is 0.22±0.10°C a decade, 15 per cent below that of the business-as-usual projection. By the year 2050, the equilibrium temperature is 3.2±1.6°C above the pre-industrial level and will continue to rise during the second half of the twenty-first century as the greenhouse effect is further enhanced.

Despite the first-step measures, there remains a sizeable warming that must be reduced by other means.

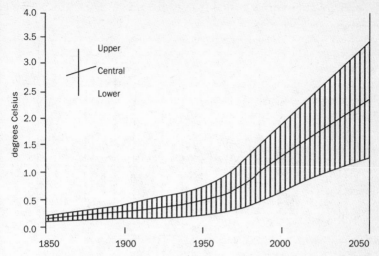

Fig. 4.7. First-step projection of the trend in global surface air-temperature for the upper (doubling temperature, 4.5°C; ocean diffusivity, 0.5 cm²s⁻¹), central (3.0°C; 1.0 cm²s⁻¹), and lower (1.5°C; 2.0 cm²s⁻¹) cases. The global temperature is expressed as a deviation from the pre-industrial norm.

4.4 The 50-per-cent recommendation

The participants at the 1988 Toronto Conference, *The Changing Atmosphere: Implications for Global Security*, recommended a series of measures to curb global warming. As far as carbon dioxide emissions from energy-related sources were concerned, they suggested that releases should be reduced to 80 per cent of the levels prevailing during the late 1980s by the year 2005, and that reduction by 50 per cent or more would be necessary to stabilize atmospheric levels.[28] No time-scale was specified for the latter reduction.

The '50-per-cent' scenario adds control of fossil-fuel emissions of carbon, along the lines suggested by the Toronto Conference, to the targets of the first-step scenario. It is based on:

■ The elimination of the production of chlorofluorocarbons and all related ozone-depleting chemicals by 1995, and the avoidance of substitutes that are greenhouse gases;

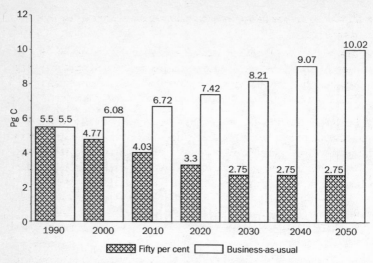

Fig. 4.8. Fossil-fuel emissions of carbon in the 50-per-cent and business-as-usual scenarios.

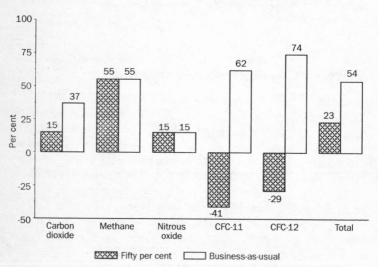

Fig. 4.9. Fifty-per-cent projection of the percentage change in greenhouse-gas concentrations over the period 1990–2050. 'Total' is the effective carbon dioxide concentration. The concentrations in the year 2050 are: carbon dioxide, 408 ppmv; methane, 2,694 ppbv; nitrous oxide, 364 ppbv; CFC-11, 167 pptv; CFC-12, 345 pptv; and effective carbon dioxide, 507 ppmv.

- A halt to deforestation (net emissions from the biosphere) by the year 2000;
- The reduction of energy-related emissions of carbon to 80 per cent of the present-day value by the year 2005 and, extrapolating beyond 2005, to 50 per cent by the year 2030, after which emissions remain constant at this level.

As noted in Section 4.1, projections based on the assumption of a constant airborne fraction may underestimate the response of atmospheric concentrations to significant reductions in carbon emissions, as envisaged in this scenario. The implications of a varying airborne fraction are summarized later in this section.[29]

As a result of the halt to deforestation and the reduction in fossil-fuel related emissions, the rise in carbon dioxide concentration by the mid-twenty-first century is limited to 15 per cent above present, as opposed to 37 per cent above the current level in the business-as-usual projection. The effective carbon dioxide concentration rises to 507 ppmv in the year 2050, and the doubling point has been delayed until late in the twenty-first century.

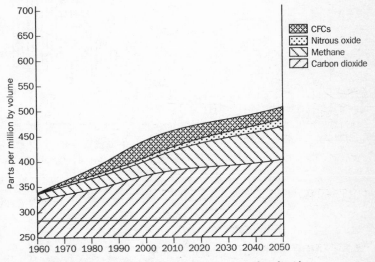

Fig. 4.10. Fifty-per-cent projection of the trend in effective carbon dioxide concentration. The relative contribution of the different gases is shown. The pre-industrial baseline is indicated by the horizontal bar.

By the year 2050, global temperature rises to 2.1±0.8°C above the pre-industrial level. This is 0.5±0.2°C below the level it would have reached as a result of the business-as-usual scenario. It represents a warming rate of 0.16±0.08°C a decade over the period to 2050, 38 per cent below that of the business-as-usual projection but still above the rate of 0.1°C a decade suggested as an interim goal by the participants at the Villach-Bellagio Workshops on the basis of the toleration level of forest communities.[30] The equilibrium temperature reaches 2.6±1.3°C above the pre-industrial level by the end of the study period, and will continue to rise as the greenhouse effect is further enhanced.

While the rate of warming has decreased significantly, it is clear that additional measures are necessary to stabilize the greenhouse effect.

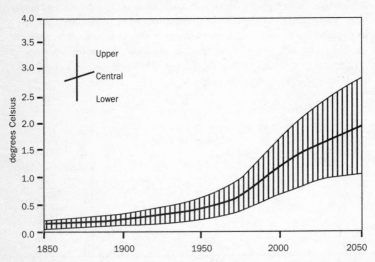

Fig. 4.11. Fifty-per-cent projection of the trend in global surface air-temperature for the upper (doubling temperature, 4.5°C; ocean diffusivity, 0.5 cm²s⁻¹), central (3.0°C; 1.0 cm²s⁻¹), and lower (1.5°C; 2.0 cm²s⁻¹) cases. The global temperature is expressed as a deviation from the pre-industrial norm.

4.5 Global warming halted

The combined effect of the elimination of chlorofluorocarbon production (and production of all related substitute chemicals) by the year 1995, a halt to deforestation by the year 2000, and a 50-per-cent reduction in fossil-fuel emissions by the year 2030 would be to reduce the future rate of warming by more than a third compared to the business-as-usual projection. But the effective carbon dioxide content of the atmosphere continues to rise. In order to reach the goal of stabilization, further measures are needed. There are a number of possibilities – but two obvious courses of action.

The first is to transform the biosphere into a sink through reforestation.[31] The carbon taken out of the atmosphere by growing trees and other forms of vegetation could then offset remaining energy-related emissions. For illustrative purposes, it is assumed that reforestation could match the carbon release into the atmosphere that would otherwise take place as a result of deforestation according to the business-as-usual projection. This amounts to around 1.65 Pg (1,650 million metric tons) of carbon a year over the first half of the twenty-first century.

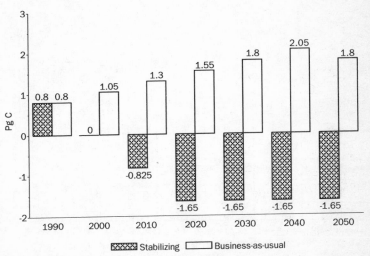

Fig. 4.12. Biospheric emissions of carbon in the stabilizing and business-as-usual scenarios

Estimates of the level of afforestation needed to achieve this degree of carbon take-up vary by a factor of 2 or more, depending on assumptions made about productivity per unit area and so on.[32] It may be necessary to create as much as 200 million hectares of new forests

(1 hectare equals 10,000 square metres), increasing the area presently covered by forest by around 5 per cent. This is equivalent to about a quarter of the forest area cleared world-wide to date.

It is assumed that the goal of absorbing 1.65 Pg of carbon a year will be achieved by the year 2020. Ten million hectares of forest – a land area equivalent to that of Guatemala, approaching that of the state of New York in the United States – would have to be created each year during the first two decades of the twenty-first century if the total area of new forest was to reach 200 million hectares by 2020.

To stabilize carbon dioxide levels, a further reduction in fossil-fuel related emissions beyond that of the 50-per-cent scenario must accompany this reforestation measure. Emissions must be reduced to 30 per cent of the current level – the 1.65 Pg of carbon a year that will be taken up by the new forests – so that a balance between source and sink is achieved and no subsequent rise in atmospheric carbon-dioxide concentration occurs. (Fig. 4.13.)

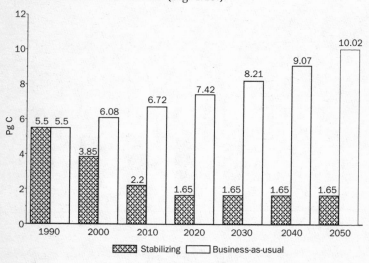

Fig. 4.13. Fossil-fuel emissions of carbon in the stabilizing and business-as-usual scenarios.

The second course of action is to balance rising emissions of methane and nitrous oxide against the decline in chlorofluorocarbon concentration, so that there is no net growth in the cumulative effective carbon dioxide concentration attributable to these gases. Over the period to 2050, chlorofluorocarbon concentrations are steadily decreasing, reducing their contribution to the greenhouse effect. This reduction in radiative forcing can be set against further rises, albeit at a slower rate than at present, in the contribution of methane and nitrous oxide. By reducing the annual increase in methane and nitrous oxide concentrations linearly to 25 per cent of the present-day figure by the year 2020, a balance could be achieved. In terms of emissions, this would mean holding methane emissions close to present-day levels and reducing nitrous oxide emissions due to human activity by more than a factor of 2.[33]

The 'stabilizing' scenario, then, consists of the following goals:

■ The elimination of the production of chlorofluorocarbons and all related ozone-depleting chemicals by the year 1995 and the avoidance of substitutes that are greenhouse gases;

■ A halt to deforestation by the year 2000, followed by extensive reforestation to offset 1.65 Pg (1,650 million metric tons) a year of energy-related carbon emissions by the year 2020;

■ A reduction in carbon emissions from fossil-fuel combustion to 30 per cent of the present value by 2020; and

■ A reduction in the annual rise in methane and nitrous oxide concentrations to 25 per cent of the present value by 2020.

The scale of these measures is broadly consistent with the targets of the 'toleration' scenario developed by Krause and others.[34] The time-scale of implementation is, however, more rapid in this study, to meet the more stringent goal of stabilizing the greenhouse effect by the mid-twenty-first century.

The net effect of this set of measures is to stabilize the concentration of carbon dioxide in the atmosphere at 375 ppmv during the 2020s, only 5 per cent above the 1990 level compared to the increase of 37 per cent in the business-as-usual projection.

The methane concentration rises to 2,148 ppbv by the year 2050, 24 per cent above the present level, in comparison to 55 per cent above the present in the business-as-usual projection. The nitrous oxide concentration reaches 337 ppbv, 7 per cent above the present level compared to 15 per cent above in the business-as-usual projection. During the final decades of the study period, the enhancement of the greenhouse effect due to the continuing rise in methane and nitrous oxide concentrations is balanced by the reduction caused by

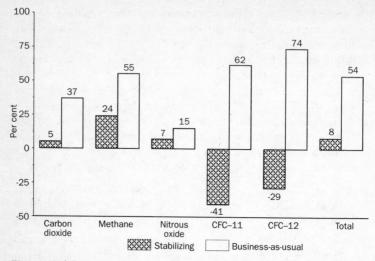

Fig. 4.14. Stabilizing projection of the percentage change in greenhouse-gas concentrations over the period 1990–2050. 'Total' is the effective carbon dioxide concentration. The concentrations in the year 2050 are: carbon dioxide, 375 ppmv; methane, 2,148 ppbv; nitrous oxide, 337 ppbv; CFC-11, 167 pptv; CFC-12, 345 pptv; and effective carbon dioxide, 445 ppmv.

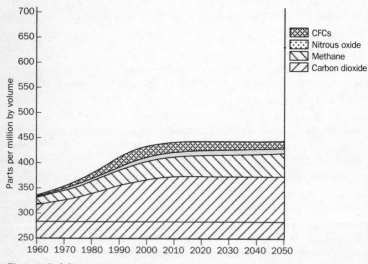

Fig. 4.15. Stabilizing projection of the trend in effective carbon dioxide concentration. The relative contribution of the different gases is shown. The pre-industrial baseline is indicated by the horizontal bar.

the decline in chlorofluorocarbon levels.

The rise in the effective carbon dioxide concentration of the atmosphere is brought to a halt by the year 2030.

The stabilization level is 445 ppmv – only 8 per cent higher than the present-day value. The goal has been achieved.

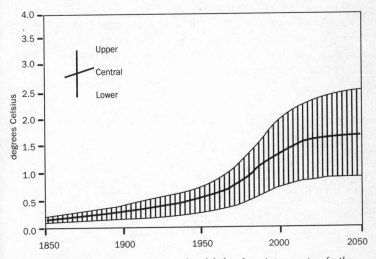

Fig. 4.16. Stabilizing projection of the trend in global surface air-temperature for the upper (doubling temperature, 4.5°C; ocean diffusivity, 0.5 cm²s⁻¹), central (3.0°C; 1.0 cm²s⁻¹), and lower (1.5°C; 2.0 cm²s⁻¹) cases. The global temperature is expressed as a deviation from the pre-industrial norm.

Although the effective carbon dioxide concentration stabilizes during the 2020s, global temperature continues to rise as the climate system slowly adjusts into equilibrium. By the year 2050, global temperature lies 1.7±0.8°C above the pre-industrial level, 0.9±0.3°C below the business-as-usual projection. By that time, though, the warming rate – 0.04±0.03°C a decade – is well below the tolerance criterion of 0.1°C a decade.

According to this projection, global temperature will eventually stabilize at 2.0±1.0°C above the pre-industrial level. The upper end of the range of uncertainty is 3°C above the pre-industrial level, close to the ceiling of tolerability defined by Krause and his colleagues.[35] The fact that radical policies are needed to meet this environmental criterion again underlines the importance of urgent action.

The results of the stabilizing projection are not particularly sensitive to the assumption of a fixed airborne fraction in the carbon-dioxide concentration model. The sensitivity studies, documented in full in the extended report of this study,[36] demonstrate that the assumption of a varying airborne fraction – dropping as emissions are reduced – has a negligible effect on the level at which climate would ultimately stabilize. Obviously, the projected carbon dioxide concentration is lower but the difference is not substantial. This is because the bulk of the additional carbon enters the atmosphere early in the emission-reduction phase when the airborne fraction is still close to 50 per cent.

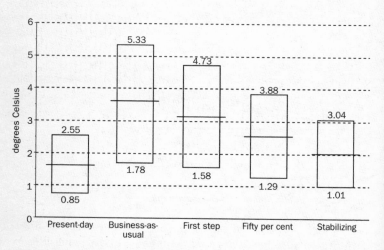

Fig. 4.17. The equilibrium global temperature in the present-day (1990) and, according to the projections developed in this study, in the year 2050 for the upper (doubling temperature, 4.5°C; ocean diffusivity, 0.5 cm²s⁻¹), central (3.0°C; 1.0 cm²s⁻¹), and lower (1.5°C; 2.0 cm²s⁻¹) cases. The global temperature is expressed as a deviation from the pre-industrial norm. The central case is indicated by the horizontal bar.

The sensitivity studies do highlight an important point as far as the emission-reduction schedule is concerned. Harvey[37] has demonstrated that the airborne fraction could drop to zero if emissions were to be reduced substantially over a short period of time. If the oceans respond slowly to the reduction in emissions, continuing to absorb close to the amount of carbon they took up before emissions were reduced, the airborne fraction would drop considerably. This means that, if immediate action were taken to reduce emissions by a substantial amount, the rate at which measures would need to be implemented in the longer term may not be as great. For example, the scale of reforestation necessary during the early twenty-first century-would be halved and the reduction in fossil-fuel emissions to 30 per cent below present could be delayed until 2050. Whether or not the real world behaves in the manner suggested by Harvey remains to be seen. The impact of an initial phase of emission reductions needs to be assessed, and models calibrated with reference to the observed effect.

The focus of this study has been the immediate future. It may be necessary to revise targets in the light of experience. Further measures will be needed during the later decades of the twenty-first century. A balance will have to be maintained between remaining carbon dioxide emissions and reforestation. Replanting will have to take place to replace trees that mature. Wood, once harvested, must not be allowed to oxidize. Moreover, the decline in chlorofluorocarbon concentrations will not counter the continuing rise in levels of methane and nitrous oxide for long after 2050. The stabilizing strategy represents only the starting point.

4.6 Conclusions

A precautionary approach to the problem of global warming is warranted on the basis of its potential impact and the scale of the response that is necessary if that impact is to be avoided. Time is of the essence.

This study has demonstrated that the effective carbon dioxide concentration of the atmosphere could be stabilized during the first half of the twenty-first century as a result of planning decisions taken over the next thirty years. It is within the power of the current generation of decision-makers to determine the course of global climate for generations to come.

According to the projections made in this report, the stabilizing strategy would limit the rise in global temperature experienced by the year 2050 to $1.7\pm0.8°C$ above the pre-industrial level. By the mid-twenty-first century, the rate of warming would be considerably less than 0.1°C a decade and global temperature would eventually stabilize at 2.0±1.0°C above the level prevailing prior to the nineteenth century.

The complete stabilizing strategy consists of:

■ First, the elimination of the production of chlorofluorocarbons and all related ozone-depleting chemicals by the year 1995, and the avoidance of substitutes that are greenhouse gases;

■ Second, a halt to deforestation by the year 2000 and reforestation to offset emissions of 1.65 Pg (1,650 million metric tons) of carbon a year by the year 2020;

■ Third, a reduction in carbon emissions from fossil-fuel combustion to 30 per cent of the present value by 2020;

■ Finally, a reduction in the annual rise in methane and nitrous-oxide concentrations to 25 per cent of the present value by 2020.

Table 4.2: Summary of the decadal targets comprising the stabilizing scenario. The targets remain constant after 2020

Year	CO_2 fossil (%)	CO_2 biosphere (Pg of carbon/year)	CH_4/N_2O (%)
2000	70	0.00	75
2010	40	−0.83	50
2020	30	−1.65	25

Notes: 1. The fossil-fuel targets for carbon dioxide (CO_2) are expressed as a percentage of current emissions, 5.5 Pg (5,500 million metric tons) of carbon a year.

2. The biosphere targets for carbon dioxide are expressed in terms of net emissions (essentially, deforestation–reforestation) in Pg of carbon a year. At present, there is a net release of 0.8 Pg (800 million metric tons). A negative value indicates the fossil-fuel emission that is to be offset.

3. The targets for methane (CH_4) and nitrous oxide (N_2O) are expressed in terms of the percentage reduction in the annual rate of increase in atmospheric concentration that would occur according to the business-as-usual projection: 16 ppbv in the case of methane; 0.8 ppbv in the case of nitrous oxide.

4. It is assumed that the production of CFCs and related chemicals is phased out by 1995.

Further measures will be needed during later decades to ensure that stabilization holds.

This particular strategy is not intended as a prescription for dealing with global warming. It serves to illustrate what is physically possible if social, economic, and political obstacles are removed. The issue of feasibility is considered elsewhere in this volume.

Targets will have to be continually reviewed in the light of experience. There are many uncertainties in current understanding of the manner in which atmospheric concentrations will respond to emission reductions and in the response of the climate system to the enhancement of the greenhouse effect. While theoretical research may resolve some of these, others will only be resolved by direct observation.

For example, a sensitivity study conducted during the course of this research suggests that the long-term targets embodied in this strategy may overestimate the rate at which measures need to be implemented during the early decades of the twenty-first century. With prompt and substantial action to reduce carbon emissions, advantage could be taken of the slow response of the oceans in order to limit the rate at which emissions need to be reduced in the longer term. In the final analysis, whether or not the theoretical basis of this possibility is correct can only be determined by experiment in the real world.

The analysis does highlight critical priorities for the present decade, targets which will ensure that society has taken the first step towards halting global warming. These measures would have a range of benefits whether or not current forecasts of global warming prove correct.[38] As understanding of the problem develops – or as unacceptable impacts occur – the decision to move to the next stage will be that much easier.

The priorities for the 'turnaround' decade of the 1990s should be:

- Prompt elimination of the production of chlorofluorocarbons and all related ozone-depleting chemicals;
- A rapid halt to deforestation; and
- A reduction in energy-related emissions of carbon to 70 per cent of the present level by the year 2000.

The primary responsibility for these measures must be taken by the industrialized world while means of assisting the Third World with its response are identified and implemented.

At the same time, a longer-term strategy must be developed to ensure further reductions in greenhouse-gas emissions and extensive reforestation in both the Third World and the industrialized nations. Given that some degree of warming cannot be avoided over the next few decades, the limitation of adverse impacts must also be considered. To be successful, this strategy must be based on new ways of thinking about policy in these areas, setting to one side conventional views of what can be achieved. If global warming is to be dealt with effectively, it will require the same commitment that confounded expectations by landing a person on the moon.

2

Impacts

" ...The Earth is slowly dying, and the inconceivable – the end of life itself – is actually becoming conceivable. We human beings ourselves have become a threat to our planet... "

Queen Beatrix of the Netherlands in her Christmas message to the people of Holland, 1988

Summary

Has the greenhouse effect arrived? This is the question we have all grown used to hearing every time there has been a drought, freak storm, major flood, or heatwave over the last few years.

But it is the wrong question to ask. The natural variability of climate is great, and – although we can safely anticipate that a warming atmosphere will generate a greater incidence of droughts, harvest failures in arid areas, greater strengths and frequencies of hurricanes and other storms, and more flooding as a result of sea-level rise and increased precipitation at mid- and high latitudes – we will never have the ability to be absolutely sure whether or not a particular extreme of climate is due to the Earth's natural climatic variability or to the enhanced greenhouse effect.

Even the fact that the five hottest years this century have all been in the 1980s could potentially be a coincidental product of natural climatic variability. The world's climate scientists conclude in their IPCC report that 'the unequivocal detection of the enhanced greenhouse effect from observations is not likely for a decade or more.' Ten years from now – quite possibly amid environmental refugees, nations on the verge of conflict over dwindling water supplies, and hosts of agricultural pests surviving increasingly warm winters – we are still likely to see scientists having difficulty putting their hands on their hearts and saying 'The impacts of the enhanced greenhouse effect are now definitely being felt.'

A more helpful question to ask is what we can anticipate the general impacts of global warming to be if we allow global average temperatures to rise as much as the world's climate scientists predict in the next century. Here there are ample lessons from studies of the natural environment to allow us to make some very robust predictions.

A common misconception is that there will be 'winners' as well as 'losers' from global warming. Those who advocate this idea point to studies which show that plants can grow more rapidly as a result of enhanced photosynthesis in an atmosphere richer in carbon dioxide, and to the supposition that agriculture will, in the future, be possible in areas – like Siberia – which are currently too cold and/or too dry. In Chapter 5 of the *Greenpeace Report*, Dr George M. Woodwell, Director of the Woods Hole Research Center in the USA, shows that the natural world is not as simple as a glasshouse experiment. Rather, we know that respiration by plants and soil microbes is stimulated more than photosynthesis by warming. Photosynthesis draws carbon dioxide down from the atmosphere; respiration returns it. Hence, Woodwell argues, we can expect the plant world to provide us with an unwelcome positive feedback – speeding global warming in ways not currently accounted for in climate models – in the next century.

Studies of the response of plants to past periods of fast and sustained natural temperature rise, as described by Dr Brian Huntley of the University of Durham in Chapter 6, show that even the 'best-guess' predictions of the IPCC scientists would herald ecological catastrophe in the decades to come. At the end of the last ice age, around 10,000 years ago, the world's average surface temperature rose by around 5°C (9°F). But it did so over several thousand years, not the 100 years – or less – that it will do in a 'business-as-usual' greenhouse world. The fossil record provides us with little hope that the plant world (and hence the creatures which depend on it) will be able to adapt to rates of change more than ten times faster than it has faced in hundreds of thousands – and quite possibly millions – of years.

What of humans? In Chapter 7, Andrew Haines, Professor of Primary Health Care at University College, London, describes the potential health impacts of warming on the scale predicted by the world's climate scientists. In addition to the health impacts of climate on agriculture and water supply, there is likely to be a poleward encroachment of diseases hitherto confined to the tropics, increased death-rates during heatwaves, and enhanced risk of epidemics among ever-growing numbers of refugees. Humans would do well to fear a 'business-as-usual' greenhouse future, and do all they can to avoid bequeathing to their children the horrors of one.

Chapter 5
The Effects of Global Warming

George M. Woodwell

" ...The possibility exists that the warming will proceed to the point where biotic releases (of greenhouse gases) from the warming will exceed in magnitude those controlled directly by human activity. If so, the warming will be beyond control by any steps now considered reasonable. We do not know how far we are from that point because we do not know sufficient detail about the circulation of carbon among the pools of the carbon cycle. We are not going to be able to resolve those questions definitively soon. Meanwhile, the concentration of heat-trapping gases in the atmosphere rises... "

If present trends continue, the atmosphere will contain in 2030–50 greenhouse gases equivalent in total capacity for absorbing radiant heat to about twice that of the carbon dioxide present in the middle of the last century.[1] This projection is based on observations of the rate of accumulation of carbon dioxide and other heat-trapping gases in the atmosphere, and on the assumption that the changes in climate will not affect the rate of accumulation of the gases. The effect of such a quantity of greenhouse gases, according to estimates of climatologists, will be to warm the Earth by an average of 1.5–4.5°C.[2] Climatologists' projections, which do not consider effects on forests and soil, are that the warming in the middle and higher latitudes in winter will be 50 to 100 per cent higher than the average for the Earth as a whole; in the tropics the warming will be slight, but there may be substantial changes in the amount and timing of rainfall.[3]

The purpose of this chapter is to examine details of the biotic implications of the warming of the Earth. I shall present evidence that the increase in respiration from warming will dominate all other biotic effects and accelerate rates of release of carbon dioxide and methane from the respiration of plants and the decay of organic matter in soils. These two gases are responsible for about three-quarters of the warming. I shall also review briefly the potential effects of global warming on agriculture, on water resources, on coastal zones, and on human settlements.

5.1 Biotic effects

The warming is expected to be continuous into the indefinite future unless checked by overt human action.[4] The scientists of the Inter-governmental Panel on Climate Change (IPCC) have shown that, in the absence of significant efforts to stem greenhouse-gas emissions, the Earth is leaving a period of substantially stable climates and entering a period of rapidly and continuously changing climates marked by a global warming of extraordinary speed.[5] While climatologists and biologists may be able to estimate the effects of changes of 1–2°C in the temperature of the Earth, greater changes will launch the world into climatic realms that reach beyond the current experience of science and scientists. No one can predict in detail, for example, how oceanic currents will be modified or what the effect of an ice-free Arctic Ocean will be on climates elsewhere. Nor can we predict in detail the effects on fish and fisheries, the distribution of arable land, the details of effects on forests, on animals, or on the distribution of human parasites and disease. The second of the three IPCC working groups, the Impacts Working Group, has made an effort so to do.[6] But their analysis, which espouses the view that there will be 'winners' as well as 'losers' from global warming, is couched only in terms of the next half-century or so, and only in terms of the warming predicted by current climatic models. It does not include an appraisal of what will happen in the event that positive feedbacks currently omitted from climatic models come into play. Nor does it take a longer view. The problem of predicting effects is the more complicated if the changes are continuous and accelerating, as they will be unless checked by human intervention. I shall argue that, if greenhouse gas emissions are not so checked, there will be no winners from global-warming, and the stakes could be higher than has usually been assumed.

5.1.1 The sources of carbon dioxide and methane

The causes of the accumulation of heat-trapping gases are complex and less well defined than is commonly recognized. The primary cause is generally accepted to be the Industrial Revolution, with its heavy reliance on fossil fuels as a source of energy. Deforestation has also, more recently, been recognized as a contributing cause,[7] with the potential for adding substantially to the total atmospheric burden of carbon dioxide and methane if the remaining forests are destroyed globally.[8] A third source of additional carbon dioxide and methane for the atmosphere is the stimulation of respiration, including the respiration (or decay) of organic matter in soils, by the warming itself.[9] This latter effect has the potential for being a positive feedback, a new source of heat-trapping gases that depends on the speed and extent of warming. The assumptions made by climatologists in estimating the rate of warming outlined above have emphasized the contribution from fossil fuels and have not accounted explicitly for either accelerating deforestation or the effect of the warming on respiration of plants and soils. The importance of this latter effect is great enough to speed the warming appreciably. Its importance is a function of the amount of carbon held in terrestrial ecosystems, especially forests, and the effect of the climatic changes on those ecosystems.

5.1.2 Stocks and flows of carbon in ecosystems

Estimates of the total amount of carbon held in plants and soils suggest that the total is about 2,000 billion tonnes,[10] nearly three times the amount in the atmosphere at present. The stocks are shown in Figure 1.3 of Jeremy Leggett's introductory chapter to this book.

The stocks of carbon held in the atmosphere and on land, principally in forests, are maintained by annual flows of carbon through terrestrial ecosystems. Carbon is absorbed as carbon dioxide from the atmosphere through gross production (the total photosynthesis of the ecosystem); it is released into the atmosphere from plants and soils through respiration. These opposing processes are commonly thought to be in approximate balance globally. The flows are large and so diffuse as to be unmeasurable in total. They are estimated here for our purposes as approximately 100 billion tonnes of carbon annually, a little less than one-seventh of the current atmospheric burden of carbon as carbon dioxide. A small change in one of these flows, amounting to 1–2 per cent, while probably unmeasurable year-by-year, has the potential for changing the composition of the atmosphere appreciably in the course of a few years. The question of how these flows may be modified by the climatic changes in ways that will effect the climate is the central issue in this analysis.

A second pair of flows connects the atmosphere and the oceans. These flows are not in balance: there is a net flow into the oceans, but the size of the net absorption by the oceans is not easily measurable. We do know that the net flow into the oceans is less than the total releases of carbon dioxide into the atmosphere. The result is the accumulation of carbon dioxide that we observe. We shall not discuss the oceanic exchanges further here.

There is a further flow of carbon through the combustion of coal, oil, and gas: the fossil fuels. The flow is one-way: fossil fuels are mined and burned with the release of carbon as carbon dioxide and methane into the atmosphere. The annual release of carbon as carbon dioxide in 1990 is thought to be 5.7 (plus or minus 0.5) billion tonnes.[11]

Deforestation also releases carbon into the atmosphere as wood is burned and as the residues of logging or other disturbances decay. The releases from this source are diffuse and difficult to estimate. They include both carbon dioxide and methane, the latter as the product of anaerobic decay, wherever it occurs. The estimated release of carbon as CO_2 from deforestation in 1990 is 1.5–3.0 billion tons of carbon annually.[12]

5.1.3 Feedbacks: positive and negative

The warming of the Earth will change physical, chemical, and biotic processes locally and globally. The central question is whether the net effect of such changes will be significant in speeding or slowing the warming. A negative feedback will reduce the severity of the warming as the warming is intensified; a positive feedback will enhance it. Such feedbacks include changes in cloud- or snow-cover that alter the reflectivity of the Earth and the energy received at the surface. Increased snow- and cloud-cover will increase reflectivity, reduce the energy retained, and reduce the warming: a negative feedback. A reduction in reflectivity works in the opposite direction, a positive feedback. These changes have been considered by climatologists in making current estimates of the warming.

There is also the possibility that changes in the patterns of circulation of the oceans[13] will change the rates of exchange of atmospheric carbon dioxide with the carbon held in various forms in oceanic water.[14] These latter changes and others involving the biota are less predictable and have not been incorporated by climatic modellers into estimates of future warming. All include the possibility of surprises well outside the current realm of systematic analysis.

There is a further set of potential negative feedbacks involving biotic interactions. The most important effect has been assumed to be the stimulation of the fixation and storage of carbon by terrestrial plants through the increase in carbon dioxide in the atmosphere. The hypothesis is that the CO_2 in the atmosphere speeds photosynthesis. Data in support of such a mechanism come largely from experiments with plants under controlled conditions,[15] and from limited field studies such as those in a salt-marsh by Drake[16] and those in tundra by Oeschel.[17] The data show that increasing concentrations of carbon dioxide often, but not always, increase the rate of growth of young plants. The effect commonly declines with time and with increasing age of the plant. It appears to have little influence on forest trees. There are no data from natural communities which confirm a general effect from the 25-per-cent increase in the concentration of carbon dioxide in the atmosphere over the past century. If such an effect exists and is large enough to add as much as 2 billion tonnes of carbon annually to plants and soils globally, the change would be 0.1 per cent of the total mass of carbon, and not detectable. Most direct appraisals of trends in the storage of carbon in forests and soils suggest a net loss year-by-year as the area of forests diminishes and as the effects of pollution and other toxins accumulate. Any stimulation of carbon storage is assumed to be small; it has not compensated for the increase in carbon dioxide in the atmosphere to date in any conspicuous or measurable way.

There is, of course, the possibility that a warming Earth will extend the area that forests can occupy and thereby increase the total carbon storage in plants and soils. The topic was examined by Woodwell,[18] and has been examined subsequently by Lashof,[19] Emanuel *et al.*,[20] and Solomon *et al.*[21] It seems doubtful that there is a circumstance in which continuous warming at rates projected for the next decades will increase the area capable of supporting forests globally. Indeed, the opposite seems more probable: the warming in continental centres will increase the arid zones globally at the expense of currently forested areas. The magnitude is difficult to appraise, but a 1°C increase in temperature at the forest-to-grassland transitions in the northern hemisphere would move the transitions 60–100 miles and replace forests covering 100–200 million hectares with grassland. Such a massive change in the distribution of forests would involve a release of carbon in the range of tens of billion tonnes, and constitute a highly significant positive feedback unbalanced by any expansion of forests into regions with newly favourable climate.

The most important consideration of biotic feedbacks is the ratio of gross production (total photosynthesis) to total respiration globally. Gross production is the total amount of photosynthesis carried out by plants. The respiration of green plants and that of all heterotrophs, including organisms of decay and all animals, is usually pooled as total respiration of the ecosystem. If gross production exceeds total respiration, carbon compounds are accumulated in the large store of carbon held in plants and soils; if respiration dominates, the store of carbon is depleted. The relationships among these sometimes confusing attributes of ecosystems have been defined in detail by Woodwell and Whittaker.[22]

The factors that affect these two processes include, in particular, light, water, nutrients, and temperature. In general, gross production is easily affected by virtually any disturbance. The effect is commonly a reduction in both gross and net production (gross production less the respiration of the green plants); it is rarely a stimulation. Specific, overt efforts are usually required to increase primary production and the effectiveness is usually limited. Light, nutrients, and water are essential. Temperature affects the process, but the effect is modest throughout a wide range of temperature.

The question is how the ratio of gross production to total respiration will shift as the Earth warms. As in most of science, absolute proof is elusive. I have suggested, on the basis of experience with measurements of the metabolism of forests over several years, that the dominant effect in the short term of years to decades will be the response to temperature: a warming will increase rates of respiration significantly without affecting gross photosynthesis appreciably.[23] If so, there will be an increasing release of carbon as carbon dioxide and methane from forests and soils, especially in the higher latitudes, and an acceleration of the warming. Evidence in favour of this hypothesis is accumulating. We can draw on three lines of evidence: (1) first principles of ecology; (2) the record of changes during the glacial period; and (3) experience in watching responses to the current warming.

First, consider basic ecology. Two changes are occurring simultaneously, and we wish to know which is the more important. There is an increase in the concentration of carbon dioxide in the atmosphere. The increase is appreciable; it has been more than 25 per cent over the past century. At the same time there is a warming, apparently of about 0.5°C globally over the same period. Which of these changes has had a greater effect on the Earth? The potential effects of increases in the concentration of carbon dioxide on rates of photosynthesis and on carbon storage in forests have been addressed above. An increase in the storage of carbon in forests or elsewhere would require that gross production exceed total respiration. If moisture is available, an increase in temperature commonly increases rates of respiration by 10–35 per cent or more per 1°C increase in temperature. This increase affects both the respiration of plants and that of the organic matter in soils. An increase in the rate of respiration of plants reduces both net primary production and net ecosystem production; an increase in the decay of organic matter in soils reduces net ecosystem production. While data from ecosystems as units are few, there is enough carbon in soils of the boreal forest for such a stimulation of decay to equal or exceed any stimulation of net primary production due to the increase in carbon dioxide in the atmosphere. There is nothing inconsistent in a circumstance in which both net primary production and total respiration are stimulated by the combination of increasing amounts of carbon dioxide in the atmosphere, additional precipitation, and higher temperatures, with the net effect being an increase in the release of carbon from the ecosystem because the stimulation of respiration dominates.

I have discussed previously the transitions to be expected at the warmer and drier limits of the distribution of forests as the climate warms. The rates of warming in these latitudes are expected to be high, possibly as high as 1°C per decade, equivalent to moving 100–150 km (60–100 miles) in latitude. There is no possibility that forests can be regenerated elsewhere at an equivalent rate. The net effect is a further release of carbon into the atmosphere as the warming progresses.

These considerations of forests and a parallel set of analyses of tundra suggest that the probability is high that a warming will stimulate the respiration of terrestrial ecosystems, including the decay of organic matter in soils, sufficiently to exceed any stimulation of net primary production. The effect will be a further release of carbon as the Earth warms and as the respiration of terrestrial ecosystems increases.

This analysis seems to be supported by data from the Vostok core,[24] a sample of ice that reached down through the glacial-age ice of the Antarctic to sample strata through the most recent 160,000 years.[25] The core has provided data on temperature and carbon dioxide and methane concentrations throughout that period (see Chapter 2, Figure 2.5). The data show that as temperature rose, the concentrations of methane and carbon dioxide rose as well; as temperature dropped, carbon dioxide and methane concentrations dropped. The observations are consistent with the suggestion of a positive feedback: a warming is correlated with an increase in the heat-trapping gases in the atmosphere; a cooling, with a decline in their concentrations. But the data do not confirm the cause of the warming or the cooling, or the reason for the shift from a warming trend to a cooling trend and back. They do, however, show that, over 160,000 years of recent time, the dominant relationship between temperature and the two most important heat-trapping gases, carbon dioxide and methane, has been a positive correlation. There is no basis in these data for assertions that the increasing carbon dioxide in the atmosphere will speed carbon storage by plants and stabilize the composition of the atmosphere, or for assumptions that any other negative feedback will dominate and stop the warming.

Analyses of the temperature of the Earth carried out at the University of East Anglia and at the Goddard Institute of Space Studies at Columbia have shown that the Earth has warmed by 0.5–0.7°C over the past century. Five of the warmest years in the record occurred in the 1980s.[26] The year 1988 was by far the warmest year on record. The warming has been abrupt and severe enough to appear as a surge in the rate of accumulation of carbon dioxide and methane in the atmosphere.

Such a surge appears to be occurring, although the data on methane are not yet available. Over the past fifteen years there has been an annual accumulation of carbon dioxide in the atmosphere of about 1.5 parts per million (ppm). This accumulation is equivalent to about 3 billion tonnes of carbon annually, slightly more than 50 per cent of the release from fossil fuels alone, but considerably less than 50 per cent of the total release of carbon due to human activities.[27]

Recently, the data from the monitoring station at Mauna Loa and at the South Pole have both recorded increases in the rate of accumulation of carbon in the atmosphere.[28] The observation has extended over eighteen months, according to Keeling, and suggests an accelerated accumulation of 2.4 ppm or about 5.0 billion tonnes of carbon per year, a 60-per-cent increase above the rate observed in the past. Such a surge is not surprising in view of the speed of the warming observed over the last decade. What is surprising is that the correlation has not been observed previously in response to earlier changes in regional and global temperatures. Whether the higher rate of accumulation will continue remains to be seen. A previous surge in 1973–4 proved transitory. The cause of the current surge will be the subject of speculation and research over the next years. Keeling *et al.*[29] and Siegenthaler[30] suggest that it is due to changes in the metabolism of forests related to drought associated with the complex series of changes in oceanic circulation of the El Nino of recent years. While there is an understandable tendency to look for subtleties in such a complicated system, the potential of a simple change in temperature for changing rates of respiration regionally or globally is great enough to swamp subtleties. The recent experience extends the immediate challenge of stabilizing the composition of the atmosphere with respect to carbon dioxide from a net cut of 3 billion tonnes of carbon per annum to one of up to 5 billion tonnes.

5.1.4 Global warming as a cause of biotic impoverishment

A general warming that may approach average changes in the temperature of the Earth of the order of 0.1–1.0°C per decade, exceeds by factors of 100–1,000 or more the capacity of natural communities such as forests to migrate.[31] The effect will be the rapid destruction of forests without their replacement. Species will be lost as climate and habitat migrate out from under them. Not only will species be lost, but the specific ecotypes – specific combinations of genes accumulated for each locale by selection through many generations – will also be lost rapidly. Under such circumstances, forests are commonly replaced by savannah, shrubland, or grassland. The patterns of impoverishment have been examined in detail recently for various ecosystems around the world.[32] The effect of such transitions is to reduce the capacity of the Earth for supporting life, including people. The reduction is not simply a reduction in the potential of the land, but a systematic reduction in the organisms on Earth, a surge in biotic impoverishment not previously anticipated or currently appraised as one of the costs of the current disruption of global climate.

The species favoured in such transitions are, first, those that are normally recognized as successional, those that occur following disturbance. As the disturbance continues, these species are replaced by smaller-bodied, rapidly reproducing species of wide distribution. These are, among plants, the widely distributed, pernicious weeds of the garden and other chronic disturbed sites; among animals, they include noxious insect pests of garden and house, all direct competitors of humans.

5.1.5 Effects on agriculture

The IPCC's Impacts Working Group concludes optimistically that 'food production at the global level can be sustained at levels sufficient to meet world demand', although at unknown cost. I wonder if this optimism is justified in the face of the uncertainties described above.

Demand for food is a function of price. Those who are hungry are not only outside the world market, but also lack a local capacity to produce their own food. While industrialized agriculture may be able to respond rapidly to the systematic changes in climate that seem probable,[33] the reality of the warming is more likely to produce a series of surprises. The summer of 1988, marked by unusual heat and drought throughout North America and elsewhere, reduced the North American grain crop by about 30 per cent, and affected the price of grain globally. Global reserves were depleted to the point where another short harvest would have produced a 'shortage' and driven prices sharply upward. The market would have continued. The starving would have been, as they are each year, those on the margin, unable to participate in the world market and unable to provide for themselves outside that market. In a world of 5.3 billion people where virtually all arable land is in use, it is difficult to envisage how a general warming of the Earth, with the increased extremes of temperature and moisture, will be easily accommodated. The probability is high that there will be erratic production over large areas and a systematic loss of production as continental centres warm further. Warmer is drier, and most appraisals suggest that soil moisture will decline as the continents warm.

Losses in production of cereals are expected in some areas of currently high production such as southern Europe, the southern United States, and western Australia. A limited warming may increase, at least in the short term, the productive potential of certain regions in mid- and high latitudes, where precipitation is expected to increase. There is, however, a dangerous and misguided school of thought which claims that Siberia will be transformed into the grain basket of the East, and that forests will be produced where no trees grow now. While there may be advantageous changes in climate in certain circumstances, neither grain nor forests will grow soon on the Canadian Shield, or in other extensive regions now covered with boreal forest or tundra. At lower latitudes, current yields will be vulnerable to increased aridity over large areas.

5.2 Other effects of global warming

5.2.1 Effects on water resources

Cities, hydro-power, irrigated agriculture, shipping, the various uses of waterways, fish and fisheries, the transport, dilution, and treatment of sewage, and the circulation of coastal and oceanic waters are all dependent on flows of fresh water from the land. The relationships are at once simple and complex: power production at Bonneville Dam is obviously dependent on a continued flow in the Columbia River, but the various rich fisheries of the Rio Negro and the Amazon are not as obviously dependent on the massive seasonal pulse of water that floods the varzea forests to a depth of 10 metres for weeks, and opens the vast resources of the forest to grazing by fish. Yet the dependence is no less real.

Predictions of surface run-off are vulnerable to the same uncertainties that afflict other aspects of the effects of a continuous warming of the Earth. Within narrow limits, perhaps within a warming of 1–2°C for the Earth as a whole, general patterns seem clear. Beyond that range uncertainty dominates. Meanwhile, long-term commitments to expensive projects that require current patterns of precipitation to continue become immediately questionable. Dams, irrigation, or other water-supply projects, that might normally be expected to have useful lives of several decades to a century or more, may well fall victim to changing patterns of precipitation in years to a decade or so.

The IPCC Working Group 2 report emphasizes that the regions that appear to be at greatest risk for 'sustaining the population' are those that are already arid and marginal. They include large and populous regions that claim a large share of the world's annual increment of 90 million new people: the Sahel, the north of Africa, southern Africa, western Arabia, South-East Asia, the whole of the Indian subcontinent, Mexico, Central America, south-western USA, parts of eastern Brazil, and the Mediterranean zone. Recent climatic models have apparently shown patterns of drought increasing in frequency from 5 per cent under the present climate to 50 per cent of the time by the year 2050.

Among the many worrying implications of these kinds of predictions are the increased threat of conflict both between and within nations, in addition to the implications for major engineering projects. One only has to consider the competition for existing water resources along the Colorado River for irrigation, hydro-power, and municipal supply, among other purposes, to see the potential for political conflict.

In other areas, excess of supply will be a problem. The IPCC Working Group 2 report points out that serious flooding could occur in many northern rivers in the USSR, for example.

5.2.2 Effects on the world ocean and coastal zones

The IPCC scientists conclude, on the basis of climatic models, that in the absence of efforts to cut greenhouse-gas emissions, sea levels will rise by between 10 and 30 cm (with a 'best guess' of 20 cm) by the year 2030, and by 30 to 100 cm (with a best guess of 65 cm) by the end of the next century. This rise is the product of thermal expansion of sea-water and the melting of glaciers, with the effect of the Greenland and Antarctic ice-sheets expected to be small over the next century. Other scientists take a less sanguine view of the prospects of a minimal contribution from the Antarctic over such a period, of course, and the stakes here are high: in the event that the West Antarctic ice-sheet were to collapse, global sea-levels would rise by more than 5 metres. Such analyses are highly speculative, of course, and local experience will hinge heavily on whether the continental plates are tipping upward or downward at that point.

But let us assume, for the purposes of this account, that the IPCC analysis is correct. The predicted increase in sea-level is two to six times more rapid than the historical rate over the last century (a 10–15 cm rise). The IPCC Impacts Working Group predicts that even a 30–50 cm rise in sea-level poses 'serious problems for the low lying nations and coastal zones.' A rise of 1 metre, such as that predicted at the upper end of the range of uncertainty for the end of the next century, 'would displace populations, destroy low-lying urban infrastructure, inundate arable lands, contaminate fresh-water supplies, and alter coastlines'. The direct effects – recession of shorelines and wetlands, increased tidal range and estuarine salt-front intrusion, and an increase in salt-water contamination of coastal fresh-water acquifers – all have profound implications for human society, especially in the many coastal areas that are densely populated. A 1 metre rise could, for example, inundate up to 15 per cent of Egypt's arable land and 14 per cent of Bangladesh's net cropped area. The problems would not be limited to the developing world. In the south-eastern USA, for example, over half the species of commercially important fishes use salt-marshes as nursery grounds. Islands would be at risk, including nations such as the Maldives, Tuvalu, and Kiribati.

5.2.3 Effects on human settlements and society

World-wide, hundreds of millions of people would be displaced by the inundation of low-lying coastal plains, deltas, and islands in the next century if efforts to reduce greenhouse-gas accumulation in the atmosphere were unsuccessful. The IPCC Impacts Working Group merely touched on the problems of environmental refugees when it mentioned that 'epidemics may sweep through refugee camps and settlements, spilling over into surrounding communities'. These would be joined by countless millions displaced from the land as aridity and biotic impoverishment spread. If political and environmental refugees are a problem in 1990 in a world of 5.3 billion people, what will the problem be in 2000 or 2010 as the population soars above 6 billion?

The implications of global warming for human health are not limited to the developing world. The IPCC Working Group 2 concluded that vector-borne diseases can be expected to shift north as the world warms. Such diseases include malaria, schistosomiasis, leishmaniasis, dengue, and Japanese encephalitis. Andrew Haines explores this problem in Chapter 7 of this book.

5.3 Implications

The restabilization of global climate is clearly desirable, even essential, for the continuation of this civilization. There is no possibility of continuing this civilization or of maintaining the current human population on an Earth that is warming at an accelerating rate. The first step in any solution requires stabilization of the composition of the atmosphere with respect to the heat-trapping gases, especially carbon dioxide and methane.

What is required? Carbon dioxide and methane are both released through use of fossil fuels; both are also products of respiration. The increases in the atmosphere have followed different patterns. Carbon dioxide concentrations have surged in the past century as industrialization has advanced and the use of fossil fuels and deforestation have burgeoned; methane concentrations have doubled over two centuries, and the gas is accumulating more rapidly now than ever previously. The amount of each gas in the atmosphere is determined by both the rate of release and the rate of removal. Carbon dioxide is removed by the processes described above; methane by oxidation to carbon dioxide. The rate of oxidation of methane is important, and may vary as other factors in the atmosphere change.

In this discussion, however, the important point is only that the sources of both gases are enhanced by any warming of the Earth. Methane production by soils is even more sensitive to a warming than carbon dioxide production. A 1°C increase in temperature may increase rates of emission of methane by 50 per cent or more.[34] Control of these gases clearly depends on limiting the increase in global temperature.

Carbon dioxide offers an example of the magnitude of the challenge. There is, at the moment, a net annual accumulation of between 1.5 and 2.4 ppm of carbon dioxide, or 3–5 billion tonnes of carbon, in the atmosphere. This amount is the excess of releases to the atmosphere, whatever they may be in total, over removal. Stabilization of the atmospheric composition of carbon dioxide today would require an immediate reduction in current annual releases of 3–5 billion tonnes of carbon as carbon dioxide. If such a step were taken suddenly, we would have a few years to observe the result, but as the diffusion-pressure gradient of carbon dioxide between the atmosphere and the oceanic surface declined, the amount diffusing into the oceans would decline as well. A further reduction in emissions would be necessary to keep the atmospheric concentration from rising. The challenge would be the greater to the extent that the warming of the Earth results in an acceleration in the rate of emission of carbon dioxide from terrestrial ecosystems.

We have limited potential for reducing emissions. We can, we assume, control the use of fossil fuels and rates of deforestation. We might shift the world to reforestation, thereby storing carbon in expanding forests. To store one billion tonnes of carbon in forests requires 1–2 million square kilometres of developing forests, more if the land is poor. Such a shift would make a significant contribution toward stabilizing the atmosphere. But there is no possibility of stabilization without controlling the use of fossil fuels, and no possibility of long-term stabilization without, for all practical purposes, abandoning fossil fuels as the source of energy for industrialization. To the extent that the Earth is allowed to warm, urgency in reducing use of fossil fuels accumulates.

5.4 Conclusions

Details of the global carbon cycle, including the various factors that determine the rate of accumulation of carbon in the atmosphere, are imperfectly known. There is a question as to the relative importance of forests as opposed to the oceans in determining the composition of the atmosphere. Current evidence suggests that the role of forests is considerably larger in the shorter term of years to decades; that of the oceans larger in the longer term of decades to centuries.[35]

An acceleration of the warming of the Earth will reduce the area of forests over large areas. A 1°C warming at the warmer and drier limit of the distribution of forest will cause the replacement of 100–200 million hectares of forest by grassland. The warming will also release, through the decay of organic matter in forests and soils, a further large amount of carbon as carbon dioxide and methane. Whether there are other still more important factors affecting the composition of the atmosphere remains to be seen, but the evidence at the moment points to effects on forests of the northern hemisphere as most important.

The most powerful evidence in favour of this analysis is the data from the Vostok core. Those data shown that, throughout 160,000 years of recent glacial history, temperature and concentrations of carbon dioxide and methane were closely correlated. While causes and effects cannot be inferred from these data, they rule out the possibility that there is any intrinsic mechanism in the global climatic system that stabilizes temperature by stabilizing the composition of the atmosphere. It is possible, of course, that there are other factors that dominate and produce this pattern. One possibility is changes in the circulation of the oceans associated with changes in their capacity for absorbing or holding carbon dioxide. The fact that methane follows closely the pattern followed by carbon dioxide is usually taken to mean that the oceans are not involved.[36]

The possibility exists that the warming will proceed to the point where biotic releases from the warming will exceed in magnitude those controlled directly by human activity. If so, the warming will be beyond control by any steps now considered reasonable. We do not know how far we are from that point because we do not know sufficient detail about the circulation of carbon among the pools of the carbon cycle. We are not going to be able to resolve those questions definitively soon. Meanwhile, the concentration of heat-trapping gases in the atmosphere rises.

A conservative action in such a circumstance is not 'steady as you go', but a definitive change of course. The problem will grow rapidly as the Earth warms further. There is no easy solution beyond reduction in the rates of emission of carbon dioxide, methane, and the other anthropogenic greenhouse gases (CFCs and nitrous oxide). Carbon dioxide has well-known large sources in fossil fuels and from the biota; methane has a smaller source in fossil fuels and a larger biotic source that is only in part associated with deforestation. Both have a large potential biotic source in the warming of the Earth. The reduction in emissions cannot be accomplished without both drastic reductions in the use of fossil fuels and cessation of deforestation. The problem can be alleviated, but not resolved, by massive programmes of reforestation. The challenge is no longer to make adjustments in the rate of warming, but an all-out effort to stabilize the composition of the atmosphere. Stabilization will require immediately a reduction in the net annual accumulation of carbon in the atmosphere of 3–5 billion tonnes. Subsequent further reductions will be required which will constitute substantial abandonment of fossil fuels. The sooner the process is under way, the greater the hope of success. If the process is not undertaken, the erosion of the human habitat will proceed rapidly, with the full panoply of ecological and political consequences.

Chapter 6
Lessons from Climates of the Past

Brian Huntley

" ...the single most important lesson, assuming that
no steps are taken to curb greenhouse-gas emissions,
is that the climate-changes forecast for the next
century will give rise to warmer climates than have
been experienced on Earth for at least several million
years, and that these climate-changes will take place
more than an order of magnitude faster than the most
rapid climate-changes of the recent geological
past... "

As increasing attention focuses upon the likelihood of substantial
and rapid climate-change in the near future, resulting from anthropogenic addition of greenhouse gases to the atmosphere, vital lessons
can be learnt from studies of environmental history.[1] Changes in various components of the global system can lead to global climate-
changes; these so-called 'forcing factors' include natural changes in
the composition of the atmosphere, the position of the continents
upon the Earth's surface, the configuration of the ocean basins, the
topography of the continents, and the quantity of radiation received
from the sun. Although all of these factors vary continually, they
change at very different rates. Thus, the first three become of real
importance only at time-scales in excess of 10 million years, whereas
the uplift of mountain ranges has had major impact during the last

5 million years, causing the climatic upheaval that marked the transition from the Tertiary to the Quaternary geological period about 2.4 million years ago.[2]

Our most detailed information about global climate-change, however, relates to the short geological time-scale of the last million years. Over this period, most climate-forcing factors have varied so little as to be virtually constant (for example, the positions and topography of the continents), and those studying past climates alternatively refer to these as climatic 'boundary conditions'. These boundary conditions determine the general state of the global climate and the extent of its variation in response to changes in the more rapidly varying forcing factors. The major climate-changes of the last million years have resulted primarily from variations in the quantity of solar radiation received by the Earth,[3] although they have been accompanied by natural changes in the concentration of some greenhouse gases in the atmosphere.[4]

The quantity of solar radiation received by the Earth varies at many different time-scales.[5] The most important variations, however, are a limited number of periodic fluctuations that include, at the shortest time-scales, the daily and annual cycles. At longer time-scales, variations in the Earth's orbit around the sun lead to variations in the amount of solar radiation that are believed to have caused the series of alternations between glacial and interglacial conditions.[6] These alternations have occurred during the past 750 thousand years with a periodicity of c.100,000 years.[7] The last glacial period ended about 10,000 years ago, and it is only during the latter part of the present interglacial period, usually termed the post-glacial, that civilization has evolved.

These geologically recent but major climate changes are recorded in considerable detail by fossils and other environmental indicators preserved in the sediments accumulating upon the floors of oceans and lakes, as well as in deposits of loess – accumulations of fine, wind-blown particles that reach great depths in some continental regions. Our knowledge of past climates and past environments – palaeoclimates and palaeoenvironments – relies upon detailed stratigraphic studies of these deposits and reconstructions of the ecosystems – the palaeoecology – of which the organisms whose fossils we study were a part. By studying these records, particularly those spanning the last 250,000 years, we can gain insights into a variety of aspects of the global system that are of direct relevance to forecasting both future climate-change and the response of ecosystems to these changes. In particular, we can learn about:

- The sensitivity of global climate both to variations in radiation balance and to natural changes in atmospheric greenhouse-gas content;

- The mechanisms of global climate-change;

- Global and regional climates at times when global average temperature has been substantially lower and/or somewhat higher than today;

- Rates of past climate-change;

- The responses of organisms and of ecosystems to climate-change; and

- The rates at which organisms and ecosystems can respond.

Although, as in most fields of scientific endeavour, much remains unknown or else is imperfectly known, what we have learned already leads to several conclusions that must not be ignored when the impact of the anthropogenic greenhouse effect is being considered. The most important of these conclusions, and the lessons that follow from them, will be discussed below. It will be argued that the single most important lesson, assuming that no steps are taken to curb greenhouse-gas emissions, is that the climate-changes forecast for the next century will give rise to warmer climates than have been experienced on Earth for at least several million years, and that these climate-changes will take place more than an order of magnitude faster than the most rapid climate changes of the recent geological past. The implications with respect to the capacity of organisms and ecosystems to respond are profound; many ecosystems will change fundamentally, and there is a real prospect that many organisms may face extinction.

6.1 Palaeoclimates: how can we profit from their study?

Several roles have been proposed for palaeoclimate studies in relation to concern about future climate-change. Perhaps the most widely cited are:

- To document warmer climates of the past that may provide analogues – so-called palaeoanalogues – for warmer climates of the future, thus enabling 'empirical forecasts' to be made not only of global but also of regional climates of the next century;

- To document past global climates that can be used, in addition to the present climate, for the validation of General Circulation Models (GCMs), and especially to investigate the reliability of climate simulations for combinations of forcing factors and/or boundary conditions markedly different from those of the present;

- To evaluate the sensitivity of global climate to changes in various forcing factors, especially greenhouse gases and solar radiation; and

- To provide insights into the mechanisms, patterns, magnitude, and rates of past climate-change.

Each of these will be discussed in turn, and a brief account given of the relevant results.

6.1.1 Palaeoanalogues

Perhaps the first application of palaeoclimate studies to receive wide attention was the possible use of warmer climates in the past as analogues for a future warmer world.[8] A great deal of accumulated evidence points to the middle of the post-glacial period, about 6,000 years ago, as a time when many higher-latitude areas in the northern hemisphere were warmer than today.[9] Similarly, several lines of evidence combine to indicate that global climate was warmer during the last interglacial period, about 125,000 years ago, than at any time during the post-glacial, and there is general agreement that the world was warmer still during the late Tertiary, some 3 to 4 million years ago. However, the use of these periods as analogues for a progressively warmer world, as Budyko in particular has proposed,[10] is beset with apparently insuperable problems, as the scientists' working group of IPCC has pointed out.

The late Tertiary period poses the greatest number of difficulties, yet is of key importance to arguments based upon palaeoanalogues because it represents the first period, moving back through the geological record, when the reconstructed global climate is warmer than today by an amount comparable to the warming forecast for an effective doubling of CO_2.[11] Amongst the most important problems posed by the use of the late Tertiary as an analogue for next century are:

- The Himalayas, Tibetan plateau, and western North American mountains were lower than today by as much as 3 km;

- The Atlantic and Pacific Oceans were connected at low latitude prior to the uplift of the Isthmus of Panama about 3 million years ago;

- There was probably no extensive Greenland ice-cap and the Antarctic ice-sheet was of much smaller and varying extent;

- There has been substantial morphological evolution in many groups of organisms since the Tertiary, rendering the quantitative reconstructions of palaeoclimate, that are based primarily upon fossil evidence of terrestrial vegetation, extremely unreliable; and

- There is evidence of marked variation in global climate during the late Tertiary, with periodicities indicating that this most likely arises from orbitally induced variations in solar radiation;[12] this variation occurs over time-scales too short to be resolved by currently available dating techniques, rendering it impossible to reconstruct global climate for any specific time and combination of forcing factors during the Tertiary.

Of these, the importance of mountain uplift alone has been demonstrated by climate-modelling results[13] that indicate that the warmer climate can be accounted for as a response only to long-term changes in the topography of the continents. In addition, an assessment of the extent of the elevation of atmospheric CO_2 levels compared to the post-glacial[14] leads to the conclusion that this was insufficient alone to account for the warmer global climate. The major differences in the state of the global system combine with the evidence of the relative importance of continental topography, as opposed to atmospheric CO_2 levels, to render the late Tertiary unsuitable for use as an analogue for future climate.

The last interglacial presents fewer problems as a palaeoanalogue than does the late Tertiary; the principal climatic boundary conditions were very similar to those of the present. However, whereas the solar-radiation forcing differed from that of the present day as well as from that of the mid-post-glacial,[15] evidence from the Vostok ice-core does not support a hypothesis that atmospheric CO_2 levels were higher during the last interglacial than they were before the Industrial Revolution.[16] Thus, this period too is an inappropriate analogue for the future because it differs in the forcing being applied to cause the higher global average temperature. The same is true for the mid-post-glacial; atmospheric CO_2 levels were apparently similar to those before the Industrial Revolution,[17] as were levels of other naturally occurring greenhouse gases,[18] whereas solar-radiation forcing was significantly different from the present day.[19] Furthermore, although average temperature was higher in many higher-latitude areas of the northern hemisphere,[20] an assessment of *global* average temperature found that this was unlikely to have exceeded the present global average.[21]

These conclusions are reinforced by palaeoclimate simulations made using general circulation models (GCMs) of the atmosphere;[22] the simulated global average temperature for the forcing factors and boundary conditions 6,000 years ago is almost the same as that at the present day. In addition, the global climates simulated for effective doubling of CO_2[23] differ in several important ways from simulated palaeoclimates for periods of greater net solar radiation; these differences arise primarily from the uneven seasonal and latitudinal distribution of the solar-radiation forcing compared to the temporally and spatially evenly distributed forcing provided by increased greenhouse-gas levels. Thus, we are forced to conclude that, however attractive the idea, palaeoclimates cannot offer acceptable analogues for warmer climates of the near future.

6.1.2 GCM validation

Denied empirical forecasts based upon palaeoanalogues, we must rely upon GCM simulations to provide the best available forecasts of future climates. GCMs, however, utilize a variety of climatic boundary conditions and forcing factors, and the simulations generated are sensitive to changes in any of these. It is insufficient to tune a GCM to simulate the present climate; this provides no assessment of the reliability with which it will simulate climate under changed boundary conditions or in response to altered forcing factors. Quantitative reconstructions of palaeoclimate for particular times in the past when boundary conditions and forcing factors are also known provide one means to validate the performance of GCMs when simulating climates different from that of the present.[24]

The work of those involved in COHMAP (Cooperative Holocene Mapping Project) has provided the most extensive of such validations.[25] Palaeoclimate simulations were made at 3,000-year intervals from the maximum of the last glacial, 18,000 years ago, to the present using the NCAR (National Center for Atmospheric Research) CCM (Community Climate Model).[26] Global syntheses of palaeoclimate indicators for the same times enabled the validity of features of the simulated climates to be assessed.[27] The results showed general support from the palaeoclimate record for the main features of the simulated climates, although some discrepancies in particular regions and/or at particular times were also identified.

More recently, pollen-climate response surfaces have been developed[28] that offer an alternative means of validating the climates simulated using GCMs. These surfaces describe the pattern of abundance of individual pollen taxa with respect to two or more principal climate variables, and can be used not only to quantitatively reconstruct palaeoclimate from the fossil-pollen record, but also to quantitatively simulate pollen data corresponding to the climate conditions simulated by a GCM.[29] This approach has been utilized to assess simulations of the eastern North American climate,[30] and more recently an equivalent study has been performed for Europe.[31] The results obtained have helped identify areas of discrepancy between the fossil record and the palaeoclimate simulations, and hence focus attention upon aspects of both the GCMs and the interpretation of the fossil record that require further investigation. The scope for continued effort, refinement of the techniques, and the extension of the approach to other palaeoclimate indicators is considerable, and offers an important avenue for further palaeoclimate research.

6.1.3 Climate sensitivity

Although the most detailed palaeoclimate reconstructions available are those for the recent geological past, they cannot readily reveal the sensitivity of global climate to changes in greenhouse-gas concentrations. Only by using palaeoclimate reconstructions for the more remote geological past, and making a range of assumptions, can this sensitivity be evaluated.[32] Despite the many difficulties associated with reconstructing not only the palaeoclimate but also the forcing factors and boundary conditions for earlier geological periods, estimates of the global-temperature sensitivity to atmospheric CO_2 levels made in this way give a comparable figure (3.0°, plus or minus 1.0°C) for doubling of atmospheric CO_2 levels to that obtained by numerical simulation.

The record of more recent palaeoclimates can, however, provide valuable indications of the sensitivity of global climate to independent changes in various boundary conditions and forcing factors other than greenhouse gases, and these can contribute to both the validation of GCMs and the understanding of mechanisms of climate change.

6.1.4 Mechanisms, patterns, magnitudes, and rates of change

The time-series of palaeoclimate information – often with high temporal resolution – available in many sedimentary sequences offers potentially invaluable information that can reveal the time-course of palaeoclimate changes, and hence the mechanisms underlying these changes. The majority of efforts to date, both in climate-modelling and palaeoclimate reconstruction, have been focused upon 'snapshots' and equilibrium responses to given boundary conditions and forcing. The same is true of most GCM simulations of future climate. More recently, however, interest has begun to focus upon the transient response of climate as the forcing is changed.[33] The modelling of such future transient responses must be securely founded upon validated simulations of past transient states, and palaeoclimate time-series will provide the validation required.

The spatial dimension and resolution of the palaeoclimate reconstructions is also important, however, because they have the potential to reveal finer-scale regional patterns in palaeoclimate. These may be important both in understanding mechanisms of climate-change and in refining future climate predictions at a regional scale. It is apparent, for example, from preliminary palaeoclimate reconstructions for Europe[34] that southern Europe was no warmer than today, and in some areas cooler, 6,000 years ago when most of northern Europe was more than 1°C warmer than today. Similarly, lake-level evidence shows very different patterns of change in the precipitation–evaporation ratio in different latitudes of western

North America since the last glacial.[35] It is also apparent in both Europe[36] and eastern North America,[37] that there was a major re-arrangement of the overall climate patterns at the time of rapid de-glacial climate-change, with consequent changes in the alignment of major ecotones – the boundaries between major vegetation types – in both continents.

The palaeoclimatic record of the magnitude and rate of past cli-mate-changes assumes importance not primarily in relation to fore-casting future climates, but rather in assessing the likely impacts of these forecast changes upon organisms and ecosystems. Forecasts for the next century give a consensus of $c.2.5°C$ average global-tempera-ture increase within 100 years. Examination of the palaeoclimate record shows that it is necessary to look back to the Tertiary period to find global average temperatures this warm; most present organisms had not evolved their present form at that time, and the global-cli-mate patterns were substantially different from those of today.[38] Rapid climate changes of a comparable magnitude occurred more recently in the geological record; the so-called 'terminations' of the Quaternary glacial stages, the last of which occurred between 15,000 and 10,000 years ago, represent global average temperature-rises esti-mated at $c.5°C$,[39] and mark the rapid transition from a preceding glacial stage to an interglacial stage. These terminations, however, although geologically rapid, none the less occupied several millen-nia; the evidence suggests that the rate of *global* warming during the most recent termination was no more than 2.5°C per millennium.[40] This is already ten times slower than the rate forecast for the next cen-tury; if one of the higher values for simulated global warming during the next century is used along with a more conservative estimate of the rate of global warming at the end of the last glacial, then the his-toric rate may be as much as 100 times slower than that projected for the future.

6.2 Palaeoecology: biotic responses to climate-change

As well as providing a record of palaeoclimates, the Quaternary fossil record reveals how organisms respond to climate change. In this way, palaeoecological data can supplement field-observational and experimental ecological studies of the response of individual species to changes in their environment[41] and simulation modelling of ecosystem-responses to changed climate.[42] Several important conclusions have emerged from examination of the record of Quaternary and especially post-glacial vegetation.

6.2.1 Migration

Organisms faced with climate-change at the rates experienced during the Quaternary period have responded by migrating.[43] Only in response to much longer-term changes has evolutionary adaptation been the primary response. Thus, during the last 12,000 years forest trees have migrated across the continents in response first to the rapid climate-changes of de-glaciation, and subsequently to the slower but continuing climate-changes of the post-glacial.[44] Other groups of organisms, including beetles,[45] vertebrates,[46] and aquatic plants[47] have shown similar responses.

6.2.2 Individualism

Each species of tree whose pollen record has been examined has shown a different post-glacial history of distribution and abundance, and hence a different migratory history.[48] This individualism of response is also observed in other groups of organisms.[49] This has important consequences for the 'history' of ecosystems; essentially, ecosystems as such do not have a history, they emerge as temporary assemblages of taxa whose ranges coincide at the time being considered.[50] Thus, when the palaeo-vegetation of Europe is mapped,[51] many of the vegetation units that have been present in Europe during the past 13,000 years are not present today, and so the vegetation history cannot be reconstructed solely by reference to modern vegetation types.[52]

6.2.3 Rates of change

The rate of change of pollen spectra through time has been assessed for various regions of eastern North America,[53] as an overall average within Europe,[54] and also at individual pollen sites.[55] Although each individual region or site shows a different pattern when examined in detail, they consistently indicate rapid change at the time of de-glaciation, centred about 10,000 years ago, and an acceleration of rates of change during the last 2,000 years, especially the last millennium.[56]

Networks of palynologically studied sites – localities where pollen analyses have been carried out – enable estimates to be made of the migration rates of higher plants, especially trees, and in particular of their maximum rates of migration. These maximum rates were achieved in most cases in response to the climatic changes during deglaciation, although some exceptions, especially in Europe, have shown their most rapid migration during the last two millennia.[57] The migration rates that are obtained are generally of a magnitude of hundreds of metres per year, that is, in the range 10–100 km per century. There is remarkable consistency in these rates with similar results obtained by different workers for Europe,[58] eastern North America,[59] and Japan.[60] Recent work upon a rapid but short-lived expansion of pine forests into the far north of Scotland about 4,000 years ago[61] concludes that the migration rates required were of the same magnitude.[62]

Three lines of evidence point to the likelihood that these migration rates are close to the maximum rates of which trees at least, if not also other groups of organisms, will be capable. First, there is the circumstantial evidence of consistency between separate continental areas[63] and of such rates being evolved as an adaptive response to the maximum rates of climate-change experienced during the recent geological past.[64] Secondly, there is the evidence that some trees may have lagged behind the most rapid de-glacial climate changes,[65] implying that the migration rates that they achieved were the maximum of which they are capable. Thirdly, there is the difficulty in accounting for even the observed rates except by recourse to relatively rare long-distance dispersal events;[66] a tree that requires twenty years to mature and produce fruits, and that is maintaining a migration rate of 300 metres per year, must rely upon regular long-distance dispersal over distances in excess of 6 km if it is to sustain its migration.

A fourth corroborative argument can finally be put forward. If it is assumed that the thermal gradient in Europe was similar at the time of de-glaciation to the present ($c.8°C$ per 1,000 km for annual average temperature), and that Europe experienced a rate of temperature-change comparable to the global rate during de-glaciation ($c.2.5°C$ per 1,000 years), then the rate of migration required to sustain a *temperature-determined* range limit in equilibrium with climate is of the order of 300 metres per year.[67] Many northern range limits are primarily temperature-determined,[68] and so migration at a rate of this order of magnitude is to be expected along many northern range margins during de-glacial climate-change if they are maintaining equilibrium with climate; this is precisely what is observed. The faster migration rates (c.1–2 km per year) estimated for some taxa[69] can be accounted for by a variety of factors, including regionally more rapid temperature-change, changes in the thermal gradient associated with the overall climate-change,[70] and/or northern range limits that are determined not by temperature directly but by some correlate of temperature, such as the accumulated warmth during the growing season, that might change more rapidly than temperature.

6.3 Ecosystems in a 'greenhouse' world

The most fundamental implications for ecosystems stem from the magnitude of the rate of climate-change forecast for the future; the palaeoclimatic record shows us that even the most rapid of geologically recent climate-changes took place between ten and a hundred times slower than the changes forecast for the next century. The palaeoecological record shows us that the response of organisms to climate-change is one of migration; we should, therefore, expect organisms at least to attempt to migrate in order to accommodate future climate-changes. However, the palaeoecological record also gives consistent indications that trees, and perhaps also other organisms, have evolved maximum migration-rates that are appropriate to sustaining their population by remaining in equilibrium with the fastest geologically recent climate-changes, those of glacial terminations.

If this interpretation of the palaeoecological record is correct, then there is little likelihood that many organisms, and trees in particular, will be able to migrate fast enough to remain in equilibrium with future climate. For many organisms the situation may be made considerably worse by patterns of human land-use and by their already depleted populations.[71] The extreme cases will be those organisms that exist today only as small populations constrained within designated reserves, whether because they themselves are subject to persecution or because their habitat has been destroyed outside such reserves. Many trees and other forest organisms will face considerable problems in migrating across the largely agricultural landscapes of western Europe. As was discussed above, they are dependent upon chance, long-distance dispersal to maintain their maximum migration-rates. In the present-day landscape the proportion of long-distance dispersal events that will carry propagules – seeds or fruits – to suitable localities for establishment and growth will be considerably less than was the case when these organisms made their great migrations in the past across a landscape of natural ecosystems largely or even entirely uninfluenced by human actions. The consequent reduction in the success-rate of long-distance dispersal events will reduce the migration-rate that can be attained.

If, as the evidence seems to indicate, many organisms may be unable to maintain their distribution in equilibrium with the changing climate, then the consequences for ecosystems will be profound. Using the concept of alternative strategies put forward by Grime,[72] we should expect the competitive species that today dominate many ecosystems to be replaced by more ruderal species – species that have shorter life-spans, a greater commitment of resources to propagule production, and are adapted to exploit disturbed situations. Ecosystems in which the previous competitive dominants are no longer able to thrive, and yet in which the competitive dominants adapted to the new environment have not arrived because they are unable to migrate quickly enough, will be exploited by such opportunistic ruderal species. The structure of these ecosystems generally will be simpler than before; they are likely to support a less diverse range of herbivores and other consumers, and the biomass will be reduced. It is also likely that a smaller proportion of the capital of nutrients in the system will be locked up in the organisms; consequently, the likelihood of leaching and resulting soil deterioration will be greater. The reduced biomass and the likely soil deterioration would both represent positive feedbacks upon the greenhouse effect.

Ecosystems that are today dominated by stress-tolerant organisms[73] may fare even worse than those dominated by competitive species. In mountain regions, cold-tolerant species at high altitudes will be relatively rapidly replaced by more competitive but less cold-tolerant species from lower altitudes as the climate warms. Seasonally dry areas today occupied by drought-tolerant organisms may become inhospitable to these species as aridity increases; amongst the higher plants, opportunistic ruderal species are likely to exploit such situations, replacing long-lived, drought-tolerant perennials. In contrast, areas that are presently occupied by competitive species may become drought-stressed but be occupied by ruderal species in the short term, because the slow growth-rates and limited propagule production that characterize stress-tolerant species are likely to render them relatively slow to migrate. If we consider also the individualism of species responses, then many ecosystems are likely to disappear in their present form and be replaced by quite different assemblages of organisms.[74]

When the fates of individual organisms are considered, then the outlook for many seems bleak. Some species will have nowhere to go; they may occupy the highest-altitude parts of a landscape or be found only within a relatively short distance of the Arctic Ocean. These species may become extinct as they are displaced upwards or northwards by more competitive species benefiting from the warmer climate. A 2.5°C warming equates to an altitudinal displacement of more than 400 m and a latitudinal displacement in northern Europe of more than 300 km; all species constrained to the upper 400 m of a landscape or to within 300 km of the Arctic Ocean face the threat of extinction. In practice, the number of species involved is relatively small, but the almost certain extinction of some must be accepted.

Other species will have a relatively limited range, and will be unable to advance fast enough into newly suitable areas to compensate for the retraction of the opposite margin of their range. In Europe, many examples of this will be found amongst species whose present northern limit is determined mainly by temperature or one of its correlates, whereas their southern limit is determined by the incidence of drought. As climate warms, the constraints upon the northern limit will be relaxed, allowing migration northwards, but at the same time the southern limit may be pushed northwards by the increased drought-incidence in warmer summers, an effect that will be amplified if, as seems likely, southern Europe also receives reduced precipitation.[75] Whereas the northern limit will advance only as fast as migration capability allows, the southern limit will be shifted northwards as fast as the climate changes and increased drought-incidence kills individuals of the species. These species will suffer an increasingly severe crisis of population reduction; if the southern limit overtakes the northern limit, then they face extinction. Even with a conservative estimate of the northward extension of drought-incidence, species whose range has a latitudinal extent of less than 200 km face likely extinction. If the predictions of increased drought-incidence in lower and mid-latitudes are taken into consideration, then southern European species with ranges extending less than 500 km from north to south may be at risk of extinction. As before, the number of species with sufficiently restricted ranges to be affected is small, but some are certain to be affected.

However, many species' range-limits and/or ecotones are determined not by temperatures directly, but by other factors such as the temperature sum. Simulation studies of the boreal forest in Fennoscandia using the temperature sums that today constrain its northern and southern boundaries suggest that it may be displaced northwards by its own breadth if it is to maintain equilibrium with the climate of the next century.[76] This represents a displacement by almost 1,000 km, more than three times the mean displacement in Europe due to temperature alone. In such a case, the actual advance of the northern boundary in the time available may be only 50 km. If some factor of summer-heat stress or drought is determining the southern limit of the dominant tree species, then the whole biome – the vegetation and all of the associated animal and other species – could be reduced in extent to only 5 per cent of its present area. Even if such an extreme reduction may be unlikely, the potential for severe reductions is real and will endanger the populations of the rarer components of many biomes; species near the apex of food-webs will be especially vulnerable, and many of these are already suffering population reductions due to persecution.

If emissions of greenhouse gases continue unabated, then many organisms will suffer severe population reductions, others will almost certainly become extinct. Many ecosystems will become less complex, less diverse, and will maintain a lower biomass, contributing a positive feedback to the greenhouse effect. The job of conservationists will become one of artificially transporting species whose capacity to migrate is insufficient to enable them to keep pace with the changing environment.[77] In the face of such threats, the conservation bodies must lobby for a new approach to conservation if the developed countries especially are not to lose many of their species. We must stop focusing upon designated reserves; the organisms that they harbour today will be unable to survive there tomorrow.[78] Instead, a network of habitats for wildlife must be incorporated into our use of the land, providing greater resilience to change through opportunities to migrate naturally along corridors.[79]

Such steps, however, should be seen only as the remedial actions necessary to cope with the climate-change to which we have already committed the world. They will be insufficient to deal with the consequences of unabated greenhouse-gas emissions. To date, the climate simulations and forecasts that are being considered relate to the time when effective CO_2 levels have doubled; this is expected to happen by c.2030 if steps are not taken to curtail emissions.[80] However, if we reach that point, then the forecast rates of emission-increase are such that we will face an accelerating rate of increase of anthropogenic greenhouse gases in the atmosphere, and consequently of global climate-change, during the second half of the twenty-first and the twenty-second centuries. In addition, the high-latitude warming that is forecast for an effective doubling of atmospheric CO_2 levels will trigger the onset of methane release, initially from the peat lands of the tundras and by melting of permafrost, and subsequently by decomposition of the vast deposits of methane hydrates beneath the permafrost zone and in the sediments on the floor of the Arctic Ocean.[81] The greenhouse properties of methane are about thirty times greater than those of CO_2, and the breakdown of methane in the atmosphere depends upon the availability of free hydroxyl ions, levels of which are reduced by reaction with the increasing concentrations of oxides of nitrogen and of tropospheric ozone. The prospect is thus one of a potentially strong positive feedback upon the anthropogenic greenhouse effect resulting from the release of methane at high latitudes;[82] this is only one of several potential feedback mechanisms that are not currently included in the GCMs used to simulate future climate. The consequences for ecosystems and organisms of the rates of climate-change forecast for the next c.60 years are extremely severe. If we continue down this path, then we are almost certain to be unable to stop there,[83] and the whole biosphere may be threatened when, during the twenty-second century, climates unlike anything since the Cretaceous or before (more than 100 million years ago) seem likely to develop.

Chapter 7
The Implications for Health

Andrew Haines

" ...The primary effects of temperature on human disease are likely to be outweighed by secondary effects on health of climate change. In particular, the adverse effects on food production, availability of water, coastal flooding, and on disease vectors should be a cause of concern... The health-impact of climate change will not, however, be limited to the Third World..."

In comparison with the large body of research on the relationship between the buildup of greenhouse gases in the atmosphere and climate change, relatively little work has been undertaken on the potential effects of climate change on health. Clearly, there must be a considerable amount of speculation involved in trying to predict the impact of climate change on disease patterns. Nevertheless, sufficient is known about the direct and indirect effects of climate on health that a number of likely consequences can be outlined. (See Fig. 7.1.) The potential health effects of climate change cannot be considered in isolation. The world's population already exceeds 5 billion, and it is projected that by the year 2000 the population will reach 6.2 billion. Much of the population-growth will occur in the Third World. Such growth in population is likely to contribute to the greenhouse effect, because greenhouse-gas emissions are mainly

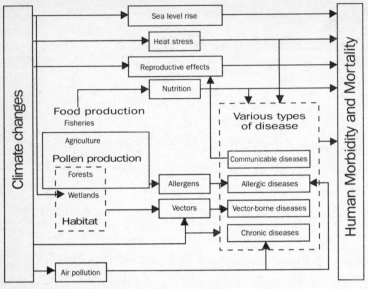

Fig. 7.1. Schematic showing how climate change can affect human health

anthropogenic, and will compound the difficulties of responding to the likely adverse effects of climate change on agricultural production, water supply, and sea-level rise. In addition, climate change will occur against a background of increasing exposure to ultraviolet radiation consequent upon the depletion of stratospheric ozone. This in itself will probably result in increased cataract formation, leading to increased requirements for operations and increasing numbers of blind people in the Third World. In addition, the incidence of skin cancer (including malignant melanoma) is likely to increase as a result of increasing exposure to ultraviolet radiation.

7.1 Effects of temperature-change on health

Temperature-change may have an impact on several major categories of disease, including cardiovascular, cerebrovascular, and respiratory diseases. (See Fig. 7.2.) The effects are likely to be particularly felt by those who are already susceptible for other reasons, in

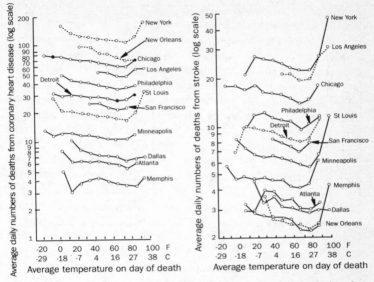

Fig 7.2 (a) Relationship of temperature to heart disease mortality; (b) Relationship of temperature to mortality from stroke. Adapted from Rogot and Padgett, n. 2.

particular the very elderly, the chronically ill, and the very young. Abrupt changes in temperature are likely to result in a higher incidence of adverse effects than gradual changes. High temperatures overload the thermo-regulatory system of the body, and in severe cases may result in frank heat-stroke. In studying the effects of climate on health, most studies have made use of mortality (death) statistics. Much less is known about changes in illness patterns (morbidity).

Attempts that have been made to predict the likely impact of climate change on mortality in the US have suggested that if acclimatization does not occur, there is likely to be a considerable rise in the number of summer deaths. An analysis of data from New York City using a regression equation incorporating nine weather-related variables, including temperature, wind-speed, and humidity, revealed a possible threshold temperature of 92°F (33°C), above which mortality increased.[1] An extension of the analysis to additional metropolitan areas in the US showed that all of the cities with the greatest average number of summer deaths were in the midwest or north-east, and those with the fewest were in the south. If no acclimatization were to occur, summer mortality in the US under a scenario in which atmospheric CO_2 doubled has been estimated to rise from a current total of around 1,150 deaths to around 7,400 deaths as a result of exposure to temperatures above the threshold. The majority of the deaths are likely to occur in the elderly. Even with full acclimatization, there is likely to be almost a doubling of summer deaths. The excess of summer deaths is likely to outweigh the small reduction in winter deaths. These figures should, however, be treated with caution, because they do not necessarily give an accurate guide as to how populations may respond in the future. A number of other factors could modify the response, including the use of air-conditioning, the availability of medical and nursing care, and the changing age-structure of the population, with increasing numbers of very elderly people.

There tends to be an inverse relationship between death from cardiovascular and cerebrovascular disease (stroke) and temperatures between the range of $-5°C$ and about $+25°C$ (that is, deaths go down as temperature goes up within this range). Above and below the range, however, increases in mortality occur which are particularly sharp in the case of stroke, with temperatures above 25°C.[2] Thus, deaths from stroke and from cardiovascular disease are likely to be major contributors to any excess mortality experienced as a result of climate change. Significant increases in premature birth and perinatal mortality in the summer months in the USA have also been recorded, probably related to the seasonality of reproductive infections.[3]

Climate may affect the respiratory tract in three ways: seasonal effects, direct effects of specific weather-conditions, such as thunderstorms and cold fronts, and combined effects of weather with other environmental or topographical factors.[4] Acute bronchitis and bronchiolitis (a viral disease which causes difficulty in breathing in young children) are more common in winter months. Individuals with chronic obstructive-airways disease are more likely to experience exacerbations of their condition in the winter, and pneumonia is also more common at that time. By contrast, asthma and hay fever tend to peak in incidence in the summer months. In the case of hay fever, pollen-release is responsible, but many patients with asthma are not pollen-sensitive and other factors may be involved, including, in some instances, levels of tropospheric ozone. There seems to be a second rise in acute asthma in the autumn, and hospital admissions are more common towards the end of the year, probably related to virus

Table 7.1: Recognized seasonal effects on respiratory illness

	Condition Affected	Possible Mechanism(s)	Source of Data
Winter	■ Acute bronchitis/ bronchiolitis	■ Colder temperature – effect on bronchial responsiveness? – increased viral replication/ transmissibility?	■ GP consultations ■ HAA ■ Mortality tables (DHSS)
	■ Acute exacerbations of chronic airflow obstruction/chronic bronchitis	■ Colder temperature – increased viral replication – permissive effect on secondary bacterial infection	■ HAA ■ Mortality tables ■ Use of the Emergency Bed Service
	■ Asthma requiring hospital admission	■ Viral-induced asthma?	■ HAA ■ Hospital attendances*
	■ Pneumonia	■ Colder temperature ■ Associated with relative humidity 1 week before?	■ HAA ■ Mortality tables
Summer	■ Asthma attacks	■ Pollen release ■ Ozone?	■ GP consultations
	■ Hay fever	■ Pollen release	■ GP consultations
Autumn	■ Acute bronchitis ■ Acute asthma	■ Viral infections? – return to school plus reduced temperature causing increased viral transmission	■ GP consultations ■ HAA ■ GP consultations ■ Hospital attendances

The data have been taken from various sources, mostly relating to the UK: HAA – hospital activity analysis (admissions); GP consultations – the Weekly Returns Service of the Royal College of General Practitioners Research Unit; mortality tables (OPCS); hospital attendances – published papers of attendances to accident and emergency departments.

* in some areas only, e.g. New York but not New Orleans.

Source: see Ayres, n. 4.

infections. Sandstorms have been associated with an increase in death-rate and symptoms from bronchitis and asthma.[5]

The mechanisms of the relationship between climate and respiratory disease are not entirely clear. There may be reduced resistance to infection or increased transmissibility of viruses in winter months, accounting for the increased incidence of bronchitis and bronchiolitis. Hot, dry summers tend to make the pollen-count high, and rainy weather reduces it. Increased ultraviolet light is likely to result in higher levels of tropospheric ozone, which have been demonstrated to cause transient reductions in respiratory function, although there are wide variations in individual responsiveness. The inhalation of concentrations as low as 0.18 parts per million may cause temporary reductions in forced expiratory volume at one second (the volume of air that can be forcibly exhaled in one second) in healthy adults.[6] In addition, there may be interactions between ozone and other pollutants. A recent study on adolescent asthmatic subjects has shown that prior exposure to low concentrations of ozone resulted in a measurable fall in respiratory function from a subsequent exposure to sulphur dioxide concentrations which would normally be insufficient to have any effect on lung function.[7]

Because of the interactions between different factors and the complexity of the relationship between respiratory disease and temperature, it is difficult to give a clear prediction of the impact of climate change. Although winter bronchitis and pneumonia may be reduced, it is quite likely that hay fever and perhaps asthma could increase. A combination of increase in temperature with increasing levels of tropospheric ozone could have clinically important effects, particularly in patients with asthma and chronic obstructive-airways disease. More work is required on the possible interactions between pollutants and temperature-change and on the possibility of long-term pulmonary damage from ozone exposure, which has been observed in animals.

7.2 Communicable diseases

The distribution of a range of diseases, currently confined largely to the tropics and including malaria, trypanosomiasis, leishmaniasis, amoebiasis, filariasis, onchocerciasis, schistosomiasis, and various worm infestations, is correlated with temperature and could in theory be affected by climate change. There are also a number of other non-parasitic communicable diseases whose distribution is related to temperature, including yellow fever, dengue and other arbovirus diseases, plague, and dysentery and other diarrhoeal conditions.[8]

The patterns of development and multiplication of malaria parasites or viruses within their mosquito hosts are temperature-dependent.[9] Extremes of the extrinsic incubation period (incubation period in mosquitoes) for yellow-fever virus, for example, are from three days to a few weeks, depending entirely on the mean ambient temperature. In Egypt, which lies partly on the edge of hot and temperate zones, water snails tend to loose their schistosome infections during January, February, and March each year when the temperature is cooler. If temperatures increase, Egyptian water snails may be able to spread schistosomiasis all the year round, increasing the already heavy parasite burden of the Egyptian peasantry.

Human activities have an important role in the transmission of many tropical diseases, for instance, many of the breeding places for the major vectors of malaria in Africa are man-made, including potholes, irrigation channels, and so on. Human behaviour has the potential for reducing or increasing the impact of climate change on a number of communicable diseases. For instance, the increase in drought may result in people and animals gathering together for increasing periods of time at limited numbers of watering holes, thus encouraging the spread of disease.

Heavy rainfall may have variable effects over a short period. Excessive rainfall may, of course, lead to flooding, with a loss of crops and an increase in breeding areas for insects that require water. It can, on occasions, have the reverse effect by flushing out residual pools of insect vectors in river systems.

The potential impact of climate change on communicable disease is not likely to be limited to the Third World. Even in an affluent country such as Australia, mosquito-borne disease may pose considerable threats to health which will probably increase as a result of the greenhouse effect.[10] The major mosquito-borne diseases in Australia are dengue fever, Australian encephalitis caused by the Murray Valley encephalitis virus, and epidemic polyarthritis caused by the Ross River virus. In the past, malaria and filariasis have also been prevalent. In tropical Australia, climate changes could increase the vulnerability to a recurrence of malaria, as well as leading to an increase in the incidence of epidemic polyarthritis and an extension of the area of distribution of the Murray Valley encephalitis virus. In the case of dengue, the influence might be limited as the mosquito vector breeds in domestic containers. In the temperate part of Australia, there could be an increased incidence of epidemic polyarthritis and also a possible increase in the number of outbreaks of Australian encephalitis. Australian encephalitis has an appreciable mortality rate, and may result in long-term effects ranging from minor personality and psychological disorders to severe paralysis and brain-damage.

Using a range of climate scenarios for the USA, it has been found that tick-borne diseases – Rocky Mountain spotted fever and Lyme disease – would spread northwards, although the distribution would also depend on the size of remaining forests and of the small mammal population. Apart from occasional outbreaks of arbovirus encephalitis, vector-control programmes and improved hygiene have virtually eradicated mosquito-borne diseases transmitted within the USA. However, the potential exists for their reintroduction because of cutbacks on the use of pesticides, and the large numbers of recent immigrants who could be sources of infection. Five of the numerous mosquito-borne diseases have been considered to be potential risks in the USA following climate change. Malaria, dengue fever, and the arbovirus-induced encephalitis were considered to be significant risks, and yellow fever and Rift Valley fever possible risks.[11]

It seems likely that climate change will result in increasing problems with communicable diseases, although other factors such as human activity, patterns of rainfall, and insecticide use will clearly be important in determining their ultimate impact.

7.3 Ultraviolet radiation and the immune system

Ultraviolet radiation is known to have effects on the immune system. For instance, coldsores not infrequently occur at the beginning of a summer holiday because of the immuno-suppressive effect of ultraviolet radiation on skin resulting in activation of the herpes simplex virus. It is possible that susceptibility to important skin infections such as leishmaniasis or leprosy might be increased by greater exposure to ultraviolet light because the expression of these diseases depends on the cell-mediated immune response.[12] The immune response to transplantation is also affected, and in animals transplantation of tumours has been shown to be more likely to be successful following exposure to ultraviolet radiation.[13] Patients who are immuno-suppressed for organ transplantation (as well as other groups, such as those with genetic diseases which impair DNA repair) are at an increased risk of the development of ultraviolet light-related skin cancer. Ultraviolet radiation induces the formation of suppressor T-cells which inhibit the normal anti-tumour response and permit the emergence and progression of tumours.[14] Thus, the effects of ultraviolet radiation on the immune response of skin may play a role in the increased incidence of skin cancer expected following the depletion of stratospheric ozone, and increased ultraviolet exposure has the potential to interact synergistically with climate change in the case of some communicable diseases.

7.4 Effects on food production

The world's food reserves are currently very sensitive to changes in the US grain harvest, which provides 90 per cent of the world's surplus; thus, any shortfall in the US harvest is likely to affect in the first instance those countries to whom grain is exported. Rice is a staple food for 60 per cent of the world's population and some countries where water management and irrigation are poorly developed, such as India and Burma, may be particularly vulnerable to changes in temperature and rainfall.

One hundred and fifty million children under 5 suffer from malnutrition, and every year 14 million children die from largely preventable causes of death. Malnutrition is a contributory cause in approximately one-third of all child deaths.[15] The proportion and absolute numbers of the world's population living in countries with average food supplies of less than 2,200 calories per head per day declined between the 1960s and around 1980. However, at that time one-third of the population in the developing world still lived in countries with daily food supplies of less than 2,200 calories. A large proportion of the population in these countries is likely to be undernourished.[16] Between the years of 1950 and 1984, the world grain-output increased 2.6-fold, but since then there has been little further increase. Since 1984 there has been no world-wide increase in per-capita grain production because of continuing population growth. In Zambia, twice as many children died from malnutrition in 1984 as in 1980. The infant-mortality rate in Brazil rose in 1983 and 1984, particularly in the poorest regions, for the first time in decades. This appeared to be a result of increasing poverty related to the heavy burden of international debt. The initial impact of any further falls in per capita food production will in the first instance probably fall principally on children in the Third World.

Currently, the small average net gain of 15 million tons world-wide in grain harvests is well below the 28 million tons required merely to keep pace with the population growth. Growth in production of food around the world has been impaired by environmental degradation, scarcity of crop-land and irrigation water, and a diminished response to the use of additional chemical fertilizers. Several pollutants, including ozone, sulphur dioxide, and nitrous oxide, may also have adverse effects on crop production.[17] In addition to effects on crop production, atmospheric change could have an impact on animal diseases. For instance, a study in North America suggests that under some scenarios of climate change there could be a major extension of the horn-fly season. This already causes considerable losses in the beef- and dairy-cattle industries. Distribution of the insect carrier of anaplasmosis, a major infection of ruminants, could extend to northern US states with climate change.[18] In addition, increased ultraviolet radiation could result in damage to the marine food-chain because of adverse effects on fish, shrimp and crab larvae, and the growing-season of invertebrate zooplankton populations, as well as on the nitrogen-fixation process in phytoplankton.[19]

7.5 Water supply

Of the estimated 41,000 cubic kilometres of water which return each year from the land to the sea, around 9,000 cubic kilometres are readily available for human use. In theory, this is enough to sustain around 20 billion people, but in practice the local availability of water varies widely because population and water supply are unevenly distributed. Withdrawal rates differ widely from country to country, for instance the average US resident consumes more than 70 times as much water per year as the average resident of Ghana.[20] Nearly three-quarters of the water used is for agricultural purposes, and the area of irrigated land is increasing steadily each year. Decreases in summer rainfall together with increases in temperature predicted for central North American, southern European, and other sites is likely to have an adverse effect on agriculture, but in the long term could also affect the availability of water for human consumption. Irrigation has increased the salinity levels in the return-water and soils of several river basins in the US, and reductions in rainfall may further exacerbate this process.[21] In the southeast and parts of the west of the USA, a large percentage of municipal water-supplies come from ground-water. These regions tend to withdraw more ground-water than can be recharged, and any increased drought caused by climate change could accelerate the mining of ground-water.

In countries with poorly developed water-supply systems, a reduction in water supply could contribute to the spread of diarrhoeal and other diseases spread by the faecal-oral route. The loss of vegetation and biomass consequent upon drought would lead to a reduction in fuel for cooking and heating water, thus further promoting the spread of disease. Sea-level rise would lead to an increase in salinization of rivers, wetlands, and aquifers, causing harm to some aquatic plants and animals and posing a threat to the use of water by humans.

7.6 Sea-level rise

Global warming could cause a sea-level rise of 0.5–2 metres by 2100. Many coastal regions are already under threat for geological reasons or secondary to extraction of ground-water and other human activities. In the case of Bangkok, for instance, local subsidence has reached 13 cms per year because of excessive extraction of ground-water.[22] The most serious implications are for those densely populated parts of the world vulnerable to small rises in sea level, such as the Nile Delta in Egypt and the Ganges Delta in Bangladesh. In the case of Egypt, around 16 per cent of the population live in a region comprising 0.4 per cent of the total area of the country, which would flood if the sea level rose by 50 cms. In Bangladesh, floods caused the deaths of 300,000 people in the 1970s. Some of the most vulnerable countries to sea-level rise include Bangladesh, Egypt, Pakistan, Indonesia, and Thailand, all of which have large, relatively poor, populations.[23] Parts of Europe could also be vulnerable. In 1953, floods killed over 1,000 people in the Netherlands. A 1-metre rise in sea level has been calculated to reduce the effectiveness of Dutch protective measures from an ability of being breached once every 10,000 years to once every 100 years. A 1-metre rise in sea level would wipe out much of England's sandy beaches, salty marshes, and mud flats.[24]

7.7 Mental health

It is likely that with climate change there will be an increasing number of disasters related either to extreme events, such as storms in conjunction with sea-level rise, or to famine. There have been a number of studies of the survivors of disasters which have suggested the potential in some cases for long-term effects on mental health.[25] In 1972, for instance, a dam collapsed in the USA leading to the deaths of 125 people and causing 4,000 to be homeless.[26] Traumatic neurotic reactions were found in 80 per cent of the survivors, and there was persistent evidence of unresolved grief, survivor shame, and feelings of impotent rage and hopelessness. Disabling psychiatric symptoms included anxiety, depression, and changes in character and life-style. Over 90 per cent of the children who were interviewed had developmental problems more than two years after the disaster. A study of individuals exposed to a cyclone in Darwin, Australia, showed that 41 per cent had psychological dysfunction at 10 weeks, but by fourteen months the level had returned to that of a controlled population.[27] The psychological reactions to disaster may depend on the magnitude of destruction, the age of the population, and the degree of support that survivors receive. There is little doubt, however, that the psychological sequelae of disaster may result in a considerable increase in contact with the medical system. For instance, following a flood in Bristol, UK, in 1968, in which 3,000 homes were inundated and one person died, there was an increase of 53 per cent in visits to doctors for the year following.[28] A similar observation was made following the effects of a flood in Brisbane, Australia, in 1974.[29]

More conjectural is the possible psychological impact of the threat of climate change. In the 1970s and 1980s a number of studies in a range of countries showed the extent of concern on the part of the public about the threat of nuclear war. There is increasing awareness by the public that major environmental threats such as climate change are also a major threat to security. For instance, a 1988 Gallup poll reported that 70 per cent of Americans saw environmental degradation as a serious problem. According to the research director of the Public Agenda Foundation, a non-profit organization in New York which surveys public attitudes, 'a lot of people think that the greenhouse effect is starting even though they don't know what to make of it'.[30] Many people are likely to react to either conscious fear or deeper uneasiness about the environment by denial. This may be partly related to guilt, because the magnitude of greenhouse effect will result from the life-style of those living in the industrialized world. Unlike the issue of nuclear war, where blame can be laid at the door of the 'enemy' or of governments, in the case of the greenhouse effect individual life-styles in aggregate will be a major determinant of how far climate change can be averted. Clearly, however, governments can play a major role in setting the legislative framework to promote such changes. Individuals may have difficulty in reacting because the threat seems nebulous and distant. It is possible, for instance, that concern and despair about the future might result in an increase in nihilistic and antisocial behaviour, but at the same time there may be an increase in activities aimed at influencing governments and individuals to prevent, as far as is possible, climate change.

7.8 Other effects

There is a range of other possible health-effects of climate change. Some are likely to be relatively minor, like an increased incidence of skin disorders such as prickly heat, and fungal skin diseases such as ringworm and athlete's foot as a result of increased temperature and humidity. More importantly, environmental degradation secondary to climate change has considerable potential for triggering armed conflicts, resulting in considerable added suffering from direct and indirect effects of military activities. For instance, 40 per cent of the world's population depends for water on 214 major river systems shared by two or more countries. Twelve of these are shared by five or more countries. Already there are a considerable number of disputes over the availability of water-supplies and pollution. Unresolved water-disputes with potential to provoke conflict include those involving the waters of the Nile, the Indus, the Ganges, the Jordan, and the Euphrates. Large movements of refugees may occur as a result of crop failure and coastal flooding. As well as provoking violence and unrest they may also promote the spread of disease both due to breakdown in sanitation and to crowding.

7.9 Conclusions

The primary effects of temperature on human disease are likely to be outweighed by secondary effects on health of climate change. In particular, the adverse effects on food production, availability of water, coastal flooding, and on disease vectors should be a cause of concern. The effects of climate change will occur against a background of steadily increasing world population, most of this in the Third World. Economic sufficiency and the education of women are important determinants of family-size, as well as the provision of contraceptive services. Thus, in addition to changes in life-style in the industrialized world, priority needs to be given to improving development, education, and health-care in the Third World if the potential impacts on health of the greenhouse effect are to be ameliorated.

The health-impact of climate change will not, however, be limited to the Third World. The populations of all countries will be affected. The potential effects which have been discussed are those which appear likely based on current knowledge. It is quite possible that a range of other consequences to health could occur which have not been predicted. This is particularly likely if governments and individuals do not respond with alacrity to calls for the limitation of greenhouse-gas emissions, and positive-feedback mechanisms (such as the release of methane from permafrost as a consequence of warming), come into play resulting in even faster warming than has been projected.

3

Policy Responses

" ... Many present efforts to guard and maintain human progress, to meet human needs, and to realize human ambitions are simply unsustainable – in both the rich and poor nations. They draw too heavily, too quickly, on already overdrawn environmental resource accounts to be affordable far into the future without bankrupting those accounts. They may show profits on the balance sheets of our generation, but our children will inherit the losses. We borrow environmental capital from future generations with no intention or prospect of repaying. They may damn us for our spendthrift ways, but they can never collect on our debt to them. We act as we do because we can get away with it: future generations do not vote; they have no political or financial power; they cannot challenge our decisions. But the results of the present profligacy are rapidly closing the options for future generations... "

The UN World Commission on Environment and Development, in Our Common Future *(the Brundtland Report, 1987)*

Summary

An understanding of the remarkable consensus among the world's climate scientists, and consideration of the impacts of the rates of global warming they predict, should surely lead any rational person to conclude that a concerted international response to global warming can no longer be delayed.

The policymakers in the Response Strategies Working Group (RSWG) of IPCC were charged with the vital – indeed historic – role of translating the scientists' appraisal of the greenhouse threat into effective policies. To conclude that they failed in this task is to understate the case. The astonishing and barely believable truth is that the IPCC policymakers could not even bring themselves to recommend a freeze in global greenhouse-gas emissions, much less the deep cuts which the scientists have shown are necessary if any attempt is to be made significantly to slow or arrest global warming. The collective view the IPCC policymakers have arrived at is that we can afford to go right on borrowing environmental capital from our children and theirs, that we are justified in carrying right on with our great global game of roulette with the future.

Yet the routes to cutting greenhouse-gas emissions are clear. They will not cost us the earth, as some people accustomed to never including environmental costs in their accountancy would have us believe. Rather, they can save us the Earth.

In this, the most important section of the *Greenpeace Report*, selected world authorities in the fields relevant to cutting greenhouse-gas emissions give us their views of the routes to survival. The concluding chapter gives the Greenpeace view.

Professor Jose Goldemberg, Secretary of State for Science and Technology in the current Brazilian government and co-author of *Energy for a Sustainable World* – one of the most influential books on energy policy ever written – argues that a key policy in the route to a low-energy future must be to help the developing world 'leap-frog' the energy-intensive mistakes already made by the industrialized countries, and shows how relatively little this would cost. In similar vein, Dr Stephen Schneider debunks the notion – advanced even in the White House – that it would necessarily cost the USA billions of dollars annually to cut its carbon dioxide emissions. Dr Amory Lovins, Research Director of a top US energy policy research institute, demonstrates that the reverse is in fact true: given the will for change, billions of dollars can be *saved* from a concerted effort to save energy. Carlo LaPorta, a past Director of Research at the US Solar Energy Industries Association, shows that it is not only environmentally imperative to replace fossil fuels with renewables, but in many cases today economically desirable – and only likely to become more so as current technological advances come to fruition in the decades to come. Michael Walsh, a past head of the US Environmental Protection Agency's motor-vehicle pollution programme, shows how great is the scope for cutting greenhouse-gas emissions in the transport sector. Dr Bill Keepin, an analyst who has held posts at a number of the world's centres of excellence in energy policy issues, demonstrates why every dollar spent on nuclear power in the fight against global warming will be a dollar wasted – even if the economics of nuclear power somehow greatly improve, and safety and waste-disposal problems somehow miraculously vanish. Next, Swedish experts from the state power board and Lund University show how the most nuclear-intensive (per capita) country in the world can implement its current plan to phase out nuclear power, cut carbon dioxide emissions, and still save money while achieving economic growth. Professor Norman Myers, a senior adviser to the Brundtland Commission, reviews the need for policies to stop global deforestation, and to promote reforestation. Dr Anne Ehrlich, Director of the Center for Conservation Biology at Stanford University in the USA, demonstrates the need to stem methane and nitrous oxide emissions from agriculture, and the routes to achieving that. Dr Kilaparti Ramakrishna, an Indian authority in environmental law, and Dr Susan George, Associate Director of the Transnational Institute, close by demonstrating the vital need for humankind, if we are to survive the greenhouse threat, to make the North–South relationship equitable.

Chapter 8
Policy Responses to Global Warming

Jose Goldemberg

" ...If the costs of the insurance against climatic change were to be divided among countries proportionally with respect to their current insurance expenditures, it would cost the US another $4.5 billion per year in insurance, or an additional 1.2 per cent on what Americans already spend on insurance ... The total amount of money needed for the operation of the fund (of the order of US$30 billion per year) could easily be amassed by setting a levy of US$1 per barrel equivalent of petroleum consumed... "

Stephen Schneider's paper on the scientific aspects of the increase of greenhouse gases (GHG) in the atmosphere due to the action of man, established clearly that important climate changes will occur in the planet (mainly in the northern hemisphere) in the next few decades. Such changes, in the absence of cuts in GHG emissions, will manifest themselves as an average global rise in temperature of the order of 1.5–4.5°C for an effective doubling of CO_2 in the atmosphere, changes in precipitation and atmospheric circulation, and a depletion of the stratospheric ozone layer.

George Woodwell's paper on the impacts of such changes

established clearly that among the many consequences there will be a rise in sea level in many areas of the world, with disastrous consequences for populations living in low coastal regions; massive changes of agriculture; and important changes in the remaining forest cover of several continents.

In the face of these prospects, it is imperative to examine what we can do to avoid such changes, and/or how to adapt to a changed climate. The policy responses to the consequences of the greenhouse effect are therefore of two broad categories: an adaptive one, in which people migrate and/or change their living conditions to adapt to a new environment; or a preventive or abatement one, in which an attempt is made to minimize man-made global climate change by removing its causes.

Numerous climate changes occurred in the past, and our present environment – and the species that exist today in nature – are the result of evolutionary changes that accompanied such changes. But what is without precedent in a world where man-made GHG emissions continue at anything like the present rate is the pace of climatic change predicted by climate simulations. We are likely to see in the next few decades average-temperature increases that took thousands of years to occur in the past. It is the speed at which such changes will come about that is without precedent, and not the absolute value of the changes.

One of the most obvious examples of an adaptive strategy would be to build dikes to protect coastal areas, as Holland has done over the centuries to reclaim areas from the sea and convert them into agricultural land. Such techniques could be applied to other countries, such as Bangladesh, where land is not much above present sea level. Another example would be to plan for switches in agricultural practice as temperatures rise. The location of fertile lands and the viability of particular crops might change drastically in several parts of the world due to changes in climate and water precipitation. As an example, one can expect the Midwest area of the United States – which is presently a large producer of grain – to become quite dry, as occurred in the mid-30s. As a result, agricultural production in the US might have to be relocated to other parts of the country, obviously at high cost.

It has been argued by some that man is a very resourceful animal with an extraordinary capacity for adaptation, and with tremendous technological resources at his disposal. The problem becomes then to a large extent a question of quantifying the anticipated changes, and the costs of adaptation. For example, could Holland afford to build the dikes required to keep the rising seas at bay in perpetuity? Even if US grain production were to be switched successfully to the northern states, what would be the costs of the net effect on US agriculture over time? Published estimates of the costs of such adaptive strategies range between a total of $500 and $1,000 billion in the next thirty years[1] if no abatement strategies are adopted in parallel. These estimates are admittedly quite rough but are based on past experiences and should not be in error by more than a factor of 2.

There are in addition other questions besides sheer costs, such as extensive relocation of populations. In some cases, these might have important geopolitical consequences, in addition to the enormous inconveniences caused to the hundreds of millions of persons involved. The prospect of enhancing the risks of regional conflicts arising from such dislocations in the Indian subcontinent, for example, should not be brushed aside.

Abatement strategies hinge on a good understanding of the causes of the greenhouse effect and of actions to eliminate the causes. Our present knowledge[2] tells us that the man-made greenhouse effect is due to energy production and use (around 57 per cent), deforestation (9 per cent), agriculture (14 per cent), and industrial non-energy activities (20 per cent) (Fig. 8.1a). The relative contributions of the several GHGs to the total effect are given in Figure 8.1b.

An obvious strategy would be to eliminate or minimize the most important contributors to the greenhouse effect: mainly carbon dioxide emissions. What of quantifying the extent of the actions needed and the cost here? As I will show later on, these costs are comparable to the costs of an adaptive strategy (500 to 1,000 billion dollars). The important point is that they avoid the enormous risks of an adaptation-only future.

It has been argued that sharp cuts in energy production would affect development and growth in developed countries.[3] On the other hand, the use of energy-efficient technologies has other benefits in addition to the reduction of carbon dioxide emissions: reducing the dependence on oil imports in many countries, avoiding the reliance on nuclear reactors with all their security problems and environmental problems, and greater self-reliance on domestic energy sources and technologies.[4]

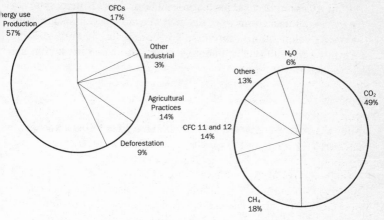

Fig. 8.1. Contributions to the enhanced greenhouse effect: (a) by activity, (b) by the principal anthropogenic greenhouse gases
(Source: *Lashof and Tirpak, n. 2*).

8.1 Decision-making in the face of uncertainties

The existence of two strategies to face the consequences of global warming leads us to the question of how decisions are taken when there are scientific and other uncertainties involved. The argument has been put forward by a number of people that the warming of the globe and other undesirable consequences of the greenhouse effect are not at all certain, and that therefore one should wait – until climate models become so sophisticated that they can predict future climate changes with certainty.

This is indeed a peculiar position to adopt, because in the realm of decision-making at high levels of government most actions are taken in the face of 'massive uncertainties'. A good example of how governments work in this respect was President Reagan's decision to go ahead with the SDI (Strategic Defense Initiative). This military initiative involved expenses of many billions of dollars in the face of very heavy criticism from many scientists sceptical that the system proposed would ever work. To request 'certainty' about the dire consequences of the warming of the globe before acting is dangerous because it might be too late – or prohibitively expensive – to act after the composition of the atmosphere changes significantly. If one acts early enough the actions required might be more acceptable to many, would cost less, and in any case are known to have positive side benefits, such as the abatement of acid rain, ozone depletion, and photochemical smog.

8.2 What is required to abate the greenhouse effect?

The anthropogenic greenhouse effect (that is, that part of the overall greenhouse effect which is due to enhancement as a result of human activities) can be considered as a sudden perturbation in a system in equilibrium. One can ask, therefore, what is needed to return to an equilibrium: to stabilize emissions? to reduce them? by how much?

To answer these questions one can use the classic climate models to find out what are the reductions in the emissions of GHGs needed to avoid atmospheric changes. This has been undertaken by the EPA (Environmental Protection Agency of the United States)[5] and by Bolin, summarizing the work of the IPCC's scientists.[6] The assumptions in these two studies do not differ much.

Since GHGs have different contributions to the total global warming, several combinations of reductions are possible to achieve the desired effect. Some arbitrariness is therefore involved in the choices made over emission-reduction scenarios, and time-scales.

The EPA estimates the emission reduction needed to stabilize atmospheric greenhouse-gas concentrations at current levels as:

50–80 per cent of carbon dioxide;
10–20 per cent of methane;
75–100 per cent of CFCs;
80–85 per cent of nitrous oxide.

Present emissions of 12.2 gigatonnes of carbon per year equivalent (Gt C/year) would be reduced by 5.4 Gt C/year by the year 2005 (Fig. 8.2). To get these numbers all emissions are converted into equivalent emissions of carbon dioxide. CFCs, although emitted in small quantities, are very effective in adding to the greenhouse effect.

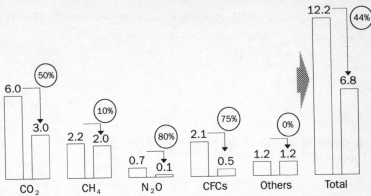

Fig. 8.2. *Drastic emission-reductions required: the minimum estimates of anthropogenic emission-reductions for stabilization of the atmospheric concentrations of greenhouse gases at present levels. Emissions are expressed as CO_2-equivalents, and given in GtC.*
(Source: See n. 16.)

8.3 Minimum EPA estimates of man-made emission-reductions for stabilization

The IPCC scientists' assessment of the effects of specific abatement actions and their likely impacts on global average temperature change are shown in Table 8.1.[7] Fig. 8.1 shows clearly the importance of energy use in causing the greenhouse effect. Table 8.1 shows equally clearly the potential role of energy use, and conservation, in abating it.

Table 8.1: Abatement strategies and their potential resultant impact on global average temperatures as advanced in the Report of the Second Session of the Steering Committee of IPCC Working Group 3, May 1989.

Strategy	Average temperature change (°C)
Ban CFCs	–0.52
Stop deforestation	–0.20
Reforestation*	–0.20
Convert from oil and coal to gas	–0.28
Energy Conservation	–0.45
Total	**–1.65**

*500–1,000 million hectares.

Table 8.2: Indicators of Energy Consumption Per Capita and Per Unit of Product (1986)

	Total population (millions)	Total energy consumption (MTEP)	TEP/Capita	TEP/US$1000	GDP(US$) /Capita
OECD	818	3,855	4.71	0.38	12,119
USA			7.2	0.41	17,480
Japan			3.2	0.20	12,840
FRG			4.5	0.30	12,080
France			3.6	0.28	10,720
UK			3.8	0.46	8,870
Italy			2.5	0.24	8,550
LDCs	3,830	1,915	0.5	0.59	680
Brazil			0.8	0.55	1,810
India			0.2	0.80	290
Mexico			1.2	0.78	1,860
Korea			1.4	0.60	2,370
China			0.6	2.12	330
CPEs	475	2,040	4.3	0.61	6,749
USSR*			4.9	0.62	7,340
GDR*			5.9	0.56	10,234
Czechoslovakia*			4.8	0.55	8,500
Total	**5,123**	**7,810**			

*Toe/1000 US$ refers to 1985.
(Sources: *British Petroleum Statistical Review of Energy; World Bank, Report on World Development* (1988); *Handbook of Economic Statistics* (CIA) (1987).)
Note: OECD = Organization for Economic Co-operation and Development;
LCDs = less-developed countries; CPEs = centrally planned economies.

Extraction of coal from underground used to be a risky and polluting business even in the fifteenth century, but the burning of such coal then represented only a minor nuisance to the environment. Today the burning of immense quantities of coal, oil, gas, and fuelwood represents a serious environmental threat. Quite apart from the greenhouse gases emitted – carbon dioxide as a result of combustion, methane from gas leakage from coal-mines and natural-gas pipelines, and so on – the sulphur and nitrogen oxides which result from the burning of fossil fuels are the main causes of smog, acid rain, and a variety of other disturbances in our environment. Carbon dioxide, which cannot be filtered or easily captured, is responsible alone for

49 per cent of the greenhouse effect.

Energy, however, is absolutely essential for development, and huge amounts are needed to achieve the present level of amenities available to people living in the industrialized nations. It is enough to recall that the average US citizen consumes 7.2 tons of petroleum equivalent (TEP) per year to realize how important energy is. In contrast to that, an average person living in the developing countries has to make do with ten times less energy (Table 8.2).

Energy consumption in the US and other developed countries (OECD as a whole) reached a level of saturation and did not increase significantly from the mid-70s to the mid-80s, although the gross domestic product (GDP) continued to grow. Recently, energy consumption has started to grow again. In the less-developed countries (LDCs), including China, however, energy consumption has been growing linearly for a long time and shows no indication of saturation, as seen in Fig. 8.3. This is also true for the Soviet Union and Eastern European centrally planned economies (CPEs).

The political leadership of LDCs, and their populations in general, believe that it is necessary to grow at all costs, and commonly operate under the assumption that energy consumption has a linear relationship with economic growth. This process involves repeating – if necessary – the same energy mixes as used in the past by the industrialized countries. In addition, in a number of LDCs intense deforestation is taking place due to changing land-use patterns. Some of the deforestation – mainly in Africa – is linked to energy uses such as cooking.[8] Deforestation of any kind contributes significantly to carbon dioxide emissions, but such action is justified by some as an inevitable result of development.[9]

It would seem at first approximation straightforward to address the greenhouse problem by measures leading to a reduction in energy consumption (and consequently reduced carbon dioxide emissions), plus a reduction in deforestation and increased reforestation where possible. Actions of this type (that is, cutting production at the source) have already been taken in the case of CFCs. Here action was taken swiftly because of the dramatic effects of CFCs on the 'ozone hole' over Antarctica. CFCs contribute not only to the warming of the globe but also to the greater transparency of the atmosphere to ultraviolet radiation. The decision to reduce drastically the amount of CFC emission – and more recently to draw up other protocols leading

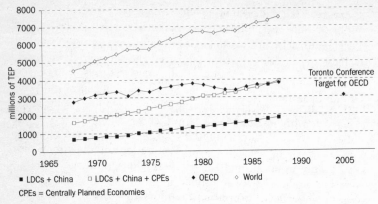

Fig. 8.3. World Commercial Energy Consumption, 1968–1987.

to their complete phase-out – is a very clear indication that international treaties can be accomplished and be quite effective. However, the phasing-out of CFCs has met stumbling blocks in some LDCs, notably India, which argues that it will comply with the Montreal Protocol only if it is compensated for the investments already made, and is supplied with adequate technology to replace CFCs on a concessional basis. Clearly more work is needed to reach the desired goal of complete phase-out of CFCs.

It is worth mentioning here that to limit emissions of other greenhouse gases might be even more difficult. Although widely used, CFCs are produced by relatively few companies around the world. The problems are different with the other greenhouse gases, because they are produced from many and various sources.

8.4 Mechanisms to cope with the greenhouse problem

8.4.1 Background on environmental protection mechanisms

Efforts have been made to induce polluters to avoid environmental degradation since the early 1970s, mainly in the OECD countries. The 'Polluter-Pays Principle'[10] was the first important effort to include the externality represented by pollution in the costs of products.

Some expected it to become a panacea and lead to the solution of all problems. But the polluter-pays approach was not very successful because, as an OECD review put it in 1989,[11]

> economic actors are normally assumed to consider costs and benefits to themselves only ... Environmental inputs and/or outputs of economic processes, and especially the wider social consequences thereof, are not fully translated into costs and benefits that bear upon the polluter ... The market mechanism has been said to arouse on the part of the individual economic actors, an inherent tendency to shift elements of social costs onto others, or into the future.

As a consequence, a very strong case was made 'for installing social institutions responsible for environmental quality and equipping such institutions with instruments to enable them to reach socially desirable environmental objectives'.

In the fifteen years between 1973 and 1988, a variety of instruments to counter environmental degradation were formulated and put into effect. Some of them rely exclusively on economic instruments and others on regulations of one sort or another. Those most commonly tried in OECD countries are the following:[12]

- Charges (such as effluent and administrative charges or tax-differentiation mechanisms towards less-polluting products);
- Subsidies (in the form of grants, soft loans, or tax allowances);
- Deposit-refund systems (to encourage people to keep polluting products from being distributed in the environment);
- Emission-trading (in which 'pollution rights' – according to current regulations – are traded among different enterprises);
- Enforcement incentives (fines or refundable bonds upon compliance).

Although environmental protection has been moderately successful in many countries, the results are very uneven. In France, for example,

> funds from the public budget are difficult to obtain, since economic and social considerations have taken precedence over the environment issue. Industry is strongly opposed to new or higher financial burdens, unless revenues return to the sector. Therefore

financial aid systems are closely linked to charge systems. Each sectorial policy (water, air, wastes, noise) has its own sources managed on the regional or local level.[13]

The application of the Polluter-Pays Principle in the case of greenhouse gases leads naturally to the idea of setting taxes on carbon emissions. The individual 'polluters' in this case are many, and even their exact identification – easy in the case of CFC producers – often poses major problems. Therefore the easiest thing to do would be to increase the price of carbonaceous fuels, such as mined coal, oil, and gas, at the source of production.

Clearly this instrument would not be a strictly economic one, and would have to be adopted by governmental decision. This would need to be by means of an international treaty among many countries, since unilateral actions are feared by some governments – mainly the US and Japan – because of the lost competitiveness they might entail for domestic industries.

The alternative would be to increase the cost of consuming fuels. The example of the cost of gasoline suggests that such a mechanism might not work. In reality, automobile owners seem quite indifferent to the costs of fuels since other expenses in purchasing, maintaining, and insuring an automobile are dominant: fuel accounts for less than 10 per cent of the total cost, and therefore the price of oil might have to double or triple before consumers started reacting to it.[14]

A variety of suggestions have been made as to how to make the 'market mechanism' work in stimulating the introduction of energy conservation in industrialized countries where the present political winds favour liberal policies. Some of them have been moderately successful in the United States, mainly in the area of energy conservation.[15] The problem here is that the price of electricity is generally established on a 'cost-plus' basis, and the large initial investments needed are obtained through particularly favoured channels, such as guaranteed municipal or state loans. To compete with such well-established financial schemes is not an easy task, and special financial schemes might be needed to give energy conservation an initial push.

8.4.2 A carbon tax

It is for this reason that the most common proposal is the creation of a general carbon tax designed to constitute a fund to curb further emissions of carbon dioxide into the atmosphere. In order to gain some insights into the size of the tax needed, estimates were made of the costs of a preventive strategy in a background report prepared for the Noordwijk Conference by McKinsey and Associates, consultants to the Dutch Government.[16] Estimates of costs were made for the three following actions:

- **Continued funding for a CFC phase-out:** of the order of US\$150–200 million per year initially, and US\$600–700 million per year should a 100-per-cent phase-out of CFCs be pursued;

- **Expanded forest-management funding:** up to a maximum of US\$10–15 billion per year (12 million hectares per year of reforested areas), at an approximate cost of US\$1,000 per hectare;

- **Funding of fossil-fuel energy conservation:** of the order of US\$10–15 billion per year; this number is based on a preliminary assessment of costs for the introduction of efficient energy-conservation measures in the developing world.

The total amount of money needed for the operation of the fund (of the order of US\$30 billion per year) could easily be amassed by setting a levy of US\$1 per barrel-equivalent of petroleum consumed. Since many forms of energy conservation have a positive return once the hurdle of incremental investment has been overcome or a marginal subsidy has been provided, funds initially committed could conceivably be higher than those cited in the McKinsey *et al.* report. For example, the replacement of old-fashioned incandescent lamps by modern fluorescent lamps has high initial costs that are returned quickly, since they require a lot less electricity to provide the same illumination.

In the US, the EPA gave an example of a tax scenario in a recent report.[17] The suggested taxes were: US\$25 per ton on coal; US\$6 per barrel on oil; US\$0.50 per million cubic feet on gas. The Global Climate Coalition, a powerful pressure group representing industrial-energy producers in the coal, gas, and oil business,[18] estimated the effects in the US of imposing such taxes. They estimated that they would raise the average tariff of electricity by 20 per cent (from the present rate of 5.8 cents per kWh); the price of gasoline by 17–20 cents per gallon; and the average residential heating costs by US\$85–100 per annum.

On the other hand, in the IPCC meetings Kaya has argued that efforts to postpone the doubling of the carbon dioxide concentration in the atmosphere will imply a reduction of GDP growth in the developed countries.[19] According to Kaya, if the growth of carbon dioxide emissions is reduced to zero, that is, if the rate of emissions is frozen at present levels, GDP growth will have to be reduced to 1.4 per cent per year from 3.1 per cent per year (the present average growth-rate of OECD countries). To reach the Toronto Conference target[20] – a reduction of 1 per cent per year in carbon dioxide emissions – Kaya estimates GDP growth would have to be reduced to 0.4 per cent per year.

Table 8.3: Carbon dioxide emissions and economic growth according to Kaya's analysis

Case	Consequence	GDP growth (%/Year)
'Business as usual'	Doubling of CO_2 in 2030	3.1
Emission of carbon dioxide frozen (0% growth/year)	Doubling of CO_2 in 2090	1.4
Toronto Conference target (–1% growth/year)	20% decrease of CO_2 in 2005	0.4

(*Source:* see n. 3.)

Representatives of Japan and the United States to the IPCC have been arguing on the basis of analyses such as Kaya's that they will be penalized if an international treaty introduces ceilings on carbon dioxide production: Japan because it believes it has done its share in emphasizing energy efficiency, and the United States because the government does not want to increase the costs of energy – particularly gasoline, which is extremely cheap in that country. Great Britain currently tends to follow this position because of a general feeling which permeates some OECD reports that the easy avenues of energy conservation have already been instigated in these countries. There was a 21-per-cent decrease in energy intensity between 1973 and 1985, while between 1985 and 1988 the decrease has only been 4.7 per cent.[21]

However, many other countries, such as Sweden and the Netherlands, have already done better than that in energy conservation, and have been pushing for limitations on carbon dioxide emissions and other anti-greenhouse actions, including the financial means to implement them.

Kaya's report, as well as more recent work along the same lines done by Manne and Richels in the US,[22] has been seriously disputed by Williams[23] on the grounds that they do not take properly into account structural changes in the economy. Such changes could accelerate considerably the decoupling of GDP growth and energy consumption which was already taking place before the oil crisis of the 1970s, as pointed out years ago by Strout.[24]

8.4.3 An insurance fund

An alternative to a carbon tax would be the establishment of an insurance fund to pay for the expenses resulting from a preventive and/or adaptive strategy. Global expenditures in insurance are given in Table 8.4. The amount of money spent on both personal and material-goods insurance in the USA in 1986 was $371 billion (43.2 per cent of the world's total insurance expenditure and approximately 8.84 per cent of the Gross Domestic Product of the US). The world total is in excess of $850 billion.

If one decided to organize a fund of $1,000 billion over a thirty-year period, it would be necessary to collect $21 billion per year (assuming a real rate of interest of 3 per cent). This amount of money corresponds to a rise in the present premium paid for insurance around the world of just 2.5 per cent.[25] If the costs of the insurance against climatic change were to be divided among countries proportionally with respect to their current insurance expenditures, it would cost the US another $4.5 billion per year in insurance, or an additional 1.2 per cent on what Americans already spend on insurance.

Table 8.4: World Insurance Expenditures 1986 *(US$ billions)*

	Premium	(% of world total insurance expenditure)	GDP
North America	390.9	(45.53)	4,554
United States	371.0	(43.20)	4,197
Europe	248.5	(28.95)	4,371
Asia	192.5	(22.43)	2,845
Oceania	9.7	(1.14)	195
Africa	8.6	(1.01)	158
Central & South America	8.1	(0.94)	401
Total	**858.5**	**(100.00)**	**12,519**

8.4.4 Equity issues and self-interest

The establishment of a carbon tax or an insurance fund of the size proposed above raises other issues. First, developing countries which at present contribute little to carbon dioxide emissions would have to be exempted until such time that the transferal of adequate technologies enables them to minimize emissions of greenhouse gases. Second, the application of the tax or fund would have to be made in concessional terms. The transfer of technology to replace CFCs or to introduce energy-efficient devices in LDCs – and to modernize the industrial sector to manufacture them – would have to be made free of charge to induce the LDCs to carry out the measures. Otherwise, the LDCs will argue that environmental considerations are subsuming their vital development considerations.

It might be appropriate to point out here that concern for the environment became very strong in developed countries before problems of poverty were completely solved in these countries. Even at present, in the United States increasingly large amounts of money are being spent on cleaning the environment while the poverty of a fraction of the population remains unsolved. This point is made by some to stress the need to separate the two problems even at the risk of having environmental concerns qualified as 'concerns of the rich'. In reality, policies to protect the environment cut across social categories and are clearly of interest to all.

Funds for development assistance of the OECD countries (including multilateral banks such as the World Bank) presently amount to $50 billion and represent 0.2–1.0 per cent of GDP of the member countries of OECD, as shown in Fig. 8.4. It is with this money that most governments in LDCs finance the construction of power plants, roads, railways and heavy industry, sanitation and education. The World Bank loans, which amount to approximately $14 billion a year in recent years, have long payback periods and somewhat attractive rates of interest. Bilateral aid, in general, is given in the form of concessional grants to the poorest countries.

Although a great effort is made every year to increase the funds destined for such activities, this task has not proved to be easy. In large countries, tight fiscal policies and a growing reliance on market mechanisms reduce the availability of public funds for development aid.

If adopted, a carbon tax or insurance fund could be proportional to the contribution of different countries to the total carbon dioxide emissions. The internal mechanism needed to collect the revenue could be left to them: in some cases it could come from the government budget (that is, from general taxes), and in others, through additional taxes to signal to the population the purpose of the new action taken. Once this is done, there could be a mechanism to increase the taxes gradually if emissions of greenhouse gases do not respond to the actions taken.

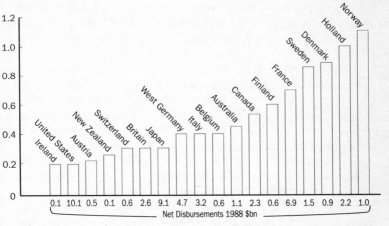

Fig. 8.4. Official aid, 1988. Net disbursements as percentage of GNP, by country.
(Source: OECD)

The new carbon tax or insurance fund would correspond to less than 0.5 per cent of the Gross Domestic Product of the richer countries, including the Soviet Union (and centrally planned economies), where energy is used rather inefficiently. Yet the absolute amount of money involved is significant, and many countries will resist this course of action. Even if approved by international treaty, some countries will not sign. The only precedent for an action of this size was the Marshall Plan – the scheme for the reconstruction of an Europe devastated by the Second World War, in which the United States invested 1 per cent of its GDP per year in the period 1948–52.

At the Conference of Foreign Ministers in Noordwijk (the Netherlands) in November 1989, proposals for a carbon tax were put forward, as discussed earlier. The proposals were not approved, due to the strong resistance of the United States, Japan, and the United

Kingdom on the grounds that the scientific knowledge on which the greenhouse effect was based was not well established, and would not be so until the IPCC reported. To be successful, a carbon tax or insurance fund would have to be based on the self-interest of the developed countries in avoiding further degradation of the atmosphere, and in stabilizing atmospheric greenhouse gases. Having the countries who provided the opposition at Noordwijk realize this is one of the main challenges to all who believe that global warming is a serious threat to environmental security. Now that the IPCC Working Group has reported, and – as Stephen Schneider points out in his paper – has given a clear warning of the potential disaster to come in a 'business-as-usual' world, surely this will now happen.

Some of the money spent on stabilizing the atmosphere undoubtedly will result in development. Reforestation will probably be the first example of that, since it avoids land degradation and generates employment. More important than that is the introduction of energy-efficient technologies as a fundamental ingredient in the process of development and not as an afterthought. To allow the LDCs to make costly mistakes in their individual development, paralleling those which we see – with the benefit of hindsight – the industrialized countries have made, is not only irrational, but will require, later on, extensive retrofitting (replacing old technology with new, where possible, *in situ*) and modernization. It is in their interest – and in the interest of industrialized countries – not to allow such a course of action to continue.

In particular, Goldemberg *et al.*[26] have shown that it is possible to achieve, in the developing countries, a level of amenities in the year 2020 similar to that of the countries of Western Europe in the mid-70s, if energy-efficient technologies are adopted early in their process of growth and development.

The amount of primary energy consumed per capita in LDCs would have to grow from the 1 kW consumed in 1980 to 1.3 kW in the year 2020, but of course such energy would be used much more efficiently than in 1980. Moreover, the continuation of present efforts in energy conservation in the industrialized countries would lead to a reduction of the total energy consumed in these countries. Consumption per capita would decrease from 6.3 kW in 1980 to 3.2 kW in 2020. All in all, total energy consumption in the scenario above would grow from 10.3 terawatts (a terawatt [TW] is a trillion watts) in

1980 to 11.2 TW in 2020, and the share of renewables would grow from 16.3 per cent to 19.0 per cent (Fig. 8.5).

More recent technical developments have led to a revision of such numbers: improvements in photovoltaics, electricity from wind machines, and, more importantly, electricity generation from biomass using advanced aeroderivative gas turbines[27] indicate that the share of renewables could be increased significantly until the year 2020, with enormous benefits from the viewpoint of reducing green-house-gaseous emissions.

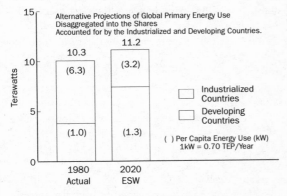

Fig. 8.5. Alternative projections of global primary energy-use dis-aggregated into the shares accounted for by the industrialized and the developing countries.

8.5 Conclusions

Although there are still scientific uncertainties on the extent of the consequences of the warming of the globe due to the man-made greenhouse gases, what is at stake is not the future of science (or self-serving arguments between scientists, as some try to make out) but the future of the atmosphere. To ruin the atmosphere in an irre-versible way might cost much more than avoiding further changes in its composition. This should be a problem of major concern not only to someone living on the seashores of the Indian Ocean in Bangladesh (one of the first countries to be hard-hit by the expected sea-level rises), but also to people living in New York or on the shores of the Gulf of Mexico.

What we all presently face is a global problem of a type not experienced before. To face it is the responsibility of all. Disregarding any considerations of philanthropy – or justification of foreign aid on humanitarian grounds – there are here very legitimate grounds for concern among the industrialized countries. Action could be justified on the grounds of enlightened self-interest alone. We have learned in the past fifteen years to fight local and regional pollution with a variety of instruments, and are meeting the bills in many ways. The time has come to pay the additional amount needed to protect the atmosphere as a whole, a problem that does not have boundaries or frontiers.

Chapter 9
The Costs of Cutting – or not Cutting – Greenhouse-gas Emissions

Stephen H. Schneider

" ... over one hundred and ten years (that is, from 1990 to 2100) even a trillion dollars in CO_2-reduction costs for the US, which sounds very expensive, is less than \$10 billion each year – only a few per cent of the US annual defence budget. Moreover... the so-called 'optimistic scenario' of \$800 billion in costs to cut CO_2 emissions is based on very pessimistic assumptions about the rapidly decreasing costs of renewable energy systems like solar, wind, or biomass power... "

The most important criticism made against those proposing action to slow global warming has been that immediate policy-steps to cut CO_2 emissions are too expensive. For example, an article in *Forbes* magazine[1] and subsequent newspaper ads attacking global-warming science and scientists suggested that CO_2-emission cuts will bankrupt developed nations and the Third World will remain impoverished. Indeed, as I discuss in many places in my book *Global Warming*,[2] there is substantial Third World opposition to the prospect that they may not be able to have their own industrial revolutions, much as the developed countries did in the Victorian period, when those then-developing western countries used cheap and dirty coal to foster their industrial growth. Since now-developing Third World countries such as India and China have abundant coal supplies, they would like to use them as low-cost routes to try to industrialize. Of course, these countries in 1990 have between them two billion people, whereas the entire world did not contain two billion people in Victorian times, so the magnitude of the global impact of developing countries' use of coal, should they choose to use coal to produce even a quarter of the western current industrial standard of living, would be greater than was that of the nineteenth-century western nations.

It is sensible, I believe, to argue that developing countries need not repeat the experience of Victorian industrialization in the west, with smog-choked cities, acidic rain, and inefficient power-production, given that modern technology has many better technical and economic solutions. Unfortunately, developing countries typically respond that high-technology, efficient power-production is initially more expensive than the traditional options that are cheaper and more available to them. This dilemma sets up the obvious need for a bargain, where developed countries with technology and capital help to provide those resources to developing countries which, in turn, develop their industries with the lowest-polluting, most efficient technologies, even if they cost more cash up front.

9.1 Options for cutting CO_2 emissions

There have been international efforts afoot to have each nation on Earth commit itself to try to decrease its carbon dioxide emissions by, say, 20 per cent by the year 2000.[3] This had been strongly opposed in November 1989 at an international meeting at Noordwijk, Holland, by the United States, echoed by Japan, UK, USSR, and some other countries. The Japanese have been unhappy since they are already twice as energy-efficient as the US, and claim it would cost them much more to cut their carbon-dioxide emissions by 20 per cent than the US, since US inefficiency gives them more opportunity to cut cheaply. Developing or Eastern European countries, being even less efficient than the US, could, with modest investments, produce vastly less growth in carbon-dioxide pollution (the principal greenhouse gas) if efficient, modern technologies were used rather than the older, cheapest technologies.

This sets up the possibility for creative international management that might not only eliminate Third World opposition to global emission reductions but could get them to compete with each other to be the venue for future emissions-limitations funded by developed countries which, in turn, could buy that developed nation out of its (say) 20-per-cent cut requirement by funding even larger CO_2 reductions in energy-inefficient developing countries.

In other words, suppose each country had to reduce its CO_2 impact on the world by something equivalent to 20 per cent of its production. Let us say, giving the Japanese as an example, that 100 million tons of CO_2 were to be cut annually. Why not structure an international agreement so that the Japanese need to be responsible either for reducing their 100 million tons of CO_2 from their own industries, or alternatively, 150 million tons in another country (or some combination of both)? The obvious candidate is China, since Japanese investment in China for efficient energy production would reduce acid rain over Japan as well as CO_2 buildup for the globe. It is likely to be much cheaper per unit of CO_2 saved for the Japanese to improve the Chinese energy efficiency, since China is starting out so inefficient, than for Japan to improve its own efficiency. At the same time the Chinese would receive extra development assistance, and the Japanese would get less acid rain and could buy out of having to cut their own emissions at home. Moreover, the Japanese would be creating friendship and markets for their products in the future, whereas the Chinese would be getting more efficient machines that would have lower operating costs over decades, thereby improving their economy and competitive posture into the twenty-first century. In other words, everybody wins. But first, we have to have a world emissions agreement that provides the incentives for such bargaining and trading to take place. That kind of agreement is what the US, UK, USSR, and Japan were balking at in 1989.

Other similar ideas include issuing 'tradeable (or leasable) permits'[4] whereby each citizen of the world gets a right to emit a certain amount of CO_2 or some other greenhouse gas. Then, these permits could be traded for cash, food, energy-efficient products, and so on. In other words, at the signing date each nation would get a fixed right to emit CO_2 based on their population size at the time. This would dramatically reduce Third World suspicion that they were being singled out to bear the immediate burden of emission controls.

9.2 The cost of emissions-reduction

Critics of emissions-reductions cite the supposed annual costs of 20-per-cent CO_2 reduction at tens of billions of dollars. But they often neglect the benefits of emissions-reductions: reduced magnitude of global warming, reduced acid rain, reduced urban air pollution, reduced balance-of-payments deficits, and lower long-term operating costs of more efficient equipment which reduces the energy costs of manufactured products, thereby enhancing competitiveness. Such critics simply cite the potential up-front capital costs of CO_2 controls or fuel taxes, write newspaper stories about how many billions or trillions it's going to cost, and scare people away from action.

For example, White House Chief of Staff John Sununu, in defending his role in convincing President Bush not to commit the US to any specific CO_2 emissions-reductions at Noordwijk, said on TV in 1990: 'There's a little tendency by some of the faceless bureaucrats on the environmental side to try and create a policy in this country that cuts off our use of coal, oil and natural gas. I don't think America wants not to be able to use their automobiles.' I agree we don't want to 'cut off our use of coal, oil and natural gas'; nor do I want to abandon our cars. But, Mr Sununu, who does? Not one proposal from any bureaucrat, National Academy of Sciences Committee, IPCC Working Group, or even environmental-action organizations I know of ever proposed such a totally sweeping policy! Rather, most are talking about giving up (or heavily taxing) gas-guzzling cars and switching to less-polluting energy equipment, regardless of the fuel used.

But some studies have suggested that switching to less-polluting energy systems could cost '\$800 billion, under optimistic scenarios of available fuel substitutes and increasing energy efficiency, to \$3.6 trillion under pessimistic scenarios ... to 2100'. This quote from the February 1990 'Economic Report of the President' to the US Congress was based on the initial results of the first wave of economic model simulations.

Because of the controversy associated with such models, the US National Academy of Sciences ran a debate in March 1990 among several economic forecasters and their critics. What came out was very revealing. First, over one hundred and ten years (that is, from 1990 to 2100) even a trillion dollars in CO_2-reduction costs for the US, which sounds very expensive, is less than $10 billion each year — only a few per cent of the US annual defence budget. Moreover, Robert Williams, an energy- technology specialist from Princeton University, pointed out that the so-called 'optimistic scenario' of $800 billion in costs to cut CO_2 emissions is based on very pessimistic assumptions about the rapidly decreasing costs of renewable energy systems like solar, wind, or biomass power.[5]

In particular, one well-cited econometric model used to project future GNP performance as a function of energy prices is calibrated by statistical methods that match GNP change over time with energy prices over time. For example, following the OPEC oil-price rise of 1973, GNP responded by decreasing for several years. Then, as economies adjusted to the higher prices and energy efficiency was encouraged by the price shock, GNP grew once again, even though total energy consumption changed very little for the next half-dozen years. Clearly, the immediate transient response of the GNP to energy-price changes will be different than the medium-term adjustment, which should be different over the very long term. Yet, this econometric model used to project GNP response to CO_2 controls (which were dealt with as an equivalent energy tax) was run over 110 years into the future based on curve-matching that included data on short-term, transient conditions. Seen in this light, it is not surprising that such a model would predict large GNP losses 100 years into the future when energy prices go up — it is built into the model by regression equations that include transient situations and then apply them over the very long term. It is also no wonder that such models were severely criticized at the US National Academy of Sciences debate.

Furthermore, with the exception of one heroic effort by Yale University economist William Nordhaus, none of the other economists' modelling simulations even attempted to estimate what direct environmental benefits we get for our supposed trillion-dollar investment in CO_2-emission controls. It is unconscionable that some critics of global-warming action could cite these already very dubious economic models' cost estimates without so much as a word on the potential benefits of slowing CO_2 emissions. Nordhaus, on the other hand, by balancing costs and benefits in his model runs, argued that cutting annual CO_2 emissions by as little as 10 per cent or as much as 47 per cent would actually produce benefits greater than the costs! However, his model, too, was admittedly crude, laden with unprovable assumptions, and simply could not by itself provide quantitatively reliable information upon which to base policy choices. But at least it laid out the framework for decision-making. Its problem is making the cost/benefit assumptions more credible.

Finally, cross-examination of the economic modellers by National Academy committee members revealed that their economic models had not even been tested to see how well they performed in predicting the economic consequences of historical events like the 1973 OPEC oil-price hike, since their structure was derived from such data and it could thus not be used for validation. I was shocked that validation tests were yet to be performed, and dismayed that some US government officials were actually citing these premature economic model results for costs of emission controls – to say nothing of the omitted benefits of controls – as an alleged rational basis for policy-making. In essence, because of the crude state of modelling, policy-making will have to be largely intuitively based, for it would not be rational to give much weight to the conclusions (that is, economic or climatic transients) of present tools – unless there were also other lines of reasoning to bolster their conclusions.

9.3 Adaptation or prevention?

Public policy responses to the advent or prospect of global climate change typically come in two categories: adaptation and prevention. With regard to adaptation, flexibility of adaptive measures needs to be considered now. Indeed, if the entire global-warming debate comes out closer to the views of the present critics and only small changes occur, what would be lost, for example, by improving the flexibility of water-supply systems? After all, nature will continue to give us wet and dry years. The 100-year flood will happen sometime, as will the 100-year drought – with or without global warming, which, of course, could change the odds of such extremes. Therefore, increasing management flexibility will pay dividends[6] even in (what I and IPCC Working Group 1 believe to be) the unlikely event that global warming proves to be minimal. This situation finds a metaphor in buying insurance. Only a foolish or desperate person would over- or under-invest in insurance. However, unlike the insurance metaphor, where a premium is 'wasted' if one doesn't collect on any damages, here we can actually get benefits for our investment in flexibility, as we buy insurance against the prospect of rapid climate change at the same time. Of course, no one gets a return on investment without making an investment, and that is true not just in the private sector, but obviously in the public sector as well.

The other category of management response is prevention. That simply means slowing down the rate at which the gases that are injected into the atmosphere that can modify the climate are produced. The principal way to do that falls primarily in the jurisdiction of energy-use and production managers. However, since deforestation is an important component of CO_2 production, halting deforestation can help to reduce the atmospheric buildup of CO_2. Thus, prevention is also in the purview of such land-management agencies. For example, domestic animals are a major source of methane, and such livestock graze extensively on public lands. Therefore, solutions to methane-emission controls will involve consideration of the use of public lands for this purpose. As another example, microbial communities in soils decompose dead organic matter into greenhouse gases, such as carbon dioxide, methane, or nitrous oxide. Since these microbes typically increase their metabolic activity when the soil warms, deforestation or grazing which removes vegetation cover and results in warmer soils could enhance the production of these greenhouse gases: a positive feedback.[7] These issues are contentious, but none the less need to be examined for their potential effectiveness as emission-control strategies.

The best strategies should have high leverage – that is, should help to solve more than one problem with a single investment. It is my personal view that such high-leverage or 'tie-in' strategies are the best approach to dealing with prevention, or at least delaying the rate of the buildup of greenhouse gases, and thus the prospect of rapid global warming.[8] It is obvious that the things to do first are the things that make the most sense regardless of whether global warming materializes. Energy efficiency, as is often mentioned and as Amory Lovins describes in detail in his chapter in this book, is the single most important 'tie-in' strategy, for using energy efficiently will not only reduce the prospect of rapid climate change, but also reduce acid rain (itself a threat to many natural lands), air pollution in cities, balance-of-payment deficits in energy-importing countries by reducing dependence on foreign supplies of energy, and in the long run can improve product-competitiveness by reducing the energy components of manufactured products.

I believe that flexibility for adaptation and high-leverage strategies for prevention are not premature policy actions. If we are to manage effectively a future with increasing uncertainty in environmental conditions, then it is imperative that management-flexibility be increased. Ideology is the enemy of flexibility. It is incumbent on both individuals and institutions – public and private – to rethink any of our ideologically rigid positions in order to fashion ways in which to enhance the flexibility of management. This can give us the opportunity to manage more effectively the potential consequences of serious climate change, as well as to improve the capacity of present systems to deal with the natural variability of the environment, itself a well-demonstrated threat to many of our abilities or resources. And in the likely event (as IPCC suggests it is) that climate-change unprecedented in the era of human civilization (that is, of more than 2°C globally) materializes, then 'planetary insurance' to slow down the rate of buildup of greenhouse gases will almost certainly prove to be a wise investment.

Chapter 10
The Role of Energy Efficiency

Amory Lovins

> " ...It is generally cheaper today to save fuel than to burn it. Avoiding pollution by not burning the fuel can, therefore, be achieved, not at a cost, but at a profit – so this result can and should be widely implemented in the market-place... "

The round-Earth theory poses ultimate limits to population growth and industrialization. Biotic and social carrying-capacities, and the finite nature of some resources, constrain the scope for 'Los Angelizing' the planet. However, even very large expansions in population and industrial activity need not be energy-constrained: energy can, in fact, be among the weakest of the many reasons for concern about indefinite population and industrial growth. This chapter first explains why energy need not limit traditional industrial expansion (at least not until very far beyond most other limits), and then explores why goals other than indiscriminate growth are worthier.

About energy there is good news and bad news. The good news is that if we simply pursue the narrowest of economic interests, the energy problem has already been solved by new technologies – primarily for more efficient end-use, secondarily for more efficient conversion and sustainable supply. In the United States, for example:

■ Full practical use, in existing buildings and equipment, of the best electricity-saving technologies already on the market would save about three-quarters of all electricity now used, at an average cost certainly below 1 cent per kilowatt hour (kWh) and probably around 0.6 cents/kWh[1] – much less than the cost of merely running a coal or nuclear power station, even if building it cost nothing. Consider one example, among the costlier that could be cited. A single 18-watt compact fluorescent lamp, producing the same light as a 75-watt incandescent lamp for approximately thirteen times as long, will over its 10,000-hour nominal lifetime avoid the emission from a typical US coal-fired power plant of 1 tonne of CO_2 and around 8 kg of SO_2, plus NO_x, heavy metals, and other pollutants.[2] Yet far from costing extra, the lamp will save about \$20-worth of ordinary lamps and their installation labour, plus about \$20–30-worth of utility fuel – far more than its approximate \$5–8 production cost or approximate \$12–18 retail price. Thus the lamp cleans up the air while creating tens of dollars' net wealth and deferring hundreds of dollars' investment in electrical-supply systems;

- Full practical use of the best demonstrated oil- and gas-saving technologies (many already on the market and the rest ready for production within about four to five years) would save about three-quarters of all oil now used, at an average cost below \$3 per barrel (bbl) – less than the typical cost of just finding new domestic oil.[3]

These savings are of a purely technical character and would entail no loss – indeed, often substantial improvements – in the quantity and quality of services provided. Efficiency technologies have already begun to sweep the market despite the many obstacles placed in their way. There is now abundant evidence that their rapid rise to complete dominance of marginal investments would be a natural outcome of free-market competition among all ways to provide desired energy services.

For these kinds of reasons, it is possible to approach the issue of energy efficiency using only the motives, methods, and criteria of orthodox neoclassical economics and conclude that saving energy will generally be desirable. But now – and especially since the completion of the IPCC Working Group 1 scientists' report – abating global warming (as well as urban smog, acid precipitation, and other results of air pollution) is widely acknowledged as an imperative rationale for dramatically reducing the amount of fossil fuel burnt. Such a step is commonly assumed to require costly technological investments or inconvenient life-style changes or both. But in reality, new developments in efficient end-use of energy can now reduce emissions of greenhouse gases and other air pollutants from fossil-fuel burning at zero or negative net internal cost to society, while providing unchanged or improved services to consumers.

The bad news, however, is that most governments and many private-sector actors are less committed to market outcomes in energy policy than to corporate socialism – to bailing out their favourite technologies, many of which are now dying of an incurable attack of market forces. So long as this ideology continues to dominate public policy and the private investments which that policy influences, energy will continue to impose intractable economic, environmental, and security constraints on even the type and degree of global development that is vital for basic living requirements.

10.1 The secret success

10.1.1 The demand side

In spite of persistent official obstructions summarized below, the genius of even a very imperfect market has been able to assert itself to a striking degree. Consider the following facts:

■ Since 1979, the US has acquired more than seven times as much new energy from savings as from all net increases in energy supply. Of that new supply, more has come from renewables (now some 11–12 per cent of total primary supply) than from non-renewables. During 1979–86 inclusive, energy savings expanded US energy-availability by seven times as much as nuclear power did, and during 1984–6, by nearly thirteenfold;

■ Because of the reductions in energy intensity achieved since 1973, the annual US energy bill has recently been around $430 billion instead of around $580 billion – a saving of about $150 billion per year (comparable to the Federal budget deficit). However, if the US were now as efficient in aggregate as its competitors in Europe and Japan, it would be saving approximately an additional $200 billion per year. And simply choosing the best energy-buys for the rest of this century could yield a cumulative net saving of several trillion of today's dollars – enough to pay off the entire National Debt;

■ During 1977–85, the US steadily and routinely saved oil four-fifths faster than it needed to do in order to keep up with both economic growth and declining domestic oil output. This 5-per-cent-per-year increase in national oil productivity cut total oil imports in half. It was achieved largely with such simple measures as caulk guns, duct tape, insulation, plugged steam leaks, and a 5-mile-per-US-gallon gain in the efficiency of the car fleet;

■ By 1986, the US energy-saving achieved since 1973 – chiefly in oil and gas – was 'producing' two-fifths more energy each year than the domestic oil industry, which took a century to build. Yet oil has rising costs, falling output, and dwindling reserves, while efficiency has falling costs, rising output, and expanding reserves;

■ The Electric Power Research Institute, the US utilities' think-tank, estimates that US electrical-intensity reductions during 1973–83 cut construction needs by some 141 GW,[4] corresponding to a marginal capacity cost of the order of $200–500 billion. Yet further potential savings are enormously larger.[5] EPRI has identified a technical potential to save 24–44 per cent of US electricity in the year 2000, not counting a further 9 per cent already in the utilities' demand forecasts or efficiency programme plans;[6]

■ Numerous utilities, by investing in more efficient use of electricity by their customers, are in fact saving large amounts of electricity at low and falling real cost; in mature programmes, the utilities' expenditures, amortized over the discounted stream of resulting savings, are typically of the order of 0.1–0.5 cents per kWh saved. For example, if all Americans saved electricity at the same speed and cost at which the roughly ten million people served by Southern California Edison Company actually did save electricity during 1983–5, then national forecast needs for long-run power supplies would decrease by about 40 GW per year (equivalent to an avoided capital cost, including its federal subsidy, of about $80 billion per year). The total cost for utilities to achieve those savings would average about 0.1–0.2 cents/kWh – about 1 per cent of the cost of new power stations.[7]

10.1.2 The supply side

Similarly striking progress is evident on the supply side. For example, life extension of conventional plants, retrofitting of combustion turbines to combined-cycle operation, packaged combined-cycle plants, and steam-injected gas turbines have virtually supplanted central steam plants as utilities' marginal supply investments of choice. With good design and favourable local conditions, small hydro-plants, hydro-upgrading, wind-power, and certain forms of geothermal and solar-thermal-electric power can be highly competitive on the margin with standard steam plants, even if the latter are subsidized while the former are not.[8] Other options, such as fuel cells and photovoltaics, are rapidly coming over the horizon of competitiveness. Even without demand-side competition, the era of the big steam plant would be over.

As proof of this, during 1981–4, US orders and firm letters of intent, minus cancellations, totalled:

- −65 net GW for fossil-fuelled and nuclear central plants,
- +25 GW for co-generation (about 20 per cent of it renewable),
- +more than 20 GW for small hydro, wind-power, and so on.

Thus, over two-thirds of lost central-station capacity was made up by smaller, faster, cheaper options which enabled investors to manage financial risks so as to minimize regret.[9] The other third was far more than made up by improved end-use efficiency. Since 1984, the conditions which produced this extraordinary shift of private capital have only intensified.

A microcosm of the power of competition is provided by California. Roughly 10 per cent of the US economy, in about 1984 the state had a peak electric load of 37 GW, supplied by 10 GW of hydroelectricity and geothermal power plus 27 GW of fossil-fuelled and nuclear plants. Around 1982, the state's utilities started offering to buy privately generated power at a fair price with roughly equalized subsidies. Within a few years of this approximation to fair competition:

- The utilities had committed around 13 GW of long-term (ten years) electrical savings, and were expecting an additional 11 GW;
- Private investors had firmly offered them more than 21 GW of new generating capacity, most of it renewable;

- More than 13 GW of that offered capacity was already built or being built;
- New offers for private generation were arriving at the rate of 9 GW, or one-quarter of total peak demand, *per year*.

Because of the resulting power glut, the California government suspended new contracts in April 1985. If the market response had been allowed to continue for another year or two, it would already have displaced *every thermal power plant in California*. Yet utilities in at least two dozen other states and provinces are still all hoping to sell their surpluses to California simultaneously. Some California utilities, unhappy with private generators' ability to out-compete their own costly central plants, are also trying to prevent or defer much of the already agreed-upon private generating capacity from coming on line – while they simultaneously complain that such capacity is 'unreliable' because it is not always completed.

During 1988–9, at least a dozen diverse US utilities ran auctions to see which private investors might wish, at their own expense and risk, to generate power for sale to the grid. Each of those utilities was offered, at very competitive prices, five to ten times as much power as it wanted.[10] Presumably they would have been even more swamped with attractive bids had they offered a similar price for energy *savings*, as some are now starting to do.

A final example: the State of Maine used competitive bidding not only to obtain large electrical savings, but also to raise the fraction of its electricity generated privately by mainly renewable sources, from 2 per cent in 1984 to 20 per cent in 1989 and to 30 per cent in 1991 (based on plants under construction in 1990).[11]

10.2 The energy-efficiency revolution

These remarkable developments reflect extremely rapid change on four related fronts:

10.2.1 Technology for extremely efficient end-use of energy

Most of the best electricity-saving technologies on the US market today were not available a year ago, and most of the best of those available then had not existed the year before that. Twice as much electricity can be saved now as could have been saved five years ago, and at only a third of the real cost – a gain in aggregate cost-effectiveness by about a factor of 6 in five years, or nearly a factor of 30 in ten years. This technological revolution shows no sign of abating. The resulting saving potential, sketched in Fig. 10.1, is based on *measured* cost and performance data.[12] Savings of similar magnitude, summarized in Fig. 10.2, can be made in oil consumption.

10.2.2 New ways to finance and deliver energy-saving technologies to the customers

Rocky Mountain Institute and others have developed,[13] and utilities are now bringing into successful use,[14] many techniques for implementing the least-cost investment strategies now demanded by the increasingly competitive energy-service market (and, in more than forty of the United States, by law). Complementing the concessionary utility loans and rebates now available to most US electric customers, these new methods include:

- Competitive bidding for all ways to make or save electricity (now beginning in at least eight states);

- Secondary-marketable covenants to stabilize or cap facilities' electric demand;

- Making electrical savings tradable within and between utilities' service territories (the first two such transactions were negotiated in 1988, whereby a utility will invest in saving electricity in another utility's territory and buy back, at a discounted price, the power thereby rendered surplus);

- Making spot, futures, and options markets in 'negawatts' (saved electricity);

- Sliding-scale hook-up fees, or 'feebates', for new buildings – fees which are positive or negative ('rebates') depending on the efficiency of each building;

- Sale of electric efficiency by electric utilities[15] in other utilities' territories (as about a dozen utilities are now profitably doing), and also by gas utilities.

These and similar innovations make saved electricity into a commodity subject to all the market mechanisms which pertain to other commodities – trading and fungibility in space and time, competitive

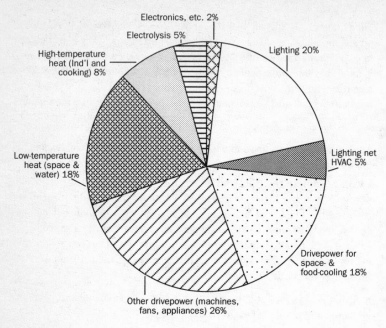

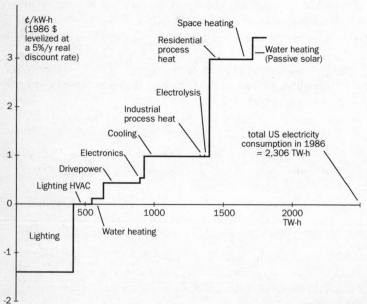

*Fig. 10.1 (shown opposite). (a) The approximate end-uses of US electricity (1985).
(b) The potential for saving electricity by full practical retrofit of the best technologies
on the market in 1988 at the costs of saved energy shown. (TW-h: terrawatt hours. 1TW
= 1,000 gigawatts). The cost and performance data shown are empirical. For simplicity,
all the measures applicable to each end-use have been bundled together as a package
rather than shown in their individual cost sequence. The list of technologies
considered, approximately 1,000, is far from complete, and no load management is
included. Significantly larger savings could be achieved at costs above those shown but
still well below long-run marginal supply costs; the marginal package costs shown here
compete with short-run marginal costs on most US utility systems. Current uncertainty
is about ten percentage points on the total quantity of savings and a factor less than 2
on its average cost. The figure shows a full practical potential to save about half of US
electricity at zero net cost, or three-quarters at a cost averaging about 0.6 cents/kWh –
many times cheaper than merely operating an existing thermal power station, even if
building it cost nothing. Evidence is emerging that the corresponding efficiency
potential in Western Europe and Japan is probably not much smaller, and in socialist
and developing countries is probably even larger.*

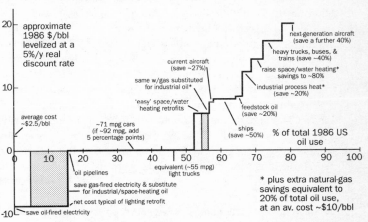

Fig. 10.2. *The approximate technical potential to save US oil consumption. Plotted in
the same manner as Fig. 10.1(b), this supply curve summarizes the approximate potential to save about four-fifths of US oil (including substitutions of saved gas for oil), with
another fifth worth of saved gas left over, at an average cost of less than $3/barrel, by
fully using the best technologies already demonstrated, roughly half of which are now
on the market.[16] The most surprising and important technology shown is the
3.3 litres/100 km (71 mpg US) car which Volvo claims to be able to make at zero
marginal capital cost.[17] A similar but less thoroughly documented claim by Peugeot at
2.6 litres/100 km (92 mpg US) would add a further five percentage points' saving.[18] Prototype cars already tested by these and around seven other manufacturers (none of
which has published a marginal production cost) variously combine superior safety
and peppiness with low emissions and normal comfort levels over a range of on-road
composite efficiencies of 1.7–3.5 litres/100 km (67–138 mpg US). Although smog-form-
ing emissions from such cars will probably not decline linearly with their fuel intensity,
major reductions are bound to occur, at a negative cost equal to the difference between
the super-efficient cars' marginal capital cost, if any, and the present-valued cost of the
fuel they save.*

bidding, secondary markets, derivative instruments, arbitrage, and so on. Similar evolution is starting to occur in savings of other forms of energy, including oil, and in other resources such as water.[19]

10.2.3 Radical changes in utilities' mission and culture, returning them to the historic roots of their business

A minority of American utilities is reinventing its mission as (in Georgia Power's phrase) 'the profitable production of customer satisfaction'. This minority is rapidly growing as these firms become noted as more profitable, and more fun to work for, than their competitors. Utilities which begin to sell both electricity and electrical savings (the main intermediate goods for providing electrical services) as commodities are shifting their orientation from being vendors of a single commodity (kWh) to being a service industry – that is, to delivering a different mix of efficiently provided commodities, including information and financing, in a way that ensures customer success. This means, among other things, learning to focus on the bottom line rather than the top line – learning that it is all right to sell less electricity and bring in less revenue, so long as costs fall even more. It used to be thought that such fundamental cultural change took a new Chair and ten years. Now some utilities are doing it in only a few years. It is difficult: it means redefining not only corporate mission but also career goals and personal identities. But it is easier than not doing it. And the threat of global warming now makes it an imperative.

10.2.4 Small but important shifts in regulatory policy to provide clear incentives which support and drive that cultural change

The most important such development is the unanimous November 1989 agreement-in-principle by the National Association of Regulatory Utility Commissioners that utilities' profits should be decoupled from their sales (so that they are at least indifferent as to whether they sell more or less electricity – which was previously true only in California), and that utilities should be rewarded for cost-minimizing behaviour (for example, by being allowed to keep as extra profit part of what they save their customers).

This progress is most prominent in, but not confined to, electric utilities. Some major vendors of fuels, including one or two of the world's largest oil companies, are now becoming seriously interested in selling all forms of energy efficiency for fun and profit.

10.2.5 Ways of thinking about future energy needs

Underlying all these developments is the post-1973 revolution in energy-policy methodology. This wrenching change is now so nearly complete that it is hard to remember the primitive methods used almost universally only a decade ago. In 1976 a memo by Herman Daly summarized how energy needs were then generally determined:

> Recent growth rates of population and per capita energy-use [or of population, per capita GNP, and energy use per unit of GNP] are projected up to some arbitrary, round-numbered date. Whatever technologies are required to produce the projected amount are automatically accepted, along with their social implications, and no thought is given to how long the system can last once the projected levels are attained. Trend is, in effect, elevated to destiny, and history either stops or starts afresh on the bi-millenial year, or the year 2050 or whatever.
>
> This approach is unworthy of any organism with a central nervous system, much less a cerebral cortex. For those of us who also have souls, it is almost incomprehensible in its inversion of ends and means ... [It says] that there is no such thing as enough[;] that growth in population and per capita energy use are either desirable or inevitable[;] that it is useless to worry about the future for more than 20 years, since all reasonably discounted costs and benefits become nil over that period[;] and that the increasing scale of technology is simply time's arrow of progress, and refusal to follow it represents a failure of nerve.

It is now widely accepted that the end-use/least-cost approach introduced in 1976[20] – asking what we want the energy for, and how much energy, of what quality, at what scale, from what source, will do each task in the cheapest way – is the best way to understand likely market developments and to plan optimal investments. It is also widely accepted that future energy needs are not fate but choice. Only the handful of analysts who have carefully examined the new technologies and delivery methods, however, realize how extremely flexibly that choice can now be exercised. The potential savings and costs shown above will surprise many. But these findings are calculated by conventional methods from documented cost-and-performance data that have been measured for real, commercially available devices. There should be little dispute about empirical data.

High-energy futures, sometimes considered inherently plausible because their extrapolation from the past requires so little thought, are in fact internally inconsistent. Their massive and costly supply expansions would require high energy prices. But those prices would in turn elicit much more efficient end-use. (High-energy futures also tend to be politically unattractive, implying greater *dirigisme* than most societies are likely to put up with. Nuclear-power advocates who suggest that America follow the example of France and Taiwan forget that, as Irwin Stelzer points out, Americans have chosen to live in a country quite unlike France or Taiwan – one whose electric-energy system is not centrally planned, but subject to political and market accountability to a substantial and highly valued degree.) I am under no illusion that any kind of energy future will be easy to achieve. But recent history teaches us that the undoubted problems of energy efficiency are much more tractable than those which will be unavoidable if it is not achieved.

10.3 Continuing blunders

The achievements of energy efficiency are all the more startling in view of the powerful forces arrayed against it. For decades, efficiency has been greatly retarded by its opponents, and has often suffered grievously even at the hands of its friends. (President Carter's public equation of saving energy with privation, discomfort, and curtailment may have set back efficiency more than his other policies helped it.)[21] At the same time, wastefully used, depletable, environmentally damaging, and egregiously uncompetitive energy options have received government succour lavishly and continuously. The triumph of narrow, private-interest expediency over macroeconomic efficiency, especially in the United States, beggars description. For example, the lopsidedness of federal subsidies to the energy sector was already severe[22] when last fully assessed in Fiscal Year 1984 (Fig. 10.3).[23] They reduced the apparent price of electricity by about 17 per cent, direct fuels by 4 per cent, and efficiency by 1 per cent. The 1986 tax reform may have modestly reduced the total amount of subsidies, which was upwards of $50 billion in FY 1984 alone, but has certainly increased their distortions of market choice.[24]

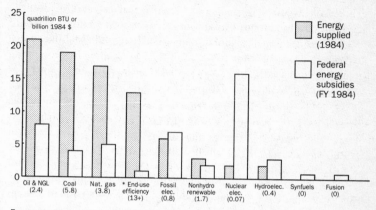

Energy resource or Technology (million BTU supplied per $ of subsidy)

*Fig. 10.3. Energy supplied and approximate federal energy subsidies in the USA in 1984 (preliminary data). The size and allocation of FY 1984 federal energy subsidies (comprising seventeen tax breaks, twenty-one agencies' budget line-item subventions, and lower marginal cost of capital from nine agencies' loans and guarantees) create the distortions shown by the 'bang-to-buck ratio' in parentheses below each set of bars. *The end-use energy-efficiency figures conservatively assume that improved end-use efficiency accounted for only half of the 1973–84 reduction in primary energy/real $ GNP; three-quarters would be a more realistic fraction, the other quarter being due to structural and behavioural changes.*

There are many other examples of such institutionally entrenched folly:

■ The Interior Department is continuing its strenuous efforts to sell or lease all public fuel resources into a glutted market at depressed prices, while counting externalities (environmental and socio-political impacts, national-security risks, and the value of wildlife, wilderness, biotic, scenic, and cultural resources) as zero.

■ The Federal Energy Regulatory Commission in the late 1980s was vigorously seeking to stifle state initiatives to introduce genuine competition into the electrical-service market.

- Federal monitoring and enforcement of existing environmental, health, safety, and anti-trust laws awkward for the energy industries has been largely gutted.[25] Building and appliance standards legislated to overcome well-known market failures have been opposed, weakened, or ignored.[26] After seven years of Reagan administration stonewalling, Congress gave up trying to operate the Conservation and Solar Bank which it had established in 1980.

- The US Department of Energy has cut real spending for efficiency research, development, and demonstration (RD&D) by 71 per cent, and long continued to press for deeper cuts – in FY 1989, for example, a further 50 per cent in RD&D and 96 per cent in the state and local programmes that deliver efficiency information to citizens – even though such investments in the past have consistently yielded returns of hundreds or thousands per cent to the national economy. Even in today's improved political climate, it will take many years to rebuild shattered research institutions to a position of sufficient strength to spend any restored funding.

- Remaining federal RD&D continues to be overwhelmingly (around 96–99 per cent) biased towards around 0–7 per cent of marginal energy needs (central-electric supply, as contrasted with generation at appropriate-scale, non-electric supply, and demand-side options).

Interventions such as these have serious, even absurd, consequences. For example, the energy wasted[27] in the United States today costs about twice as much as the federal budget deficit, or more than the entire $10,000-a-second military budget. The amount of crude oil wasted in 1986[28] by that year's rollback of US light-vehicle efficiency standards[29] equalled 1985 US imports from the Persian Gulf. It also equals the average annual oil output which the Interior Department hoped to achieve over thirty years from beneath the Arctic National Wildlife Refuge. In effect, the Administration thereby 'undiscovered' one potential ANWR's worth of oil – even as it sought Congressional consent to lease for exploration in the Refuge, at great environmental cost and very probably at a financial net loss to the lessees.

Similarly, the Electric Power Research Institute (EPRI) estimates that the approximate 56 GW of base-load savings to be achieved by the year 2000 by utilities' efficiency programmes will be largely undone by some 35 GW of on-peak, and 41 GW of off-peak, new demand deliberately created by today's power-marketing programmes, probably none of which, in my view, is economically rational.

These and other interventions have probably played a more important role than price fluctuations in stalling, during 1988–9, previously steady reductions of several per cent per year in the US energy/GNP ratio, although these have since partially resumed.

Shielding potentially hazardous industries from market and political accountability encourages sloppy operations which incur enormous future costs – as we are now discovering with the roughly $100-billion clean-up bill starting to be presented by the US military nuclear sector. This nasty surprise seems likely to be dwarfed by a similar bill, similarly created, from the civilian nuclear sector.[30]

Electricity in FY 1984 (the last reliable data available) received upwards of $35 billion in federal subsidies – two-thirds of all federal energy subsidies, going to only 14 per cent of the delivered energy.[31] This distortion made electricity look nearly a fifth cheaper than it really was, thereby artificially increasing demand, and, by effectively financing new power plants at approximately zero (or negative) interest rates, leveraged most or all of the roughly $30 billion of annual private investment in expanding electrical supply. (The impact on national capital allocation was large, because marginal central-electric systems are about a hundred times as capital-intensive as the traditional oil, gas, and coal systems on which today's American economy was built.) The total investments still being made for new US electric supply – some $60 billion a year, half private and half public – equal the total investment in US durable-goods manufacturing industry. Thus, electricity savings only fast enough to keep up with growth in service demand and plant retirements would leave nearly twice as much capital to keep those manufactures competitive.

Just the difference in aggregate energy intensity between the US and Japanese economies now creates an automatic cost-advantage of the order of 5 per cent for the typical Japanese export. This gap is widening, especially with regard to electrical productivity: the Japanese GNP in 1986 was 36 per cent less electricity-intensive than the US GNP, and this gap is officially projected to become 45 per cent by 2000. In particular major industries, such as cars, paper, and cement, electricity intensity per ton is falling in Japan – proof that such falling intensity can accompany, even increase, competitiveness – yet it is rising in the US, following the official US dogma that rising electric intensity is essential to economic health and must therefore be further subsidized.

Large expenditures are being contemplated to mitigate or respond to such problems as CO_2 emissions, acid rain, and nuclear proliferation – all of which are artefacts of an economically inefficient energy policy, and could be abated not at extra cost but at a profit (as is discussed below).

Twice in the past fifteen years, the US government has responded to an oil shock by spurring supply and ignoring demand. Both times, the supply initiatives have collapsed while the market quietly produced a gush of efficiency, sticking the supply industries with unsaleably costly surpluses. Today, the US government continues its efforts to repeat this mistake for a third time. To be sure, it has learnt the lesson that 'balance' is required between supply- and demand-side investments, albeit in roughly the proportions of the classic recipe for elephant-and-rabbit stew – one elephant, one rabbit. This 'balance' rests not on the neoclassical calculus of marginal costs and benefits, but rather on the 'Chinese-restaurant-menu theory' of energy policy – pick one option from Column A, one from Column B, and so on, to please the major constituencies – and on the hand-waving claim that more supply is needed as 'insurance' in case efficiency somehow fails to work. The result of trying to buy both, of course, would be to stint both (since they compete for the same resources), and hence could be to get neither. Worse, as in the recent past, we could *get* both – and hence further bankrupt the supply industries, which need increased demand to pay for costly new supplies.

In short, successive US administrations have been acting out Abba Eban's remark that people and nations 'behave wisely once they have exhausted all other alternatives'. We are certainly working our way well down the list.

10.4 Environmental bonuses

It is at least conceivable that the confluence of environmental problems now stirring such deep public anxiety may help to rebuild energy policy on a foundation of economic rationality. This is far from certain – virtually every news-magazine except *Business Week*, for example, has fallen for the fallacious argument that nuclear power can help to abate global warming[32] – but it offers a new opportunity to reframe the basic arguments.

Fuels which are not mined and burnt have no environmental impacts. It is generally cheaper today to give away efficiency[33] than to dig up and burn the fuels to do the same task. Most environmental impacts associated with obtaining, converting, and using energy can thus be abated at negative net internal cost to society.

For example, rather than raising people's electric bills to put nappies on dirty coal plants to reduce acid-gas emissions, one can use well-established delivery methods to help the same customers to get super-efficient lights, motors, appliances, and building components. They will then need less electricity to obtain the same services. The utility can burn less coal and emit less CO_2 and sulphur (preferably using 'environmental dispatch' to back out the dirtiest plants first). But the main effect will be that the utility saves a great deal of money, because efficiency is cheaper than coal.[34] The utility can then use part of its saved operating cost to clean up the remaining plants by any method of its choice, part to reduce its tariffs, part, if desired, to compensate displaced coal-miners, and part to reward its investors for having hired such smart managers. On very conservative assumptions,[35] one analysis of this approach found that the Midwest region responsible for a third of all US power-plant sulphur emissions could achieve a 55-per-cent sulphur reduction at a net-present-valued 1985-2000 cost of about *minus* \$4–7 billion, rather than the *plus* \$4–7 billion of conventional abatement without end-use efficiency improvements – a net saving of \$11+ billion.

Similar economic considerations apply to the more complex issues of abating nuclear proliferation,[36] improving domestic energy security against accidental or deliberate disruption,[37] and reducing dependence on Middle Eastern oil.[38] Achieving these benefits by improved end-use efficiency *lets one make money on the deal*. In a variant on Marv Goldberger's memorable phrase, this is 'spherically sensible' energy efficiency: it makes sense no matter which way you look at it. It should be done to save money, even if we are not concerned about such issues as global warming.

In most cases, the environmental benefits of energy savings can be achieved most quickly and profitably by saving electricity, because this energy form uses several units of fuel at the power plant per unit delivered, the generation and delivery system are extremely expensive, and electricity, for both these reasons, is by far the costliest form of energy.[39] This high environmental and economic leverage puts a premium on saving electricity, even though virtually all official and private effort has so far focused instead on saving directly used oil and gas. The leverage is highest in countries like the Soviet Union, where low-grade coal is inefficiently mined and burnt, then around 30–40 per cent of the power is lost in long-distance transmission to inefficient end-uses. From this perspective, among the most attractive ways to head off global warming will be saving electricity in the USSR, China, and India.

10.5 International applicability

The astonishing and little-noted progress in electric efficiency has been fastest in the United States because of its immensely diverse utility system. Among some 3,500 enterprises in around fifty major and hundreds of minor regulatory jurisdictions (along with substantial unregulated operations), a great many experiments have already been tried somewhere. This has occurred with little help, and despite overt and covert opposition, from the federal government; most of the initiative has come from the utilities themselves, from other private-sector actors, and from state and local governments.

Unfortunately, most other countries have a much more monolithic structure in their electric and energy industries[40] – often nationalized, usually centrally planned, generally devoid of market or political accountability, and hence with no incentive and little inclination to innovate. This discouraging picture is starting to change rather rapidly, however, as political (and, especially in developing countries, financial) constraints hamper traditional supply expansion and as public concern rises about global warming, acid rain, and nuclear safety. In country after country – even those previously most immune to innovation, such as the UK and USSR – new incentives are starting to bring the entrepreneurs out of the woodwork.

Naturally, there are important differences between end-use structures, behavioural patterns, and capital stocks in different countries.

None the less, it is becoming apparent in the roughly forty countries in which I am active in energy policy, and in others where my colleagues work, that the technical (and usually the institutional) opportunities for major savings are strikingly similar even in countries with quite different levels of overall energy efficiency. For example, Jørgen Nørgård at the Technical University of Denmark has recently found a potential to save about half of the electricity now used in Danish buildings, at an average cost of around 0.6 cents/kWh, or three-quarters at an average cost of 1.3 cents/kWh.[41] Several other European analysts are converging on similar results: doubling Swedish end-use electric efficiency in all end-uses and sectors, for example, was found to cost only 1.3 cents/kWh.[42] To be sure, Europeans generally light their offices less intensively, and turn the lights off more, than Americans do, but that does not affect the percentage-savings available in the lighting energy that is used – a function only of the lighting technology itself, which is quite similar on both continents.

Contrary to the common but fallacious view that developing countries can save little energy because they use so little (at least in commercial forms), the same is true there too. Replacing an incandescent with a compact-fluorescent lamp will save about 70–85 per cent of the energy per unit of delivered light regardless of whether the original lamp is in Belgium or Bihar. Superwindows[43] cut cooling loads by the same (or a greater)[44] percentage in Bangkok as in Bakersfield.

Efficiency opportunities may well turn out to be smaller and costlier in Europe and Japan than in North America, but on current evidence, the differences will probably be unimportant; and they may well be offset, or more, by even bigger and cheaper opportunities for savings in the socialist[45] and developing countries. (Table 10.1 summarizes one aggregated measure of how very far many such countries have to go, and why.) Perhaps the most encouraging analysis so far, for Sweden (see Chapter 14), showed how doubling electric end-use efficiency, coupled with fuel-switching to gas and biofuel and with environmental dispatch (operating most plants which emit the least carbon), could simultaneously displace the nuclear half of that nation's power supply, support a 54-per-cent larger GNP, reduce the utilities' CO_2 output by a third, and reduce the cost of electrical services by nearly $1 billion per year. This finding implies that practically any other country should be able to do even better, because Sweden has a severe climate, a heavily industrialized economy, and the world's highest aggregate energy efficiency to begin with.

Table 10.1: Some comparative national energy intensities
(primary megajoules per 1983 $ of 1983 GNP)

Market-oriented nations

Sweden	8.6
France	8.6
Japan	9.7
Spain	11.8
FRG	11.8
Italy	12.9
UK	17.2
USA	19.3

Centrally planned nations (at least in the industrial sector)

Yugoslavia	21.5
Poland	26.9
GDR	29.0
Czechoslovakia	30.1
USSR	32.3
Romania	37.6
People's Republic of China	40.9
Hungary	49.5

(Source: Worldwatch Institute, *State of the World 1987.)*

The exact values shown are of course sensitive to the exchange rates assumed (which are based on an authoritative comparison of purchasing power) and cannot substitute for careful comparisons of the technical intensity of each sector and product, but are still qualitatively indicative of a major difference between market and non-market economies. Possible reasons for these striking disparities are:

(1) Poor price formation: e.g. most Soviet prices are at 1928 levels, with no effective regulatory substitute (however, many Soviet commodity prices are currently proposed to float to market-clearing levels in the next few years);

(2) Some countries, e.g. Hungary, use cost-plus industrial accounting which creates a perverse incentive to maximize inputs per unit output;

(3) Obsolete, often 1930s-vintage, technologies, especially in basic-materials industries such as steel-making; poor controls and maintenance;

(4) Greater emphasis on basic-materials industries than on manufacturing. In the US in 1978, per dollar of value added, the former were about fourteen times as energy-intensive and about five times as electricity-intensive as the latter;

(5) A small services sector. In the US this sector typically uses only a quarter as much electricity per worker as does the industrial sector.

There is considerable room for argument about how much energy can be saved, both in theory and in practice. Most debates in this sphere turn out to arise from differences in the modernity and thoroughness of characterization of the technologies assumed, or in the degree of disaggregation of the end-uses analysed (since excessive aggregation omits many opportunities for savings which are individually small but collectively large). In round numbers, however, a four- to tenfold (or greater) aggregate efficiency gain, compared with 1973 levels, seems to represent the practical and cost-effective potential. The lower figure is broadly consistent with a careful, technically conservative, clearly presented analysis by Goldemberg *et al.*,[46] based on case-studies for Brazil, India, Sweden, and the United States. The upper figure is consistent with an earlier analysis for the German Federal Environmental Agency, based on 1980 end-use patterns, efficiency levels, technologies, and costs in the Federal Republic of Germany, cross-checked against a variety of case-studies from other countries and regions.[47]

The latter study assumed a world with eight billion people roughly a century hence, uniformly industrialized to the level of the Federal Republic of Germany in 1973, when it was the most heavily industrialized country on Earth, and one of the most energy-efficient. This assumed level of industrialization corresponds to global economic activity nearly five times that of 1975, and a tenfold increase in the developing countries. (Of course, this may well be impossible or undesirable for reasons other than energy.) None the less, if such a world used energy in a way that would have saved money under 1980 FR German conditions, then its total primary energy use would have been approximately 3.5 terawatts (3.5 x 10^{12} W), or less than half of the actual 1973 level, or about a third of the actual 1990 level. Moreover, except for one instance of modest inter-regional trade in biofuel, each of the world's major regions (classified on the IIASA scheme) would be independently able to meet all or virtually all of its resulting needs for energy in each form using only renewable sources which in 1980 were already available and cost-effective on the long-run margin. In short, no energy problem – even on economic-growth assumptions that most would consider implausibly high. And complete implementation over some decades would require only a rate of efficiency improvement (and, for some countries like the US, renewable-supply deployment) somewhat *below* that actually achieved since 1973.

The energy-supply system required in such low-energy futures differs strikingly from that of conventional projections, and so do the corresponding costs and impacts. Even the low IIASA scenarios, for example, imply world energy-use in 2030 some two-and-a-half times that of 1983. That projection is about two to three times lower than was in vogue in the late 1970s, but still requires thousands of nuclear reactors (with a new one commissioned around every four to six days), a three- to six-fold increase in the rate of coal-mining, fossil-fuel supplies increased at a rate equivalent to about an Alaska (about 2 million barrels per day) every one or two months, and hence largely depleted global conventional hydrocarbon resources. The resulting atmospheric CO_2 concentration in 2030 is, in consequence, about 450 parts per million by volume (ppmv), rising by 50 ppmv every decade or so.

In contrast, the 'efficiency scenario', assuming the same economic and population growth but using energy in a way that saves money (under 1980 conditions, which are probably less favourable than today's), uses four to five times less energy, costs much less, stretches oil and gas for centuries, dispenses with reliance on both the Middle East and the atom, and by 2030 has attained an atmospheric CO_2 level barely above today's and rising by 5 ppmv every three decades or so, making this part (about 40 per cent) of future global warming virtually vanish. Many other problems would also disappear, such as those associated with the million bombs'-worth of plutonium proposed to be annually extracted and put into global commerce under the IIASA scenarios.

In view of the well-known institutional barriers to using energy efficiently in developing countries, some will ask whether this technical potential has any practical force. I believe the real issue is just the opposite: how can such countries develop *without* a high degree of efficiency? Consider these small examples:

- A colleague formerly in charge of Haitian energy policy estimated that giving away quadrupled-efficiency light-bulbs throughout Haiti could increase the average household's disposable income by as much as a fifth – because so much of the cash economy goes to electricity, chiefly for lighting. (Southern California Edison Company has in fact given away more than 800,000 such lamps to its low-income residential customers and their neighbourhood shops, because that is cheaper than operating the utility's existing power stations.)

- Ashok Gadgil at the Tata Energy Research Institute has shown by a Bombay case-study that lighting is responsible for about 37 per cent (about 9 GW) of India's evening peak load, which over-stresses the grid and is often responsible for rotating blackouts.

These in turn greatly hamper economic output and competitiveness, both directly by shutting down production and indirectly by forcing factories to install very costly back-up diesel generators. Again, giving away efficient lamps could largely solve the problem.[48] (Such giveaways in an Alaskan village recently reduced the peak lighting load by a factor exceeding 7.)

■ The People's Republic of China recently decided it was time that people had refrigerators, and built more than 100 refrigerator factories. The fraction of Beijing households owning a refrigerator rose from 2 per cent to more than 60 per cent during 1981–6. Unfortunately, however, through mere inattention, an inefficient refrigerator design was chosen – thereby committing China to billions of dollars'-worth of electric capacity to serve those refrigerators, and creating shortages of both electricity and capital.

These examples are especially striking when one recalls that at least a quarter of the world's total development capital goes to electrification; that a large, even dominant, fraction of many developing countries' debt service is energy-related; that inadequate electricity supplies already severely constrain the development of many countries which lack the capital to build (or the skills to operate reliably) more plants and grid; and that such expansions of electrification in developing countries are officially forecast (by the World Bank and others) to need between 8 and 10 times as much capital as is expected to be available for this purpose.

In energy, as in water, minerals, and many other resources, it appears that developing countries can achieve their economic goals only by building comprehensive resource-efficiency into their infrastructure from scratch. This is easier than the developed nations' task of having to retrofit trillions of dollars' worth of obsolete stocks, and in principle could therefore give developing countries a comparative advantage. In practice, most developing countries so far lack the technical and commercial sophistication to ensure that they are buying the best options – especially in the face of developed countries' often strenuous efforts to sell them equipment so inefficient that it is obsolete on their home markets (a dangerous and immoral export akin to that of deregistered pesticides, but not yet subject to any international constraints). The continued fixation of major international lenders on central generating plants, and the greater opportunity for decision-makers to receive large 'commissions' on such projects, also make it as difficult as in the industrialized countries for the political process to accommodate efficiency gains which would discommode the vendors of uncompetitive energy-supply technologies. But if developing countries hope to break the cycle of poverty in a capital-constrained world, they have extremely strong incentives to overcome these daunting barriers. They *must* 'do it right the first time', because they cannot afford to do it twice.

Another hidden advantage of energy efficiency in a technologically dynamic world is that it buys *time*. Time can be used, among other things, to develop and deploy better technologies for both supply and demand. The former type of progress, of which we have lately seen dramatic examples (such as the 40-per-cent cost reduction in the technology used to bring in Royal Dutch/Shell's Kittiwake oilfield in the North Sea)[49] stretches supply curves, expands reserves, and slows depletion. This yields more time in which to deploy efficiency, which has similar effects. Both kinds of progress reduce real resource costs, freeing capital for more productive investment elsewhere, while demand-side efficiency-gains reduce sensitivity to supply costs. Buying time and using it to advantage for developing and deploying better technologies, taken together, thus make many problems recede very far into the future, or go away altogether.

10.6 Whose development path?

The deeper question of whether energy need, may, or should constrain development cannot be addressed in isolation from what kind of development is contemplated, by and for whom, chosen how and by whom. These questions in turn rest on still deeper questions of social purpose.

Consider, for example, the data on the past five centuries' Danish patterns of primary energy-use for heating and cooking (Table 10.2). If, looking at the last three lines, one made a facile identification of energy-use with well-being, one would then have to conclude that Danes have only recently regained the standard of living which they enjoyed in the Middle Ages. What actually happened was that in 1500 and 1600 Danes burned a lot of wood and peat in very inefficient open fires, similar to the situation in many developing countries today; by 1800, more Danes were burning wood in fairly efficient wood and ceramic stoves; by 1900, they burned mainly coal in very efficient stoves, and in 1950 mainly oil (incurring refinery losses) in fairly inefficient furnaces. By 1975 they had added the Carnot and grid losses of expanded electrification. This example shows that simply equating energy-use with social benefits telescopes together several distinct relationships which are best kept separate:

- How much primary fuel is fed into the energy system does not determine how much useful energy is supplied – that depends on the system's conversion and transmission efficiency;

- How much useful energy is supplied does not determine how much service is performed – that depends on end-use efficiency;

- How much service is provided does not determine whether what was done with the energy was worth doing.

Table 10.2: Average per-capita primary energy used in Denmark for heating and cooking (kW)

1500	0.9–1.9
1800	0.9
1900	0.4
1950	0.9
1975	2.3

(Source: 'Energy in Denmark 1990–2005: a case study', Report 7 (survey by the Work Group of the International Federation of Institutes for Advanced Study, Sept. 1986).)

This last question is an important one. Mimicry of traditional development paths via normal industrialization ignores both industrialized countries' mistakes and developing countries' new opportunities. It is by no means clear that the industrial countries' development path must, even if it can, be repeated by other countries striving for similar material wealth. Hong Kong and Singapore have parlayed skilled, well-educated, hard-working people into a global economic force without any significant heavy industry; they simply earn enough to buy materials and manufactures from abroad, much as many American communities or states (like Vermont) or even sizeable 'industrialized' countries (like Denmark) do. To be sure, heavy industries no longer competitive or attractive in the 'advanced' countries are moving offshore to other countries desperate for any kind of investment; but it is not at all obvious that such low-value-added enterprises are advantageous to them either.

The technologies that can create wealth today are very different, and generally far less materials- and more information-intensive, than they were when the OECD countries built their infrastructure. No sensible country today, building an urban sanitary system from scratch, would build Western-style sewers and treatment plants; if it used flush toilets at all (rather than advanced composters), it would probably do better with ones five or more times as water-efficient,[50] feeding into a relatively localized biological wastewater-treatment system.[51] Similarly, no sensible country would imitate Los Angeles' car-dependence or its freeway system, together with their costs, fuel-intensity, greenhouse gases, and smog; instead, it would encourage people to live near where they want to be, work nearer home, tele-commute more, and use sophisticated public transport.[52] No sensible country would try to extend electric grids into rural areas when, even competing with cheap US grid-power, the break-even distance to the grid, beyond which it becomes cheaper to use photovoltaics and super-efficient appliances, is already typically less than 400 metres and falling fast. Such examples are almost endless. In short, much of the money- and resource-intensive infrastructure which we think of as central to development, simply because we ourselves live with it, is in fact obsolete – unable to compete with newer, smarter ways to do the same thing better.

By a happy coincidence, at a time when many countries are seek-ing to develop on the strength of few resources other than people and sunlight, the combination of very efficient energy-use with advances in many kinds of solar technologies is bringing modern energy ser-vices within economic reach.[53] This is a pattern of 'eco-development' which integrates energy, water, waste, food, and other services at a village scale, providing a sound alternative to migrating to urban slums.

The very assumption that development requires large increments of certain basic-materials industries' capacity (the most energy-inten-sive kind)[54] – whether in one's own country or elsewhere – is itself up for review. US steel consumption per dollar of GNP is now below its 1860 level and falling; we still use steel, but much less of it,[55] and the same is true for virtually all basic materials. Does a country which builds with local materials[56] need many cement plants? Does one which jumps straight to advanced materials need much steel? Does one which 'goes electronic' early need much paper? Does one which makes an *ab initio* commitment to product-longevity, recycling, re-use, re-manufacture, scrap-recovery, minimum-materials design, near-net-shape processing, limited packaging, and so on need so much of any kind of material to maintain an ample stock (not flow) of material artefacts? What are the industrial underpinnings required for systematic 'eco-development' on a national or regional scale? Nobody knows, but certainly the answer will be very different than what the OECD countries require today.

10.7 Conclusion

Energy need not constrain global development, nor need it engender 'great experiments' with the environmental security of future generations – but it may well do so, much more widely than it is doing at present, if some of our major institutions don't start learning faster and practising the economic rationality they preach. Whether for energy-derived CO_2, SO_x, or NO_x, advanced techniques for energy end-use efficiency can pay for very large direct and indirect reductions in emissions, usually with money left over. This permits much more complete abatements than are often analysed, and not at a cost but at a large profit.

The order of *economic* priority, however, is also the order of *environmental* priority. Choosing the best buys first maximizes abatement per dollar; choosing anything else first thus reduces abatement per dollar. In this opportunity-cost sense, nuclear power makes global warming worse by diverting investment away from electric end-use efficiency, which would displace far more coal-burning per dollar spent. To achieve the largest, fastest abatement, therefore, requires that instead of buying a bit of everything, one adopt the least-cost approach. The powerful supply-curve method of identifying priorities, as used in the figures for this paper, is therefore valid only if pollution-*prevention* is considered together with, and allowed to precede and even displace as well as to augment, the more traditional 'end-of-pipe' technologies.

The physically explicit nature of supply-curves of energy-efficiency potential, based as they are on engineering/economic analysis from measured data for real devices, offers a valuable counter-weight to the econometric theory that often passes for fact nowadays.

Many of the world's leading newspapers, for example, have carried headlines along the lines of 'Abating global warming will cost trillions, experts say', reporting conclusions by distinguished economists. But on closer examination, those newspapers turn out to have been hoodwinked by an *assumption* masquerading as a fact. The assumption – that saving fuel costs far more than burning it – simply ignores the enormous body of empirical experience flatly to the contrary.

How can this be? In essence, it turns on a difference of temperament between econometricians and physical scientists or engineers. Econometricians believe that truth resides in coefficients, such as historic price-elasticities of demand, which are shorthand representations of how large numbers of people behaved in the past. This behaviour, econometricians suppose, is a kind of revealed economic truth that essentially determines the future. In contrast, analysts grounded in physical design disciplines consider the future to be not fate but choice: they believe that past behaviour, under conditions which no longer exist and which it is often a goal of policy to change as much as possible, is a severely limiting and grossly inaccurate guide to future possibilities, especially when new technologies or delivery mechanisms radically expand what is possible.

Thus econometricians, reviewing historical experience, ask when was the last time the rate of burning fossil fuel sharply decreased. 'Aha!', they say: 'That is what happened after the 1973–4 Arab oil embargo, and the decrease was driven by quadrupled energy prices, accompanied by recession, unemployment, and misery. So if we want to decrease fossil-fuel burning once more, as would be necessary to meet (say) the Toronto CO_2 goals, then we must again have dramatic increases in the price of energy. Now let us crank our econometric models to see how high the price must go, with how much accompanying recession, unemployment, and misery, to achieve the desired result.'

Strange, but true. That is exactly how the often quoted models work, and where those silly headlines come from. Despite their undoubted eminence and skill, these econometricians have somehow failed to observe that numerous utilities and industries are *in fact* continuing to save ever more energy with payback times under two years – paybacks which would not exist if saving fuel actually cost more than burning it.

So obsessed are these economists with the *theory* of perfect markets that they *assume* that if it were cost-effective to save a lot of energy at present prices, we would already have done so. They turn a blind eye to the reality of the major market failures (and proven ways to correct them) which are the everyday activity of energy-efficiency experts: poor information, immature delivery infrastructure, perverse regulation which penalizes efficient utility investment, sparse markets in saved energy, and discount rates ten times lower for energy-supplying than energy-saving options (thus diluting price signals tenfold). By supposing that such issues either do not exist or at least are immaterial – that what is real (major market failures) is hypothetical, and what is hypothetical (energy-savings cost-effective only at prices far above today's) is real – those economists conceal real problems and potentials behind a curtain of theory, and thus hide the truth even from themselves. This is reminiscent of the economist who was taking his mannerly little granddaughter for a walk. She spied a ten-pound note lying on the ground, and asked, 'Please, Grandpa, may I pick that up?', to which he replied, 'Don't bother. If it were real, somebody would have picked it up already.'

It is precisely this theory-bound attitude, so foreign to common-sense and everyday experience, that has propagated as fact the falsehood that saving large amounts of energy will cost money instead of saving money. It led the Chairman of President Bush's Council of Economic Advisors, in a recent White House conference on global warming, to estimate costs of up to $200 billion per year for the US economy to meet the Toronto CO_2 goals. The amount may in fact be about right, but he got the *sign* wrong: such an efficiency-gain would *save* the US economy roughly $200 billion per year (excluding the avoided costs of trying, or failing, to adapt to climatic change).

It is a supreme irony that precisely the governments most committed to markets and economic rationality are today stalling progress on abating global warming, and gravely embarrassing themselves, by not taking economics seriously – the *practical*, field-proven economics of energy efficiency. And it is not a quaint scholastic oddity, but an intellectual scandal, that public policy on a matter of enormous importance is being grounded on invalid theory whilst governments ignore the actual data demonstrating the availability of abundant and cheap efficiency resources.

Unfortunately we still need technology transfer to policy-makers, few of whom appreciate the modern efficiency potential. If they did, they would eschew many international conferences on global warming, which devote perhaps 1 per cent of their agenda to energy efficiency, and use it to say that although important and desirable, efficiency gains will of course be slow, small, costly, inconvenient, and authoritarian – so let us get on with the real business of setting up new bureaucracies to tell people how to live. In this bizarre way do many governments seek to substitute *dirigisme* for markets, penury for development, risks for rewards, and costs for profits.

The antidote is to satisfy oneself about a simple truth: *it is generally cheaper today to save fuel than to burn it. The pollution avoided by not burning the fuel can, therefore, be achieved not at a cost but at a profit – so this result can and should be widely implemented in the market-place.*

I am originally a physicist, not an economist, and, despite my neoclassical perspective, have some sympathy with the view that economists are those people who lie awake at night worrying about whether what works in practice can possibly work in theory. But the biggest evolution in my thinking over the fifteen years since the first modern oil shock has been an increased respect for how well even very imperfect markets can work. Efficiency and renewables have swept the US energy market despite a formidable array of officially erected obstacles meant to achieve the opposite result. How much better would we have done – can we yet do – with an even-handed policy, should we ever get a truly conservative government that takes markets seriously? My main residual concern here, beyond helping the market to work better (via better information, fair access to capital, real competition, and so on), is that amidst the dramatic global shift now underway towards market mechanisms, we do not forget that markets are meant to be efficient, not fair; that while they can be superb short-term allocators of scarce resources,[57] there are many other important things that they do badly or were never designed to do; and that if markets do something good for whales or wilderness, for God or grandchildren, it is purely accidental.

My conclusions here will already have suggested to many readers a charming historical irony. In the days of *Limits to Growth* – a prescient work still maligned by those who haven't read it or who missed its central message of the importance of adaptation – there were those whom my colleagues and I called 'cornucopians'. The cornucopians said 'Not to worry' about the problems of population, resources, and environment; these would be solved, they said, by the intelligent application of advanced technology. Some of us, however, pointed out that technology, though no doubt very powerful (as my practice of it had taught me), was not omnipotent, had costs, and often had side-effects – in Garrett Hardin's definition, 'consequences we didn't think of, the existence of which we will deny as long as possible'. For this caveat, we were derided as 'technological pessimists' – not in James Branch Cabell's sense ('The optimist proclaims we live in the best of all possible worlds; the pessimist fears this is true'), but as ignoramuses denying the reality of technological progress.

Today, however, it is we former 'technological pessimists' who are pointing out that new technologies – albeit of a more mundane, vernacular, and 'transparent' kind than those anticipated by the cornucopians; such as loft insulation rather than fusion reactors, and microelectronic motor controls rather than solar-power satellites – have indeed proved far more powerful than anyone, including us, thought possible. These relatively small, accessible, and cheap technologies even seem powerful enough to solve the energy problem, the water problem, many strategic-minerals problems, and probably a good many other thorny problems, such as agriculture and national security, to boot.[58] For saying this, we are berated by the former cornucopians, now turned 'technological pessimists', who successively assert that our proposed technological innovations don't exist, or won't work, or aren't cost-effective, or won't sell, or won't remain popular in the long run.[59]

Thus the role-reversal is complete. But it reminds us born-again technological optimists not to overlook – as our partners in this debate long did – the limits of technical fixes, the restricted relevance of markets to achieving justice, the ever-shifting tapestry of social values, the importance of surprises, and the inherent frailty of the human design.

Chapter 11
Renewable Energy: Recent Commercial Performance in the USA as an Index of Future Prospects

Carlo LaPorta

" …technology exists that can produce electricity, or any temperature heat (up to 1,400°C) directly from natural resources available at a remote location in nearly any country. The demand can be satisfied without transporting a continuous, long-distance stream of fuel or running long-distance electric-power transmission lines – or emitting vast quantities of greenhouse gases…There is no qualification needed for these statements. Technically, it is possible. Economically, it is a more limited situation, but not nearly as limited as most observers and analysts believe… "

Since the dawn of the Industrial Revolution, economic development among nations has depended on substitution of modern forms of energy for human labour. In the years to come, growing population and rising economic expectations could accelerate demand for energy even faster. But as it becomes more evident that planet Earth needs to be treated more carefully to safeguard it, older economic development paths need to be modified. In this context, it is essential that humankind uses available energy resources much more efficiently, and relies more on cleaner sources of energy than the fossil fuels that now dominate global energy supplies. Nearly every international forum in recent years that has dealt with the threat of global warming has come to this conclusion.

This chapter reports on the recent performance of renewable energy in commercial markets – stressing examples from the USA. The aim is to illustrate the potential of renewable-energy technologies to contribute more energy to global energy-supply in a shorter time-frame than is commonly expected.

While they agree that renewable-energy technologies are desirable and acknowledge that numerous systems have been successfully demonstrated, many policy-makers do not believe that renewable-energy technologies can appreciably reduce fossil-energy consumption in the next three decades. The recently published Cairo Compact from the Cairo Conference on Preparing for Climate Change, December 1989, spoke of the need to 'develop and deploy' renewable-energy technologies.[1] These words reveal an opinion of the final drafters of the Compact that renewable-energy technologies still need to be developed before they can compete. This is simply not true.

Calling continually for further technological development is a delaying tactic for those who do not believe that alternatives to fossil energy are reliable or less expensive now. Yes, some technologies will require further refinements or major cost-cutting development to compete more widely; but economies can safely seek greater reliance on technologies ready and capable of deployment today. Recognition of this near-term potential, and taking action to realize it, will channel resources to building up the industrial infrastructure that will deliver more advanced versions of these technologies in the future.

The Intergovernmental Panel on Climate Change (IPCC) Working Group 3 on Response Strategies refers to renewable energy and reveals some knowledge of the capability of renewable-energy systems. But the references in the IPCC Report do not do justice to how much renewable energy can do in the near term. They ignore the fact that tens of millions, and ultimately hundreds of millions, of renewable-energy systems could dramatically alter energy balances on Earth.

11.1 Why turn to renewable energy?

Besides the trauma of severe dislocations and high-cost adjustments should worse-case scenarios regarding global warming occur, there are many other environmental reasons why reliance on cleaner sources of energy should be expanded as quickly as possible. People know that dirty air is choking cities throughout the world, that rainclouds contaminated with sulphur dioxide threaten forests, and that processing petroleum creates many toxins. The solution is simple: more reliance on renewable energy will lessen the amount of fossil fuels used, and these associated health and environmental problems. Further, besides environmental gains, a shift to cleaner sources of energy can also mean lower energy costs. More affordable sources of energy are essential in countries desperately attempting to raise their standards of living. Farmers and their food-processing co-operatives in rural areas in developing countries just cannot afford diesel oil at US$1.60 per gallon. Just as climate has changed throughout history, change in the energy resources that fuel humankind's development will bring on cheaper, better alternatives.

The IPCC has identified a three-pronged course of action for reducing carbon dioxide releases to the atmosphere. The three elements are:

(1) Efficiency improvements in energy supply, conversion, and end use;
(2) Fuel substitution by energy sources lower in greenhouse-gas emissions;
(3) Reduction in greenhouse gases by removal, recirculation, or fixation.[2]

Renewable-energy technologies are capable of contributing significantly in each of these areas. Depending on their locations, users who insist on high efficiency can demand buildings that extensively incorporate solar energy and natural ventilation to reduce energy demand by 40 to 80 per cent compared with conventional buildings. A more efficient electricity generation-and-transmission network will increasingly rely on renewable sources of power that match demand-requirements closely and can be added in small increments. Decomposition rates of organic compounds in aqueous solutions increase in the presence of concentrated sunlight. Metal treatment (surface hardening) has been postulated and demonstrated with concentrated solar flux. Researchers in the USA have found that photochemical enhancements in the destruction of dioxin occur in the presence of concentrated sunlight due to the presence of solar photons (known as the 'solar bullet') between 300 and 400 nanometres in wavelength.

Because renewable-energy technologies can make liquid fuels and produce heat or electricity, substitution for fossil-fuel consumption can occur in every economic sector for nearly every application. Commercial experience with already-deployed renewable-energy technologies confirms the ability of these systems to compete shoulder-to-shoulder with fossil-energy systems in certain applications today. Indeed, in some applications, renewable-energy technologies have become the preferred system, for example, small remote power systems using solar photovoltaic panels. These solar-energy systems are preferred because they require fewer resources – money, material, and manpower – than would otherwise be needed to furnish the electrical energy to perform the desired service. A wide range of new technologies, and improvements in older ones, promise even further competitiveness for renewable energy, as fossil-fuel prices rise in the future.

Finally, renewable-energy technologies can figure in carbon fixation and sequestering strategies. For example, technology has been developed that will harvest and combust whole trees from energy plantations. (Note that the use of trees, plants, and indeed any organic products or wastes for fuel is known as 'biomass' fuel). Using genetically selected strains of fast-growing trees, such a system eliminates the need for chipping or chunking wood (thereby lowering wood-fuel cost), and the net effect of this energy from biomass cycle is carbon dioxide absorption, plus elimination of sulphur dioxide emissions that cause acid rain.[3]

Fortunately, the call for revisions in the conventional energy-supply system comes a decade after the energy crisis in the 1970s stimulated tremendous investment in alternatives to petroleum. The cleanest of these were renewable-energy technologies which convert natural energy-flows powered by the constant radiation from the sun. At the Earth's outer atmosphere, the solar constant – the supply of energy from the sun – is 1,353 watts of energy per square metre, and on the Earth's surface the maximum amount of this solar energy available on a clear day is 1,000 watts per square metre.[4]

Solar radiation, both direct and diffuse, can be captured directly with solar-energy technologies to make thermal energy or electricity, or indirectly through biomass, wind, and hydro technologies. Trees and plants – commonly collectively referred to as the 'biota' – use solar radiation to run nature's chemical factories, which furnish biomass for direct combustion to thermal energy, or feedstocks for conversion into any of the same chemical products now extracted from crude petroleum, natural gas, or coal. Uneven distribution of radiation stimulates air-flow, generating wind, which may also be converted to mechanical, thermal, or electrical energy. And finally, solar energy powers the water evaporation and condensation cycle that creates precipitation and ultimately hydro-power.

Table 11.1 lists most of the renewable-energy technologies available and the applications for which they are used. The list is comprehensive, for renewable-energy technologies are capable of supplanting fossil energy in most applications. Indeed, in some applications, renewable-energy technologies offer superior performance attributes that exceed the capabilities of fossil-energy systems.

While no energy technology is totally harmless to the environment, environmental-impact monitoring of many renewable-energy projects has documented these effects. They are well understood, and it is clear that many classes of renewable-energy system, particularly solar-energy conversion, have much less environmental impact than conventional energy systems. The US Department of Energy calculated the difference in a recent study of several electric-power generation technologies. This assessment determined net releases of carbon dioxide in a cradle-to-grave analysis that took account of the emissions released to build, source the fuel, and operate the electric-power systems. The results, shown in Table 11.2, indicate how much less harmful renewable-energy technologies are when it comes to greenhouse-gas emissions.

Table 11.2 indicates why policies implemented to combat the release of greenhouse gases will give high priority to substitution of renewable-energy systems for fossil-fuelled ones. A solar thermal electric-power peaking plant emits 134 times less carbon dioxide than a natural gas-fired peaker per gigawatt-hour of delivered energy (a gigawatt-hour is a billion watts supplied for 1 hour). The US Department of Energy has postulated that a wood-fired electric power plant, using a short-rotation (rapid-growth) managed forest to

Table 11.1: Renewable-energy technologies and applications

Technology and Typical Size System	Application
Photoconversion with solar technologies	
Active solar (1 to 500 + kW$_{th}$)	
Flat plate collectors	Water-heating
Evacuated tube collectors	Pool-heating
Seasonal storage systems	Space-heating and -cooling
	Industrial-process heat
	Crop-drying
Passive Solar (1 to 500 + kW$_{th}$)	
Solar gain and control	Day-lighting
Thermal storage and distribution	Space-heating
Natural ventilation	Space-cooling
Solar Thermal (4 kW$_e$ to 100 MW$_e$)	
Parabolic troughs	Industrial-process heat
Parabolic dishes	Building energy needs
Central receivers	Electricity
Solar ponds	Irrigation-pumping
	Chemical and fuel production
	Desalination
	Destruction of toxic wastes
Photovoltaic (watts to megawatts)	
Flat plate collectors	Consumer electronics
Concentrating collectors	Remote power systems
	Utility grid power
Photoconversion with biomass (kW$_{th}$ to 100s megawatts)	
Anaerobic digestion	Thermal energy
Fermentation/distillation	Electricity through cogeneration and utility power plants
Chemical reduction and distillation	Liquid and gaseous fuels
Pyrolysis, liquefaction, gasification	Feedstocks for chemicals
Hydrogenation	
Direct combustion	
Wind (100 watts to megawatts)	
Horizontal axis turbines	Mechanical pumping
Vertical axis turbines	Electricity for remote and utility grid applications
	Thermal energy
Geothermal (kilowatts to 10s of MW$_e$)	
Hydrothermal	Utility-scale electricity
Dry rock	Commercial and residential heating
Geopressured	
Magma	Methane production from geo-pressured brine
Hydroelectric (watts to 1000s MW$_e$)	
Containment dams	Remote electric power
Run-of-river systems	Utility-scale electricity
	Industrial power

Ocean

Wave (3 to 500 kW$_e$)	Utility-scale electricity
Tidal (megawatts)	Mechanical energy
Ocean Thermal Energy	Aquaculture
Conversion (10s to 100 MW)	Distillation
	Small-scale electric power

Source: International Energy Agency.[5]
(Explanation of Units: '1 to 500+kWth' means systems from one kilowatt thermal to more than 500 kilowatt thermal in size. 'kW$_e$' is kilowatt electric.)

provide its fuel, could absorb 159.9 tonnes of carbon dioxide for each gigawatt hour of electricity produced over the lifetime of the plant. This net-absorption calculation assumes new strains of fast-growth trees that re-grow from root systems. Actual performance has yet to be determined, but the potential exists to create a renewable-energy biofuels system that can reabsorb nearly all the carbon dioxide it releases.

Table 11.2: Carbon dioxide emissions of electric power plants given fuel extraction, construction and operation *(metric tons of CO_2 per GW/hour output)*

Technology	Fuel extraction	Construction	Operation	Total
Conventional Coal	1.0	1.0	962.0	964.0
Atmospheric fluidized bed combustion	1.0	1.0	960.9	962.9
Integrated gasification combined cycle	1.0	1.0	748.9	750.9
Oil-fired	–	–	726.2	726.2
Gas-fired	–	–	484.0	484.0
Ocean-thermal energy	n/a	3.7	300.3	304.0
Geothermal steam	0.3	1.0	55.5	56.8
Small hydro-power	n/a	10.0	n/a	10.0
Boiling water nuclear*	1.5	1.0	5.3	7.8
Wind energy	n/a	7.4	n/a	7.4
Photovoltaics	n/a	5.4	n/a	5.4
Solar thermal	n/a	3.6	n/a	3.6
Large hydro-power	n/a	3.1	n/a	3.1
Wood (sustainable harvest)	–1509.1	2.9	1346.3	–159.9

Source: US Department of Energy.[6]
* The figure for nuclear powerare subject to debate (see Chapter 19).

Tables 11.1 and 11.2 support the contention that renewable-energy technologies can deliver the energy modern economies require, while emitting much lower amounts of greenhouse gases. Why, then, is there so much scepticism about the future of renewable energy?

11.2 The future for renewable energy

How much renewable-energy displacement of fossil fuels is possible, or feasible? World-wide, renewable energy accounts for approximately 20 per cent of total primary energy supply, mainly from biomass energy and hydro-power.[7] In the highly industrialized economy of the United States, renewable energy contributes about 9 per cent to national primary energy supply. In Austria, Australia, Sweden, Denmark, Canada, and Switzerland, renewable-energy resources, excluding hydro-power, provide between 1 and 5 per cent of total primary energy.[8] While modest in the total energy balance, these shares are significant, and the potential exists for them to expand widely.

Considering the modest renewable-energy contributions in most countries and the huge amount of capital invested in fossil-energy infrastructure, suggestions that renewable energy could exceed the output of the conventional energy system seem irresponsible. Thus, it is unusual to find energy forecasts that project anything but small rises in renewable-energy supply over the next decades. This seems more true in developing countries, where substantial growth in energy-use is expected over the next thirty years, and where fossil fuels are predicted to be the source most likely to meet this new demand.

But is it irresponsible to suggest that an economy should begin to shift to renewable-energy resources when they far exceed fossil-energy reserves? In every country, the combined solar, biomass, geothermal,[9] hydroelectric, and wind-energy potential overshadows reserves of petroleum, natural gas, coal, and uranium. For the United States, one of the richest countries in terms of fossil-energy reserves, renewable energy dominates the total energy-resource base projected into the next century. Using billions of barrels of oil equivalent (BBOE) to gauge its energy resources, Table 11.3 shows that more than 614,000 BBOE are available in renewable resources in the USA compared to 44,000 BBOE for conventional energy resources.

Total resources expressed in Table 11.3 represent the sum of identified and undiscovered resources that can be economically extracted with current or future technology in a projected time-frame. (Renewable energy resources are based on yearly output over a set period of time corresponding to the conventional resource projections established by the federal government agencies that performed the resource assessments.) A more realistic determination of energy resources can be derived by limiting the estimate of energy reserves to only those that are 'accessible'; that is, the resources that can be delivered with current technology or with technologies to be available in the very near term.

Table 11.3: US total resource base of energy *(billions of barrels of oil equivalent)*

Energy source	BBOE
Geothermal	258,263
Photoconversion (solar and biomass)	178,438
Wind	176,910
Shale oil	27,518
Coal	15,079
Petroleum	477
Natural gas	294
Peat	244
Uranium	203
Hydro-power	170

Source: Meridian Corporation, for US Department of Energy. [10]

To inject limitations, the calculations of accessible resources presented in Table 11.4 eliminated land areas already occupied by urban and suburban development, or for which other competing uses would preclude renewable-energy conversion. Furthermore, laws that restrict energy operations in parklands are taken into account, and hydroelectric potential is severely curtailed by assuming that objections to it by groups concerned about dam impacts govern policy on expansion of hydro at new sites. As can be seen, these and other assumptions curtailed geothermal and wind-energy potential greatly. Energy potential from photoconversion (solar and biomass energy systems) remains very high, overwhelmingly dominating all other future US energy sources.

Conforming to a practice of only counting energy resources that are 'proven' to exist, and are economically exploitable with technology already commercialized (standard practice among US government agencies that tally energy resources), the Meridian Corporation analysts who conducted this study placed still more limits on their resources-assessment in order to classify them as 'energy reserves'. Based on the level of US energy consumption in 1987, the reserves-total in Table 11.5 would supply the US with energy for a period of seventy-eight years. Renewable resources amount to 10.4 per cent of the total, just a few per cent larger than the contribution that already exists.

Table 11.4: US accessible resources of energy *(billions of barrels of oil equivalent)*

Energy Source	BBOE
Photoconversion (solar and biomass)	101,153
Coal	6,577
Geothermal	3,928
Shale oil	2,018
Wind	870
Petroleum	190
Natural gas	153
Uranium	126
Peat	61
Hydro-power	27

Source: Meridian Corporation, for US Department of Energy.[11]

Table 11.5: A conservative analysis of US reserves of energy *(billions of barrels of oil equivalent)*

Energy Source	BBOE
Coal	908.0
Photoconversion (biomass)	57.7
Geothermal	42.5
Natural gas	39.9
Petroleum	26.9
Hydro-power	10.0
Uranium	7.3
Photoconversion (solar)	3.0
Wind	less than 1.0
Shale oil	less than 1.0
Peat	less than 1.0
Total	**1,096.2**

Source: Meridian Corporation, for US Department of Energy.[12]

The analysis that estimated the reserves listed in Table 11.5 was fairly conservative because it factors in prevailing market-prices for fossil fuels, and thereby assumes limited market-penetration of renewable-energy technologies. Because of the prices assumed in the study, no new solar-thermal or photovoltaic installations are assumed in the reserves, only the output of existing systems. More-over, the reserves include no additional hydroelectric capacity, and quite pessimistic values for the delivered cost of solar heat (for example, $28 per gigajoule, a figure that is at least two to three times too high given current costs of parabolic trough concentrators being installed at favourable sites in the United States today).

Even though such assumptions have limited the amount of renew-able energy in the reserves, Table 11.5 still indicates that, after coal, the second most abundant US reserve is biomass, followed by geothermal energy. These two categories of reserves are greater than natural gas and petroleum reserves. Moreover, comparing the energy reserves of Table 11.5 with accessible energy resources in Table 11.4 reveals that very large potential for renewable forms of energy exists in the future.

Such an assumption is supported by the data in Table 11.4, which show that accessible resources of biomass and solar energy amount to 101,153 BBOE, nearly 111 times the amount of coal counted as reserves in Table 11.5. Furthermore, the accessible renewable-energy resources are essentially infinite. Solar radiation will continue to fall uninterrupted for millions of years to come, while coal resources will ultimately be expended. Should policies evolve that place limits on coal combustion, renewable reserves will rise even further in importance.

This summary of the United States energy future was used to point out that renewable-energy resource-bases in any country dominate the available supply of fossil energy. A difficult issue for policy-makers, however, is deciding how quickly the pace of technological and economic change will move renewable-energy resources from an accessible-energy to an energy-reserves table.

A case can be made for forecasting that renewable energy will expand in the market much faster than analysts have predicted. Sup-port for this statement can be found in the experience of the last fifteen years, a period in which more than a few renewable-energy technologies have proved successful in both technical and economic performance.

11.3 Wind energy

Wind energy illustrates a renewable-energy technology that has achieved economic competitiveness in a short time. Five decades ago, wind systems were fairly common in many countries for water-pumping and mechanical power, and some small-scale electric-power generation. Then, except in certain limited locations, cheap fossil fuels wiped them from the market.

Fortunes changed again when wind-energy research and development revived in the 1970s, and high costs for oil and natural gas in California created a market opportunity in the utility sector. Federal legislation in the United States in 1978 allowed independent power producers to escape burdensome utility regulations,[13] and federal- and state-government tax incentives provided investors with attractive tax breaks for investment in renewable energy systems. This combination of factors stimulated a rapid market expansion of wind-power in California, where wind-resource availability tracked closely with utility needs for peak power in summer months.

Spurred by an aggressive industry and private investors, total installed wind-energy capacity in California grew from virtually nothing to 16,000 wind turbines, totalling 1,400 megawatts of capacity. Utilities did not pay for the capital cost of installing the new capacity, only for a capacity credit and the energy delivered to them under standard contracts the state government had helped create. Through 1989, these turbines had generated 5,693 gigawatt-hours of electricity, saving California the equivalent of 10,041,000 barrels of oil. In a state with 11 per cent of the US population and an economy about sixth-largest in the world, wind-power was producing 1 per cent of the electric power. This 1-per-cent contribution has occurred in less than a decade. And since 1985, no federal or state investment tax incentives (credits for a portion of the capital invested) have been available for these installations.[14]

California is not alone. In Hawaii and Denmark, wind energy is also providing 1 per cent of electric power, and several countries are now investing to create wind-energy companies and buying wind-energy power plants. In the years to come, wind-power will expand to other US states (mainly in the Plains), where the wind-resource available far exceeds that in California.

The rapid commercialization of wind energy in the United States and Denmark has confirmed key attributes of renewable-energy systems. First, they exhibit substantial economies of scale. Learning-curve gains among manufacturers and increases in system sizes[15] lowered production and installation costs from $3,500 per kilowatt to between $1,000 and $1,200 per kilowatt for rated peak capacity for wind-farm turbines being installed today. Over the 1980s, the output per installed capacity unit has risen dramatically from 200 kilowatt hours per kilowatt to 1,300 kilowatt hours.[16] Technical improvements still on the horizon will further improve these figures.

A proper comparison of wind-energy technology with other electric-power systems must also take into account the capacity factor of a wind turbine. It is a characteristic of renewable-energy systems that they perform intermittently. A utility or user must know how much output it can expect in a year, measured by the capacity factor. For wind turbines, the machine must be available over 95 per cent of the time the wind reaches adequate speed to produce power. Such reliability levels are now common, and in the many wind-plant installations in California, measured performance has shown that overall capacity factor for the entire collection of wind turbines in the state has risen to 16 per cent. This figure includes performance of early systems with poorer reliability and output. Newer systems are recording a capacity factor of 20 per cent, and the best plants have achieved a capacity factor of 30 per cent.[17]

These figures mean that wind turbines can deliver competitively priced electricity, in the range of 8 to 9 cents per kilowatt hour, and wind plants are out-performing the most expensive electric-utility power plants in the United States, invariably nuclear facilities. Industry analysts point out that at least one-fourth of the wind-energy industry present in California is competitive with new nuclear capacity in the United States.[18]

The large number of wind turbines, and ten years of monitored performance, have given electric-power utilities in the United States, Denmark, and several other countries a thorough understanding of wind-energy capacity and performance. In California, they have concluded that wind-energy plants in many sites match their system power-management requirements well and offer the utility reliable, firm capacity or load-carrying capability.[19] Some utilities in the USA and abroad have estimated that their system could accept wind energy for 5 to 20 per cent of their power, without significant adjustments due to the intermittent nature of the resource. Affordable energy-storage systems (for example, batteries and fuel cells) can raise this figure further.

The environmental benefits from wind energy in California are already significant. In 1988, it has been estimated that 1.8 billion kilowatt-hours of wind-power delivered to utility grids in California eliminated 62,000 tons of air pollutants and 2.2 million tons of carbon dioxide from the atmosphere. Industry analysts have predicted that in a high-growth scenario over the next ten years, wind-power could eliminate up to 50 million tons of carbon dioxide emissions per year in the United States.[20]

Wind-energy experience in the US and Denmark has led numerous developing countries to begin planning for incorporation of wind-energy in their electric-power planning. India and Egypt have contracts with suppliers from Europe and the USA for wind farms, and licence agreements to manufacture wind turbines are in place or contemplated in these and other developing countries. A few developed countries have brought this technology to the threshold of worldwide market acceptance, and have created opportunities for export and highly beneficial technology transfer.

11.4 Renewable-energy technologies' expansion in the power sector

Wind energy is just one renewable-energy technology making major inroads in electric-power sectors. Public Citizen, a consumer advocacy group in the United States, conducted a study on renewable-energy development in the US over the last decade that documents how quickly renewable-energy capacity has grown in the electric-power market. Excluding hydroelectric power plants, in 1980, it found that total capacity of renewable-energy electric plants amounted to 1,109 megawatts. By 1989, this figure had grown to 9,543 megawatts. In addition, 11,700 megawatts of new hydroelectric capacity were added over the same nine years.[21]

Including all existing hydroelectric capacity, at the end of 1988, 97,443 megawatts of renewable-energy electric power were on-line in the United States. This is slightly more than the 97,220 megawatts of nuclear energy capacity that also existed in 1988.[22]

In the United States, national primary energy consumption is measured in quads, or quadrillion British thermal units. Based on the growth-rates exhibited in the 1980s, and projections it gathered from industry utilities and government, the authors of the Public Citizen study suggest that renewable energy could contribute 14 quads of energy in the United States by the year 2000 (1 quad being 1.055 exajoules, or 10^{15} BTU), a doubling of the current contribution. Depending on US growth in energy-demand and the pace of improvements in energy efficiency, 14 quads could represent from 15 to 19 per cent of US energy supply by the year 2000. For the world's largest national economy that annually consumes 83 quadrillion BTU, this contribution represents a quite large number of installations and a rapidly maturing industry.

The projection of 14 quads is based on the current energy-policy climate, continued low fossil-fuel costs, and the results of severe cuts in the government renewable-energy research and development budget that occurred in the 1980s. To gauge how large a contribution renewable energy could make in the United States under a more favourable policy environment, industry representatives have compared market growth over the next decade in business-as-usual and accelerated scenarios. As reported at the Forum on Renewable Energy and Climate Change, held in Washington, DC, 14–15 June, 1989, these industry estimates of growth were up to five times larger than the business-as-usual scenarios if certain policies were enacted to favour accelerated expansion.

The estimate for wind energy revealed that market acceleration would expand the wind-energy contribution by a factor of 3 to 5 in the next decade, and that 50 million tons of carbon dioxide emissions, rather than ten million tons, could be eliminated each year. For biomass, the industry estimate for more rapid market expansion was 14.6 quads in 2000 versus a business-as-usual expansion of 4.14 quads. (The biomass energy starting-point was an estimated 2.95 to 3.8 quad contribution in 1989.) Thus, for biomass energy, an accelerated market-penetration scenario would increase the energy contribution three- to four-fold compared to business as usual.

In order to assure accelerated market expansion for renewable energy, industry suggested several policy initiatives. For wind energy, they were:

■ An increase in federal research-and-development funds, with a commitment to a multi-year programme with funding between

$20 million and $50 million over five years, primarily to develop a new class of more-efficient, cost-effective turbines, and improve technological knowledge;

■ Construction of utility interconnections to facilitate transmission (wheeling) of wind-produced electricity to high-density population centres;

■ Financial incentives for the private sector, which could include: $0.02 to $0.04 per kilowatt-hour premium for energy generated by non-polluting renewable resources, and internalizing hidden costs of energy generation from conventional energy sources.

For biomass, industry policy recommendations were to:

■ Create a fund for interest rate buy-downs to finance biofuels facilities;

■ Provide technical assistance to businesses identified as candidates for conversion to biofuels;

■ Develop tax or regulatory incentives proportional to environmental benefits;

■ Continue/extend an excise-tax exemption for ethanol fuels;

■ Reinstate the 10-per-cent energy tax credit for biofuels facilities;

■ Extend a tax credit for production of non-conventional gas;

■ Require federal facilities and vehicles to use biofuels at specified levels;

■ Mandate nation-wide use of biofuels at target levels (for example 50 per cent of all gasoline to contain 10 per cent ethanol).

These policy suggestions relate primarily to incentives to support commercialization of renewable energy. They testify to the fact that, even though continued research and development will improve competitiveness in the future, ample opportunities exist in current markets with present-day renewable-energy technologies for significant market expansion to occur. Furthermore, as environmental policies are enacted which raise the cost of energy from the conventional technologies which cause most pollution in order to reduce their emissions, the competitive environment will dramatically improve.

The future looks especially promising for many renewable-energy technologies because only modest price-increases in fossil fuels are needed for them to cross those economic and institutional acceptance-hurdles that currently hinder their diffusion. One such technology is new, light-weight parabolic troughs for industrial-process heat systems or commercial building energy. In favourable climates, parabolic-trough concentrators can deliver a gigajoule for between $6.00 and $9.00, with a system-life of only fifteen years. With natural gas priced near $4.00 per gigajoule, and considering the efficiency of a conventional gas boiler (anywhere from 55 to 80 per cent is typical), solar thermal energy systems without storage are very close to a competitive positon in locations with good solar energy resources.

Another technology poised for rapid market expansion is solar thermal electric-power systems that also use parabolic troughs. Luz International Ltd. is a California- and Israel-based manufacturer/ developer of solar electric-power systems. Since 1984, this company has installed over 275 megawatts of hybrid solar/natural-gas electric-power systems in southern California. Through technical development and larger-scale production, Luz has lowered the cost of solar electric power plants from 25 cents to 8 cents per kilowatt-hour for a thirty-year plant life.[23] This figure is a levellized cost, that is, it offers the buyer a nearly fixed price for the power over thirty years. According to Luz, the portion of electric power fuelled by combusting natural gas, up to 25 per cent of the electric-power output annually, will actually be the most expensive energy portion of the plant output as the price of natural gas rises over thirty years. Solar and other renewable power plants which offer a long-term, nearly fixed price for the delivered energy, escape the fuel-price escalation factor.

Luz's system, constructed in 80 megawatt units, is gaining competitiveness in the United States, and will be suitable in Australia or northern Africa for locations with high insolation levels and utilities that face substantial peak-power requirements in summer months. These systems will also find markets in developing countries, where the cost of diesel electric power for utility grids is high, especially as Luz and other companies continue to raise efficiency of these systems while finding new, less costly materials. Too often critics of the ability of these types of systems to expand in the market make no allowance for future technological advances.

Another factor which aids the competitiveness of solar thermal electric-power plants is their capability to track daily peak-demand curves closely. With a solar electric plant, a utility can develop a more efficient dispatching strategy for its grid, since the plant output occurs in afternoons when demand is highest, and they are designed to cycle on and off daily. These plants can also be added in small increments. Finally, with a modest amount of thermal-energy storage, one of the least expensive ways to store energy, a solar thermal electric facility can offer capacity factors in excess of 30 per cent.

To summarize, solar, geothermal, biomass, and wind-power systems are rapidly gaining acceptance among utilities. The costs of competing fossil-energy systems need only rise modestly over the next few years for these systems to become more attractive. As a result, order-of-magnitude changes in cost and performance are no longer required for these technologies to expand quickly in the electric-power market or in the industrial, commercial, and building sectors.

11.5 Solar energy for buildings and industry

Besides renewable-energy technologies to produce electric power, using solar collectors to provide thermal energy for industry and building applications is another example of technology that will require only modest price-increases in fossil fuel to expand competitively. Called distributed renewable-energy systems, because the energy output does not feed into a centralized utility grid for transmission and distribution, their potential is being overlooked. This may be why the Energy and Industry Subgroup of the IPCC anticipates that commercial renewables in solar energy will not make substantial inroads in energy markets by 2025.

Solar water-heaters and other solar heating technologies for buildings seem to be discounted because the energy savings and pollution reductions they provide are considered too small to make a difference. It seems that energy or environmental policy-makers turn too quickly to the electric-power sector when they consider options for reducing energy consumption. This is short-sighted, because combining active solar and passive solar systems and designs can reduce a consumption of conventional energy in buildings from 30 up to 80 per cent, and these savings will accumulate year after year.[24]

Passive solar building design, using sunlight and natural ventilation, has extensive potential in countries with temperate climates.

For example, in the United States in 1985, buildings consumed 37 per cent of primary energy supplies. Heating, cooling and ventilation, and lighting took 54.4 per cent of the primary energy needed for residential buildings, and 84.2 per cent of primary energy for commercial buildings. Considering the national fuel-mix furnishing energy for residential buildings in the United States and the geographical distribution of the building inventory, a conservative estimate calculates that 6.7 million solar-design buildings would eliminate annually the following levels of atmospheric emissions:

- 67.5 million short tons of carbon dioxide;
- 284,000 tons of sulfur dioxide;
- 165,000 tons of nitrogen oxides;
- 10,000 tons of particulate matter.[25]

This level of pollution reduction from just under 7 per cent of the housing stock represents a significant target of opportunity.

Another opportunity for solar design and solar thermal systems is in commercial buildings in developing countries. In Kingston, Jamaica, the national petroleum company headquarters building, a solar-designed structure, uses 377 megajoules of purchased energy per square metre per year, while the next most efficient building consumes over 908 megajoules per square metre. For most other commercial buildings in the city, the figure exceeds 1,136 megajoules.[26] Since the IPCC anticipates that the share of carbon dioxide emissions from the developing world will rise from 25 per cent of the world total to fifty per cent by the year 2025, solar technologies must be incorporated in the expanding infrastructure in these countries. Constructing a solar-energy-efficient building may add up to 15 per cent to the original cost, but the additional costs can be recovered by the energy savings in one or two years.

11.6 Realizing the potential of solar-heat technologies

A brief review of the status of solar water-heating technology will illustrate the history and status of distributed solar technologies and their potential. In the late 1800s in the United States, solar water-heaters were introduced commercially because they offered hot water conveniently inside a building without the trouble of heating it on a stove or on a fire out of doors. Despite cheap fossil fuel and the invention of the domestic water-heater, solar water-heaters enjoyed commercial viability well into the 1940s. After the energy crises of the 1970s, solar thermal systems for buildings were re-engineered and manufactured using more modern materials, and a whole new range of technologies and applications developed.

Since the revival of interest in this technology in the mid-1970s, government and industry research has improved the thermal output of solar collectors by about 30 to 35 per cent. At the same time, the costs to manufacture collectors has fallen somewhat more than the rate of inflation. In 1978, the wholesale selling-price for a high-quality collector (in 1978 dollars) was about $120 to $130 per square metre. The wholesale price of a solar collector manufactured today with the same design remains about $120 per square metre, but in 1989 dollars. Producing medium-temperature flat-plate collectors at a rate approaching 12 million square feet per year in the mid-1980s allowed industry to become highly skilled in production.[27] The few manufacturers that exist today have retained the production knowledge, even without achieving mass-production levels, and the real price of solar collectors has dropped by nearly half over the last decade.

These gains, plus a tougher market created by lower prices for fossil fuels and efficiency improvements in conventional systems, have forced the US solar industry to reduce the installed cost of solar water-heating systems to $2,000 to $2,500, nearly half the price in the early 1980s.

What can the 'lowly' solar water-heater contribute towards the reduction of greenhouse-gas emissions? For a family in an advanced industrial country, besides ceasing to use its car (or cars) every day, the solar water-heater offers one of the largest energy savings available. A solar water-heater that saves the owner a net 2,300 kilowatt-hours of electricity per year in the United States can eliminate emission of 1770 kilograms of carbon dioxide into the atmosphere per year every year of its life.

A solar water-heater saves more than just carbon dioxide emissions. The United States Environmental Protection Agency reviewed the pollution-reduction potential of solar water-heating if this application were to expand in the United States. Based on greenhouse-gas and air-pollution emission values for the national fuel-mix generating electric power, each year five million solar water-heaters would eliminate:

- 9.72 million metric tons of carbon dioxide;
- 41,000 tons of sulphur dioxide;
- 356,000 tons of nitrogen oxides;
- 2,403 tons of particulate matter.[28]

The market for solar water-heating and other solar building technologies must expand to realize this potential, but how extensively can solar water-heaters penetrate the market? In the past, some analysts estimated that the maximum market-penetration of solar water-heaters in the United States would be about 10-per-cent. It has already reached approximately 1 per cent, since over 1 million solar water-heaters have been installed in a total housing stock of 90 million dwelling-units.[29]

Considering the status of the technology and the growth in the housing stock, plus the potential to retro-fit existing homes with solar water-heaters, a 10 per cent market-penetration level could be too modest. Forty-four per cent of new, single-family homes built in the United States in 1986 had electricity as their heating fuel.[30] Electricity is the most expensive source of energy for buildings, and presents the most favourable market-opportunity for solar water-heaters. Furthermore, annual sales of homes in the United States exceed 3 million units per year. Should air-pollution regulations mandate solar-heating systems on all homes sold or resold, then the market could expand by more than 4 million units per year.

The economic return of investing in a solar water-heater will also become more attractive. With current technology, a net saving of 2,300 kilowatt hours per year is common. At a cost of 8 cents per kilowatt hour for electricity from a utility, and a $2,000 investment to install a solar water-heater, the owner can achieve a cash-on-cash return of 9.2 per cent in the first year. This return will improve as electricity prices rise. Consequently, some home-builders have discovered that adding solar energy to a home sells it faster, since it offers lower energy bills and increases the amount of money that can be borrowed while still meeting monthly payment/income guidelines of lenders. In addition, installation of solar-energy systems on existing buildings is not complicated. Thus, the overall market potential should exceed 20 million units in the next twenty years. (The United States will probably add 14 million new, single-family homes between 1990 and 2010.)[31]

Several other countries offer evidence that market-penetration rates much above 1 to 10 per cent are likely. Barbados offers a case where the market for residential solar water-heaters may have saturated at about the 30 to 35 per cent level. These systems generally compete against natural gas, sold at a price near $5.00 per gigajoules, but which has an effective price nearly double that given the inefficiency of most gas-fired water-heaters. In Barbados, a combination of a good, locally manufactured product, sound marketing, high energy prices, and government support for consumers resulted in installation of more than 20,000 water-heaters on an island with about 65,000 dwellings.[32] Consumers in this medium-income country have found that the solar water-heater represents an excellent energy-conserving investment.

Instrumentation studies of commercially installed solar water-heaters have confirmed that they most often substitute for between 50 and 70 per cent of the conventional energy used for water-heating.[33] If more energy output is desired, one or more collectors can be added to a system. Moreover, the Florida Solar Energy Center found cases where consumers in warm climates shut off any fossil-fuel or electricity back-up for their solar water-heaters and make a few minor adjustments to their living pattern so as to rely 100 per cent on solar to meet their energy need. Such systems amortize in enough time that a strong income flow becomes available to the owner, easily justifying the initial investment. Apparently, the ability to amortize solar water-heaters in high-cost energy areas has stimulated a program in Tunisia, where a low-interest loan for seven years from the utility is used to pay for a solar installation. The borrower saves more energy per month than the cost of the loan, and then realizes 100 per cent of his energy earnings after the loan is paid off.[34]

One of the findings of the IPCC was that water-heating in developing countries would expand to a level exceeding 90 per cent of dwellings. For example, the IPCC Energy and Industry Subgroup assumes that, by 2025, 100 per cent of households in Brazil and Mexico will have hot-water service. Consumers in all countries desire hot water in their homes. With little incentive, they can be presented with an option that substitutes solar heaters for fossil-energy ones and gives them a better economic choice. Such programmes will help renewable energy expand more rapidly in developing countries and reduce reliance on fossil fuels, while satisfying a fundamental economic desire.

Since water-heating in an industrialized country such as the United States accounts for 16 per cent of residential energy demand, and 6 per cent of overall demand for primary energy, the potential for saving energy by paying attention to this application should not be ignored. For example, a 20-per-cent market share for solar water-heating in the United States has the potential to reduce energy consumption about 500 trillion BTU per year, equal to 85 million barrels of crude oil per year, or 235,000 barrels of crude oil per day for one year. Any initiative that replaces a significant number of water-heaters with solar units over the next two decades has the potential to reduce fossil-energy consumption by 1 or more per cent. This 1 per cent is a goal worth achieving, because it chips away at the total problem and, combined with other small-scale measures, helps us gain control over greenhouse-gas emissons.

Experience in several countries show that market-penetration rates for solar water-heaters can reach or exceed 50 per cent in current markets. As fossil-fuel prices continue to rise and solar-energy systems continue to improve technically and economically, such market-penetration rates will be found in more and more countries. Thus, even though today it appears that a solar-energy contribution for water-heating is too small to matter, in time, solar-energy systems will substitute completely for fossil fuels in such applications.

11.7 Measuring competitiveness

Are there applications where renewable energy that displaces a fossil-energy system is not a justifiable investment? Considering rational allocation of resources to provide needed goods and services, yes – in many instances renewable-energy systems remain too costly compared to fossil-energy ones. Often, however, energy competitiveness, actually a complex concept, is judged with the wrong measures. One faulty evaluation-approach used too often is simple payback, where a decision-maker compares the value of energy savings with the investment cost, and calculates the number of months it takes to recover the investment. Other approaches, such as levellized energy costing or life-cycle costing, are better indicators of the value of an energy system. However, one of the best tools for decision-making about energy choices is net present-value analysis.

In net present-value analysis, all the costs associated with owning and operating an energy system are discounted to the present day. In addition, such analysis accounts for price-escalation of fuels, and operation and maintenance requirements are also discounted to the present day. It is a preferred method for analysing energy choices because it assesses the value of competing investment opportunities. Choosing to conserve energy or purchase a renewable-energy system will often out-perform other investments when analysed using proper discount rates and realistic fuel-cost inflation rates.

When treated to net present-value analysis, renewable-energy systems will deliver a positive return more frequently than many would suspect. Certainly, this has proved to be the case when it comes to the use of photovoltaic systems for small remote power applications. In the communications field, or for cathodic protection of structures in remote locations, a photovoltaic array and battery is more reliable and requires much less service than a small generator or battery-only system. Thus, even though the cost per delivered kilowatt-hour appears high, when the transportation, fuel, maintenance, and man-power requirements are all added together over the lifetime of the system and discounted, the net present value for solar electricity is superior, and choosing this technology represents proper resource allocation. A serious effort at re-education will be required for net present-value analysis to extend to energy decision-making on a wide scale, but no one can be confident since the financial types have mastered it. Unfortunately, most of those making energy choices today reveal that they often do not use a realistic or accurate discount rate. (The discount rate expresses the future value of money in the present day.) Indeed, research is showing that consumers choose appliances with practically no thought to future energy costs to run them. A correct discount rate is an important key variable in net present-value analysis that can turn purchasers away from higher capital cost energy systems that actually represent a more sound investment of capital than making a commitment to an unpredictably priced stream of fossil fuel for many years in the future.

Another factor beginning to affect energy comparisons is the incorporation of the societal or external costs associated with supplying energy with conventional or renewable energy systems. This concept is just beginning to take hold in several countries. They are finding that when subsidy, health, environmental, energy security, and diversity of supply factors are incorporated in price determinations, fossil energy will appear to be more costly, and the results of economic analysis will begin to shift in the direction of energy technologies with lower external costs.

Until consideration of externalities in energy assessments is common, in the real world companies, governments, and individuals will continue to make decisions every day that forgo energy-conservation investments. They seem to be fixated on simple paybacks of less than one or two years, and solar-energy and energy-conservation companies around the world encounter this discouraging barrier daily. They must convince decision-makers to use a more rational method for determining how they invest their capital. Unless a sense of urgency develops, it will be years before these concepts are widely accepted and externalities are fully incorporated in net present-value analysis and other energy decision-making methods.

A related issue, but also very relevant to capital-investment decisions, is the choice between investment in energy conservation and renewable energy. Two key points stand out. First, many analysts argue that conservation investments should be made before any investment is made in renewable energy. The renewable-energy industry itself advocates this position, yet points out that in the future the returns on investment for renewable-energy systems will become more attractive than conservation options. Decision-makers will find that, in their analysis, curves comparing returns on investment between conservation and renewable energy will cross as an economy gains in energy-efficiency and the marginal cost of saving the next energy-unit rises. Secondly, unlike conservation, a renewable-energy system delivers a true unit of energy supply. Although to a utility the output of a dispersed renewable-energy system appears as demand reduction, to the owner or user it is a supply addition.

Renewable systems that produce liquid fuels for transportation or electricity for utilities are obvious supply additions as well. In these cases, the renewable-energy industry suggests that non-polluting, renewable-energy systems be considered a gain in energy-efficiency. Consequently, when policies are developed to increase energy-efficiency in an economy, the industry suggests that they include renewable-energy supply technologies. In the near future, and certainly in the long run, the energy supply characteristic of renewable-energy technologies will become quite important in a world that will need additional supplies of energy to sustain economic development.

While waiting for acceptance of methods for making more rational energy decisions that will overcome institutional resistance to investment in renewable energy, independent energy-producer and shared-savings energy-conservation companies have developed new energy-marketing approaches. One of the more successful is the third-party energy-sales contract. Project developers attract third-party investors to furnish capital for the new energy systems, and charge the energy users (business or utility) for the output or savings achieved. The energy purchaser, who makes no capital outlay for the energy savings or new supply, faces practically no risk. Third-party energy systems can also answer concerns of such institutions as the lodging industry, which worries about personnel requirements to maintain new, unfamiliar systems, or utilities, which worry about reliability of new technologies. The disadvantage is that such contracting mechanisms add overhead burdens that increase the cost to the economy of the renewable energy. This situation will improve, however, as energy users discover that they should be retaining the full returns for themselves from investment in greater efficiency through renewable-energy systems.

It must be said that claims that investing in clean, renewable-energy technologies will bankrupt economies are just not valid. Furthermore, when new sources of energy are needed and no retirements of existing systems occur, consideration of externalities and lower energy-costs will swing more and more decisions to renewable energy.

The need for 'innovative' marketing techniques reveals how institutional barriers unrelated to economic performance, block more-rapid expansion of renewable energy. Increased knowledge about the positive economic- and environmental-performance characteristics of these systems will help break down these barriers. This familiarization, a process that requires time for transfers of technology and experience, can be accelerated if civil authorities actively encourage and promote use of renewable energy. Civil authorities also need to review their own energy decisions, and in light of external social and environmental costs associated with continued reliance on fossil energy, encourage the private sector to come forward with projects that will make government itself more energy-efficient.

This raises an important observation. To date, in many energy markets, renewable-energy companies that negotiate energy-sales contracts for thermal or electric power have usually had to undercut the price of conventional energy in order to be accepted as a substitute supplier. To break into these markets, the renewable-energy vendor has offered discounts, often of 10 to 20 per cent for a solar heating-system, over the cost of a competing fossil fuel. As noted above, for young companies with new technologies, higher overhead costs make competition with entrenched conventional suppliers difficult.

Given a chance, renewable-energy companies will write long-term energy sales contracts to deliver energy to a government facility at a lower price than petroleum or natural gas that is tied to the future price of the replaced fuels. If government has the social responsibility to encourage use of cleaner sources of energy, and it can do so while reducing its energy costs, then it should make such energy-sales contracts easy to negotiate. Instead, the contrary is true. A simple three-page agreement with a government agency may take two years to negotiate. If government is going to impose its own barriers on the use of cleaner, cheaper sources of energy, then perhaps it should reward the vendors of such energy with higher prices for renewable energy than it pays for fossil energy. Later, when the market matures, and selecting a renewable-energy system is no more difficult than buying building supplies, government can sign contracts for lower energy costs.

11.8 One hundred per cent substitution of fossil fuels by renewables

Besides outright purchases or entering into third-party energy-sales contracts with renewable-energy vendors and developers, government has other ways to encourage faster development of renewable energy. Since numerous renewable-energy systems can completely substitute for fossil fuels, one policy-option is to search for applications where fossil fuels can be completely replaced with a renewable-energy system under economically favourable conditions. Already, in certain applications, 100-per-cent replacement of fossil-fuelled systems is technically quite feasible and, in many countries, quite within the bounds of any reasonable economic test.

In many countries, small, diesel-engine generators are used where small, portable, and temporary supplies of energy are needed. These fossil-fuel generators run 24 hours a day, spewing out carbon dioxide and other pollutants. Granted, the engines are small, and the quantity of pollutants seemingly insignificant. However, a completely clean, quiet alternative is available in a system that uses batteries recharged with photovoltaic panels. The replacement solar-energy technology is actually more reliable, and over time will prove to be a more economical choice. Consequently, civil authorities can specify that these systems be used in their jurisdictions to eliminate 100 per cent of certain greenhouse-gas emissions associated with fossil-fuel combustion. They will also lower costs in the long run, because the fuel and maintenance costs for these small engine systems will ultimately exceed the cost of purchasing and maintaining the solar-energy/battery system.

Photovoltaic-powered refrigerators for vaccine storage in medical clinics in remote Third World locations is another application where concerned agencies can safely mandate a renewable energy system to replace one driven by fossil fuel. The higher reliability of the photovoltaic system compared to a diesel- or kerosene-powered unit prevents more vaccine from spoilage when the fossil powered unit fails to operate due to mechanical malfunction or lack of fuel. The reduced losses in medicines can justify the cost of the more expensive photovoltaic energy system.

Another example where solar energy can economically replace fossil-fuel combustion is swimming-pool heating. In both the residential and commercial/institutional sectors, pool heating is an ideal application for solar thermal-energy panels. The heat required is at a low temperature, which allows the solar-energy panels to operate most efficiently. (The laws of thermodynamics dictate that, as the operating temperature of a solar collector increases, heat losses accelerate, and overall efficiency in converting sunlight to thermal energy decreases.) A solar collector heating a swimming-pool can approach 80 per cent efficiency under ideal conditions.[35] In lower latitudes in the northern hemisphere, unglazed panels made of plastics are specified. In more temperate climates, glazed panels may be required, especially if a system is to operate twelve months per year.

In countries where private and public swimming-pools are common for recreation, or in tourism facilities vital to many developing-country economies, solar-energy systems may completely eliminate combustion of fossil fuels. In tropical and sub-tropical climates where resorts heat their pools, solar-energy systems have proved that they offer the property-owner a much more cost-effective alternative than continued reliance on fossil fuel.[36] A civil authority in a developed or developing country can simply mandate that no, or very little, fossil energy be used to heat swimming-pools. The private sector will manage the rest.

The greenhouse-gas emission savings for the two applications described above might seem too insignificant to stimulate government to design and implement a 100-per-cent substitution programme. However, these micro-approaches offer opportunities for completely eliminating reliance on fossil fuels while still providing fully the services these fuels offer. They show that fossil energy can be replaced. Moreover, in the long term, the owners of the 100 per cent renewable energy systems will have made a more sound energy investment. The aggregate impact of many such micro-economically justified decisions offers a cleaner environment and a more rational energy system.

From a policy perspective, finding and mandating 100-per-cent applications has the added benefit of strengthening renewable-energy companies by opening markets more quickly, and reducing expensive marketing overhead. When a civil authority requires that specified applications for certain classes of consumers must use a renewable-energy system, it will partially reduce often burdensome and expensive sales efforts that now accompany renewable marketing, allowing manufacturers and installers to concentrate on delivery of the technologies.

A key premise behind the 100-per-cent substitution concept for fossil fuels in selected applications is that, in a warming-globe scenario, no percentage of fossil-energy savings offered by a competitive alternative will be too small to consider and implement. For the companies in the early stages of market development, as they successfully capture new, small, incremental markets, the firms make more product, lower costs, earn more, and become more capable of delivering technology into other new markets. If civil authorities help economic decision-makers decide for 100-per-cent substitution of fossil fuel with renewable-energy systems where an economic and environmental case favouring such installations can be made, these small gains will instil a sense of the commonplace for the technologies, making the reach into additional markets less difficult.

11.9 Renewable energy in environmental policy

On a global scale, policy to protect the environment is in many stages of development and implementation. Adding control of greenhouse-gas emissions will broaden the scope and reach of environmental policies already in effect to protect health, air and water quality, and natural ecosystems. In some countries, environmental policies have already begun to have a positive effect on development of renewable energy, and as reduction of greenhouse-gas emissions gains priority, the impact will grow stronger. A concept referred to above, the external or social costs associated with conventional energy systems, will help guide these policies in the future.

This concept gained attention in late 1988, when Olav Hohmeyer of the Fraunhofer-Institut fur Systemtechnik und Innovations-forschung in West Germany completed a study for the Commission of the European Communities on the social costs of producing energy with coal and nuclear power-stations compared to wind and photovoltaics.[37] The hypothesis was that society bears the cost of environmental impacts from reliance on fossil- and nuclear-energy technologies that are not borne by the energy suppliers or directly by consumers in the price paid for the energy delivered. Society as a whole covers the cost of subsidies, less-healthy citizens, and damage to forests and waterways, or reduced agricultural output due to atmospheric emissions.

Hohmeyer attempted to calculate what these social costs were in West Germany, and offered a suggested value for the first time. He pointed out that 'research efforts to estimate the full costs of energy systems to society are necessary. The knowledge of these full social costs for energy could enable government to take corrective action to help the market mechanism achieve an optimal allocation of resources.'[38] Hohmeyer believes that, with such a value available, energy policy-makers could reconsider the merits of the energy-supply choices they were making, and accelerate lagging market diffusion of more desirable energy technologies.

Today, governments in several countries are seeking to incorporate in their energy analysis the concept of identifying, calculating, and then finding ways to internalize hidden social costs of energy. The net effect may be decisions to reward cleaner energy-producing technologies with higher prices for the energy they deliver, or recovering more of the costs society bears from the producers of conventional energy, most simply by raising the price paid for the energy, or cutting subsidies, or by tightening health and environmental control requirements.

In West Germany, the federal government decided to grant investors in wind-energy plants a payment of about 8 pfennigs (4 US cents) per kilowatt-hour of wind energy delivered.[39] The amount selected is within the band of estimated external or hidden costs which Hohmeyer calculated for coal and nuclear power. Tied to a specific technology the government wishes to see enter the market more strongly, this environmental subsidy was planned to support faster wind-industry development. The wind-energy industry in the United States has suggested a similar subsidy of about 2 to 4 cents per kilowatt-hour, contending that with current technology, such a subsidy will raise wind to a truly competitive status, accelerate the market, and attract investment for further research and development.

Besides subsidies directly tied to the output of renewable-energy systems, or tax incentives applied to capital costs of such systems, another avenue being considered for accelerating development of environmentally attractive technologies is to mandate their use. In the Los Angeles basin in California, the multi-jurisdictional authorities responsible for regional air quality have produced a comprehensive plan to reach compliance with federal government air-pollution standards over the next decade. One option considered in the plan is to mandate replacement of gas- and electric-powered water-heaters with solar water-heaters. The US solar-energy industry in southern California pointed out that water-heating and swimming-pool heating were actually significant contributors to the air-quality problem, and that installing solar heaters was a way in which the consumer could help air quality and save money at the same time.[40]

The South Coast Air Quality Management District in Los Angeles has not, to date, mandated the solar water-heating option, apparently because representatives of the natural-gas industry intervened saying that new gas burners would eliminate the nitrogen-oxide emission problems and would cost less than mandating use of solar-energy systems. Still, several small communities in the Los Angeles basin require that solar water-heaters be installed on all new residential construction in their jurisdictions.[41]

The trade-off between redesigned gas-heater burners and solar water-heaters defines an important environmental debate. The solar industry suggests that the local economy make a larger investment in solar water-heaters rather than burner replacement, since this will nearly eliminate combustion of fossil fuel for a key application. With natural-gas prices as low as $4.00 per gigajoule for the consumer, the value of energy savings in the near term seems low. It should be noted, however, that a Public Utility Commission study in California of solar water-heaters installed on commercial projects revealed that gas water-heaters commonly in use in California were only 55 per cent efficient. This raises actual fuel cost for natural gas to $8.00 per gigajoule, and the economics become more favourable. Anticipating large price-increases for natural gas that would double the well-head price of this fuel in the next ten years, a case can be made to consumers for considering a solar option.

Industry addressed this situation as a marketing problem by approaching the consumer on a cash-flow basis. In Arizona, for example, a solar company originated a programme with home-builders that offered solar water-heaters on new homes at a price of $1,800 to $2,200 completely installed. When added to the home-buyer's mortgage, the cost of the solar-energy system increased the monthly loan-payment by approximately $12 to cover principal and interest. For a home with a conventional electric water-heater, the solar unit saves the home-buyer more than $20 per month, so the cash-flow return is immediately positive. According to the manufacturer who developed this marketing approach to ease entry into the home-building industry, a majority of home-owners will select the solar option when presented with this scenario.[42]

Still, such marketing programmes have had difficulty gaining widespread acceptance. Often, it is an institutional barrier associated with organizations that finance home sales. Conventional bank lenders have shied away from solar energy in the United States, because of a bad reputation surrounding the solar industry when some unscrupulous firms misused federal and state tax credits that had been meant, in effect, to stimulate solar-energy sales. Government-accepted lending agencies, however, when educated about the solar-energy option, have supported marketing programmes such as the one in Arizona. Indeed, lenders favoured them, because the lower monthly energy costs for a solar-equipped home meant that the borrower could qualify more easily for the loan or afford a larger loan.

If greenhouse-gas emissions related to global warming are added to the air-quality issues in Los Angeles, the weight of a double concern over the environment should stimulate a wider range of policy options that encourage faster development of renewable-energy technologies. The process, still slow, will ultimately lead to much-more-favourable market prospects. The end result is a constantly brightening future for all renewable-energy technologies.

11.10 Conclusions

Today, new energy technologies present wider investment choices and offer many countries an opportunity to break from historic patterns, where heavy investment in centralized, highly capital-intensive energy infrastructure was a prerequisite for economic development. Indeed, in the same way that new technologies eroded the AT&T telephone company's monopoly in the United States, new energy technologies are threatening the fossil-energy monopolies that exist throughout the world. The results are positive, and more competition will create more efficiency and lower costs for consumers. Research and experience in the USA has shown that growth of renewable-energy companies will generally create more jobs than those lost in the fossil-energy sector. Analysts found this to be true in New England when they studied the biofuels industry supplying wood-fired cogeneration systems, and the Solar Energy Industries Association used a short-hand input–output model to study the comparative employment and gross domestic product impacts of solar-thermal electric and gas-fired electric power plants. Finally, countries that rely on renewable energy can achieve a greater degree of international independence.

Technologies available in 1990 make it possible to deliver energy, including electricity, anywhere that a society establishes demand for it. Until recently, when demand for heat, motive power, or electricity existed far from established energy-delivery channels, the high-energy content and easy transportation of petroleum fuels made them the only choice. Now, technology exists that can produce electricity, or any temperature heat (up to 1400°C) directly from natural resources available at a remote location in nearly any country. The demand can be satisfied without transporting a continuous, long-distance stream of fuel, or running long-distance electric-power transmission lines – or emitting vast quantities of greenhouse gases. A solar-energy company can place a solar collector and energy-storage system anywhere, to furnish as much electricity or heat as a user requires. A biomass company can use local resources to produce solid, liquid, or gaseous fuels for power. There is no qualification needed for these statements. Technically, it is possible. Economically, it is a more limited situation, but not nearly as limited as most observers and analysts believe.

A case can be made that, had the solar-energy conversion technologies been available a hundred years ago that are available today, many regions of the world would not be putting in place centralized electric-power grids using large thermal-electric conversion systems and long-distance transmission systems. Of course, where well-managed extensive grids exist, they can be used to transmit renewable energy from resources to where the energy is needed. None the less, when the costs are considered of starting to build a modern energy system-mines and wells, pipelines, and so on, where no infrastructure exists it can be more cost-effective to install a remote solar-power, or wind, or biomass-energy system.

The option to forgo extensive investment in conventional energy-supply infrastructure does not apply to the Andes, African savannah, or Australian Outback alone. Even in the United States, electric utilities have found that home-owners in remote locations can install a complete solar electric-power system to satisfy all the energy needs of a large modern home more cheaply than paying the utility to install the transmission system to deliver power several miles from an existing grid. In other words, for that building, $20,000 investment in a self-sufficient solar-energy system is the most cost-effective option. To repeat, in certain locations it can be less costly to an economy to choose solar energy than to rely on the electric-power generation-and-delivery system which a modern utility company would employ to service customer needs.

In developing countries where no electric-power grid exists, or where transport of diesel fuel is haphazard, extending electric power to remote villages is expensive. Moreover, utility companies in developing countries find that they may never recover the cost of extending their power lines with the revenue generated by electricity sales. Often, communities in these remote areas will rely on small diesel generators to create a micro-grid. Such electric power is also expensive, often exceeding 20 cents to 50 cents per kilowatt-hour when the maintenance and fuel costs are added over the life of the system. Given enough economic potential to provide a long-term earnings stream to pay for the energy, then a renewable-energy system may well be the most cost-effective option.

While these remote locations are not typical of the bulk of energy use, they underscore the point made above, that renewable-energy systems available today are capable of delivering energy in locations that up to now would choose conventional fossil-energy systems. If renewable energy technologies can find economically viable markets in developed countries with low-priced fossil fuels, then their prospects can be even greater in developing countries. In these nations, rapidly growing demand, less developed infrastructure that makes energy more dear to deliver, and greater government power in energy markets can all contribute to faster expansion of renewable energy. Furthermore, electric power networks have not reached many of the remote rural locations that characterize much of the developing world, and in these areas, renewable energy is more competitive. For it to advance in developing countries, however, government will have to decide in favour of removing barriers to expansion of renewable energy and encourage the private sector to invest in the capability to deliver these technologies, and profit from the businesses created. Therefore, two points emerge:

- Technically, renewable-energy systems can deliver energy reliably; and

- Renewable-energy systems can be the preferred economic choice, even with today's seemingly expensive solar-energy technologies and historically low costs for conventional energy.

This chapter has focused on renewable-energy performance in markets that exist today, and only touched on a few technologies and their applications. (Wood energy, small hydroelectric plants, and bio-fuels would provide additional successful examples of renewable-energy applications.) This concentration was chosen to emphasize that renewable-energy technologies can make a difference in the nearer term. Furthermore, by omitting consideration of new technological breakthroughs and unimagined renewable-energy systems yet to be developed, we escape the criticism that proponents of renewable energy are misguided optimists. With technologies in hand, very large numbers of small systems offer substantial opportuntity to increase energy-efficiency and substitute for fossil fuels, while still maintaining adequate supplies of energy to sustain economic development. Policy-makers must not overlook renewable energy because the systems appear small. One million installations will expand to two, then twenty, and ultimately hundreds of millions.

To summarize, with perfect knowledge and unencumbered choice, each individual actor will select the least-costly energy commodity needed to satisfy his or her particular service needs. Driven in part by a wider array of technological choices, the energy economics governing these decisions are changing. For example, in several countries, utility companies are finding that an investment in energy conservation by its customers can be a more profitable choice than a decision to produce and sell additional kilowatt-hours to satisfy the higher level of demand. This is a somewhat radical proposition for an industry that, since its birth a hundred years ago, has known nothing but uninterrupted demand for its product; where selling the next kilowatt-hour produced by the company did not seem to require anything like a choice at all.

In this changing environment, the pace of technological advance continues to accelerate. Utility regulators and utility owners in the United States are now seeking ways to decouple a utility's revenue stream from increases in energy production. A healthier utility and economy will result from this recognition that the economic framework that stimulated reliance on fossil-energy systems in the last hundred years has changed. These lessons must and will expand globally. Renewable resources offer safe, clean, reliable, and economic energy. The challenge in a world that must address global-climate issues is to understand the changing energy economy, appreciate the potential of alternative energy strategies and technologies, recognize that exponential growth in renewable-energy capacity is on the horizon, and put the wider range of energy choices in the hands of individual decision-makers, wherever they are.

Chapter 12
Motor Vehicles and Global Warming

Michael P. Walsh

" ...based on projected increases in vehicles and their use around the world, motor-vehicle CO_2 emissions will skyrocket over the next forty to fifty years ... Experience gained during the 1970s and 1980s suggests that the dual goals of low emissions (CO, HC, and NO_x) and improved energy efficiency (and therefore lower CO_2) are not only compatible but mutually reinforcing. However, significant gains in either area are dependent on forceful government requirements. Mandatory fuel-efficiency standards throughout the world are feasible and necessary ... the potential exists not only to offset the global impacts of expected vehicle growth over the next half century but also to start an emissions downturn... "

Motor vehicles generate more air pollution than any other single human activity. Greenhouse gases emitted by (or attributable to) motor vehicles include chlorofluorocarbons (CFCs), carbon dioxide (CO_2), nitrous oxide (N_2O), methane (CH_4), and the precursors to tropospheric ozone – hydrocarbons (HC) and nitrogen oxides (NO_x).[1] Motor vehicles are also the major source of carbon monoxide (CO), which plays a critical role in methane and tropospheric ozone accumulations. In this chapter I outline where, how, and in what quantities greenhouse gases are emitted from motor vehicles, and review the other pollutants emitted. I go on to consider trends in the growth of motor vehicles world-wide, and the likely impact on global warming if these trends are left to follow their course without efforts either to reduce emissions further, or to reduce growth in vehicle numbers – or both.

12.1 Greenhouse gases from motor vehicles

CFCs are the most potent greenhouse gases on a per-unit mass basis, now contributing about 24 per cent of the total global warming effect.[2] About 40 per cent of the United States' production of CFCs and 30 per cent of European production is devoted to air-conditioning and refrigeration. Mobile air-conditioning accounted for 56,500 metric tons of CFCs – 28 per cent of the CFCs used for refrigeration in the United States, or about 13 per cent of total production. In contrast, home refrigerators accounted for only 3,800 metric tons or about 1 per cent of total US production.[3] Thus, approximately 1 out of every 8 pounds of CFCs manufactured in the US is used, and emitted, by motor vehicles. (CFCs are also used as a blowing agent in the production of seating and other foamed products, but this is a considerably smaller vehicular use.)

Carbon dioxide is the other major greenhouse gas. A single tank of gasoline produces between 300 and 400 pounds of CO_2 when burned. Overall, the transport sector uses approximately 55 quads [1 quad = 1.055 Exajoules] of energy each year, varying considerably between regions of the world. The US is far and away the largest consumer, using over 35 per cent of the world's transport energy. Transport consumes almost one-third of the total energy consumed in the world, again highly dependent on region.

Because of this high overall energy consumption, it is not surprising that motor vehicles emit almost 1,100 teragrams (Tg) of carbon, approximately 25 per cent of the world's output; in the US, transport is responsible for almost 30 per cent of the total CO_2 emissions.[4] Finally, the US accounts for more than one-third of the global transport budget, emitting almost as much CO_2 from the transport sector as Eastern Europe, Asia, China, Africa, Latin America, and the Middle East combined.

In 1985, in the US, transportation sources were responsible for 70 per cent of the carbon monoxide, 45 per cent of the NO_x, and 34 per cent of the hydrocarbons (HC) emitted. Including transportation sources other than highway vehicles (such as air, rail, and marine transport), the Congressional Office of Technology Assessment (OTA) concluded that mobile sources were actually responsible for almost 40 per cent of total nation-wide volatile organic compounds; the only other major source category which OTA found to be responsible for even close to mobile-source emissions in 1985 was organic solvent evaporation.[5] (Based on recent data regarding evaporative 'running losses', the HC contribution from vehicles may actually be 5 to 10 per cent higher.)[6]

Motor vehicles also dominate the emissions inventories of most European countries. OECD has found that: 'The primary source category responsible for most NO_x emissions is road transportation roughly between 50 and 70 per cent ... Mobile sources, mainly road traffic, produce around 50 per cent of anthropogenic VOC [volatile organic compounds] emissions, therefore constituting the largest man-made VOC source category in all European OECD countries.'[7]

Beyond the US and Europe, Table 12.1 shows that, for OECD countries as a whole, motor vehicles are the dominant source of carbon monoxide, oxides of nitrogen, and hydrocarbons.[8]

Table 12.1: Motor-vehicle share of OECD pollutant emissions (1000 tons, 1980)

Pollutant	Total emissions	Motor-vehicle share (plus %)
NOx	36,019	17,012 (47)
HC	33,869	13,239 (39)
CO	119,148	78,227 (66)

The role of motor vehicles as an emissions source in less-developed countries is more variable. However, it is clear that in many of these countries, the significance of vehicle emissions as a proportion of total emissions may be even greater than in the OECD. For example, in Mexico City, rapidly becoming the most heavily populated urban area in the world, vehicles are responsible for as much as 80 per cent of total emissions by weight.

12.2 Indirect enhancement of global warming by motor vehicles

It is easy to understand the significance of motor-vehicle emissions as a contributor to global warming when they act directly (for example, as CO_2 or CFCs). However, in a number of cases, the impact is more indirect, as with carbon monoxide, or occurs as a result of secondary transformations (such as photochemical smog or ozone resulting from NO_x and HC). These will be discussed below.

Carbon monoxide is not generally thought of as an important greenhouse gas, because it does not trap heat directly. However, it tends to react with other compounds, notably hydroxyl radicals (OH), thereby reducing their presence in the air. Reduction of hydroxyl radicals is important, because they normally react with and remove other greenhouse gases such as methane; as hydroxyl radicals are removed by CO, more methane is allowed to survive and rise to the upper atmosphere where it can increase the global warming.[9] As summarized by Ramanathan,

> The highly reactive OH is the primary sink for many tropospheric gases and pollutants including O_3 [ozone], CH_4, CO, and NO. Hence, increases in CH_4, such as those during the last century (135-per-cent increase) could have caused a substantial (20- to 40-per-cent) reduction in OH, which in turn, could cause an increase in tropospheric O_3 by as much as 20 per cent. Since CH_4 oxidation leads to the formation of H_2O, an increase in CH_4, an important greenhouse gas, can lead to an increase in H_2O in the stratosphere. Likewise, an increase in the CO concentration can tie up more OH in the oxidation of CO. Thus, through chemical reactions, an increase in either a radiatively active gas such as CH_4 or even a radiatively inactive gas such as CO can increase the concentration of several important greenhouse gases.[10]

Thus, carbon-monoxide emissions are very important for climate modification. This point was reinforced by MacDonald:

> Carbon monoxide could thus be indirectly responsible for increasing greenhouse warming by 20 to 40 per cent through raising the levels of methane and ozone ... Carbon monoxide participates in the formation of ozone, and also in the destruction of hydroxyl radicals, which are principal sinks for ozone and methane green-

house gases. Because carbon monoxide reacts rapidly with hydroxyl, increased levels of carbon monoxide will lead to higher regional concentrations of ozone and methane. Measures to reduce carbon monoxide emissions will assist in controlling greenhouse warming.[11]

At least one analyst who specializes in the chemistry of radicals in the atmosphere believes that the destruction of hydroxyl by carbon monoxide contributes more to rising amounts of methane in the air than any increase in sources.[12] This is especially significant in view of the evidence that global CO levels are now also increasing. As recently noted by Khalil and Rasmussen: 'the average tropospheric concentration of CO is increasing at between 0.8 and 1.4 per cent per year, depending on the method used to estimate the trend, and the 90-per-cent confidence limits of the various estimates range between 0.5 and 2.0 per cent per year.'[13]

A recent analysis concludes that the global-warming potential (GWP) of a gram of CO is greater than that of a gram of CO_2. This is because CO impacts on the atmosphere in two ways. First by increasing methane's average atmospheric residence time by an additional 20 per cent, it has a methane impact. This gram of methane has a greater impact on global warming than a gram of CO_2. Further, each gram of CO is eventually converted to CO_2. Thus, combining these two effects, the overall impact of CO is estimated by the authors to be 2.2 times as high as that of CO_2 emissions.[14] The significance of this is that controlling CO emissions from vehicles is a much better strategy for global warming than is allowing the carbon to be emitted as CO_2 directly.

Vehicles are also a direct source of methane emissions, although it is not possible to quantify fully the overall proportion from vehicles. One can also note that as a general matter, over the past two decades, as total hydrocarbons have been reduced from vehicles in many countries – at least on a per-mile-driven basis – methane emissions have been reduced roughly proportionately.

Photochemical smog or ozone results from chemical reactions involving both hydrocarbons and nitrogen oxides in the presence of sunlight. Tropospheric ozone is a greenhouse gas. While tropospheric ozone is only responsible for about 8 per cent of global-warming gases, its significance may be somewhat greater because of the short lifetime of these gases compared to other greenhouse gases. Once formed, ozone has an atmospheric lifetime of only hours to days, rather than decades to a century, as is true with most other greenhouse gases. Therefore, eliminating the precursors of ozone may have a more immediate short-term effect than eliminating similar amounts of other greenhouse gases.

need to stop depleting O₃ by eliminating depleters!

12.3 Other pollution by motor vehicles

Many of the same pollutants which cause or contribute to global warming also contribute substantially to adverse health effects in many individuals, in addition to harming terrestrial and aquatic ecosystems, causing crop damage, and impairing visibility. In most cases, these effects alone are more than sufficient reason to minimize their emission. Some of these other effects will be described below.

Ozone (which results from emission of hydrocarbons and nitrogen oxides) is a special concern. First, the problem is widespread and pervasive and appears likely to be a long-term one in many areas of the world unless significant further controls are implemented. For example, over 100 million Americans currently reside in areas which fall below the current air-quality standard.[15] Many of these individuals suffer eye irritation, coughs and chest discomfort, headaches, upper respiratory illness, increased asthma attacks, and reduced pulmonary function as a result of this problem.

In addition, the current air-quality standard tends to understate the health effects. For example, as noted in testimony before the US Congress in 1987 by the US Environmental Protection Agency (EPA), new studies indicate:

> that elevated ozone concentrations occurring on some days during the hot summers in many of our urban areas may reduce lung function, not only for people with preexisting respiratory problems, but even for people in good health. This reduction in lung function may be accompanied by symptomatic effects such as chest pain and shortness of breath. Observed effects from exposures of 1 to 2 hours with heavy exercise include measurable reductions in normal lung function in a portion (15–30 per cent) of the healthy population that is particularly sensitive to ozone.[16]

Other studies presented at the 1988 US-Dutch Symposium on ozone indicate that healthy young children suffer adverse effects from exposure to ozone at levels below the current air-quality standard.[17] Numerous studies have also demonstrated that photo-chemical pollutants inflict damage on forest ecosystems and seriously impact the growth of certain crops.[18]

It is important to note that ozone-layer depletion may have a significant impact on local ozone air-pollution episodes. As pointed out by the American Lung Association,

> the increase in ultraviolet B radiation resulting from even a moderate loss in the total ozone column can be expected to result in a significant increase in peak ground based ozone levels ... these high peaks will occur earlier in the day and closer to the populous urban areas in comparison to current experience, resulting in a significant, though quantitatively unspecified, increase in the number of people exposed to these high peaks.[19]

Exposure to carbon monoxide results almost entirely from motor-vehicle emissions. (In some localized areas, wood stoves also significantly affect CO levels.) While there has been progress in reducing ambient CO levels across Europe, Japan, and the United States, the problem is far from solved. For example, approximately forty-four major metropolitan areas in the US with a population approaching 30 million currently exceed the carbon-monoxide air-quality standard.[20] In fact, EPA indicated in Congressional testimony (February 1987) that as many as fifteen areas in the United States may have intermittent carbon-monoxide problems that could prevent attainment for many years.[21]

The CO problem is important because of the clear evidence relating CO exposure to adverse health effects. For example, in a recent assessment conducted under the auspices of the Health Effects Institute, it was concluded that:

> The results of this study confirm the hypothesis that elevation in blood COHb levels accompanying exposure to CO decreases the time to the onset of myocardial ischemia in exercising males with coronary artery disease. The decrements in the time to onset of electrocardiographic ST-segment changes provide the best evidence in support of this hypothesis. The time to the onset of angina is also decreased in response to elevations in COHb levels. The results are convincing, even though the magnitude of the

effect is small and is superimposed on considerable biological variability.[22]

Further, in another recent study of tunnel workers in New York City, the authors noted: 'Given the magnitude of the effect that we have observed for a very prevalent cause of death, exposure to vehicular exhaust, more specifically to CO, in combination with underlying heart disease or other cardiovascular risk factors could be responsible for a very large number of preventable deaths.'[23] In addition, as noted earlier, recent evidence indicates that CO may contribute to elevated levels of tropospheric ozone.[24]

Emissions of nitrogen oxides from vehicles and other sources produce a variety of adverse health and environmental effects. NO_x emissions also react chemically with other pollutants to form ozone and other highly toxic pollutants. Next to sulphur dioxide, NO_x emissions are the most prominent pollutant contributing to acidic deposition.

Exposure to nitrogen-dioxide (NO_2) emissions is linked to increased susceptibility to respiratory infection, increased airway resistance in asthmatics, and decreased pulmonary function.[25] Further, short-term exposures to NO_2 have resulted in a wide-ranging group of respiratory problems in schoolchildren (cough, runny nose, and sore throat are among the most common) as well as increased sensitivity to broncho-constrictors by asthmatics.[26]

The World Health Organization concluded that a maximum one-hour exposure of 190–320 micrograms per cubic metre (0.10–0.17 parts per million) should be consistent with the protection of public health, and that this exposure should not be exceeded more than once a month. The State of California has also adopted a short-term NO_2 standard, 0.25 ppm averaged over one hour, to protect public health.

Oxides of nitrogen have also been shown to affect vegetation adversely. Some scientists believe that NO_x is a significant contributor to the dying forests throughout central Europe.[27] This adverse effect is even more pronounced when nitrogen dioxide and sulphur dioxide occur simultaneously. Further, nitrogen dioxide has been found to cause deleterious effects on a wide variety of materials, including textile-dyes and fabrics, plastics, and rubber, and is responsible for a portion of the brownish colorations in polluted air or smog.

Acid deposition results from the chemical transformation and transport of sulphur dioxide and nitrogen oxides. Emissions of nitrogen oxides are responsible for approximately one-third of the acidity of rainfall. Recent evidence indicates that the role of NO_x may be of increasing significance with regard to this problem:

> Measurements of the nitrate to sulphate ratio in the atmospheric aerosol in southern England have shown a steady increase since 1954. The nitrate content of precipitation averaged over the entire European Air Chemistry Network has steadily increased over the period 1955 to 1979. The nitrate levels in ice cores from South Greenland have continued to increase steeply from 1975 to 1984, whilst sulphate has remained relatively constant since 1968. The 'Thousand Lake Survey' in Norway has recently revealed a doubling in the nitrate concentration of 305 lakes over the period 1974 –1975 to 1986, despite little change in ph [acidity] and sulphate.[28]

Several acid-deposition control plans have targeted reductions in NO_x emissions in addition to substantial reductions in sulphur dioxide. Furthermore, the ten participating countries at the 1985 International Conference of Ministers on Acid Rain committed themselves to 'take measures to decrease effectively the total annual emissions of nitrogen oxides from stationary and mobile sources as soon as possible'.[29]

Motor-vehicle emissions of HC, CO, and NO_x, therefore, can be seen as a major source not only of climate modification but also of adverse health and other environmental effects from ground-level pollution. On the basis of these latter effects alone, substantial reductions of these pollutants are justified. In addition, tropospheric pollution and climate modification are directly linked by a variety of mechanisms. To deal with these problems in a co-ordinated fashion requires the minimization of carbon monoxide, carbon dioxide, hydrocarbons, nitrogen oxides, and chlorofluorocarbons.

On a global scale, emissions of these pollutants depend on the number of vehicles in use and their emission-rates. In turn, their actual emission-rates depend on their fuel efficiency and their use of control technologies which are available.

Increased population and economic activity in the future holds the potential to increase the problem. Whereas the number of people in Europe and the US is increasing slowly, the global population is expected to double (compared to 1960 levels) by the year 2000, driven by more than a doubling of population in Asia and an almost 150-per-cent increase in Latin America. Beyond the overall growth in population, an increasing portion of Asia's and South America's people are moving to cities, driving up the global urban population. One result is that, without active intervention to encourage patterns of economic development not dependent on motor vehicles, global automobile production and use are projected to continue to grow substantially over the next several decades.

12.4 World motor vehicle registrations

Fig. 12.1 shows the overall trends in vehicle registrations around the world since 1930. Since 1950, the average annual growth-rate for cars has been 5.9 per cent; for trucks and buses, it has been only slightly less, 5.6 per cent per year. Most recently the trends have remained quite high, but commercial vehicles have actually been growing more rapidly than cars. For example, since 1970, annual car-growth has averaged 4.7 per cent per year, while truck and bus registrations averaged 5.1 per cent per year. Overall, as a result of this growth, the total world-wide vehicle population in 1985 was 500 million, with cars just slightly under 400 million.

Europe and North America each have slightly more than a third of the world's car population, with the remainder divided between Asia, South America, Oceania, and Africa, in that order. With regard to trucks and buses, on the other hand, North America has about 40 per cent, followed closely by Asia, and then Europe.

It is important to emphasize the dominant role of North America and Western Europe as potential vehicle markets. While the percentage growth in vehicle production is quite high in other countries, and to a lesser extent the percentage growth in vehicle registrations is also quite high, the 'highly industrialized' market is so large as to dominate the world, and it is likely to continue to do so for the foreseeable future.

The significance of this is that, to a large extent, vehicle characteristics in the highly industrialized countries will have a significant impact on vehicle characteristics in other areas. For example, it seems likely that increased stringency of emissions- or fuel-economy requirements in Western Europe and the United States would lead to similar improvements in other vehicle markets, especially those where vehicle production is increasing with an eye toward export to the highly industrialized markets. The converse is, of course, also true – weak requirements in the highly industrialized areas probably means weak controls in the developing areas.

Beyond new vehicles, it also appears that much of the vehicle-population growth in some rapidly industrializing developing countries comes from imports of used vehicles from highly industrialized areas. In this way fundamental designs which are either high or low in emissions or fuel consumption are perpetuated and can increase or decrease overall emissions and fuel consumption in these countries.

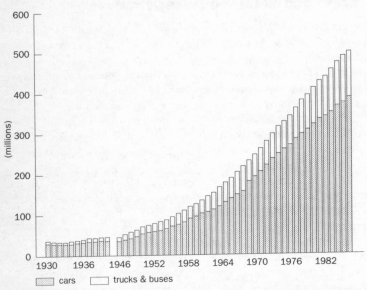

Fig. 12.1. Global vehicle-population growth since 1930

12.5 Fuel consumption and CO_2 emissions

The degree of control of fuel consumption exercised by governments varies throughout the world. In the USA and Japan, improvements in fuel consumption are being enforced. In Europe, government control is limited to mandatory publication of vehicle fuel-consumption data (in France and the United Kingdom); voluntary commitments have been made by motor manufacturers in several countries for improvements in fuel consumption. Other measures which have been taken by some countries to reduce fuel consumption include lower speed-limits and higher taxes on vehicles with high fuel consumption. In addition, voluntary agreements have been made with car manufacturers in several countries for reductions in consumption of around 10 per cent. Sweden has specified limits in terms of litres per 100 km which each manufacturer should meet, averaged over all cars produced in a given year.

Table 12.2: European agreements for reductions in vehicle fuel consumption

UK	Compulsory reporting of fuel-consumption data. 10% increase in mpg (9.1% reduction in fuel consumption) from 1978 levels, by 1985, for passenger cars.
France	Compulsory reporting of fuel consumption data. Mean fuel consumption to be less than 7.5 litres per 100 km by 1985.
West Germany	10–12% lower consumption (5% for heavy trucks) from 1978 levels, by 1985.
Italy	10% lower consumption from 1978 levels, by 1985.
Sweden	Fleet average 8.5 litres per 100 km by 1985; 7.5 litres per 100 km by 1990.

Despite the absence of regulatory programmes like those in the United States, Europeans consume considerably less motor-fuel per person than do Americans, in part at least because of higher fuel prices. Most European countries have motor-fuel prices that are at least twice those of the United States (as the result of taxes) and in a number of countries they are more than three times higher. The corresponding per-capita motor-fuel use in these countries is less than half that of the United States.

The US Energy Policy and Conservation Act, passed in the United States in December 1975, amended the Motor Vehicle Information and Cost Saving Act to require improvements in passenger-car fuel consumption up to a level of 27.5 miles per US gallon (8.55 litres/100 km) by 1985, as shown in Table 12.3, as measured by EPA test procedures. (The Federal standards were administratively relaxed by the Reagan administration in Model Years 1986, 1987, and 1988, and restored slightly in 1989 by the Bush administration.) Vehicle manufacturers are required to test sufficient vehicles to allow a fuel-consumption figure to be assigned to each product line produced by them. From these figures a sales-weighted average fuel-consumption level is calculated for all the passenger cars produced by the manufacturer concerned. This value must be below the standard specified for the appropriate Model Year. The standards are based on the combined city/highway fuel-consumption figures, and are known as the CAFE standards (Corporate Average Fuel Economy). Since the 1979 Model Year the programme has been expanded to cover Light Duty Trucks as well as passenger cars.

Table 12.3: US fuel-consumption standards
(litres/100 km, and miles/US gallon in brackets)

Model year	Passenger cars		Light trucks		Light trucks § (2-wheel drive)		Light trucks § (4-wheel drive)	
1978	13.07	(18.0)	–	–	–			
1979	12.38	(19.0)	–	–	13.68	(17.2)*	14.89	(15.8)*
1980	11.76	(20.0)	16.80	(14.0)+	14.70	(16.0)†	16.80	(14.0)†
1981	10.69	(22.0)	16.22	(14.5)+	14.08	(16.7)†	15.68	(15.0)†
1982	9.80	(24.0)	–	–	13.07†	(18.0)†	14.70	(16.0)
1983	9.05	(26.0)	–	–	12.07	(19.5)†	13.45	(17.5)
1984	8.71	(27.0)	11.76	(20.0)	11.59	(20.3)†	12.72	(18.5)
1985	8.55	(27.5)	10.94	(21.5)	11.94	(19.7)†	12.45	(18.9)
1986	9.05	(26.0)	11.76	(20.0)	11.47	(20.5)†	12.06	(19.5)
1987	9.05	(26.0)	11.47	(20.5)	11.20	(21.0)	12.06	(19.5)
1988	9.05	(26.0)	11.47	(20.5)	11.20	(21.0)	12.06	(19.5)
1989	8.88	(26.5)	11.24	(20.5)	11.20	(21.0)	12.06	(19.5)

Notes: * up to 6,000 lbs GVW.
† up to 8,500 lbs GVW.
+ a relaxation was granted for vehicles produced in small numbers and not based on passenger-car engines, for 1980 and 1981 only.
§ separate 2-wheel/4-wheel-drive standards are optional from 1984.
In 1977, before the introduction of fuel-consumption standards, passenger cars in the USA averaged 13.36 litres per 100 km.

A manufacturer whose fleet-average fuel consumption does not meet the standard is subject to a fine of $5 for each vehicle produced, for every 0.1 miles per US gallon that the standard is exceeded. These fines may be offset by credits accrued in other model years, however.

The *Gas Mileage Guide* published annually by the EPA and the Department of Energy lists the city fuel-consumption test results of each vehicle model, and is intended to provide information to the new-car buyer. In addition, each vehicle must carry a label specifying the vehicle fuel consumption as determined by EPA, an estimate of the annual fuel cost based on 15,000 miles of operation, and the range of fuel economy achieved by similar-sized vehicles of other makes. The values posted are not intended to give an accurate estimate of the fuel consumption that the owner will achieve under normal driving conditions, but to allow a relative comparison between different models of vehicle.

In calculating the CAFE, a manufacturer may include in the fleet-average figure any electric or hybrid vehicles produced. The procedures defined by EPA for calculating the equivalent fuel economy of electric vehicles takes account only of the petroleum energy used to produce the electricity which powers the vehicle, and ignores other sources of energy in power generation such as coal. The calculated fuel-economy figures are, therefore, high (around 195 miles per US gallon), giving an incentive for development of such vehicles. Similar credits will be possible for flexible-fuelled vehicles (that is, vehicles which can operate on either methanol or natural gas as well as conventional gasoline) as a result of legislation adopted in 1988.

In addition to the average fuel-economy figure required of each manufacturer, taxes are levied on vehicles which do not achieve certain minimum fuel-economy figures. These standards are:

1984	19.5 miles/US gallon	(12.1 litres/100 km)
1985	21.0 "	(11.2 ")
1986	22.5 "	(10.5 ")

Vehicles which fail to meet these figures are subject to a 'gas-guzzler' tax ranging from $500 for a 0.1 mile/US gallon shortfall to a maximum of $3,850 (1986 figures).

The Japanese Government has legislated for mandatory improvements in fuel consumption of passenger cars of up to 11.2 per cent by 1985, compared with 1978 levels (Table 12.4). Standards have been specified by vehicle weight, and the measurements are made on the basis of the 10-mode test procedure. With the increased availability of low-cost oil in the world market today, average new-vehicle fuel economy in Japan has started to decrease.

In response to an Australian Government report, *Proposals for an Australian Conservation of Energy Programme*, the Federal Chamber of Automotive Industries (FCAI) has proposed a voluntary *Code of Practice for Passenger Car Fuel Consumption Reduction*. Under this code, the FCAI set annual goals for a National Average Fuel

Consumption (NAFC) and from this a sales-weighted Corporate Average Fuel Consumption (CAFC) target was derived for each manufacturer. The base-level NAFC for 1978 was 11.2 litres/100 km, and the FCAI goal for 1983 was 9.0 litres/100 km.

Table 12.4: Japanese fuel consumption standards

	Inertia weight category (kg)			
	625	750–875	1,000–1,250	1,500–2,000
1978 Actual fuel consumption (litres/100 km)	5.38	6.94	9.01	13.16
1985 Legislated fuel consumption (litres/100 km)	5.05	6.25	8.00	11.76
% improvement	6.10	9.90	11.20	10.60

The US fuel-consumption experience provides useful insights into future policy options. Figure 12.2 shows that auto CAFE rose during the 1970s but has remained fairly flat since the early 1980s. It is important to note that during the 1970s, when emissions standards were substantially tightened, average miles per gallon improved markedly. (This observation is also true even if fuel-economy improvements due to vehicle-weight reductions are not included.) However, during the 1980s, when vehicle-emission and fuel-efficiency standards have generally stabilized, and gasoline prices have plunged, fuel-economy gains have been minimal. Further, without the stimulus of regulatory requirements or market incentives due to higher fuel prices, manufacturers quickly reverted to historical patterns of competing on the basis of horsepower and acceleration rather than fuel economy or low emissions. As the regulatory forcing of the CAFE standards has waned in recent years, US new-car fuel efficiency is now slipping more rapidly. According to recent EPA data, the fuel efficiency of new US cars declined by 4 per cent between 1988 and 1990 (projected). Over this same period, new cars showed a 6-per-cent weight gain and a 10-per-cent increase in horsepower. The lesson seems to be that, just as with emissions, stringent regulation is the surest path to the desired goal. Regulations alone, however, are not sufficient; they must be supplemented by rising fuel prices to increase public demand for efficient vehicles.

On a world-wide basis at present, very little, if any, fuel-efficiency improvement is occurring. The governmental push of the late 1970s and early 1980s has stalled, and market competition now appears to be focused primarily on performance improvements rather than fuel-economy gains. As a result, road transport is responsible for a steadily increasing portion of oil consumption in the OECD region and other countries. In OECD member countries, for instance, the share of total oil consumed by the transport sector has risen from less than 40 per cent in 1973 to nearly 60 per cent in 1989, with road transport accounting for over 70 per cent of total transport-fuel use. With production down in major non-OPEC oil-producing countries such as the USSR and the US, and consumption increasing rapidly in the developing world, the risk of a serious global oil crisis is potentially as great or greater than that which existed in the early 1970s. That fact alone, with its economic, energy-security, and balance-of-payments implications, should be sufficient reason substantially to improve vehicle efficiency. OECD automobile and other light vehicles have by far the largest share of OECD oil consumption. This trend toward more and more oil consumption by the transport sector, coupled with greater and greater emissions, has become a serious threat to future generations.

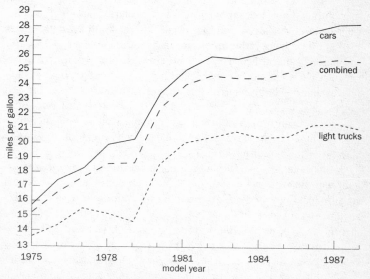

Fig. 12.2. Trends in fuel efficiency in US motor vehicles, as measured by the US Environmental Protection Agency

12.6 Future motor-vehicle emissions

12.6.1 Emissions of CO, HC, and NO$_x$

To estimate emissions, the world vehicle population was subdivided into several vehicle categories, according to the level of emission control which was judged likely to apply at a given point in time:

- European Community (EC);
- European Free Trade Association (EFTA);
- North America;
- Japan/Australia;
- Rapidly industrializing countries (RIC); and
- the rest of the world (ROW).

Emissions standards for each country category in the base case were those which have already been adopted and either are in effect or are estimated to come into effect in the next several years.

A second scenario was also assumed for each group of countries, which is referred to as the state of the art. In this case all vehicles in the world are estimated to adopt the most stringent set of requirements considered technologically feasible today. These include currently adopted Californian standards for cars and light trucks, a further 50-per-cent reduction in these requirements for CO, HC, and NOx shortly after the turn of the century (as currently proposed in US Clean Air Act amendments adopted by the US Senate), heavy-truck requirements scheduled to be introduced during the 1990s in the US, volatility controls on petrol to reduce evaporative and refuelling hydrocarbon emissions, and enhanced inspection and maintenance programmes to maximize the actual effectiveness of emissions standards and refuelling controls.

A third scenario was added which, in addition to the more stringent requirements of the state of the art, included lower growth-rates in vehicle miles travelled. The baseline and modified growth-rates by region are summarized in Table 12.5.

Fig. 12.3 shows the likely future global CO, HC, and NO$_x$ emissions trends if we continue current patterns. Recently adopted requirements in Western Europe, combined with further tightening of US standards along the lines of current US Congressional debates, are shown to continue a gradual but steady reduction in emissions throughout the 1990s. By the turn of the century, however, each of these pollutants will have bottomed out and will start to increase unless further controls are introduced. Figs. 12.4, 12.5, and 12.6 show that, while the highly industrialized areas of the world remain the dominant source of motor-vehicle emissions, the greatest growth is in the rapidly industrialized areas of the world, and the remainder of the world where vehicle-pollution controls are virtually non existent. Fig. 12.7, which summarizes the vehicle-miles travelled by region of the world, shows that these regions are becoming an increasingly important contributor to global mileage.

Table 12.5: Growth rates in vehicle miles travelled from 1985

Area	Base (%)	Low Growth (%)
European Community*	2.50	1.50
European Free Trade Association†	2.50	1.50
North America‡	2.50	1.50
Japan/Australia	3.50	2.00
Rapidly Industrializing Countries§	5.00	3.00
Rest of the World	4.00	3.00
Global	3.23	1.97

* All member countries except Denmark.

† Sweden, Norway, Finland, Denmark, Switzerland, Austria.

‡ Canada and the United States.

§ Taiwan, S. Korea, Mexico, Brazil, and the Eastern European Countries including the USSR.

Results from the second scenario, under which it was assumed that all vehicles around the world introduce state-of-the-art emission controls, are summarized in Figs. 12.8, 12.9, and 12.10. They show that this alternative has the potential to offset the global vehicle-population growth. In other words, if it were possible to introduce state-of-the-art emissions controls across the entire planet, it would be possible to start to reduce global emissions of CO, HC, and NO_x from the vehicle population while simultaneously absorbing an approximately 3-per-cent annual vehicle motor transport (VMT) growth (only 2.5-per-cent in the industrialized world, but higher rates in the rapidly industrializing and other areas of the world).

Further growth, however, will continue to put pressure on these levels. After 2030, emissions will start to turn up again unless growth is constrained or technology advances sufficiently to lower emissions per mile driven even more. Figs. 12.11, 12.12, and 12.13 illustrate that emissions controls in several regions are not sufficient to keep pace with projected VMT growth.

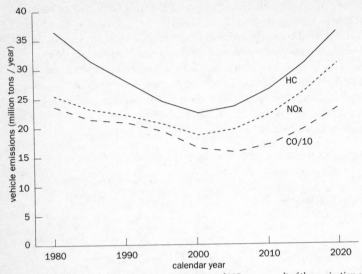

Fig. 12.3. Trends in vehicle emissions of HC, CO, and NO$_x$ as a result of the projection of currently adopted requirements (for CO, multiply vertical scale by 10)

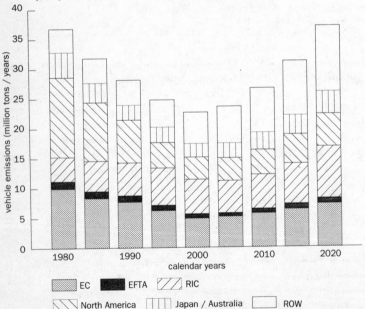

Fig. 12.4. Trends in total vehicle emissions of HC by region as a result of the projection of currently adopted requirements

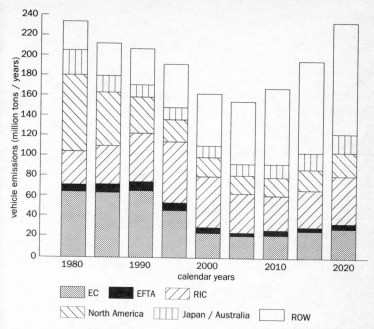

Fig. 12.5. Trends in vehicle emissions of CO by region as a result of the projection of currently adopted requirements

The third scenario, which reduces projected mileage-growth modestly (see Table 12.5 and Fig. 12.14), shows the benefits which can result. Therefore, it is encouraging to see countries such as the Netherlands beginning to pursue strategies such as road-pricing to restrain vehicle growth.

12.6.2 Global CO_2 emissions

As noted earlier, the specific fuel consumption of automobiles tends to remain high. Since the early 1980s, the rate of improvement in new-vehicle fuel efficiency has declined significantly in response to low oil-prices. Although maximum speeds are now limited in most countries of the world, new models are generally able to attain higher performance, and such increasingly powerful cars consume more fuel. New light-duty vehicles' fuel consumption per kilometre driven in most OECD countries is now actually increasing.

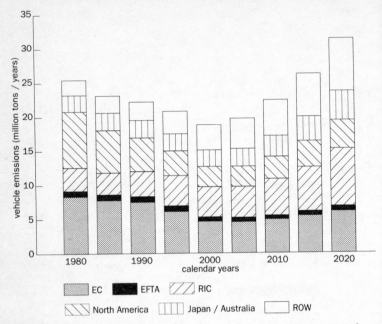

Fig. 12.6. *Trends in vehicle emissions of NO$_x$ by region as a result of the projection of currently adopted requirements*

Further, the stock of vehicles is also continuing to increase world-wide, at a rate of more than 3 per cent per year. The increase is mainly due to socio-economic development and demographic change, and will likely be accelerated as Eastern European countries develop more market-based economies.

Yearly mileage per vehicle is growing in several countries. This seems to be a consequence of low fuel prices, lack of effort in promoting energy efficiency, and problems with urban planning and mass transportation. So the amount of driving in congested urban and suburban areas is also constantly increasing, and leads to much higher fuel consumption per kilometre.

The Toronto Conference on global warming concluded that in the short term, that is, over the next fifteen years, CO$_2$ reductions of the order of 20 per cent of current emissions rates will be necessary to stabilize the global climate; over the longer term, reductions of approximately 50 per cent will be needed. The Intergovernmental Panel on

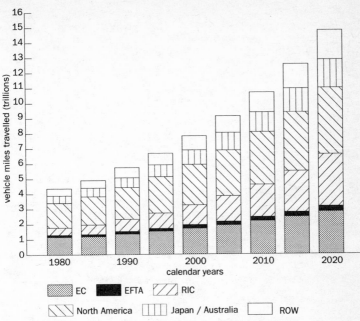

Fig. 12.7. *Trends in vehicle-miles travelled by region (base case)*

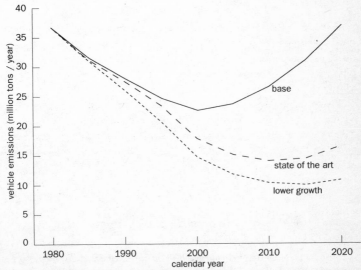

Fig. 12.8. *Trends in vehicle HC emissions if all vehicles around the world used state-of-the-art emission controls*

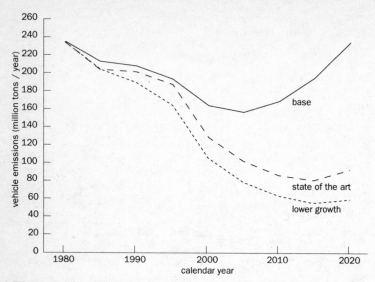

Fig. 12.9. Trends in vehicle CO emissions if all vehicles around the world used state-of-the-art emission controls

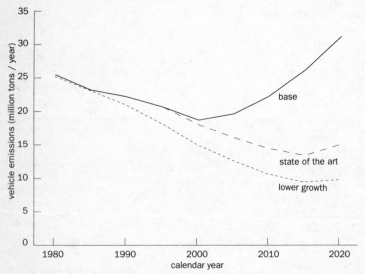

Fig. 12.10. Trends in vehicle NO_x emissions if all vehicles around the world used state-of-the-art emission controls

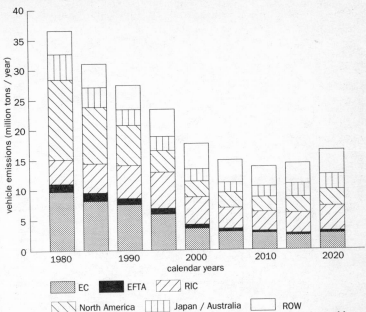

Fig. 12.11. *Trends in vehicle HC emissions by region if all vehicles around the world used state-of-the-art emission controls*

Climate Change has shown that, if the goal is to stabilize greenhouse-gas concentrations in the atmosphere at present levels, cuts in CO_2 emissions of more than 60 per cent are needed immediately. Both targets seem daunting to say the least in the face of the inexorable growth in vehicle numbers and the relatively slow rate at which emissions controls are being introduced and vehicle fuel-efficiency improved.

Experience gained during the 1970s and 1980s in the US suggests that the dual goals of low emissions (CO, HC, and NO_x) and improved energy efficiency (and therefore lower CO_2) are not only compatible but mutually reinforcing, as illustrated in Fig. 12.15. However, significant gains in either area are dependent on forceful government requirements. Left to its own devices, the motor-vehicle industry shows no inclination to adopt state-of-the-art pollution controls or advanced-efficiency technology. Simultaneously, governments around the world have shown themselves to be extremely fickle in terms of adopting stringent vehicle-efficiency targets and sticking to

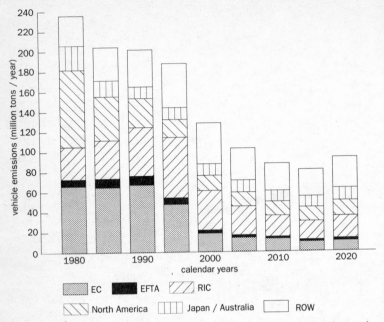

Fig. 12.12. Trends in vehicle CO emissions if all vehicles around the world used state-of-the-art emission controls

those targets through the cyclical variations in the global oil market. Industrialized countries have actually begun to slip backward in terms of new-vehicle efficiency.

Since consumption of each gallon of gasoline results in the emission of about 6 pounds of carbon or 22 pounds of CO_2, it is easy to see why CO_2 overall is increasing. As illustrated in Fig. 12.16, based on projected increases in vehicles and their use around the world, motor-vehicle CO_2 emissions will skyrocket over the next forty to fifty years. Reducing the global growth in vehicles and their use, however, could substantially lower, though not eliminate, this increase.

Less fuel consumption for the global fleet is the real key to lower CO_2 emissions. This energy conservation can take the form of less miles driven per vehicle per year, or less total vehicles, or more efficient vehicles; ultimately, it will probably require some combination of all these measures. Fig. 12.17 illustrates the potential impact of a 2-per-cent annual improvement in new-vehicle fuel-efficiency

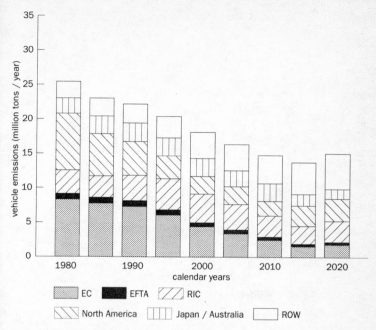

Fig 12.13. Trends in vehicle NO_x emissions by region if all vehicles around the world used state-of-the art emission controls

starting this year. The increase in global vehicle fuel consumption can begin to be reversed, and as shown in Fig. 12.18, CO_2 emissions can start to turn down. Merely holding the line at today's high CO_2 emission levels, as noted earlier, however, is far from sufficient to address global-warming concerns. Conversion of 2 per cent of the new vehicle fleet to operate on fuel cells (to cite just one option), which attain 50-per-cent better fuel-efficiency than conventional systems, and increasing this conversion at a rate of 2 per cent per year after 2000 (3 per cent after 2010), in conjunction with the 2-per-cent improvement in conventional vehicle efficiency, can start to lower CO_2 emissions after the turn of the century.

Fig. 12.18 also shows the potential impact of this combination of strategies. Specifically, if 'conventional' new vehicles were to improve at a rate of 2 per cent per year, starting in 1990, and 3 per cent of the fleet were to convert to fuel cells and achieve twice the efficiency of conventional vehicles starting in the year 2000, it would be

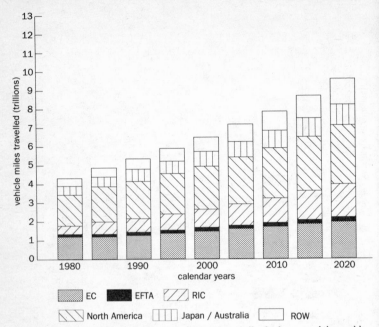

Fig. 12.14. Trends in vehicle-miles travelled, by region, if all vehicles around the world used state-of-the-art emission controls

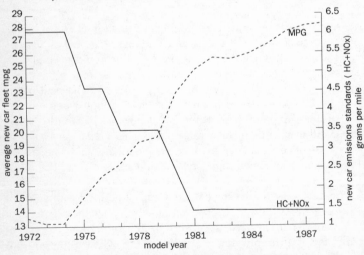

Fig. 12.15. US vehicle emissions- and fuel-economy trends since 1972

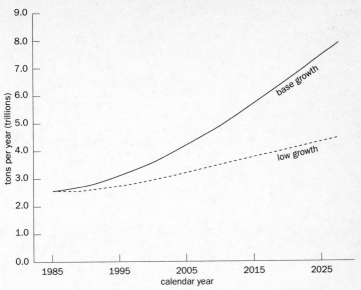

Fig. 12.16. *Global vehicle CO$_2$ emissions assuming no improvements in vehicle efficiency*

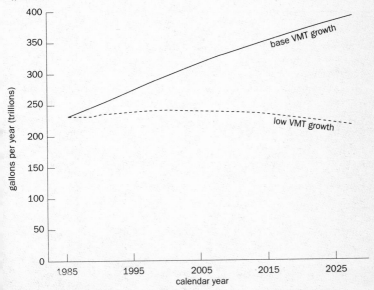

Fig. 12.17. *Global vehicle fuel consumption assuming 2-per-cent annual vehicle-efficiency gain*

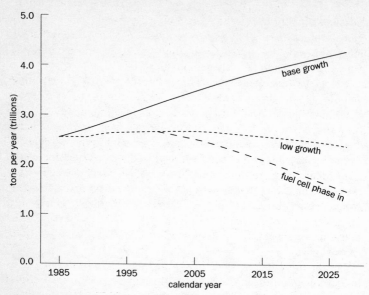

Fig. 12.18. Global vehicle CO$_2$ emissions assuming 2-per-cent annual vehicle-efficiency gain, showing impact of fuel cell phase-in

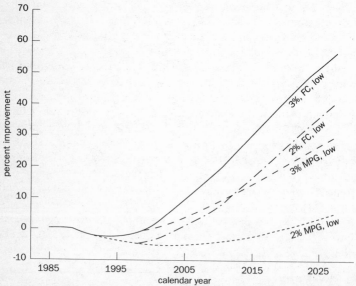

Fig. 12.19. Global vehicle CO$_2$ emissions in the different scenarios used in this chapter, as a percentage improvement from 1985 performance

possible actually to start to reduce global CO_2 emissions from the global vehicle fleet. (Fuel cells, in addition to improving vehicle efficiency, have the potential to dramatically lower 'conventional emissions' beyond currently demonstrated levels.)

Fig. 12.19 illustrates the percentage improvement in global motor-vehicle CO_2 emissions from a variety of strategies. It shows that only a combination of lower growth in the global vehicle population and the miles they drive, coupled with steady significant improvement in conventional new-car efficiency, and a gradual shift to advanced technologies such as fuel cells, holds the promise for achieving the goals identified in Toronto. And, of course, we must go well beyond these. To the extent that growth is constrained even more, the pressure on conventional-vehicle fuel economy is lessened; conversely, to the degree that conventional vehicles are made cleaner and more fuel efficient, there is less pressure to convert to alternative advanced technologies.

For the present generation of automobiles, significant reductions in fuel consumption and pollution from vehicles is both feasible and necessary. Progress in reducing fuel consumption can be achieved by focusing first on the engine and transmission, on weight reductions, on aerodynamic improvements, and on increasing use of electronics. Computer models, and the actual construction of prototype automobiles with fuel economies in the range of 60–120 mpg, have demonstrated that it is possible to approximately double the average fuel economy of current automobiles without sacrificing interior space, and preserving adequate performance. Such large improvements are possible because of the multiplicative effects of improvements in the efficiency of the power plant and reductions in power requirements.

The energy efficiency of the propulsion system can also be improved by ensuring that the engine will be operated at its most efficient speed for each specific power-demand at the wheels. This requires a transmission with a wide ratio (gear)-range within which the ratio can be varied continuously or in relatively modest steps, and with electronic controls or a system that indicates to the driver when to change the ratio for optimal fuel economy. Such transmissions have an additional energy-efficiency benefit, in that they make available the peak engine power at all road speeds, and therefore make possible a reduction in unused peak engine power.

Many different improvements are possible to reduce power requirements at the wheels, including continued reductions in weight (through materials substitutions) and aerodynamic drag. Unfortunately, some of the progress which has already been achieved in reducing power requirements has been offset by a shift toward more powerful engines which operate with high fuel consumption in ordinary driving conditions.

After the year 2000, other low-pollution and energy-efficient technologies appear feasible if encouraged by government regulatory or other incentives. These include two-stroke engines, hybrid vehicles with thermal and electric engines functioning together, and fuel cells using methanol or hydrogen.

A variety of policy instruments are necessary to assure the introduction and acceptance of fuel-efficient technological advances in the market-place. Included among these are vehicle-efficiency standards, economic instruments directed at both vehicle and fuel manufacturers and consumers, as well as much more focused public-information efforts. The economic instruments should be directed toward lower low-fuel-consumption vehicle taxes and concurrently increased taxes on high-consumption vehicles. It would probably include some combination of:

- Fuel taxes;
- Vehicle taxes related to fuel consumption, both at time of sale and annually;
- Road pricing and/or permanent barriers in some areas based on vehicle fuel consumption; and
- Parking taxes and/or restrictions based on efficiency.

At current fuel prices – and even much higher prices – large opportunities for automotive fuel-economy improvements will remain untapped if the decisions are left to ordinary market forces, because there is only a relatively modest impact on the overall cost of driving at higher fuel prices, and even this is partially offset as the vehicle's fuel economy increases. Increased fuel taxes *alone* will, therefore, not be sufficient to bring about the necessary reductions in vehicle fuel consumption.

The most effective policy is an integrated one which includes elements of both vehicle standards and economic instruments. Only if governments decide to pursue this objective through early and significant action can important progress be expected by the end of the century.

It is possible to bring about significant improvements in the short term and even more in the longer term. Through a combination of engine-efficiency improvements, better aerodynamic design, modification to accessories, reduced weight, less rolling resistance, and advances in electronics, vehicle consumption improvements of 30 to 40 per cent beyond today's vehicles are possible over the next five to seven years. Improved fuels and more widespread vehicle inspection and maintenance could increase these gains. Over the longer term, significant additional gains – perhaps of the order of 60 per cent – are possible.

12.7 Linkages between CO₂ and conventional emissions

Ever since vehicle emissions have been regulated, vehicle manufacturers have argued that such controls would inevitably result in poorer fuel economy. This issue is now being raised again by manufacturers and their lobbies in the context that more stringent CO, HC, and NO_x standards will impair efforts to address global warming by increasing CO_2 emissions. It is, therefore, useful to examine the available data. Past and present data do not support these allegations.

As noted earlier, experience gained during the 1970s and 1980s in the US suggests that the dual goals of low emissions (CO, HC, and NO_x) and improved energy efficiency (and therefore lower CO_2) are not only compatible but mutually reinforcing, as illustrated in Fig. 12.15. In spite of this historical record, one of the arguments being put forth by the vehicle manufacturers is that it would be a mistake to tighten tailpipe standards for conventional pollutants, because such standards will lead to increased CO_2 and more global warming. The specific focus is with regard to the oxides of nitrogen, where it is argued that tighter standards would result in a fuel-economy penalty and therefore increased CO_2. To investigate this issue, a data set of 1989 model-year cars was obtained from the US EPA. The analysis consisted of regressing the actual CO_2 emissions per mile against the NO_x, HC, or CO emissions per mile. The results suggest that, in fact, CO_2 emissions will tend to go down as NO_x, HC, or CO are reduced. This tends to support the observation that more stringent emissions-standards tend to encourage the more advanced air-fuel and spark-management systems, with the result that overall fuel economy also tends to improve.

12.8 CFCs

Significant reductions in CFC releases could be achieved through improvements in air-conditioner seals, and especially through changes in repair-shop work-practices, because CFCs are intentionally vented to the air when air-conditioners are repaired. CFC consumption in the US has been estimated as shown in Table 12.6.

Table 12.6: Estimated US consumption of CFC-12 for mobile air-conditioners

Use	CFC consumption (1,000 tonnes)	% of Total
Initial charge of units		
US	14.7	27.2
Imported	2.8	5.2
After market	1.0	1.8
Recharge of units		
After leakage	13.5	25.0
After service venting	18.2	33.6
After accident	3.9	7.2

What is needed is cradle-to-grave controls designed to eliminate CFC emissions from vehicles. Elements of a comprehensive strategy could include:

■ A full-life, useful-life requirement on hoses, seals, and fittings, such that it would be the manufacturers' responsibility to design vehicles so that no leakage would be allowed over the actual vehicle life;

■ Where maintenance is required, limiting it to qualified, licensed facilities which have appropriate equipment, catalysts, and so on, to prevent leakage or venting of CFCs;

■ An immediate ban on sales of 'do-it-yourself' kits to recharge existing auto air-conditioners;

■ A ban on all new sales of CFCs as quickly as possible.

12.9 Conclusions

Motor-vehicle emissions of HC, CO, and NO_x are a major source of climate modification as well as adverse health and other environmental effects from ground-level pollution. In addition, tropospheric pollution and climate modification have been found to be directly linked by a variety of mechanisms. To deal with these problems in a coordinated fashion requires the minimization of carbon monoxide, carbon dioxide, hydrocarbons, nitrogen oxides, and chlorofluorocarbons. Control of these pollutants from vehicles will be mutually reinforcing with regard to the dual problems of global warming and urban air pollution.

On a global scale, emissions of these pollutants depends on the number of vehicles in use and their emissions-rates. In turn, their actual emissions-rates depend on their fuel efficiency and their use of control technologies such as catalytic converters. Mandatory fuel-efficiency standards throughout the world are feasible and necessary to slow the growth in CO_2 emissions. In conjunction with stringent HC, CO, and NO_x requirements, the potential exists not only to offset the global impacts of expected vehicle growth over the next half century but also to start an emissions downturn.

The correct policy to address local and global environmental problems from vehicles would have the following elements:

- Stringent emission standards for CO, HC, and NO_x such that all new vehicles sold in the US (and ultimately around the world) are equipped with state-of-the-art emissions controls;

- Carbon dioxide emission standards which will be sufficient to lower global-fleet emissions by 20 per cent in the short term and 50 per cent in the longer term (taking into account not only the direct emissions but also the emissions associated with the entire extraction, manufacture, and distribution of the fuel). This likely means fuel-efficiency levels for future vehicles approaching 40 mpg by the year 2000 and 90 mpg by 2030, unless growth in vehicle-miles travelled is constrained;

- Minimizing the potential for continued growth in the number of vehicles and their use. At a minimum, this should include the adoption of government policies which will provide attractive alternatives to the use of private cars. As another important element, energy prices should gradually be significantly increased, so encouraging individuals to purchase highly efficient vehicles and fuels, and to make life-style decisions which will tend to minimize vehicle travel as well as other energy uses.

Chapter 13
Nuclear Power and Global Warming

Bill Keepin

"…given business-as-usual growth in energy demand, it appears that even an infeasibly massive global nuclear power programme could not reduce future emissions of carbon dioxide. To displace coal alone would require the construction of a new nuclear plant every two or three days for nearly four decades …

… in the United States, each dollar invested in efficiency displaces nearly seven times more carbon than a dollar invested in new nuclear power … even if the nuclear dream cost of around 5 cents/kWh were realized, electric efficiency still displaces between two-and-a-half and ten times more carbon than nuclear power per dollar invested. And these numbers may be conservative…**"**

Global warming looms as perhaps the most serious environmental threat the world has ever faced. Meanwhile, acid rain damage is spreading, and air pollution has afflicted all metropolitan areas in the world, reaching catastrophic proportions in some industrial regions.

The principal culprit in all these problems is the burning of coal, oil and natural gas, and international pressure to reduce fossil fuel consumption is now mounting year by year.

For this reason, nuclear power has received much attention recently. Nuclear power is widely portrayed as one of the best means for achieving substantial reductions in future fossil-fuel consumption. In particular, given the threat of global warming, nuclear power is viewed by some people as the only realistic or practical response to this dilemma. As the former Environment Minister for the United Kingdom said in 1988: 'If we want to arrest the greenhouse effect we should concentrate on a massive increase in nuclear generating capacity.'[1] At first sight, it is perhaps natural to expect that nuclear power might be the best substitute for fossil fuels. Nuclear power stations produce no direct emissions of carbon dioxide (CO_2), and the nuclear fuel-cycle releases only negligible quantities of carbon dioxide, acidifying gases, and other air pollutants associated with fossil-fuel combustion.[2]

However, upon closer analysis, it turns out that nuclear power cannot meet this expectation. This chapter examines the nuclear option from several viewpoints, and reaches the following conclusions. First, rapid expansion of nuclear power is not a viable response to the threat of global warming. Second, energy efficiency can abate future carbon dioxide emissions more quickly and for much less cost than nuclear power. Third, renewable energy sources offer greater promise than nuclear power for a long-term sustainable energy future. Finally, several problems with nuclear power remain unresolved.

The following section explores a hypothetical scenario of rapid expansion of nuclear power. While this exercise is carried out for the sake of analysis, the actual chances of substantial nuclear expansion seem remote in most countries, given recent developments. Six countries of the European Community have either decided not to develop nuclear power, or have had referenda forcing its phase-out (for example, Italy).[3] A Swedish referendum requires that nuclear power be phased out there by 2010, and following Chernobyl, the Swiss parliament commissioned a study that demonstrates the feasibility of phasing out Switzerland's nuclear power by 2025.[4] In the United States, no order has been placed for a nuclear plant since 1978, and the American business magazine *Forbes* has opined that 'the failure of the US nuclear power program ranks as the largest managerial disaster in business history'.[5] Nuclear programmes in most Third World nations have been cancelled or scaled back drastically.

Even in Britain, where the government has historically supported the nuclear industry, recent developments suggest that this support may have ended. The British government is privatizing the previously nationalized electric power utilities. Nuclear power proved unacceptable for the investors to purchase, and so it will remain nationalized, and the government will require all utilities to purchase at least 20 per cent of their electricity from non-fossil (effectively nuclear) sources. To subsidize the high cost of nuclear power, a tax will be levied on fossil-fuelled power, and the government has declared that it does not expect to assist any new nuclear power plant.[6]

13.1 Can nuclear power solve global warming?

What are the prospects for eliminating the threat of global warming by large-scale expansion of nuclear power? To address this question, this section explores the effects of launching a massive nuclear power programme world-wide to 'solve' the greenhouse problem. For this purpose, a typical scenario of the world's energy future is modified to simulate rapid global nuclear expansion under assumptions favourable to nuclear power, and the effects on future carbon dioxide emission levels are assessed. Full technical details of this analysis are published elsewhere.[7]

The global energy scenario chosen for analysis here is a typical middle-of-the-road projection published by the United States Department of Energy.[8] Numerous long-term business-as-usual projections could be used for this purpose; however, the conclusions would be roughly the same in all cases, and thus a representative scenario is analysed here.[9] The selected scenario is produced from a global energy/carbon dioxide model that is one of the most widely used and thoroughly tested models available.[10] Principal inputs include assumptions about population and labour-productivity growth, supply and demand schedules for each fuel type, and initial conditions. The scenario was obtained by setting all model parameters to median estimates, and the results are typical of mainstream baseline energy/

CO_2 projections. The projected global energy growth is considered moderate, with primary energy demand reaching 21.3 terawatts by the year 2025 (TW: a terawatt is a thousand billion watts), of which 9.4 TW are supplied by coal, 4.0 TW by oil, 3.6 TW by gas, 2.9 TW by hydro-power, and 0.7 TW each by nuclear power and renewable energy.[11] Carbon emissions grow steadily to reach 10.3 gigatonnes per year by 2025, approximately double today's levels (Gt/y: a gigatonne is a billion tonnes). This scenario is roughly comparable to the IPCC reference scenario, although the latter is somewhat more energy-and carbon-intensive than the scenario analysed here.[12] Thus, an even more extreme nuclear programme would be required in the IPCC reference case to achieve the same carbon emission levels discussed below.

13.1.1 Optimistic nuclear assumptions

To explore the best hope for a nuclear response to the greenhouse threat, economic and political conditions are deliberately assumed below to be highly favourable to a nuclear strategy. First, since coal is the 'dirtiest' fossil fuel, this hypothetical nuclear programme is aimed at displacing coal. This assures the greatest reduction in carbon emissions per unit of nuclear power installed.[13] Also, coal is the most substitutable fossil fuel, because it is used largely for electricity generation and process heat. Second, the hypothetical nuclear programme is assumed to begin immediately and to be implemented relatively quickly. This is because climatologists believe there is an inherent time lag in global climate response to radiative forcing.[14] Thus, the sooner a given reduction in CO_2 is implemented, the greater its effect will be in retarding global warming.

For these reasons, the optimistic assumption is made that the world vigorously pursues a full transition from coal to nuclear power – completing it by the year 2025. This strategy offers the greatest possible reduction in CO_2 emissions for a given amount of nuclear power,[15] and it provides for the greatest ameliorating effect on climate warming.[16] In addition, several assumptions must be made about the technology of nuclear power. These too are chosen to be highly optimistic:

■ *Assumption 1.* Nuclear power is very *inexpensive.* Assumed costs are consistent with estimates put forth by the most optimistic nuclear proponents: capital cost is assumed to be $1,000 per kilowatt (kW) of capacity installed (compared with $3,000/kW in the United States today), and electricity generation cost from new plants is assumed to be 5 cents per kilowatt-hour (kWh)[17] (compared with 13.5 cents/kWh in the United States today).[18] These figures are consistent with reported costs in France, which builds standardized plants in a stable regulatory environment.[19]

■ *Assumption 2.* Nuclear plants can be *built relatively quickly.* Construction time for a 1,000 megawatt plant is assumed to be just six years (MW: a megawatt is a million watts),[20] which has been achieved in France (compared with ten to twelve years in the United States today).

■ *Assumption 3.* Nuclear power is perfectly *clean and safe.* All problems with nuclear power are assumed to disappear or be readily solved, including (a) nuclear waste treatment and storage, (b) all health and safety concerns, (c) decommissioning of retired plants, and (d) the possible impact on the proliferation of nuclear weapons.

Taken together, these hypothetical assumptions are extreme indeed, but they embrace the nuclear dream and its utmost hope for eliminating the greenhouse threat.[21] This nuclear programme is simulated in the scenario described above by incorporating a transition from coal to nuclear power that starts now and is completed by the year 2025.[22] Apart from this, the scenario remains unchanged.

13.1.2 Infeasible economics

What are the implications of this global nuclear programme? As illustrated in Figure 13.1, the world must build more than *five thousand* large nuclear power plants between now and the year 2025 – nearly half of which would be located in the Third World. This means, on average, a new nuclear plant (of 1,000 MW capacity) must be built every two-and-a-half days from now until 2025. Total capital cost is $5.3 trillion (1987 $), or an average of $144 billion annually, of which developing countries are responsible for $64 billion per year. Total electricity generation cost would average $525 billion per year, of which the developing countries' share would be $170 billion annually. By 2025, the global installed nuclear capacity would reach 5,200 gigawatts (GW: a gigawatt is a billion watts), an 18-fold increase over today's capacity.[23] Of this, 2,330 GW are in the Third World, which would mean a staggering 155-fold increase over today's installed capacity of 15.02 GW.[24] In Latin America alone, which has only 1.7 GW operating today, the required capacity is 334 GW by 2025 – substantially more than all the nuclear power in the world today.[25]

Such a scenario appears infeasible. The economic strain on the rich industrialized nations would be extreme, if not disastrous. Developing countries could not even consider this scenario, which entails building 2,351 large nuclear power plants in the Third World. For perspective, the World Bank lent $3 billion in 1987 to the electric-power sector[26] – less than 5 per cent of the $64 billion that would be required annually. Indeed, the current Third World debt burden would roughly double – just to build the required plants.

13.1.3 Future carbon emissions still grow

Despite the impossibility of such an extreme nuclear scenario, suppose for the sake of argument that it could be implemented. What would the effect be on future carbon dioxide emissions? Remarkably, it turns out that global carbon emissions would still continue to *grow*, reaching 6.5 billion tonnes by the year 2000, and thereafter emissions would remain at or above today's level.[27] This is due to the projected expansion in use of oil and natural gas.[28]

Other studies reach similar conclusions. For example, a recent analysis carried out for the International Energy Agency (IEA) examines a scenario of massive nuclear expansion in OECD countries, assessing the implications for future carbon dioxide levels. Utilizing analytical tools developed by the IEA Secretariat,[29] the scenario assumes that all OECD nations shift to 70 per cent nuclear electricity generation within twenty years. Thus, by 2010, all OECD nations would have the same share of nuclear electricity that France has today. The extreme implausibility of this scenario is acknowledged. It turns out that 800 GW of new capacity must be built in OECD nations (equivalent to 800 large nuclear plants, meaning a new 1,000 MW plant in the OECD every nine days from now until 2010). Despite this aggressive programme, the resulting environmental benefit is minimal. Global carbon dioxide emissions continue to grow substantially, and by 2005 emissions are only 6.7 per cent less than they would have been without the accelerated nuclear program. By 2050, atmospheric concentration of carbon dioxide is reduced by a mere 1.0 to 1.6 per cent.[30]

Fig. 13.1. Infeasibility of a nuclear response to global warming

(a) Today: approximate geopolitical distribution of the world's nuclear power plants in 1990. Each dot represents the equivalent of ten large nuclear power plants (1,000 MW each). (Exact locations of plants have been altered somewhat for graphical clarity. In some developing regions, actual capacity installed is substantially less than indicated.)

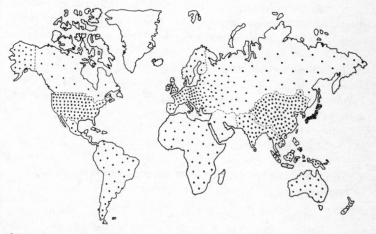

(b) 2025: approximate geopolitical distribution of 5,346 new nuclear power plants to be built by 2025 in a hypothetical massive nuclear response to the threat of global warming. As in Fig. 13.1(a), each dot represents the equivalent of ten large nuclear plants (1,000 MW each). Even under this infeasibly extreme nuclear scenario, global carbon dioxide emissions from fossil fuel combustion remain at or above 1988 levels. (Plants have been evenly distributed for graphic clarity.)

Key for Fig. 1(b)
Nuclear capacity to be built by 2025
(Each GW is equivalent to one large nuclear plant.)

USA	1,071 GW
W. Europe/Canada	564 GW
E. Europe/USSR	957 GW
Japan/Australia/New Zealand	403 GW
Centrally Planned Asia	1,147 GW
South and East Asia	511 GW
Africa	329 GW
Middle East	29 GW
Latin America	335 GW
Total	**5,346 GW**

In sum, given business-as-usual growth in energy demand, it appears that even an infeasibly massive global nuclear power programme could not reduce future emissions of carbon dioxide. To displace coal alone would require the construction of a new nuclear plant every two or three days for nearly four decades, and even then, future growth in oil and natural-gas consumption would still be sufficient to keep carbon dioxide emissions at or above today's levels until supplies are exhausted. These startling results follow from the simple fact that nuclear power today provides only a few per cent of the world's energy supply, and so it would have to expand very dramatically to increase its share substantially. Moreover, nuclear power is currently only practical for electricity generation, which is responsible for just one-third of fossil-fuel consumption. Thus, nuclear power's scope for reducing fossil-fuel dependence in the coming decades is fundamentally limited.

13.2 The near term: nuclear power versus energy efficiency

We have just seen that nuclear power cannot solve the global warming problem. Nevertheless, it is still true that nuclear power stations produce almost no carbon dioxide, and thus they can contribute to displacing CO_2. How effective is nuclear power for this purpose? How does it compare with other options for abating carbon dioxide emissions? Such questions are taken up in this section, which summarizes detailed results published elsewhere.[31]

The two most widely discussed options for reducing fossil-fuel carbon dioxide emissions in the near term are nuclear power and energy efficiency. While nuclear power is currently practical only for displacing fossil-fuelled electricity generation, energy efficiency improvements are available for the entire range of fossil-fuel uses. Indeed, despite tremendous gains already achieved via energy efficiency, the 'efficiency reserves' remaining to be tapped are enormous in both industrialized and developing nations. One detailed global analysis indicates that, given sufficient investment in existing energy-efficient technologies, the entire world could achieve living standards at or above those of Western Europe by the year 2020, while sustaining an increase in global energy consumption of only 10 per cent.[32] For discussions of policies to promote energy efficiency and state-of-the-art efficiency technologies, see Chapters 8 and 10.

13.2.1 Nuclear versus efficiency in the United States

What is the relative effectiveness of investments in nuclear power and energy efficiency for displacing carbon dioxide emissions? To explore this question, we consider the particular case of displacing coal-fired electricity, because this is the arena in which the nuclear option could have its greatest impact on future carbon dioxide emissions. The economic data utilized here reflect today's conditions, rather than the optimistic costs assumed in the scenario above. We begin with data for the United States, which is of particular interest, because the United States releases more carbon dioxide than any other nation, and it also has the largest nuclear power programme in the world.

To compare efficiency and nuclear investments, we need estimates of today's cost of saving electricity via improved efficiency, and today's cost of generating electricity from new nuclear power plants. Under present conditions, the cost of generating electricity from new US nuclear plants is around 13.5 cents/kWh (in 1987$).[33] This figure assumes a capital cost of $3,000 per kW, which is the average capital cost for the twenty-three US plants completed between 1984 and 1987. Meanwhile, a number of recent studies analyse the cost and savings potential of electrical efficiency improvements. Several technologies are considered, including solid-state ballasts, compact fluorescent lamps, improved refrigerators and water-heaters, motor improvements, and so on. While the best electric-efficiency

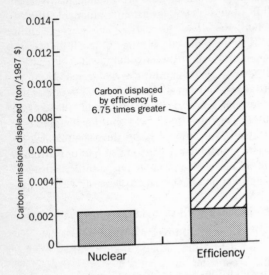

Fig. 13.2 Nuclear power and energy efficiency compared. Bars show the cost-effectiveness of today's investments in nuclear power and electric efficiency for abating carbon emissions from coal-fired power plants in the USA. Note that a dollar invested in efficiency displaces nearly seven times more carbon than a dollar invested in new nuclear power. Similar results hold in other countries.

investments cost less than 1 cent per kWh of electricity saved, the average cost weighted over a wide range of electric efficiency improvements is around 2 cents per kWh of electricity saved. For example, Lawrence Berkeley Laboratory (LBL), and the American Council for an Energy-Efficient Economy (ACEEE) have documented large potential electrical savings at average costs of 2 cents/kWh.[34]

Assuming a strategy of displacing coal-fired power, the reciprocals of these unit costs give the amounts of coal-fired electricity that can be displaced for each dollar invested: 7.4 kWh/$ for nuclear electricity and 50 kWh/$ for electric efficiency. Thus, at the present time in the United States, *each dollar invested in efficiency displaces nearly seven times more carbon than a dollar invested in new nuclear power*. The comparison is shown in Figure 13.2.

Some critics contend that in this analysis, the cost assumed for nuclear power should reflect, not its full cost, but only the *additional* cost over and above what it would cost to generate electricity from a new coal-fired power plant.[35] However, the resulting comparison with electric efficiency would be misleading, because it implicitly assumes that the equivalent investment in coal-fired electricity would have to be made in either case. One of the major benefits of electric efficiency improvement is that it offers the opportunity to *avoid* building many such coal plants in the first place. Thus, the analysis here compares the *full* costs of displacing coal-fired electricity in both cases, as follows. The full cost of providing the next kWh of carbon-free electricity services is 13.5 cents if it is supplied by nuclear power, and 2 cents if it is supplied by electric efficiency. Or, equivalently, the full cost of displacing one kWh of electricity from an existing coal-fired power plant is 13.5 cents if it is displaced with a new nuclear plant, and 2 cents if it is displaced with electric efficiency.

To the extent that nuclear power and electric efficiency compete for the same funds, this analysis indicates that choosing the nuclear option entails a significant environmental penalty. This is illustrated in Figure 13.2, where the difference in height between the two bars represents the additional carbon that is released into the atmosphere by investing in nuclear power rather than electric efficiency.[36] This 'environmental opportunity cost' is substantial: for every $100 invested in new nuclear power, one metric tonne of carbon is effectively released into the atmosphere that could have been avoided, had that $100 been invested in electric efficiency instead.[37]

13.2.2 Other estimates

The foregoing results are based on today's actual costs of nuclear power and electric efficiency. However, some analysts argue that electric efficiency can be provided at a considerably lower cost, while others contend that the cost of nuclear electricity can also be greatly reduced in the future. For example, nuclear advocacy groups, such as the United States Council for Energy Awareness (USCEA), argue that building standardized plants in a stable regulatory environment could bring down the cost of new nuclear electricity to around 5 cents/kWh.[38] Advocates of smaller, passively safe reactor designs, such as the modular gas-cooled reactor, believe that such designs could eventually produce electricity for 4.5 cents/kWh.[39]

Meanwhile, advocates of energy efficiency at the Rocky Mountain

Institute (RMI) argue that large potential electrical savings are available for 0.5 cents/kWh or less.[40] To give a remarkable example, a recent thorough study of motors in the United States concludes that motors consume more than half of all US electricity, and that there is a combined technical potential to save 44 per cent (plus or minus 16 per cent) of all electricity now used in US drive systems, at an average net cost of 0.49 cents/kWh saved (plus or minus 0.14 cents/kWh).[41] Even if this cost estimate is optimistic, it can be doubled or even quadrupled, and motor improvements still represent an opportunity to save roughly as much electricity as the entire US nuclear programme produces, for less than 2 cents/kWh. Since operating costs for all US nuclear plants exceed 2 cents/kWh, then in principle this suggests that it might be cost-effective to shut down the entire US nuclear programme today, and replace it with improvements in motors and drive systems.

To give fair representation to these divergent views on the future economics of nuclear and efficiency investments, Figure 13.3 illustrates the cost-effectiveness of abating carbon emissions for a wide range of cost estimates. The spread in the data in Figure 13.3 represents current uncertainty ranges in the literature. Note that electric efficiency is uniformly more cost-effective for abating carbon dioxide emissions. In fact, *even if the nuclear dream cost of around 5 cents/kWh were realized, electric efficiency still displaces between two-and-a-half and ten times more carbon than nuclear power per dollar invested.* And these numbers may be conservative; a recent study by the Worldwatch Institute estimates that the total cost of avoiding carbon emissions from coal-fired power plants is some thirty-two times more expensive with nuclear power than with energy efficiency.[42]

13.2.3 Similar results in other countries

The foregoing analysis applies to the United States. Detailed studies are not as widely available for other countries, though it appears that the same general conclusion will hold in most cases. For countries where nuclear power is less expensive than in the United States, the ratio of cost-effectiveness may be somewhat less, though still favouring efficiency. For example, representative calculation for the United Kingdom shows that investment in compact fluorescent lighting is four to five times more cost-effective than nuclear power for

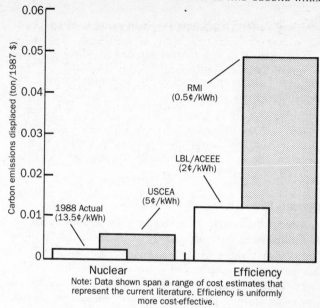

Fig. 13.3. Nuclear power and energy efficiency compared. Bars show the cost-effectiveness of nuclear- and efficiency-investments for abating carbon emissions from coal-fired power plants. Data shown span the range of estimates and projections in the current literature. Note that efficiency is uniformly more cost-effective than nuclear power.

abating carbon dioxide emissions.[43] In fact, the UK Department of Energy's own data show that nuclear power is one of the most expensive control options available for substantial carbon reduction,[44] and this has been confirmed by independent assessments.[45] A recent study for India and Brazil shows that under conservative assumptions, the cost of electric efficiency from lighting improvements in the domestic and commercial sectors is four to six times less than the long-range marginal cost of electricity in the two countries.[46] A detailed study for Brazil concludes that investing $8 billion in electric efficiency would save the country's utilities at least $38 billion, by avoiding the need to construct 19 GW of new electricity-generation capacity.[47]

13.3 The long term: nuclear versus renewable energy

Many proponents of nuclear power concede that energy efficiency offers the most important opportunities for carbon abatement in the near future. However, energy efficiency is not a panacea, and no matter how efficiently electricity is used, it must still be generated somehow. Thus, some people believe that nuclear power will be required in the future. Once again, it is important to compare the likely future developments in nuclear technologies with developments in other areas, which is the focus of this section.

13.3.1 Prospects for new nuclear technologies

Today's light-water reactor is recognized by spokespersons within the nuclear industry to be '...inherently an exceedingly complex, unforgiving device'.[48] However, some analysts foresee a 'Second Nuclear Era' in which nuclear power will make a come-back, utilizing improved 'passively safe' reactor designs.[49] Current research is focused in several areas. Advanced light-water reactors incorporate design improvements such as reduced power density (via increased core size) and improved emergency cooling. Such changes would tend to make a core melt-down much less likely. Some designers hope for plant lifetimes of sixty years, capacity factors of 87 per cent, and construction periods of four-and-a-half years – though current designs are far from achieving such targets.[50]

Another prototype design is the modular high-temperature gas-cooled reactor (MGR), which utilizes small spheres of uranium oxide as fuel, embedded in successive shells of graphite and other moderating materials. The small power density would ensure that temperatures remain below 1,600°C under any circumstances. Some analysts hope that the MGR will be the 'pollutant free energy source' of the future,[51] while others point out that this design is particularly suitable for tritium production, which would increase the risks of nuclear-weapons proliferation.[52]

Most research on 'passively safe' designs focuses primarily on reactor safety, and does not address many of the other problems associated with nuclear power, such as nuclear waste and the possible enhancement of the proliferation of nuclear weapons. The research emphasis is primarily on reducing the risk of major nuclear accidents, especially core melt-downs (loss of coolant). Moreover, it is not even clear that the new designs would achieve this very well. According to a study by the UK Atomic Energy Authority, some of the new designs may be just as vulnerable to structural failures as conventional plants are.[53] An article in *Nucleonics Week* states that 'experts are flatly unconvinced that safety has been achieved – or even substantially advanced – by the new designs'.[54]

13.3.2 Nuclear versus renewable technologies

There is a widespread belief that renewable energy will never provide a significant share of energy supply in the foreseeable future. However, this view is based on experience and data that are now way out of date. Renewable energy technologies have made dramatic progress over the past several years. Wind power has matured rapidly, and the cost of electricity generated from wind in the United States has dropped from 25 cents/kWh in 1980 to 7 to 9 cents/kWh in the late eighties, making wind competitive for intermediate and peak power.[55] The Danish Ministry of Energy reports that wind-power costs just 5.3 cents/kWh.[56] In a scenario for the United Kingdom that most closely reflects today's conditions, the UK Department of Energy's own data show that wind power can save almost as much carbon dioxide as nuclear power by the year 2005 – for nearly one-quarter the cost.[57] Electricity generated from biomass currently costs about 5 cents/kWh, and the commercialization of biomass-gasification co-generation technology is expected to generate electricity from sugar wastes for 3.3 cents/kWh within five years.[58] For a thorough review of the promise of renewable energy technologies, see Chapter 11.

Solar photovoltaic (PV) technology produces electricity from sunlight with no moving parts and no fuel. Recent improvements in solar PV technology have been dramatic, and the cost of PV electricity has plummeted from $1.50/kWh in 1980 to between 20 and 40 cents/kWh today (depending on the particular system employed).[59] The potential for solar PV was recently assessed by the United States Department of Energy (USDOE). The USDOE is hardly a solar-advocacy group, yet its conclusions are remarkable: PV can be used effectively anywhere in the United States, including under the grey skies of the north east. No cooling water is required, and contrary to widespread belief, land requirements per kWh of electricity produced are very similar to those for coal production and combustion.[60] PV sales are currently expanding at 30 per cent per year, and the cost of PV electricity (with storage for supplying electricity at night) is expected to fall to 4 cents/kWh by 2030, or sooner.[61] Rather than the usual incremental growth, there is a likelihood of explosive growth in the PV market when the price reaches about 8 cents/kWh, which could happen as early as the year 2000. Thus, according to the USDOE assessment, 'the ultimate role of PV may be far larger than most assume', and 'PV appears to be a long-term and desirable solution to U.S. and global concerns for energy and environment'.[62]

Critics of the USDOE assessment have argued that its time frame for PV cost reduction is too conservative. An optimistic assessment of the potential for a solar hydrogen economy from Princeton University/World Resources Institute suggests that cheap PV electricity could be available much sooner.[63] Based on detailed examination of current laboratory and field experience, the Princeton study concludes that by the year 2000, DC electricity could be produced in sunny regions for 2 to 3.5 cents/kWh, and that baseload AC electricity, with underground pumped hydro storage, could be produced for 5 to 8 cents/kWh.

The Princeton study draws a striking comparison between PV technology and nuclear power. The allure of nuclear power is that small quantities of fuel can produce large quantities of energy. Cycled through fast-breeder reactors (the most efficient nuclear technology), a single gram of uranium can produce 3,800 kWh of electricity. However, a uranium atom can only be fissioned once, whereas a silicon solar cell can absorb photons repeatedly and convert them to electricity. The amorphous silicon solar cell requires a thin film of silicon about one micron thick, which means that 3 grams of silicon are required per square meter of cell area. Over its lifetime in 15 per cent efficient thin-film PV solar cells, one gram of silicon produces 3,300 kWh of electricity. Thus, gram for gram, silicon and uranium produce comparable amounts of electricity, and silicon is 5,000 times more abundant in the earth's crust. Silicon accounts for half the mass of ordinary sand, and the electricity that could be produced from one tonne of sand is equivalent to that from burning over half-a-million tonnes of coal.[64]

The USDOE and Princeton assessments of the potential for solar photovoltaic energy pose a serious challenge to conventional thinking about solar PV electricity. Taken together, the two assessments project that the cost of solar PV electricity with storage will fall to around 4 cents/kWh sometime between the year 2000 and the year 2030. While the manufacture of early PV cells entailed significant toxic wastes, large-scale implementation of less hazardous silicon-based solar systems are expected to cause no greater environmental damage than the production of conventional energy systems, and disposal of silicon-based solar power systems should not cause any significant environmental problems.[65] Such auspicious prospects for solar energy were unthinkable even a few years ago, and they suggest that solar energy may become far more attractive than nuclear power in the relatively near future.

13.3.3 Nuclear phase-out?

Some analysts have suggested that even if the public were to demand a phase-out of nuclear power in the near to intermediate term, there would be no practical way to achieve it in countries that have substantial nuclear power programmes. Sweden is often cited as an example, where 50 per cent of the electricity is generated from nuclear power, and a Swedish referendum requires that nuclear power be phased out by 2010. However, the analysis of the Swedish electricity sector in Chapter 14 shows that not only is a nuclear phase-out possible in Sweden, but it can be achieved with a 50 per cent *increase* in electrical services. This is accomplished via investment in a range of end-use efficiency, substitution, and new supply technologies. Moreover, the average cost of a unit of electricity services decreases by 18 per cent between 1987 and 2010, even though the average cost of electricity increases by 11 per cent over the period and actual electricity consumption declines by 25 per cent from 1987 levels.[66] The study also shows that it would be feasible to reduce carbon dioxide emissions from the heat and power sectors in Sweden by 34 per cent over the period, and all of this is achieved with no increase in hydropower (as required for environmental reasons).

Seemingly counter-intuitive results such as these demonstrate the importance of integrated energy demand/supply planning, and they also suggest that the supply-side economic calculus that dominates most energy-economic planning may obscure optimal energy strategies. In any case, results similar to the Swedish case may be applicable to potential phase-outs of nuclear power in other countries.

13.3.4 Total social costs of nuclear and renewable energy technologies

In the future, the costs of environmental degradation and other 'externalities' will likely be included in the prices of energy supplied by different technologies. A first glimpse of the possible implications was provided in a recent study of the total social costs of electricity generation in West Germany.[67] The study examined general economic effects, employment, environmental impacts, health effects, and government subsidies – quantifying only those externalities which lent themselves to monetization. Four electricity generation technologies were considered: fossil fuels, nuclear, photovoltaics, and wind power.

The basic results were as follows. Measured in monetary terms, social costs for fossil fuels (2.4 to 5.5 cents/kWh) and nuclear power (6.1 to 13.1 cents/kWh) were approximately equal to their market costs, so that total costs for these technologies were roughly twice the market prices. However, social costs for the two renewable technologies represented a net social benefit, owing to employment gains and resulting wage and tax benefits. For wind power the benefit was 0.3 to 0.6 cents/kWh, and for photovoltaics 0.9 to 3.3 cents/kWh. When all external effects were accounted for, both wind and photovoltaic electricity cost substantially less than fossil or nuclear power.[68]

This assessment is a first-cut analysis, and some of its assumptions were necessarily crude.[69] Nevertheless, if similar findings are borne out in more detailed and refined assessments, they could have significant impact in shifting future investment priorities away from nuclear power and toward renewable energy technologies.

13.4 Unresolved problems with nuclear power

'Nuclear power is safe, non-polluting, ...[and] the question of nuclear waste is no problem at all', according to recent assurances from physicist Edward Teller.[70] The United States Council for Energy Awareness proclaims that 'Every day is Earth Day with nuclear energy'.[71] However, despite the negligible carbon and particulate emissions from nuclear power, several environmental, health, and security problems continue to plague the industry. Most of these issues are well known and have been widely publicized; hence only a brief overview is warranted here, emphasizing recent developments.

The nuclear accident at Chernobyl in the Soviet Union on 25 April 1986 resulted in the greatest release of radioactivity ever recorded in one technological disaster. Measured in terms of the dangerous radionuclide Cesium137, the release was equivalent to the fall-out from a large nuclear explosion.[72] Even more than 1,500 km away, fall-out in some places far exceeded the levels recorded during the period of atmospheric nuclear-weapons testing. Although only thirty-one people died in the accident itself, Chernobyl will lead to as many as 28,000 fatal cancers and 40,000 thyroid tumour cases world-wide, half of them in non-Soviet Europe.[73] Chernobyl demonstrated that large-scale toxic releases to the atmosphere can have extensive trans-national impacts for which no country is adequately prepared. World-wide, more than 700 million people live within 160 km of a nuclear plant.[74] Recently, a team of experts from West Germany, France, and other nations completed a study of nuclear plants in Eastern Europe, concluding that the reactors fall far short of Western safety standards, and in many cases should be radically modified or closed down.[75] Based on the accident rate established by Three Mile Island and Chernobyl, another study concludes that there is a 70 per cent chance of another nuclear accident in the next 5.4 years.[76] Should it occur in the Third World, consequences could be far more severe, as the emergency infrastructures and medical facilities are less adequate in many developing countries.

Nearly 400 nuclear power plants are operating world-wide, and there is still not a single long-term waste disposal programme in place.[77] Radioactive waste is steadily accumulating, as battles rage over what to do with it.[78] A recent review reaches the conclusion that we may end up doing what the previous generation did: pass the problem on to our children, unsolved.[79] In the United States, the two principal candidate sites for long-term waste storage have encountered increasing technical difficulties, as well as growing public opposition in the affected states (New Mexico and Nevada). The total cost of cleaning up US defence waste has been estimated at $150 to $200 billion over the next 30 years. In July 1990 the US Department of Energy announced that clean-up operations over the next five years will cost $28.6 billion, an increase of 50 per cent over its previous estimate made eight months earlier.[80]

Exposure to radioactivity may be more dangerous than previously believed. Estimates of cancer-risk from low-level radiation exposure have been revised upward about twofold, based on a re-examination of data from Hiroshima and Nagasaki.[81] More recently, startling results were announced in a study of childhood leukaemia near the Sellafield (formerly Windscale) re-processing plant in Britain. It has been known for some time that childhood leukaemia is unexpectedly high in the village of Seascale where the Sellafield plant is located. However, a study just completed reports that the increased incidence of leukaemia is correlated with paternal employment at the plant.[82] The results suggest that a father's exposure to routine low-level radiation on the job may increase his children's risk of contracting leukaemia by six- to eight-fold. Critics contend that the results may be due to chance, or that there is no evidence of a hereditary component to leukaemia. However, many specialists are grappling with new questions raised by the study. For example, while the new results appear inconsistent with bomb-data from Hiroshima and Nagasaki, it is possible that a heretofore unknown mechanism of genetic mutation has been identified that is associated with low-level radiation exposure during the months just prior to conception, or the ingestion of miniscule quantities of radioactive substances.[83] In any case, as the debate continues over the significance of the findings and the possible impact on radiation standards, public disenchantment in Britain is mounting as Sellafield workers are having difficulty obtaining health insurance, and the younger workers agonise over whether it is safe for them to have children.[84]

A major problem associated with the spread of nuclear power is that it substantially increases the risk of proliferation of nuclear weapons. Commercial nuclear reactors provide both the technological know-how and the necessary materials to make nuclear weapons. The typical 1,000 MW light-water reactor produces about 250 kg of plutonium each year, enough to make some twenty-five nuclear weapons.[85] (In the nuclear scenario analysed earlier, annual plutonium production in the year 2025 would be 1.3 million kilograms, enough to make 130,000 nuclear weapons each year.) As hopes for large-scale breeder programmes fade, the question of what to do with the plutonium is becoming ever more urgent. France and the United Kingdom currently have operating re-processing facilities, and West Germany and Japan plan to construct them. Both France and the UK have contracts to process spent reactor fuel from several countries, including Japan and West Germany. This activity raises the proliferation risk considerably, because the separated plutonium is ready for use in weapons.

13.5 Conclusions

Several questions have been addressed in this chapter. Can nuclear power avert the threat of global warming? Is nuclear power an economic means for reducing fossil-fuel dependence? Will nuclear power be necessary in the long term? Are the problems with nuclear power moving clearly toward effective resolution?

The answer to each of these questions appears to be negative. First, global expansion of nuclear power, even to absurd proportions, cannot prevent future fossil-fuel carbon dioxide emissions from growing. Thus, nuclear power does not provide a solution to the threat of greenhouse warming induced by fossil-fuel combustion. Second, energy efficiency offers much greater potential than nuclear power for abating carbon dioxide emissions, at much lower cost. For example, in the US, a dollar invested in electrical efficiency displaces nearly seven times more carbon than a dollar invested in new nuclear power. Third, in the long term, renewable energy sources, including solar, wind, and biomass technologies, offer greater promise than nuclear power for clean, inexpensive generation of electricity. Finally, nuclear power continues to be plagued by serious, unresolved health, safety, and security risks. Nuclear waste remains an unprecedented challenge, the potential for proliferation of nuclear weapons is aggravated by commercial nuclear power, and a possible link has just been reported between routine low-level radiation exposure among nuclear-plant workers and increased incidence of leukaemia in their children.

When weighed against the alternatives, nuclear power appears increasingly irrelevant to a sustainable energy future for the world. Given the bright prospects for energy efficiency today and renewable energy in the near to long term, it is unlikely that substantial nuclear power will be needed in the future – either as fission or fusion. Renewable sources already produce more energy than nuclear power in the United States, which has the largest nuclear programme in the world.[86] Some analysts argue that the proper role for nuclear power is one of transition: something to fill the gap until a sustainable renewable energy economy becomes possible. Perhaps – but this role already lies more in the past than the future. Nuclear power production has peaked and is beginning to decline in most countries. Energy efficiency is filling in the gap, and renewable technologies are rapidly coming of age. By the time today's new reactors come up for de-commissioning, renewable energy can take up the slack. The only prerequisite is that sufficient resources be allocated to renewable development over the next few decades.

Nuclear proponents are still hopeful about prospects for future passively safe reactor designs, smaller modular reactors, and the ultimate promise of thermonuclear fusion. However, these efforts appear increasingly unnecessary, because by the time they are developed (if ever), they will not be needed. Indeed, today's solar photovoltaic technology already achieves every dream of nuclear technology research: the solar PV resource potential is unlimited, its energy source is fusion (with a self-containing 'reactor' located a comfortable 93 million miles away), it is clean, it needs no fuel, it is passively safe, its waste and safety problems are relatively minor, it comes in all sizes from rooftop to utility-scale, and the necessary materials are effectively infinite (sunlight and sand). The only thing left to do is to bring down the cost, which will not be difficult according to informed assessments by the United States Department of Energy and Princeton University. In the meantime, electricity generated from wind and biomass already achieves the nuclear dream cost of a few cents per kilowatt hour.

Three areas of nuclear power research remain formidable obstacles to a global sustainable future: nuclear waste, de-commissioning nuclear plants, and preventing the diversion of nuclear materials. While these may not seem like glamorous research areas, future generations have a tremendous stake in our taking these challenges seriously. The vision of a sustainable energy future free of all fossil and nuclear fuels is now appearing on the horizon. A vital co-requisite is the responsible closure of the nuclear era.

Chapter 14
The Challenge of Choices: Technology Options for the Swedish Electricity Sector

Birgit Bodlund, Evan Mills, Tomas Karlsson, and Thomas Johansson

" ...This landmark study shows that Sweden's three goals – carrying out the Referendum decision to phase out nuclear power by the year 2010, not exploiting Sweden's four remaining wild rivers, and not adding to carbon dioxide emissions – can be achieved with a mixture of energy efficiency and an expanded role for renewables, and at lower cost than a business-as-usual scenario. In the most nuclear-intensive country in the world (on a per-capita basis), emissions of carbon dioxide and other substances can be lowered while switching completely away from nuclear power... " (Editor).

The power-production industry in Sweden is facing a major change. Following a public referendum in 1980 and several subsequent Parliamentary decisions, nuclear power, which now provides about one-half of the country's electric energy and one-third of its generating capacity, will be phased out by the year 2010. Other related national objectives include continued economic growth, improved environmental quality, reduced oil consumption, and increased use of sustainable, preferably renewable and domestic energy sources.

Environmental goals place strict demands on the electricity system in Sweden, some of which are potentially conflicting in nature. Hydroelectric power now provides the other half of Sweden's electricity. After some minor expansion, the construction of additional hydro-power capacity will be forbidden by law. Fossil fuels are not an easy alternative in light of a Spring 1988 decision by Parliament to set general guidelines restricting carbon dioxide emissions to their present level, and encouraging their overall reduction. Meanwhile, official forecasts of electricity-demand indicate continued growth from today's value of 130 TWh/year to 145 TWh/year in 2010, including losses,[1] with a broad range of uncertainty.[2] (Electricity demand is commonly expressed as terawatt hours [TWh]. 1TW is one trillion watts used for one hour.) This forecast implies a 0.5-per-cent/year demand growth-rate, much reduced from the 3.9-per-cent annual rate in the 1970–82 period and the 5.2-per-cent/year rate between 1982 and 1987.

All the above-mentioned factors will have great implications for the strategy of utilities in Sweden as they plan for the future. The global importance of the CO_2 problem could lead to a much larger-scale planning challenge involving many countries If nations follow the recommendations of the 1988 Toronto Conference – to reduce CO_2 emissions by 20 per cent by the year 2005 – key strategies will address the end-use efficiency of energy as well as the choice of primary energy sources and conversion technologies.[3]

Around the world, development of technologies for electricity production and end-use efficiency is proceeding, and consumer-oriented efficiency-improvement programmes are emerging. Most of the existing experience with demand-side management lies with the North American utilities. However, in Sweden, Vattenfall (the Swedish State Power Board) is conducting the 'Uppdrag 2000' project to help demonstrate efficient end-use technologies and identify the country's efficiency potential by working directly with power and heat customers, suppliers, and equipment manufacturers.

14.1 Conceptual approach

One way to gain perspective on the current situation is to construct scenarios that shed some light on the various possibilities and their implications. This chapter presents scenarios that focus especially on the technological options. Our objective is to examine the technologies and strategies that could be chosen to meet the multiple objectives, that is, with respect to the nuclear phase-out, keeping CO_2 emissions constant, and maintaining economic growth. Our analysis makes use of the assessments provided in the other analyses in the book *Electricity* from which this chapter is reprinted, and draws as well on other state-of-the-art studies of electricity-efficient end-use and generation technologies.

We begin with the simple observation that electricity *per se* is not of interest, but rather that the demand for electricity is a reflection of the demand for the *services* it can provide: hot showers, cold herring, clean clothes, illumination, motive power, maintenance of a comfortable indoor climate, data storage/retrieval, and so on. This perspective has led us to adopt end-use oriented methods in the preparation of our scenarios. Framing the analysis in terms of energy services helps to identify options and constraints that affect the electricity demand–supply balance, while delivering all of the energy services demanded by electricity users in a growing economy. This was in fact the perspective of Thomas Edison in starting the first electric utility. His ambition was to sell *illumination*, rather than electricity, realizing that as the efficiency of lamps inevitably increased his profits would also increase.

The boundary conditions of our study include all present (1987) electricity services from the direct uses of electricity in Sweden, and, because of the linkages in the supply sector, the energy services from district heating and from the heat produced in industrial co-generation. (Co-generation involves finding a use for the waste heat produced when electricity is generated.) Our analysis, then, does not include the energy services derived from fuel presently used in transportation, space heating, and industry, except that consumed in co-generation. Today's interruptible power (about 10 TWh/year, consumed in large electric boilers used in the district heating systems and industry), is also excluded from the analysis.

The scenarios developed below are all based on the same growth in these services, resulting from projections of 1.9-per-cent real growth in gross national product over the 1987–2010 period. This growth-rate reflects average growth, which is the same as that used in the long-term economic forecasts made by the Swedish Ministry of Finance.[4]

Our approach employs electricity-demand models and techniques that are used in the planning work at Vattenfall, with the exceptions noted below. We make use of the same future activity levels in all sectors and changes in life-style as those used in a recent Vattenfall demand-scenario study.

The demand-side scenarios are constructed in the following way:

■ **Reference Scenario.** This is one of several scenarios developed by Vattenfall for use as input into the planning of future power-production needs.[5] We chose a scenario close to the middle of the current official forecast interval for 2010.[6] This scenario is based on past Swedish experience of the market's behaviour, and assumes no policy measures (for example, incentives, standards, information) beyond those already existing, and an anticipated 50-percent real electricity price increase. Thus, adoption of efficient end-use technologies is based on the assumption that the decision-makers – for example, electricity consumers, retailers, consultants, and utilities – will act on their own accord and invest when motivated to do so by their individual perceptions of payback time, discount rates, and non-economic factors.

To prepare for developing the remaining scenarios, we employ a computational aid that we call the 'Frozen-Efficiency baseline'. The demand level corresponding to frozen efficiency is a projection of demand as it would develop given the increase in long-term economic activity and associated structural change within the anticipated GDP growth, but no improvement in efficiencies compared to the base-year levels. The Frozen-Efficiency baseline thus represents the 'electric energy service' level in the target year, based on efficiencies in 1987. With the following three scenarios, we then explore potential impacts of existing and emerging technological opportunities discussed in *Electricity*. The efficiency levels of electricity-efficient technologies are assumed to become average efficiency levels in the stock at the rate of capital turnover and expansion. Fuel switching, from electricity to oil and natural gas, is also incorporated. In contrast to the Reference Scenario, these scenarios utilize efficient end-use technologies that are cost-effective from a societal perspective (6-percent real discount rate), rather than from a private perspective.

■ **Efficiency Scenario.** This scenario is based on high penetration of the most efficient end-use technologies commercially available,[7] and cost-effective in comparison with new electricity supply.

■ **High-Efficiency Scenario.** This scenario is based on the previous scenario plus adoption of selected end-use technologies for lighting, motors, and several household appliances, in advanced stages of development or already developed but not yet commercialized.

■ **Advanced-Technology Scenario.** This scenario is intended to show the effect of adopting additional technology measures and strategies, still at the research-and-development stage, that cannot at this time be judged to be cost-effective.

It must be stressed that scenarios are not forecasts. The last three scenarios represent in no way what *will* happen, but rather what *could* happen if information, education and training, regulations, and incentives are orchestrated to steer the decisions of the many electricity users as well as investors and designers in this direction.

On the supply side, we determine the amount of new generation necessary to meet the difference between the demand levels resulting from each scenario and the existing non-nuclear capacity. We adhere to Sweden's standards of electrical-system reliability, ensuring that it remains at or above today's criteria for reliable operation. The power-generation technologies are assumed to be among the most efficient available and meet Sweden's environmental guidelines planned for 1995. Various options to provide the required electricity are then organized into three generation scenarios:

■ **Economic Dispatch.** The first scenario is based on the traditional notion of economic dispatch – new power-plants are constructed and utilized in order of increasing costs per kilowatt-hour supplied, including all costs for complying with present environmental regulations.

■ **Natural Gas/Biomass.** The second scenario includes currently unutilized forest-residue resources and some wind, and then proceeds with economic dispatch, excluding coal-based technologies.

■ **Environmental Dispatch.** The final generation scenario specifies new power-plants in order of increasing net carbon emissions per unit of electricity supplied. Biomass fuels from energy plantations are utilized in this scenario.

To facilitate comparisons between investments in conservation and in new generating capacity, all economics evaluations of the scenarios are made using a 6-per-cent real discount rate and do not incorporate the effects of direct energy taxes. For efficiency improvements, we use the annualized investment cost divided by annual savings as our cost-effectiveness indicator. For traditional power-plants and wind, we adopt cost-estimates used by the Swedish power industry. For new technologies, cost-estimates (which by definition have higher uncertainty due to lack of experience) are taken from other chapters in *Electricity*. We use the 1987 world prices for oil and coal. The price of natural gas is selected to equalize the busbar costs from gas- and coal-fired condensing power-stations – the costs of electricity 'at the gate' of a power station, before it goes into the electricity grid – based on the assumption that future gas prices will be negotiated this way. The cost-estimate for domestic biomass is also based on a 6-per-cent real discount rate, and is therefore below the present market price. Real energy prices are assumed to be constant during the 1987–2010 planning period. The basic assumptions are presented in Table 14.1.

Finally, by integrating our analyses of the demand- and supply-side options, we describe a range of choices and their key economic and environmental implications.

14.2 Electricity-demand scenarios

14.2.1 Methodology

To develop scenarios of future electricity demand, we employ four overview electricity-demand models used at Vattenfall: one each for residential appliances, services, industry, and space-plus-water heating. These models are end-use oriented and are essentially based on the notion that total electricity demand is the product of specific use (efficiency) and activity level (structure and utilization), summed over all activities in society. The models incorporate many sources of data on the structure and intensity of electricity demand in Sweden.

Table 14.1: Key economic, demographic, and structural assumptions in the scenarios
(all growth statistics are for the 1987–2010 period)

General

Population growth (million): from 8.41 to 8.60 (0.1%/y).

Gross domestic product: 1.9% real annual growth (index: 10–154).

Private consumption: 1.5% real annual growth (index: 100–141).

Public consumption: 0.9% real annual growth (index: 100–123).

Nuclear power phase-out period: 1995–2010.

Energy prices: real world market oil prices, $20/barrel crude (equals $26 heating oil)
  [the Reference Scenario uses $30/barrel crude in 2010].

  Fuel prices for power generation (fuel basis, lower heating value):

  Coal, 0.60 cents/kWh$_{th}$; natural gas, 1.10 cents/kWh$_{th}$; biomass, 1.25 cents/kWh$_{th}$.

  All energy prices reflect costs to Sweden, net of direct taxes.

  US$1 = 6.3865 Swedish kronor.

Household Appliances

The number of households (million): single-family – grows from 1.77 to 1.88; multi-family –
  grows from 1.95 to 2.24.

Persons/household: decline from 2.82 to 2.67 (single-family) and from 1.75 to 1.60
  (multi-family).

Degree of appliance saturations: Trends in saturation reflect life-style changes that include
  the increased consumption of white goods.

Service Sector

Floor area (million m^2): 148 existing in 1987, 23 additions, 5 demolitions.

1987 end-use shares and annual increase in electricity service to 2010:

  lighting (31%, 2.3%)

  motors, pumps, fans, etc. (37%, 3.1%)

  food preparation and refrigeration (17%, 1.6%)

  office electronics (14%, 4.5%)

  other (1.5%, 4.5%)

Industry

Structure: overall output increases by 2.6%/year (value added).

  The output of mining and textiles declines, respectively, by 1.5% and 1.0% annually.

  The greatest growth is in the engineering sector – 3.6% annually; chemicals 2.2%/year.

  Steel industry output 0.8%/year.

  The largest electricity use is in paper and pulp, where output grows at 1.6% annually.

Electric Space Heating and Domestic Hot Water

Electric heating equipment, GWh and million m^2 in 1987: [Electric resistance; electric
  boilers; heat-pumps; multi-fuel furnaces]

  Single-family homes – 8,700 (69.0); 4,300 (31.0); 390 (5.9); 5,800 (76.6).

  Multi-family homes – 900 (5.1); 500 (2.5); 500 (3.6); 2,600 (19.5).

  Service sector – 1,600 (8.0); 720 (4.4); 100 (1.7); 860 (15.7).

Multi-fuel heating equipment in single-family homes: net conversions, 13.5 million m^2; new
  homes, 20.5 million m^2; demolitions, 9 million m^2 (Reference Scenario only).

Total electricity demand is obtained by adding the results from the four models. When forecasting, Vattenfall uses these models plus more detailed material and supplementary models. Where possible, the results of interviews with energy users, large buyers, and firms supplying energy-using equipment are also incorporated. The size of Sweden makes it possible to incorporate customer-specific data, especially within the industrial sector.

The models vary, however, in their suitability for estimating the impacts of changes in end-use efficiency. The residential-appliance model is the best-suited for this purpose because it explicitly accounts for the efficiency of many different appliance end-uses and degree of saturation, life-style factors affecting them, and for their lifetimes in the stock. Because of lack of data, the service-sector model is the least developed; it provides only minimal end-use breakdowns without explicitly separating efficiency and structural-change factors.

This section will briefly describe the concept and structure of each model. Section 14.2.2 will then describe the scenarios that we have developed using the models.

14.2.1.1 Residential-sector appliance model In this model, appliance saturation, stock turnover, and efficiency are specified for thirty-five residential end-uses, including 'cottage industry', well-pumps on farms, and even 'weekend apartments' rarely occupied. Trends in private consumption, home area, persons per household, mix of single- and multi-family homes, utilization, saturation, and technical improvements are all specified in the model. In addition, small adjustments are made to account for a slight deterioration of efficiency as individual appliances age, and for product-change factors such as the anticipated increased use of microwave ovens.[8]

For some of the major appliances (refrigerators, freezers, and combination units), a separate stock/vintage model is used to trace each year's cohort of new appliances through their lifetime in the stock. A logit function reflects that some appliances remain in use for much longer than the average lifetime.

Surveys conducted by the National Bureau of Statistics, and interviews with large buyers (for example, housing-management companies) are used to incorporate consumer preferences into the estimates of future appliance type, saturation, and efficiency. The most attention is given to refrigeration, especially in multi-family buildings where it represents 40 per cent of non-heating electricity use. Price effects are not accounted for explicitly and are assumed to play a much smaller role in determining efficiency than does techno-logical change.

14.2.1.2 Service-sector model In this model, electricity demand in seventeen sectors is separated into lighting, motors, food preparation and refrigeration, general office electronics, and 'other' end-uses.[9] Future demand is estimated based on official projections of changes in employment, floor area per employee, number of firms, and so on.[10] Sub-calculations are made for floor-area-independent demand (for example, trains). The existing end-use and sub-sector data are so limited that no clearly separable efficiency effects are included in the forecasts made with this model. Instead, trended projections based on historic electricity-per-employee statistics are the determining factors. The growth-rates prior to 1982 – when the promotion of elec-tric heating was escalated in Sweden – are used by Vattenfall to esti-mate non-heating electricity trends for the future. Price effects are not formally included in the model.

14.2.1.3 Industrial-sector model Industrial electricity demand is modelled using a series of linked matrices, each containing parame-ters relevant to electricity demand. The matrices include fuel share, efficiency improvement, and production. For each matrix, different rate-of-change assumptions are made for four time-periods between 1987 and 2010. The model distinguishes among ten sectors plus 'small industry', defined as firms with five or fewer employees. End-uses include transport, lighting, processes (four sub-categories), and a space-heating and 'other' category for offices. Demand for each end-use is assumed to grow in direct proportion to production and is then modified by an efficiency parameter. Production is measured in mon-etary terms, but for the paper-and-pulp and steel industries produc-tion is also measured in physical units. Price effects are not explicitly accounted for in the model. (When used for forecasting, high future prices are assumed to result in the elimination of some electricity-intensive processes, for example certain electric arc furnaces, and sometimes to precipitate the closure of entire firms.)

14.2.1.4 Space-heating and domestic hot-water model Space- and water-heating in all sectors, except industry, are incorporated into one model. Single-family homes, multi-family homes, vacation homes, the service sector, and large heat-pumps are treated separately. Virtually no detail is included on water-heating for domestic purposes, an end-use that represents roughly 5 TWh$_e$ per year in single-family homes. For space- heating, an attempt is made to separate the effects of projected stock additions, demolitions, efficiency improvements, and price-induced conversions to and from electricity. In addition, about 50 per cent of all efficiency improvements in the appliance model are counted as increased electric heating in homes that have electric heating, because the reduced waste heat from these appliances will increase the need for electric space-heating during part of the year.

There is a large quantity of 'hidden heating' in Sweden, that is, electric heating used by customers that are counted as fuel-heating customers in the national statistics but in fact use electric heaters as well as (or instead of) fuel. Vattenfall estimates that single-family homes had at least 2.1 TWh of hidden heating in 1986[11] and multi-family homes 1 TWh.[12] This special type of heating is included in the heating model. Electric space-heating in industry is included as an end-use in the industrial model, rather than in the space-heating model.

14.2.2 The demand scenarios

The scenarios we develop in the following pages are intended to illustrate a range of choices. The demand scenarios differ in the assumptions made about end-use efficiency and the choice of energy-carrier for heating, and in the conservation-investment criteria used, as explained in Section 14.1. All other economic-growth, demographic, and structural factors are held at values based on long-term studies from the Ministry of Finance (see Table 14.1). The choice of the year 2010 as an 'end-point' is made because considerable attention is focused on this date in other energy studies and discussions in Sweden. Of course, the technology changes described here are ones that would occur gradually, and the exact year of full implementation would be a function of many factors.

In the following scenarios, we allow ample time for capital turnover. Net additions to the buildings stock are taken directly from those assumed in the Vattenfall model. The twenty-three-year time-horizon of each scenario (1987–2010) is longer than the lifetime of household appliances and is well within the time necessary to formulate and deploy programmes, incentives, and so on, designed to stimulate adoption of more efficient technologies at the time when replacement decisions are being made. This time-period is also longer than the lifetime for many technologies in the industrial sector, especially given that equipment is often replaced because there is an economic gain from doing so, rather than because it is 'worn out'. Aside from these considerations of capital turnover, the exact shape of the path from 1987 to 2010 is not analysed.

All calculations and assumptions are shown in a technical support document for this chapter, available from Lund University.[13] Brief supporting information and sources are given in the notes at the end of the chapter. The assumptions are based on chapters in *Electricity* and other published sources.

14.2.2.1 Frozen-Efficiency electricity demand The level of electricity services required in 2010 can be thought of as today's activity-level plus all growth in activity that would occur if the economy expanded as shown in Table 14.1 and end-use electricity efficiency remained at its 1987 level – for example, a 10-per-cent increase in steel production and no change in electricity use per ton of steel yields a 10-per-cent increase in the electricity services provided and a 10-per-cent increase in the electricity required. New technologies are thus assumed to have the same electricity efficiency as the present average.[14]

This 'Frozen-Efficiency' baseline is included as an analytical tool only, in order to be able to isolate the impact of efficiency in the scenarios from that of other factors embedded in the models.

The resulting level of electricity services (measured for the remainder of the chapter in units of TWh equivalent, TWh_{eq}) forms a basis from which to measure prospective efficiency improvements, without double-counting those embedded in any previous forecast or scenario. Table 14.2 contains the efficiency assumptions used in each of the following scenarios.

14.2.2.2 Reference Scenario The Reference Scenario estimates electricity demand in 2010, assuming market-driven conservation behaviour in an environment with real electricity prices 50 per cent higher than today's.[15] Conservation effects are included, based on individuals' investment perspectives. Fuel-switching in homes is based on an economic comparison of electric-resistance heating only, multi-fuel systems, or oil-only systems. Given time-of-use rate structures, customers are assumed to switch heating systems if there is at least a $85/year net benefit from doing so.[16] This is intended to reflect historic consumer behaviour. The scenario assumes the implementation of 90 per cent of those changes fulfilling this criterion. An average tariff is used for those with only electric-resistance systems. The scenario results in a net 3 TWh of conversions to electricity, mostly as a result of rate structures that favour the use of electricity for summer-time water-heating. An additional 0.6-TWh increase in space-heating demand results from the net demolition/ construction of buildings.

New buildings in the service sector are assumed to use 140 kWh/m^2-year (excluding electric space-heating), due to the increased number of electric end-uses. As a result of retrofits in existing buildings, the stock average remains at the present level of about 100 kWh/m^2-year in 2010. Developments in the industrial sector are quite varied. Efficiency as well as production-volume decline in some sectors and increase in others. The average efficiency of household appliances in 2010 is expected to be near today's best, due to technological change that is only partly driven by design-changes intended to reduce electricity use.

14.2.2.3 Efficiency Scenario In this scenario, we retain all of the structural factors from the Reference Scenario and explore the effect of high penetration of the best commercially available and cost-effective efficiency technologies described below and in greater detail in Table 14.2. Where household appliances are concerned, we assume that the efficiencies of presently best-available appliances become average in the stock.

In the service sector, we estimate the potential efficiency improvements from new lighting technologies; adjustable-speed drives for motors, pumps, fans, compressors (and more efficient motors and systems design); and retrofit of food-refrigeration and preparation equipment in existing buildings, and from high-efficiency office electronics. Measured results from 206 US buildings show median electricity savings of 19 per cent from retrofits, roughly 90 per cent of which had payback times of five years or less.[17] New buildings are assumed to be constructed with electricity intensities comparable to

Table 14.2: Efficiency assumptions in the Scenarios *(except where noted otherwise, the numbers shown refer to the % of base-year intensity)*

('Reference'), 'Efficiency', 'High-Efficiency', and 'Advanced-Technology' Scenarios

Appliances
Food storage (69), 49, 24, 24
Food preparation (86), 85, 69, 69
Lighting (61), 60, 59, 59
Dish and clothes washing/drying (56), 55, 19, 19
Miscellaneous appliances (89), 89, 76, 76

Services
Lighting (55), 36, 30, 30
Motors, pumps, fans, compressors (70), 65, 60, 60
Refrigeration and food preparation: 60 in all cases
Office electronics (65), 32, 20, 20
New buildings 140 kWh/m², 50 kWh/m² in all other cases (excludes space-heating)

Industry
Lighting (71), 45, 40, 40
Motors, pumps, fans, compressors (85), 70, 60, 50
Mechanical pulping: (included in total motors), 90, 80, 70
Process heating: (60)*, 80, 80, 80
Electrolysis: (75)*, 85, 85, 85
Steel scrap-melting: (included in process heat), 80, 25, 25
Conversions from electricity to natural gas (TWh$_e$) (0), 2.1, 3.6, 3.6

Space- and water-heating
Multi-fuel furnaces – conversion to oil (CO) or earth-source heat-pumps (HP)
[COP 2.7 Efficiency Scenario, 3.3 High-Efficiency and Advanced-Technology]:
  (0 (CO) and 0 (HP)), 72 and 18 penetration in all other cases.
Existing heat-pumps estimated to have COPs approx. 2.3 and are replaced (over 23 years)
  with the efficient models described in the previous note.
Electric boilers – earth-source heat-pumps in homes with electric boilers:
  (0), 90 penetration in all other cases.
Large heat-pumps:
  (60 conversion), 80, 80, 100.
Envelope retrofits in homes with direct electric resistance heating (penetration):
  (not indicated), 50 roof retrofits, 20 wall retrofits in all other cases.
New homes:
  (8,000 kWh/year for space and water heating), 2,500 kWh/year space heat and
  2,500 kWh/year water heat in all other cases

*Includes price-induced plant closures (Reference Scenario only).
Note: The Reference-Scenario values are enclosed in parentheses to distinguish them from those for the other scenarios. The Reference Scenario numbers are implied by the Frozen-Efficiency results, i.e. they were not used to derive the scenario. For detailed notes to the Table, see Johansson *et al.*, *Electricity*, notes to box 2, pp. 940–3.

the values described by Abel in *Electricity*[18] and from the measured performance for several hundred of the best buildings known.[19]

In industry, we estimate the increased energy-productivity opportunities from improved lighting, adjustable-speed drives and more efficient motors, used in well-designed systems moving gases or liquids, process-heat conservation measures and fuel switching (2.1 TWh$_e$), and efficiency improvements in 'office' equipment.

Savings in space-heating and domestic hot water in this scenario are derived from a combination of building-envelope and heating-system retrofits, plus fuel switching. For this purpose, we segment the stock into four parts, based on annual surveys by the national bureau of statistics in Sweden. The first segment has electric resistance heating and no ability to use an alternative fuel. The second segment heats with hydronic electric-only systems. Other buildings use electric heat-pumps. The fourth segment currently has the ability to heat with two or more fuels, including electricity.[20]

To estimate penetration in households, we assume, as in the Reference Scenario, that 10 per cent of the homes do nothing whatsoever. For those remaining: electric-resistance homes install insulation and upgrade their glazing if other renovation work is performed.[21] The very-high-use homes (over 30,000 kWh/year) install ground-source heat-pumps (COP 2.7); homes with electric-only boilers install heat-pumps; homes that can switch fuels are assumed to do so or to install heat-pumps.

To be conservative, we assume that all new homes use electric heating. These homes conform to the state-of-the-art performance described by Elmroth.[22] Triple-pane windows with coatings or gas fill, described in a paper by Granqvist in *Electricity*,[23] are included in new energy-efficient homes in the scenario. The current Swedish construction standard requires triple-glazing, but not coatings or gas fill.

We do not analyse envelope-efficiency improvements in buildings that switch fuels. There is a potential quick increase in electricity demand due to reconversion if the electricity-to-oil price ratio for any reason decreases (and policies do not respond).

14.2.2.4 High-Efficiency Scenario In this scenario, we assume (in addition to the previous scenario) slightly more effective lighting system retrofits in services and industry, adjustable-speed drive applications, and several advanced household appliances that are not commercialized at this time but can be designed using existing components. Heat-pump COPs increase from 2.7 to 3.3, based on a paper by Berntsson in *Electricity*.[24] We make a special scenario for steel, based on the Plasmascrap process described in studies by Eketorp and Santen and Feinman.[25] Plasma-beam heating is discussed more generally in a paper by Schaefer and Rudolf in *Electricity*.[26] Conversions to natural gas in industrial-process heating increase from 2.1 to 2.8 TWh$_e$ in 2010.

14.2.2.5 Advanced-Technology Scenario The final scenario makes use of measures that are technically possible but cannot necessarily be judged cost-effective at present. We convert to oil and conserve a total of 0.5 TWh of electric heating in vacation homes (out of a total of 2.4 TWh), 0.5 TWh of electricity used in large heat-pumps, and an additional 1 TWh of electric heating in single-family homes. In the steel industry, we assume the introduction of direct casting,[27] which saves 1.3 TWh by eliminating 75 per cent of the estimated need for motor power in the rolling process.

14.2.3 Electricity demand results

14.2.3.1 Overview The level of electricity services corresponding to the Frozen-Efficiency baseline is equivalent to 194 TWh/year by 2010. The Reference Scenario estimates generation at 140 TWh$_e$ – which means that 54 TWh$_{eq}$ equivalent of the required services will be provided with increased end-use efficiency and alternate fuels. In the Efficiency, High-Efficiency, and Advanced-Technology Scenarios, electricity generation falls to 111 TWh, 96 TWh, and 88 TWh, respectively.

The historic and projected sectoral components of total supply and demand are shown in Fig. 14.1(*a* and *b*). In light of the policy to phase Sweden's nuclear plants out of operation by 2010, the question immediately arises as to when new capacity will be required. The stepped curves in Fig. 14.1(*a*) reflect three possible nuclear phase-out programmes.[28] The middle case reflects a linear phase-out plan, and faster and slower cases are included for comparison. These three curves have clearly distinct impacts on the schedules for the construction of new generating capacity, which is required when demand rises above the stepped curve.

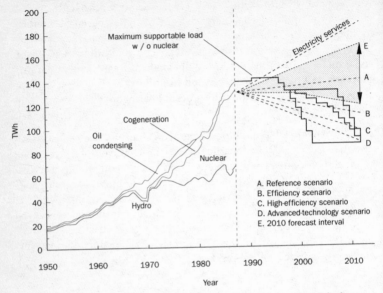

Fig. 14.1(a and b). Historic electricity generation and demand scenarios for the future. Figure 14.1(a) shows the evolution of Sweden's generation mix up to 1987. Peaking turbines have provided only about 0.1 TWh/year since the late 1960s. The three stepped curves represent the range of proposed schedules for phasing out Sweden's twelve nuclear reactors. The curves show the level of electricity demand acceptable with the current system reliability levels and no new capacity additions. The small vertical gap between 1987 and the scenario starting-point represents interruptible power. As shown in Fig. 14.1(b), since the beginning of the nuclear building period electric space-heating has risen from almost zero to over 30 TWh/year.

The sectoral breakdown for each of the four scenarios is shown in Fig. 14.2. Additional detail on the sector-specific supply of electricity is shown in Table 14.3 and in Figs. 14.3 through 14.6. Following are some key observations for each sector, and the overall reduction in specific needs (Efficiency, High-Efficiency, and Advanced-Technology scenarios):

- Substantial increases in efficiency occur in the household-appliances sector. Yet structural changes (increased numbers of appliances) offset much of the savings. Food-storage appliances offer perhaps the greatest efficiency potential. Overall specific needs decline to 66 per cent, 47 per cent, and 47 per cent of their 1987 levels.

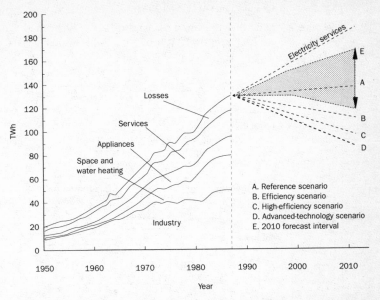

- In the service sector, demand falls, due mostly to improvements in existing buildings. New buildings represent 15 per cent of the total floor area in 2010. The greatest efficiency gains are in motors and so on, and in lighting. Overall specific needs decline to 50 per cent, 44 per cent, and 44 per cent of their 1987 levels.

- In the industrial sector, electricity demand in the Efficiency Scenario remains about the same as in 1987. Motors, fans, pumps, and so on are by far the most important end-use (64 per cent of all industrial electricity in 1987) and paper and pulp is by far the most important sub-sector. Overall specific needs decline to 70 per cent, 60 per cent, and 53 per cent of their 1987 levels.

- Existing fuel and equipment flexibility in the space-heating sector contributes to substantial electricity reductions via fuel substitution and the use of heat-pumps in existing hydronic systems. The Reference Scenario also includes conversions to electricity of 3 TWh$_e$ (because a crude-oil price of \$30/barrel is assumed). The Efficiency Scenario incorporates 6.9 TWh$_e$ of fuel-switching in buildings, which would increase Sweden's 1987 total oil imports by 4 per cent.[29] Overall specific needs decline to 39 per cent,

37 per cent, and 32 per cent of their 1987 levels.

■ Transmission and distribution losses are 9.2 TWh in the Efficiency Scenario, versus 10.6 TWh in 1987. Both numbers are based on losses equal to 9 per cent of demand.

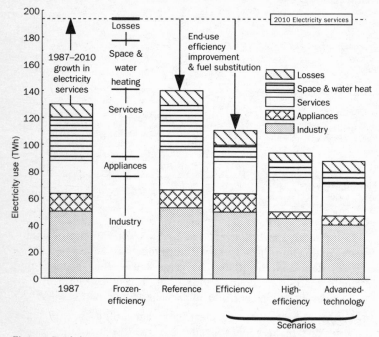

Fig. 14.2. Total electricity demand plus losses for 1987 and for the four scenarios in 2010. The level of electricity services supplied (from the Frozen-Efficiency calculations) is shown as the horizontal dotted line. The height of the bars represents electricity use and the gap between the top of each bar and the horizontal line represents the electricity services provided with efficiency improvements and fuel substitution.

Our results are consistent with those from a number of other similar studies in Nordic countries and elsewhere. Recent scenarios made for Denmark resulted in overall end-use electricity intensities at 66 per cent of the 1986 level for presently commercialized technology and 51 per cent for advanced technologies that could be made available within ten years.[30] A similar, and more detailed, study has been completed for Finland.[31] The authors identify a potential to reduce demand to 60 per cent of the level forecast for the year 2020.

Table 14.3: Summary statistics for the scenarios

Scenario	Energy used (TWh$_e$) 1987	2010	Average %/year growth rates (23 yrs)
Frozen-Efficiency baseline			
Industry	49.3	73.9	1.8
Household appliances	13.2	18.1	1.4
Services	24.2	46.9	2.9
Space- and water-heating*	31.3	38.7	0.6
Losses	10.6	16.0	1.8
Total	**128.6**	**193.6**	1.8
Reference Scenario			
Industry		54.2	0.4
Household appliances		13.2	0.0
Services		30.5	1.0
Space- and water-heating		30.0	−0.2
Losses		11.5	0.4
Total		**139.5**	0.4
Efficiency Scenario			
Industry		51.4	0.2
Household appliances		11.9	−0.4
Services		23.5	−0.1
Space- and water-heating		14.9	−3.2
Losses		9.2	−0.6
Total		**110.9**	−0.6
High-Efficiency Scenario			
Industry		44.2	−0.5
Household appliances		8.5	−1.9
Services		20.7	−0.7
Space- and water-heating		14.5	−3.3
Losses		7.9	−1.3
Total		**95.9**	−1.3
Advanced-Technology Scenario			
Industry		39.0	−1.0
Household appliances		8.5	−1.9
Services		20.7	−0.7
Space- and water-heating		12.5	−3.9
Losses		7.3	−1.6
Total		**88.0**	−1.6

*In 1987, the end-use shares were: single-family homes (61.0%), multi-family homes (14.3%), vacation homes (6.3%), services (10.4%), municipal heat-pumps for district heating (8.0%). Values may not add perfectly due to rounding errors.

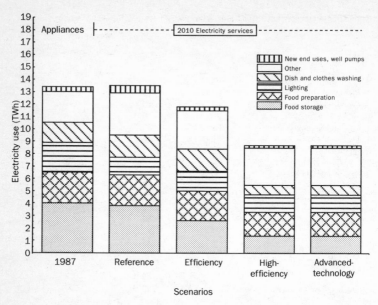

Fig. 14.3. Residential-appliance electricity-demand results for 1987 and for the four scenarios in 2010. Six end-uses are shown.

There are many examples from the United States, most of which focus on the residential sector and include both energy and peak-demand potentials.[32] At the state level, studies have been done for Michigan,[33] Texas,[34] the four-state Pacific Northwest Region,[35] and California.[36] Studies of electricity-demand potentials have also been conducted in Canada.[37] Many of these analyses employ supply curves of conserved electricity to rank the various conservation measures in order of levelized cost per kilowatt-hour.

14.2.3.2 Efficiency economics For most demand-side technologies in the Efficiency Scenario, we used the cost of conserved electricity (CCE) statistic to calculate cost effectiveness.[38] The CCE is the annualized investment in increased efficiency (and incremental operations and maintenance, if any) divided by the annual reduction in electricity use required to provide the same service. Thus, the result has the same units as the price of electricity (cents/kWh) and can be easily compared with retail prices or with the busbar cost of new supply.[39] Table 14.4 summarizes the results. Note that several

Table 14.4: Selected cost-effectiveness calculations for the Efficiency Scenario

End-use technology or strategy	Annual savings (TWh)	Cost of conserved or switched electricity (cents/kWh)
Measures requiring incremental investment		
Lighting (all sectors):	12.0	
compact fluorescents (3,000 h/y)		1.0
fluorescent systems (2,000 h/y)		1.6
Motors and pumps, compressors, etc.	18.5	1.4
Commercial food refrigeration	2.4	2.5
Residential heat-pumps:	5.7	
of which electric-resistance home	(2.0)	6.8
of which electric-boiler home	(3.7)	4.5
Appliances (excl. lighting)	5.1	0.6
Subtotal	43.7	1.9
Measures requiring little or no investment		
New home construction	0.6	very low
Miscellaneous office equipment	6.4	very low
Large heat-pumps	2.0	0.0
Fuel-switching for space-heating	6.9	0.0
Transmission and distribution losses	6.8	0.0
Subtotal	22.6	
Total	**66.3**	**1.2**
Residual non-monetized savings	16.3	?

(For notes to the Table, see Johansson *et al.*, *Electricity*, pp. 906–7.)

measures are shown at zero cost because they involve fuel-switching. The cost of the new fuel is counted instead in the final economic assessment in Section 14.4.

From the table, we can see that substantial cost-effective efficiency resources are available in Sweden, that is, are available at a fraction of the cost of new electricity supply. In Section 14.4.1 the demand-side resources we have identified will be ranked along with electricity-supply technologies in a grand supply curve for the year 2010.

Although capital investment is commonly required to achieve savings, some efficiency-improving technologies can increase electricity efficiency at zero or even negative cost. This can result from:

■ Gains derived from no- or low-cost changes in operations of existing technology;

- More careful selection among appliances available in the market-place;

- Technological change that has a 'side-effect' of improved efficiency;

- Reductions in labour and/or replacement costs that exceed the investment; or

- Complex engineering interactions that create 'bonuses' by reducing the energy demand in an end-use other than that targeted with the efficiency technology.

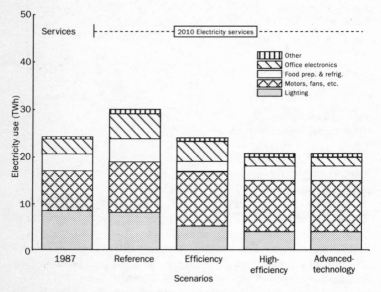

Fig. 14.4. Service-sector electricity-demand results for 1987 and for the four scenarios in 2010. Five end-uses are shown.

Today's market-place for refrigerators and freezers in Sweden provides a clear example of the sometimes imperceptible incremental cost for selecting the best available appliances (second point in the list above). As shown in Fig. 14.7(*a* to *c*), there is no correlation between the price and the energy-efficiency of refrigerators in Sweden.[40] This also holds for freezers and combination refrigerator-freezers.

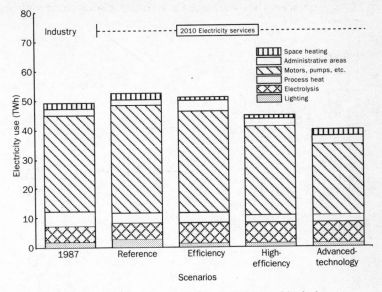

Fig. 14.5. Industrial-sector electricity-demand results for 1987 and for the four scenarios in 2010. Six end-uses are shown.

14.2.3.3 Electricity and economic well-being

Assuming that Sweden's GDP continues to grow at 1.9 per cent per year, electricity demand would decline at 0.6 per cent per year, according to the Efficiency Scenario. Thus, the ratio of electricity use to GDP would decline sharply while economic growth continues.[41] Sweden, like Canada and Norway, has enjoyed relatively low electricity prices and, partly as a result of this situation, many electricity-intensive industries and widespread use of electric space-heating in their cold climates have contributed to a high level of electricity use. However, assuming the development shown in the Efficiency Scenario, Sweden's 2010 electricity intensity will be similar to today's values for many other industrialized countries, as shown in Fig. 14.8.[42]

Comparisons of electricity use per capita are also interesting. In 1987, the intensity was about 17,400 kWh/capita. This may be compared with that of Japan (5,600 kWh/capita), West Germany (6,700 kWh/capita), or the US (11,000 kWh/capita). The comparison is shown in the left-hand set of bars in Fig. 14.8 for the OECD as a whole and for thirteen member countries.

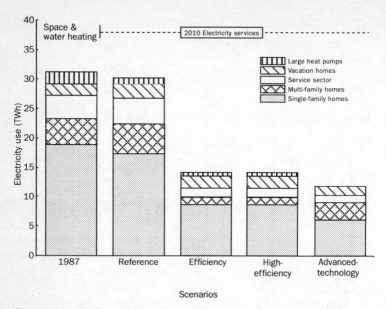

Fig. 14.6. Space- and water-heating electricity demand results for 1987 and the four scenarios. Five sub-sectors are shown. The main source of the difference between the Reference and the two Efficiency scenarios is fuel-switching and use of heat-pumps.

Fig. 14.9 puts each of the four scenarios in perspective with historic electricity demand and GDP. An interesting characteristic of the Frozen-Efficiency baseline is that the aggregate result for all sectors shows electricity use per unit of GDP as almost the same in the year 2010 as in 1987. This is in line with our assumptions insofar as electricity use per GDP can be considered a measure of national electricity use. This implies a break in the historic trend of increasing electricity use per unit of economic activity. This comes about because of structural changes in the economy towards less electricity-intensive activities, and in much-reduced growth in electric space-heating. In the 2010 Reference Scenario, electricity/GDP has fallen by 30 per cent; in the Efficiency Scenario it falls by about 50 per cent.

14.2.3.4 Factors that could lead to other scenarios No forecast or scenario can incorporate every determinant of energy use, nor can it account for all of the possible permutations of its assumptions. The

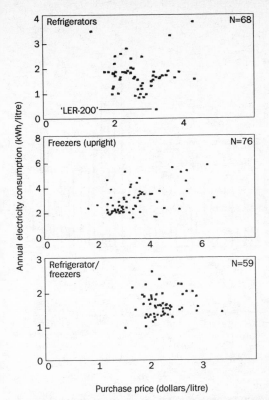

Fig. 14.7(a–c). *The non-correlation between appliance retail price and energy-efficiency. Each data point is a refrigerator, freezer, or combination refrigerator-freezer model sold in Sweden as of August 1987. Note that for a single price-level, efficiency, measured as kWh/litre-year, can vary by a factor of 2 or 3. Each model is government-tested according to a standard procedure (25 °C ambient, no door openings, no auto-defrost cycle). To compensate for varying freezer volumes in refrigerators with small freezer compartments and in combination units, freezer volumes are adjusted to their refrigerated-volume equivalents according to the US Department of Energy testing methodology. No such adjustment is made for freezers. A number of specialty models are excluded. The 200-litre Danish LER-200 (now marketed in Denmark by Brdr. Gram A/S) is shown for reference. A model of nearly identical size and price, but with twice the electricity use, is made by the same manufacturer.*

scenarios in this chapter are constructed within a given set of assumptions about the economy and about technologies. We add here a list of factors that could contribute to scenarios of either higher or lower electricity use. Some factors reflect differences in energy

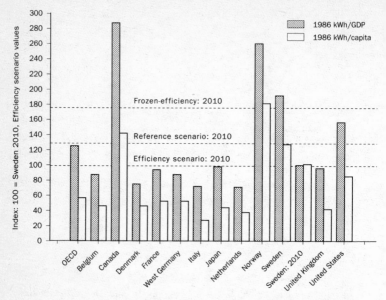

Fig. 14.8. Comparison of electricity intensity (measured as kWh/capita and kWh/GDP) in the Efficiency Scenario with that of other industrialized countries. The results for Sweden in 2010 are transformed into an index = 100 (third pair of bars from the right). Sweden's intensities in 1986 as well as those in the other countries are thus compared with the Swedish 2010 values. Horizontal lines for two other 2010 demand levels – relative to the Efficiency Scenario – are also shown.

service levels that would be associated with different developments of society and the economy:

- Alternate levels of energy services demanded by consumers;
- Alternate GDP growth trends;
- Changes in life-style other than those assumed in the structural and utilization factors in the appliance model and implied in the growth of electricity services in the Frozen-Efficiency baseline for the service sector;
- Alternate levels of immigration and domestic population growth;
- Different patterns of structural change in industry, for example a larger shift to more thermo-mechanical pulping in the paper-and pulp industry than the 44-per-cent increase in production assumed in the scenarios.

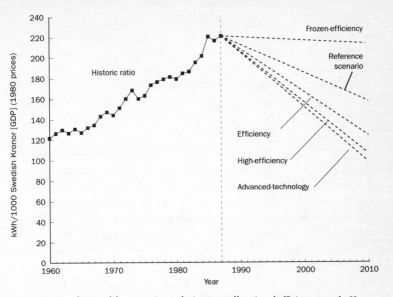

Fig. 14.9. Translation of the scenario results into overall national efficiency trends. Here, efficiency is defined as electricity use per unit of gross domestic product. The historic trend shows how electricity use increased much more rapidly than overall economic growth up to 1987, due in part to the steady growth of electric heating. All scenarios are based on annual GDP growth of 1.9 per cent. The values shown exclude interruptible power, up to 10 kWh/1000 kronor in recent years.

Other factors relate to the end-use technologies. The Efficiency and High-Efficiency scenarios are conservative insofar as a less-than-exhaustive list of efficiency technologies and strategies is included. There are many unexplored efficiency opportunities. The factors that could reduce electricity use further than in these scenarios include:

■ Technological change can bring entirely new efficiency opportunities, for example aerogel window materials or electrochromic smart windows. Only a few such improvements are included in the Advanced-Technology Scenario;

■ Half of the double-paned windows in electric-resistance homes are upgraded to triple-glazing, but only those constructed up to 1981. Greater savings could be attained by installing a third pane treated with a low-emissivity coating;

■ No operations-and-maintenance measures are included for the industrial and service sectors;

- Increased automation and controls can save large amounts of electricity but are not included here. Power-integrated Circuits (PICs) will lead to a new generation of 'smart motors' with efficiencies above those we have assumed;[43]

- Increased use of pollution controls can reduce waste and thus indirectly increase efficiency due to increased material productivity;

- Due to lack of data on the existing stock, no low-cost measures such as water-efficient showerheads and thermostat controls are included. Also not included are heat-pump water-heaters;

- The only building-insulation retrofits considered are those in homes heated with electric-only systems. Not only might additional retrofits be cost-effective in other buildings, but they would also reduce the risk of unexpected demand-growth if multi-fuel homes re-convert to electric heating;

- Except for the Advanced-Technology Scenario, no electric space-heating savings-potential is assumed for vacation homes;

- No fuel-switching is assumed for residential electric appliances, although a potential exists (stoves use 1.4 TWh, clothes-washing and drying use 1 TWh, and water-heating uses about 5 TWh in the Reference Scenario). No natural-gas substitution is assumed for commercial cooking equipment;

- Air-conditioning is an emerging end-use in new and existing service-sector buildings. We assume no efficiency improvement, although many options exist.[44]

Just as the factors described above could contribute to efficiency gains beyond those incorporated in our scenarios, a similar list may be constructed to enumerate factors that could work to push demand upwards:

- Technological change could introduce new electricity end-uses or processes, for example microwave drying of lumber in industry;

- Of the buildings that have converted from electricity to fuel, some could later convert back to electricity for heating following higher fuel-prices and the absence of balancing policies. The size of this 'virtual load' is 6.9 TWh, in the Efficiency Scenario;

- We have incorporated only to a small extent the 'take-back' of electricity savings in the form of increased energy services, for example increased lighting intensity or lamp on-time, higher interior temperatures, larger refrigerators, and so on;

- Persistence of savings. The deterioration of technology efficiency has been taken account of in the residential-appliances model (refrigerator and freezer efficiency declines by 1 per cent annually) but not elsewhere;

- Increased utilization of pollution-control equipment or increased ventilation to make 'buildings healthier' over what is already assumed could require additional electricity use;

- Additional waste-heat recovery in industry could conserve fuel but drive electricity use upwards more than assumed.

There are distinct differences in the potential magnitude of impacts from the uncertainties in the factors listed above. Uncertainties related to the factors pertaining to the development of society as a whole could lead to scenarios of significantly higher or lower electricity demand. The latter two groups of factors – concerning specific technologies and their performance – would affect national electricity use less.

14.3 Electricity/heat supply scenarios

14.3.1 Methodology

In this section, we develop electricity-supply and heat scenarios to couple with the demand scenarios described above. We take the same conceptual approach to supply-side technology as we did in our demand-side analysis. Here the goal is to illuminate some of Sweden's supply options by incorporating best available technologies as well as some which are still in the research-and-development phases but could be brought to the market well within the timeframes of a 1987–2010 planning period. We adhere to the system boundary, described earlier, that includes all of the services today provided by electric heating and other electric end-uses, industrial co-generation of electricity and process heat, and district heating.

An important objective in electricity planning is to obtain a production system that supplies power at the lowest possible cost, given the accepted reliability requirements.[45]

The stepped curves shown in Fig. 14.1(*a*) show Sweden's current reliability criterion and the generating capacity available in Sweden as the nuclear plants are phased out. The planning task is to bring new generating capacity on-line by the year when the demand curve rises above the stepped curve. Depending on the assumed demand scenario and which phase-out schedule is assumed, new capacity would be required some time between 1995 and 2010.

For new capacity, we utilize technology relevant to the Swedish context. To account for existing generation capacity, we use costs reported by Vattenfall and from the literature.

The integrated nature of heat-and-power production necessitates the explicit inclusion of district heating in our analyses. We assume that municipal district-heating demand in 2010 is the same as that in 1987 (38 TWh_{th} including losses). This is based on efficiency improvements in existing buildings being offset by the entry of new customers. The district heating today provided by refuse-derived fuel (RDF) incineration, waste heat, grey-water heat-pumps, and so on (5 TWh, or 13 per cent of the total) is included in the preceding estimate. In industry, we include 15 TWh of industrial-process heating, to be provided by a mixture of co-generation and boilers.[46] The electricity-production cost for a year is credited for the heat *sales* from co-generation during the year (that is, 35 TWh in the scenarios).

14.3.2 Electricity supply technologies

This section briefly describes the existing generating mix and various generation options and their economics. The variable cost estimates indicated for today's capacity are those used by Vattenfall.

14.3.2.1 Condensing power Today's non-nuclear condensing power in Sweden is based on oil. There is currently a generation capacity for 20 TWh/year, but less than 1 TWh is typically utilized. The variable cost of this oil-fired capacity is 3.9 cents/kWh. There are currently no gas- or coal-fired condensing power plants in Sweden. The total busbar costs for constructing and operating coal- and natural gas-fired plants in Sweden are estimated at 4.2 cents/kWh.

14.3.2.2 Combined heat and power (CHP) and industrial co-generation Today there is an installed CHP capacity in district-heating systems of 6.5 TWh$_e$/year, and about half of this is utilized based on a mixture of oil and solid fuels (peat and coal), with variable costs of 1.7 cents/kWh$_e$. The busbar costs for new capacity are estimated at 3.2 cents/kWh$_e$ in Sweden. Pressurized fluidized bed combustion (PFBC) systems may provide both electricity and useful heat while emitting less sulphur oxides than in conventional coal-fired power systems. Discussion of the state of the art in PFBC is provided by Pillai.[47]

Industrial back-pressure co-generation systems have been in the Swedish system since before 1950. Today's installed capacity can produce 5 TWh$_e$/year, much of which is in the paper-and-pulp industries. Production in 1987 was 3 TWh and the variable production costs are 1.6 cents/kWh. We estimate the total busbar cost at 3.1 cents/kWh.

Steam-injected gas turbines (STIG) fuelled with gasified biomass could potentially supply large quantities of power and heat in Sweden. As described in *Electricity* by Larson *et al.*,[48] such systems can be configured with absorption heat-pumps or as combined cycles to attain relatively high overall efficiencies. The total busbar costs of electricity generated by biomass-gas-driven turbines for Sweden are estimated at between 4.5 and 5.6 cents/kWh, assuming fuel prices of $3 per gigajoule including the costs of drying, chipping, and delivery to the power plant. This range is based on an avoided fuel cost of $2.0–$5.0/GJ in determining the heat credit; the natural gas prices in Table 14.1 correspond to about $3/GJ. In our analysis, we assume a higher fuel cost of $3.6/GJ,[49] and that the busbar cost of this option will be 5.6 cents/kWh.

Due to the small size of many district-heating systems in Sweden, turbine systems smaller than the 53 MW$_e$ ones assumed in these calculations would have to be used in many cases. A similar situation holds for the 25 MW$_e$ circulating fluidized bed (CFB) coal systems that we specify for co-generation. For the biomass CHP systems, this effect increases the capital cost by up to 60 per cent (at 5 MW$_e$), or approximately 0.7 cents/kWh. However, a higher heat credit is also attained by smaller systems and this will partially offset the cost increase. This effect is much smaller than the 50-per-cent increase of total busbar costs that we calculate in a sensitivity analysis of biomass cost in Section 14.4.2.

14.3.2.3 Gas turbines The installed capacity in the Swedish system is currently 1,800 MW. These oil-fired turbines are used as peaking capacity only. Total busbar costs are 9.7 cents/kWh.

New technologies make it possible to use natural-gas-fired turbines in baseload applications. The steam-injected gas turbines
(STIG) and intercooled steam-injected gas turbines (ISTIG) described
in *Electricity* by Williams and Larson[50] have busbar costs that are
competitive with traditional generating technologies and can be used
in electric-only or combined heat-and-power configurations.
Advanced gas-fired combined cycles are also an important technology, and may be based on natural gas, gasified coal, or gasified
biomass.

14.3.2.4 Wind power Sweden has sufficiently strong winds to institute the increased use of wind power. Land-use restrictions favour
the use of offshore plants. Cost estimates vary widely, depending on
siting and the quality of the wind-resource at the site. Experimental
wind stations exist and provide some indication of the investment
requirements.

According to a recent governmental committee report, sites have
been identified that would permit a generation of 1.5–7 TWh/year at
land-based sites and 22 TWh/year offshore.[51] However, this report
does not include any economic analysis. Vattenfall's current belief is
that the likely utilization of wind is 0–3 TWh/year at a cost of 7.0
cents/kWh.[52]

14.3.2.5 Fuel cells and photovoltaics Electricity and heat could be
provided with fuel cells during the scenario time-frame. Also, photovoltaic solar cells could perhaps provide some electricity during the
summers late in the scenario time-frame. Blomen and Carlson have
discussed the state of the art and prospects for the future.[53]

14.3.3 Resource constraints and potentials

Many new types of power-generation systems could be constructed
in Sweden. The introduction of systems based on natural gas is constrained by gas availability, prices, and the current lack of a gas-
transport network.

The potential for biomass-fired generation is also constrained by
fuel availability. Approximately 50 TWh/year of existing presently
unused biomass fuel could be recovered and utilized for power generation.[54] Gasified and then converted to electricity and heat in gas
turbines, this resource could generate about 15 TWh of electricity and

about 15 TWh of district heating. An additional 12–40 TWh of fuel could be cultivated in the form of coniferous mixed or deciduous forests on agricultural land that has either already been abandoned or is no longer needed (0.5–1.0 million hectares of fields and pasture land).[55] Field trials in Sweden indicate a higher sustainable biomass production rate (40–80 TWh/year) from this same land area.[56]

The industrial co-generation potential is a function of the need for process heat in industry. The heat need is in turn based on the introduction of heat-efficient processes. An estimate of the potential has been provided by Johansson *et al.*[57] We assume that half of this potential would be utilized by 2010, and that the systems used would have power-to-heat ratios of 0.7, based on steam-injected gas turbines. This will yield a potential electricity production of 3.5 TWh/year beyond today's level of 5 TWh.

14.3.4 The supply scenarios

To formulate various supply scenarios, it is necessary to adopt some decision-rules governing the selection and ranking of electricity-generation technologies and fuels. The key objectives are to minimize direct costs as well as non-economic factors such as emissions and energy-import dependency. To illustrate a range of possible outcomes, we construct three types of generation scenarios and apply them to the four demand scenarios developed above. In each scenario, we begin with an existing mix of 65 TWh hydro; 1 TWh each oil condensing and gas turbines; 5 TWh of industrial back-pressure.[58] In the Economic-Dispatch Scenario 6.5 TWh existing CHP is incorporated. In the other scenario existing CHP systems would be rebuilt/ replaced using new technology with improved power-heat production ratios. This supply mix includes an excess production capacity of 20 TWh that is needed to ensure the conventional planning criterion of 3-per-cent risk of energy shortage.

To the already existing generating capacity, we then add, in the specified order, additional capacity to satisfy the energy-and-power performance criteria. For co-generation we assume that up to three-quarters of the municipal district-heating needs are supplied through steam-injected gas turbines operated in CHP mode. The amount of electricity co-generated is determined by the system's annual average alpha value. When full heat output is not needed for district heating,

Table 14.5: Generation scenarios: power and heat production, fuel use

	Alpha (Power/ heat)	Busbar Cost (¢/kWh)	Economic-Dispatch scenario			
			Reference Scenario	Efficiency Scenario	High-Efficiency Scenario	Advanced-Technology Scenario
Existing Capacity (TWh$_e$)						
Hydro		2.01	65.0	65.0	65.0	65.0
Combined heat and power (CHP)	0.5	4.94	6.5	6.5	6.5	6.5
Oil-condensing power stations		5.85	1.0	1.0	1.0	1.0
Gas turbines		9.71	1.0	1.0	1.0	1.0
Industrial co-generation (gas)	0.5	3.10	5.0	5.0	5.0	5.0
New Capacity (TWh$_e$)						
Industrial co-generation (biomass)	0.7	5.30	0.0	0.0	0.0	0.0
Fluidized bed/CHP (coal)	0.5	3.19	5.3	5.3	5.3	4.8
Steam-injected cycle CHP (gas)	1.1	3.19	5.3	5.3	5.3	4.8
Steam-injected cycle CHP (biomass)	1.1	5.60	0.0	0.0	0.0	0.0
Central station (coal)		4.17	25.2	10.9	3.4	0.0
Combined cycle (gas)		4.17	25.2	10.9	3.4	0.0
Wind generators		7.00	0.0	0.0	0.0	0.0
Total Electric Generation (TWh$_e$)			139.5	110.9	95.9	88.0
Combined Heat and Power, Industrial Process Heat						
Industrial co-generation (TWh$_{th}$)			10.0	10.0	10.0	10.0
Municipal CHP (TWh$_{th}$) [includes 5 TWh RDF, etc.]			33.4	33.4	33.4	31.8
Supplemental district heating or process heat (TWh$_{th}$)			9.6	9.6	9.6	11.2
Second-Order Fuel Use						
Fuel-switching, to oil from electricity (TWh$_e$)			–3.0	6.9	6.9	7.9
Fuel-switching from electricity to natural gas in industry (TWh$_e$)			0.0	2.1	3.6	3.6
Total Fuel Use (all energy services) (TWh)						
Coal			96	60	41	31
Oil			17	29	29	32
Gas			86	55	42	33
Biomass			0	0	0	0
Total			199	144	112	96

the excess heat is used to raise steam which is injected into the gas turbine to enhance power production.[59] The alpha value just cited refers to the ratio of total annual electricity produced to the total heat produced for district heating.

Detailed descriptions of the scenarios, economics, and emissions are shown in Bodlund *et al.*,[60] and the generation mix for each scenario is shown in Table 14.5.

Natural Gas/Biomass scenario				Environmental-Dispatch scenario			
Reference Scenario	Efficiency Scenario	High-Efficiency Scenario	Advanced-Technology Scenario	Reference Scenario	Efficiency Scenario	High-Efficiency Scenario	Advanced-Technology Scenario
65.0	65.0	65.0	65.0	65.0	65.0	65.0	65.0
0.0	0.0	0.0	0.0	0.0	0.0	0.0	0.0
1.0	1.0	1.0	1.0	1.0	1.0	1.0	1.0
1.0	1.0	1.0	1.0	1.0	1.0	1.0	1.0
5.0	5.0	5.0	5.0	5.0	5.0	5.0	5.0
3.5	3.5	3.5	3.5	3.5	3.5	3.5	3.5
0.0	0.0	0.0	0.0	0.0	0.0	0.0	0.0
18.3	18.3	4.4	0.0	5.0	5.0	0.0	0.0
13.0	13.0	13.0	9.5	26.3	26.3	17.4	9.5
0.0	0.0	0.0	0.0	0.0	0.0	0.0	0.0
29.7	1.1	0.0	0.0	29.7	1.1	0.0	0.0
3.0	3.0	3.0	3.0	3.0	3.0	3.0	3.0
139.5	110.9	95.9	88.0	139.5	110.9	95.9	88.0
15.0	15.0	15.0	15.0	15.0	15.0	15.0	15.0
33.4	33.4	20.8	13.6	33.4	33.4	20.8	13.6
4.6	4.6	17.2	24.4	4.6	4.6	17.2	24.4
–3.0	6.9	6.9	7.9	–3.0	6.9	6.9	7.9
0.0	2.1	3.6	3.6	0.0	2.1	3.6	3.6
0	0	0	0	0	0	0	0
4	17	31	31	4	17	11	12
124	60	32	23	96	32	23	23
50	50	50	50	90	90	84	68
178	127	113	104	190	139	118	103

14.3.4.1 Economic-Dispatch Scenario In order of increasing busbar cost, new power-plants are constructed and used to meet the demand in excess of that provided by the existing plants. Here, the usage of the term Economic-Dispatch refers to long-term planning and is analogous to the short-term decision rule about which plants to operate. We assume a 50-per-cent coal, 50-per-cent natural-gas generation mix. This is based on the assumption that market forces will cause gas prices to adjust until there is parity with the costs of gas-fired and between coal-fired electric power generation.

14.3.4.2 Natural Gas/Biomass Scenario In this scenario, Sweden's existing *non-utilized* biomass resources (50 TWh fuel) are used to produce heat and electricity. The biomass is gasified and used first in steam-injected gas turbines to produce useful heat and electricity, and then in district-heating boilers if the electricity demand has been satisfied, and there are remaining biomass fuel resources. For industry, this includes 3.5 TWh_e of new biomass-fired co-generation systems with alpha values of 0.7 as described by Larson *et al.* for steam-injected systems operating almost year-round at full heat output. We also include 3 TWh_e of wind-generated electricity to represent Vattenfall's estimate of the resource that might be exploited. Natural-gas generation is then introduced according to economic dispatch, that is, combined heat and power until the district-heating demand is met and then conventional power stations.

14.3.4.3 Environmental-Dispatch Scenario In this scenario, new power-plants are constructed and used to meet the electricity and district-heating demand in order of increasing CO_2 emissions. Biomass residues plus up to 40 TWh (fuel) production from 'energy plantations' are utilized in combined heat-and-power stations, industrial co-generation systems, and for district heating. Wind-power is utilized as in the previous scenario (3 TWh). If needed, electricity and heat are then generated with natural gas according to economic dispatch.

14.4. Integrated resource planning

This section integrates the final supply-and-demand scenarios. We determine the total cost of operating the system in the various supply/demand scenarios just described, i.e. the combined cost of supplied and conserved electricity.

14.4.1 The integrated resource supply curve

The concept of supply curves is commonly used in energy planning, and is especially useful when a diversity of resources are to be considered. In a supply curve, the available resources are ranked in order of increasing cost. We use the concept of the traditional supply curve in a new way by combining *conserved* and *supplied* electricity – the sum of these two components is the total electric-energy service of 194 TWh$_{eq}$ defined earlier by the Frozen-Efficiency baseline.

A supply curve can be presented as a series of steps, with cumulative supply on the horizontal axis and the incremental cost of each supply addition on the vertical axis. For supply-side resources, the *y*-axis value is the levelized busbar cost (cents/kWh) and for demand-side resources it is the cost of conserved electricity (also cents/kWh). We developed supply curves that combine these two kinds of resources, based on a ranking of their costs.

Twelve different supply curves could be drawn for various combinations of the four supply scenarios and three generation scenarios presented in this chapter. Each would supply 194 TWh$_{eq}$ of electricity services, but would do so with varying mixes of efficiency measures and types of power plants. Two such 'integrated supply curves' are shown in Fig. 14.10(*a* and *b*). The first figure represents the Reference Scenario for demand and the Economic-Dispatch Scenario for supply, and the second figure shows the Efficiency Scenario and the Environmental-Dispatch Scenario. (Note that the supply curve is used here to rank and compare changes in electricity use resulting from some sort of capital investment. Therefore, the costs of fuels that replace electricity are included below instead of in the supply curves.) Sweden's district heating and industrial back-pressure heat-needs are also met in the scenarios but are not shown explicitly in the curves.

To present another aspect of the results, in Fig. 14.11(*a* and *b*) we show the monthly electricity demand for the same supply/demand scenario combinations shown in the previous two figures.[61] In Fig. 14.11(*b*), electricity is supplied mostly with domestic resources. The decreased seasonality of demand is also notable, mainly due to the assumed switching from electricity to fuel, primarily oil, for space-heating. Hydro capacity is utilized differently in the two scenarios, in order to operate the CHP systems efficiently.

14.4.2 Scenario economics

Many types of economic costs are included within the system boundary that we have defined for the scenarios. We have tabulated the annualized costs of existing electricity capacity, new electricity

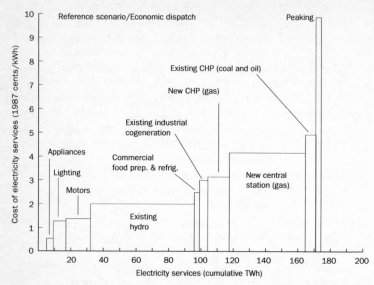

Fig. 14.10(a and b). 'Integrated electricity' resource supply curves for Sweden. The curves rank scenario end-use technologies and new supply technologies (described in the chapter) according to their levelized per-kWh costs (6-per-cent real discount rate). The x-axis measures cumulative electricity conserved or supplied by 2010 with respect to the Frozen-Efficiency baseline and the y-axis measures the levelized cost for each technology. Fuel-switching is shown at zero cost because this is electricity use in buildings with existing multi-fuel systems that have an operating cost reduction at essentially no capital cost. The operating costs for fuel are counted in the section on total societal economics. The supply curves shown exclude efficiency savings for which we have not determined the investment cost.

capacity, district heating, natural-gas transmission, fuels used in switching away from electric space-heating and electric-based process heating in industry, and the investments in improved efficiency. Focusing first on electric-energy services, we can define the total cost of these services as the annual investment in generating capacity, efficient end-use technology, and fuel switching, divided by 194 TWh_{eq} (Table 14.6). In every case, total costs tend to decline as efficiency increases. This is because the average cost of conserved electricity is lower than the average supply cost.[62]

All of the energy services in our system (obtained by combining district heating and process heat with the results just discussed) amount to 247 TWh_{eq} (194+53). The costs per kilowatt-hour

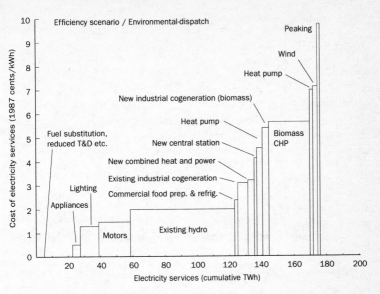

equivalent of these energy services are comparable to today's busbar costs of electricity and district heating in Sweden, both about 2.8 cents/kWh. This busbar cost is, by definition, equal to the costs of electricity services in 1987. The annualized societal costs are summarized in Fig. 14.12. The costs lie between $5.5 and $7.0 billion per year (2.2–2.8 cents/kWh$_{eq}$) over the full range of supply-and-demand scenarios.

The average cost of the new electricity supply would range from 3.2 cents/kWh to 5.8 cents/kWh$_e$ (including wind) (Table 14.7). The marginal cost would be up to 5.6 cents/kWh, when biomass is the marginal resource.

We tested the sensitivity of the results shown in Table 14.6 to alternate assumptions about the cost of conservation:

- By increasing the cost of conserved electricity by 50 per cent, the cost of electric energy services for the High-Efficiency/Environmental-Dispatch Scenario rises from 2.3 to 2.7 cents/kWh$_{eq}$, still less than the 1987 value of 2.8 cents/kWh$_{eq}$;
- The Reference Scenario/Economic-Dispatch result rises from 2.6 to 2.8 cents/kWh$_{eq}$ given the same assumption.

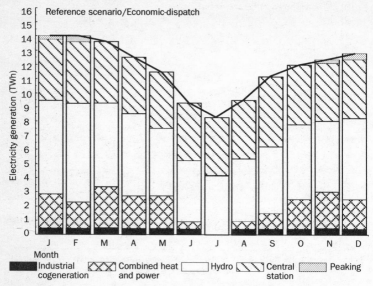

Fig. 14.11(a and b). Monthly electricity generation and supply mix corresponding to two demand scenarios. Fig. 14.11a shows the Reference Scenario demand level and the Economic-Dispatch supply mix. Fig. 14.11b shows the Efficiency Scenario and the Environmental-Dispatch supply mix with 90 TWh of biomass fuel availability. The demand for lighting and space-heating (including that in industry) is allocated to the months according to average-year heating degree-days in Stockholm. Water-heating in one-fuel systems is spread evenly over the months. Because of the presence of time-of-use rates, electric water-heating in multi-fuel systems is assumed to occur in the six-month summer period March–August. Based on historical statistics, industrial demand during the national holiday month (July) declines by 33 per cent. Monthly hydro production in 2010 is based on Vattenfall's estimates for an average rainfall year. Power generation by co-generation systems is curtailed during the summer because of minimal need for district heating.

We also tested the impact of 50-per-cent higher biomass fuel costs. This would result in biomass-STIG busbar costs of 7.6 cents/kWh, up from the base case value of 5.6 cents/kWh:

■ For the Environmental-Dispatch Scenario, the total electricity-service costs for the Reference Scenario and High-Efficiency Scenario demand levels were 3.2 cents/kWh and 2.6 cents/kWh, respectively, up from the base case values of 2.9 cents/kWh and 2.3 cents/kWh;

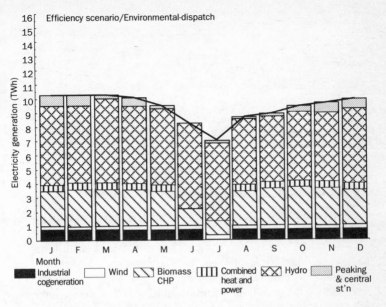

Efficiency scenario/Environmental-dispatch

Electricity generation (TWh) — Month: J F M A M J J A S O N D

Legend: Industrial cogeneration | Wind | Biomass CHP | Combined heat and power | Hydro | Peaking & central st'n

■ For the Reference/Environmental-Dispatch Scenario, the average cost for new electricity supply will rise from 4.9 to 5.8 cents/kWh$_e$. For High-Efficiency/Environmental-Dispatch, the cost will rise from 5.7 to 7.5 cents/kWh$_e$.

Even given these assumptions, the fact remains that costs for electricity services in the Efficiency scenarios are lower than in the Reference scenario, as does, of course, the fact of the higher costs of biomass-using scenarios in relation to fossil-fuel-only scenarios.

Table 14.6: Total annualized costs for all 194 TWh$_{eq}$ electric energy services; generating capacity, efficient end-use technology, and fuel-switching *(cents/kWh$_{eq}$)*

Supply scenario	1987	Reference Scenario	Efficiency Scenario	High-Efficiency Scenario	Advanced-Technology Scenario
		<———————— Demand scenario ————————>			
Electric energy services (TWh$_{eq}$)		194	194	194	194
of which electricity supply (TWh$_{eq}$)	129	140	111	96	88
Economic-Dispatch (ckWh$_{eq}$)	2.8	2.6	2.3	2.1	—
Natural Gas/Biomass (ckWh$_{eq}$)		2.7	2.4	2.3	—
Environmental-Dispatch (ckWh$_{eq}$)		2.9	2.6	2.3	—

Table 14.7: Average cost of new capacity *(cents/kWh$_{eq}$)*

Supply scenario	<--- Demand scenario --->			
	Reference Scenario	Efficiency Scenario	High-Efficiency Scenario	Advanced-Technology Scenario
Electricity Generation (TWh$_e$)	68	39	24	15
Economic-Dispatch	4.0	3.8	3.6	3.2
Natural Gas/Biomass	4.4	4.5	5.3	5.8
Environmental-Dispatch	4.8	5.3	5.7	5.8

14.5 Carbon dioxide and other emissions

The quantitative assessment of the emissions associated with power and heat generation is playing an increasingly large role in energy systems analysis and energy policy. The most ominous manifestation of energy-related emissions is global warming, commonly known as the greenhouse effect. For each demand-and-supply scenario, we have assessed the output of carbon dioxide, the main greenhouse gas.[63] In addition, we have tabulated the airborne emissions of certain heavy metals (cadmium and mercury), hydrocarbons, sulphur, and NO$_x$, plus solid waste materials (for example, ash) left behind.

For each generation mix in the supply scenarios, we apply emissions factors for state-of-the-art combustion technologies.[64] All new generating capacity in the scenarios complies with Sweden's 1995 guidelines for sulphur, NO$_x$, and particulates emissions.[65] In the Economic-Dispatch Scenario, we assume today's fuel-mix in existing central heat and power production: approximately 70 per cent coal, 30 per cent heavy fuel oil. For the purpose of estimating emissions from the district-heating sector and from industrial-process heat, we assume a fuel conversion efficiency of 85 per cent and exclusive use of natural gas, where biomass is not used.

Because each efficiency scenario incorporates some fuel substitution, we include the associated emissions from this increase in fuel use. Most of the effect is due to conversions from electricity to heating-oil (6.9 TWh$_e$) and the replacement (upon retirement) of large-scale heat-pumps with fuel-based district-heating systems (2 TWh$_e$), but there is also increased natural-gas use in the steel industry that displaces electricity now used in electric arc furnaces and other

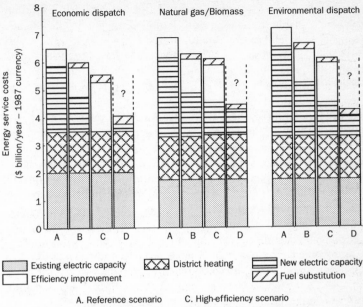

Fig. 14.12. *Energy service costs in 2010. The total annualized costs for 247 TWh$_{eq}$ energy services today provided by direct electricity production, combined heat and power, industrial co-generation, efficiency investments, and the costs of substitute fuels are included in the diagram. No conservation investment has been estimated for the Advanced-Technology Scenario. The values for existing capacity vary in some cases because some existing CHP capacity and industrial back-pressure are replaced with biomass-fired generators in those scenarios. Costs are based on constant real fuel prices shown in Table 14.1.*

process-heating tasks (about 4 TWh$_e$).[66] In order not to underestimate the CO_2 effects, we assume that all conversions from electric space-heating are to oil (while in reality some will likely be to wood fuel, which makes no net CO_2 additions to the atmosphere, or to natural gas). The Reference Scenario includes some switching from fuel to electricity, and we credit this to lower emissions from oil-fired heating systems.

As mentioned earlier, a present national goal is to freeze current CO_2 emissions. The current levels from the power and heat sector are low, due to an electricity production mix that is based almost entirely on nuclear and hydroelectric power. Were there interest in constructing fossil-fuel-based power plants, the option always exists to seek offsets outside the power and heat sector, but this strategy may be unacceptable in the long run. Natural gas might be allowed as a transitional fuel if carbon dioxide emissions can be correspondingly reduced in other sectors. The same holds for other fossil fuels, although the reduction of CO_2 emissions in other sectors would then have to be larger because of the higher amounts of CO_2 released when using these other fuels.

In Fig. 14.13(a–d) the carbon emissions from the heat and power sector (247 TWh_{eq}) are shown for each generation and demand scenario. The curves show the total annual costs of providing the energy services. The results for carbon reveal an extremely broad range of emissions and yet very similar costs, regardless of the generation mix. The set of bars accompanying the Economic-Dispatch Scenario show that efficiency will indeed reduce carbon, but not nearly enough to meet the target. On the other hand, the Environmental-Dispatch Scenario may not suffice either. A combination of substantial efficiency improvement *and* low-carbon generation technologies is the only solution among the twelve combinations shown. And, as shown in Fig. 14.13, the total societal economic costs of the high-CO_2 scenarios may be *higher* than the costs of the low-CO_2 scenarios.

As shown in Table 14.8, only four of the twelve scenario combinations result in per-capita carbon emissions – including those emissions outside the power and heat sector – equal to or lower than those in 1986.[67] However, even the best case is nearly twice the world average of about 1 ton/capita annually.[68]

In the highest emissions case, total carbon emissions increase to over 150 per cent of their 1986 levels and those from the heat and power sector alone increase to about 500 per cent. In contrast, the High-Efficiency/Environmental-Dispatch case results in a 10-per-cent reduction in CO_2 from today's levels. Emissions from the power and heat sector alone decline by 35 per cent from today's levels (Table 14.9). In 1986, the power and heat sectors accounted for 15 per cent of Sweden's CO_2 emissions whereas – assuming constant emissions from other sectors – in 2010 with coal/gas economic dispatch and efficiency improvements corresponding to the Reference Scenario, it would be the source of 50 per cent of national emissions.

No CO_2 emissions from the transportation of fuels are included. For domestic biomass they will be very small, but this is not necessarily the case for the import of coal.

We calculated the offsets required for each scenario if carbon emissions from the power and heat sector are to remain at their present levels. In all but three of the twelve cases, substantial offsets would be necessary. For reference, total 1986 carbon emissions from industry were approximately 4.2 megatons/year; from residential space-heating 3.8 Mtons/year; and from road transport 4.7 Mtons/year. Based on the emissions shown in Fig. 14.13, achieving the highest offset of about 10.5 Mtons/year does not seem conceivably possible. Attaining full offsets in any of the Economic-Dispatch cases would be quite difficult, as it would for the Reference Scenario demand for any of the three generation strategies. Substantial improvements in automobile efficiency and additional efforts to conserve heating-oil in the buildings sector could in principle achieve sufficient offsets for some cases where the natural gas/biomass systems are used. However, it must be kept in mind that these offsets may be needed to meet future agreements, such as those outlined in the recent Toronto and Hamburg recommendations that call for 20–50-per-cent reductions in CO_2 emissions by 2005 and 2015, respectively.[69]

Table 14.8: Per-capita carbon emissions – all sectors *(tons/capita-year)*

		<---	Demand Scenario	--->	
Supply Scenario	1986	Reference Scenario	Efficiency Scenario	High-Efficiency Scenario	Advanced-Technology Scenario
Economic-Dispatch	1.91	3.10	2.67	2.40	2.27
Natural Gas/Biomass		2.26	1.99	1.96	1.89
Environmental-Dispatch		2.10	1.83	1.73	1.74

Table 14.9: Carbon emissions in 2010 – power and heat sector *(Mtons/year)*

(Mtons/year)		<---	Demand scenario	--->	
Supply Scenario	1986	Reference Scenario	Efficiency Scenario	High-Efficiency Scenario	Advanced-Technology Scenario
Economic-Dispatch	2.9	13.6	9.9	7.6	6.5
Natural Gas/Biomass		6.4	4.1	3.8	3.3
Environmental-Dispatch		5.0	2.7	1.9	2.0

Another alternative – the control of CO_2 emissions from fossil-fuelled power plants – has been proposed, but in coal plants it is estimated that 16 per cent of the power plant's capacity would be required to operate the control system, and overall production costs

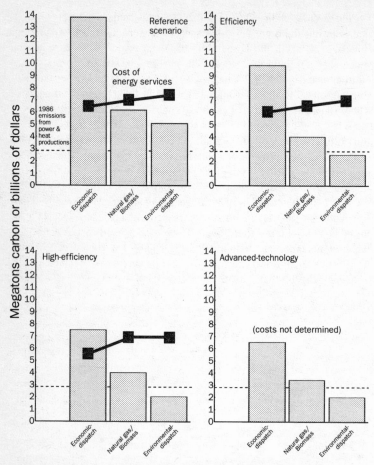

Fig. 14.13(a–d). Annual carbon emissions from the production of heat and power within the system boundary, plus the use of substitute fuels in 2010. Results are shown for each generation scenario and demand scenario. The total costs of energy services from Fig. 14.12 are given by the curves.

would increase by 56 per cent to 100 per cent. The capital investment would range from 70 per cent to 150 per cent of the existing capital investment.[70]

Some additional carbon reductions will occur over the short run if biomass plantations are used. These plant materials will absorb carbon from the atmosphere for as many years as the size or intensity of plantation area is being increased. We have not included this 'biomass buffering' effect in our analysis.

We also evaluated other emissions. Fig. 14.14(a and b) present a comparison of carbon dioxide and other emissions by showing an index for each by-product for each demand level, where 100 equals the Reference Scenario/Economic-Dispatch combination. In the fossil-based Economic-Dispatch generation scenario, nitrogen oxides, polyaromatic hydrocarbons, and heavy metals (cadmium and mercury) are approximately 40–70 per cent lower in the Efficiency scenarios than in the Reference case. Cadmium levels are only slightly lower in the Environmental-Dispatch Scenario because those in coal are replaced by those in biomass. There is an important difference, however, in that coal-mining mobilizes heavy metals otherwise bound in mineral form (and the greenhouse gas methane), thereby increasing the amount of heavy metals circulating in the bio-geological system.

For all pollutants, emissions will vary between years, primarily depending on the annual hydro-power production. Seen as an average over many years, the emissions presented here would be largely representative, but we have not made a detailed analysis of this.

Before concluding, we note that it is important to guard against adverse environmental effects that might result based on the assumptions of the scenarios. For example, it would be necessary to make use of environmentally acceptable ways of growing the biomass beyond that already available as waste products, improving buildings, designing gas-turbine exhaust-cleaning systems, avoiding CFCs and other greenhouse gases in all applications. The strategy described in this chapter is not in conflict with these guidelines. Concerning CFCs from heat-pumps, we assume successful development of benign alternatives.[71]

14.6 Policy implications

14.6.1 The challenge of choices

The preceding scenarios illustrate some of the choices available to Sweden in determining her electricity future. It is possible from a

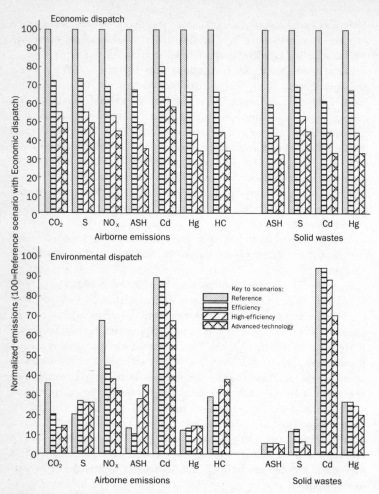

Fig. 14.14(a and b). *Emissions indices. The height of the bars is shown as an index. In this way, the relative changes for many different materials can be easily compared. The following waste-product data are for the Reference Scenario/Economic-Dispatch Scenario case, i.e., the one indexed to equal 100 in Figure 14.14(a). They can thus be used to estimate directly the corresponding values for the other bars, according to their respective indices. Annual Airborne Emissions: net carbon emissions, 13,644 kilotons [C]; sulphur emissions, 19 ktons [S]; NO_x emissions, 89 ktons; airborne ash, 6 ktons; cadmium emissions, 52 kg [Cd]; mercury emissions, 278 kg [Hg]; polyaromatic hydrocarbon emissions, 390 kg. Annual Solid Waste Production: ash waste material, 1,720 ktons; sulphur waste material 105 ktons [S]; cadmium waste material 3,459 kg [Cd]; mercury waste material 1,106 kg [Hg]. (Note: NO_x emissions are computed here as their NO_2 equivalents.)*

technical standpoint to find paths that satisfy the demand for electricity services associated with continued economic growth, uphold environmental quality standards, and expedite the phase-out of nuclear power as planned. The scenarios have very different CO_2 emissions, while other environmental aspects meet present environmental standards. These low-CO_2 scenarios would require the increased use of efficient end-use technology in all sectors as well as the installation of new low-CO_2 generating facilities. Use of coal and natural gas would lead to large increases in CO_2 emissions compared with present levels. The economic differences are much smaller. In fact, the costs of the Efficiency and High-Efficiency/Environmental-Dispatch scenarios would be similar to or lower than those for the Reference/Economic-Dispatch scenario, as calculated in this chapter, based on today's knowledge about costs and prices.

Experience suggests that such a development would not happen by itself. Individual decision-makers tend to optimize for themselves rather than for society at large. By definition, the Reference Scenario illustrates the development that one could expect under present operation of the market-place. The difference between the Reference Scenario and the High-Efficiency Scenario – 44 TWh/year – can be thought of as one measure of the opportunities for alternative market dynamics. To capture some or all of these savings, policies would have to be shaped to make markets work better and stimulate actors in all sectors to make use of the technical opportunities we have described in the preceding pages. Information, education and training, rules and regulations would have to reflect this by making the national good also be the actor's good.

The chapters by Geller,[72] Williams,[73] and de la Moriniere[74] in *Electricity* describe how such policies might be designed, markets organized, and the necessary financing arranged, and the chapter by Geller *et al.*[75] describes the potential for research and development to help accelerate the introduction of new technologies into the market-place. These four chapters discuss many policy options, and the experiences that are available from testing some of them in the US and France.

It is evident that electricity prices are only one of several significant factors in the process of achieving a cost-effective total development of the energy system, or the electricity system, and that there is great uncertainty in price/demand relationships.[76]

Electricity costs are often not very significant, and consumers lack influence over how the equipment they purchase is designed. It is therefore not surprising to find that the effective rates-of-return demanded by consumers are often 50–100 per cent or higher,[77] much above the interest rates commonly used in evaluating supply investment options. This suggests that the total system will not develop in a least-cost direction. Reflecting long-run marginal costs in rate structures (for example, in inverted-block tariffs that convey the marginal cost-incentive without increasing the total cost of electricity) is probably necessary but not sufficient to bring the options discussed in this book into reality.

Policy measures would also have to be formulated on the supply side, because costs of new generating capacity are higher than average generating costs. This is due to the large, low-cost hydro-power production in Sweden. The average costs of new supplies would range up to 5.8 cents/kWh$_e$, well above the new system-wide average cost of about 3 cents/kWh$_e$. The problem is most pronounced in the High-Efficiency/Environmental-Dispatch scenario. The extent of policies required to stimulate new generation under these circumstances depends on electricity-pricing principles. With marginal cost pricing, costs would be covered, but otherwise one could not expect non-hydro-owning utilities or industries to invest in, for example, co-generation. An arrangement where central utilities purchase power from independent power-producers on an avoided-cost basis would be one way to approach this dilemma.

As discussed in other chapters in *Electricity*, research-and-development work remains to be done on many complex issues related to some technologies included in the scenarios. This work should be done now, and not postponed, if these technologies are to contribute significantly by 2010.

14.6.2 Lead times

A perceived dilemma in selecting the end-use efficiency improvements as a major component of an overall electricity strategy is the lack of data on the effectiveness of various policy mechanisms intended to secure these resources. Can power-supply planning that fulfils the usual reliability criteria be accomplished without investing so much in supply capacity that the economic imperative to utilize this excess capacity becomes an obstacle for continued efficiency improvement?

The answer to this question lies partly in the fact that the new supply technologies have short lead times, as compared with traditional central-station generating facilities. Both combined cycles and the advanced gas turbines (described by Williams and Larson in *Electricity*) would require about three years for construction and two years for licensing, assuming fuel supplies such as natural gas and biomass are available on the market in the relatively small quantities that would be needed for each additional unit. Coal and oil are readily available, and can by and large be transported to the point of use with the existing infrastructure. Natural gas would require a transmission system, and biomass is presently available only at the levels specified in the Natural-Gas/Biomass Scenario. A large natural-gas transmission system would require five to ten years to build. To implement the Environmental-Dispatch scenario would involve a five- to seven-year lead time for energy plantations. For both natural gas and biomass, time is needed to establish a market.

To the extent that electricity plans utilize short lead-time strategies, the traditional problem facing utilities having to forecast electricity demand eight or ten years into the future – and increase the generating capacity sufficiently to mitigate the forecasting uncertainties – can be reduced. It thus becomes possible to follow load growth and the effectiveness of efficiency-improvement policies, and to respond to the realities as they develop, while maintaining the traditionally high reliability standards, but with far lower uncertainty (and thus expense) than has been the case historically.

Although all scenarios have abundant excess capacity, the use of steam-injected gas turbines offers an additional route to winter-time extra reserve-power production capacity. If heat normally supplied in co-generation using these units is shifted to the stand-by oil-fired boilers needed for backup in every district-heating system for reliability reasons, this makes available steam that can augment power production. In this way, reserve boilers contribute to an improved reserve margin in the power system.

Demand-side opportunities can be utilized at the rate of capital turnover and expansion. This often means ten to twenty years for full penetration. Fuel-switching, on the other hand, can be much faster (a property that is disadvantageous if the switching is reversed at a later date).

When utilizing demand-side resources, it becomes necessary to account for the lead time involved with programmes or other mechanisms intended to accelerate the introduction of end-use technologies. For scenarios that rely on commercially available technologies, a key component is the speed with which a given programme can achieve a targeted participation rate. For scenarios that rely on technologies still under development, the key factor is the rate at which research and development proceed and thus bring new technologies to the market-place.

In any case, developing demand-side resources begins with identifying them. This chapter has provided an assessment that could be expanded upon. Vattenfall has initiated a market-research project called 'Uppdrag 2000' to identify the cost-effective conservation opportunities in Sweden.[78] Over the next few years, the project will spend $60 million and have a staff of roughly seventy people. The work will focus mostly on demonstration projects intended to obtain actual data on technical and behavioural issues in each sector. There remains a three- to four-year period of continued investigations before implementation begins.

14.6.3 Balance of payments

Some of the preceding scenarios would improve the balance-of-payment situation in Sweden. In recent years, Sweden's balance of payments has oscillated from year to year between net debts and net credits, with an annual balance of plus-or-minus $1 billion/year between 1983 and 1986.[79] The size of the impact for the scenarios would be primarily a function of the difference between the cost of no-longer-imported uranium and newly imported coal, gas, and/or oil. We find for a demand-level corresponding to the Reference Scenario, and a fossil-based supply mix, that the impact on balance of payments would be adverse whereas the two Efficiency plus Environmental-Dispatch scenarios indicate strong benefits.[80] At one extreme (Reference/Economic-Dispatch) the costs of imported coal for power generation and of oil for district heating would be $1.4 billion/year. At the other extreme (High-Efficiency/Environmental-Dispatch) the cost of imports would be $0.25 billion/year.

The cost of electricity services, especially to industry, is an important component of competitiveness and the balance-of-payments equation. The closure of some industrial firms in the Reference

Scenario is intended to reflect their sensitivity to the cost of electricity. In Table 14.6 we saw that for several of the scenarios, the costs of producing electricity services were comparable to or lower than today's.

14.7 Summary and conclusions

We have presented four electricity-demand scenarios for Sweden in the year 2010, based on different levels of electricity end-use efficiency. We combined the results with three generation scenarios, based on the utilization of various fuels and generation technologies. All of the scenarios assume 1.9-per-cent annual growth in gross domestic product and the corresponding amount of new buildings construction, industrial output, appliances purchased by households, and so on. Each scenario combination provides all the energy services associated with this economic growth. Based on the final demand levels and supply mixes, we evaluated the total costs of energy services and the associated emissions of carbon dioxide and other by-products of heat and power generation. We did not evaluate the impact of higher or lower GDP trends, nor we did we test the implications of different life-style developments.

There is a conceptual difference between some of the demand scenarios. The Reference Scenario is based on expectations of market behaviour in the absence of new policy measures but with a 50-per-cent increase in real electricity prices. This scenario also assumes some price-induced industrial-plant closures in the steel and electrolysis sub-sectors. Two other scenarios illustrate the results of more intensive use of electricity-efficient end-use technologies. These technologies are cost-effective in comparison with new electricity generation, based on a 6-per-cent real discount rate, and no direct taxes. In the last scenario, 'Advanced-Technology', we assume the use of technologies still under development.

In the scenarios, direct use of electricity contributes between 88 and 140 TWh of Sweden's 194 TWh-equivalent demand for electric-energy services in 2010. The reductions in electricity use are brought about largely by improvements in lighting, motors, miscellaneous office equipment, and (except in the Reference Scenario) substitution of electric space-heating by fuel. The additional oil use from fuel conversions is equivalent to 4 per cent of Sweden's total oil imports in 1987 (based on replacing 6.9 TWh of electricity).

All the scenarios satisfy present environmental guidelines, but, obviously, some of these scenarios do not meet the environmental ambition of keeping CO_2 emissions constant. Given presently known technologies, we find that to achieve the economic growth mentioned above, fulfil national ambitions of keeping CO_2 emissions at or below their present level, and provide energy services requires a *combination* of energy-efficiency and low-carbon electricity-supply strategies. Depending only on one or the other will not suffice.

In order to keep carbon emissions at or below the present level, bio-fuels have to be used to avoid the fivefold increase in carbon emissions from the power and heat sector that would result from using natural gas and coal to meet a demand level of 140 TWh. Furthermore, with two of the low-electricity scenarios, Sweden could provide a large fraction of its heat and power with domestic resources. A prerequisite for using bio-fuels in this way is completion of biomass-gasification technology development.

These Efficiency scenarios could be attained by 2010 at an overall cost of electricity services of 2.6 cents/kWh_{eq} or less, versus a busbar cost of 2.8 cents/kWh in 1987, and a marginal cost of 4.2 to 5.6 cents/kWh_e (depending on whether natural gas or biomass is the marginal resource), including all investment in end-use technologies. On the supply side, the use of biomass is more expensive than that of natural gas or coal, and this extra cost can be seen as a price for reducing CO_2 emissions. On the other hand, we have chosen measures on the demand side that reduce all emissions (including CO_2) and deliver the electricity services at a cost *less than* that of constructing and operating fossil-fuel power plants.

In evaluating the economic costs and considering the uncertainties, we are reluctant to say that one scenario is more expensive than the others in supplying all the energy services within the system we study. However, we submit that the societal costs per unit of energy services in the Efficiency scenarios do not increase from their current levels, and CO_2 emissions are 35 per cent lower in two cases.

Because the development of the preceding scenarios is based on a national perspective, the associated benefits would not necessarily be attractive to individual actors. These actors may or may not find it in their interest to pursue the technical opportunities that comprise the scenarios, for example industrial co-generation and biomass recovery. To deal with this, policies will have to be shaped to bring individual actors' interests in line with the national interest. Some policy mechanisms could be implemented by the Swedish utilities as they become full energy-service companies in the sense that Edison intended, but many other entities also have key roles to play.

From the point of view of a utility, a new type of uncertainty enters the supply-planning process because future demand-side policies and their impacts are hard to predict. Whereas US utilities and local governments have gained considerable experience with demand-side planning – thereby reducing the associated planning uncertainties – there is a great lack of experience in the Swedish context. Also, many of these policies would have to be formulated and implemented by non-utility actors, while the utilities would retain responsibility for providing the required electricity.

The problems and opportunities we have described here are not unique to Sweden. Bringing down primary energy-use by increasing end-use efficiency is the key strategy to deliver society's desired energy services and at the same time contribute to the amelioration of major global problems.[81] The efficient use of energy illustrated in the scenarios would enable Sweden to develop her energy system in ways compatible with solving global problems.

As the twenty-first century approaches, Swedish society is planning for an expanding use of services from electricity and energy. The great business opportunity for utilities and entrepreneurs is to make the electric-energy services their business activity. This will be an exciting era, with a key role for high technology in both the supply and demand arenas. The new challenges are in policy-making and in the market-place.

Chapter 15
Tropical Forests

Norman Myers

" ...As long as the overall context of economic relations between North and South reflects a reverse resource flow ... there can be little hope that tropical-forest governments, which owed $562 billion, or 58 per cent of all Third World debt, in 1987, will direct enough investment toward one of the most neglected of all development sectors, namely subsistence agriculture as practised by the poorest of the poor... "

By the late 1970s the humid tropics were losing forest cover at a rate estimated to be around 75,000 km² per year.[1] This chapter reviews the situation ten years later, assesses the future outlook and implications for global warming, and analyses the scope for grand-scale reforestation as a policy-response to global warming. This chapter is a summary review of a report, *Deforestation Rates in Tropical Forests and their Climatic Implications*, prepared by the author (with a climate-analysis chapter by Richard A. Houghton) for Friends of the Earth UK.[2]

15.1 Defining terms

Tropical forests are defined here as 'evergreen or partly evergreen forests, in areas receiving not less than 100 mm of precipitation in any month for two out of three years, with mean annual temperature of 24-plus degrees Celsius, and essentially frost-free; in these forests some trees may be deciduous; the forests usually occur at altitudes below 1300 metres (though often in Amazonia up to 1,800 metres and generally in South-east Asia up to only 750 metres); and in mature examples of these forests, there are several more or less distinctive strata'.

As for deforestation, this term refers to the complete destruction of forest cover through clearing for agriculture of whatever sort (cattle-ranching, smallholder agriculture, whether planned or spontaneous, and commodity-crop production through, for example, rubber and palm-oil plantations). It means that hardly a tree remains, and the land is given over to non-forest purposes. There are certain instances too where the forest biomass is so severely depleted – notably through the very heavy and unduly negligent logging of dipterocarp forests in South-east Asia, resulting in removal of or unsurvivable injury to the great majority of trees – that the remnant ecosystem is a travesty of natural forest as properly understood. Decline of biomass and depletion of ecosystem services are so severe that the residual forest can no longer qualify as forest in any practical sense of the word. So this particular kind of over-logging is included under the term 'deforestation'.

As for agents of deforestation, it is not necessary to define the commercial logger or the cattle-rancher. But it is appropriate to distinguish between various forms of slash-and-burn cultivator. Until roughly the mid-1960s, the small-scale farmer was usually a shifting cultivator of traditional type, one who practised a migratory sort of agriculture. As long as there were not many of these cultivators and there was plenty of forest to shift around in, they made sustainable use of forest ecosystems. But during the past quarter-century there has been an influx into the forests of what can be called 'shifted' cultivators. These are farmers who have formerly made a living in long-established farmlands of the countries concerned, often in territories far distant from the forests. For various reasons – population growth, maldistribution of established farmlands, lack of agrotechnologies for intensive cultivation, and inadequate rural development generally – they have increasingly been squeezed out of their erst-while homelands. Perceiving no alternative way to sustain them-selves, they head for the only unoccupied lands available to them, namely tropical forests.

These shifted cultivators have grown exceptionally numerous in recent decades. Advancing upon the forest fringe in vast throngs, they penetrate deeper into the forest season by season. Behind them come still more multitudes of displaced and usually impoverished peasants. With scant understanding of how to make sustainable agri-cultural use of forest ecosystems, these shifted cultivators now cause more forest destruction than all other agents of deforestation combined.

More than seventy countries of the humid tropics feature moist forest. But only thirty-four countries (Table 15.1) account for almost 7.8 million km^2 of forest, or 97.5 per cent of the present biome, esti-mated to total 7,783,500 km^2; and these are the countries covered in the original Friends of the Earth report.[3] In turn, this means that there is no consideration of forty-plus countries with small amounts of tropical forest that may none the less be important for values such as environmental services and biodiversity. These countries include Liberia, Ethiopia, Uganda, Kenya, Tanzania, Sri Lanka, Nepal, China, and certain countries of the Caribbean, as well as the United States (Hawaii and Puerto Rico) and Australia (Queensland). These non-included countries encompass around 200,000 km^2 of forest, or 2.5 per cent of the biome-wide total of almost 8 million km^2. For purpose of calculation of the overall deforestation rate in the entire biome, it is assumed that these subsidiary countries are experiencing the same amount of deforestation as the countries analysed.

The survey on which the original report, and hence this chapter, was based was perforce undertaken as a 'desk research' investigation. While it drew upon the author's twenty years of travel and work throughout the biome, it relied primarily on an extensive survey of the recent professional literature. The survey's findings have depen-ded heavily, moreover, upon remote-sensing data, whether satellite imagery, side-looking radar, or aerial photography. This constitutes a methodical and comprehensive form of documentation, provided it incorporates an appropriate degree of ground-truthing, backed in turn by careful interpretation of survey findings.[4] In short, remote sensing constitutes by far the best mode of determining deforestation rates.

Table 15.1: Tropical moist forests: present status in select countries *(areas in km²)*

Country (plus area)	Original forest cover	Present forest cover	Present primary forest	Current deforestation per year (plus %)	
Bolivia (1,098,581)	90,000	70,000	45,000	1,500	(2.1)
Brazil (8,511,960)	2,860,000	2,200,000	1,800,000	50,000	(2.3)
Cameroon (475,442)	220,000	164,000	60,000	2,000	(1.2)
Central America (522,915)	500,000	90,000	55,000	3,300	(3.7)
Colombia (1,138,891)	700,000	278,500	180,000	6,500	(2.3)
Congo (342,000)	100,000	90,000	80,000	700	(0.8)
Ecuador (270,670)	132,000	76,000	44,000	3,000	(4.0)
Gabon (267,670)	240,000	200,000	100,000	600	(0.3)
Guyanas (French Guiana, Guyana and Suriname) (469,790)	500,000	410,000	370,000	500	(0.12)
India (3,287,000)	1,600,000	165,000	70,000	4,000	(2.4)
Indonesia (1,919,300)	1,220,000	860,000	530,000	12,000	(1.4)
Ivory Coast (322,463)	160,000	16,000	4,000	2,500	(15.6)
Kampuchea (181,035)	120,000	67,000	20,000	500	(0.75)
Laos (236,800)	110,000	68,000	25,000	1,000	(1.5)
Madagascar (590,992)	62,000	24,000	10,000	2,000	(8.3)
Malaysia (329,079)	305,000	157,000	84,000	4,800	(3.1)
Mexico (1,967,180)	400,000	166,000	110,000	7,000	(4.2)
Myanma (Burma) (696,500)	500,000	245,000	80,000	8,000	(3.3)
Nigeria (924,000)	72,000	28,000	10,000	4,000	(14.3)
Papua New Guinea (461,700)	425,000	360,000	180,000	3,500	(1.0)
Peru (1,285,220)	700,000	515,000	420,000	3,500	(0.7)
Philippines (299,400)	250,000	50,000	8,000	2,700	(5.4)
Thailand (513,517)	435,000	74,000	22,000	6,000	(8.4)
Venezuela (912,050)	420,000	350,000	300,000	1,500	(0.4)
Vietnam (334,331)	260,000	60,000	14,000	3,500	(5.8)
Zaire (2,344,886)	1,245,000	1,000,000	700,000	4,000	(0.4)
Totals	**13,626,000***	**7,783,500†**	**5,321,000‡**	**138,600**	**(1.8)**

Notes

* = 97 per cent of estimated total original extent of tropical forests, around 14 million km²

† = 97.5 per cent of present total extent of tropical forests, 8 million km²

‡ = 67 per cent of total remaining tropical forests, 8 million km²

15.2 Three key countries

There is not space in this paper to review the thirty-four countries covered in the original report. But it is pertinent to take a detailed look at three countries that make up more than half of remaining tropical forests, namely Brazil, Zaire, and Indonesia. The treatment of these three countries also serves to illustrate the analytic methodologies deployed for the other thirty-one countries dealt with in the main report.

15.2.1 Brazil

Of Brazil's 8,511,960 km^2, almost 2.9 million km^2 were covered with Amazonian forest as recently as the late 1960s – or 3.6 million km^2 if one includes transitional or 'fringe forests'.[5] Today the forest expanse has declined to around 2,200,000 km^2. Reduced as it is, this still leaves Brazil with 27.5 per cent of all tropical forests. So the situation deserves to be treated in extended detail.[6]

The deforestation pattern in Brazilian Amazonia is highly differentiated. Some parts are losing forest cover rapidly, others hardly at all. The best-known case of progressive deforestation is the southern state of Rondonia, with an area of 243,044 km^2. By 1980, less than 8000 km^2 of forest had been eliminated, but by 1985 the amount had expanded to almost 28,000 km^2, and by 1987 to almost 60,000 km^2.[7] There is prospect that deforestation in Rondonia could eventually spread even more rapidly, and still further beyond government control, than has been the case to date in the wake of construction of the BR 429 highway. Until late-1988 there were only 140 forest guards in Rondonia, or less than one to every 1300 km^2. Fortunately there has been a substantial attempt by the government in 1989 to regulate forest-land farming and to enforce settlement laws. But in light of the continuing massive influx of settlers, both official and spontaneous, into Rondonia, the escalating land conflicts, and lack of law-enforcement, it is far from certain that the government will be able to control deforestation to the extent it now proclaims.

Likewise, in the neighbouring state of Mato Grosso to the east of Rondonia there has been progressive loss of forest: by 1975 only a little over 10,000 km^2, but by 1985 almost 57,000 km^2, and by 1988, 208,000 km^2.[8] In the state of Acre to the west of Rondonia, the 1975 deforestation total amounted to less than 1200 km^2, and by 1980 it was still less than 2500 km^2. But by 1985 it had soared to 5269 km^2, and by 1988 to almost 20,000 km^2.[9]

Within the context of these state-by-state assessments, some recent remote-sensing reports from the Brazilian Space Research Agency present an estimate of 81,000 km^2 of forest burned in just four states of southern Amazonia – Acre, Rondonia, Mato Grosso, and Para – during the dry season of 1987,[10] followed by a further 96,000 km^2 in 1988. Subsequent analyses[11] suggest that these 1987 and 1988 estimates were probably on the high side, due to somewhat indiscriminate interpretation of remote-sensing images. A more realistic, albeit conservative, assessment for these four states (leaving aside the rest of Amazonia) would be some 50,000 km[2] burned in 1987, and 48,000 km[2] in 1988.[12] Even when thus reduced, these totals are to be compared with the amount deforested in Brazil in 1979, an area between 14,500 km[2] and 14,800 km[2].[13] They are also to be compared with the annual amount deforested throughout the entire tropical-forest biome during the late 1970s, an aggregate figure around 75,000 km[2].[14]

As for the whole of Brazilian Amazonia, the accumulated deforestation total by 1975 was estimated to be only 29,000 km[2], and by 1980 no more than 125,000 km[2].[15] But a number of observers,[16] drawing on latest remote-sensing data, indicate that the amount cleared by 1988 totalled almost 400,000 km[2] or 11 per cent of originally forested Amazonia.[17] Of this forest-clearing, roughly 69 per cent has occurred since 1980.

Given the extent to which deforestation increased markedly in the four southern states during 1987 and 1988, it is heartening news that during the early part of the 1989 dry season the burning seemed to have been curtailed somewhat, due to a combination of policy changes, better controls on burning, and most important of all an exceptionally wet 'dry' season. After the first two months of the dry season, July and August, total deforestation in these four states is estimated to have amounted to roughly 33,000 km[2]; and the eventual total for 1989 could turn out to have been as low (*sic*) as 40,000 km[2], by contrast with 48,000 km[2] in 1988.[18] Note that the figure of 40,000 km[2] proposed for 1989 reflects the fact that while timber-burning was reduced somewhat, the area of forest-felling overall was higher than the area burned: much forest was felled and the trees left on the ground until such time as they became dry enough to be burned, perhaps not until the dry season of mid-1990.

At the same time, there has been increased deforestation in other states. In Roraima, for instance, along the northern perimeter of Amazonia, there was a loss of almost 10,500 km[2] of forest between 1978 and 1985.[19] Since 1985 there has been an influx of migrants from Rondonia, plus a sudden outburst of gold-prospecting; there are now reports of fast-expanding deforestation in Roraima. In addition, there has been growing deforestation in other states, notably Amapa, Maranhao, and Amazonas.

When we take account of all deforestation in whatever part of Brazilian Amazonia, whether documented in detail or not, the 1989 total for the region could well have amounted to around 45,000 km². This estimate is to be compared with the latest figure from the Instituto Nacional de Pesquisas Espaciais, 40,000 km² of primary forest eliminated in 1989 (note: for primary forest alone),[20] this being a figure for demonstrated and recorded deforestation. True, the estimate of 45,000 km², based on the less-than-comprehensive evidence adduced in the review above and reflecting the author's calculations (based in turn on discussions with a host of scientists involved), must remain an interim estimate until such time as more detailed data and analyses become available. The estimate is advanced here with the sole purpose – no more and no less – of helping us to 'get a handle' on the situation in Brazilian Amazonia, albeit a handle that constitutes a far-from-conclusive understanding of a situation that forms a sizeable portion of deforestation throughout the humid tropics.

The uncertainty issue is so important that it deserves further consideration. Despite the remote-sensing technologies employed and the large quantity of reports and evaluations published in recent years, the situation remains clouded with a regrettable degree of uncertainty. In the author's judgement, the findings above reflect a consensus of informed opinion among most professionals and institutions involved. Moreover, and in light of the big-picture implications for climate-change world-wide, it is scarcely significant whether deforestation in Brazilian Amazonia has eliminated 11 per cent or 8 per cent, or indeed 9.682 per cent, of forest cover.

True, some observers may object that in the absence of conclusive evidence and analyses, one should stick with lower estimates on the grounds that they are more 'responsible'. But this raises a key factor, that of asymmetry of evaluation. A lower estimate, ostensibly 'safe' because it takes a conservative view of such limited evidence as is to hand in documented detail, may fail to reflect the real situation just as much as does an 'unduly' high estimate that is more of a best-judgement affair based on all available evidence, with varying degrees of demonstrable validity. As in other situations beset with uncertainty, it will be better for us to find we have been roughly right than precisely wrong.

In turn, these considerations are exceptionally germane to the prospect for the future. Whatever the final figure for deforestation in 1989, deforestation in future years may well increase by virtue of government hopes to develop and otherwise 'open up' Amazonia. For instance, there are ambitious plans to create new settlement territories in several sectors of Para, Mato Grosso, Rondonia, Acre, and Amapa. The same applies even to parts of Amazonas State, the most remote portion of Brazilian Amazonia and one that has remained little affected to date, with only 12,000 km^2 eliminated.[21] As we have seen, there is growing settlement in the territory of Roraima in the far north. In Maranhao State, some 24,000 km^2 had already been deforested.[22]

So while we can welcome the ostensibly better news of reduced deforestation in 1989, we must consider that additional pressures – of road-building and settler immigration, as well as mining, dam-construction, and commercial logging – are likely to mount and stimulate yet greater deforestation in the future. All too easily they could prove to be pressures that the government would find ever-more difficult to contain through orderly development. Consider, for instance, some recent fossil-fuel discoveries. In 1987 a 20-billion-cubic-metre deposit of natural gas came to light west of the Jurua River, stimulating drilling over much of the entire region. It also revealed a 20-million-barrel deposit of high-quality oil in the Urucu River basin, considered to be part of what could turn out to be a 1.2 million-km^2 oil reservoir.[23] Initial development of just a single sector of these new discoveries is already leading to a gross spread of infrastructure, while exploitation of the Urucu oil-deposit will, it is officially anticipated, lead to the deforestation of 10,000 km^2. Perhaps more significant still, fossil-fuel development will result in the early influx of perhaps 50,000 people into western Amazonia – an area virtually unsettled to date.

There are other, similarly extensive, development plans envisaged for Amazonia, as set out in a mid-1980s regional-development strategy.[24] While certain of these plans may have been reduced in scope in light of subsequent analyses of Amazonian ecology and socio-economics, they illustrate the scale of development intended. According to the regional strategy, the government aims to flood an eventual area totalling between 65,000 km^2 and 150,000 km^2 for hydroelectric development. Timber-harvesting is scheduled to ultimately account for anywhere between 200,000 km^2 and 500,000 km^2. Smallholder settlements are projected to extend across an eventual total of between 200,000 km^2 and 430,000 km^2. The Grande Carajas project in eastern Amazonia could entail the logging of natural forests, to supply charcoal for the pig-iron smelters, accounting for 240,000 km² of forest-lands (it accounts for around 550 km² per year already).[25] Finally, plantations of softwood trees, in addition to the plantations associated with Grande Carajas, are scheduled to eliminate at least 36,000 km², possibly a great deal more, much of it by the mid-1990s.[26]

In sum, these diverse activities, together with fossil-fuel exploitation, are planned to ultimately deforest somewhere between 750,000 km² and 1,366,000 km² of Brazilian Amazonia. Even if the government holds to its new-found and more circumspect approach to Amazonia, and even if it can manage to apply its regulations more stringently across the huge expanse of the region (in mid-1989 there were only 500 staff and five helicopters to police an area larger than Western Europe), one still finds it hard to see how the scale and pace of deforestation will not continue to increase progressively.

In addition to this planned deforestation of Amazonia, there will surely be much 'incidental' deforestation due to the activities of already established farmers and ranchers. One of the most adverse features of settlement to date has been the tendency for settlers to abandon their designated sites after just a few years, and to take up a life-style of slash-and-burn cultivation or 'shifting ranching'.[27] Worse yet, there could well be an outburst of 'spontaneous' (as opposed to planned) settlement on the part of smallholder migrants from north-eastern and southern Brazil. The figure given above for the area of official smallholder settlement in the foreseeable future, between 200,000 km² and 430,000 km², could accommodate no more than a total somewhere between a quarter-of-a-million and 1 million farming families, or 1.5 to 6 million people in all, given the amount of land each farmer has been deforesting to date in Rondonia and elsewhere in the main settlement zones. Yet between 1975 and 1988, the smallholder communities flooding into Rondonia alone totalled 1.5 million persons. These are the communities who not only do most damage to the forests, but are the most difficult to control.

The pressures that have been driving the colonists into Rondonia, Acre, and other settlement areas – skewed land distribution and inadequate land-tenure systems in farming territories elsewhere in Brazil, plus the shaky Brazilian economy and the debt burden, along with population growth – show no sign of abating within the foreseeable future. Rather, they are likely to become exacerbated unless both the

Brazilian government and outside bodies (foreign governments, international development banks, private commercial banks, aid agencies) take a much more constructive approach to Brazil's myriad problems. In the absence of such a seismic change in attitude, there is likely to be a growing tide of landless peasants and other settlers migrating towards Amazonia.

All in all, there is every reason to suppose that deforestation could well work out at a little above recent levels, namely around 50,000 km^2 per year. Moreover, this figure should be regarded as a cautious and conservative assessment; it could all too easily be exceeded.

The prospect of a growing urge to 'develop' Amazonia, and of the increased deforestation it will entail, cast light on the 1989 phenomenon of a drop in the recent deforestation rate. Will this prove to be a transient affair, that is, will it turn out to be a non-sustainable dip in a longer-term trend? In view of the prognosis presented above, it is surely realistic to anticipate that the average deforestation rate for the last years of the 1980s and the early 1990s will be more in accord with the years 1987 and 1988, when deforestation in just the four southern states amounted to (a conservative calculation of) 50,000 km^2 and 48,000 km^2 respectively. For purposes of this paper, then, the 'current' deforestation rate, meaning a trend-rate over a period of several years, should be considered to be higher than the postulated 1989 amount of 45,000 km^2. Hence, an estimate is advanced – a tentative but informed and considered estimate – of 50,000 km^2 per year for the next several years, or 2.3 per cent of remaining forest cover.

15.2.2 Zaire

Zaire's 2,344,886 km^2 encompass a major portion of the Zaire basin. Since its forest cover extended to almost 1 million km^2 or thereabouts in 1980,[28] it comprised roughly one-eighth of the entire biome. So its situation is worth dealing with in as much detail as is feasible. Unfortunately, this is not much: despite the significance of the country's forest cover, the Zaire government appears to have produced only rudimentary statistics on its forest estate, less than any other African country.

Zaire possesses only 35 million people in its huge territory, albeit a total growing at a rate of 3.1 per cent per year. The populace is mostly rural, depending for livelihood on underdeveloped agriculture that consists largely of slash-and-burn cultivation. Thus, disruptive pressures of population growth and economic expansion have not been exerting much impact as yet on the bulk of the country's forests.

But in view of the bankruptcy of the national economy, there are plans to extract a much greater harvest from the timber resource. To date, lumbering is confined to areas close to the few communications that exist, mainly river networks. This situation is scheduled to change markedly, however, if the government can attract enough foreign investment for its timber sector – and capital is reportedly starting to flood into the country.[29] As much as 60 per cent of the forests are considered to be loggable. Whereas only half-a-million cubic metres of timber were cut, with 150,000 cubic metres exported, in 1984, the government aims to increase this volume to 6 million cubic metres, with 5 million cubic metres exported, by the year 2000.[30] Logging operations are very wasteful: in some areas every one tree cut for commercial timber entails the cutting of twenty-five other trees for road-building.

More significantly, the throng of slash-and-burn cultivators has been increasing rapidly in numbers. This reflects not so much population growth as run-down of the national economy and greater marginalization of the country's poorest people. According to recent reports,[31] there has been a marked expansion in subsistence farming in forests during the 1980s – a trend that is likely to increase unless the high rate of population growth is swiftly slowed and the national economy picks up solidly. While the total of forest-land farmers is still low in proportion to the forest estate, they affect three times as much forest each year as do their counterparts in West Africa.

Various figures have been proposed for the late-1970s extent of Zaire's forests.[32] While some estimates have been as high as 1,100,000 km², others have proposed only 900,000 km², while an authoritative UNESCO study (1978) has suggested only 750,000 km². It has proved exceedingly difficult to ascertain which of these estimates accorded best with the real situation on the ground. Fortunately a recent mapping project, combining aerial photography with satellite imagery, has come up with preliminary findings to the effect that forest cover of all kinds still amounts to just over 1 million km²[33] out of an original total estimated at almost 1,244,600 km². But much primary forest is interspersed with patches of secondary forest of various ages[34] to the extent that primary forest is now estimated to cover no more than 700,000 km^2.

Slash-and-burn farming is widespread, especially in the wake of a flood of impoverished peasants overtaking forests during the 1980s.[35] In some forest-fringe areas it now causes outright destruction of forest cover, so heavy have the localized pressures of numbers become. In many other areas it causes significant disruption of forest ecosystems, to the extent that it ranks as gross degradation.

The deforestation rate, based on the reports cited above, is estimated at 4000 km^2 of remaining forests per year (0.4 per cent). This amount is double the Food and Agriculture Organization estimate for 1979,[36] which, being based almost entirely on government reports rather than on remote-sensing surveys, seems to have been a considerable under-estimate.[37] The 0.4-per-cent figure is to be compared with a 1950–85 average figure of 0.35 per cent per year.

15.2.3 Indonesia

Possessing the second largest forest expanse after Brazil, and almost 10 per cent of the entire biome, Indonesia is specially important to this paper. Moreover, forest products are significant for Indonesia's economy, timber being the second largest export after oil and natural gas combined, and supplying $2.5 billion in foreign-exchange earnings in 1987.

Of the country's 1,919,300 km^2 of national territory, some 1,440,000 km^2 are officially considered to rank as forest-lands. But this refers to lands under the aegis of the Ministry of Forestry, and many of them have long featured no forest cover at all. As a result of the logging boom beginning in the mid-1960s, the Transmigration Programme underway by the mid-1970s, and a recent expansion of plantation agriculture (especially oil-palm and rubber), much forest has been grossly degraded or destroyed outright.[38]

During the late 1980s some systematized assessments, drawing largely on satellite imagery and aerial photography, were undertaken by the Land Resources Department of the United Kingdom's Overseas Development Administration, in conjunction with the Indonesian Ministry of Transmigration and the National Body for Mapping and Surveys. The report, known as the Regional Physical Planning Programme for Transmigration, or RePPProT (1989), has aimed to determine the extent of forest-covered lands.[39] It shows that in, for, instance, Kalimantan – the Borneo sector of Indonesia, encompassing more than 1 million km^2 – at least 16 per cent of production forests' area featured no forest cover at all by 1981–2, and a good part more had been subjected to exceptionally heavy logging; and even more remarkably, a full 8 per cent of conservation and protection 'forests' area no longer possessed any tree cover. In 1983, moreover, a fire in East Kalimantan eliminated 36,000 km^2 of forest; and in subsequent years there has been much further destruction.

Nation-wide, the total area featuring forest of any sort can be esti-mated to have amounted to no more than 1 million km^2 and more likely as little as 914,000 km^2 by 1981–2. During the period 1980–7 the World Bank[40] has postulated an average annual deforestation rate of 9,000 km^2 a year (in contrast with a recent Food and Agriculture Organization estimate[41] of 6,000 km^2). This means that during 1983–8 a further 54,000 km^2 of forest were eliminated. As a result, there were only 860,000 km^2 of forest left in 1988.

But the estimate of 9000 km^2 deforested on average each year may now be on the low side. The World Bank[42] accepts that a 'reasonable' estimate for the late 1980s could be anywhere from 7,000 km^2 to 12,000 km^2 a year. When this writer was in Jakarta for government consultations in August 1988, he presented the higher figure to the Vice-President and eight Cabinet ministers; five of the nine agreed (albeit informally) that in light of expanding logging and growing encroachment on forest by slash-and-burn cultivators, the figure could well be correct for 1988.[43] Moreover, the Indonesian Develop-ment Plan for mid-1989 to mid-1994 (Ministry of Forestry, 1989) pre-sents an estimate of 11,550 km^2 of forest eliminated per year. So a deforestation rate of 12,000 km^2 per year is accepted as valid for the position today. It amounts to 1.4 per cent of remaining forest. It fur-ther means that Indonesia is losing a larger expanse of forest each year than any other tropical-forest country except Brazil.

15.3 Analysis of overall findings

15.3.1 Summation of country-by-country reviews

The thirty-four countries concerned are estimated to be losing forest cover at a collective rate of 138,600 km^2 per year, as indicated in Table 15.1.[44] If we also consider the forty-plus countries omitted from the country-by-country analysis, comprising approximately 200,000 km^2 of forest, and if we suppose that they too are losing their forest at the same rate, this adds another 3,600 km^2 of forest destroyed each year. (True, this is a large generalization, covering more than forty countries. But it appears valid in light of progressive deforestation reported in countries as diverse as Ghana, Ethiopia, Uganda, Kenya, Sri Lanka, Bangladesh, Nepal, and China.) So the deforestation total for the biome is estimated to be 142,200 km^2, or 1.8 per cent of remaining forest comprising 7,783,500 km^2.

As noted, the deforestation total for 1979 was estimated to be around 75,000 km^2.[45] So, during the course of the last ten years there has been an increase in the annual deforestation rate of 67,200 km^2, that is, almost 90 per cent. On a biome-wide basis, the 1989 deforestation of 142,200 km^2 works out to 390 km^2 per day, 16 km^2 per hour, and 27 hectares per minute.

It is important to recognize, however, that patterns and trends of deforestation are far from even throughout the biome. In South-East Asia it is likely – supposing the present situation persists unvaried – that virtually all forest will be eliminated by the end of the century in Thailand and Vietnam, and virtually all primary forest in the Philippines and Myanma (Burma). Little forest of whatever sort is likely to remain in another twenty years' time in most of Malaysia, and in Indonesia outside of Kalimantan and Irian Jaya. But in Papua New Guinea, with its low population pressures (fewer than 4 million people in an area of 461,700 km^2, almost the size of Spain or California), there could well be sizeable tracts of forest remaining for several decades into the next century.

A similarly differentiated picture emerges in Africa. Supposing – though this is a big 'if' (see below) – that recent deforestation patterns and trends persist unchanged, one can realistically anticipate that hardly any forest will remain in Madagascar, East Africa, and West Africa beyond the end of the century, if only due to the combined pressures of population growth and impoverished peasantry. But in the Zaire basin, comprising Gabon, Congo, and Zaire, there are only 38 million people occupying an area of 3 million km^2; and these countries are so well-endowed with mineral resources that their governments sense little urgent need to exploit their forest stocks in order to fund development, although with the opening of the Trans-Gabon Railway and the increased foreign investment for commercial logging in Zaire, the situation may change rapidly. Recall, moreover, that the population total is projected to reach 98 million as early as the year 2020. (For more on the linkages between population growth and deforestation, see Section 15.4.2 on Population Pressures.)

As for Latin America (and subject to the same qualifications), it is difficult to see that much forest in Mexico and Central America can persist beyond the end of this century. The Colombian Choco may survive a while longer. Amazonia presents a mixed picture. The sectors in Ecuador, Peru, and Bolivia may be largely eliminated within another two decades at most. By contrast, the Venezuelan sector is hardly affected thus far, and much of it may well remain intact for a good while to come. Of course the Amazonia situation is dominated by Brazil. There has been creeping attrition of Brazil's Amazonian forest throughout the past two decades, with a sharp acceleration in the deforestation rate during much of the past three years. While the peripheral states along the southern, eastern, and even northern borders of Brazilian Amazonia may well continue to experience extensive deforestation, the west-central bloc could conceivably survive with scant depletion for a good while to come. There is even better hope for the Guyanas, with more than 400,000 km^2 of forest and only 2 million people. Until the road linking Guyana south to Brazil is built, little deforestation appears likely.

All in all, then, deforestation presents a decidedly mixed picture, not only now but as concerns the future. This makes it all the more unrealistic to generalize, let alone to project, from the biome-wide deforestation rate of 1.8 per cent per year. Many, if not most, countries will have little forest left in just another few decades. A few could well expect – if we make a simple extrapolation of the recent past – to retain sizeable expanses for at least several decades more. But this raises a key question: will the future be a simple extension of the recent past? Will deforestation rates continue in linear manner, or will there be a geometric increase in certain sectors of the biome – and might some areas even experience a decline in deforestation rates? This central issue is considered further in Section 15.4.

15.3.2 Degradation of forests

In addition to outright destruction of forests, there is a good deal of disruption to a degree that leads to significant degradation of forest tracts without eliminating all forest cover. While this aspect of forest 'conversion' is important with respect to forest values such as bio-diversity and watershed functions, it is not so critical for considerations of biomass, and hence for carbon-storing capacity and climate-regulation mechanisms of tropical forests. But since it is often viewed as a salient aspect of tropical-forest depletion, and it relates to the question of forest regrowth and thus of secondary forests (see below), it deserves a brief mention here.

It is easier to determine how much of a forest area has been destroyed than how much has been degraded. (For some country-by-country assessments, see the original report.)[46] These assessments reveal that the overall degradation rate is often about the same as the deforestation rate, if not rather more in a good number of countries. Thus, the amount of degradation in 1989 can be estimated – as a strictly preliminary estimate – at a minimum of 150,000 km^2.

15.3.3 Regrowth and secondary forests

It has been supposed by some observers that most deforestation is quickly compensated for by regrowth, and that areas cleared and then abandoned are soon covered with secondary forest. This conclusion is questionable, according to the survey's[47] findings.

For one thing, deforested areas are not usually abandoned nowadays. As we have seen, the bulk of deforestation is due to the activities of slash-and-burn cultivators, who, operating in huge numbers (as many as 300 million by the early 1980s, according to a range of authorities), hardly ever practise a rotatory form of agriculture any more. Rather, as described above, vast throngs of 'shifted' cultivators impose huge pressures on forest fringes, clearing extensive areas before pressing deeper into the remaining forest year after year. Behind them come still more waves of shifted cultivators, allowing the forest no chance to re-establish itself.[48]

Such is now the pattern in much of West Africa, East Africa, and Southern and South-East Asia, where population pressures are greatest. True, in parts of Latin America, and especially in Amazonia, it is often the case that abandoned crop-lands and pastures feature forest regrowth. For instance, in Brazilian Amazonia in 1988, between 20 and 40 per cent of deforested lands were starting to feature secondary-forest recovery.[49] But this is far from the invariable outcome. Indeed, there are many instances in Amazonia where regrowth does not occur at all. It seems to be more difficult than is sometimes supposed for successional processes to get underway in a manner that leads to secondary forest. In the Bragantina Zone in eastern Amazonia, an area of some 35,000 km^2 was abandoned after a short-lived effort at agricultural settlement early this century. Fifty years later there was still little vegetation beyond scrub and brush-growth, together with some scattered patches of secondary forest.[50] There is scant forest regrowth in many parts of the Amazonian sectors of Colombia,[51] Ecuador,[52] and Peru.[53]

This outcome, that is, of no secondary-forest regrowth, is even more pervasive in Asia. Indonesia features at least 160,000 km^2 of alangalang (*Imperata*) grasslands that have colonized deforested areas; the grass proves so competitive that forest growth simply cannot establish itself. There are similar tracts of fire-climax grasslands in the Philippines, totalling some 70,000 km^2,[54] and in Thailand,[55] Malaysia,[56] and Papua New Guinea,[57] making up 450,000 km^2 in all. In Africa too a parallel phenomenon is widespread, due in the main to sheer pressure of numbers of small-scale farmers, for instance in Cameroon and Ghana,[58] Ivory Coast,[59] and Madagascar.[60]

Moreover, even in cases where secondary forest manages to establish itself, the forest's stature and biomass are often smaller than in primary forest – with all that that implies for their carbon-storing capacity and hence their linkage to the global carbon budget. In Malaysia, secondary forests usually achieve only half to three-quarters the height of primary forest.[61] Near Altamira in Para, Brazil, they have been found to possess less than half the original biomass.[62] Secondary forest on abandoned pasture-lands in Brazilian Amazonia proves much slower to take hold than would occur on crop-land sites abandoned as part of shifting-cultivator cycles.[63] Furthermore, the success of secondary forest varies according to the degree of cattle-use before abandonment, with only half as much biomass on heavily used sites (the predominant type) than on more lightly used sites.[64]

In some parts of the humid tropics, deforested lands are used for tree plantations, whether coffee, tea, rubber, oil-palm, and other agricultural crops based on trees, or for commercial timber and fuel-wood. The first category has little relevance here, since their biomass is generally too slight to make much difference to factors of biomass and hence of carbon-cycling. As for commercial-timber plantations and fuel-wood lots, these now amount to a little over 200,000 km^2. They have mostly been established since the early 1970s, and the current rate of establishment is some 11,000 km^2 a year, of which roughly two-thirds, or 7,300 km^2, are in the humid tropics.[65] So for considerations of tree cover in the humid tropics, this latter total, 7,300 km^2, should be deducted from the figure for 1989 deforestation, 142,200 km^2, making a net total of 134,900 km^2 in 1989.

15.4 Future outlook

Should we anticipate a simple extension of recent trends and patterns of deforestation? Or should we reckon with discontinuities, such as a still-greater acceleration of the deforestation rate in certain countries – or perhaps even a decline in the rate in certain other countries? Clearly, the 1989 rate cited for Ivory Coast, 15.6 per cent, or for Nigeria, 14.3 per cent,[66] cannot be maintained for more than another five years, since there would hardly be any forest left. Equally clearly, the rates are likely to decline before then as remaining forests are reduced to fragments in inaccessible localities such as ultra-steep hillsides or ravines. In Ivory Coast, indeed, the rate has declined a good deal during the 1980s; so too in Central America and the Philippines.

How far, then, can we engage in a realistic prognosis of the future situation, given the many variables at work? Consider a number of salient factors.

15.4.1 Planned deforestation

Certain governments have formulated plans to exploit their remaining forests on a broad scale. The most notable example cited is Brazil.[67] Here we shall briefly consider the case of Indonesia, by way of illustration of specific intent to deforest.

All timber concessions in Indonesia, accounting for the great bulk of remaining lowland forests, are scheduled for exploitation within twenty-five years at most.[68] In addition, the government plans that during the period 1988–2000 a forest expanse of at least 60,000 km^2, and conceivably three times as much, will be converted to planned agriculture, primarily through the Transmigration Programme (which, however, has recently slowed down, though due to lack of funds rather than doubts about its effectiveness). In addition, there will surely be a sizeable amount of forest taken for unplanned agriculture by 'spontaneous' settlers and other types of slash-and-burn cultivators. These three deforestation factors could well eliminate a total of at least 200,000 km^2 of forest during the 1990s, possibly much more, for an average of 20,000 km^2 per year, by contrast with the 1989 deforestation estimate of 12,000 km^2.

15.4.2 Population pressures

Population pressures are often supposed to be the prime factor behind deforestation (for details of present population numbers and projected growth, see Table 15.2). But while this is true in many respects, there is much more to the situation.[69] Note, for instance, that while tropical-forest countries' populations have expanded by amounts ranging from 15 to 36 per cent during the 1980s, deforestation has expanded by 90 per cent.

As mentioned, the single largest agent of tropical deforestation is the 'shifted' cultivator.[70] With fast-growing numbers, these people find themselves squeezed out of traditional farmlands in the countries concerned, whereupon they head for the last unoccupied lands they are aware of, the forests. Driven significantly by population growth and sheer pressure on existing farmlands (albeit often cultivated with only low or medium levels of agrotechnology, hence cultivated in extensive rather than intensive fashion), slash-and-burn farming is the principal factor of deforestation in Colombia, Ecuador, Peru, Bolivia, Nigeria, Madagascar, India, Thailand, Indonesia, and the Philippines, and also (though to lesser extent) in Mexico, Brazil, Myanma (Burma), and Vietnam.

Populations of these cultivators are often increasing at annual rates far above the rates of nation-wide increase. In Rondonia in Brazil, the numbers of small-scale settlers have been growing at a rate that has surpassed 15 per cent per year for much of the period since 1975, whereas the population growth-rate for all Brazil has averaged only 2.1 per cent.[71] There are similar mass migrations into tropical forests, albeit at lower rates, in Colombia, Ecuador, Peru, Bolivia, Ivory Coast, Nigeria, India, Thailand, Vietnam, Indonesia, and the Philippines. In all these instances, population growth is a significant if not the predominant factor in deforestation.

Moreover, there is vast scope in population growth of the future for still larger throngs of shifted cultivators to accelerate deforestation in

Table 15.2: Population growth in selected tropical-forest countries

	Population in millions		Growth of population 1989 (%)	% of population in rural areas	Projected population (millions)		stationary population	Per-capita GNP (US$)
	in 1950	in 1989			in 2000	in 2020		
Latin America								
Brazil	53	147	2.0	29	180	234	280	2020
Central America	9	28	2.8	n/a	37	54	88	1240
Colombia	12	31	2.0	33	38	49	57	1220
Ecuador	3	11	2.6	56	14	20	24	1040
The Guyanas	n/a	1.6	2.1	52	2	3	n/a	1050
Mexico	27	87	2.4	34	107	142	170	1820
Peru	8	21	2.1	31	26	35	46	1430
Venezuela	5	19	2.4	17	24	33	42	3230
Asia								
India	362	835	2.2	74	1042	1374	1766	300
Indonesia	77	185	2.0	74	222	287	345	450
Kampuchea	4	7	2.3	89	9	12	n/a	n/a
Laos	n/a	4	2.5	84	5	7	n/a	n/a
Malaysia	6	17	2.5	65	21	27	37	1800
Myanma (Burma)	18	41	2.3	76	51	69	97	n/a
Papua New Guinea	2	4	2.7	87	5	8	12	730
Philippines	20	65	2.8	59	86	131	127	590
Thailand	20	56	1.7	83	66	82	98	840
Vietnam	24	67	2.6	81	86	121	168	n/a
Africa								
Cameroon	5	11	2.6	58	15	24	67	960
Congo	1	2	3.4	52	3	6	17	880
Gabon	n/a	1	1.9	59	1.6	2.6	6	2750
Ivory Coast	3	12	3.6	57	19	35	83	750
Madagascar	5	12	3.1	78	17	30	49	200
Nigeria	41	115	2.9	72	161	274	500	370
Zaire	14	35	3.1	60	49	89	200	160

(Sources: *Population Reference Bureau, 1989; World Bank, 1989.*)

many parts of the humid tropics. By the year 2030 or thereabouts, 80 per cent of the world's projected population of 8 billion people are expected to be living in tropical-forest countries. This translates into 6.4 billion people, or more than 1 billion people more than now live on Earth. Given the 'demographic momentum' built into population-growth processes in countries concerned, and even allowing for expanded family-planning programmes, population projections (Table 15.2) suggest that in those countries where economies appear likely to remain primarily agrarian, there will surely be progressive pressures on remaining forests, extending for decades into the future. For instance, Ecuador's population is projected to increase from 10.5 million today to 24 million (129 per cent greater) before it attains zero growth in about a century's time; Cameroon's from 11 million to 67 million (509 per cent); Ivory Coast's from 12 million to 83 million (592 per cent); Madagascar's from 12 million to 49 million (308 per cent); Nigeria's from 115 million to 500 million (335 per cent); Myanma's from 41 million to 97 million (137 per cent); India's from 835 million to 1766 million (112 per cent); Indonesia's from 185 million to 345 million (87 per cent); and Vietnam's from 67 million to 168 million (151 per cent).

Of course, one must be careful not to overstate the case on a biome-wide basis. In much of the island of New Guinea, population pressures are slight to date, and appear unlikely to become significant within the foreseeable future. Much the same applies in the countries of the Zaire Basin in Central Africa; in the countries of the Guyanas, namely Guyana, Suriname, and French Guiana; and in the western sector of Brazilian Amazonia.

15.4.3 The special role of the shifted cultivator

Slash-and-burn cultivation, usually practised by the shifted cultivator of recent form rather than the shifting cultivator of traditional type, accounts (roughly calculated) for rather more than 60 per cent of all deforestation, a proportion that is likely to increase rapidly.[72] A 'marginal' person by virtue of his lack of economic, social, political, and institutional status, the shifted cultivator feels he has no alternative but to encroach on to the marginal environments of tropical forests. His needs can be addressed only through a broad-scope effort to bring him into the development process through redistribution of existing farmlands, reform of land-tenure systems, buildup of agricultural-extension services, improvement of credit facilities, and provision of agrotechnologies that enable him to practise more intensive and sustainable farming in established farming areas, namely the areas from which he now feels obliged to migrate.

Most important of all, the slash-and-burn cultivator should not be viewed as some sort of 'culprit'. He is no more to be held responsible for felling the forest than a soldier is to be blamed for fighting a war. His life-style is driven by a host of factors – economic, social, legal, insitutional, political – of which he has scant understanding and over which he has virtually no control.

Regrettably, there seems limited prospect of the shifted-cultivator problem being resolved within a time-horizon that will assist tropical forests, unless there is much more attention directed by governments concerned, and by international development agencies, to the particular development challenges he poses. It is a measure of how far his cause is systematically neglected that we have no basic idea of how numerous he is: we simply do not know how many forest-land farmers there are, beyond estimates that range from 300 million to 500 million. If the latter estimate is correct (it may even be an underestimate), he accounts for almost one-in-ten of humankind. Yet he remains a forgotten figure.

It is also a measure of how far Third World development is systematically neglected by the developed world that, in 1988, the indebted countries of the South paid $54 billion more to their Northern creditors in debt repayments, than they received in aid, public loans, and private investment. As long as the overall context of economic relations between North and South reflects a reverse resource flow of this inequitable sort, there can be little hope that tropical-forest governments, which owed $562 billion, or 58 per cent of all Third World debt, in 1987, will direct enough investment toward one of the most neglected of all development sectors, namely subsistence agriculture as practised by the poorest of the poor.

Meantime, the consequence is that the predominant factor in tropical deforestation continues to increase in scope, with little likelihood that it will be diminished within the foreseeable future. If it is not addressed with the comprehensive effort and the urgency it deserves, the destructive processes will build up too much momentum to be halted before vast tracts of tropical forests are eliminated. Herein lies the number-one question about the future of tropical forests – a question that is rarely raised, let alone answered.

15.4.4 Likely acceleration in deforestation rates

On the basis of the problems presented by the shifted cultivator alone, there is solid reason to suppose there will be a continued acceleration in deforestation rates in much, if not most, of the biome. That is to say, deforestation will increase not in a linear manner, but in an exponential fashion. But by how much? Could we reasonably anticipate that, whereas there has been a 90-per-cent increase in the annual deforestation rate during the 1980s, the 1990s could well see the rate soar as high as 150 per cent, meaning the amount of forest being lost in the year 2000 would expand to almost 213,000 km^2? If so, the total of forest remaining would meantime have declined from today's 8 million km^2 to only a little over 6 million km^2. So a loss in the year 2000 of 213,000 km^2 of forest would work out at 3.4 per cent of remaining forests. In other words, it would take far less than a doubling in the annual rate of loss to produce more than a doubling of the expanse lost.

This finding applies, of course, at the level of the individual country (though with a qualifier – see below). Even were the depletive pressure exerted on a forest-stock to remain unchanged, the proportion of remaining forest eliminated each year would increase due to a 'tightening' effect. But the depletive pressure is likely to increase, if only through growing human numbers and growing human demands (in tropical-forest and non-tropical-forest countries alike). So the tightening effect becomes compounded. This all means that the last tracts of tropical forest could be eliminated far faster than one might expect.

15.4.5 Additional sources of deforestation

There are still further possible sources of deforestation, these being atmospheric and climatic in nature. True, they are not likely to make their impact felt until early next century, whereas the factors described are already powerful causes of deforestation. But these additional factors could eventually prove to be some of the most harmful of all. They include regional-scale climatic feedbacks,[73] global-warming feedbacks,[74] and acid rain, all of which could serve to induce pronounced depletion of tropical forests. Here we shall consider just one instance by way of illustration: acid rain.

Acid rain, more correctly known as acid precipitation, is usually thought to be a phenomenon confined to temperate-zone forests of North America and Europe. But increasingly it is becoming a threat to tropical forests.[75] Already it is demonstrably causing widespread damage to forests of southern China.[76] Soon it may well overtake forests elsewhere, notably in those regions with large and growing populations, high numbers of motor-vehicles, a fast-expanding industrial base, and naturally acidic soils. These regions include extensive sectors of western Indonesia, peninsular Malaysia, Vietnam, Thailand, India, the eastern part of West Africa, south-eastern Brazil, north-western Venezuela, and northern Colombia.

How fast this further form of deforestation will overtake the areas in question, is not known. But evidence to date suggests it could eventually (or soon?) cause widespread degradation, if not destruction, of large tracts of forest, even as much as 1 million km², within just a few decades.

15.5 Implications for global warming

Deforestation leads to the release of large amounts of biomass carbon into the global atmosphere, where it combines to form carbon dioxide – the gas that is accounting for almost half of the greenhouse effect. It also releases significant quantities of two other potent greenhouse gases, methane and nitrous oxide.[77]

So far as we can discern from modelling analysis, the 1989 release of carbon from deforestation as documented in Myers' report[78] was in the order of 1.4 billion tonnes per year. This figure is to be compared with a 1979 amount in the order of 0.8 billion tonnes (range, 0.4 to 1.4 billion tonnes). In turn, this means there has been an increase of 75 per cent in carbon emissions. (For a country-by-country breakdown of carbon emissions, see Table 15.3.)

But these figures apply only to closed forests, that is, dense forests with continuous canopy. If we include open forests, the total carbon release in 1989 is estimated to be in the order of 2.4 billion tonnes (range, 2.0 to 2.8 billion tonnes). This is an increase of 0.7 billion tonnes over the 1979 total of 1.7 billion tonnes, that is, an increase of 41 per cent. Note too that the 1989 deforestation of closed forests is estimated to have contributed 58 per cent of carbon emissions from all tropical forests.

The present release of carbon from tropical forests of all types is to be compared with the total from combustion of fossil fuels world-wide (though mostly in developed nations), estimated at 5.6 billion tonnes in 1989. Thus, tropical forests are now contributing 30 per cent of the buildup of carbon dioxide in the global atmosphere, which in turn is considered to be accounting for roughly half of global warming. When we add other greenhouse gases emitted by tropical deforestation, namely methane and nitrous oxide, the overall contribution

Table 15.3: Country-by-country estimates of the deforestation release of carbon, 1989

Country	Deforestation (km2)	Carbon Release (million tonnes)	(% of total)
Brazil	50,000	454	32.1
Indonesia	12,000	124	8.9
Myanma (Burma)	8,000	83	5.9
Mexico	7,000	64	4.6
Thailand	6,000	62	4.4
Colombia	6,500	59	4.2
Nigeria	4,000	57	4.1
Zaire	4,000	57	4.1
Malaysia	4,800	50	3.6
India	4,000	41	2.9
Vietnam	3,500	36	2.6
Papua New Guinea	3,500	36	2.6
Ivory Coast	2,500	36	2.6
Peru	3,500	32	2.3
Central America	3,300	30	2.1
Philippines	2,700	28	2.0
Cameroon	2,000	28	2.0
Madagascar	2,000	28	2.0
Ecuador	3,000	27	1.9
Bolivia	1,500	14	1.0
Venezuela	1,500	14	1.0
Laos	1,000	10	0.7
Congo	700	10	0.7
Gabon	600	9	0.6
Kampuchea	500	5	0.4
Guyanas	500	4	0.3
Total	**1,386,000**	**1,398**	**100.0**

of tropical deforestation to global warming can be estimated to be around 18 to 19 per cent, possibly more.

Moreover, the tropical-forest contribution to the buildup of carbon dioxide in the global atmosphere appears to be expanding more rapidly than that of fossil fuels. Extrapolation of recent trends shows the tropical-forest component could reach a peak of 5 billion tonnes by early next century – whereafter it would rapidly decline, on the grounds that there would not be much forest left to burn.

15.6 Grand-scale reforestation as a response to global warming

A potential response to global warming could well lie with tropical reforestation, undertaken on a scale to restrict the buildup of carbon dioxide in the global atmosphere. Thanks to trees' photosynthesis, grand-scale reforestation would sequester substantial amounts of carbon from the atmosphere. Of course, this measure would work only if it were accompanied by efforts to reduce tropical deforestation, and thereby to stem the current release of carbon dioxide (also of methane, nitrous oxide, and other greenhouse gases) from the tropical-forest zone.

As we have seen in Section 15.5, carbon releases from all sources now amount to some 8 billion tonnes per year. Of this, slightly less than half remains in the atmosphere, the rest ostensibly disappearing into the oceans or being absorbed by plants (through the so-called fertilizer effect) or by other 'sinks'. So the current net annual buildup of atmospheric carbon dioxide is around 4 billion tonnes. But if tropical deforestation were to be reduced by, say, one-third forthwith (more should surely be feasible in the longer-term future), the present annual buildup of carbon would theoretically be cut by 0.8 billion tonnes (out of 2.4 billion tonnes of carbon emitted through deforestation today), leaving the net carbon amount in question at 3.6 billion tonnes. In practice, however, the amount remaining in the atmosphere would be larger, because the oceans, experiencing a lesser 'load' of carbon to be taken up, would tend to absorb a smaller proportion of the airborne volume.

How fast can tropical trees absorb atmospheric carbon dioxide? A tree plantation can readily accumulate between 15 and 25 tonnes of biomass per hectare per year, with a working mean figure of 20 tonnes.[79] To be sure, there is much variability in figures adduced for growth rates and yields, according to climatic conditions, soil types, and the like. But as a measure of the conservative nature of these figures, note that eucalyptus plantations in southern Brazil have been regularly averaging over 30 tonnes per hectare per year, with occasional top yields of over 70 tonnes.[80] Since half of plant growth is made up of carbon, a plantation can assimilate 10 tonnes of atmospheric carbon per hectare per year. In turn, this means that planting trees in 100 million hectares, or 1 million km^2, could take up 1 billion tonnes of carbon from the atmosphere per year for as long as the trees continued to grow rapidly, that is, for thirty years at least.[81]

One million km^2 is a lot of land. It is equivalent to Britain, France, and West Germany together, or an expanse larger than California, Oregon, and Washington combined. In tropical terms, it is more than three times the size of the Philippines, and almost one-third the size of Brazil's sector of the Amazonian forest. Fortunately, a lot of already deforested lands remain available, that is, they have not been taken for permanent settlement by human communities.[82] Tree-planting labour would, it is hoped, be provided free, in light of the many local goods and services (construction materials, soil conservation, wind-breaks, and so on) that would be supplied by trees.

Note, moreover, that there need be no eventual wood-storage problem. Trees can continue to grow, and store carbon, for thirty or even forty years. This should surely give us enough time to move beyond a fossil-fuel-based economy, in which case the tree-planting measure becomes a stopgap affair to help us through an energy/climate bottle-neck. In these circumstances, carbon-sequestering wood is continuously 'stored' as it keeps on growing in plantations.

As for cost, we can reckon that at 1988 prices for seedlings and the like, an agroforestry or social-forestry plantation – such as would be suitable for the bulk of the programme – costs between $200 and $500 per hectare. By contrast, a commercial-timber plantation, generally established without free inputs, costs around $2000 a hectare. Suppose the costs average, as a reasonable 'working' estimate,[83] $400 per hectare. This means that planting 1 million km^2 with trees would cost $40 billion. Were the programme to be spread out over, say, ten years, the average annual cost would be $4 billion at present prices. While this sum is well over twice the annual amount required for the most ambitious tropical forestry programme to date, the Tropical Forestry Action Plan, it would represent an exceedingly positive investment compared with the concealed costs of inaction as concerns the greenhouse effect's impacts on agriculture and coastal communities alone. The tree-planting concept has already been accepted in principle by the Intergovernmental Panel on Climate Change, which proposes planting an area of 120,000 km^2 per year for twenty years in various parts of the world, making an ultimate total of 2.4 million km^2.

Who would pay for grand-scale reforestation in the humid tropics? Those countries that most need watershed rehabilitation, fuel-wood supplies, and commercial timber would reap a sizeable benefit, so they would presumably be inclined to assume much of the cost. The fact that they have not yet undertaken tree-planting activities of sufficient scale is explained partly by their lack of understanding of the pressing need for tree-planting (this lack is being made good in several countries), and partly by sheer shortage of funds. This second factor argues for a greater injection of financial support on the part of the industrialized nations, partly on conventional grounds of development needs, and partly in light of the industrialized nations' emergent stake in mitigating the greenhouse effect. Indeed, the industrialized nations should surely cover the bulk of the costs, on the grounds that they have been the main source of the greenhouse-effect problem.

15.7 Conclusion

Tropical deforestation has accelerated markedly during the 1980s. As a result, it is now contributing around 30 per cent of buildup of carbon dioxide in the global atmosphere. Moreover, there is every prospect that in the absence of much more vigorous and urgent efforts to tackle the problem, the deforestation rate will continue to accelerate, and that the proportionate emission of greenhouse gases will expand.

Fortunately, there is a positive aspect to the tropical forests' situation. It now appears that one of the most cost-effective and technically feasible ways to counter the greenhouse effect lies with grand-scale reforestation in the tropics as a means to sequester carbon dioxide from the global atmosphere – provided, of course, that the strategy is accompanied by greatly increased efforts to slow deforestation. The infusion of support-funding and technical expertise would transform the outlook for tropical forests.

Chapter 16
Agricultural Contributions to Global Warming

Anne Ehrlich

" ...If, in a global movement toward controlling greenhouse-gas emissions, the agricultural sector and the underlying driving force of population growth are forgotten or neglected, heroic efforts to convert the energy sector might be negated as the more potent methane and nitrous oxide emissions build up in place of carbon dioxide. In that circumstance, agriculture's fairly modest 14-per-cent share of the greenhouse buildup could quickly double... "

Agriculture makes important contributions to global warming from enhanced greenhouse-gas emissions, being responsible for an estimated 14 per cent of the total.[1] This estimate by IPCC Working Group 3 may include the fraction of carbon dioxide produced by the world agricultural sector, some 3–8 per cent of total commercial energy use in most nations,[2] but apparently does not include (or understates) the carbon dioxide released in tropical deforestation for agricultural land. Also ascribed to agriculture are substantial portions of the global emissions of two important greenhouse gases, methane (CH_4) and nitrous oxide (N_2O), as well as minor amounts of two other relevant gases – carbon monoxide (CO) and nitric oxide (NO). Carbon dioxide emissions are dealt with in other chapters and will not be discussed here. Carbon monoxide is important primarily because of its influence on atmospheric concentrations of methane. This chapter focuses mainly on agricultural emissions of methane and nitrous oxide, their potential impacts, and appropriate policy responses.

Agriculture is an indispensable activity for supporting the growing human population, now about 5.3 billion and projected to pass 6 billion by 1998 and 8 billion before 2020.[3] Since the activities that generate the greenhouse emissions are central to the agricultural enterprise, complete elimination of greenhouse emissions from this sector clearly will not be possible. Rather, continued expansion of global food production will surely lead to increased emissions unless concerted efforts are made to prevent them. The mechanisms underlying releases of both methane and nitrous oxide are poorly known, unfortunately, and the degree to which they could be manipulated by changes in farming and livestock-management practices is even less well understood. Nevertheless, significant reductions do seem possible.

In view of their potency as greenhouse gases, serious efforts to reduce emissions of both gases without impairing agricultural productivity should be an important goal. It must be remembered, however, that in the long run, control of all greenhouse gases, including agriculture-related ones, will ultimately depend on success in controlling population growth.[4]

16.1 Methane

Methane (CH_4) is some twenty times as potent a greenhouse gas as carbon dioxide, molecule for molecule, and its concentration in the atmosphere has been rising faster – by about 1 per cent per year – in this century.[5] Concentrations in the atmosphere have increased about 2.5-fold since they began rising over a century ago. Methane ranks second in importance behind CO_2, accounting for about 17 per cent of the radiative forcing effect of greenhouse gases since the dawn of the industrial age.[6] For the decade of the 1980s, the estimated radiative forcing of methane fell behind that of the rapidly rising CFCs and was only about 11 per cent. If the trends in accumulation of both CO_2 and CH_4 continue unchanged (and CFCs are curbed), the greenhouse effect from methane could exceed that of CO_2 by 2040.[7]

Methane's concentration of 1,720 parts per billion (ppb) in the atmosphere in 1990 is more than twice as high as occurred in previous interglacial periods over the past 160,000 years, according to recent polar ice-core studies.[8] Total global emissions of methane are estimated to be in the range of 350 to 600 teragrams (Tg) per year, most of which is destroyed in the atmosphere, resulting in an average annual accumulation of around 40–50 Tg.[9]

16.2 Sources of methane

Methane is distinguished in having a large number of significant sources (unlike, for instance, CFCs). Substantial uncertainty surrounds the sizes of various methane sources and even more so their likely emission rates in the future, several of which may change in response to global warming itself and/or to changes in concentrations of other greenhouse gases.[10] Most major sources appear evident, and their contributions have been at least roughly estimated. Table 16.1 compares the estimates of the IPCC panel on greenhouse-gas emissions with those of Lashof and Tirpak's study for the United States Environmental Protection Agency (EPA) in 1989.[11] Isotopic studies have established that at least 80 per cent of emissions are from recent biological origin, not fossil sources.[12]

Anaerobic fermentation is the primary source of methane emissions from contemporary biological sources, both natural and agricultural. Natural sources include all kinds of wetlands, especially peatbogs in northern latitudes, which are responsible for perhaps 50 per cent of wetland emissions. Peatbogs in particular, as well as other wetland sources, may increase their releases of methane in response to global warming as higher temperatures boost the activity of the methane-producing bacteria. Even more worrying, a huge but unmeasured potential source is methane hydrates, now locked in sediments under permafrost and on continental margins, which also may be destabilized and released as temperatures rise.[13] Other relatively minor natural sources include termites (now, after some controversy, estimated at 10–20 Tg per year) and gas exchanges between the atmosphere and oceans and lakes (about the same magnitude).[14]

Table 16.1: Current emissions of methane by source *(Tg = 10^{12} grams or 10^6 tonnes)*

	Lashof/Tirpak	Watson *et al.*
Natural sources (wetlands)	115–345	100–200
Rice production	60–170	25–170
Domestic animals	65–100	65–100
Fossil-fuel production	50–95	40–100
Biomass burning	50–100	20–80
Landfills	30–70	20–70
Termites	–	10–100
Oceans and freshwaters	–	6–45
CH_4 hydrate destabilization	–	0–100

Sources: D. A. Lashof and D. A. Tirpak (eds.), *Policy Options for Stabilizing Global Climate* (EPA, Washington, DC, 1989); Watson *et al.*, IPCC Working Group 1, Section 1, *Greenhouse Gases and Aerosols*, Peer Reviewed Assessment for Working Group 1 Plenary, 25 Apr. 1990.

The principal anthropogenic sources of methane arise from agriculture. Others include incomplete combustion in burning of biomass, as in tropical deforestation and forest fires as well as agricultural burning; releases from landfills; and leakage of natural gas from pipelines, venting from oil- and gas-wells, and escape of gas from coal in mining and processing. All these sources are highly variable over time (especially that from biomass burning) and/or have been only roughly estimated.[15]

In the agricultural sector, the leading sources of methane releases are emissions from rice paddies, enteric fermentation in ruminant animals, and biomass burning, respectively contributing roughly 21, 15, and 8 per cent of all methane releases.[16]

The largest agricultural source of methane production is anaerobic bacteria associated with rice cultivation in paddies – analogous to emissions from natural wetlands.[17] The estimates are subject to huge uncertainties, ranging from a global annual total of 25 to 170 Tg,[18] that is, by a factor of 7. Very few field measurements have been made, including only one published study in Asia, where more than 85 per cent of the world's rice is produced.[19] The handful of field studies that have been made produced widely divergent results because of differences in measuring methods, cropping patterns, and crop varieties. Measured methane flux rates per season (or per crop, if multi-cropped) in studies up to 1989 varied from 28 grams to over 120 grams per square metre of paddy surface.[20] Additional factors found to affect the rate of methane emissions from paddies include soil properties, temperature, fertilizer use, and irrigation practices.

Mammals digest their food with the aid of anaerobic bacteria in their digestive tracts, which produce methane. Ruminants such as cattle and sheep are especially dependent on bacteria to digest the cellulose in their diets, and they emit large amounts of the gas. Table 16.2 compares the average quantities emitted by different species.[21] Of the animals that emit significant amounts of methane, including a few non-ruminants such as horses and pigs, cattle are by far the most important, because they are among both the most methane-productive beasts and the most numerous. Some 4–9 per cent of the energy in their food is converted to methane. In the late 1980s, there were some 1.26 billion head of cattle world-wide,[22] collectively producing about three-quarters of the total estimated ruminant contribution of some 65–100 Tg per year.[23] Table 16.3 compares the world-wide numbers of leading animal emitters.

Table 16.2: Methane emission rates from animals (Kg per animal per year)

Cattle (developed country)	55
Cattle (less developed country)	35
Buffalo	50
Sheep	5–8
Goats	5
Camels	58
Pigs	1–1.5
Horses	18
Mules/asses	10
Human beings	0.05

Source: Adapted from P. H. Gleick and C. Shirley, Greenhouse Gas Emissions for Agricultural Activities (report for the Office of Technology Assessment, Pacific Institute, 1988); information from P. J. Crutzen, I. Aselmann, and W. Seiler, 'Methane production by domestic animals, wild ruminants, other herbivorous fauna, and humans', Tellus (1988), vol. 38B, pp. 271–84.

The world's cattle population in recent decades has been growing more slowly than the human population – about 1.2 per cent annually (compared with 1.8 per cent for humanity). Since 1980, the rate of growth has slowed even further; the increase in eight years from 1980 to 1988 was only 3.7 per cent – less than 0.5 per cent per year. Since then, given the tightening of global grain supplies thanks to several dismal world harvests,[24] the cattle population is unlikely to have expanded significantly; and with changing consciousness in rich nations about the dangers of high-fat, high-meat diets, demand for beef and dairy products may not increase as rapidly in the future as it did in the 1950s and 1960s, which is good news for the atmosphere as well.

The third largest agriculture-related source of methane is biomass burning, much of which occurs in forest-clearing for conversion to agriculture in the tropics. An unknown fraction of total global emissions (an estimated 20–80 Tg of methane per year) is produced in burning of harvested fields or crop residues.[25]

Table 16.3: Numbers of livestock species world-wide *(millions)*

	1980	1988
Cattle	1,218	1,263
Horses	64	65
Mules/asses	52	57
Buffalo	124	136
Camels	17	19
Sheep	1,097	1,173
Goats	465	520
Pigs	780	823

Source: *1988 Production Yearbook* (Food and Agriculture Organization, Rome, 1989).

16.3 Methane sinks, feedbacks, and interconnections with other gases

While human activities have evidently increased global emissions of methane, changes in natural sinks may also be included in its buildup. The principal sink for atmospheric methane is through reactions with hydroxyl (OH) radicals in the troposphere. Approximately 90 per cent of annual methane emissions are destroyed in this way, leading to methane's relatively short atmospheric-residence time of about ten years. The amount of OH available in the atmosphere to destroy CH_4 is contingent on several factors, including the abundance of carbon monoxide, which competes with methane and other hydrocarbons in reacting with OH. Moreover, about a quarter of the CO is itself a product of methane photochemical oxidation.[26] The rapid rise in CH_4 concentrations, therefore, may be due in part to impairment of the hydroxyl sink as CO concentrations from incomplete combustion have risen, thus lengthening the residence time of methane.

In addition, methane contributes to the formation of ozone in the troposphere, which is another greenhouse gas. Along with other hydrocarbons and CO, methane can be photo-oxidized in the presence of oxides of nitrogen to form ozone. A doubling of methane emissions could increase tropospheric ozone if oxides of nitrogen also continue to increase through human activities. And ozone also competes for destruction in part by OH radicals.[27]

About 10 per cent of the methane escapes destruction in the lower atmosphere and rises into the stratosphere, where it is oxidized, forming water molecules. About half of the water vapour in the stratosphere today is estimated to have originated as methane. Thus increased methane concentrations in the atmosphere could lead to more stratospheric water vapour, which, besides enhancing the greenhouse effect, could in turn increase the polar stratospheric clouds that have been linked to the dramatic ozone destruction in polar regions.[28]

An additional minor sink for methane is soils, which may remove some 15–45 Tg per year.[29] Although little seems to be known about this sink, it appears that it too is being impaired, ironically by inputs of nitrogen, which can lead to production of nitrous oxide emissions.[30] In forest and farmland soils in New England, nitrogen enrichment from acid precipitation as well as from fertilizers was found to be suppressing methane destruction.

Besides its direct action as a greenhouse gas, methane can contribute indirectly to global warming through various chemical reactions in the atmosphere. Simply curbing anthropogenic methane emissions may not suffice to reduce its greenhouse effects; control of other atmospheric gases and pollutants with which it interacts (especially gases that compete for destruction by OH radicals) must be considered as well. And the potential positive-feedback effect of increased methane emissions due to warming itself, as higher temperatures stimulate more rapid fermentation in systems from northern peatbogs to rice paddies to the guts of tropical termites, should be a serious concern to policymakers.[31] Nevertheless, the IPCC Working Group 1 concluded that, because of its short residence time (other things being equal, presumably), methane concentrations could be stabilized by reducing current anthropogenic emissions by only 15–20 per cent.[32]

16.4 Opportunities for emissions reductions

Opportunities for reductions in emissions of methane in human-controlled areas are significant, although in some cases the best way to achieve them may not be immediately clear. Emissions from biomass burning, of course, can best be reduced by forgoing burning when possible (see discussion below).

Emissions of methane from rice production probably could be reduced significantly,[33] but much more needs to be learned about the mechanisms of emission, and the effects on it of different cultivation and irrigation practices, rice cultivars, and fertilization strategies, in order to do this intelligently. A particular challenge will be achieving production-increases through use of higher-yield crop varieties and faster-maturing ones, allowing more crops per year without greatly increasing methane emissions. Much experimentation with different varieties and cultivation methods is needed to determine the best approach in different situations.

But other complications attend such changes. For example, raising yields often requires increased fertilizer applications. Synthetic fertilizers seem to cause lower methane emissions than natural ones, yet they might boost emissions of nitrous oxide and cause other environmental problems.[34] Similarly, multiple cropping (growing more crops per year) may result in year-round flooding of paddies instead of only a few months per year, thus increasing CH_4 emissions.

Efforts to raise rice-yields without increasing greenhouse-gas emissions should focus on more-efficient fertilizing practices, including examination of the relative emissions of both methane and nitrous oxide resulting from use of natural nitrogen-fixing organisms in place of, or to supplement, synthetic fertilizers.

Another goal might be development of rice strains with a higher ratio of grain to non-grain biomass, leaving less residue to decay and emit methane or be burned. Alternatively, using crop residues in biogasification units, to produce methane as an energy source and the residue from that process as livestock feed or fertilizer, might be an efficient way to use them in many developing countries. In China and some other Asian regions, aquaculture is commonly combined with rice cultivation; the fish help control weeds and insects, contribute nutrients to the paddy, and provide a food source for the farmer. It would be useful to know what the greenhouse-gas emissions from such systems might be.

Methane emissions from livestock may be controllable through improved management.[35] It is known that the fraction of food energy that is converted to methane varies with the quality and quantity of feed, with a smaller fraction converted to methane in high-quality feed containing a high proportion of starch relative to cellulose. Grain-fed cattle emit five or more times less methane per pound of meat produced than do range-fed cattle with a high cellulose diet.[36] In general, a well-fed animal is substantially more productive than a poorly fed one, even on a forage diet diet resulting in more meat or milk produced per animal.

The importance of better feeding purely for reasons of efficient production is known and heeded in most developed nations (especially the market economies), which had about 405 million head of cattle in 1988 and 338 million sheep.[37] These numbers represent roughly a 5-per-cent reduction in cattle herds since 1980 and a slight increase in sheep. In recent years, enhanced productivity, achieved through biotechnology, selective breeding, and optimized feeding has permitted a steady reduction of herds. And, as mentioned, consumption of meat and dairy products has been declining for health reasons in the United States and some European nations for the past decade or so. Continuation of both trends would certainly help in reducing methane emissions.

An additional opportunity for reducing emissions in dairy cattle may be high-tech feeding supplements, such as methane-inhibiting bacteria, charcoal, or other substances such as halogenated organics and fatty acids.[38] Their potential effectiveness is unknown, but clearly deserves exploration. So does the potential for different feeding regimes.

The greatest scope for reducing methane emissions through improved livestock management obviously lies in developing regions. There, numbers of both cattle (860 million in 1988) and sheep (484 million)[39] have been rising steadily, and feeding levels are in most cases quite poor. But in poor nations, most cattle do not compete significantly with people for food; they subsist on forage on marginal lands generally unsuitable for sustained farming. Overgrazing and resultant desertification are common problems, not limited to poor countries. Unquestionably, better management, including reduction of many herds and perhaps limited supplemental feeding, would result in fewer, more-productive animals in many regions. But making such changes is difficult in societies where people are struggling day by day to survive.

Achieving significant improvements in livestock management must overcome the barriers of poverty, tradition, and sometimes varied goals of maintaining herds. In parts of Africa, for instance, cattle are kept primarily as embodiments of wealth and only secondarily for meat, milk, and leather products. The animals' condition is of little consequence; numbers are what count for wealth. Changing this tradition to value productivity over numbers will be no easy task.

India has the world's largest cattle population, around 200 million in the mid-1980s. India's cattle are considered sacred and are valued more as traction and sources of fertilizer and fuel (in the poorest areas) than for meat or milk, especially among the vegetarian Hindus. Numbers are not controlled, nor is feeding-quality a concern. In a region where 50 per cent of the human population is significantly underfed,[40] the outlook for improved feeding of cattle is not very bright. The first order of business in this situation almost certainly should be to rationalize the cattle population – reduce herds to supportable levels based on the real needs for animal power, manure, and animal foods – but tradition again will present obstacles.

Clearly, to achieve reductions in methane emissions from livestock and rice production in developing nations, assistance from the developed world will be needed. Moreover, more questions than answers are available for solving the problem at this point; far more comparative research on specific rice-growing and livestock-management practices in different settings is needed. For efficiency, studies and monitoring programmes could be set up in tandem with the introduction of new practices, but this would require a quite intensive effort in agricultural extension and information exchange – something that is lacking in many developing nations. Specific programmes, however, could be set up in the network of United Nations-affiliated agricultural research institutes, such as one that has been initiated at the International Rice Research Institute to develop and disseminate effective, feasible, and economically sensible methods for both sectors that can be applied under the wide variety of soil/climate regimes and socio-economic systems found in the developing world.

In any case, improvements in sustainable production-efficiency in all agricultural sectors are needed for their own sake as the world population continues to grow and natural constraints on expanding food production increasingly manifest themselves.[41] It should be possible to integrate research-and-development projects focused on alternative agricultural methods that curb greenhouse-gas releases into more generalized agricultural development programmes, if the urgency of doing so is accepted.

But a broader, more interdisciplinary approach will be required than most agricultural research and extension programmes are accustomed to using, either in developed or in developing nations. Openness to change and flexibility will be needed not only to reduce greenhouse emissions from the agricultural sector, but also to enable that sector to adapt with minimal losses to adverse weather and climate changes caused by global warming. Fortunately, the growing recognition that the conventional agriculture practised since about 1950, and transferred (often unwisely) to developing nations, has serious drawbacks may make agricultural institutions more open now than in the past few decades to new ideas and practices.

16.5 Nitrous oxide

As with other greenhouse gases, concentrations of nitrous oxide (N_2O) began to increase in the atmosphere as industrialization progressed. Nitrous oxide is an even more powerful greenhouse gas than methane, being about 230 times as effective per molecule as CO_2.[42] Its cumulative contribution to increased radiative forcing to date is estimated at about 4 per cent, and about 6 per cent during the 1980s.[43] The 1990 concentration is about 310 parts per billion, some 8 per cent above the pre-industrial level, and is rising by about 0.2 to 0.3 per cent per year, amounting to an addition of some 3 to 4.5 Tg.

The principal sink for nitrous oxide is destruction by ultraviolet light in the stratosphere, which accounts for its long atmospheric-residence time of roughly 150 years. Soils and aquatic systems may provide small additional sinks of unknown size. The stratospheric sink destroys only about two-thirds of annual emissions; consequently, the scientific panel of IPCC estimates that an immediate reduction of 70–80 per cent of excess emissions (about 23 per cent of total emissions) would be required to stabilize atmospheric concentrations at the current level.

16.6 Sources of nitrous oxide emissions

Of the estimated 14 Tg of nitrous oxide emitted to the atmosphere each year, only a small fraction is now thought to come from fossil-fuel use, primarily coal.[44] The rest arises from gas exchanges with the oceans, from biomass burning and deforestation, and is emitted from soils through the processes of denitrification or nitrification, both of which are connected to the use of agricultural fertilizers.[45]

The sizes and relative values of nitrous oxide sources are even more uncertain than those for methane, and the portion of emissions ascribable to human activity, mainly the use of fertilizers, biomass burning, land-use changes, and fossil-fuel use, is not clear. Table 16.4 shows the most recent estimates, which in several cases (oceans, fossil-fuel combustion, and biomass burning) represent substantial reductions from earlier estimates. Since both the atmospheric build-up and the main sink are reasonably well quantified, perhaps 4 Tg N per year remain unaccounted for from the estimated sources, although the IPCC scientific working-group presumes much of the 'missing' emissions to be anthropogenic in origin. As much as half the gap may prove to be natural, possibly from coastal ecosystems and estuaries.[46]

Table 16.4: Estimated sources and sinks of nitrous oxide *(range in Tg N per year)*

Source	
Fossil fuel use	0.1–0.3
Oceans	1.4–2.6
Soils (tropical forests)	2.2–3.7
(temperate forests)	0.7–1.5
Biomass burning	0.02–0.2
Fertilizers/groundwater	0.01–2.2
TOTAL	**4.4–10.5**

Sinks	
Soils	?
Photolysis in the statosphere	7–13
Atmospheric increase	3–4.5

Source: as Table 16.1, Watson *et al.*

The IPCC scientists' estimate of annual emissions from tropical forests, however, is only about half that of an earlier estimate, by McElroy and Wofsy, of 7.4 Tg N.[47] Moreover, the panel mentions, but does not incorporate, small-scale studies that indicate accelerations of N_2O releases from recently cleared pastures in lowland tropical-forest areas of up to threefold.[48] Other studies have found different results.[49] What is clear is that emissions may vary widely with different soil types and moisture levels. Based on their measurements of nitrous oxide fluxes in tropical forest converted to pasture, and the extent of such conversions up to 1980, Luizao *et al.* estimated that an additional 0.8 to 1.3 Tg N per year of nitrous oxide might arise from this source. Since the rate of tropical deforestation has increased by some 50 to 90 per cent since 1980,[50] their estimate of emissions from cleared land might also be low. Of course, the emissions represent a loss of valuable nutrient from the soils as well, and accord with widely observed rapid declines in fertility of many tropical forest soils after clearing.

16.7 Nitrous oxide and fertilizers

The principal agricultural source of nitrous oxide is from the use of fertilizers, accounting for an estimated 5–20 per cent of total emissions. Both natural (animal or human manure and crop residues: 'green manure') and manufactured fertilizers make contributions, mainly through the biological process of denitrification (reduction of nitrate) in soil. Nitrification, the process of converting ammonia to nitrate, also can produce nitrous oxide. Both nitrification and denitrification are important parts of the global nitrogen cycle, which is heavily dependent on biological systems.[51] Nitrogen, an essential nutrient, must be converted from its atmospheric form (N_2) to ammonia or nitrate before plants can absorb it, a chemical transformation (called fixation) performed by bacteria in soil and aquatic systems.

In recent decades, the intensification of agriculture to support the growing human population has been accompanied by a massive increase in the use of synthetic fertilizers to boost crop yields. By the mid-1980s, over 70 million metric tons of nitrogen per year were being applied to the world's crops.[52] The global rate of industrial fixation of nitrogen to make fertilizers now approaches that of natural fixation, representing a large perturbation in a natural cycle. Excess nitrate in soil that is not taken up by plants often leaches out or runs off to pollute surface waters and ground-water. The accumulated nitrate in soil is also available for denitrification, thereby releasing nitrous oxide into the atmosphere. In view of the great increase in nitrogen compounds applied to soils world-wide, a substantial fraction of which cannot be used by the crops even under the best circumstances, it is no surprise that nitrous oxide emissions have risen.

While both natural and synthetic fertilizers contribute N_2O emissions, synthetics are assumed to be the main offenders, largely because they comprise the 'extra' nitrogenous elements added to the system. Beyond that, synthetic fertilizers are often applied at less appropriate times and in too-large amounts at once, and therefore may be less efficiently utilized and more likely to cause excess releases of N_2O. To the extent that over-use of synthetic ferilizers with too little return of organic matter to soil accelerates nitrate losses, the problem is exacerbated. Synthetic-fertilizer use in the tropics, which has risen explosively in the past fifteen years, may account for some of the 'missing' N_2O source. More nitrous oxide is released from tropical soils per unit of nitrogen circulating in tropical forests than in temperate ones. There is reason to suspect that the same may occur when fertilizers are applied to tropical soil.[53] Emissions from both natural and synthetic fertilizers are known to vary with such factors as timing of applications, soil moisture, soil type, surface temperature, timing of rainfall, tillage methods, and crops.

16.8 Opportunities for nitrous oxide emissions reductions

Since anthropogenic sources account for roughly a quarter to a third of nitrous oxide emissions (and possibly all of the excess causing the atmospheric buildup), ample opportunities should exist for reducing them, despite the handicaps of inadequate information and incomplete understanding of the processes involved. Forest preservation (especially in the moist tropics) and improved forest management are obvious measures to be taken, but are discussed in other chapters.[54]

While agricultural burning is a minor source of N_2O, it clearly is an activity that could be substantially reduced, with the result of lowering not only emissions of nitrous oxide but also other greenhouse gases, including CO_2 and CH_4. The practice is widespread, especially in the tropics and subtropics, and is employed for various reasons, including weed and pest control. Alternative methods to accomplish the goals of burning need to be found for different settings and traditions, and the new practices introduced to farmers.[55] The IPCC Working Group 3 subgroup on agriculture suggests, among other possibilities, removing crop residues that otherwise would be burned to use as an alternative fuel. Better choices would be to plough it into the soil to serve as green manure, or to feed it to livestock. Changing traditional farming practices is not easy, but it can be done, especially if the new measures prove profitable.

Reductions of nitrous oxide emissions from agricultural soils may be accomplished by more-judicious fertilizing practices, which would have the added benefits of reducing farmers' costs and society's pollution problems. Synthetic fertilizers, if used extensively without adding organic matter to soil, can undermine its long-term fertility and nutrient-retention capacity and impair the ability of crops to utilize the fertilizers. To compensate, fertilizer applications must be increased, and, no doubt, nitrous oxide emissions also rise.[56]

It should also be noted that the manufacture of nitrogen fertilizers is very energy-intensive; the feedstock on which the process is based is natural gas, and distribution of fertilizers to dispersed farms and their application require additional energy. So any reduction of synthetic nitrogen fertilizer-use is also a reduction in energy-use (and thus of CO_2 emissions).

For sundry reasons, then, increased use of natural fertilizers and less reliance on synthetic ones is advisable. In the United States, about 25 per cent of the manure produced by livestock is not returned to soil but is discarded, often creating serious water-pollution problems,[57] and very possibly also causing significant nitrous oxide emissions (as well as methane releases). Simply making the effort to reclaim this wasted material for fertilizer would have a positive effect on greenhouse releases. Similar opportunities doubtless exist in many countries, especially industrialized ones that practise intensive livestock production.

In situations where synthetic fertilizers are needed to supplement natural ones, N_2O emissions can probably be lowered by using alternative forms or methods of application. Several different forms of synthetic nitrogen fertilizers are in use, which produce nitrous oxide emissions at very different rates (Table 16.5).[58] Since measurements have been obtained from only a few single-site tests in the United

States, conclusions based on them should be viewed with scepticism; but they do indicate that different emission-rates offer an opportunity, if they are verified under an appropriate variety of conditions, to reduce emissions simply by switching fertilizer types. Again, since high emission-rates presumably reflect higher soil-nutrient losses, such switches are likely to improve fertilizing efficacy as well.[59]

Table 16.5: Emission coefficients for N_2O from agricultural fertilizers
(% of N evolved to atmosphere as N_2O)

Anhydrous ammonia	1 to 5
Aqua ammonia	1 to 5
Urea	0.05 to 0.5
Ammonium nitrate	0.04 to 0.5
Ammonium sulphate	0.04 to 0.5
Diammonium phosphate	0.1
Nitrogen solutions	0.05
Sodium nitrate	0.05

Source: Gleick and Shirley, as Table 16.2, based on information from J. M. Bremner and A. M. Blackmer, 'Nitrous oxide: emission from soils during nitrification of fertilizer nitrogen', *Science* (1978), vol. 199, pp. 295–6; G. A. Breitenbeck, A. M. Blackmer, and J. M. Bremner, 'Effects of different nitrogenous fertilizers on emissions of nitrous oxides from soils', *Geophysical Research Letters* (1980), vol. 7, no. 1, pp. 85–8; F. Slemr and W. Seiler, 'Field measurements of NO and NO_2 emissions from fertilized and unfertilized soils', *Journal of Atmospheric Chemistry* (1984), vol. 2, pp. 1–24; I. Fung, E. Matthews and J. Lerner, 'Trace gas emissions associated with agricultural activities', EPA Workshop on Agriculture and Climate Change, Washington DC, 29 Feb.–1 Mar. 1988.

While much more research needs to be done to determine which fertilizer forms and application methods produce lower emissions under which circumstances and with which crops, enough is known to make some preliminary suggestions.[60] Deep injection of fertilizer pellets below the surface can reduce nitrogen volatilization, but may not lower N_2O releases. Slow-release forms of nitrogen fertilizers do result in decreased nitrogen losses, especially in rice paddies, and have the added benefit of being available when needed by crops in appropriate quantities. Careful timing and placement of fertilizer applications can make a significant difference in decreasing denitrification losses (and N_2O emissions); such efficient application would also diminish the total amount needed.

Besides manipulation of fertilizer applications, other cultivation methods may prove useful in controlling N_2O emissions. Soil moisture and aeration are factors of some importance in governing emissions; both might be subject to some control, especially in irrigated fields. No-tillage or minimum-tillage treatments also may reduce the need for synthetic fertilizers while improving the texture and organic content of the soil, although no-till cultivation appears to enhance nitrous oxide emissions. Much more study is needed of the relative effects and interactions of different cropping systems, fertilizing practices, and tillage in different settings.

Among long-term technological possibilities is the development of nitrogen-fixing capabilities for cereals and some other crops, and enhancement of those capacities in crops that have them (mainly legumes).[61] Obviously, any avenue that might provide more-efficient fertilization and maintains or boosts crop yields without degrading soil should be pursued.

The emphasis in agricultural development in all nations should be on sustainable, soil-preserving practices, particularly increased reliance on natural fertilizers and crop rotation (nitrogen-fixing leguminous crops alternating with non-leguminous crops), with the goal of enhancing long-term productivity.[62] In the United States, serious problems with soil erosion, rising costs of inputs (fertilizers and pesticides) as well as pollution problems from their use, increasing resistance to pesticides, and competition from other food-exporting nations have induced farmers to begin seeking more sustainable, less costly, alternative methods of production. Many of the methods that best answer these problems may also help to reduce greenhouse-gas emissions.

A special committee of the US National Research Council has noted that the US agricultural system would benefit in myriad ways by adoption of a less energy- and chemical-intensive, more ecologically oriented farming regime.[63] The committee recommended working in that direction, focusing on three goals: keeping US farm exports competitive; cutting production costs; and reducing the environmental costs of farming (although there is no indication that agricultural contributions to global warming were among their concerns).

Clearly, significant reductions in nitrous oxide will not be easily achieved, given the vital importance of continuing to expand food production and the central role that fertilizers play in that endeavour. The obstacles are great, not least the lack of solid information and understanding of the complex systems involved, and the technical difficulties of research and monitoring. Beyond those are the institutional and economic problems of rapidly deploying new practices, especially in developing countries but also in rich ones.

16.9 Projected trends

The policymakers of IPCC Working Group 3 appropriately note the continuing expansion of the human population and the consequent necessity of continuing to expand food production for decades to come.[64] But the policymakers' cited projections for average population growth of 1.3 per cent per year from 1990 to 2025, reaching 8.2 billion by then, are inexplicably lower than most recent projections.[65] Current estimates are for the world population to reach 8.2 billion before 2020, an increase of about 55 per cent in thirty years, implying an average annual growth-rate of about 1.5 per cent – only a small decline from the current 1.8 per cent.

The IPCC Working Group 3 report also makes a series of projections about the world food system that seem unduly optimistic or unrealistic. Unfortunately, no details on the assumptions behind these projections are given in the report. Estimates of future changes in land use,[66] including a 50-per-cent increase in cultivated land in developing nations by 2025, would indicate a reversal of recent trends. The area of crop-land planted in grain (the principal human feeding base) reached a peak in 1981, some 24 per cent above that of 1950; since then it has been declining as the amount of deteriorating farmland taken out of production has exceeded that of new land brought under the plough. (Indeed, the agricultural subgroup itself recommends taking marginal lands out of annual crops and replacing them with perennials for fodder or fuel-wood.) The world-wide acreage of cropland per person has fallen steadily for decades; by 2000 it will be half that of 1950.[67] Nearly all the 2.6-fold gain in annual food production since 1950 has been from increased yields on a very slowly expanding, and recently shrinking, land base.

Similarly, one wonders where the IPCC Working Group 3 projection of a 34-per-cent increase in rice-growing area is to come from, since nearly all rice is grown in Asia, a continent generally recognized as having the least remaining land available for new cultivation. The only possibilities are an increase in multiple cropping, possibly facilitated by extensive irrigation development in South Asia, or an expansion of rice-growing in Africa or Latin America. In Africa, other crops would undoubtedly be displaced by the rice, and water-availability might be a serious constraint. In Latin America, such expansion would most likely occur in the Amazon region, a development that should be undertaken only with due consideration for its sustainability and balanced against the need to preserve the forest.

The IPCC Working Group also projects a 45-per-cent increase in meat and dairy production by 2025, with a similar increase in methane emissions. Apparently, no account is taken of potential increases in productivity per animal, especially in developing nations, which might boost production without a corresponding rise in methane emissions. Such an increase is at variance with recent trends of slowing production. Moreover, it seems unlikely that herds in developing countries can long continue to expand, given the already serious problems from over-grazing and desertification.[68]

The projection of quadrupled fertilizer use in developing nations (and doubled for the world) by 2025 is dubious as well, in part because of the likelihood that fertilizer prices will rise as Middle Eastern oil-production curves pass their peak, thus adding to the very real economic obstacles already felt by poor farmers. Another reason to doubt the projection is that, in many developing nations, diminishing returns from increased applications are being realized.[69] Finally, synthetic fertilizers are even more environmentally disruptive and soil-damaging, and less effective, in the tropics than in temperate regions. While increases in fertilizer use undoubtedly will and should occur, they must be used judiciously and with care in the tropics; the reasons for emphasizing natural fertilizers are even more compelling in these settings.[70]

Whether the tightening constraints on increasing world food production (leaving out the problems that global warming and changed climatic conditions might bring to slow-responding agricultural systems) will themselves lead to higher emissions of greenhouse gases is unpredictable, but should be a matter for concern. Unquestionably, food-production systems will be subject to heightening intensification (including more use of synthetic fertilizers where economics permit), and environmental problems can be expected to assert themselves more and more.[71]

16.10 The bottom line

In short, the IPCC Working Group 3 projections must be viewed with some suspicion; reality presents a much grimmer picture. The population is growing faster, and the scope for increasing food production is considerably narrower, than the IPCC policymakers cheerily assume.[72] Nevertheless, IPCC projections for rising emissions of both methane and nitrous oxides, in the absence of any change in policy from business as usual, are hardly reassuring. Indeed, the projected increases over thirty-five years from all sources – about 43 per cent for methane and 70–110 per cent for nitrous oxide – might turn out to be low if positive feedbacks and synergistic interactions (such as nitrogen fertilizing acting to suppress the methane soil sink) come into play. Far from the reductions of 15–20 per cent in human-caused methane emissions and 70–80 per cent of the excess nitrous oxide which the scientists of IPCC Working Group 1 say are needed if the goal is to stabilize greenhouse gases in the atmosphere, the built-in pressures of an expanding population and agricultural enterprise will cause rapid rises.

If, in a global movement toward controlling greenhouse-gas emissions, the agricultural sector and the underlying driving force of population growth are forgotten or neglected, heroic efforts to convert the energy sector might be negated as the more potent methane and nitrous oxide emissions build up in place of CO_2. In that circumstance, agriculture's fairly modest 14-per-cent share of the greenhouse buildup could quickly double, assuming no significant change in sinks.

With a concerted global effort, 15–20-per-cent reductions for methane might be attainable, especially if accompanied by control of other gases that compete for the OH radical sink. Since the larger share of agricultural methane-emission sources is in the developing world, a major effort must concentrate on assisting developing nations to improve livestock management and discover and deploy alternative rice-growing practices. Of course, if global warming itself is found to be stimulating emissions from natural methane sources, such as northern peatbogs and offshore hydrates, much larger reductions in the agricultural sector might well become necessary.

Nitrous oxide emissions present a more difficult challenge, partly because a much greater fraction must be reduced, and partly because it may simply be harder to accomplish without setbacks in food production. Moreover, the scientific challenge of overcoming the myriad uncertainties in the system and determining effective ways to achieve reductions will cause some delay before appropriate measures can be implemented.

Policymakers may be faced, not only in the case of these two gases but for others as well, with finding ways to compensate for difficulty in reducing emissions of one gas by making greater reductions in others. If reducing methane emissions, for instance, proves to be much easier than reducing nitrous oxide, it may pay to reduce it more than is needed for stabilization to make up for nitrous oxide emissions that cannot be eliminated. Methane's short residence time, indeed, may make it an emission of choice to reduce in compensation for long-lived gases such as nitrous oxides or CFCs, whose slow removal from the atmosphere will cause effects long after emissions have been reduced. Such trade-offs undoubtedly will become increasingly necessary as civilization moves into the greenhouse century.

But unless the driving force of human population expansion is recognized and seriously addressed by the world community, no amount of tinkering with emission sources and sinks will prevent substantial global warming and climatic disruption in the long run. The IPCC report confines itself to projections to 2025, but human population at that point will still be increasing (and food and energy needs along with it) at a rate of more than 1 per cent per year. Undoubtedly, the most effective single measure humanity could take to slow global warming and avert the most tragic consequences is to reduce birth-rates as rapidly as possible.

Chapter 17
Third World Countries in the Policy Response to Global Climate Change

Kilaparti Ramakrishna

" ... We have been sustained by the ocean for two million years, and it has been bountiful and continues to yield to us its bounty. We have now learned that this harmony could be interrupted by the actions of nations very distant from our shores ... We, the peoples of the South Pacific Region, appeal to you in a common voice, the voice of those who may become the first victims of global warming ... to ensure the survival of our cultures and our very existence and to prevent us from becoming 'endangered species' or the dinosaurs of the next century ... **"**

(Ernest Beni, Vanuatu's principal delegate, addressing the IPCC Response Strategies Working Group, Geneva, Oct. 1989.)

The First World Climate Conference[1] held in 1979 pointed out in the following words that the accumulation of carbon dioxide in the atmosphere deserves the most urgent international attention:

The long-continued reliance of society on fossil fuels as a principle energy source in the future, along with continued deforestation, is seen as likely to result in massive atmospheric carbon
dioxide increases in future decades and centuries ... The present
understanding of climate processes leads to the recognition of the
clear possibility that these increases in carbon dioxide may result
in significant and possibly major long-term changes of global-scale
climate; and ... Carbon dioxide added to the atmosphere by man's
activities would be removed slowly by natural processes, and
therefore the climatic consequences of increased carbon dioxide
concentrations would last for a long time.

Conferences held subsequent to this have reinforced the need to
determine the effects of increasing carbon dioxide on global and
regional climates and on the carbon cycle within the atmosphere-
ocean-biosphere system, and to ascertain the socio-economic consequences of these effects. Several recent workshops, seminars, and
symposia attended by scientists from around the world have not only
reinforced the concern expressed in 1979, but have generated a scientific consensus – possibly without precedent – on the threat posed by
global warming.

Of particular importance among these were meetings that discussed the potential effects of global warming as well as policies to
prevent, mitigate, and adapt to this phenomenon. Some notable
meetings were held in Villach, Austria, in 1980, 1983, 1985,[2] and
more recently in 1987.[3] The 1987 Villach meeting, which continued
at Bellagio, Italy, in November 1987,[4] and the Toronto Conference in
1988,[5] were the first ones that devoted their attention to developing
policy options for responding to climatic change.

The Toronto Conference pointed out in its final statement that:

Humanity is conducting an unintended, globally pervasive experiment whose ultimate consequences could be second only to a
global nuclear war. The earth's atmosphere is being changed at an
unprecedented rate by pollutants resulting from human activities,
inefficient and wasteful fossil-fuel use, and the effects of rapid
population growth in many regions. These changes represent a
major threat to international security and are already having harmful consequences over many parts of the globe ... Far-reaching
impacts will be caused by global warming and sea-level rise,

which are becoming increasingly evident as a result of continued growth in atmospheric concentrations of carbon dioxide and other greenhouse gases. Other major impacts are occurring from ozone layer depletion, resulting in increased damage from ultraviolet radiation. The best predictions available indicate potentially severe economic and social dislocation for present and future generations; this will worsen international tensions and increase the risks of conflict among and within nations. It is imperative to act now.

17.1 Policy formulation

Two months after the Toronto Conference, the Maltese delegation to the United Nations took the initiative to have the global climate declared a common heritage of humankind. This draft proposal was discussed in the General Assembly of the United Nations, which, in December 1988, adopted a resolution on the protection of climate for present and future generations of humankind.[6] The resolution recognized that climate change is a concern of humankind and requested immediate action leading to a comprehensive review and to recommendations. Discussions since then have focused on appropriate legal and policy measures to be adopted by the international community.

Implicit in this recognition is the fact that the potential legal and policy responses to climatic change differ greatly from the richer industrialized nations to the poorer Third World nations. The richer nations realize that the adverse consequences of global warming will be damaging to their economies and life-styles. They are on the threshold of adopting appropriate national and regional policies within the Organization for Economic Co-operation and Development (OECD) and the European Community (EC).

On the other hand, the poorer nations find, initially at least, that the warming of the Earth may be an additional burden, potentially slowing further the economic growth that all want. They see an urgent need for sustainable economic development, for relief from balance-of-payments deficits and foreign debts, for a need to stabilize currencies and build their economies. Until recently they have had little time or opportunity to contemplate the potential effects of the warming of the Earth, despite the implications of such powerful environmental changes for those nations.

17.2 The Intergovernmental Panel on Climate Change

At about the same time as the General Assembly resolution was debated, the World Meteorological Organization (WMO) and the United Nations Environment Programme (UNEP) established the Intergovernmental Panel on Climate Change (IPCC).[7] Before its establishment, governmental interest in the climatic change issue was evident at best among industrialized countries. It is even fair to say that the interest of industrialized countries' governments in the IPCC was largely due to the powerful statement adopted at the Toronto Conference in 1988.

At its first session IPCC divided its work among three working groups. Working Groups 1 and 2 are concerned with science and socio-economic impacts of climatic change, and Working Group 3 is looking at response strategies. International legal and policy options form part of Group 3's priorities. Structured in this manner, the IPCC has several features to distinguish itself from initiatives launched by international organizations in the past. First, the inner workings of the IPCC represent a mixture of processes borrowed from scientific organizations and characteristics unique to political institutions. For example, although the Terms of Reference emphasize the peer review process – a process uncommon in political organizations – and although participation in the various Working Groups and Sub-Groups is expected to be at a technical level, the participants essentially either were chosen by the governments or are working in various governmental departments in the member countries.

The second and third sessions of the IPCC with all of its Working Groups took place in Nairobi[8] and in Washington, DC,[9] on 28–30 June 1989 and 5–7 February 1990 respectively. At the intergovernmental level before the Nairobi IPCC session, confusion as to the appropriate agency responsible for initiating the first steps toward an international convention to stabilize the greenhouse-gas composition of the atmosphere inhibited real progress in solving the climate change problem. At the Nairobi session, however, the chairman of the IPCC resolved the issue when he announced that the IPCC will prepare the background for a draft of an international convention on greenhouse gases. This decision does not exclude other international organizations from working on this issue, but does establish the IPCC as an international focal point with a clear agenda and timetable for progress.

A major change adopted at the Nairobi session was with reference to the concept of core membership. In November 1988, thirty-two nations had core membership. For the June 1989 session, the chairman invited all the members of UNEP and WMO and several international organizations to attend and participate in the proceedings. The session in its plenary decided to abandon the core-membership concept. The representatives of forty-four nations and of several Intergovernmental Organizations and Nongovernmental Organizations (NGOs) that attended the Nairobi session applauded the decision.

Among the various recommendations made for the IPCC, the following merit particular attention:

- The IPCC should consider the possibility of arranging conferences and seminars in developing countries to help mobilize national and regional action. For example, it was pointed out that a conference to heighten the awareness of climatic change among scientists from developing countries would contribute to the objectives of the IPCC. Roving seminars held on a regional basis have proved to be a cost-effective method of reaching a wide audience and stimulating valuable national action in developing countries.

- The development of an indigenous intellectual and scientific base backed by appropriate technologies is a key factor in the medium- to long-term capacity of developing countries to participate fully in international programmes on climatic change.

These issues have since become the rallying points around which both the less-developed and the industrialized countries have continued their discussions.[10] In 1989 these forums included: the ministerial conference hosted by the British prime minister in March; the meeting of heads of state and government organized by the governments of Norway, France and the Netherlands in The Hague in March; the first meeting of the contracting parties to the Vienna Convention for the Protection of the Ozone Layer and the Montreal

Protocol in Helsinki in April; the biennial session of the governing council of the United Nations Environment Programme in May; the economic summit of the Group of Seven, held in Paris in July; a conference in Tokyo in September; the ninth Conference of Heads of State or Government of Non-Aligned Countries meeting in Belgrade in the same month, where the Indian prime minister advocated the establishment of a Planet Protection Fund; IPCC Working Group 3 meeting in October, where forty-five governments for the first time decided that it is time to begin work on a framework convention; a meeting of the heads of state and government of the Commonwealth in Kuala Lumpur in the same month; a meeting of the ministers of environment organized by the Netherlands government in November; and others.

A significant aspect of the growing importance of the IPCC process relates to the participation of developing countries. Despite an occasional comment in newspapers to the contrary, there has been a tremendous surge of interest among the developing countries in their participation, expressions of concern, and recommendations to adopt appropriate measures to deal with the issue of climate change. This new interest is reflected not only in the IPCC process, but also in several other conferences at the ministerial and head-of-state and government levels organized in various parts of the world.

The sense of urgency with regard to increasing international co-operation is reflected in several pronouncements made in the United Nations. Mikhail Gorbachev addressed the UN General Assembly in December 1988, and said that 'national and regional problems [economic, food, energy, environmental...] have been turned into global problems. The world is more visible and tangible.' He also pointed out that 'our time and the realities of today's world call for internationalizing dialogue and the negotiating process', and that states must review their attitude to the United Nations, 'without which world politics would be inconceivable today'. Speaking for the British government, Sir Crispin Tickell addressed the issue of global climate change, and pointed out before the UN Economic and Social Council that a special committee of the General Assembly should be created that would have environmental matters as its prime responsibility. He also recommended that the UN Security Council should take up environmental issues periodically.

Geoffrey Palmer, the prime minister of New Zealand, addressed the UN General Assembly in October 1989 and spoke primarily on global environmental problems. He felt that there is a need for the establishment of a new organ in the United Nations system called the Environmental Protection Council. The then prime minister of India, Rajiv Gandhi, speaking at the Ninth Non-Aligned Summit in Belgrade in September 1989, responded to the need for global co-operation in the field of global environmental protection with a suggestion that the world community establish a Planet Protection Fund under the aegis of the United Nations. It is this combination of interests from both the developed and the developing countries that is responsible for the amount of attention paid to the IPCC.

Despite the growing desire of the Third World countries to participate in the IPCC process, the IPCC had, at best, only limited success in facilitating such participation. To correct this, a report was prepared by the *ad hoc* Sub-Group on Ways to Increase the Participation of the Developing Countries in IPCC Activities. Saudi Arabia chaired this Sub-Group, with Brazil, Senegal and Zimbabwe as members. The Report[11] was circulated before the second session's meeting to China, India, the chairman of the IPCC, the chairmen of the IPCC Working Groups, and to Mostafa K. Tolba (Executive Director of UNEP) and G. O. P. Obasi (Secretary-General of WMO). The Sub-Group pointed out that, among the most widely accepted scenarios, the area of the globe occupied by developing countries will be most affected by adverse climate changes. At the same time, the developing countries are not economically or technologically equipped to implement some of the practical policy measures that are necessary in order to find and implement appropriate solutions. Of the recommendations made on actions to be taken in the short term and in the medium and long term in order to increase participation by developing countries, the following merit particular attention:

- The work of IPCC requires the involvement of disciplines beyond the normal scope of the WMO and UNEP, especially in relation to Working Group 3. Therefore, the Working Groups, with the support of the WMO and UNEP Secretariats, should seek to identify possible funding-sources beyond those traditionally associated with the work of WMO and UNEP.

- The IPCC should consider the possibility of arranging conferences and seminars in developing countries to help mobilize national and regional action and heighten the awareness of scientists from developing countries of climatic change.

■ A critical issue for the medium- to long-term capacity of developing countries to participate fully in international programmes on climate change is the development of an indigenous intellectual and scientific base backed by appropriate technologies.

■ A special emphasis needs to be placed on developing the capacity and infrastructure from within the developing nations, using appropriate technology. This idea needs to be linked with the development of centres such as the African Centre of Meteorological Applications for Development and WMO Regional Specialized Meteorological Centres, and systems such as Climate Computer Systems and the Global Resource Information Database Geographic Information Systems.

Reacting to the suggestions, Executive Director Tolba and Secretary-General Obasi suggested that a system[12] whereby (a) countries that could be seriously affected by global warming and the consequent sea-level rise, and (b) countries whose actions could have a major impact on carbon dioxide emissions and uptake would be selected as natural candidates and must be ensured full participation in IPCC activities. Tolba and Obasi estimated that about twenty countries would meet either of these two criteria, and that the total resources needed would be about one million dollars. But the total pledged in response did not achieve even this modest figure.

On the whole, the IPCC proceedings moved slowly. The discussions revealed a surprising lack of understanding among many, perhaps most, of the official delegates of the technical details of the issues of climatic changes and what might be done to limit the problem. While the delegates from the less-developed nations complained at being excluded from discussions, they were not sufficiently well-versed in the topic to advance arguments as to specific threats to their interests or to advance proposals for solutions. Nor were the delegates of the richer nations sufficiently well-versed in the details to offer technical judgements or specific insights. The only time there was any sign of animation was when the question of financial assistance was discussed.

Presented thus, the task of addressing global climate change is a daunting one, perhaps beyond the means or scope of the IPCC or any other single subsidiary or specialized agency of the United Nations. In hindsight it is clear that the founders of the IPCC did not realize that environmental protection and the urgency of addressing global climate change would be so high on the political agendas of countries from both East and West as well as from North and South. If either of the sponsoring institutions of the IPCC (WMO and UNEP) had realized that this topic would be so central to political debate in all conceivable forums, they would have staffed the organization better and would not have dreamt up the idea of core-membership.

17.3 Developing countries

Historically, powerful nations were able to protect their interests well. In modern times, however, nations must form alliances to protect and promote their interests. Developing countries that have recently emerged from the decolonization process learned this lesson fairly quickly. They formed a caucus known as the Group of 77, and tried to articulate their interests on the global level. With the horizontal expansion of the international community, the size of the Group of 77 grew to contain more than 120 countries.

It is customary to believe that environmental issues were articulated in the international community primarily because of the concerns of the industrialized countries. If one were to look at the time immediately preceding the organization of the 1972 Stockholm Conference on Human Environment, that may indeed hold true. But since then, and particularly in global climate change debates, the developing countries have closely identified their interests with the adoption of appropriate international environmental policies. There are many reasons why developing countries have espoused a seemingly similar position on the international level. But it is important to keep in mind that, even among the developing countries, the reasons for the existence of what appears to be a common platform are not always the same.

The newly industrializing countries articulated the developing country position at the international level. They maintained that the debate about and the demand for a New International Economic Order pervade the entire gamut of international relations. When environmental issues were addressed, they focused on the same economic issue, namely: how does participation in an international debate help hasten their economic development? Principal questions emerging from such a focus ask what economic assistance would be available under this scheme, what form of technology transfer could be expected, and so on.

However, it would be inappropriate to assume that the position articulated by the newly industrializing countries accurately reflected that held by other developing countries. Several countries, often described in the United Nations terminology as the least-developed or the geographically disadvantaged states, have viewed their participation in the international arena and the debate about environmental issues differently from the newly industrializing countries. For these countries, the adoption of appropriate preventive and adaptive policies on environmental issues, not just within their own countries but in the world at large, is crucial for their very survival. Islands are vulnerable to environmental changes, and especially to the effects of global warming. However, their contributions to the buildup of greenhouse gases in the atmosphere are very minimal. Island states, therefore, do not see participation in international environmental debates as an opportunity to attain quicker economic development. Nor do they perceive the international environmental policy arena as one more forum in which to try to set right all the injustices perpetuated through the period of colonization. They would obviously like quicker economic development, but overshadowing this is their concern for their very existence.

The first international conference on global warming and climatic change to take place in the developing world[13] was held in New Delhi, on 21–23 February 1989. Attended by well over 150 scientists, policy-makers, and government officials, mainly from nations of the Indian subcontinent, the conference focused on the scientific evidence for, the impacts of, and policy responses to the problem of global climatic change. The participants approved a comprehensive statement which pointed out that:

> Global warming is occurring at a time when many of the world's life-support systems are already stressed by the growth of population, industrial development and the need for agricultural land and the unsustainable exploitation of natural resources. These stresses are caused both by careless and short-sighted actions and as a consequence of poverty and underdevelopment. They include

increasing air and water pollution, deforestation, soil erosion and salination, among others.

Maldives, an island state, became the first to voice concern at the head-of-state level in the United Nations General Assembly about the growing threat of sea-level rise due to global warming. A number of other island nations, such as the Bahamas, Jamaica, and Iceland, have expressed their serious concern at the same phenomenon. But the most significant set of nations to come together, form an alliance, and articulate their points with one voice is probably the South Pacific island states.

Ernest Beni of Vanuatu, speaking on behalf of the twenty-two island governments of the South Pacific region put it best:

> We have been sustained by the ocean for two million years, and it has been bountiful and continues to yield to us its bounty. We have now learned that this harmony could be interrupted by the actions of nations very distant from our shores ... We, the peoples of the South Pacific Region, appeal to you in a common voice, the voice of those who may become the first victims of global warming ... to ensure the survival of our cultures and our very existence and to prevent us from becoming 'endangered species' or the dinosaurs of the next century.

In this light, it is quite understandable why the developing island countries are actively pursuing, within the IPCC and other forums, the advancement of the scientific understanding of and formulation of policies on the climate change and sea-level-rise topics.

While the contributions from all developing countries to the increase of greenhouse gases is minimal at the present time, a number of developing countries will, in the next several years, reach a level of industrial development which will result in the emission of a significant amount of greenhouse gases. These are, by and large, the newly industrializing countries, and countries such as Brazil, China, and India. The South Pacific islands in particular, and a number of other developing countries, do not have a plan of industrial expansion of similar magnitude and, as a result, still will not generate a significant amount of greenhouse gases in the near future. However, these nations are subject to all of the adverse consequences of global warming.

17.4 A look ahead

Put in the context of the north–south dialogue on international environmental issues, this ready acceptance, for one reason or another, of
a global problem is rather remarkable. The problem of the accumulation in the atmosphere of radiatively-active trace-gases responsible
for global warming was persuasively articulated by the world's
climate scientists in IPCC Working Group 1's report, published in
June 1990. In addition, the environmental groups in the developing
world are perhaps more vocal and effective now than at any other
time in their relatively recent history. But it would be simplistic to
conclude either that the grave dangers forecast by the scientists have
transformed the ruling élite or that the NGOs have taken it upon
themselves to give priority to the global climate change issue in their
deliberations with the governments in the developing world.

After all, it was not so long ago that several Third World countries
suspected that the wave of environmental concerns amongst the
developed countries and the consequent urgings for effective environmental policies was a ploy to keep the Third World in a perpetual
state of dependence.[14] Few have tried to understand the reasons or
present a logical explanation for the interest evinced by Third World
countries in finding appropriate solutions to the problem of global
climate change. Unless this change in perspective and the reasons for
it are clearly understood, and unless the developing countries' expectations in obtaining access to new technologies and additional monetary resources are met to a satisfactory degree, the interested
communities in both the industrialized and the developing countries
run the risk of losing the support of the developing world.

Mostafa Tolba[15] pointed out that global warming and climate
change present a window of opportunity for both the industrialized
and the developing countries to address a host of priority items,
including trade imbalances, debt relief, technology transfer, and
technical and financial assistance. Sir Shridath Ramphal, former
Secretary-General of the Commonwealth, inaugurating the Cambridge Lectures on Environment and Development in 1989, stated
that the Report of the World Commission on Environment and Development, *Our Common Future*,[16] addressed the close connection
between environmental protection and economic-development
issues of critical importance for developing countries. He also pointed out that a succession of disasters all over the world triggered

intellectual awareness of the possibility of some underlying pattern of causality.

Perhaps more credit than this passing reference should be given tc *Our Common Future*. The Chairperson of the Commission that authored this report, the then prime minister of Norway, drew from it much of the time in her keynote address at the Toronto Conference, the first large-scale discussion of policy options for climate change,[17] in June 1988. She pointed out that there is 'a need for a fresh impetus in international co-operation. Development aid and lending must be increased, and the debt crises must be resolved.' She also said that 'the ultimate goal must be to forge an economic partnership based on equitable trade and to achieve a new area of growth, one which enhances the resource base rather than degrades it'. She concluded by saying that 'the mission must be to make nations return to negotiations on the global issues after years of decline into real multilateralism'. It is sentiments of this nature that effectively warded off possible large-scale criticism and rhetoric from the Third World participants and from NGOs attending the Toronto Conference.

The Toronto Conference document stated that:

> The countries of the industrially developed world are the main source of greenhouse gases and therefore bear the main responsibility to the world community for ensuring that measures are implemented to address the issues posed by climate change. At the same time they must see that the developing nations of the world, whose problems are greatly aggravated by population growth, are assisted and not inhibited in improving their economies and the living conditions of their citizens. This will necessitate a wide range of measures, including significant additional energy use in those countries, and compensating reductions in industrialized countries. The transition to a sustainable future will require investments in energy efficiency and non-fossil energy sources. In order to ensure that these investments occur, the global community must not only halt the current net transfer of resources from developing countries, but actually reverse it. This reversal should embrace the relevant technologies involved, taking into account the implications for industry.

The Toronto Conference called upon governments to establish a World Atmosphere Fund financed in part by a levy on fossil-fuel consumption in the industrialized countries. This recommendation has been endorsed in varying forms by every single conference on this subject held around the world. The governments of Brazil, India, and Mexico have made proposals along these lines. A large number of governmental representatives, environment ministers from sixty-eight countries, have subscribed to this in principle at the Noordwijk Ministerial Conference on Atmospheric Pollution and Climate Change in November 1989.[18] The Norwegian government endorsed the idea by announcing that it will contribute a tenth of 1 per cent of its gross domestic product to the global fund if other industrialized countries follow suit.

The only other time when environmental concerns and development needs were addressed as one package was during the early 1970s. Though the developing world was initially reluctant, it subsequently endorsed the Stockholm Conference on Human Environment in 1972. The United Nations Environment Secretariat, established in 1971 to pursue the objectives of the conference, succeeded in convincing the developing countries that environmental issues are not conflicting but compatible with their compelling needs.[19] The other, more important, reasons given were that the developing countries would experience significant social and economic repercussions as a result of environmental measures taken in the industrialized world; that they should be informed and equipped to avoid the type of environmental degradation which the industrialized countries were only beginning to recognize and remedy; and finally, that it would be in their own interest that they be party to decisions that would directly affect their futures.

Several important questions needed to be answered to obtain the participation of the developing countries. They were: How would actions taken by the more-industrialized nations affect them? What technical assistance would be available? What would happen to the markets they required for their own development? What attention was likely to be given to the kind of environmental problems which directly affected them? All these questions were addressed in the Founex Report, commissioned by the secretary-general of the United Nations Conference on Human Environment by convening a panel of twenty-seven experts in the fields of development and environment.[20] It became a central document in the deliberations of the developing countries in the four regional seminars held in Bangkok,

Addis Ababa, Mexico City, and Beirut.

The Founex Report at the outset pointed out that the 'concern for environment must not and need not detract from the commitment of the world community...to the overriding task of development of developing regions of the world', and that the developing countries should 'avoid as far as feasible the mistakes and distortions that have characterized the patterns of development of the industrialized societies'. The report made it clear that adequate safeguards and standards were necessary. However, 'these standards must necessarily be those that are appropriate to the specific conditions of these countries and be capable of being observed within the resources available to them'. Warning that 'environmental issues may come to exercise growing influence on international economic relations', the Report stated: 'Unless appropriate economic action is taken, there are a number of ways in which the developing countries could suffer rather than profit from the new emphasis on environment. The latter could have implications for aid, trade and transfer of technology.'

The points made by the report from the point of view of the developing countries, which found their place in the Declaration and Action Plan for the Human Environment adopted at the end of the 1972 Conference, affirm that additional funds will be required: to subsidize research in environmental problems for the developing countries; to compensate for major dislocations in the exports of developing countries; to cover major increases in the cost of development projects owing to higher environmental standards; and to finance restructuring of investment, production, or export patterns necessitated by the environmental concerns of developed countries. These recommendations resulted in the establishment of the concepts of additionality and compensation. Unfortunately, in subsequent years the United Nations system deemed it appropriate to separate the economic development aspects from the environmental agenda.

The special circumstances of the developing world, however, have been recounted in all of the international environmental conferences since then. Special provisions were made to accommodate pollution control strategies that take into account their current lack of development – effectively introducing and endorsing 'double-standards' and bringing it into common parlance. Assurances of technical and financial assistance and technology transfer were likewise written into the texts of several international legal instruments. The urgency for assisting developing countries has never before been stated with more seriousness. For example, Mostafa Tolba, speaking at the closure of the ministerial conference on ozone-layer protection in London in March 1989, stressed that in helping the Third World 'we must stop talking in generalities', and that 'there is a need for international mechanisms to compensate them for forgoing the use of CFCs and some of their natural resources in the interest of environmental safety'. Similar sentiments were expressed by the administrator of the United States Environmental Protection Agency earlier at the same conference, both from the official platform and at a private meeting with the delegations of India, China, and Brazil.

Even the World Bank, which was slow in according environmental work within the Bank a prominent position until recently, came forward with a proposal to create a new environmental lending facility. The Bank's document, *Funding for the Global Environment*, released in draft form in February 1990, recognizes that additional financial and technical assistance from industrialized countries will be crucial in helping developing countries address global environmental problems. The Bank's basic analysis of the need for increased resource transfers to limit emissions of greenhouse and ozone-depleting gases, as well as to preserve biodiversity and water-quality, is based on another document released by the Bank (Discussion Paper no. 78, April 1990) called *The Greenhouse Effect: Implications for Economic Development*. This paper also makes a very persuasive case for why the development community should be concerned:

> The development community needs to outline a policy and research program for sustainable economic development which addresses the implications of possible climate effects of greenhouse gases. The greatest opportunities lie in the energy sector, which should be the primary focus of attention, notwithstanding that energy efficiency options are substantial in sectors such as agriculture and urban systems. Indeed, the opportunities for public and private energy efficiency gains are compelling and suggest that the threat of global warming can be reduced primarily by concentrating present efforts on improving the energy efficiency of the global economy.

17.5 Conclusions

It is this renewed interest and determination to assist the Third World in their economic development that is responsible for the wave of support from the developing countries. The scientific certainty over global warming sought by the United States and other industrialized countries was dismissed by developing countries as delaying what needs to be done by the world community anyway. The foreign minister of Brazil, Dr Jose Francisco Rezek, inaugurating the Regional Conference on Global Warming and Sustainable Development in São Paulo, Brazil, on 18 June 1990, put it best:

> There is no reason why action should be conditioned to a definite scientific proof, which perhaps will never be attained or might be reached only when it becomes too late adequately to tackle the problem. It is unlikely that the continuous increase in carbon concentration in the atmosphere, which is taking place since the industrial revolution, can occur without consequences to the global environment.

All concerned agree that the appropriate responses needed to address global warming will have to be global in nature. This is where the industrialized countries need to show the required resolve to help the developing countries adopt a development strategy away from dependence on fossil fuels, otherwise there is no incentive for the developing countries to try the alternative technologies that are currently being developed.

If anyone were to argue that, since developing countries had a very small role in bringing the current situation into existence, they should be kept completely out of any discussion of global measures, they would be failing to take into consideration the efforts made up to now in trying to obtain a just and equitable international economic order, and the opportunities that global climatic change affords both in promoting efforts to protect the global environment and in realizing many of the developing countries' demands for quicker economic development.

Chapter 18
Managing the Global House: Redefining Economics in a Greenhouse World

Susan George

“ ...the South cannot stay marginalized for long in the environmental debate ... biospheric solidarity may yet be forced upon the governments of the North; like it or not, they may finally have to recognize that debt relief and real contributions to sustainable development in the South are vital to their own survival... **”**

'Economics' stems from the Greek *oikos*, house, and a derivative of *nemein*, to manage. We now know that our house is the world. Yet this house is filthy, growing virtually unfit for human habitation. Its air is increasingly unbreatheable, its water foul, its rooms and gardens full of refuse. No one takes overall charge of its management, the householders are forever squabbling. Most of them – individuals, corporations, or nation-states – feel no particular responsibility for the mess to which they have contributed; each expects the others to clean up. Present-day 'economics' has strayed far indeed from its classical origins.

In its modern sense, economics is generally defined as the science (disputable) that deals with the laws (also disputable) of the production, consumption, and distribution of wealth. This definition falls well short of the Greek idea, and conveys no sense of comprehensive management. It also represents a step backward from the wisdom of a more recent past. If human beings are to deal with the urgent problems of the late twentieth century and make their global house fit to live in, the (social) science they need to apply is less neo-classical economics as practised in the late twentieth century than 'political economy' as understood in the eighteenth or nineteenth century.

Adam Smith wrote that 'political economy ... proposes two distinct objects ... to provide a plentiful revenue or subsistence for the people ... and ... to supply the state ... with a revenue sufficient for the public services'. His definition is a good starting-point, stressing as it does popular welfare and sound management on behalf of the citizens. A more explicit concept of political economy for our own time would also require that we analyse (1) the management of resources, (2) the production and distribution of wealth, and (3) the exercise of power. The last is most important, since the exercise of power determines who will benefit and who will lose from the management of resources and the production and distribution of wealth.

These three areas also bear overwhelmingly on the quality of the environment and lie at the heart of the ecological crisis. Indeed, one can forcefully argue, with no offence to the 'hard' sciences, that there *are* no ecological problems – only the economic and political problems that underlie them. Unless we look to these political-economic roots, there is little hope that the pace of environmental destruction can be stemmed, much less reversed.[1]

18.1 Managing and pricing resources

As the environmental movement has been pointing out for decades, the management of resources, the initial element in this concept of political economy, is in crisis. Every year an unsustainable 50 billion tonnes of minerals are extracted from the earth's crust.[2] Soils are being over-cultivated, eroded, and washed away, forests are rapidly disappearing. The ocean margins, constituting 'a membrane between the land and sea that is essential to the well-being of the planet', are everywhere being polluted, perhaps to the point of no return. Irreversible 'flips' in the biology of these coastal waters and the subsequent death of all the life-forms they contain are a significant threat.[3] Further, as several chapters of the present volume amply demonstrate, the indiscriminate release of greenhouse gases into the atmosphere will necessarily result in climate-change: the questions still awaiting answers are 'when', 'how much', and 'with what consequences' – not 'whether'.

And yet, at the close of the twentieth century, our economic practice still proceeds as if nature were passive, infinitely exploitable, and indefinitely pollutable, whereas any sensible person already knows that this is not the case. National and corporate balance sheets are, in particular, mythical constructions because they do not take into account the real, longer-term costs to nature or to society. As an economic wit once remarked, the best way to increase your Gross National Product is to have a war – the more resources consumed, the higher growth will be, or, rather, will appear. GNP figures, still the preferred indicators of national well-being, tell us nothing about what is growing, who is gaining or losing, nor about stresses placed on the earth in the process.

Financial accounting systems, including those of corporations underpaying inputs, governments calculating their national output, or major public development institutions intervening in dozens of Third World economies, are narrowly based on annual figures. Irreplaceable resources that took aeons to constitute are squandered in an instant, according to the 'laws' of supply and demand. What is a commodity's 'price', if not this point at the temporal intersection between a resource and someone's immediate use for it? In the case of raw materials – food, agricultural products, or minerals – this intersection is sometimes quite graphically and accurately called a 'spot' price. In a similar way, the line for 'depreciation' in financial accounts concerns only already-constituted physical plant and equipment – never the wearing down and the wearing out of the resource base itself nor the costs of restoring the environment (always assuming this is still possible).

Although neo-classical economics pretends to apply 'truth in pricing', the real costs of production, pollution and the disposal of industrial wastes, are infrequently charged to the industries concerned: society at large is expected to assume the burden of these costs, as well as many others presently unaccounted for, both upstream and downstream from production.

Low taxes or no taxes are the rule for the heaviest energy and raw-material users, particularly in those countries, like the United States, where consumption is highest. In the US, gasoline/petrol fetches a lower price than anywhere else in the industrialized countries. Partly because of this policy of underpricing non-renewable resources, every American's energy-use amounts to over 7,200 kgs of oil equivalent per year. According to World Bank figures, each inhabitant of the wealthy OECD nations consumes on average twenty-two times as much energy as a person in a low-income country: 6,573 kg as opposed to 297 kg of oil equivalent. If (relatively) prosperous China and India are excluded from the 'low-income' group, the contrast is even more stark: a citizen of the twenty-four OECD countries 'weighs' on average fifty-six times more on the energy scales than a person living in one of the forty poorest countries.[4] The United States also holds dubious first-place honours in carbon emissions from fossil fuels per capita: five tonnes per person, amounting to 1.2 billion tonnes in all. This total is twice as large as China's carbon emissions, even though China's population is five times as large and the country relies almost entirely on coal-burning to supply its energy requirements.[5]

18.2 Production and distribution of wealth

As a logical outgrowth of resource mismanagement, our present profligate modes of *production and distribution of wealth*, the second element in a modern concept of political economy, also contribute heavily to environmental stress. Some Marxists argue that capitalism *per se* will be to blame if the looming ecological disaster they foresee actually takes place. One of the more florid passages in this modern Marxist literature holds that 'Today, human society, and the biosphere itself, cannot survive the organised greed and environmental ruination that the system demands for its continued vampire-like existence. Hot under the collar, America? It's *their* (the capitalists') fault. And don't let anyone forget it.'[6]

No one, least of all its practitioners, can deny that capitalism's goal is the maximization of profit; in the life of a corporation, whatever contributes to this goal is deemed by definition good, whatever does not, bad. Dirty, unsustainable, unsafe, disposable production is almost invariably cheaper – at least in the short term – the only term the market understands – than clean, sustainable, safe, recyclable production. Consequently, the first alternative is generally chosen over the second because profit, not the well-being of citizens or of society and the earth at large, is the objective of production. Such choices should thus not be surprising, though they have been and should be targets for action. Only when popular protest is followed by public action is this very real economic law infringed or modified.

It would, however, be dangerously simple-minded to blame capitalist production methods and short-term profit orientation for all the ecological woes of the planet. The most cursory look at the state-socialist nations of Eastern Europe ('socialist', at least, until quite recently) is enough to show that environmental destruction in these countries has attained levels unheard of even in the free-market heartland. Ecology, a 'bourgeois science', was not taught in the universities. The results of the few environmental-impact studies that were carried out were often suppressed as too alarming. Protest against pollution and environmental hazards was considered tantamount to the crime of state-subversion. With neither a free press nor a free electorate, no democratic checks or balances, feedback mechanisms, or opportunities for publicizing abuses existed. Furthermore, COMECON countries' economies could not rival capitalist efficiency. The drive for efficiency can, under some circumstances, lead to cleaning up one's environmental act; such pressures were wholly absent in Eastern Europe. Indeed, the only constraint on environmental destruction here has been far lower levels of private consumption than in the West; surely that is cold comfort.

As the Hungarian environmental activist Janos Vargha has explained: 'Under the command economies of "socialism", the more aggressive technologies – those which need a great deal of energy and natural resources and cause extensive environmental pollution – represent a large percentage of industrial production.' Unfortunately, the transition to democracy and political pluralism is no magic bullet for ecological problems. Vargha sees such pluralism as a necessary but not sufficient condition for environmental sanity: 'Eastern Europe still has to learn by experience that parliamentary democracy will not in itself solve today's global ecological problems. Even those societies which are more successful in guarding their democratic traditions are mainly concerned with the non-human and non-biological effects of technology – like profit, for example.'[7]

Eastern Europe will need a great deal of hard cash for damage control alone. The figures for greenhouse-gas emissions and energy intensities confirm the extent of the problem where global warming is concerned (see Fig. 8.3 and Table 8.2 in chapter 8). The new Polish minister for the environment, Bronislaw Kaminski, has drawn up a list of two hundred large industrial plants that threaten the environment and should be closed down. Such plant-closures could only contribute to the massive unemployment already foreseen for Poland. Furthermore, according to one Polish expert's estimate, Poland would need to spend 'US$60 billion for pre-treatment installations alone to limit deadly emissions from coal-fired power plants. Who [he asks] will make such a sum available in a country that owes over US$40 billion to foreign creditors?'[8] Who indeed? The key word in his question is 'foreign', and leads us directly to the third element of a modern concept of political economy: the exercise of power.

18.3 The exercise of power

Economic analysis alone will be unsuccessful unless it asks 'Who is in charge? Who has the power to make decisions, including those decisions which, for good or ill, will have an enormous impact on the environment?' Here the crucial question is: *What are the political conditions that make ecological responsibility possible?*

Although this theme is clearly too broad to be fully explored in a paper of this length, it is still important to point out that power is not only political in the narrow sense, that is, not merely the province of states or other public entities. Trans-national corporations (TNCs) and banks wield far more power than many, indeed most, governments, and their influence is increasing yearly. As scarcely needs pointing out, these huge international bodies are guided solely by the profit motive. The annual turnover of the top two hundred TNCs was estimated in 1984 at $3 trillion – fully 30 per cent of Gross World Product. This is power indeed.[9]

An examination of such power, which necessarily bears on the environment and the Earth's climate, leads one to assess the ecological impact of different economic blocs as a function of their capacity to intervene world-wide. Although state socialism has proved itself an environmental disaster in all the countries where it has been applied, these disasters have usually been confined to the national territories of the states concerned. Obviously a catastrophe like

Chernobyl respects no frontiers, but what is meant here is that the Eastern bloc has not, for complex reasons and with rare exceptions, been in a position to export its own industrial development model. Compared to the OECD countries, Eastern Europe has sold few replicas of its Chernobyls or its smoke-stack industries to the Third World. The Eastern bloc accounts for less than 9 per cent of 'world' trade, and over half of that is in intra-bloc exchanges.[10]

The market-economy, industrialized (OECD) countries, on the other hand, have extended their economic and commercial power and, consequently, their ecological impact far beyond their own borders. Their presence, and thus their responsibilities in the Third World are overwhelmingly greater than those of the state-socialist countries, whatever criterion one may choose to measure this involvement by – trade, aid, loans, investment, and so on. We will not examine here the environmental impact and the influence on the climate of trans-national corporations present in the Third World because their activities there are analagous to those already described, only more so. Safeguards against dirty, unsustainable, unsafe, disposable production are even fewer in poor countries than in rich ones; the Third World has offered corporations greater scope for environmental damage and pollution.

Similarly, we can devote only passing mention to the (indirect) environmental impact of the Third World activities of commercial banks. Throughout the 1970s, in particular, those banks made huge and, many argue, reckless loans to Third World governments on the principle that there was no real risk since 'countries do not fail to exist', as the then Chairman of Citicorp put it. Unfortunately, these loans were overwhelmingly devoted to financing current consumption, purchases of military hardware, huge, ecologically destructive projects, or simply fuelled capital flight. Private banks, with the full and enthusiatic co-operation of public lending agencies, borrowing governments, and commercial interests on both sides, thus prepared the ground for the debt crisis of the 1980s – referred to by UNICEF and many others as the 'lost decade for development'. As a result of this crisis, whatever care for the environment Third World governments might previously have exercised – never a priority in the Southern hemisphere to begin with – went by the boards. Environmental ministries were among the first casualties of cost cutting, while natural resources were rapidly cashed in to earn hard currency for interest payments.[11]

The debt crisis, in turn, brought to far greater prominence than they had hitherto enjoyed two major international economic and financial agencies; the International Monetary Fund and the World Bank. These two organizations, sometimes called 'Keynes' twins' or the 'Bretton Woods' institutions, now exercise enormous power over a great many Third World economies and consequently on their environment. Chronically indebted countries unable to borrow from any source without the IMF 'seal of approval' must undertake 'structural adjustment' programmes overseen by the Fund, and, increasingly, by the Bank as well. The IMF furnishes credits conditional on adoption of structural adjustment programmes, while the Bank contributes its own so-called 'structural adjustment' or 'non-project' loans ($6.5 billion in 1989).

Although technically part of the United Nations system, both the Bank and the Fund are in fact chiefly managed by and accountable to the rich-country governments. Their voting structures do not follow the 'one country, one vote' principle of other UN agencies, but are proportional to capital subscriptions; their policies, therefore, mostly reflect those of their most powerful members – in particular the United States, Japan, Germany, Britain, and France. These policies have a disproportionate effect on the world's environment because they are applied to so many countries at once. It is, therefore, important that we examine here the ecological and climatic impact of the Bank and the Fund.

18.4 The role of the World Bank

By 1989, the World Bank had cumulative commitments to the Third World (including those of its 'soft loan' window, the International Development Association) of $225 billion. In 1989 alone, it made over $21 billion of new commitments.[12] These sums make the Bank by far the world's largest 'development' lender, yet even these figures understate the reality, for the Bank has an impact in the Third World far surpassing its own capacity to provide capital. It also acts as a catalyst, a mobilizer, and an architect of co-financing packages. Its 'seal of approval' is often vital for bringing other donors to pursue joint projects. In 1989 alone, outside donors contributed nearly $10 billion to co-financing packages for 131 projects designed by the Bank.[13] For some critics, the Bank's development philosophy and practice tend to the 'hegemonic'.[14] Hegemonic or not, few governments of poor countries can choose to do without the Bank's huge lending capacity and its ability to mobilize other funds; nor are they in a position to ignore the Bank's economic advice when they avail themselves of its loans. This is the reality which would face any government seeking funds for technological 'leap-frogging' , of the kind described by Jose Goldemberg, in the event that they wished to pursue a 'greenhouse-friendly' route to development.

Several of the Bank's projects have led to massive destruction of tropical forests in countries as different as Brazil and Indonesia. One of these, the Polonoroeste scheme, would perhaps never have been undertaken were it not for the extreme inequality of land tenure in Brazil (where 400 large landowners reportedly control an area equivalent to 85 per cent of Great Britain). Heavily skewed land-ownership is not, after all, the World Bank's fault. The Bank did, however, join forces with the Brazilian (military) government, which had consistently refused meaningful land reform, in order to deal with the sheer numbers of unemployed, landless peasants streaming into the cities. A stopgap measure was conceived to entice them to settle instead in Amazonia, where they were promised a better future and title to land. From 1982, the Bank financed the paved highway that allowed thousands of settlers to stream into Amazonia, simultaneously increasing the penetration of the region by timber, mining, and cattle-ranching companies,[15] with all the additional problems that has posed for the anthropogenic loading of greenhouse gases in the atmosphere.

Between 1982 and 1985, deforestation in the Brazilian state of Rondonia increased from 5 per cent of the total area to 11 per cent. 'Since then, NASA space surveys show that the area of deforestation has doubled approximately every two years.' The neighbouring state, Mato Grosso, once contained over 300,000 square miles of virgin forest. By 1987, virtually all of it was gone, and that same year 'satellite photographs showed 6,000 forest fires burning across the entire Amazon basin – every one of them started deliberately by land clearers. Many of the fires were burning close to the [Bank-financed] Highway BR-364.'[16]

Opportunities for land speculation have accelerated the rate of forest destruction. The Bank and its partners ought normally to have foreseen these consequences, since 'the granting of the right of possession to whoever deforests a piece of land is a centuries-old legal practice in the Brazilian Amazon. Such rights of possession are eventually transformed into ... full rights of ownership. Pasture represents the easiest way to occupy an extensive area, thus considerably increasing the impact of a small population on deforestation.'[17] In this process of deforestation, small subsistence producers or squatters – *posseiros* – are far less destructive than large land-grabbers – *grileiros* – who have every economic interest in destroying the forest, particularly since government incentives for ranching have, contrary to many reports, been maintained. As Susanna Hecht explains:

> A whole industry ... has developed around clearing land for pasture, selling that land as quickly as possible, pocketing the gains and then moving on into new forest zones. Indeed, more than 20 million hectares of the Amazon have shifted from public to private lands in the past decade – an enclosure movement unmatched in speed and size. As a result, pasture lands throughout Brazil have experienced immense rises in value, rises which also reflect large-scale infrastructure investment patterns – the development of extensive highway systems – and the clear commitment by the Brazilian government to sustain investment in Amazonia through such mega-projects as Grande Carajas and the Tucurui dam.[18]

The World Bank is also a major financial partner for the Carajas and Tucurui schemes. Both involve widespread destruction of forests, foreseen, understood, and condoned by the financiers from the outset. Grande Carajas, a huge iron-ore strip-mining and smelting project, can only be economically viable if energy for the pig-iron smelters is provided by charcoal made from the surrounding forest. The Tucurui dam, whose first stage was inaugurated in 1984, has already flooded 216,000 hectares of forests. Over 13 million cubic metres of hardwood were left to rot underwater, having first been sprayed with dioxin (Agent Orange), of which several barrels may have been lost in the reservoir during the flooding.[19]

In Indonesia, the same grim tale of out-migration and forest destruction has been repeated, with over $600 million worth of assistance from the Bank. The Indonesian Transmigrasi programme has deported several million Javanese settlers to the 'Outer Islands'.[20] As in Brazil, roads are built into the forests to facilitate settlement. What then happens is predictable and is described by tropical botanist

Nicholas Guppy:

> Logging (on Kalimantan) has been proceeding at the rate of over 800,000 hectares a year, while shifting cultivators following behind cut about 200,000 hectares of mostly previously logged and damaged or secondary forest. Extrapolating current clearing rates, there will be no trace of these forests left in thirteen years...Visiting such areas, it is hard to view without emotion the miles of devastated trees, of felled, broken and burned trunks, of branches, mud and bark crisscrossed with tractor trails... Such sights are reminiscent of photographs of Hiroshima... Indonesia might be regarded as waging the equivalent of thermonuclear war upon its own territory.[21]

So-called 'development' financing agencies use standard accounting practices, taking note only of those elements which can be expressed in monetary terms. The long-term costs of forest destruction, including climate-change, the loss of biological diversity, which disappears with the forests, and the disruption or death of indigenous forest-dwelling communities is not quantifiable and is therefore not quantified.

For the past several years, the Bank has been under constant pressure from environmental activists because so many of its projects have proved to be environmental disasters. In May 1987, Mr Barber Conable, president of the Bank, conceded that the experience of Polonoroeste had been 'sobering'; that the Bank 'had misread the human, institutional and physical realities of the jungle and the frontier'.[22] The Bank has also recently hired a much larger environmental staff and made ecological sensitivity a cornerstone of its public-relations policy. Its most recent annual report devotes several pages to describing environmental activities, and claims that 'these [environmental] concerns now pervade Bank operations, policy and research evaluation, training and information activities'.[23] The Bank has also made a $117 million loan to Brazil for 'environmental education, research and protection'.[24] Its critics still say that the Bank will need to be very 'green' indeed if it is to make up for the ecological damage to which it has so often directly contributed in the past.

For one thing, it is now extremely difficult to halt forest destruction in the Third World, if only because the settlers have nowhere to go but further into the forest. Until at least 1988, people were still flocking to Amazonia at an average rate of 13,000 per month. They can eke out a meagre harvest on the cleared land for two years at most. And because this land quickly becomes sterile and barren when stripped of its forest cover, they will then move further into the forest. For the settlers, their day-to-day survival is at stake and they cannot afford the luxury of thinking about the future consequences of their present actions, even though they may well understand them.

Meanwhile, the effects of this kind of 'development' are only beginning to be calculated. *Science News* reports a 'growing body of evidence that intentionally lit fires over the globe also contribute significantly to pollution levels and could play a major role in changing the earth's climate'. Paul Crutzen, an atmospheric chemist at the Max Planck Institute for Chemistry, explains that '[fires related to] agricultural practices and land-use conversion have a very large impact on the overall chemistry of the atmosphere. That is something that has come as a surprise.' In the same article, Crutzen stresses that chemists used to believe biomass fires produced some 2.5 billion tons of carbon annually, but have now revised this estimate upwards to 3–4 billion tons. Nor can wholesale damage done to forests ever be undone: we now know that a decimated forest will not grow back. New computer models of the Amazonian ecosystem show that 'cutting the entire forest would severely alter the climate in the Amazon basin, causing temperatures to rise and precipitation levels to fall – a shift that would severely hinder development of a new rain forest…'.[25]

Despite all the evidence, the World Bank has not yet accepted that the most important cause of 'development'-induced destruction in the Third World is the alliance between local and foreign capital seeking short-term profit through the exploitation of all resources, both natural and human. On the contrary, the Bank's view that economic growth-rates are the best indicators of development has been strengthened by events in Eastern Europe and the collapse of state-socialist economies. The now familiar 'triumph of capitalism' argument was repeated in early 1990 by Bank President Conable, who told the *New York Times:* 'If I were to characterise the past decade, the most remarkable thing was the generation of a global consensus that market forces and economic efficiency were the best way to achieve the kind of growth which is the best antidote to poverty.'[26]

Yet whether or not the Bank chooses to recognize the fact, 'market forces' will continue to do what they have always done when left unchecked by popular activism or state action. The playing-field is not level, the market is tilted to those who have, and it will continue to concentrate economic power in the hands of the few – large landowners, wealthy business élites, exploiters of natural resources – with increasingly catastrophic consequences for the Earth. 'Economic efficiency', as Conable defines it, cannot and will not produce democratic or sustainable development.

18.5 The Tropical Forestry Action Plan

In its relentless pursuit of economic growth, the World Bank has contributed, and now admits as much, to destroying the world's remaining tropical forests. Yet its latest strategy with regard to these forests shows no sign that it has really changed course. Its new strategy is called the Tropical Forestry Action Plan (TFAP), undertaken in co-operation with the Food and Agricultural Organization of the United Nations, the World Resources Institute, and the United Nations Development Programme.[27] Most environmental Non-Governmental Organizations (NGOs) regard this plan as an illusion at best; at worst, as another ecological disaster in the making.

At the more moderate end of the critical spectrum are the Washington, DC, Environmental Policy Institute and US Friends of the Earth. They see the proposed guidelines of TFAP as 'quite good. Most NGOs find no fault with them. On the ground, however, there often appears to be little relationship between the Guidelines and reality.' The EPI-FOE then proceed to list fourteen major things wrong with TFAP in practice, including lack of involvement of local NGOs, disenfranchisement of indigenous forest-dwellers, scant attention to sustained-yield forest-management systems or ecosystem conservation, thin or non-existent research, and so on.[28] In a memo to the French Treasury on environmental issues, EPI Senior Attorney James Barnes states: 'In short, the record to date of the TFAP, in terms of complying with its own guidelines, is abysmal.'[29]

More radically critical are groups like the World Rainforest Movement and environmentalists close to *The Ecologist*, the British monthly with a well-established track-record of documenting and exposing the forces behind environmental destruction. *The Ecologist* denounces 'official solutions' (to deforestation, including TFAP), calling them 'as ecologically and socially bankrupt as the policies driving deforestation are suicidal'. Indeed, far from stemming the tide of deforestation, the proposed "solutions" will effectively seal the fate of the forests and the peoples who depend on them for their livelihoods.'[30]

The Ecologist affirms that this dire prediction is warranted because TFAP, and the Bank, refuse to recognize that 'development' projects like those we have described in this paper – large dams, huge resettlement schemes, and so on – are precisely the ones that lie at the heart of present deforestation. Instead, say the critics, TFAP blames the victims of the crisis: smallholders, settlers, landless peasants, forest-dwellers, and the poor in general. Because TFAP does not address the primary causes of most deforestation, it 'thus effectively ensures that the destruction can only continue'.

The Bank is likely to provide upwards of $420 million a year for TFAP, not counting funds it will mobilize from other donors, yet only 10 per cent of the budget is earmarked for protection of forest ecosystems. The needs of people now dependent on forest resources are barely considered. In fact, *The Ecologist* claims, TFAP is not really concerned with forests at all, but rather with setting up commercial timber plantations of fast-growing species like eucalyptus. One such TFAP scheme is being imposed in north-east Thailand, where *Eucalyptus camaldulensis* is already taking its toll. Thai villagers call it 'selfish' because it monopolizes nutrients, is useless for fodder, damages soil and water regimes, supplies little firewood, provides no employment, and, worst of all, pushes rural forest-dwellers off their communal lands and forces them to encroach on the little remaining natural forest.[31]

Under TFAP, supported by the Bank and other UN agencies, a modern 'enclosure movement' is taking place, removing resource-management from local communities, handing concessions over to local or foreign entrepreneurs, and placing even greater stress on dwindling natural forests.

TFAP is to be applied throughout the Third World, and the inroads it has already made are alarming, as a case study by the Environmental Policy Institute of its implementation in Ghana makes clear.[32] Ghana has attracted particular attention from the World Bank and the IMF in recent years, and has received per-capita aid unequalled by that to any other country undergoing structural adjustment (for instance, the Programme of Action to Mitigate the Social Costs of Adjustment, or PAMSCAD). Ghana has also received quite massive economic aid, notably for the timber industry. As a result, EPI notes that: 'The value of timber exports increased from $30 million in 1983 to nearly $100 million in 1987. However, the vastly accelerated logging rates occurred at a time when national economic readjustment had greatly reduced Ghana's forestry administration capability. Consequently, according to the World Bank, the country's forests are presently being cut at more than double the sustainable rate.'

But TFAP in Ghana won't help and will very likely worsen this situation, because it will withdraw from poor rural people the very forest resources on which their survival depends – not just wood, but bush-meat, medicines, tree cover vital for protecting cocoa and other crops, and so on. Even the economic (monetary) value of non-industrial exploitation of the forest as practised by the rural population represents as great or greater value to Ghana than that generated by commercial timber exports. Yet only 14 per cent at most of Ghana's TFAP budget will be targeted to rural forestry, according to the EPI.

Moreover, logging concessions as planned by the Bank must cover at least 10,000 hectares and will be granted to the highest bidder. According to EPI, such measures are 'aimed at ensuring only large and efficient operators will be able to obtain concessions'; they will encourage the 'formation of cartels' and 'favour foreign operators'. Ghana must also pay the recurrent costs for huge amounts of imported foreign equipment at 'precisely the time when foreign exchange earnings [from the forestry sector] may even decline'.[33] The Bank will, however, doubtless continue to argue that 'economic efficiency' has been respected and growth-rates increased.

The climate is already changing in Africa as a result of forest destruction. French agronomist René Dumont writes that 'from Casamance (Senegal) to Zaire, the coastal forests of Western Africa, "the ever-green", have been reduced by half since 1950. In the Ivory Coast, 15 million hectares of forests have become 3 million, and even these are full of "holes" made by plantations. This forest destruction has contributed, along with the greenhouse effect, to reduced rainfall in the coastal forest itself and especially in the Sahel: 20 to 25 per cent less rain since 1968.'[34]

18.6 Development and debt

The environmental impact of large and powerful international agencies like the World Bank is straightforward: they support ecologically devastating projects, including those that destroy forests, in the name of economic development based on a spurious conception of unlimited growth. The long-term, hard-to-quantify environmental and social costs of this growth are glossed over or negated. Most of the 'aid' programmes sponsored by individual OECD donor countries, particularly the largest ones like the United States and Japan (now, with $10 billion, the largest national-aid donor), are based on the same principles. Japan's insatiable appetite for woodchips and pulp is, in particular, contributing heavily to forest destruction in Malaysia, Indonesia, Thailand, and more recently in Amazonia. The logging roads and bridges are built with 'development' money; the corporations can then proceed to remove the forests to Japan.[35]

Pressures on the environment and on remaining forests have been further exacerbated by the debt crisis of the 1980s. Heavily indebted countries practising structural adjustment under the aegis of the IMF are all being told the same thing: Export. Most tropical-rainforest destruction is taking place in countries with heavy debt burdens – Brazil, Columbia, Peru, Indonesia, Malaysia, Mexico, Ivory Coast, Nigeria, the Philippines, Thailand, and Zaire. Although other forces besides debt have clearly been at work over the past decade, the annual rate of tropical-forest destruction none the less closely mirrors mounting debt service.[36]

18.7 The limitations on growth

The doctrine of the development Establishment, led by the Bank and the IMF, holds that the whole of the developing world – even including the poorest African countries – must imitate the supposed 'success' of Newly Industrialized Countries (NICs) like South Korea and Taiwan, or mini-dragons Hong Kong and Singapore. To reach NICdom, one must follow the road of export-led growth and structural adjustment. While no one denies that nations, like individuals, cannot live indefinitely beyond their means and must 'adjust' to economic reality, the idea that dozens of indebted countries can all become

NICs if they only try hard enough is patently absurd. The first result of this mistaken doctrine is a glut on the market. These dozens of countries all try to export the same limited range of raw materials or small manufactures, which leads to depressed prices, which in turn trigger the need to export even more just to keep revenues stable; and so on, in a vicious spiral. Export-led growth as a development strategy is a recipe for resource depletion, including the decimation of forests.

Simple arithmetic shows just how bizarre the 'NIC-dom for all' argument really is. In 1987, South Korea's per-capita exports amounted to $1,120, Hong Kong's to $8,650, Singapore's to $11,000. What would happen if Thailand or Indonesia – often mentioned as apprentice NICs – were to attain similar levels? If Indonesia, whose population is 171 million, were to export as much per capita as Singapore, this single country would take over fully 75 per cent of world trade! (The largest present exporter, the Federal Republic of Germany, accounts for under 12 per cent of world trade.) A less extreme example: if Thailand, with 54 million people, were to equal South Korea's per-capita performance, it would export 2.4 per cent of world trade; whereas the two biggest dragons, Taiwan and South Korea, today export respectively 2.2 per cent and 1.9 per cent.[37] Tropical timber would necessarily rank high on their lists of exports.

Clearly the dominant development paradigm will accelerate deforestation, and TFAP is almost certain to make matters worse. How, then, could forests be sustainably managed, and by whom? One thing we know is that traditional forest-dwellers, when allowed to practise their own time-tested systems and given enough space per person, do manage the forest sustainably – if only because they must do so in order to survive. One hopeful recent development in forest management is the policy of the Colombian government. In a far-sighted move, it has given more than 18 million hectares of the Colombian Amazon over to the collective care of Indians belonging to some fifty ethnic groups. Between Indian lands and national parks, Colombia is now protecting an area of the Amazon forest nearly as large as Britain.

Indians are the best forest-managers because their whole lives are based on a complex economic, but also religious and profoundly ecological system of giving to and receiving from the forest. In the words of Peter Bunyard, 'the traditional economy of the Indians is almost the exact opposite of a market economy, in which a person's status increases with his wealth and possessions. In the Indian community, a person who accumulates is evidently one who lacks social relations with others and has no one with whom to share.'[38] Such values are diametrically opposed to those expressed by the dominant development Establishment.

Citizens' groups can also help to impose sustainable forest management. Thai peasants are resisting the spread of eucalyptus. A group in Palawan, the Filipino island with the country's most extensive rainforests, has taken on the wealthy logger whose concession covers 61 per cent of Palawan's forests. This group, like hundreds of others, belongs to the Filipino ecological association Haribon, whose president explains that: 'in the past 15 years we have had only 470 logging concessionaires who [exploit] all the resources of the forests... the process created poverty for 17 million people around the forest areas.'[39] During this same period, the World Bank loaned nearly $5 billion to the Philippines.

18.8 The North's new dependency

In the face of the intensifying momentum of destruction, what hope can one hold out, if any? With the receding threat of nuclear war, the state of the Earth, and climate-change in particular, is becoming what one analyst has called the 'global dread factor'. Recent events in Eastern Europe have tended to marginalize the Third World and to make the South seem less important to Northern policy-makers – even though 80 per cent of the world's population lives there! But the South cannot stay marginalized for long in the environmental debate. If China chooses to produce, say, 300 million refrigerators with CFCs; if India starts to burn twice as much coal; if the last tree is felled, then we can say goodbye to the world as we know it.[40]

Biospheric solidarity may yet be forced upon the governments of the North; like it or not, they may finally have to recognize that debt relief and real contributions to sustainable development in the South are vital to their own survival. They must take the lead in correcting the deep flaws which prevent the 'science' of economics from telling us the difference between money and wealth, between assumed efficiency and actual waste, between short-term profit for the few and global sustainability.

The growing popular environmental movements in the North and the South also have a crucial role to play. In the North, they must insist that their own governments set the example in the campaign against global warming; they must demand that the World Bank and the IMF become publicly accountable. In the South, thousands of popular organizations are struggling for sustainable development, synonymous with survival. If North and South join hands, we can together begin to practise real economics: the economics that cares for our global house.

Chapter 19
Global Warming: A Greenpeace View

Jeremy Leggett

" ...The uniquely frustrating thing about global warming – to those many people who now see the dangers – is that the solutions are obvious. But there is no denying that enacting them will require paradigm shifts in human behaviour – particularly in the field of co-operation between nation states – which have literally no precedents in human history. That is the challenge for the 1990s. There is no single issue in contemporary human affairs that is of greater importance... "

Global warming is a problem which cannot be considered outside the the historical context of atmospheric pollution as a whole. We humans have long treated the atmosphere as a dumping ground for pollutants, and have never been able to predict the exact harm (though harm we have often known it to be) of our emissions.

19.1 The precautionary principle

Many readers will be familiar with the long and sad story of acid rain, a form of pollution which, though now the subject of international agreements – has yet to be addressed with the needs of the natural environment as the first priority.[1] When coal and oil were first burned on a large scale, in the early days of industry and of motorized transport respectively, those responsible had no idea that the sulphur dioxide and nitrogen oxides emitted would lead to large-scale acidification, with all its threats to the health of forests, fisheries, and other aspects of the environment. But even after the scientific evidence linking acidification with emissions from the burning of fossil fuel became clear, vested interests such as power companies dragged their feet appallingly as the first legislative efforts were made to cut emissions. They continue to do so – aided by governments in many cases – to this day.[2]

The ozone story is similar. Chemical companies insisted that chlorofluorocarbons (CFCs) could not be depleting the ozone layer – first when the link between CFCs and ozone-depletion was only a theory,[3] and then even after the ozone hole was discovered in 1985.[4] Only after NASA scientists proved, in 1986, that CFCs were responsible for ozone-depletion by measuring chlorine levels in the ozone hole over Antarctica did companies like ICI and DuPont accept that CFC production – a $1 billion per year industry[5] – would have to be cut. But given the long lifetimes of CFCs in the atmosphere, scientists soon demonstrated that a complete cessation of CFC production would be necessary if ozone-depletion was to be arrested.[6] The chemical multinationals lobbied to have this phase-out delayed as long as possible. And even today, with an international agreement to phase-out CFCs and some other ozone-eating industrial gases agreed – but only on the basis of a phase-out date fully ten years hence – the chemical companies have lobbied to have other ozone-depleters like methyl chloroform excluded from regulation.[7]

We have known for many years that forests, fish, and wildlife were dying as a result of acid rain, and we have tinkered rather than dealt with the causes. We have known for several years that CFCs and related gases are harming life on Earth as a result of the extra ultraviolet radiation the depleted ozone layer lets through, and we have again allowed vested interests to come before the needs of the environment. Now, with the emergence of the global-warming threat, there is a widespread and justified belief that industrial and other human activities have thrown a shadow over the very future of our species. Yet still, amazing as it may seem, we appear to be witnessing the same order of priorities that we adopted for acid rain and ozone-depletion. The concerns of oil companies, chemical companies, power companies, and a host of other vested interests, including the primacy of governments' favoured economic models, are weighed against the need to safeguard the environmental capital of future generations and given the same or even greater priority.

This, then, is the heart of the matter. For organizations like Greenpeace, what comes first must be the needs of the environment – ahead of the expectation of multinationals to make billion-dollar profits, ahead of the idea that freedom involves the right to pollute with impunity unless there is categorical evidence that you are swelling hospital waiting lists. The *modus operandi* we would like to see is: 'Do not emit a substance unless you have proof that it will do no harm to the environment' – the precautionary principle. The *modus operandi* of the modern world is, of course, the reverse: 'You can emit what you like – especially if the proceeds contribute to our Gross National Product – until there is proof of harm to the environment.' The fact that proof of harm might come too late – or that proof is invariably hard to demonstrate with absolute certainty – only augments the licence given the polluters.

These contrasting philosophies, in a very real sense, come to a head with the greenhouse effect. Absolute proof that harm is being done to the environment cannot be achieved – certainly not before there is a very grave risk of it being too late. And – if the likes of President Bush's Chief-of-Staff, John Sununu, are to be believed, making serious efforts to cut greenhouse-gas pollution will not just impinge on the profits of oil and chemical multinationals and other vested interests, but will bring in their train economic chaos and dramatic reductions in standards of living for all.

Reading the *Greenpeace Report* will show that the 'economic ruin' notion – given collective human will to square up to change – is wrong. In this final chapter, I argue that we have no choice but to adopt the precautionary principle where greenhouse-gas emissions are concerned; that to do so will not cost us the earth, but may well in fact save it; and that the anti-greenhouse future which is now an imperative need not involve dramatic cuts in standards of living for all, but rather can involve maintaining economic activity in the industrialized countries, expanding economic activity in the developing countries – and improving quality of living for all, while achieving the goal of greenhouse-gas emissions which leave the atmosphere subject only to natural levels of radiative forcing.

I will support a number of main conclusions, summaries of which are given in italics below, with arguments and examples from within the *Greenpeace Report*. I will then summarize the principal inadequacies of the Intergovernmental Panel on Climate Change (IPCC) policy recommendations, as represented in the report of the IPCC Response Strategies Working Group, and compare the vision of the future outlined there with the one advanced in the *Greenpeace Report*. Finally, I will consider the role of the individual in winning the fight against global warming.

19.2 Greenpeace's response to the greenhouse threat

1. The prospects of future environmental security being compromised by global warming are now so real as to make adoption of a precautionary response imperative – in other words, policy should focus on buying insurance, and policymakers should be clearly aware that waiting in perpetuity for better scientific data entails the real risk of waiting until it is too late.

The radiative forcing of greenhouse gases is well known – based as it is on physical principles.[8] The buildup of greenhouse gases in the atmosphere is also a fact: established by measurement in recent decades, and by ice-core analysis back into the historic past.[9] 'All' that is at issue for scientists is the extent to which, in Earth's complex climate system, the increased radiative forcing of the increasing content of greenhouse gases in the atmosphere will translate into actual temperature rise and other perturbations of Earth's natural climate. The IPCC scientists predict, based on their computer models of climate, increases of temperature more than ten times faster than life on Earth has experienced in at least 100,000 years, and probably much longer. Stephen Schneider, George Woodwell, and Brian Huntley give a graphic picture of the ecological devastation which would arise if we allow such global warming to occur.

But the IPCC scientists may be wrong. They are more than 300 of the world's most eminent climate scientists – in government service as well as in universities. According to Dr John Houghton, the chair of the IPCC scientists group, the IPCC Report involved every serious researcher in the world in the field of climate-modelling, and 'less than ten' would disagree with its conclusions.[10] But such are the uncertainties of the climate system that they could, nonetheless, – just conceivably – be wrong. The response of climate to radiative forcing in the next century could be less than they predict. At least one eminent climatologist, Professor Richard Lindzen of the Massachusetts Institute of Technology, believes it will be. (See Stephen Schneider's chapter on the science of climate-modelling for a critique of Lindzen's ideas).

But do we want to gamble on that tiny possibility? If the world's climate scientists are in virtual unanimity that unprecedented global warming will occur if we do nothing about greenhouse-gas emissions, would we not best serve our children and theirs if we took heed – even if there are uncertainties? And when we hear that the climate scientists also believe that it is 'likely' that their predictions are underestimates – because of the feedbacks described in the chapters by myself, Stephen Schneider, David Schimel, and George Woodwell in the *Greenpeace Report* – should we not be even more impelled to take a precautionary approach?

We should also bear in mind that – even in the unlikely event that the scientists are wrong about the unprecedented and dangerous climate changes to come – by acting, we would have cleared up acid rain, dramatically cut photochemical smog with all its attendant health problems, and eased a host of other environmental problems such as oil-spills at sea as well.

Those who take the view that 'models are invariably wrong' should first of all recall that there is a world of difference between economic models and models based on proven physical principles. If they still choose to baulk at the idea of tackling the ingrained energy profligacy of the world community, and related greenhouse-unfriendly activities, they would be well advised to think of the concept of insurance. Nobody – repeat, nobody – can deny that there is at the very least a prospect of ecological disaster on the horizon where the greenhouse effect is concerned. Those who choose to ignore the prospect, therefore, willfully elect to ignore the environmental security of future generations.

Humans routinely insure themselves and their families against contingencies which are only remote possibilities – death in an air crash, for example. Even in the unwise eventuality that people – and governments – should choose to be sceptical of the world's climate scientists ('after all, many of them will benefit with huge research grants from the current crisis') they would do well – unless they care nothing for their children's and grandchildren's view of them – to apply the principle of insurance.

2. The main routes to surviving the greenhouse threat are energy efficiency, renewable forms of energy production, an immediate and total ban on the production of all CFCs and related gases, less greenhouse-gas-intensive agriculture, stopping deforestation, and reforestation.

This much is clear from a perusal of the suite of greenhouse gases which come from human activities, and the types of human activity that they involve, as described in Chapter 1 of the *Greenpeace Report*. Well over half of all greenhouse-gas emissions can be ascribed to production and use of energy via the extraction, transport, and burning of fossil fuels – coal, oil, and gas. As Jose Goldemberg, Amory Lovins, Michael Walsh, Bill Keepin, and Birgit Bodlund and her colleagues describe, the world has been profligate with fossil fuels since first they were utilized to provide energy in industry, the home, and transport. The opportunities for a 'low-energy' future – as these chapters demonstrate – are legion, and have barely been tapped as yet.

But energy must be produced somehow, as environmentalists are constantly reminded – as though they do not care what happens to the electricity supply to schools, hospitals, and the like. Herein lies the first of several paradigm-shifts which will have to be engendered if humankind is to fashion an anti-greenhouse future. As Carlo LaPorta and Bill Keepin argue in their chapters, there are many viable ways to produce energy other than from fossil fuels and nuclear fuel. They involve renewable sources – sources which produce little or no carbon dioxide and which can, in most cases, be used in perpetuity. Even without the additional dynamic of global warming, these methods of energy production could be facing a glittering future in the decades to come, due to a combination of technological advances and falling costs per kilowatt-hour (this despite considerable stinting on research-and-development over the years). With the greenhouse dynamic, no effort should be spared to speed development of the renewables.

Even if there was no such thing as the greenhouse effect – or if CFCs were not greenhouse gases – there would be an imperative for an immediate CFC phase-out: their known depletion of the ozone layer. The fact that CFCs are greenhouse gases whose additional potency when compared against carbon dioxide is measured in thousands[11] makes their immediate removal from production all the more imperative. The replacements which the chemical industry is developing for CFCs – the HCFCs and HFCs, are also potent greenhouse gases, a fact which the industry seeks either to hide or play down in its advertising.[12]

Around 14 per cent of greenhouse gas emission can today be ascribed to agricultural practices: primarily methane production from ruminants and rice paddies, and nitrous oxide production from fertilizer use. This proportion is only likely to grow as human population grows. Yet, as Anne Ehrlich describes in her chapter of the *Greenpeace Report*, there are agricultural methods available which can achieve reductions of emissions in this area, and additional research into non-intensive methods of agriculture should lead to still-further reductions in the future. We can, in principle, feed the world without mortgaging the future. Concerted efforts at population control, aimed at slowing and eventually stopping population growth globally, would bring concomitant slowing of methane and nitrous oxide egress.

The significant contribution of deforestation to greenhouse-gas emissions is well known. Though absolute amounts of carbon dioxide emitted – globally and from individual countries – are the subject of some dispute, there is no disagreement that deforestation provides a huge component of greenhouse-gas emissions. If the world community could but find a way to stop people destroying their own forests, a great advance would have been made in the fight against global warming. Norman Myers and Susan George describe how this can be done in their chapters.

Just as burning trees release carbon dioxide into the atmosphere, so living trees take carbon dioxide down from the atmosphere as a result of their photosynthesis. If extra trees could be planted in sufficient quantities, as Norman Myers and Mick Kelly show in their chapters, the burden of carbon dioxide in the atmosphere could be reduced.

3. The world community should strive to achieve a 'low energy' future of the kind spelt out by the End-Use Global Energy Project, with a world energy-consumption of not much more than around 12 ter- awatts (TW) by 2025, but spread through the world more equitably than the 10 TW consumed today, so that developing countries can enjoy standards of living akin to those enjoyed in the industrialized countries.

Jose Goldemberg and Thomas Johansson, authors of chapters in the *Greenpeace Report*, were two of four world authorities on energy pol- icy who published, in 1988, a landmark volume on how a low-energy future could be achieved. This study, *Energy for a Sustainable World*, was the product of a long research programme, the End-Use Global Energy Project (EUGEP); it is widely recognized as one of the classics of energy policy.[13] In it, Goldemberg, Johansson, and their colleagues considered the problem of supplying the world with sufficient energy to allow a much-improved average level of amenities to all, while simultaneously reducing the average global per capita energy consumption in the interests of environmental sustainability.

The 70 per cent of humanity which lives in developing countries accounts for only 30 per cent of global energy consumption currently; a person from a developing country consumes, on average, less than one-tenth as much energy as the average US citizen. It would be ruinous if the governments of the developing countries continued to perceive – as many of them still do today – that providing their people with the same average standard of living as the USA's necessitates a tenfold increase in per-capita energy provision. Fortunately, of course, it doesn't. Goldemberg and his colleagues calculated that, by using modern, energy-efficient technologies, such a linear linkage between energy consumption and standard of living can be compre- hensively broken: by supplying an amount of energy equivalent to only 1 kW per person of power (from both commercial and non-com- mercial sources), a level of amenities similar to that enjoyed in Euro- pean countries in the 1970s could be sustained throughout the world. By spreading that level of demand among a global population of seven billion, a total demand of around 12 TW could be arrived at in the year 2020 – a level of energy-demand only 20 per cent higher than today's global energy-demand as assessed by the World Bank.[14]

This is the kind of vision of the energy future which humankind must strive for. There is no other choice.

4. *This pattern of consumption should be achieved by massive investment in energy efficiency in the industrialized countries, and large-scale transfer of up-to-date energy-efficient and non-CFC-dependent technologies from the industrialized countries to the developing countries, to enable them to 'leap-frog' the kind of energy-intensive, polluting, routes which the developed countries took during industrialization.*

Such a world would require a radical rethink of how we view technology. Today, the products of technology are jealously guarded, patented, and competitively marketed. But, as Kilaparti Ramakrishna and Susan George describe in their chapters, commerce must be reshaped to take more cognizance of the global commons. If the industrialized countries continue to sell their energy-inefficient cast-offs to the developing world, the global-warming problem will never be solved. Consider China. With 730 billion tonnes of proven coal- and oil-reserves (measured against the 750 billion tonnes of carbon in the carbon dioxide in the current atmosphere; see Chapter 1), with a uniquely high 76 per cent of its energy currently coming from coal, with a population of more than 1 billion, and a stated government intention of putting a refrigerator in every Chinese home, what is likely to be the burden of carbon dioxide emissions from that single country in the early decades of the next century? Add to that the CFC emissions if – as is currently the prospect – all the new, but technologically antiquated, Chinese fridges use CFCs and leak them into the atmosphere. The solution to this sum is depressing in the extreme.

Regarding the carbon dioxide, energy analysts have calculated that if China were to put a small fridge and a small freezer in each home and employ current fridge technology, it would require thirty 1 gigawatt (billion watt) power-stations – presumably almost entirely coal-fired – just to power them. But if the Chinese were to produce their fridges using the best available, energy-efficient western technology, only three such power stations would be necessary – a 90 per cent improvement in the situation.[15] For such a possibility to come to fruition, however, the industrialized world is clearly going to have to rethink its approach to aid and international co-operation, and to accept the limitations of market forces in an environmentally interdependent world.

And the example of Chinese fridge technology only scratches the surface of the 'new economics' which Susan George describes in

Chapter 18. Again, we are talking about paradigm shifts.

In his chapter of the *Greenpeace Report*, Jose Goldemberg argues that such a rethink towards technological development in poor countries is an imperative. He shows how little it would cost – relatively speaking – using the examples of global insurance expenditures and a levy of $1 on every barrel-equivalent of petroleum consumed, to create the necessary international fund for a viable anti-greenhouse regime to be implemented.

5. *Given suitable investment of funding and resources, the goal should be for the world's entire energy requirement to be produced by renewable forms of energy production as soon as possible in the next century.*

What of the future for fossil fuels? Consider the recent words of a past president of Shell Oil Company: 'world energy needs likely will require a better-than-50 percent increase in the fossil fuel production rate over the next 40 years ... beyond 40 years, the projection is for an accelerating gap between the growing energy demand and the ability of today's fossil fuel resources to respond to this demand.'[16] These are the words of a man who cannot have given much thought to the radiative forcing of carbon dioxide in the atmosphere.

Greenpeace has a different vision of the future: we believe that it is imperative to phase out fossil-fuel use completely, and as soon as possible. The imperative is provided not just by the question of global warming, but by acidification and by aspects of pollution of the type described by Michael Walsh in his chapter on motor-vehicle emissions.

A visionary view? Maybe, in the current frame of reference. But a view which we believe will yet come to be seen as a routine imperative.

So how will the world's energy-demands be met? They can be met sometime in the next century – given a far less energy-intensive world than the present one – by the many forms of renewable energy production. This is manifestly not a visionary view. Carlo LaPorta's chapter gives a taste of the plummeting economic costs and exciting technological advances in the area of renewables. Yet to date, only relatively little has been spent on research and development on these technologies, compared to fossil-fuel and nuclear R&D.[17] Indeed, there is reason to believe that the oil and nuclear industries, and their

supporters in legislatures, have systematically stifled the development of renewables wherever the opportunity has presented itself
over the years.[18]

Many experts speak of a potential forthcoming 'explosion point'
for renewables, where market forces alone would become such that it
would be irrational not to expoit them at the expense of fossil fuels.
All that the world has to do is speed the arrival of that explosion point
by legislating to foster the development of renewables, and by putting
research-and-development funding where common sense – and not
the lobbying of strong and entrenched vested interests like the oil and
nuclear industries – dictates.

6. *Expansion of the nuclear-power industry, or replacement of existing nuclear-power stations when they come to the ends of their operating lifetimes, would involve diverting funds from cost-effective
energy-solutions to the greenhouse crisis (energy-efficiency and most
forms of renewable-energy production), and therefore – especially
when viewed in concert with safety, waste disposal, decommissioning, and nuclear-weapons proliferation problems - should have no
role to play in the international policy response.*

It might seem at first sight common sense to think of replacing coal-
fired power with nuclear if the goal is to cut greenhouse-gas emissions. After all, nuclear power does not give rise – directly – to
appreciable greenhouse-gas emissions. (Note, however, that appreciable CO_2 emissions are generated as a result of mining and milling
uranium, and during various other phases of the nuclear cycle.) But,
as Bill Keepin makes clear in Chapter 13 of the *Greenpeace Report*,
the economics of nuclear power alone (much less the environmental
considerations) exclude it from a sensible portfolio of policy responses to the greenhouse effect. If the goal is to replace all coal-fired
power-stations, the proposal is particulary incredible: thousands of
new nuclear-power stations would have to be built – one every few
days for the next three decades or more – by an industry which, in the
United States, has had every order for a reactor placed in the last 16
years (more than 100) cancelled or indefinitely deferred, and which
takes ten to twelve years to build a new nuclear-power station.

But even the goal of allowing a limited expansion of the nuclear-
power sector – or even replacement of existing nuclear plants at the
end of their lives – makes no sense. In the USA, the average cost of

generating nuclear electricity is 13.5 cents per kilowatt-hour (in 1987 dollars). This compares against a host of potential energy-saving investments averaging around 2 cents per kWh or less. In global-warming terms, each dollar invested in energy-efficiency, therefore, buys nearly seven times more carbon dioxide emissions-savings than a dollar invested in nuclear.

But we cannot mine the energy-efficiency potential – deep though it is – forever. Again, our future energy must come from somewhere. And here renewables win over nuclear too. As Bill Keepin describes, a number of renewable technologies are available now at prices ranging from around 3 to 9 cents/kWh. And with widely projected reductions in the cost of solar photovoltaic-energy production from the present level of 20 to 40 cents per kWh to less than 10 by the early years of the next century, the nuclear industry – currently generating electricity costing more than 13 cents per kWh – is clearly heading for long-deserved retirement from the inventory of energy options. This would happen even if nuclear operating costs somehow fell dramatically (whereas the overall costs of nuclear are likely only to increase still further as a result of a host of still-unaddressed waste-disposal and decommissioning problems).

Birgit Bodlund and her colleagues provide detailed arguments which underline Keepin's conclusion. Sweden is the most nuclear-intensive country in the world, on a per-capita basis. Fully half of Swedish electricity currently comes from nuclear power. Yet, in a 1980 referendum, the Swedish people voted to phase out nuclear power. Bodlund's chapter is a Swedish electricity plan, formulated by researchers at the Swedish State Power Board (Vattenfall) and Lund University. It finds that the Swedish government's goal of carrying out the referendum decision and not expoiting Sweden's four remaining rivers for hydroelectric power can be achieved, while cutting carbon dioxide emissions from today's electricity-related and district-heating-related emissions. The prescription involves strong emphasis on energy-efficiency in new technologies, and increased use of renewables, particularly biomass. Bodlund and her colleagues find that, despite anticipated economic growth of 54 per cent (1.9 per cent per year) by the year 2010 (as projected by the Swedish Ministry of Finance), total Swedish electricity-demand could decline by fully 25 per cent. The necessary replacement of equipment with 'high-efficiency' technologies would cost as much as $500 million *less* than a 'business-as-usual' plan which places little emphasis on energy conservation and which uses traditional fossil fuels for producing electricity.

Shortly after this landmark study was first printed in a Swedish publication (it is reprinted in the *Greenpeace Report*) the Swedish State Power Board established a programme costing more than $300 million to finance efficiency improvements and biomass-power generation.

The only miracle left in the nuclear dream is that more people have not awakened to the fact that nuclear power is economically – and increasingly, in that it takes much-needed funds away from renewables and efficiency – ethically, redundant.

7. The detailed mix of policy prescriptions, and their quantification, should be subject to scientific research results during the 1990s, but essential first steps are as follows:

■ *implementation of immediate cuts in carbon dioxide emissions and the drawing-up of integrated strategies aimed at the phase-out of fossil fuels as early as possible in the next century;*

■ *no effort be spared to arrest deforestation and halt the production or use of CFCs, and related compounds such as HFCs.*

Our goal should clearly be to stabilize the concentrations of greenhouse gases in the atmosphere. But even this simple statement is fraught with scientific uncertainties. By how much would we need to cut emissions to do this? The IPCC scientists say that to stabilize carbon dioxide at present levels in the atmosphere (353 parts per million), an immediate global cut of more than 60 per cent would be needed. That would be difficult to the point of impossibility, unless global burning of coal, oil, and gas could somehow be more-than halved overnight. So what should the goal be?

The modelling study by Mick Kelly in Chapter 4 of the *Greenpeace Report* shows that, even if we stop deforestation by the end of the century, reforest an area of 200 million hectares in the first two decades of the next century (adding the equivalent of around 5 per cent to the area presently covered by forest), phase out CFCs and related chemicals by 1995, and slow the growth of agricultural emissions of methane and nitrous oxide appreciably, we would still need to cut carbon dioxide emissions globally by 70 per cent to stabilize greenhouse-gas concentrations in the atmosphere in the first half of the next century. If Kelly's model is accurate, we would have stabilized at a greenhouse-gas concentration of 445 ppm carbon dioxide-equivalent: a level only 8 per cent higher than today.

This is only an example of the mix of policies which might be attempted in the decades to come. Clearly, any policies decided in this field will have to be reviewed on a continuous basis. What is needed at this stage is for the world community to decide on the basics. The Greenpeace conclusion is that the goal must be elimination of fossil fuels from the energy inventory, and that that goal should be reflected in the target for the year 2000. The goals of stopping deforestation and phasing out CFCs can almost be taken as read if the goal is to be stabilization of greenhouse-gas concentrations in the atmosphere.

Where it comes to narrowing the many scientific uncertainties involved in climate models, there is much left for scientists to do. A priority for the future must clearly be expanding international research and monitoring efforts. But this should not be – as some world leaders would seem to like – a substitute for policy actions. Scientists are generally confident that they can narrow down some of the uncertainties with time. But, as the IPCC scientists concluded in their report, 'considering the complex nature of the problem and the scale of the scientific programmes to be undertaken we know that rapid results cannot be expected. Indeed further scientific advances may expose unforeseen problems and areas of ignorance.'[19] The leader of the Princeton University climate-modelling team, Professor Suyukuro Manabe, put it more graphically at the 1990 American Association for the Advancement of Science Meeting: 'we are never going to have a perfect model. And even if we had one, we wouldn't know we had it.'[20]

8. The large sums needed to fund these and other anti-greenhouse strategies, plus the expanded scientific-research effort which is essential in the 1990s to narrow down the remaining scientific uncertainties, can come from diverting the greater part of the $1,000 billion spent on armaments annually by the world community, as befits the changing concepts of global security which the late 1980s have heralded.

The world spends a trillion dollars a year on its weapons. The USA alone spends almost $300 billion each year, and the Soviet Union probably around the same figure.[21] As Stephen Schneider points out in Chapter 9, there have been recent estimates of the 'cost' of cutting greenhouse-gas emissions which talk of sums of more than 3 trillion dollars over the next century. Even if such sums were correct (and they are not – as Schneider recounts, they have been strongly attacked by the US National Academy of Sciences and others) the world would be spending at least two orders of magnitude more than this on weapons alone if it maintained business-as-usual in the defence arena in the twenty-first century. If concepts of security do not change among the small community of men who control the purse-strings of the world's militaries in the decade to come, they will certainly be changing – indeed already are changing – among populations.[22] Three trillion dollars can come to seem a very small price-tag indeed for saving the planet from ecological disaster.

The anachronisms of military spending in the modern, ecologically threatened world are legion. Take the price-tag for safeguarding two-thirds of the Amazon rainforest: $3 billion according to a 1989 estimate.[23] Cancel just six US 'Stealth' bombers and you have the necessary cash to do it. You would have cut human greenhouse-gas emissions overnight by several percent – at least – by this simple act of survival-motivated 'altruism' towards the people of Brazil.

It is difficult to believe that the hard sell on 'military threats' can be maintained for much longer in support of defence budgets on the scale currently in force in the OECD and Eastern-bloc countries. Additionally, if those countries were to embrace the paradigm-shift from military security of the 1980s to environmental security in the 1990s, with all its budgetary implications, it is difficult to believe that the arms trade from North to South would survive for long in all its current extravagance. As the UN's World Commission on Environment and Development noted in the Brundtland Report, 'the recent destruction of much of Africa's dryland agricultural production was more severe than if an invading army had pursued a scorched earth policy. Yet most of the affected governments still spend far more to protect their people from invading armies than from the invading desert.' With a significant 'peace dividend' emerging in the north, and a shrivelling arms trade, Third World governments would abruptly find themselves with expanded – and altogether more sustainable – options for investing their GNP.

19.3 The IPCC vision of the future versus the Greenpeace vision of the future

The undoing of the Intergovernmental Panel on Climate Change, in its vital role of providing guidance to world leaders on how to frame effective policies to fight global warming, has been the work of the Response Strategies Working Group (Working Group 3) – hereafter referred to interchangeably as the RSWG or the policymakers working-group. In their final report,[24] completed in June 1990, the policymakers consistently ignored or glossed over the major conclusions of the scientists' working-group (Working Group 1) in their final report, completed in May.

The scientists' report – in plain language – made the assessment that the remaining scientific uncertainties, though huge, translate to a question, not of whether the human-enhanced greenhouse effect will be bad, but of how bad, and by when. They stated clearly that global warming will occur in a business-as-usual world with no policies to stem emissions of greenhouse gases. The uncertainties concern only the degree of that warming. They recognized that both positive feedbacks and negative feedbacks can come into play in a warming climate system, that few of these feedbacks are incorporated in existing climate models, and that those which are incorporated in models are only crude approximations of nature. In the context of this uncertainty, they further pointed out that positive feedbacks, such as a decreasing carbon sink in the oceans, increase of microbial respiration in warming soils, depletion of the atmospheric hydroxyl reservoir, and release of methane from expanding wetlands, melting tundra, and hydrates, are more likely to dominate than negative feedbacks. This means – as the scientists' report pointed out clearly – that the 'best guesses' for future temperature-rise produced by the computer models (2°C above pre-industrial levels by by 2030 and 4°C above pre-industrial levels by 2090) are likely underestimates – and possibly major underestimates – of next century's reality.

Though the scientists had been making their developing text available to the policymakers' working group throughout the IPCC process, the penultimate version of the policymakers' report, in contrast, never even mentioned the words 'global warming'. It referred to 'climate change' forty-six times, rarely qualifying this phrase, and on the one occasion where it did, used the word 'potential' climate change, flatly ignoring a main conclusion of the scientists' report.

Adjectives like 'formidable' and 'significant' appeared in the RSWG report, but only in the context of the difficulties facing policymakers, or the remaining scientific uncertainties.

The RSWG report also glossed over major conclusions of the Impacts Working Group (IPCC Working Group 2). The geo-historical record shows that a 1.5–4.5°C (2.7–8.1°F) rise in global average temperature, as predicted at equilibrium for a doubling of greenhouse gases in the atmosphere by Global Circulation Models, is many times faster than any past temperature-rise experienced during the tenure of humankind on the planet. This rate of temperature-rise would itself – notwithstanding the risk from positive-feedback enhancements – herald unprecedented stresses on ecosystems. The Impacts Working Group report stated accordingly, in its penultimate draft, that 'these rates [of temperature-rise] are likely to be faster than ecosystems can respond. Major vegetation zones could, therefore, face severe disturbances and disruptions.' Working Group 2 spoke, for example, of the potential for 'substantial reductions in biological diversity', and extended geographical ranges for some insect pests and diseases, 'allowing the expansion of these pests, at present limited to tropical countries, to current subtropical and temperate regions', with consequent harm to crops. Also, where agriculture is concerned, it concluded that 'soil moisture will decrease' in some areas, '...particularly those that are already in marginal situations such as in Africa'. Where human health is concerned, it concluded that 'major impacts are possible on large urban areas', and that the climatic changes 'could radically alter the patterns of vector-borne diseases by shifting them to higher latitudes and thus put large populations at risk'. Throughout the Working Group 2 report, the tenor was that the many remaining uncertainties entail massive risks to humankind, just as George M. Woodwell, Brian Huntley, and Andrew Haines make clear in the Impacts section of the *Greenpeace Report*.

The policymakers' report, in contrast, contained no language which would give any impression that the stakes are this high. Instead, it said in six separate places that climate change can only 'potentially' result in significant impacts.

Without even discussing the merits or demerits of a suite of policies designed to buy insurance against the global-warming scenarios which the first two IPCC working-groups described, the policymakers' working-group report dwelt disproportionately on the need for increased research. The summary of the report referred to scientific research, using qualifiers such as 'careful' or 'substantial', twelve times. This it did despite a section of the scientists' Summary which clearly describes how additional research – essential though it is – stands little chance of narrowing scientific uncertainties appreciably over the next decade or so.

The IPCC policymakers did recommend negotiation of a Climate Convention, but only one which 'lays down general principles and obligations for addressing climate change'. Nowhere did it recommend – or even discuss – specific cuts in greenhouse-gas emissions. The US Environmental Protection Agency and the IPCC scientists both argue that stabilization of the greenhouse-gas content of the atmosphere would require cuts of global carbon dioxide emissions of as much as 60–80 per cent. Implicit in this conclusion, in the light of the IPCC scientists' conclusion about the likelihood of positive feedbacks dominating in a greenhouse world, is that not to attempt such a policy goal – or something at least approaching it – is to gamble willfully with the environmental security of future generations.

Instead, the policymakers' report did not even advocate a freeze on emissions. It described itself as 'an important interim assessment for policymakers', yet found that 'it was not possible to complete such an analysis [of quantitative targets] by the time of this report's publication'. Yet in that same time-frame, a host of eminent scientists and research groups have researched and published specific emission-reduction scenarios - including the study by Mick Kelly presented in Chapter 4 of this volume.

The IPCC policymakers' report persistently aired the perceived costs of policy action, and never considered the costs of inaction.The impression generated was one of potential crisis for the world economy if serious attempts are made to cut greenhouse-gas emissions. For example, the report justified its failure to advocate – or even to consider – specific emissions targets thus: 'the primary constraint on conducting the analysis is the serious lack of data on the economic and social costs of the various response options', noting with dazzling myopia where the qualitative implications of the work of the first two IPCC working-groups are concerned, that, 'an adequate understanding of the benefits, in terms of climate changes that can be avoided, is also lacking'.

Nowhere was there a discussion of responsibility, or equity, in the past and present pattern of emissions of greenhouse gases. The IPCC scientists clearly showed that the great majority of greenhouse gases historically have come from the developed countries, and – though the developing countries are beginning to catch up – the dominance of the rich countries in the emissions league-table continues. Because of the delay in the response of the climate system to the radiative forcing of these greenhouse gases, it is the emissions of the rich countries which, in a very real sense, will be the cause of the warming in the poor countries in the decades to come. Hence, it would seem only fair that the developed countries take on the lion's share of the necessary cuts. Not only was this obvious conclusion eschewed as a recommendation of the IPCC Response Strategies Working Group Summary, it was not even discussed. The RSWG advocated policies which 'reflect the obligations of both developed and developing countries', and rightly argued that 'there is a need for the transfer of technologies for limiting climate change to the developing countries', yet chose to erect – in the face of a basic common-sense (not to say humanitarian) approach to equity – a 'number of impediments' including in the list of these impediments 'lack of financial resources'.

The IPCC policymakers' report was firmly rooted in a frame of reference which refuses to countenance appreciable change from present conditions. For example, where transport is concerned, the economic and market potentials of alternatives 'are very low because petroleum fuels are relatively cheap', and constrained by 'consumer demand and preference for larger, more powerful and better equipped cars'. The mandate of RSWG clearly allowed the policymakers to make reference to – and, indeed, recommend – particular legislative inducements which would allow such obstacles to a sustainable, anti-greenhouse future to be combated. But the report contained no such recommendations. An inappropriate and unsubstantiated conclusion that 'the most effective response strategies, especially in the short term, are ... in particular those which use market-based mechanisms' is flatly contradicted by the transport example above.

19.4 The individual and global warming

Most of the Policy section of the *Greenpeace Report* has focused on the role of government and of industry, the interfaces between these two, and the relationships between nations or national groupings. It is in these areas that the paradigm-shifts which we must achieve in order to survive the greenhouse threat must come to fruition. But individuals, of course, are just as important. Governments respond to people. Industries respond to people. And over and above the ability of the individual to insist on governmental or corporate change comes the ability of each of us to strive for an anti-greenhouse way of living. How this can be done will be fairly self-evident to anyone who has read the *Greenpeace Report*. Below, we describe guide-lines for living an individual 'greenhouse-friendly' life. Such guide-lines are covered in more detail in a number of excellent popular books published recently.[25] We emphasize that this is just a 'starters' list for anyone seriously concerned about global warming.

Some anti-greenhouse actions for the concerned citizen
(Not necessarily in order of amount of greenhouse-gas emissions saved)

- Replacing conventional light bulbs with compact fluorescents in the home.
- Insulating the roof, the water tank, and the walls.
- Fitting draught-stripping and/or double-glazing, and use of radiator thermostats.
- Replacing electric appliances with best-available energy-efficient products.
- Recycling of paper and avoidance of excess packaging and disposable products.
- Active pursuit of personal ways out of the 'great car economy' trap: use of public transport wherever possible, avoidance of car-use wherever possible.
- Favouring organically farmed produce over intensive-farming products.
- Favouring vegetarian produce over meat.
- Exercise of consumer discretion concerning the products of companies whose activities add to the greenhouse threat.

■ Use of the power of the pen in exerting pressure for anti-green-house changes in society.

The starting-point is to make the home as energy-efficient as possible. Huge savings in greenhouse gases could be achieved at the power-station if householders simply insulated their roof, walls, hot-water tank, doors, and windows. A super-insulated house can save each year quantities of carbon dioxide measured in tonnes. A fringe benefit is that households accustomed to paying annual fuel bills of several hundreds of dollars can reduce their bills to just tens of dollars.[26] Bigger savings still – of both greenhouse-gas emissions and money – are available in the areas of radiator thermostats and other methods of heating-control, in gas-condensing boilers, in the use of heat-reflecting or heat-retaining windows, and a host of other techniques, many of which are discussed in Amory Lovins's chapter of the *Greenpeace Report*.

Replacing electric appliances with best-available energy-efficient products at the end of their lifetimes (or earlier) is essential, because the range in energy-efficiencies among products currently on the market is enormous. Amory Lovins and Birgit Bodlund and her colleagues give many examples in their chapters. Only rarely are such differences made clear to consumers in labelling of products, however. Given mandatory energy-efficiency labelling, consumer-pressure can be brought to bear so that energy-efficient, greenhouse-friendly goods can be favoured over energy-profligate goods.

In the interim, the concerned consumer can always ask for guidance. If people display such concerns in sufficient numbers, news soon filters back to manufacturers from shopkeepers, so adding to pressure for corporate change. The time is probably not far off when manufacturers will be competing with each other to market goods and services on the basis of how 'greenhouse friendly' they are, both in final performance of the product and in the process by which it was manufactured. Though there is no substitute for the consumer asking whether he or she really needs a particular product in the first place, there is no doubt that in the provision of essential products the role of anti-greenhouse-motivated consumerism can make a big impression in the fight against global warming.

Recycling of paper and avoidance of excess packaging and disposable products is necessary because paper and packaging can end up in landfills, where methane is generated. The more paper and packaging, the more methane. Again, much could be done to help achieve the necessary increases in domestic and municipal recycling were governments to take a more interventionist stance than is commonly the case today, and deploy judicious fiscal inducements to encourage good anti-greenhouse practices.

There is no choice but for us to seek ways out of the 'great car economy'. As Michael Walsh describes in his chapter of the *Greenpeace Report*, the contribution of motor vehicles to the enhanced greenhouse effect is measured in double figures. This, more than any other field of human activity, is a clear symptom of humankind's collective complacency over atmospheric pollution. Fully in the face of the emergence of the scientific consensus about the global-warming threat, and despite growing public concern, auto manufacterers the world over daily spend millions in seeking to persuade us that status, quality of living – even sexuality – are all tied in with the performance of the cars we own. The oil companies, whose business depends in large measure on those cars, spend similar sums persuading us that theirs is the fuel which will give us that little bit of extra edge over the rivals'. Yet whenever a litre of petrol is burned, whether from an Exxon or Shell garage, whether in a ritzy BMW or an artisan's Citroen, two-and-a-half kilograms of carbon dioxide go into the air. The average car pours four times its own body-weight of carbon dioxide into the air each year.[27]

It goes without saying that the anti-greenhouse citizen will use public transport wherever possible, and think very carefully about use of the car.

It seems only a matter of time before the first alternatives to the internal-combustion engine become widely available for powered personal transportation. But electric cars will only push the carbon dioxide emissions down the line to the power-station if the power-stations still burn fossil-fuels. The paradigm-shift in transport must come hand-in-glove with a paradigm-shift in energy supply.

Favouring organically farmed produce over intensive-farming products is necessary because of the additional nitrous oxide emissions which come from using chemical instead of natural fertilizers. Other aspects of pollution from fertilizers, such as nitrate buildup in drinking-water, and increasing evidence that intensive agriculture is not sustainable and ruins land in the long run,[28] are additional reasons for favouring organically farmed produce. Similarly, favouring vegetarian produce over meat is an inevitable conclusion when the citizen concerned about the greenhouse threat looks at the figures for methane emissions from ruminants, as described by Anne Ehrlich in her chapter of the *Greenpeace Report*.

Exercise of consumer discretion is a very important option for the individual. The products of companies involved in deforestation can be avoided. So, too, can those of companies who show evidence of favouring greenhouse-gas-related profits over early changes to an anti-greenhouse corporate strategy. Making the reasons for rejecting their products known to the companies concerned in writing is even more powerful. If enough people do this, a company has no choice but to change course, or face lost profits. In fact, persistent use of the power of the pen is possibly the most important option available to the concerned citizen. As any Greenpeace campaigner will tell you, politicians, government employees, and companies alike are quick to take a serious look at any issue which attracts a heavy post-bag. In exerting pressure for anti-greenhouse changes in the way a society operates, letter-writing is a must for anyone who worries about the threat of global warming. Any national Greenpeace office will be able to give you information on how to go about this.

19.5 Conclusions

In a recent paper quoted elsewhere in this concluding chapter, a former president of Shell Oil advocated an expansion of the use of fossil fuels into the next century. If the world's climate scientists are to be believed he was, in effect, advocating what could prove to be – within just a few short generations – a great global suicide pact. In that same paper, he also used these words: 'One reason for the slow penetration of any new energy source is the significant inertia in the system, including social, economic and technological inertia. Lifestyles and personal preferences are slow to change and often take two or more generations to take effect.'[29]

This is the first and most important of the profound shifts we are going to have to bring about if we are to ensure that humankind and the bulk of the natural world are not to succumb to the greenhouse threat. Human beings are not predisposed to collective suicide. The danger, though – given the time-scales on which we plan the routine

operations of our lives – is that the threa
enough people in time to achieve the col;
uniquely frustrating thing about global wa
ple who now see the dangers – is that the
there is no denying that enacting them will
human behaviour – particularly in the field
nation states – which have literally no prece..
That is the challenge for the 1990s. There is no single issue in contemporary human affairs that is of greater importance.

Notes

Introduction Jeremy Leggett

1　W. Booth, 'Action urged against global warming: scientists appeal for curbs on gases', *Washington Post*, 2 Feb. 1990.

2　J. Leggett, 'The New Manhattan Project: America's weapons labs are turning to a new enemy', *New Scientist*, 16 Sept. 1989.

3　Intergovernmental Panel on Climate Change, Report to IPCC from Working Group 1: Policymakers' Summary of the Scientific Assessment of Climate Change (June 1990). Note that scientists discuss temperatures in degrees Celcius. To convert to Fahrenheit, multiply by 9 and divide by 5, adding 32 to the result if the value quoted is absolute ($0°C = 32°F$; $10°C = 50°F$ etc.). The average surface temperature on Earth today is $15°C$ ($59°F$).

4　See n. 3, p. 10. See also chapters by Jeremy Leggett and David Schimel in this volume.

5　For a good summary of these events, see.S. Boyle and J. Ardill, *The Greenhouse Effect: A practical guide to the world's changing climate* (New English Library, 1989).

6　Statement issued by the participants at the World Conference on 'The Changing Atmosphere: Implications for Global Security', Toronto, 30 June 1988.

7　W. Schwarz, 'Stirrings of hope in the forest', *Guardian*, 14 Mar. 1989.

8　B. Bolin, speech to Third Plenary of the Intergovernmental Panel on Climate Change, Washington, DC, Feb. 1990.

9　R. Sivard, *World Military and Social Expenditures*, 1989.

10　Editorial, *Wall Street Journal*, 6 Feb. 1990.

11　Intergovernmental Panel on Climate Change, Report to IPCC from Working Group 3: Policy-makers' Summary, Response Strategies Working Group (June 1990).

12　D. A. Lashof and D. A. Tirpak (eds.), *Policy Options for Stabilizing Global Climate*, draft report to Congress, US Environmental Protection Agency (completed Feb. 1989, in press).

13　P. M. Kelly, *Halting Global Warming* (Greenpeace International Climate in Crisis Series, no. 1, Feb. 1990).

14　See n. 3.

15　Margaret Thatcher, address to the United Nations General Assembly, 8 Nov. 1989, and see also her speech at the Royal Society, Sept. 1988.

16　W. Keepin and M. Barrett, *Critique of the UK case study for IPCC* (Greenpeace Special Report, June 1990).

17 G. Lean, 'Revealed: the will to fight', *Observer*, 15 Apr. 1990.

18 Research/Strategy/Management Inc., *Global warming and energy priorities: a national perspective* (A study for the Union of Concerned Scientists, Nov. 1989).

19 See n. 3, p. 10.

Chapter 1: The Nature of the Greenhouse Threat Jeremy Leggett

The author is grateful to Mick Kelly, Dan Lashof, John Mitchell, and
Stephen Schneider for comments on all or parts of this chapter.

1 Intergovernmental Panel on Climate Change, *Scientific Assessment of Climate Change* (Report of Working Group 1, and accompanying Policymakers Summary, June 1990).

2 Global Warming Potential is the capacity for a kilogram (or other mass unit) of greenhouse gas to warm the atmosphere, relative to the same mass unit of carbon dioxide, taking account of the different lifetimes (residence times) of the gases in the atmosphere. See IPCC, n. 1, section 2.

3 The cryosphere comprises the ice caps and glaciers of the world, its seasonal snow-cover, and permanently frozen ground (permafrost).

4 The biosphere is the zone at and adjacent to the surface of the Earth where all life exists, comprising all living organisms.

5 The geosphere is the solid portion of the Earth.

6 See IPCC, n. 1, section 2.

7 An aerosol is a dispersion of fine solid or liquid particles in the atmosphere.

8 Albedo is a term used for the capacity of the ground, vegetation, ice , snow, water, clouds, or particulates in the atmosphere – individually or together – to reflect solar radiation. The higher the albedo, the higher the reflectivity.

9 The physics of the greenhouse effect, and the likely implications for the atmosphere of heat-trapping gases, were calculated by Swedish scientist Svante Arrhenius at the turn of the century.

10 See J. Gribbin, 'The end of the ice ages?', *New Scientist*, 17 June 1989, 48–52, for a popular account. Also: J. Imbrie, J. Hays, D. Martinson, A. McIntyre, J. Mix, N. Morley, N. Pisias, W. Prell, and N. Shackleton, 'The orbital theory of Pleistocene climate: support from a revised chronology of the marine ^{18}O record', in A. Berger *et al.* (eds), *Milankovitch and Climate*, part 1 (Dordrecht, Riedel), pp. 296–306.

11 See, for example, comments by J. Smagorinsky, 'Strengths and weaknesses of GCMs', introductory paper to the symposium on 'Climate Change – models and policies', AAAS meeting, New Orleans, 19 Feb 1990.

12 See IPCC, n. 1.

13 The main centres are: University of Illinois; Goddard Institute for Space Studies, NASA; Geophysical Fluid Dynamics Laboratory, NOAA, Princeton University; National Center for Atmospheric Research, Colorado; the Lawrence Livermore National Laboratory in California; the UK Meteorological Office; Hamburg in the FRG; the Canadian Climate Centre; and CSIRO in Melbourne, Australia .

14 See IPCC, n. 1.

15 Ibid.

16 See IPCC, n. 1, Section 5.

17 See IPCC, n. 1, Section 7.

18 S. Schneider, 'The changing global climate', *Scientific American* (Sept. 1989), vol. 261, no. 3, pp. 38–47.

19 See IPCC, n. 1, Policymakers Summary, p. 16.

20 C. Lorius *et al.*, 'Antarctic ice core: CO_2 and climate change over the last climatic cycle', *Eos* (June 1988), vol. 79, no. 26, pp. 681–4.

21 See Gribbin and Imbrie *et al.*, n 10.

22 See Lorius *et al.*, n. 20.

23 See Gribbin and Imbrie *et al.*, n. 10.

24 F. I. Woodward, *Climate and Plant Distribution* (Cambridge University Press, 1987).

25 H. and E. Stommel, 'The year without a summer', *Scientific American*, June 1979.

26 See IPCC, n. 1, Policymakers Summary, p. 10.

27 See section 1.5.7 on ocean circulation.

28 See IPCC, n. 1, Policymakers Summary.

29 See Scheider, n. 18.

30 See *Biota and Palaeotemperatures*, a collection of papers in the *Journal of the Geological Society of London* (1989), vol. 146, pp. 145–86.

31 J. Hansen, testimony to US Congress, 1988.

32 See, e.g., correspondence in *Science*, 4 Aug. 1989, pp. 451–2.

33 R. A. Houghton and G. M. Woodwell, 'Global climatic change', *Scientific American*, Apr. 1989, pp.36–44.

34 C. Clover, 'Thin ice alert by polar scientists', *Daily Telegraph*, 1 Sept. 1989. See also: A. Coghlan, 'American Navy witholds "greenhouse" data', *New Scientist*, 9 September 1989, p. 46.

35 R. Highfield, 'Global warming melts polar ice at British Antarctic base', *Daily Telegraph*, 27 September 1989.

36 See IPCC, n. 1, Policymakers Summary, p. 22.

37 W. S. Broecker, 'Unpleasant surprises in the greenhouse?', *Nature* (July 1987), vol. 328, pp. 123–6.

38 See IPCC, n. 1, Section 1.

39 But note caveats arising from the work of Tans, Takahashi, *et al*: see later section on carbon dioxide fertilization.

40 R. A. Berner and A. C. Lasaga, 'Modelling the geochemical carbon cycle', *Scientific American*, Mar. 1989, 54-61.

41 IPCC, n. 1, puts the range at 0.6 to 2.5 Gt carbon from deforestation, following R. P. Detwiler and C. A. S. Hall, 'Tropical forests and the global carbon cycle', *Science* (1988), vol. 239, pp. 43–7. See also F. Pearce,'Felled trees deal double blow to global warming', *New Scientist*, 16 Sept. 1989, p. 25. In this article, based on an interview, Charles Keeling of Scripps Institution of Oceanography posits that 4 Gt of carbon, not 2 as is commonly assumed, is coming from deforestation each year.

42 See Houghton and Woodwell, n. 33.

43 B. Bolin, 'How much CO2 will remain in the atmosphere? The carbon cycle and projections for the future', in B. Bolin, B. R. Doos, J. Jager, and R. A. Warrick, (eds), *The Greenhouse Effect, Climate Change, and Ecosystems* (Scope Report no. 29. John Wiley), pp. 93–155.

44 J. F. Bookout, 'Two centuries of fossil fuel energy', *Episodes* (Journal of the International Union of Geological Sciences), (Dec. 1989), pp. 257–62.

45 See Schneider, n. 18.

46 World Resources Institute, *World Resources 1988–89* (Washington DC).

47 See Bookout, n. 44.

48 Z. Jiaheng and H. Gulian, 'The development of energy and its influences on environment', paper submitted for the 39th Pugwash Conference on Science and World Affairs, Cambridge, MA, 23–8 July 1989.

49 Barron, *et al.*, cited in n. 33.

50 V. Ramanathan, B. R. Barkstrom, and E. F. Harrison, 'Climate and the Earth's radiation budget', *Physics Today* (May 1989), pp. 22–32.

51 See IPCC, n. 1, Policymakers Summary p. 2.

52 Ibid., p. 10.

53 Ibid., p. 19.

54 A. Raval and V. Ramanathan, 'Observational determination of the greenhouse effect', *Nature* (1989), vol. 342, pp. 758–61.

55 See IPCC, n. 1, section 3.3.3, p.9.

56 The troposphere is the 'weather zone' of the atmosphere – the lower 10–15km.

57 R. D. Cess, *et al.*, 'Interpretation of cloud climate feedback as produced by 14 atmospheric general circulation models', *Science* (1989), vol. 245, pp. 513–6.

58 See Ramanthan *et al.*, n. 50.

59 See IPCC, n. 1, section 3.3.4.

60 W. J. Ingram commenting at the AAAS meeting in New Orleans, Feb. 1990, on the UK Met. Office model. J. F. B. Mitchell, C. A. Senior, and W. J. Ingram, 'CO_2 and climate: a missing feedback?', *Nature* (1989), vol. 341, 132–4.

61 Michael Schlesinger and Anthony del Genio, presentation on behalf of the OSU/UI and GISS modelling teams, respectively, at the symposium on 'Climate Change – models and policies', AAAS meeting, New Orleans, 19 Feb. 1990.

62 S. Hameed and R. Cess, 'Impact of a global warming on biospheric sources of methane and its climatic consequences', *Tellus* (1983), vol. 35B, pp. 1–7.

63 See n. 58 and D. A. Lashof, 'The dynamic greenhouse: feedback processes that may influence future concentrations of atmospheric trace gases and climate change', *Climatic Change* (1989), vol. 14, pp. 213–42

64 The average concentration of hydroxyl in the troposphere is 3×10^{-14} according to Paul Crutzen, 'Global changes in atmospheric chemistry', paper presented at the First General Assembly of Academia Europeae, in press. See also J. Lelieveld and P. Crutzen, 'Influences of cloud photochemical processes on tropospheric ozone', *Nature* (1990), vol. 343, pp. 227–33.

65 See IPCC, n. 1, section 2.2.3.

66 See IPCC, n. 1, section 2, and T. Wigley, 'Possible climate change due to SO_2-derived cloud condensation nuclei', *Nature* (1989), vol. 339, pp. 365–7.

67 See IPCC, n. 1, section 8.

68 T. Takahashi, 'The carbon dioxide puzzle', *Oceanus* (1989), vol. 32, no. 2, pp. 22–9.

69 See IPCC, n. 1, section 1.2.7.1.1.

70 Ibid., section 1.

71 Ibid., section 1.2.7.1.1, and see Lashof, n. 63.

72 Natural Environment Research Council, *Oceans and the global carbon cycle* (NERC, 1989).

73 See Takahashi, n. 68.

74 See IPCC, n. 1, section 1.2.7.1.2.

75 Ibid. Note that the ocean comprises essentially three layers, in vertical profile. They are the Seasonal Boundary Layer, in which the water is completely mixed. This is generally less than 100 metres deep in the tropics, extending to hundreds of metres deep in most of the sub-polar sea areas of the world. The Cold Water Sphere is the deep ocean layer, filling the bottom 80 per cent of the volume of the world ocean, and ventilated by cold surface water down-welling at the poles. Between them is the Warm Water Sphere, or permanent thermocline, which is ventilated from the Seasonal Boundary Layer (See IPCC, n. 1, section 3.2.2).

76 B. H. Stauffer *et al.*, 'Atmospheric CO_2 concentrations during the last glaciation', *Annals of Glaciology* (1984), vol. 5, pp. 760–4, and W. S. Broecker, 'Unpleasant surprises in the greenhouse?', *Nature* (1987), vol. 328, pp. 123–6.

77 See Broecker, n. 76, and IPCC, n. 74.

78 See Takahashi, n. 68.

79 See IPCC, n. 1, section 1.2.7.1.3.

80 Ibid., section 1.2.7.1.4.

81 B. R. Strain and J. D. Dure (eds.), *Direct effect of increasing carbon dioxide on vegetation* (DOE-ER-0238, US Department of Energy, Washington, DC, 1985), and IPCC, n. 1, section 1.2.7.2.1.

82 IPCC, ibid.

83 See Bolin, 43.

84 See IPCC, n. 1, section 1.

85 See Takahashi, n. 68, p. 29, and P. P. Tans, I. Y. Fung, and T. Takahashi, 'Observational constraints on the global atmospheric CO_2 budget', *Science* (1990), vol. 247, pp. 1431–8.

86 See Takahashi, n. 68.

87 See IPCC, n. 1, section 1.2.7.2.2.

88 See, e.g., the report of a recent Dahlem conference: J. Cherfas, 'The fringe of the ocean – under siege from land', *Science* (1990), vol. 248, pp. 163–5.

89 See IPCC, n. 1, section 1.2.7.2.2..

90 Ibid., section 1.2.7.2.3.

91 Ibid., section 1, fig. 1, and references in caption.

92 G. Woodwell, 'Global warming: and what can we do about it', *Amicus Journal* (Fall, 1986), vol. 8, pp. 8–12.

93 See Lashof, n. 63.

94 See IPCC, n. 1, section 1.2.7.2.4.

95 Ibid., section 1.2.7.2.5.

96 J. T. Overpeck, D. Rind, and R. Goldberg, 'Climate-induced changes in forest disturbance and vegetation', *Nature* (1990), vol. 343, pp. 51–4.

97 See Lashof, n. 63, p. 227.

98 R. Cess, 'Biosphere-albedo feedback and climate modelling', *Journal of Atmospheric Science* (1978), vol. 35, pp. 1765–9.

99 See IPCC, n. 1, section 1.2.7.1.5.

100 UNEP, *Environmental effects of ozone depletion*, report of the panel for Environmental Assessment (UNEP / 0ZL. Pro. Asmt. 1/Inf. 2, 1989)

101 See IPCC, n. 1, section 1.3.3.2.

102 Ibid., table 2.8.

103 See Lashof, n. 63, p 233–5.

104 See IPCC, n. 1, section 1.3.4.1.

105 See Lashof, n. 63, p. 235.

106 See IPCC, n. 1, section 1.3.4.1.

107 See Lashof, n. 63, p. 235.

108 See IPCC, n. 1, section 1.3.4.2.

109 Ibid.

110 See Lashof, n. 63.

111 E. G. Nisbet, 'Some northern sources of atmospheric methane: production, history, and future implications', *Canadian Journal of Earth Sciences* (1989), vol. 26, pp. 1603–11.

112 See IPCC, n. 1, section 1.3.4.2.

113 See Nisbet, n. 111.

114 K. A. Kvenvolden, 'Methane hydrates and global change', *Global Biogeochemical Cycles* (Sept. 1988), vol. 2, pp. 221–9.

115 G. J. MacDonald, 'Role of methane clathrates in past and future climates', paper presented at the Second North American Conference on 'Preparing for Climate Change: A Cooperative Approach', sponsored by the Climate Institute, Washington, DC, 6–8 Dec. 1988.

116 See Berner and Lasaga, n. 40..

117 See Kvenvolden, n. 114, p. 224.

118 See MacDonald, n. 115.

119 See Nisbet, n. 111.

120 Ibid., pp. 1603 and 1608.

121 Note also that significant quantities of methane are often trapped as free gas below the impermeable hydrate layers in many offshore areas (see refs. Kvenvolden, n. 114, and MacDonald, n. 115, and papers cited therein). If convection of fluids did breach a significant hydrate-plus-free-gas accumulation, large emissions would result. If these were offshore, they would produce plumes of gas.

122 J. W. Clarke, P. St. Armand, and M. Matson, 'Possible causes of plumes from Bennett Island, Soviet Far Arctic', *American Association of Petroleum Geologists Bulletin* (1986), vol. 70, p. 574.

123 See Nisbet, n. 111, p. 1608.

124 See IPCC, n. 1, Policymakers Summary, p. 8.

125 D. A. Lashof and D. A. Tirpak (eds.), 'Policy Responses for Stabilizing Global Climate', draft report to Congress (US Environmental Protection Agency, Office of Policy, Planning and Evaluation. Washington, DC, 1989).

Chapter 2: The Science of Climate-Modelling and a Perspective on the Global-Warming Debate Stephen H. Schneider

Any opinions, findings, conclusions, or recommendations expressed in this article are those of the author and do not necessarily reflect the views of the National Center for Atmospheric Research or its principal sponsor, the National Science Foundation.

1 Intergovernmental Panel on Climate Change (IPCC), *Scientific Assessment of Climate Change* (2nd Draft) (World Meteorological Organization, Geneva, 1990).

2 S. H. Schneider, 'Climate Modelling', *Scientific American* (1987), vol. 256, no. 5, pp. 72–80.

3 M. O. Andreae and D. S. Schimel (eds.), *Dahlem Workshop on Exchange of Trace Gases between Terrestrial Ecosystems and the Atmosphere* (John Wiley and Sons, New York, 1989).

4 A. Raval and V. Ramanathan, 'Observational Determination of the Greenhouse Effect', *Nature* (1989), vol. 342, p.758.

5 L. O. Mearns, S. H. Schneider, S. L. Thompson, and L. R. McDaniel, 'Analysis of climate variability in general circulation models: Comparison with observations and changes in variability in $2xCO_2$ experiments', *Journal of Geophysical Research* (in press); D. Rind, R. Goldberg, and R. Ruedy, 'Change in Climate Variability in the 21st Century', *Climatic Change* (1989), vol.14, pp. 5–37.

6 K. C. Land and S. H. Schneider, 'Forecasting in the Social and Natural Sciences: An Overview and Analysis of Isomorphisms', *Climatic Change* (1987), vol. 11, pp. 7–31.

7 J. E. Kutzbach and P. J. Guetter, 'The Influence of Changing Orbital Parameters and Surface Boundary Conditions on Climate Simulations for the Past 18,000 Years', *Journal of Atmospheric Sciences* (1986), vol. 43, pp. 1726–59.

8 COHMAP Members (P. M. Anderson *et al.*), 'Climatic Changes of the Last 18,000 Years: Observations and Model Simulations', *Science* (1988), vol. 241, pp. 1043–52.

9 R. E. Dickinson and R. J. Cicerone, 'Future global warming from atmospheric trace gases', *Nature* (1986), vol. 319, pp. 109–15.

10 W. M. Washington and G. A. Meehl, 'Climate Sensitivity Due to Increased CO_2: Experiments With a Coupled Atmosphere and Ocean General Circulation Model', *Climate Dynamics* (1989), vol. 4, pp. 1–38; R. J. Stouffer *et al.*, 'Interhemispheric asymmetry in Climate Response to a Gradual Increase of Atmospheric CO_2', *Nature* (1989), vol. 342, pp. 660–2.

11 S. H. Schneider and S. L. Thompson, 'Atmospheric CO_2 and Climate: Importance of the Transient Response', *Journal of Atmospheric Science* (1981), vol. 37, pp. 895–900.

12 George C. Marshall Institute, *Scientific Perspectives on the Greenhouse Problem* (Washington, DC, 1989).

13 See IPCC, n. 1.

14 W. T. Brookes, 'The Global Warming Panic', *Forbes*, 25 Dec. 1989, pp. 96–102.

15 R. Peters (ed.), *Proceedings of the Conference on the Consequences of the Greenhouse Effect for Biological Diversity* (Yale University Press, New Haven, in press).

16 'Loads of Media Coverage', *Detroit News* editorial, 22 Nov. 1989; S. H. Schneider, 'News Plays Fast and Loose With the Facts', *Detroit News*, 5 Dec. 1989.

17 See George C. Marshall Inst., n. 12.

18 H. W. Ellsaesser, 'The Climatic Effect of CO_2: A Different View', *Atmospheric Environment* (1984), vol. 18, pp. 431–4; R. Lindzen, 'Some coolness concerning global warming', *Bulletin of the American Meteorological Society* (1990), vol. 77, pp. 288–99.

19 See Raval and Ramanathan, n. 4.

20 J. F. B. Mitchell, W. J. Ingram, and C. A. Senior, 'CO_2 and Climate: A Missing Feedback?', *Nature* (1989), vol. 341, pp. 132–4.

21 See IPCC, n. 1.

22 National Academy of Sciences, *Current Issues in Atmospheric Change* (National Academy Press, Washington, DC, 1987).

23 See George C. Marshall Inst., n. 12.

24 J. Hansen, D. Johnson, A. Lacis, S. Lebedeff, P. Lee, D. Rind, and G. Russell, 'Climate Impact of Increasing Atmospheric Carbon Dioxide', *Science* (1981), vol. 213, pp. 957–66; R. L. Gilliland and S. H. Schneider, 'Volcanic, CO_2 and Solar Forcing of Northern and Southern Hemisphere Surface Air Temperatures', *Nature* (1984), vol. 310, pp. 38–41; T. M. L. Wigley and S. C. B. Raper, 'Natural Variability of the Climate System and Detection of the Greenhouse Effect', *Nature* (1990), vol. 344, pp. 324–7.

25 See Chap. 8, n. 1.

26 R. W. Spencer and J. R. Christy, 'Precise Monitoring of Global Temperature Trends from Satellites', *Science* (1990), vol. 247, pp. 1558–62.

27 J. Hansen and S. Lebedeff, 'Global surface air temperatures: Update through 1987', *Geophysical Research Letter* (1988), vol. 15, pp. 323–6.

Chapter 3: Biogeochemical Feedbacks in the Earth System David Schimel

1 S. H. Schneider, 'Global climate and trace gas composition: From atmospheric history to the next century', in M. O. Andreae and D. S. Schimel (eds.), *Exchange of Trace Gases between Terrestrial Ecosystems and the Atmosphere* (John Wiley & Sons, New York, 1989), pp. 281–90.

2 V. Ramanathan, 'The radiative and climatic consequences of the changing atmospheric composition of trace gases', in F. S. Rowland and I. S. A. Isaksen (eds.), *The Changing Atmosphere* (John Wiley & Sons, New York, 1988), pp. 159–86.

3 W. S. Broecker, 'Glacial to interglacial changes in ocean and atmospheric chemistry', in A. Berger (ed.), *Climate variations and variability: facts and theories* (D. Reidel, Dordrecht, 1981), pp. 109–20; J. M. Barnola, D. Raynaud, Y. Korotkevich, and C. Lorius, 'Vostok ice core provides 160,000-year record of atmospheric CO_2', *Nature* (1987), vol. 331, pp. 675–9.

4 T. E. Graedel and P. J. Crutzen, 'The Changing Atmosphere', in *Managing Planet Earth*, Scientific American special publication (W. H. Freeman and Co., New York, 1990), pp. 13-23.

5 W. C. Oechel and B. R. Strain, 'Native species responses to increased atmospheric carbon dioxide concentration', in B. R. Strain and J. D. Cure (eds.), *Direct effects of increasing carbon dioxide on vegetation* (U S Department of Energy ER0238, Washington, DC, 1985).

6 W. J. Parton, D. S. Schimel, C. V. Cole, and D. S. Ojima, 'Analysis of factors controlling soil organic matter levels in Great Plains grasslands', *Soil Science Society of America Journal* (1987), vol. 51, pp. 1173–9; J. M. Melillo, R. J. Naiman, J. D. Aber, and A. E. Linkins, 'Factors controlling mass loss and nitrogen dynamics of plant litter decaying in northern streams', *Bulletin of Marine Science* (1984), vol. 35, no. 3, pp. 341–56.

7 See Parton *et al.*, n. 6.

8 D. S. Schimel, W. J. Parton, T. G. F. Kittel, D. S. Ojima, and C. V. Cole, 'Grassland biogeochemistry: links to atmospheric processes', *Climatic Change* (1990), in press.

9 See n. 8.

10 See Parton *et al.*, n. 6.

11 A. F. Bouwman, 'Background', in A. F. Bouwman (ed.), *Soils and the Greenhouse Effect* (John Wiley and Sons, New York, 1990).

12 See Parton *et al.*, n. 6; S. E. Trumbore, G. Bonani, and W. Wolfi, 'The rates of carbon cycling in several soils from AMS 14C measurements of fractionated organic matter', see A. F. Bouwman (ed.) (n. 11), pp. 407–14.

13 See n. 8.

14 See Parton *et al.*, n. 6.

15 J. Pastor and W. M. Post, 'Influence of climate, soil moisture and succession on forest carbon and nitrogen cycles', *Biogeochemistry* (1986), vol. 2, pp. 3–27.

16 D. H. Ehhalt, 'How has the atmospheric concentration of CH_4 changed?', in F. S. Rowland and I. S. A. Isaksen (eds.) (n. 2), pp. 25–32.

17 See nn. 16 and 4.

18 See n. 11; H. U. Neue, P. Becker-Heidmann, and H. W. Scharpenseel, 'Organic matter dynamics, soil properties and cultural practices in rice lands and their relationship to methane production', A. F. Bouwman (ed.) (n. 11), pp. 457–66.

19 H. U. Neue, personal communication.

20 H. Schutz, W. Seiler, and R. Conrad, 'Processes involved in formation and emission of methane in rice paddies', *Biogeochemistry*, vol. 7, pp. 33–54.

21 See Neue *et al.*, n. 18.

22 E. G. Nisbett, 'Some northern sources of atmospheric methane: production, history, and future implications', *Canadian Journal of Earth Sciences,* vol. 26, pp. 1603–11; see n. 1.

23 See Parton *et al.*, n. 6.

24 See n. 8.

25 J. O. Wilson, P. M. Crill, K. B. Bartlett, D. I. Sebacher, R. C. Harriss, and R. L. Sass, 'Seasonal variation of methane emissions from a temperate swamp', *Biochemistry*, vol. 8, pp. 55–72.

26 J. M. Melillo, P. A. Steudler, J. D. Aber, and R. D. Bowden, 'Atmospheric deposition and nutrient cycling', in *Exchange of Trace Gases between Terrestrial Ecosystems and Atmosphere* (John Wiley & Sons, New York, 1989), pp. 263–80; J. M. Melillo and P. A. Steudler, 'The effect of nitrogen fertilization on the CO_2 and CS_2 emission from temperate forest soils', *Journal of Atmospheric Chemistry*, in press.

27 See n. 11.

28 Anonymous, 'Conclusions and recommendations of the conference working groups', see A. F. Bouwman (ed.), n. 11., pp. 1–24.

29 A. R. Mosier, W. J. Parton, and D. S. Schimel, 'Rates and pathways of nitrous oxide production in a shortgrass steppe', *Biogeochemistry* (1988), vol. 6, pp. 45–58; P. A. Matson, P. M. Vitousek, and D. S. Schimel, 'Regional extrapolation of trace gas flux based on soils and ecosystems', in M. O. Andreae and D. S. Schimel (eds.), *Exchange of trace gases between terrestrial ecosystems and the atmosphere*, report of a Dahlem Conference (John Wiley and Sons, New York, 1989), pp. 97–108.

30 R. J. Charlson, J. E. Lovelock, M. O. Andreae, and S. G. Warren, 'Oceanic phyto-plankton, atmospheric sulphur, cloud albedo and climate', *Nature* (1987) vol. 326, pp. 655–661.

31 M. O. Andreae, 'The global biogeochemical sulfur cycle: a review', in D. S. Schimel and B. Moore (eds.), *Trace gases and the biosphere: Proceedings of the 1988 Global Change Institute* (Office for Interdisciplinary Earth Studies, Boulder, Colorado, 1990), in press.

32 M. O. Andreae and H. Raedmonck, 'Dimethylsulfide in the surface ocean and the marine atmosphere: a global view', *Science* (1983), vol. 221, pp. 744–7.

33 See n. 31.

34 See nn. 30, 31.

35 Intergovernmental Panel on Climate Change, *Scientific Assessment of Climate Change* (IPCC Working Group I Report, June 1990), in press.

36 R. E. Dickinson, 'Uncertainties of estimates of climatic change: A review', *Climatic Change* (1989), vol. 15, pp. 5–13.

37 S. H. Schneider, 'The Changing Climate', in *Managing Planet Earth*, as n. 4, pp. 23–6.

38 See Melillo *et al.*, n. 26.

39 J. Roughgarden, S. Gaines, and H. Possingham, 'Recruitment dynamics in complex life cycles', *Science* (1988), vol. 241, pp. 1460–6.

40 See n. 28.

41 H. Rodhe, 'A comparison of the contribution of various gases to the greenhouse effect', *Science* (1990), vol. 248, pp. 1217–19.

Chapter 4: Halting Global Warming Mick Kelly

This chapter is based on a research project funded by Greenpeace International. The author thanks Tom Wigley of the Climatic Research Unit and all those who took part in the peer review of this study for their invaluable contribution. The use of methodologies and models developed in the Climatic Research Unit by Sarah Raper, Dick Warrick, Tom Wigley, and Angela Wilkinson is acknowledged with appreciation.

1 Department of Energy, Washington, DC, *State of the Art Report on the Carbon Dioxide Research Programme* (series of vols., 1985); B. Bolin, B. R. D. Döös, J. Jäger, and R. A. Warwick (eds.), *The Greenhouse Effect, Climatic Change and Ecosystems* SCOPE 29 (Wiley, Chichester, 1986).

2 D. A. Lashof and D. A. Tirpak (eds.), *Policy Options for Stabilizing Global Climate* (Environmental Protection Agency, Washington, DC, 1989).

3 World Meteorological Organization/United Nations Environment Programme, *Intergovernmental Panel on Climate Change* (Geneva, 1990), 3 vols..

4 P. M. Kelly, 'Halting Global Warming', *Climate in Crisis*, no. 1 (Greenpeace International, Amsterdam, 1990).

5 J. R. Trabalka (ed.), *Atmospheric Carbon Dioxide and the Global Carbon Cycle* (Department of Energy, Washington, DC, 1985); B. Bolin, 'How much CO_2 will remain in the atmosphere?', in Bolin *et al.*, *The Greenhouse Effect*, pp. 93–155; H.-J. Bolle, W. Seiler, and B. Bolin, 'Other greenhouse gases and aerosols', ibid. 157–203.

6 See Bolin, n. 5.

7 T. M. L. Wigley, 'Future CFC concentrations under the Montreal Protocol and their greenhouse-effect implications', *Nature* (1988), vol. 335, pp. 333–5.

8 See Bolle *et al.*, n. 5.

9 A. Wilkinson and R. A. Warwick, 'Greenhouse-Gas Policy Model. User's Guide' (Report to the Central Electricity Generating Board, Climatic Research Unit, Norwich, 1989).

10 T. M. L. Wigley and S. C. B. Raper, 'Thermal expansion of sea water associated with global warming', *Nature* (1987), vol. 330, pp. 127–31.

11 R. E. Dickinson, 'How will climate change?', in Bolin *et al.*, *The Greenhouse Effect*, pp. 206–70.

12 Ibid.

13 T. M. L. Wigley, 'Relative contribution of different trace gases to the greenhouse effect', in *Climate Monitor* (1987), vol. 16, no. 1, pp. 14–28.

14 V. Ramanathan, R. J. Cicerone, H. B. Singh, and J. T. Kiehl, 'Trace gas trends and their potential role in climate change', *Journal of Geophysical Research* (1985) vol. 90, D3, pp. 5547–66; see also Wigley, n. 13.

15 See Kelly, n. 4.

16 J. A. Edmonds, J. M. Reilly, R. H. Gardner, and A. Brenkert, *Uncertainty in Future Global Energy Use and Fossil Fuel CO_2 Emissions 1975 to 2075* (TR036, Department of Energy, Washington, DC, 1986).

17 See Lashof and Tirpak, n. 2. Note that 1 Pg is equivalent to 1 gigatonne (Gt), a unit used in other chapters in this volume.

18 The projection is based on scenario (2) in Wigley, n. 7.

19 See Edmonds *et al.*, n. 16.

20 See Bolin, n. 5.

21 R. A. Houghton, W. H. Schlesinger, S. Brown, and J. F. Richards, 'Carbon dioxide exchange between the atmosphere and terrestrial ecosystems', in Trabalka (ed.), *Atmospheric Carbon Dioxide and the Global Carbon Cycle*, pp. 113–40.

22 See Wigley, n. 7.

23 See Lashof and Tirpak, n. 2.

24 It is impossible to establish how much of the observed warming that has occurred since the late nineteenth century is due to enhancement of the greenhouse effect, rendering impracticable the use of the present-day level of global temperature as a baseline. See T. M. L. Wigley, P. D. Jones, and P. M. Kelly, 'Empirical climate studies', in Bolin *et al., The Greenhouse Effect*, pp. 271–322.

25 Intergovernmental Panel on Climate Change, *Scientific Assessment of Climate Change* (Report of IPCC Working Group 1, United Nations, June 1990).

26 F. Krause, W. Bach, and J. Koomey, *Energy Policy in the Greenhouse* vol. 1, *From Warming Fate to Warming Limit: Benchmarks for a Global Climate Convention* (European Environmental Bureau, Brussels/International Project for Sustainable Energy Paths, El Cerrito, California, 1989).

27 World Commission on Environment and Development, *Our Common Future* (Oxford University Press, 1987).

28 Conference Statement, *The Changing Atmosphere: Implications for Global Security*, Toronto, 27–30 June 1988 (Environment Canada, 1988).

29 See Kelly, n. 4.

30 J. Jäger *et al., Developing Policies for Responding to Climatic Change* (WMO Report TD-No. 225, World Meteorological Organization, Geneva, 1988).

31 G. Marland, *The Prospect of Solving the CO_2 Problem through Global Reforestation* (TR039, Department of Energy, Washington, DC, 1988).

32 Ibid; K. F. Wiersum and P. Ketner, 'Reforestation, a Feasible Contribution to Reducing the Atmospheric Carbon Dioxide Content', document submitted by the Delegation of the Netherlands to the DAC meeting of the Working Party on Development Assistance and Environment, Paris, 15–16 Nov. 1989.

33 See Lashof and Tirpak, n. 2.

34 See Krause *et al.*, n. 26.

35 Ibid.

36 See Kelly, n. 4.

37 L. D. D. Harvey, 'Managing atmospheric CO_2', *Climate Change* (1989), vol. 15, no. 3, pp. 343–81.

38 J. H. W. Karas and P. M. Kelly, *The Heat Trap* (Friends of the Earth, London, 1988).

Chapter 5: The Effects of Global Warming George M. Woodwell

1 The gases involved are carbon dioxide (CO_2), methane (CH_4), nitrous oxide (N_2O), the chlorofluorocarbons (CFCs), ozone (O_3), and water (H_2O). Their influence has

been reviewed in the IPCC report and in various recent reviews, such as *Changing Climate, Report of the Carbon Dioxide Assessment Committee, NAS-NRC* (National Academy Press, Washington, DC, 1983); *Conference Statement, International Assessment of the Role of Carbon Dioxide and of Other Greenhouse Gases in Climate Variations and Associated Impacts*, Villach, Austria, (UNEP/WMO/ICSU, 1985).

2 The magnitude of the warming is commonly expressed as the amount expected from the equivalent of a doubling of the carbon dioxide content of the atmosphere above what was present in the middle of the last century, about 270 parts per million. The emphasis on a doubling suggests that climates will shift to a new stability under a warmer circumstance. This impression is misleading. The Earth will continue to warm unless definite steps are taken to avoid a further accumulation of heat-trapping gases.

3 The topic is treated in detail in *Developing Policies for Responding to Climatic Change: a summary of discussions and recommendations of workshops held in Villach and Bellagio, 1987* (WMO/UNEP, 1988); evidence of changes in patterns of rainfall has been presented by R. S. Bradley, H. F. Diaz, J. K. Eischeid, P. D. Jones, P. M. Kelly, and C. M. Goodess, 'Precipitation fluctuations over Northern Hemisphere land areas since the mid-19th century', *Science* (1987), vol. 237, pp. 171–5.

4 The question of whether there are limits to the warming that will become effective as carbon dioxide accumulates and effects of the warming spread globally is clearly answered in the negative. See n. 2 and 3.

5 See n. 3.

6 Intergovernmental Panel on Climate Change, Working Group 3 Report, Response Strategies Working Group (June 1990).

7 Deforestation was the major cause of the accumulation of carbon dioxide until the middle of this century, when a global surge in the use of fossil fuels pushed that source above the still-accelerating releases from deforestation. For a discussion of the importance of deforestation, see R. P. Detwiler and C. A. S. Hall, 'Tropical forests and the global carbon cycle', *Science* (1987), vol. 239, pp. 42–50; R. A. Houghton, J. E. Hobbie, J. M. Melillo, B. Moore, B. J. Peterson, G. R. Shaver, G. M. Woodwell, 'Changes in the carbon content of terrestrial biota and soils between 1860 and 1980: a net release of CO_2 to the atmosphere', *Ecological Monographs* (1982), vol. 53, pp. 235–62; R. A. Houghton, 'Emissions of Greenhouse Gases', in N. Myers (ed.), *Deforestation Rates in Tropical Forests and Their Climatic Implications* (Friends of the Earth, London, 1989); G. M. Woodwell and R. A. Houghton, 'Biotic influences on the world carbon budget', in W. Stumm (ed.), *Global Chemical Cycles and Their Alterations by Man* (Dahlem Konferenzen, Berlin, 1977); G. M. Woodwell, R. H. Whittaker, W. A. Reiners, G. E. Likens, C. C. Delwiche, and D. B. Botkin, 'The biota and the world carbon budget', *Science* (1978), vol. 199, pp. 141–6; G. M. Woodwell, J. E. Hobbie, R. A. Houghton, J. M. Melillo, B. Moore, B. J. Peterson, G. R. Shaver, 'Global Deforestation: Contribution to Atmospheric Carbon Dioxide', *Science* (1983), vol. 222, pp. 1,081–6; G. M. Woodwell, 'Biotic effects on the concentration of atmospheric carbon dioxide: A review and projection', in *Changing Climate*, n. 1.

8 The amount of carbon held in forests and their soils globally is approximately three times the amount held in the atmosphere currently. The amount in plants is commonly thought to be 500-600 billion tonnes; the amount in soils is about 1,500 billion tonnes. The atmosphere currently contains about 750 billion tonnes.

9 Various discussions of this possibility have been advanced. See in particular Woodwell, n. 7.

10 See n. 8.

11 IPCC Working Group 1 report, *Scientific Assessment of Climate Change* (June 1990).

12 See Houghton, n. 7.

13 W. S. Broecker, 'Unpleasant surprises in the greenhouse?', *Nature* (1987), vol. 328, pp. 123–6.

14 The total annual flux between atmosphere and oceans involves the diffusion of approximately 100 billion tonnes of carbon as CO_2 in each direction. Any change in this flux has the potential significantly to affect the composition of the atmosphere in a short time. A similar flux exists between the atmosphere and the terrestrial ecosystems. See R. A. Houghton and G. M. Woodwell, n. 9, and G. M. Woodwell, 'Biotic effects of climatic change: surprises in store?' *Oceanus* (1986), vol. 29, pp. 71–5.

15 B. R. Strain and J. D. Cure, (eds.), *Direct Effects of Increasing Carbon Dioxide on Vegetation* (US Department of Energy, National Technical Information Service, Springfield, Virginia, 1985).

16 B. G. Drake, *Elevated atmospheric CO_2 concentration increases carbon sequestering in coastal wetlands*, (Carbon Dioxide Information Analysis Center, Environmental Sciences Division, ORNL, Oak Ridge, Tennessee, 1989).

17 W. C. Oechel and G. H. Reichers, 'Impacts of increasing CO_2 on natural vegetation, particularly the tundra', in Proceedings of the Climate-Vegetation Workshop, (NASA/GSFC, Greenbelt, Maryland, Jan. 1986); B. G. Drake, R. J. Luxmoore, H. A. Mooney, W. C. Oechel, and L. F. Pitelka, 'How will terrestrial ecosystems interact with the changing CO_2 concentration of the atmosphere and anticipated climatic change?' (unpublished manuscript, 1990).

18 See Woodwell, 1988–9, n. 9.

19 D. A. Lashof, 'The dynamic greenhouse: Feedback processes that may influence future concentrations of atmospheric trace-gases and climatic change', *Climatic Change* (1989), vol. 14, pp. 213–42.

20 W. R. Emanuel, H. H. Shugart, and M. P. Stevenson, 'Climatic change and the broad-scale distribution of terrestrial ecosystem complexes', *Climatic Change* (1985), vol. 7, pp. 29-44.

21 A. Solomon, 'Transient response of forests to CO_2-induced climate change: simulation modeling experiments in eastern North America', *Oecologia* (1986), vol. 68, pp. 567–79.

22 G. M. Woodwell and R. H. Whittaker, 'Primary production in terrestrial ecosystems', *American Zoologist* (1968), vol. 8, pp. 19–30.

23 See Woodwell, n. 7.

24 J. M. Barnola, D. Reynaud, Y. S. Korotkevich, and C. Lorius, 'Vostok ice core provides 160,000-year record of atmospheric CO_2', *Nature* (1987), vol. 329, pp. 408-18.

25 Before the availability of this core and the development of techniques for detecting the concentration of carbon dioxide and methane in the air trapped in the ice at the time of formation, there was no way of determining the composition of the atmosphere with respect to the heat-trapping gases for times before 1958, the

beginning of the Mauna Loa record established by Keeling. See R. Bacastow and
C. D. Keeling, 'Atmospheric carbon dioxide and radio carbon in the natural carbon
cycle; changes from A. D. 1700 to 2070 as deduced from a geochemical model',
in G. M. Woodwell and Pecan, *Carbon and the Biosphere* (USAEC, Washington,
DC, 1973).

26 J. Hansen and S. Lebedeff, 'Global surface air temperatures: update through 1987',
Geophysical Research Letters (1988), vol. 15, no. 4, pp. 323–6; P. D. Jones,
T. M. L. Wigley, and P. B. Wright, 'Global temperature variations between 1861 and
1984', *Nature* (1986), vol. 322, pp. 430–4.

27 The total release of carbon from all human activities is not known. The amount
released from use of fossil fuels annually is about 5.6 billion tonnes of carbon as
carbon dioxide; the amount from deforestation, 1.5–3.0 billion tonnes. A further
increment is probably being released through the stimulation of the decay of
organic matter globally by the warming already experienced. This increment
could easily be 1–3 billion tonnes or more.

28 C. D. Keeling (personal communication).

29 A detailed analysis of factors affecting the concentration of carbon dioxide in the
atmosphere has been offered by Keeling and his colleagues in 'Aspects of Climate
Variability in the Pacific and Western Americas', D. H. Peterson (ed.), *Geophysical
Monograph* (1983), vol. 55, pp. 165-363, (American Geophysical Union).

30 U. Siegenthaler, 'El Nino and atmospheric CO_2', *Nature* (1990), vol. 345,
pp. 295–6.

31 The topic has been addressed in various ways and with varying intensities of
analysis. One of the most direct analyses is by M. B. Davis, 'Climatic change and
survival of forest species', in G. M. Woodwell (ed.), *The Earth in Transition*,
(Cambridge University Press, New York ,1990).

32 Ibid.

33 IPCC Working Group 2 Report, *Impacts* (June 1990); see also P. Crosson in a paper
prepared for the WMO/UNEP Conference, 1988, n. 3.

34 M. K. Burke, R. A. Houghton, and G. M. Woodwell, 'Progress toward predicting the
potential for increased emissions of CH_4 from wetlands as a consequence of global
warming', in A. F. Bouwman (ed.), *Soils and the Greenhouse Effect* (John Wiley &
Sons, London, 1990), pp. 451–5.

35 Oceanographers and climatologists have assumed in the past that the major control
of atmospheric composition is through interactions between the atmosphere and
the oceans. While this assumption may be correct over the longer term of centuries
to millenia, it is probably not correct over periods of years to decades. The most
powerful evidence of the influence of forests is their capacity for affecting the
carbon dioxide content of the atmosphere over a few weeks by several per cent
through the annual cycle of photosynthesis. Other evidence is presented here. The
discussion has been intensified recently by the following paper, which suggests
that the forests of the northern hemisphere are absorbing carbon from the
atmosphere, despite abundant direct evidence that the size and stature of forests
over large areas are decreasing: P. P. Tans, I. Y. Fung, and T. Takahashi,
'Observational constraints on the global atmospheric CO_2 budget', *Science* (1990),
vol. 247, pp. 1,431–8.

36 Carbon dioxide is highly soluble in ocean water, where it enters the complicated
interactions of the carbonate–bicarbonate system. Methane, on the other hand, is
not highly soluble in water, and tends to be released directly as a gas into the

atmosphere. The parallel behaviour of the two gases throughout glacial time suggests that the dominant exchanges do not involve the oceans.

Chapter 6: Lessons from Climates of the Past Brian Huntley

1 H. Oeschger and J. A. Eddy, *Global Changes of the Past* (IGBP Global Change Report no. 6, 1989); B. Huntley, 'Studying global change: the contribution of Quaternary palynology', *Palaeogeography, Palaeoclimatology, Palaeoecology* (1990), vol. 82 (Global and Planetary Change Section); id., 'Historical lessons for the future', in I. F.Spellerberg, F. B. Goldsmith, and M. G. Morris (eds.), *Scientific Management of Temperate Communities for Conservation*, (British Ecological Society Symposium, no. 31, Blackwell Scientific Publications, in press).

2 W. F. Ruddiman and M. E. Raymo, 'Northern Hemisphere climate régimes during the past 3Ma: possible tectonic connections', *Philosophical Transactions of the Royal Society of London* (1988), ser. B, vol. 318, pp. 411–30; W. F. Ruddiman and J. E. Kutzbach, 'Forcing of Late Cenozoic Northern Hemisphere Climate by Plateau Uplift in Southern Asia and the American West', *Journal of Geophysical Research* (1989), vol. 94, pp. 18409–27.

3 J. Imbrie and K. P. Imbrie, *Ice ages: solving the mystery* (Macmillan, London, 1979); P. J. Bartlein, 'Late-Tertiary and Quaternary paleoenvironments', in: B. Huntley and T. Webb III (eds.), *Vegetation History* (Kluwer Academic Publishers, Dordrecht, 1988), pp. 113–52; J. D. Hays, J. Imbrie, and N. J. Shackleton, 'Variations in the Earth's Orbit: Pacemaker of the Ice Ages', *Science* (1976), vol. 194, pp. 1121–32.

4 J. M. Barnola, D. Raynaud, Y. S. Korotkevich, and C. Lorius, 'Vostok ice core provides 160,000-year record of atmospheric CO_2', *Nature* (1987), vol. 329, pp. 408–14; C. Lorius, N. I. Barkov, J. Jouzel, Y. S. Korotkevich, V. M. Kotlyakov, and D. Raynaud, 'Antarctic Ice Core: CO_2 and Climatic Change Over the Last Climatic Cycle', *Eos* (1988), vol. 69, pp. 681, 683–4; D. Raynaud, J. Chapellaz, J. M. Barnola, Y. S. Korotkevich, and C. Lorius, 'Climatic and CH_4 cycle implications of glacial–interglacial change in the Vostok ice core', *Nature* (1988), vol. 333, pp. 655–7; id., 'Atmospheric CH_4 record over the last climatic cycle revealed by the Vostok ice core', *Nature* (submitted).

5 J. M. Mitchell, 'An overview of climatic variability and its causal mechanisms', *Quaternary Research* (1976), vol. 6, pp. 481–93; B. Huntley and T. Webb III, 'Migration: species' response to climatic variations caused by changes in the earth's orbit', in *Journal of Biogeography* (1989), vol. 16, pp. 5–19.

6 See n. 3.

7 Ibid. See also W. F. Ruddiman, M. Raymo, and A. McIntyre, 'Matuyama 41,000-year cycles: North Atlantic Ocean and northern hemisphere ice sheets', *Earth and Planetary Science Letters* (1986), vol. 80, pp. 117–29; G. G. Start and W. L. Prell, 'Evidence for two Pleistocene climatic modes: data from DSDP Site 502', in A. L. Berger and C. Nicolis (eds.), *New Perspectives in Climate Modelling* (Elsevier, Amsterdam,1984), pp. 3–22.

8 I. I. Borzenkova and V. A. Zubakov, 'The late-Atlantic climatic optimum of the Holocene as a model of global climate of the early 21st century' (unpublished paper presented to the Joint US/USSR Meeting on Anthropogenic Climatic Change, 3–9 July 1983; T. Webb III and T. M. L. Wigley, 'What past climates can tell

about a warmer world', in M. C. MacCracken and F. M. Luther (eds.), *DOE State of the Art Report: Climatic Effects of Increasing CO_2 Concentrations* (Department of Energy, Washington, DC, 1985), pp. 239–57; T. Webb III, *A Global Paleoclimatic Data Base for 6000 yr B.P.* (Department of Energy, Washington, DC, 1985); V. A. Zubakov and I. I. Borzenkova. 'Pliocene palaeoclimates: Past climates as possible analogues of mid-Twenty-first century climate', *Palaeogeography, Palaeoclimatology, Palaeoecology* (1988), vol. 65, pp. 35–49; T. J. Crowley, 'Are there any satisfactory geological analogs for a future greenhouse warming?', in M. E. Schlesinger (ed.), *Greenhouse-gas-induced Climatic Change: A Critical Appraisal of Simulations and Observations* (Elsevier, Amsterdam, in press); M. I. Budyko, 'Climatic Conditions of the Future' (unpublished paper presented to the IPCC Working Group 1 Discussion Meeting on 'Paleo-analog Forecasting', Bath, 20–21 Nov. 1989).

9 P. J. Bartlein, T. Webb III, and E. Fleri, 'Holocene climatic change in the northern Midwest; pollen-derived estimates', *Quaternary Research* (1984), vol. 22, pp. 361–74; P. J. Bartlein and T. Webb III, 'Mean July temperature estimates for 6,000 yr B.P. in eastern North America; regression equations for estimates from fossil pollen data', in C. R. Harrington (ed.), *Climatic Change in Canada 5, Syllogeus* (1985), vol. 55, pp. 301–42; B. Huntley and I. C. Prentice, 'July temperatures in Europe from pollen data, 6000 years before present', *Science* (1988), vol. 241, pp. 687–90.

10 See Budyko, n. 8.

11 See Zubakov and Borzenkova, Crowley, n. 8.

12 See Ruddiman and Raymo, n. 2; N. J. Shackleton *et al.*, 'Oxygen isotope calibration of the onset of ice-rafting and history of glaciation in the North Atlantic region', in *Nature* (1984), vol. 307, pp. 620–4.

13 See Ruddiman and Kutzbach, n. 2; W. F. Ruddiman, W. L. Prell, and M. E. Raymo, 'Late Cenozoic Uplift in Southern Asia and the American West: Rationale for General Circulation Modeling Experiments', *Journal of Geophysical Research* (1989), vol. 94, pp. 18379–91; J. E. Kutzbach, P. J. Guetter, W. F. Ruddiman, and W. L. Prell, 'Sensitivity of Climate to Late Cenozoic Uplift in Southern Asia and the American West: Numerical Experiments', *Journal of Geophysical Research* (1989), vol. 94, pp. 18393—407; W. F. Ruddiman and J. E. Kutzbach, 'Late Cenozoic Plateau Uplift and Climate Change' (unpublished manuscript).

14 N. J. Shackleton, unpublished results reported to the IPCC Working Group 1 Discussion Meeting on 'Paleo-analog Forecasting', Bath, 20–21 Nov. 1989.

15 See Bartlein, n. 3; W. A. Watts. 'Late-Tertiary and Pleistocene vegetation history – Europe', in B. Huntley and T. Webb III (eds.), *Vegetation History* (Kluwer Academic Publishers, Dordrecht, 1988), pp.155–92.

16 See Barnola *et al.*, Lorius *et al.*, n. 4.

17 See Barnola *et al.*, n. 4; A. Neftel, E. Moor, H. Oeschger, and B. Stauffer, 'Evidence from polar ice cores for the increase in atmospheric CO_2 in the past two centuries', *Nature* (1985), vol. 315, pp. 45–7; H. Oeschger, 'The Ocean System –/Ocean/Climate and Ocean/CO_2 Interactions', in T. Rosswall, R. G. Woodmansee, and P .G. Risser (eds.), *Scales and Global Change* (Wiley, New York, 1988), pp. 319–52.

18 C. J. Lorius, 'Polar ice cores and climate', in A. Berger *et al.* (eds.), *Climate and Geo-Sciences* (Kluwer Academic Publishers, Dordrecht, 1989), pp. 77–103.

19 See Bartlein, n. 3; J. E. Kutzbach and P. J. Guetter, 'The influence of changing orbital parameters and surface boundary conditions on climate simulations for the

past 18,000 years', *Journal of Atmospheric Science* (1986), vol. 43, pp. 1726–59; COHMAP members, 'Climatic changes of the last 18,000 years: Observations and model simulations', *Science* (1988), vol. 241, pp. 1043–52.

20 See n. 9.

21 See Webb and Wigley, n. 8.

22 See Kutzbach and Guetter, COHMAP members, n. 19.

23 S. Manabe and R. J. Stouffer, 'Sensitivity of a global climate model to an increase in the CO_2 concentration in the atmosphere', *Journal of Geophysical Research* (1980), vol. 85, pp. 5529–554; C. A. Wilson and J. F. B. Mitchell, 'A 2 x CO_2 climate sensitivity experiment with a global climate model including a simple ocean', *Journal of Geophysical Research* (1987), vol. 92, pp. 13315–43.

24 T. Webb III, J. Kutzbach, and F. A. Street-Perrott, '20,000 Years of global climatic change: Paleoclimatic research plan', in T. F. Malone and J. G. Roederer (eds.), *Global Change* (Cambridge University Press, Cambridge, 1985), pp. 182–218; T. Webb III, F. A. Street-Perrott, and J. E. Kutzbach, 'Late-Quaternary paleoclimatic data and climate models', *Episodes* (1987), vol. 10, pp. 4–6.

25 See COHMAP members, n. 19.

26 See Kutzbach and Guetter, n. 19.

27 See COHMAP members, n. 19.

28 P. J. Bartlein, I. C. Prentice, and T. Webb III, 'Climatic response surfaces from pollen data for some eastern North American taxa', *Journal of Biogeography* (1986), vol. 13, pp. 35–57.

29 See COHMAP members, n. 19.

30 See COHMAP members, n. 19; T. Webb III, P .J. Bartlein, and J. E. Kutzbach, 'Climatic change in eastern North America during the past 18,000 years; comparisons of pollen data with model results', in W. F. Ruddiman and H. E.Wright Jr. (eds.), *The Geology of North America, VolK-3, North America and Adjacent Oceans during the Last Deglaciation* (Geological Society of America, Boulder, Colorado, 1987), pp. 447–62.

31 B. Huntley, 'Pollen–climate response surfaces and the study of climate change', *Applied Quaternary Research*, Proceedings of the Quaternary Research Association Discussion Meeting, Jan. 1990 (submitted).

32 M. I. Budyko, A. B. Ronov, and A. L. Yanshin, *History of the Earth's Atmosphere L.:Gidrometeoizdat* (1985; English trans.: Springer-Verlag, 1987).

33 J. Hansen, I. Fung, A. Lacis, S. Lebedeff, D. Rind, R. Ruedy, G. Russell, and P. Stone, 'Global climate changes as forecast by the GISS 3-D model', *Journal of Geophysical Research* (1988), vol. 93, pp. 5385–412.

34 See Huntley and Prentice, n. 9.

35 S. P. Harrison and S. E. Metcalfe, 'Variations in lake levels during the Holocene in North America: An indicator of changes in atmospheric circulation patterns', *Géographie physique et Quaternaire* (1985), vol. 39, pp. 141–50.

36 B. Huntley, 'Glacial and Holocene vegetation history – Europe'. in B. Huntley and T. Webb III (eds.), *Vegetation History* (Kluwer Academic Publishers, Dordrecht, 1988), pp. 341–83.

37 T. Webb III, 'Glacial and Holocene vegetation history – Eastern North America', ibid, 385–414.

38 See Ruddiman and Raymo, Ruddiman and Kutzbach, n. 2; Ruddiman and Kutzbach, n. 13; W. F. Ruddiman *et al.*, 'Late Miocene to Pleistocene evolution of climate in Africa and the low-latitude Atlantic: Overview of Leg108 results', *Proceedings of the Ocean Drilling Program, Scientific Results* (1989), vol. 108, no. 29, pp. 463–84.

39 S. Schneider, 'The changing global climate', *Scientific American* (1989), vol. 261, no. 3, pp. 38–47.

40 See Schneider, n. 39.

41 C. D. Pigott, 'Biological Flora of the British Isles. *Cirsium acaulon* (L.)Scop', *Journal of Ecology* (1968), vol. 56, pp. 597–612; F. I. Woodward and C. D. Pigott, 'The climatic control of the altitudinal distribution of *Sedum rosea* (L.)Scop and *S. telephium* L. i. Field Observations', *New Phytologist* (1975), vol. 74, pp. 323–34; F. I. Woodward, 'The climatic control of the altitudinal distribution of *Sedum rosea* (L.)Scop and *S. telephium* L. ii.The analysis of plant growth in controlled environments', ibid. 335–48; C. D. Pigott and J. P. Huntley, 'Factors controlling the distribution of *Tilia cordata* at the northern limits of its geographical range. i. Distribution in north-west England', *New Phytologist* (1978), vol. 81, pp. 429–41; Id., 'Factors controlling the distribution of *Tilia cordata* at the northern limits of its geographical range. ii. History in north-west England', *New Phytologist* (1980), vol. 84, pp. 145–64; id., 'Factors controlling the distribution of *Tilia cordata* at the northern limits of its geographical range. iii. Nature and cause of seed sterility', *New Phytologist* (1981), vol. 87, pp. 817–39; C. D. Pigott, 'Nature of seed sterility and natural regeneration of *Tilia cordata* near its northern limit in Finland', *Annales Botanici Fennici* (1981), vol. 18, pp. 255–63; F. I. Woodward, *Climate and plant distribution* (Cambridge University Press, Cambridge, 1987).

42 A. M. Solomon, 'Transient response of forests to CO_2-induced climate change: simulation modeling experiments in eastern North America', *Oecologia* (1986), vol. 68, pp. 567–79; J. T. Overpeck and P. J. Bartlein, 'Assessing the response of vegetation to future climate change: Ecological response surfaces and paleoecological model validation ', in *The Potential Effects of Global Climate Change on the United States* (Appendix D: Forests) (United States Environmental Protection Agency, 1989)

43 See Huntley and Webb, n. 5.

44 See n. 36; n. 37; M. B. Davis, 'Pleistocene biogeography of temperate deciduous forests', *Geoscience and Man* (1976), vol. 13, pp. 13–26; id., 'Holocene vegetational history of the eastern United States', in H. E. Wright Jr. (ed.), *Late-Quaternary environments of the United States* (University of Minnesota Press, Minneapolis, 1983), pp. 166–81; B. Huntley and H. J. B. Birks, *An atlas of past and present pollen maps for Europe: 0-13000 years ago* (Cambridge University Press, Cambridge, 1983).

45 G. R. Coope, 'Climatic fluctuations in northwest Europe since the last interglacial indicated by fossil assemblages of Coleoptera', *Geological Journal Special Issue* (1975), vol. 6, pp. 153–68.

46 A. J. Stuart, *Pleistocene vertebrates in the British Isles* (Longman, London, 1982).

47 See Huntley and Birks, n. 44; J. Iversen, 'The Late-glacial flora of Denmark and its relation to climate and soil', *Danmarks geologische Undersögelse* (1954), ser. 2, vol. 80, pp. 87–119.

48 See Huntley and Webb, n. 5; n. 36; n. 37; Davis 1976, 1983, Huntley and Birks, n. 44; B. Huntley, 'European post-glacial vegetation history: a new perspective',

Proceedings of the XIX International Ornithological Congress, Ottawa, 1986 (University of Ottawa Press, Ottawa, 1989), pp. 1060–77.

49 R. W. Graham and E. C. Grimm, 'The paleobiological perspective for the response of terrestrial biological systems to global warming', *Trends in Ecology and Evolution*, vol. 5 (in press).

50 See Huntley and Webb, n. 5; n. 36; n. 49; R. G. West, 'Inter-relations of ecology and Quaternary palaeobotany', *Journal of Ecology* (1964), vol. 52 (suppl.), pp. 47–57; B. Huntley, 'European vegetation history: palaeovegetation maps from pollen data – 13,000 B.P. to present', *Journal of Quaternary Science* (1990), vol. 5; id., 'How plants respond to climate change: migration rates, individualism and the consequences for plant communities', *Annals of Botany* (suppl. *Global Change and the Biosphere*) (submitted); id., 'European forests since the last glacial: compositional changes in response to climatic change', *Journal of Vegetation Science*, vol. 1 (in press).

51 See n. 36; Huntley and Birks, n. 44; Huntley 1990 (in press), n. 50.

52 See n. 49.

53 G. L. Jacobson, T. Webb III and E. C. Grimm, ' Patterns and rates of vegetation change during the deglaciation of eastern North America', in W .F. Ruddiman and H. E. Wright Jr. (eds.), *The Geology of North America, VolK-3, North America and Adjacent Oceans during the Last Deglaciation* (Geological Society of America, Boulder, Colorado, 1987), pp. 277–88.

54 B. Huntley, 'Dissimilarity mapping between fossil and contemporary pollen spectra in Europe for the past 13,000 years', *Quaternary Research* (1990), vol. 33, pp. 360–76.

55 M. G. Kelly and B. Huntley, 'An 11,000-year record of vegetation and environment from Lago di Martignano, Latium, Italy', *Journal of Quaternary Science* (in press).

56 See n. 54.

57 See Huntley and Birks, n. 44.

58 See n. 36; Huntley and Birks, n. 44.

59 See Davis 1976, n. 44.

60 See Huntley, n. 48.

61 A. J. Gear, 'Holocene vegetation history and the palaeoecology of *Pinus sylvestris* in northern Scotland (Ph.D. Thesis, University of Durham, 1989).

62 A. J. Gear and B. Huntley, 'Rapid changes in the range limits of Scots Pine four thousand years ago', *Science* (submitted).

63 See Huntley and Webb, n. 5; Huntley, n. 48.

64 See Huntley and Webb, n. 5.

65 See Huntley and Birks, n. 44; H. J. B. Birks, 'The use of pollen analysis in the reconstruction of past climates: a review', in T. M. L. Wigley, M. J. Ingram, and G. Farmer (eds.), *Climate and History* (Cambridge University Press, Cambridge, 1981), pp. 111–38; I. C. Prentice, 'Postglacial climatic change: vegetation dynamics and the pollen record', *Progress in Physical Geography* (1983), vol. 7, pp. 273–86; M. B. Davis, 'Climatic instability, time lags, and community disequilibrium', in J. Diamond and T. J. Case (eds.), *Community ecology* (Harper and Row, New York, 1984), pp. 269–84; K. D. Bennett, 'The rate of spread and population increase of forest trees during the postglacial', *Philosophical Transactions of the Royal*

Society of London (1986), ser. B, vol. 314, pp. 523–31; M. B. Davis, K. Woods, S. L. Webb, and R. P. Futyama, 'Dispersal versus climate: expansion of *Fagus* and *Tsuga* into the Upper Great Lakes region', *Vegetatio* (1986), vol. 67, pp. 93–103; W. A. Pennington (Mrs T. G. Tutin), 'Lags in adjustment of vegetation to climate caused by the pace of soil development', ibid. 105–18; I. C. Prentice, 'Vegetation response to past climatic variation', ibid. 131–41; T. Webb III, 'Is vegetation in equilibrium with climate? How to interpret late-Quaternary pollen data', ibid. 75–91.

66 See Huntley and Birks, n. 44.

67 See Huntley (submitted), n. 50.

68 See Woodward 1987, n. 41.

69 See Huntley and Birks, n. 44.

70 See Huntley and Prentice, n. 9.

71 See Huntley (in press), n. 1; Huntley (submitted), n. 50; M. L. Hunter, G. L. Jacobson, and T. Webb III, 'Paleoecology and the coarse-filter approach to maintaining biological diversity', *Conservation Biology* (1988), vol. 2, pp. 375–85; B. Huntley and T. Webb III, Discussion in B. Huntley and T. Webb III, (eds.), *Vegetation History* (Kluwer Academic Publishers, Dordrecht, 1988), pp. 779–85.

72 J. P. Grime, *Plant Strategies and Vegetation Processes* (Wiley, Chichester, 1979).

73 See n. 72.

74 See n. 49; Huntley (submitted), n. 50.

75 D. Rind, 'Climate variability and climate change' (unpublished manuscript and figures presented at the 1989 Global Change Institute: *Explaining records of past global changes*, Snowmass, Colorado); Department of the Environment, *Global Climate Change* (Central Office of Information, HMSO, London, 1989).

76 M. L. Parry, T. R. Carter, and N. T. Konijn, 'Climate impact analysis in cold regions', *Nordia* (1984), vol. 18, pp. 67–79.

77 See Huntley (submitted), n. 50.

78 See Huntley (in press), n. 1; Huntley (submitted), n. 50; Hunter *et al.*, Huntley and Webb, n. 71.

79 See Huntley (in press), n. 1.; n. 49; Huntley (submitted), n. 50; Huntley and Webb, n. 71.

80 See Department of the Environment, n. 75.

81 J. Leggett, Chap. 1 of this volume.

82 See Chapellaz *et al.*, n. 4; n. 81.

83 S. H. Schneider, 'Climate Modeling', *Trends in Computing* (May 1987), pp. 132–9.

Chapter 7: The Implications for Health Andrew Haines

1 L. S. Kalkstein, R. E. Davis, J. A. Skindlov, and K. M. Valimont, 'The Impact of Human-Induced Climate Warming Upon Human Mortality: A New York Case Study', in *Proceedings of the International Conference on Health and Environmental Effects of Ozone Modification in Climate Change* (Washington, DC, 1986).

2 E. Rogot and S. J. Padgett, 'Associations of Coronary and Stroke Mortality with Temperature and Snowfall in Selected Areas of the United States 1962–1966',

American Journal of Epidemiology (1976), vol. 103, pp. 565–75.

3 C. A. Keller and R. P. Nugent, 'Seasonal Patterns in Perinatal Mortality and Pre-Term Delivery', *American Journal of Epidemiology* (1983), vol. 118, pp. 689–98.

4 J. G. Ayres, 'Meteorology and Respiratory Disease', *Update* (1990), pp. 596–605.

5 E. G. Brown, 'Dust Storms and their Possible Effects on Health', *Public Health Report* (1935), vol. 50, pp. 1369–83.

6 W. F. McDonnell, D. H. Horstman, S. Abdul-Salaam, and D. E. House, 'Reproducibility of Individual Responsiveness to Ozone Exposure', *American Review of Respiratory Diseases* (1985), vol. 131, pp. 36–40.

7 J. Q. Koenig, D. S. Covert, Q. S. Hanley, G. Van Belle, and W. E. Person, 'Prior Exposure to Ozone Potentiates Subsequent Response to Sulphur Dioxide in Adolescent Asthmatic Subjects', *American Review of Respiratory Diseases* (1990), vol. 141, pp. 377–80.

8 J. D. Gillett, 'Increased Atmospheric Carbon Dioxide and the Spread of Parasitic Disease', in *Parasitological Topics; A Presentation Volume to P C Garnham FRS, on his 80th birthday* (Society of Protozoologists, special publication, 1981), vol. 1, pp. 106–111.

9 P. C. Garnham, 'Factors Influencing the Development of Protozoa in their Arthropodan Hosts', in A. E. R. Taylor (ed.), *Host Parasite Relationships in Invertebrate Hosts* (Blackwell Scientific Publications, Oxford, 1964).

10 P. Curson, 'Human Health in the Greenhouse Era', in *Planning for the Greenhouse* (School of Earth Sciences, MacQuarie University, MacQuarie University Continuing Education Programme, Australia, 1989); P. F. S. Liehne, 'Climatic Influences on Mosquito-Borne Diseases in Australia', in G. R. Pearman (ed.), *Greenhouse – Planning for Climate Change* (Division of Atmospheric Research CSIRO, Australia, 1989).

11 J. A. Longstreth, 'Human Health', in J. B. Smith and D. Tirpak, *The Potential Effects of Global Climate Change on the United States* (United States Environmental Protection Agency, 1989).

12 M. Giannini, 'Suppression of Pathogenesis in Cutaneous Leishmaniasis by UV Irradiation' *Infection Immunology* (1986), vol. 51, pp. 831–43.

13 C. Spellman and R. Daynes, 'Modification of Imunological Potential by Ultraviolet Radiation, II Generation of Suppressor Cells in Short-Term UV-Irradiated Mice' *Transplantation* (1977), vol. 24, pp. 120–6; M. Fisher and M Kripke 'Systemic Alterations Induced in Mice by Ultraviolet Light, Irradiation and its Relationship to Ultraviolet Carcinogenesis' *Proc. Nat. Acad, Sci*. USA (1977), vol. 74, pp. 1688–92.

14 L. K. Roberts, W. E. Samlowski, and R. A. Daynes, ' The Immunological Consequenses of Ultraviolet Radiation Exposure, *Photodermatology* (1986), vol. 3, pp. 284–98.

15 *State of the World's Children 1990* (UNICEF, Oxford University Press, 1990).

16 D. Grigg, *The World Food Problem 1950–1980* (Basil Blackwell, Oxford, 1985).

17 L. R. Brown and J. E. Young, 'Feeding the World in the Nineties', in L. R. Brown (ed.), *State of the World 1990*, A Worldwatch Institute Report on progress toward a sustainable society (W. W. Norton & Co., New York/London, 1990).

18 C. Rosenzweig and M. M. Daniel, 'Agriculture', in Smith and Tirpak, n. 11.

19 D. M. Damkaer, D. B. Day, G. A. Heron, and E. F. Prentice, 'Effects of UV-B radiation on near surface zooplankton of Puget Sounds', *Oecologia* (1980), vol. 44, no. 1, pp. 49–58; G. Dohler, 'Effect of UV-B radiation (290-320nm) on the nitrogen metabolism of several marine diatoms', *Journal of Plant Physiology* (1985), vol. 118, pp. 391–400, .

20 J. W. Maurits la Riviere, 'Threats to the World's Water', *Scientific American* (1989), vol. 3, pp. 48–55.

21 N. W. Mugler and M. C. Rubino, 'Water Resources', in Smith and Tirpak, *n. 11*.

22 J. L. Jacobson, 'Holding Back the Sea', in Brown, *State of the World 1990*.

23 United Nations Environment Programme, *Criteria for Assessing Vulnerability to Sea Level Rise; A Global Inventory of High Risk Areas* (Delft Hydraulics Laboratory, Delft, Netherlands, 1989).

24 L. A. Boorman, J. D. Goss-Custard, S. McGrorty, *Climatic Change Rising Sea Level and The British Coast* (Institute of Terrestrial Ecology Report no. 1, London: HMSO, 1989).

25 B. C. Chamberlin, 'Mayo Seminars in Psychiatry: The Psychological Aftermath of Disaster', *Journal of Clinical Psychiatry* (1980), vol. 41, pp. 238–44.

26 J. L. Titchener and T. K. Frederic, 'Family and Character Change at Buffalo Creek', *American Journal of Psychiatry* (1976), vol. 133, p. 3.

27 E. Parker, 'Cyclone Tracy and Darwin evacuees: on the restoration of the species', *British Journal of Psychiatry* (1977), vol. 130, pp. 548–55.

28 G. Bennet, 'Bristol floods 1968: controlled survey on effects on health of local community disaster', *British Medical Journal* (1970), vol. 3, pp. 454–8.

29 M. J. Abrahams, J. Price, F. A. Whirlock, *et al.*, 'The Brisbane Floods, January 1974: their impact on health', *Medical Journal of Australia* (1976), vol. 2, p. 936.

30 S. E. Davis, 'Greenhouse Effect: The Human Response', *Washington Post*, 17 Apr. 1990.

Chapter 8: Policy Responses to Global Warming Jose Goldemberg

1 Dean Abrahamson and Peter Ciborowski (eds.), *The Greenhouse Effect: policy implications of a global warming* (Proceedings of a Symposium held in Minneapolis, Minnesota, on 29–30 May 1984); Michael C. Barth and James G. Titus (eds.), *Greenhouse Effect and Sea Level Rise – a challenge for this generation* (McGraw Hill Book Co., 1984).

2 D. A. Lashof and D. A. Tirpak (eds.), 'Policy Options for Stabilizing Global Climate', (US EPA Office of Policy, Planning and Evaluation; draft completed Feb. 1989, as yet unpublished); A. J. Streb, 'Energy Efficiency and Global Warming', in *Energy Technologies for Reducing Emissions from Greenhouse Gases* (2 vols., OECD, Paris, 1989).

3 Y. Kaya, K. Yamaji, and R. Matsuhashi, 'A Grand Strategy for Global Warming' (Tokyo Conference on the Global Environment and Human Response toward Sustainable Development, 11–13 Sept. 1989).

4 J. Goldemberg, T. B. Johansson, A. K. N. Reddy, and R. H. Williams, *Energy for a Sustainable World* (Wiley Eastern Ltd., 1988).

5 See Lashof and Tirpak, n. 2.

6 B. Bolin, 'Preventive Measures to Slow Down Man-Induced Climate Change' (Report of the Second Session of the Steering Committee of IPCC Working Group 3, Geneva, 10–12 May 1989).

7 Ibid.

8 E. S. Kalapula, 'Woodfuel Situation and Deforestation in Zambia', *Ambio*, vol. 18, no. 5, p. 293, and *Énergie Internationale* (1989–90).

9 'Amazonia: facts, problems and solutions', International Symposium on the Amazon (University of São Paulo, Brazil, July 1989; Coordinator: J. Goldemberg) .

10 OECD, *The Polluter-Pays Principle* (OECD, Paris, 1975).

11 OECD, *Economic Instruments for Environmental Protection* (OECD, Paris, 1989) pp. 11–12.

12 Ibid. 31.

13 Ibid.

14 F. von Hippel and B. G. Levi, 'Automotive Fuel Efficiency: the opportunities and weakness of existing market incentives', *Resources and Conservation* (1983), vol 10, no. 103, pp. 103–24.

15 R. H. Williams, 'Innovative Approaches to Market Electric Efficiency', in T. B. Johansson, B. Bodlund, and R. H. Williams (eds.), *Electricity-Efficiency End-Use and New Generation Technologies and Their Planning Implications* (Lund University Press, Sweden, 1989); C. J. Cichetti and W. Hogan, *Including Unbundled Demand Side Options in Electric Utility Bidding Programs* (Energy and Environmental Policy Center Report no. E-88-07, J. F. Kennedy School of Government, Harvard University, Cambridge, Mass, 1988); A. B. Lovins, 'Saving Gigabucks with Megawatts', *Public Utilities Fortnightly* (1985), pp. 19–26.

16 McKinsey and Company Inc., Background paper on funding mechanisms, prepared for the Ministerial Conference on Atmospheric Pollution and Climate Change, Noordwijk, 6–7 Nov. 1989.

17 See Lashof and Tirpak, n. 2.

18 Center for Strategic and International Studies, *Implications of Global Climate Policies* (Washington, DC, 27 June 1989).

19 See n. 3.

20 Conference on the Changing Atmosphere: *Implications for Global Security* (Toronto, June, 1988).

21 See n. 3.

22 A. S. Manne and R. G. Richels, 'CO_2 Emission Limits: an economic cost analysis for the USA – November 1989', *The Energy Journal* (submitted).

23 R. H. Williams, 'Energy Policy', *The Energy Journal* (submitted).

24 A. M. Strout, 'Energy-Intensive Materials and the Developing Countries', *Materials and Society* (1985), vol. 9, no. 3, pp. 281–330.

25 Geraldo Barbieri and Alecseo Kravec, Faculty of Economics and Administration, University of São Paulo, Brazil, private communication, 1989.

26 See n. 4.

27 See n. 23.

Chapter 9: The Costs of Cutting – or not Cutting – Greenhouse-gas Emissions Stephen H. Schneider

Any opinions, findings, conclusions, or recommendations expressed in this article are those of the author and do not necessarily reflect the views of the National Center for Atmospheric Research, or its principal sponsor, the National Science Foundation.

1 W. T. Brookes, 'The Global Warming Panic', *Forbes*, 25 Dec. 1989, pp. 96–102.

2 S. H. Schneider, *Global Warming: Are We Entering the Greenhouse Century?* (Sierra Club Books, San Francisco, 1989, also Lutterworth, London, 1990, revised edition).

3 Environment Canada, Conference Proceedings: *The Changing Atmosphere: Implications for Global Security* (World Meteorological Organization, Geneva, 1988).

4 M. Grubb, *The Greenhouse Effect: Negotiating Targets, Energy and Environmental Program* (Royal Institute of International Affairs, 1989).

5 R. H. Williams, 'Will Constraining Fossil Fuel Carbon Dioxide Emissions Really Cost So Much?', a critique of: A. S. Manne and ᴵ . Richels (Draft),'Global CO_2 Emissions Reduction – the Impacts of Rising Energy Costs', Feb. 1990.

6 P. E. Waggoner (ed.), *Climate Change and US Water Resources* (John Wiley and Sons, New York, 1990).

7 D. A. Lashof, 'The Dynamic Greenhouse: Feedback Processes That May Influence Future Concentrations of Atmospheric Trace Gases and Climatic Change', *Climatic Change* (1989), vol. 14, pp. 213–42; M. O. Andreae and D. S. Schimel (eds.), *Dahlem Workshop on Exchange of Trace Gases between Terrestrial Ecosystems and the Atmosphere* (John Wiley and Sons, New York, 1989).

8 See Schneider, n. 2, chapter 8.

Chapter 10: The Role of Energy Efficiency Amory Lovins

This paper is an edited and updated version of two earlier papers: one presented at the Hoover Institution conference on 'Human Demography and Natural Resources' at the Hoover Institution, Stanford University, Stanford, California, 1–3 Feb. 1989; The other a plenary address at the Air and Waste Management Association at its Anaheim Conference, 26 June 1989. They are respectively Rocky Mountain Institute's publication nos. E89-1 and E89-33.

1 This potential is exhaustively documented by the technical reports of Rocky Mountain Institute's *Competitek* quarterly-update service, currently provided to more than 160 subscribers (chiefly electric utilities and governments) in 30 countries. The application of those technical and economic data to a practical case is illustrated by RMI's June 1988 analysis *Negawatts for Arkansas* (Publication no. U88-30), vol. 1. No inter-fuel substitution (for example, of gas for electricity) is assumed here, although it is often worthwhile. For citations to comparative international results, see A. B. Lovins, 'End-Use/Least-Cost Investment Strategies', World Energy Conference (Montréal, Sept. 1989) (RMI Publication no. E89-35).

2 If it is displacing nuclear power instead, it will typically avoid producing half-a-curie of strontium-90 and caesium-137, plus about 25 mg of plutonium, equivalent

in explosive power to about 385 kg of TNT (see A. B. Lovins, 'Nuclear weapons and power-reactor plutonium', *Nature* (28 Feb. 1980), vol. 283, no. 5750, pp. 817–23); if it is displacing an oil-fired plant (now very uncommon in the US), it will typically avoid burning about 200 litres (1.25 barrels) of oil – enough to run a US family car for 1000 miles, or to run a super-efficient prototype car coast-to-coast and back. All these calculations include distribution losses and net space-conditioning effects. For details see A. B. Lovins, 'Factsheet: How a Compact Fluorescent Lamp Saves a Ton of CO_2' (RMI Publication no. E90-5).

3 A. B. Lovins, 'Drill Rigs and Battleships Are the Answer! (But What Was the Question?)', in R. Reed and F. Fesharaki (eds.), *The Petroleum Market in the 1990s* (Westview, Boulder, 1989); RMI Publication no. S88-6. Modest gas-for-oil substitution is assumed here, but only where the gas has also been saved (rather than representing an increase in demand), and no inter-fuel or inter-modal substitution is assumed in the transport sector. For the plotted supply-curve, see A. B. Lovins, 'Abating Air-Pollution at Negative Cost via Energy Efficiency' (RMI Publication no. E89-33), or Fig. 10.2 in this chapter.

4 One GW, or 1,000 megawatts, or 1 million kilowatts, is the nominal capacity of a single giant power-station.

5 A. Fickett, C. Gellings, and A. B. Lovins, 'Efficient Use of Electricity', *Scientific American* (Sept. 1990), in press.

6 *Efficient Electricity-Use: Estimates of Maximum Energy Savings* (EPRI, CU–6746, Mar. 1990).

7 Specifically: when its peak load was 14 GW, SCE was reducing its long-term forecast peak by nearly 1.2 GW/year: around 45 per cent through its own programmes, costing 0.3 cents/kWh for efficiency and about \$31 peak/kW for load management, and around 55 per cent through state programmes, such as the Title 24 building code, which cost the utility nothing. Without that state action, SCE could have achieved similar results at costs ranging from zero (for sliding-scale hook-up fees replacing building codes) to about 0.6 cents/kWh (for seller rebates replacing appliance standards). The average of all these costs to the utility would have been about 0.1–0.2 cents/kWh. The corresponding cost to society, including participating customers' contributions, would have been several-fold larger, but still less than 1 cent/kWh.

8 During 1975–85, more new US capacity was ordered from small hydro-plants and wind-power than from coal and nuclear plants, not counting their cancellations, which collectively exceeded 100 GW. At the time, all these options enjoyed significant subsidies, though those to the renewables were probably smaller per unit of energy supplied (see n. 23).

9 Because the dispersed investments are small, modular, and relatively cheap, and have very short lead times, fast paybacks, and high velocity of cash-flow, they thus avoid playing 'You Bet Your Company' that demand forecasts a decade ahead will be accurate enough to ensure amortization of a multi-billion-dollar central station.

10 Most, though not all, of the proposals could be relied upon to produce actual, reliable capacity if accepted; many utilities have also found that private co-generation is typically more reliable than their own central plants.

11 D. Moskovitz (former Chairman, Maine Public Utilities Commission), personal communications, 1989.

12 The first step in the supply curve – the around 92-per-cent potential saving in lighting energy, displacing about 120 GW of US generating capacity – has a

negative cost (which balances the positive cost of subsequent steps up to about 50 per cent of total consumption). That is because the efficient new lighting equipment often lasts longer than the inefficient equipment it replaces, or less of it is needed, to the extent that the new equipment more than pays for itself by avoided customer maintenance cost, making its electrical savings better than free (by about $30 billion a year). See A. B. Lovins and R. Sardinsky, *The State of the Art: Lighting* (RMI/*Competitek*, Mar. 1988). The quantity of 'drivepower' savings shown, representing thirty-five classes of improvements to motor systems, is probably understated by a factor of up to two (see A. B. Lovins *et al.*, *The State of the Art: Drivepower* [RMI/*Competitek*, May 1989]),but increasing it would significantly decrease other terms such as space-cooling, so as to avoid double-counting.

13 For a lay summary see A. B. Lovins, 'Making Markets in Resource Efficiency' (RMI Publication no. E89-27).

14 As documented and elaborated by the Implementation Papers of RMI's *Competitek* service.

15 In the form of any combination of financing, information, design services, project management, equipment, installation, commissioning, training, operation, monitoring and maintenance. A utility which sells such elements can, but need not, bill the results according to the energy services delivered.

16 See n. 13.

17 The car's efficiency depends substantially on its light weight, obtained partly by composites and plastics. But these permit large, complex assemblies to be moulded as a unit. The extra cost of the moulding dies and the more exotic material is less than the saving from not making and assembling many small parts. The leftover money is spent on smarter chip controls for the engine, better aerodynamics, and so on, yielding a net marginal cost of about zero. Extrapolation from conventional incremental improvements, of course, gives a far less favourable but invalid result.

18 Additional efficiency at some positive marginal cost is doubtless available but is conservatively omitted here, as is the prospect of further major advances from fundamental redesign, for example with series hybrid drives, switched-reluctance drive-motors, or crushable metal-foam bodies.

19 K Menke and J. Woodwell, *Water Productivity and Development: Strategies for More Efficient Use* (RMI Publication no. W90-10).

20 A. B. Lovins, 'Energy Strategy: The Road Not Taken?', *Foreign Affairs* (Oct. 1976), vol. 55, no. 1, pp. 65–96; the concept was later clarified, and the term 'least-cost' introduced, in a series of pioneering quantitative analyses by my colleague Roger Sant. Interestingly, while the 'soft-path' diagram in that *Foreign Affairs* article was meant to be illustrative, not a forecast, it accurately represents actual renewable supply in 1988 (a quarter of the way through the half-century shown), and shows total 1988 energy demand at least a tenth above actual.

21 Similarly, his solar tax credits rewarded effort rather than success – they rewarded people for spending money, not for saving or supplying energy, and most of the rent was captured by the vendors. The credits therefore encouraged the proliferation of charlatans, preserved the uncompetitive at the expense of the honest and clever, and removed incentives to cut costs. Waiting for the credits to be implemented destroyed roughly half the solar industry; their removal eliminated most of the other half by drying up distribution channels for many viable products. Unfortunately, Congress scrapped the credits rather than improving them – even though it retained and even increased most of the far larger subsidies given throughout to competing energy forms, leaving the playing-field even less level than before.

22 For example, electricity was eleven times as heavily subsidized per unit of energy supplied as were direct fuels; nuclear power was around eighty times as heavily subsidized as were efficiency improvements and non-hydroelectric renewable sources; and the subsidies per unit of energy supplied were at least 200 times as great for nuclear power as for efficiency.

23 H. R. Heede, *A Preliminary Analysis of Federal Energy Subsidies in FY 1984* (RMI Publication no. CS85-7, 1985), summarized in H. R. Heede and A. B. Lovins, 'Hiding the True Cost of Energy Sources', *Wall Street Journal* (17 Sept. 1985), p. 28 (RMI Publication no. CS85-22). Heede's far more detailed final report, updated to contrast recent data, is to be published by RMI in 1990–1.

24 Chiefly by removing most subsidies for efficiency and renewables. But other policy actions are expanding the damage. In 1988, for example nuclear power was offered a new, approximately $9 billion subsidy in the form of a write-off of enrichment debts. The US Department of Energy ignored warnings by, among others, me, when I served on the department's senior advisory board in 1980–1, that those debts would prove unpayable.

25 Among the most recent examples to come to light are the dismantling of most enforcement of coal-stripping restoration rules, the pervasive lack of monitoring of Arctic oil operations (especially with regard to pollution, for example by drilling muds) and numerous nuclear problems, such as the late-1988 removal of promised funding for Nevada's independent assessment of nuclear-waste disposal operations, or the NRC's adoption of backfit rules so bizarre that, on its figures, a cost-benefit break-even would be achieved by new pressurized-water reactors with no containments and an even chance of a Chernobyl-sized release every few years. See J. Harding, *A Current Appraisal of Reactor Safety and Risk Issues* (MHB Associates, San Jose, California, 1990). The major national environmental groups have thoroughly documented dozens of such issues.

26 This is still going on, for example in the US Department of Energy's proposed rules on appliance standards. The proposed national Building Energy Performance Standard (BEPS) was made voluntary rather than mandatory, and even the voluntary residential standards were never issued.

27 'Wasted' in the sense that it is used instead of being displaced by cheaper efficiency options now commercially available and practically applicable and deliverable for doing the same task.

28 The equivalent waste in each subsequent year is probably even larger.

29 Together, in unknown degree, with the simultaneous 70-per-cent cut-back in the print-run of the government's *Gas Mileage Guide*, so that two-thirds of new-car buyers could not get a copy.

30 The pervasive self-deception involved in promoting the latter sector is discussed in A. B. Lovins, 'The Origins of the Nuclear Power Fiasco', *Energy Policy Studies* (1986), vol. 3, pp. 7–34 (RMI Publication no. E86-29).

31 See n. 23.

32 This is fallacious because of the *opportunity* cost of buying any option costlier than efficiency. Because nuclear power (for example) costs much more on the margin than efficiency does, it can displace proportionately less coal-fired electricity per dollar invested. Buying nuclear power instead of efficiency thus makes global warming worse. It is not very practical anyhow – see papers by W. N. Keepin and G. Kats, 'Greenhouse Warming: comparative analysis of nuclear and efficiency abatement strategies', *Energy Policy* (Dec. 1988), vol. 16, no. 6, pp. 538–61, and 'Global Warning', *Science* (1988), vol. 241, p. 1027; and by A. B. Lovins, 'Energy Options', *Science* (6 Jan. 1989), vol. 243, p. 12.

33 And cheaper still to deliver efficiency by the many proven methods which share the cost between the energy vendor and the customer: electric utilities' rebates, for example, typically pay around 15 per cent of the cost, while the customer puts up the remaining 85 per cent in the expectation of avoiding the retail tariff.

34 For example, *Negawatts for Arkansas* (see n. 1) found in that state a full technical potential to save around $5-7 billion (1986 net present value) against an avoidable short-run marginal cost of only 2 cents/kWh.

35 Including electricity savings only a quarter as big and several times as costly as RMI estimates to be now available. The study is H. Geller *et al.*, *Acid Rain and Electricity Conservation* (American Council for an Energy-Efficient Economy, Washington, DC, 1987).

36 A. B. and L. H. Lovins and L. Ross, 'Nuclear Power and Nuclear Bombs', *Foreign Affairs* (Summer 1980), vol. 58, no. 5, pp. 1133–77; A. B. and L. H. Lovins, *Energy/War: Breaking the Nuclear Link* (Harper & Row Colophon, New York, 1980) – out of print in English but available in several other languages; P. O'Heffernan, L. H. and A. B. Lovins, *The First Nuclear World War* (W. W. Norton, New York, 1983; RMI Publication no. S83-14).

37 A. B. and L. H. Lovins, *Brittle Power: Energy Strategy for National Security* (originally written for the US Defense Civil Preparedness Agency) (Brick House, Andover, MA, 1982); about 1200 refs., summarized in 'The Fragility of Domestic Energy', *The Atlantic* (Nov. 1983), vol. 252, no. 5, pp. 118–26 (RMI Publication no. S83-8). See also more broadly RMI's *Energy Security Reader*, 2nd edn. (Publication no. S88-45, Oct. 1988), an anthology including many papers cited here.

38 See n.3; A. B. and L. H. Lovins, 'The Avoidable Oil Crisis', *The Atlantic* (Dec 1987), vol. 260, no. 6, pp. 22–30 (RMI Publication no. S87-25), and letters (Apr. 1988), vol. 261, no. 4, pp. 10–11, and (June 1988), vol. 261, no. 6, pp. 10–12, (RMI Publication no. S88-15), and 'Oil-Risk Insurance: Choosing the Best Buy', *GAO Journal* (US General Accounting Office, Washington, DC, Summer 1988), vol. 2, pp. 52–60, RMI Publication no. S88-26).

39 Each cent per kilowatt-hour is equivalent in heat content to oil at $17 per barrel, so typical US retail electricity costs about 7 times as much per unit of heat contained as does current world-market oil.

40 At least in function if not in outward appearance: Switzerland, for example, has some 1,200 utilities, mostly very small distribution companies, but capital allocation to the Swiss electric industry is chiefly made by a few people in a small handful of large generating companies.

41 J. S. Nørgård, 'Low Electricity Appliances – Options for the Future', in T. B. Johansson *et al.* (eds.), *Electricity* (Lund University Press, Lund, Sweden, 1989). Nørgård's calculation does not yet include space-heating or commercial lighting. Including them should make his result more favourable, since space-heating, though a relatively costly saving, is rarely done with electricity in Denmark and hence is unimportant amongst all the other kinds of savings, while

commercial lighting savings contribute a substantial additional saving with a strongly negative net cost.

42 B Bodlund *et al.*, 'The Challenge of Choices:Technology Options for Swedish Electricity Sector', in *Electricity* (op. cit., n. 41), pp. 883–947.

43 An important new class of technologies; they insulate two to four times as well as triple-glazing, cost about the same, passively keep buildings cooler in summer and warmer in winter, pay back in around two to three years, and are equivalent just in US oil- and gas-saving potential to two Alaskas or two North Seas, at a cost equivalent to a few dollars per barrel.

44 Because the cooling equipment is probably less efficient and less well maintained to start with, and the Thai climate and average building-size are more favourable for such shell measures.

45 A Soviet energy economist who recently launched a for-profit co-operative selling energy-efficiency services in Moscow reports that energy prices are about a third of actual cost, but that efficiency is also roughly three times worse than in the West, so the economics of saving energy work out about the same.

46 J. Goldemberg, T. B. Johansson, A. K. N. Reddy, and R. H. Williams, *Energy for a Sustainable World* (World Resources Institute, Washington, DC, 1987, and Wiley-Eastern, New Delhi, 1988).

47 A. B. and L. H. Lovins, F. Krause, and W. Bach, *Least-Cost Energy: Solving the CO_2 Problem* (Brick House, Andover, MA, 1981, reprinted in 1989 by RMI as Publication no. E89-17; summarized in *Climatic Change* (1982), vol. 4, pp. 217–20 (RMI Publication no.E82-2). Recalculating the results with today's efficiency technologies would yield slightly larger savings at much lower costs – lower by a factor probably greater than the concomitant decline in real energy prices.

48 Dr Gadgil, now at Lawrence Berkeley Laboratory, and M. Anjali Sastry, of Rocky Mountain Institute, in co-operation with the Bombay utility and other Indian institutions, have now launched a large-scale demonstration project to this general effect.

49 When it was planned to bring in the field at costs implying a retail crude-oil price of about \$20 per barrel, Shell planners, seeing the 1986 crash coming, said the project would not be pursued unless the price could be cut to \$12 per barrel. The engineers at first said this would be impossible. It took them a year to do. Apparently they had previously been told only to bring in new fields as quickly as possible, with cost no object. This time, they were asked to bring in a field as cheaply as possible, even if it took a little longer – so they invented a completely different design approach. In how many other supply technologies have we got the wrong answer by assigning the wrong task?

50 See RMI's *Catalog of Water-Efficient Technologies for the Urban/Residential Sector* (Publication no. W87-30, 1988).

51 Such as those now being commercialized by Dr John Todd *et al.* at Four Elements Corporation (Falmouth, Massachusetts), which use a sophisticated greenhouse-enclosed 'swamp' to turn raw sewage into ultra-pure polished drinking water, crops, and flowers, with no hazard, no odour, and a third of the capital cost of a chemical-based plant.

52 Perhaps such as the brilliant bus-system innovations developed by Jaime Lerner in Brazil.

53 Surprisingly, this is also true even in the most industrialized, densely populated, cold, and cloudy countries. In terms of renewable energy, as my analyses have found since 1972, Japan probably has the most – and clearly the most ample – supply options of any major OECD country. The climatic range of solar technologies has been greatly extended by Dr David Mills of Sydney University: his highly selective solar absorbing surfaces, in a hard vacuum, could yield about 600°C on a cloudy winter day in Stockholm.

54 See Table 10.1's exegesis. But this too is a function of technology. As Ernie Robertson (then at the Biomass Institute in Winnipeg) once remarked, there are three ways to make limestone into a structural material: (*a*) Cut it into blocks. That is not vey interesting. (*b*) Bake it at thousands of degrees into Portland cement. That is inelegant. (*c*) Feed chips of it to a chicken. Twelve hours later it emerges as eggshell, several times stronger than Portland cement. Evidently the chicken knows something we do not about ambient-temperature technology.

55 This is also true per capita: during 1975–84 alone, per-capita consumption of steel fell by 11.5 per cent, parallelling a trend in many other countries, both industrialized (UK, –32 per cent, Sweden, –43 per cent, etc.) and developing (Brazil, –40 per cent, Argentina, –46 per cent, Philippines, –50 per cent, and so on). This is partly because of increased net imports of steel-intensive products such as cars, but also in substantial part because of, for example, lighter-weight cars.

56 The many advantages of adobe, caliche, rammed earth, and so on, are now being rediscovered in even the most advanced countries, for example through the work of Pliny Fisk in Austin, Texas, and the late Hassan Fathy in Egypt.

57 So long as we bear chiefly in mind that market costs and prices are neither revealed truth nor *per se* a meaningful test of desirable behaviour, because they depend largely on tacit accounting and philosophical conventions – such as whether depletable resources are valued at extraction cost or at long-run replacement cost.

58 These are the main areas of Rocky Mountain Institute's detailed research in support of its mission, which is to foster the efficient and sustainable use of resources as a path to global security. Naturally, achieving security ('freedom from fear of privation or attack'), while it has an important technological component, also requires other kinds of advances to achieve a sufficient mix of conflict prevention, conflict resolution, and effective but non-provocative defence. See H. Harvey, M. Shuman, and D. Arbess, *Reclaiming Security: Beyond the Controlled Arms Race* (Hill and Wang, New York, Aug. 1990), in press.

59 The last of these responses – the only one left now that the others have proved groundless – is essentially a theological argument which cannot be settled on technical merits. It dominates much of today's energy-policy debate, in the superficially plausible form: 'We must buy more power plants in case people don't go on buying efficiency as consistently as they have done so far.' Of course, buying the plants creates strong economic incentives (at least for the top-line thinkers) to sell more energy, not less.

Chapter 11: Renewable Energy: Recent Commercial Performance in the USA as an Index of Future Prospects Carlo LaPorta

1 *Cairo Compact*, report of the Cairo Conference on Preparing for Climate Change, Dec. 1989 (Climate Institute, Washington, DC, 1990).

2 Draft report, Energy and Industry Subgroup of IPCC Working Group 3, 26 Mar. 1990, p. E-4.

3 L. D. Ostlie, 'Creating Production Economies of Scale Through Government Action: The Case of Biomass Energy from Whole-Tree Burning', Forum on Renewable Energy and Climate Change, Washington, DC, 14 June 1990.

4 J. A. Duffie and W. A. Beckman, *Solar Energy Thermal Processes* (John Wiley & Sons, New York, 1974), p. 4.

5 Adapted from International Energy Agency, *Renewable Sources of Energy* (International Energy Agency, Paris, France, 1987), p. 29.

6 R. San Martin, 'Environmental Emissions from Energy Technology Systems: The Total Fuel Cycle', *Forum on Renewable Energy and Climate Change*, 14 June 1989 (US Department of Energy, Washington, DC, 1989), p. 5.

7 See IPCC, n. 2, pp. 2–14.

8 See IEA, *Renewable Sources*, n. 5, p. 24.

9 Even though geothermal energy reserves are finite, they are counted among renewable-energy resources because of the massive amount of thermal energy available beneath the surface.

10 Meridian Corporation, for US Department of Energy, Characterization of U.S. Energy Resources and Reserves (Washington, DC, June 1989), p. 19.

11 Ibid., p. 25.

12 Ibid., p. 30.

13 Public Utility Regulatory Policies Act (PURPA) of 1978.

14 P. Gipe, 'Wind Energy Comes of Age in California', paper for American Society of Mechanical Engineers and the National Aeronautical and Space Administration, 1989.

15 C. LaPorta and K. Porter, 1984 Wind Energy Market Status Survey, American Wind Energy Association, Alexandria, Virginia, 1985.

16 L. J. Rogers, 'The U.S. Department of Energy Wind Technology Research Program', Presentation to the American Wind Energy Association R&D Committee, 5 Dec. 1989.

17 See Gipe, n. 14.

18 Ibid.

19 D.R. Smith *et al.*, *PG&E's Evaluation of Wind Energy* (Pacific Gas & Electric Company Department of Research and Development, San Ramon, California, 1989).

20 R. Lynette, ' Wind Energy Systems', *Forum on Renewable Energy and Climate Change* (Washington, DC, 14 June 1989).

21 N. Rader, *Power Surge* (Public Citizen, Washington, DC, 1989).

22 Ibid.

23 M. Lotker, Luz Development and Finance Company, presentation at SOLTECH 90, Austin, Texas, Mar. 1990.

24 *Five Year Research and Development Plan, Solar Buildings* (US Department of Energy, Washington DC, 1986).

25 C. LaPorta, unpublished analysis for US Environmental Protection Agency Division of Global Change, Washington, DC, 1990.

26 Personal communication from Marvin Goodman, Architect, Kingston, Jamaica.

27 *Solar Collector Manufacturing Activity Report* (Energy Information Administration, US Department of Energy, Washington, DC, 1988).

28 See LaPorta, n. 25.

29 Statistic provided by the Solar Energy Industries Association, Washington, DC.

30 *Statistical Abstract of the United States* (US Government Printing Office, Washington DC, 1989).

31 Private communication with Department of Energy staff developing the US National Energy Strategy.

32 Interview with Solar Dynamics, Bridgetown, Barbados.

33 *Solar Water Heating* (California Public Utility Commission, San Francisco, California, 1985).

34 Interview with staff, Volunteers in Technical Assistance, Arlington, Virginia, 1989.

35 Power Systems Group, Ametek, *Solar Energy Handbook: Theory and Applications* (Chilton Book Company, Radnor, Pennsylvania, 1979), p.82.

36 'Taking Charge of Your Energy Costs', draft report for US Department of Energy, CBY Associates (Washington, DC, 1990).

37 O. Hohmeyer, *Social Costs of Energy Consumption* (Springer-Verlag, Berlin, 1988).

38 Ibid.

39 Interview with O. Hohmeyer, Washington, DC, 1989.

40 Interview with L. Nelson, president, California Solar Energy Industries Association, Mar. 1990.

41 L. Nelson, CALSEIA.

42 Interview with R. Bingman, president, Ramada Energy Company, Phoenix, Arizona, 1988.

Chapter 12: Motor Vehicles and Global Warming Michael P. Walsh

1 M. A. DeLuchi *et al.*, 'Transportation Fuels and the Greenhouse Effect', submitted to the *Transportation Research Record*.

2 Intergovernmental Panel on Climate Change, *Scientific Assessment of Climate Change*, (Report of Working Group 1, June 1990).

3 *Regulatory Impact Analysis: Protection of Stratospheric Ozone* (Environmental Protection Agency, Washington, DC, Dec. 1987).

4 'The Transport Sector and Global Warming', background study for OTA Report, Parsons, 31 May 1989.

5 US Congressional Office of Technology Assessment, Apr. 1988.

6 US EPA Mobile 4 Emissions Model, 1989.

7 B. Lubkert and S. de Tilly, *An Emission Inventory For SO_2, NO_x and VOCs in North-Western Europe* (Organization for Economic Cooperation and Development, Paris, 1987).

8 'OECD Environmental Data' (Organization for Economic Cooperation and Development, Paris, 1987).

9 A. M. Thompson and R. J. Cicerone, 'Atmospheric CH_4, CO and OH from 1860 to 1985', *Nature* (1986), vol. 321, pp. 148–50; G. J. MacDonald, 'The Greenhouse Effect and Climate Change', paper presented to US Senate Environment and Public Works Committee, 28 Jan. 1987.

10 V. Ramanathan, 'The Greenhouse Theory of Climate Change: A Test by an Inadvertent Global Experiment', *Science*, 15 Apr. 1988.

11 See MacDonald, n. 9.

12 'Methane: the hidden greenhouse gas', *New Scientist*, (6 May 1989).

13 M. A. K. Khalil and R. A. Rasmussen, 'Carbon Monoxide in the Earth's Atmosphere: Indications of a Global Increase', *Nature* (1988), vol. 332, pp. 242–5.

14 D. A. Lashof and D. R. Ahuja, 'Relative contributions of greenhouse gas emissions to global warming', *Nature* (1990), vol. 344, p. 529.

15 *National Air Quality and Emissions Trends Report, 1988* (US Environmental Protection Agency, Mar. 1990).

16 L. M. Thomas, Testimony before the Subcommittee on Health and the Environment, Committee on Energy and Commerce, Washington, DC, 19 Feb. 1987.

17 'Tighter Ozone Standard Urged By Scientists' *Science*, (24 June 1988).

18 J. J. Mackensie and M. El-Ashry, *Ill Winds Pollution's Toll on Trees and Crops* (World Resources Institute, Sept. 1988).

19 American Lung Association, Comments to EPA, 1988.

20 See n. 16.

21 *Acute Effects of Carbon Monoxide Exposure on Individuals with Coronary Artery Disease* (Health Effects Institute Research Report no. 25, Nov. 1989.)

22 F. B. Stern *et al.*, *Heart Disease Mortality Among Bridge and Tunnel Officers Exposed to Vehicular Exhaust* (National Institute for Occupational Safety and Health (NIOSH), Cincinnati, Ohio).

23 See n. 10.

24 Lindvall, *Health Effects of Nitrogen Dioxide and Oxidants* (Department of Environmental Hygiene, National Institute of Environmental Medicine and Karolinska Institute, Mar. 1982).

25 Orehek *et al.*, 'Effect of Short-Term, Low-Level Nitrogen Dioxide Exposure on Bronchial Sensitivity of Asthmatic Patients', *The Journal of Clinical Investigation* (Feb. 1976), vol. 57; Mostardi *et al.*, 'The University of Akron Study on Air Pollution and Human Health Effects', *Archives of Environmental Health* (Sept.–Oct. 1981), vol. 36, no. 5.

26 G. S. Whetstone and A. Rosencranz, *Acid Rain In Europe And North America* (Environmental Law Institute, 1983).

27 International Conference of Ministers on Acid Rain, Ottawa, Canada, Mar. 1985.

28 R. A. Derwent, 'A Better Way To Control Pollution', *Nature* (1988), vol. 331.

29 International Conference of Ministers on Acid Rain, Ottawa, Canada, Mar. 1985.

Chapter 13: Nuclear Power and Global Warming Bill Keepin

1 Nicholas Ridley, quoted in C. Flavin, 'Slowing Global Warming' in *State of the World 1990* (W. W. Norton, New York, 1990).

2 The nuclear fuel-cycle releases small quantities of carbon dioxide (for example, the mining and transport of uranium entails some fossil-fuel combustion). According to US data, the boiling water reactor (BWR) fuel-cycle emits approximately ninety times less carbon dioxide than a conventional coal-based power plant: see Meridian Corporation, 'Energy System Emissions and Material Requirements', prepared for the US Department of Energy, draft version, Nov. 1988. According to data from the Federal Republic of Germany, the pressurized water reactor fuel-cycle emits twenty times less carbon than the coal fuel-cycle: see U. Frische, L. Rausch, K. H. Simon, *Environmental Analysis of Energy Systems: The Total-Emission-Model for Integrated Systems* (Oeko Institut, Darmstadt, Sept. 1989). According to the latter report, renewable alternatives have considerably lower emissions than nuclear: photovoltaic systems emit about 10 per cent and small-scale wind systems about 20 per cent of the carbon emissions from the nuclear fuel-cycle.

3 S. Boyle, *Limiting Climate Change: An Assessment of Global/Regional/National Energy-CO_2 Scenarios* (Association for the Conservation of Energy, 9 Sherlock Mews, London, 1990).

4 H. L. Schmid, *Energy Scenarios, Technologies and Strategies and Their Impact on CO_2 Emissions* (Federal Energy Office, Berne, Switzerland, Mar. 1989).

5 J. Cook, 'Nuclear Follies', *Forbes*, 11 Feb. 1985.

6 D. Fishlock, 'Lord Marshall Attacks U-Turn on Reactors', *Financial Times*, 29 Jan. 1990.

7 B. Keepin and G. Kats, 'Greenhouse Warming: Comparative Analysis of Nuclear and Efficiency Abatement Strategies', *Energy Policy* (Dec. 1988), vol. 16, no. 6, pp. 538–61.

8 'Scenario B' in J. A. Edmonds, J. Reilly, J. R. Trabalka, and D. E. Reichle, *An Analysis of Possible Future Atmospheric Retention of Fossil Fuel CO_2* (United States Department of Energy DOE/OR/21400-1, Washington, DC, Sept. 1984).

9 In the published technical version of this analysis (see Keepin and Kats, n. 7), a second scenario is also analysed, and together the two scenarios provide a range of results that reflect future uncertainty in business-as-usual energy futures. Since the conclusions are similar in both cases, only the less extreme scenario is analysed here.

10 For detailed description of the model, see J. Edmonds and J. Reilly, 'Global Energy and CO_2 to the Year 2050', *Energy Journal* (1983), vol. 4, no. 3, pp. 21–47, and J. Edmonds and J. Reilly, 'A Long-Term Global Energy-Economic Model of Carbon Dioxide Release from Fossil Fuel Use', *Energy Economics* (1983), vol. 5, pp. 74-88. Detailed sensitivity and uncertainty analyses have been conducted with this model, including a probabilistic scenario analysis utilizing sophisticated Monte Carlo techniques. See J. M. Reilly *et al.*, 'Uncertainty Analysis of the IEA/ORAU CO_2 Emissions Model', *Energy Journal* (1987), vol. 8, no. 3, pp. 1–30.

11 Technically, the TW is a unit of power, and the TW-year is a unit of primary energy. The precise unit here is TW-year per year, but since the 'year' appears in both the numerator and denominator, this is commonly abbreviated in the literature as simply TW.

12 In the IPCC 'Country Study Base Case', primary energy demand in 2025 is 24.2 TW, with carbon emissions of 12.2 Gt/y: from 'Energy and Industry Subgroup Report', draft report for IPCC, pp. 2-42, Mar. 1990.

13 Coal is the most carbon-intensive fossil fuel, followed by oil and then natural gas. Carbon emissions per unit primary fuel burned are 0.75 Gt/TW-y for coal, 0.62 Gt/TW-y for oil, and 0.43 Gt/TW-y for gas: from G. Marland, 'The Impact of Synthetic Fuels on Global CO_2 Emission', in W. Clark (ed.), *CO_2 Review 1982* (Oxford University Press, Oxford, 1982).

14 The time-lag is attributed primarily to the thermal inertia of the oceans, which can warm only slowly.

15 This assumes no major contribution from shale oil or tar sands. Note that emissions of the greenhouse gas N_2O from coal combustion are also displaced.

16 Given that most studies of the greenhouse warming problem look forward 100 years or more, the reader may wonder why we consider only the next few decades here. The purpose is to explore the prospects for a nuclear response to the green-house problem under the most promising assumptions, and this requires a major transition to nuclear power over the next few decades. Beyond this time horizon, it is simply assumed for the sake of argument that all further growth in energy demand would be supplied by nuclear power (or some other CO_2-benign source). Hence, the calculations do not extend beyond 2025 (if they did, the resulting average rates of nuclear capacity installation would be even higher than those calculated below).

17 Cost data are in 1987 US dollars; see 'A Comparison of Future Costs of Nuclear and Coal-Fired Electricity: An Update' (Study Group of the Committee on Financial Considerations, US Council for Energy Awareness, July 1987). A kilowatt-hour is 1,000 watts used for one hour.

18 This figure is explained in section 13.2.1.

19 Private communication, French Embassy, Washington, DC, Oct.1987.

20 From this point onwards, the terms kW, MW, and GW refer to electricity, or to electric capacity. Note that 1 GW=1,000 MW=1,000,000 kW.

21 As a further optimistic assumption, this analysis ignores the energy (and associated carbon emissions) that it would take actually to build the nuclear plants. A recent study concludes that large nuclear power systems would yield only a relatively small amount of net energy under optimistic assumptions, and negligible-to-negative net energy under less optimistic assumptions. (The study also cites an earlier report that wind-powered electrical generating systems are not producers of net energy, though this was for designs prior to 1985, and considerable advances have been made since then.) See G. Tyner Sr., R. Costanza, and R. G. Fowler, 'The Net-Energy Yield of Nuclear Power,' *Energy* (1988), vol. 13, no. 1, pp. 73-81.

22 In all cases, primary-to-secondary conversion efficiency for coal is assumed to be 33 per cent, nuclear-plant capacity factors are assumed to be 65 per cent (the world-wide average has been around 63 per cent for twenty years), and plant life-times are assumed to be thirty years. These are typical averages, and while they could change over time due to technological improvement, this cannot be predicted. Moreover, such changes could offset one another; for example, improved conversion efficiency for coal would tend to increase the nuclear capacity required to displace coal, whereas improved nuclear-plant capacity factors would tend to decrease the required capacity. Rather than attempt to guess

the future evolution of these details, values known to be reasonable today are assumed.

23 Using data from *Nucleonics Week*, 4 June 1987.

24 In developing countries, plant capacity factors have tended to be low, which would mean that even more installed capacity might be required in practice.

25 See Keepin and Kats, n. 7.

26 J. Van Domelen, *Power to Spare: The World Bank and Electricity Conservation* (The World Wildlife Fund, Washington, DC, 1988).

27 Carbon dioxide emissions by 2025 would be roughly the same as today's level, and emissions thereafter in this scenario would grow steadily due to increased oil and gas combustion. See Keepin and Kats, n. 7.

28 In principle, it would be possible for nuclear power to substitute for oil and gas also (for example, cars and trucks could be run on electricity or nuclear electrolytic hydrogen). However, maximum carbon reduction would result from displacing coal, so this would presumably be done first, and the point here is that even to displace coal would require more plants than could feasibly be built over the next several decades.

29 N. Kouvaritakis, *Exploring the Robustness of Energy Policy Measures Designed to Reduce Long-Term Accumulations of Carbon Dioxide: An Approach* (International Energy Agency, Paris, June 1989).

30 N. Kouvaritakis, *Policy Measures and their Impact on CO_2 Emissions and Accumulations* (International Energy Agency, Paris, Dec. 1989).

31 See Keepin and Kats, n. 7.

32 J. Goldemberg, T. B. Johansson, A. K. N. Reddy, and R. H. Williams, *Energy for a Sustainable World* (Wiley Eastern Ltd, New Delhi, 1988).

33 Calculated using approximate empirical values of $3,000 per kW installed (1987 $), 20 per cent per year nominal fixed-charge rate (including capitalized interest during construction), 0.65 capacity factor (which is optimistic for US plants), and 1 cent/kWh each for fuel operation and maintenance, and net capital additions (data are from Komanoff Associates, New York, USA). This calculation gives busbar cost (the cost before the electricity enters the grid). A delivered kWh costs about 5 per cent more, due to grid losses incurred in transmission and distribution. Such losses are much higher in developing countries – up to 40 per cent (this is not accounted for in the scenario). Note that electricity saved through end-use efficiency is automatically 'delivered', because it is already on site. Thus, strictly speaking, the analysis should compare the cost of efficiency savings with the cost of delivered electricity, but this is not done here (which means that the results in Figures 13.2 and 13.3 are biased slightly toward nuclear power).

34 See e.g., H. Geller *et al.*, *Annual Review of Energy* (1987), vol. 12, p. 357, where the weighted average cost of electricity-saving measures in Table 4 is 2 cents/kWh. A detailed study of the residential sector in Michigan showed that 29 per cent of electricity consumption forecast for the year 2005 could be saved at an average cost of 2 cents/kWh. The average cost of the first 75 per cent of savings is only 1.1 cents/kWh: F. Krause, A. Rosenfeld, and M. Levine, Analysis of Michigan's Demand-Side Electricity Resources in the Residential Sector (Lawrence Berkeley Laboratory, Berkeley, CA, Apr. 1988).

35 This is apparently the argument in P. M. S. Jones, 'Greenhouse Warming – A Comment', *Energy Policy* (Dec. 1989), vol. 17, no. 6, pp. 613–4, and in F. Conrad,

'Kernenergie-Ausbau vs. rationellere Energienutzung zur Loesung des CO_2-Problems?' *Atomwirtschaft* (Aug./Sept. 1989).

36 Money not invested in nuclear power will not necessarily be invested in efficiency instead, but money invested in nuclear power certainly cannot be invested in efficiency, and may create contrary incentives. For example, in an effort to recover their over-investment in nuclear and coal-fired power plants, many US utilities discontinued efficiency programmes in favour of power marketing. The Electric Power Research Institute estimated that this will create, by 2000, roughly 35 GW of new on-peak national electric demand: *Impact of Demand-Side Management on Future Customer Electricity Demand* (Palo Alto, CA, EPRI EM-4815-SR, Oct. 1986), p. 4-9. Investments in power plants and in efficiency are thus not merely neutral competitors for resources; they are antithetical to some extent, because utilities require increased demand to pay for new plants.

37 See Keepin and Kats, n. 7.

38 See e.g., *A Comparison of Future Costs of Nuclear and Coal-Fired Electricity: An Update* (Study Group of the Committee on Financial Considerations, US Council for Energy Awareness (USCEA), Washington, DC, July 1987).

39 P. E. Gray, 'Nuclear Reactors Everyone Will Love', *Wall Street Journal*, 17 Aug. 1989.

40 For example, Amory Lovins of Rocky Mountain Institute (RMI) argues that the US can save 75 per cent of its electricity consumption for approximately 0.5 cents/kWh. Reported in RMI's *Competitek* Update Service (Rocky Mountain Institute, Snowmass Colorado).

41 A. B. Lovins *et al.*, *The State of the Art: Drivepower* (Rocky Mountain Institute, Snowmass, Colorado, Apr. 1989).

42 C. Flavin, *Slowing Global Warming: A Worldwide Strategy* (Worldwatch Paper 91, Worldwatch Institute, Washington, DC). From Table 4 on p. 47, 'Carbon Avoidance Cost' is $19/ton for efficiency and $617/ton for nuclear power; the ratio is thus 617/19=32.5.

43 B. Keepin and G. Kats, 'The Efficiency-Renewable Synergism', *Energy Policy* (1989), vol. 17, pp. 614–6.

44 B. Keepin and M. Barrett, 'Critique of UK IPCC Case Study,' June 1990.

45 T. Jackson and S. Roberts, *Getting Out of the Greenhouse: An Agenda for UK Action on Energy Policy* (Friends of the Earth, London, Dec. 1989).

46 A. Gadgil and G. de M. Jannuzzi, 'Conservation Potential of Compact Fluorescent Lamps in India and Brazil' (draft version, Lawrence Berkeley Laboratory, 2 May 1989).

47 Figures given are undiscounted 1985 dollars. H. Geller *et al.*, 'Electricity Conservation in Brazil: Potential and Progress', *Energy* (1988), vol. 13, no. 6, pp. 469-83.

48 L. M. Lidsky, 'Safe Nuclear Power', *The New Republic*, 28 Dec. 1987.

49 A. M. Weinberg and I. Spiewak, 'Inherently Safe Nuclear Reactors and a Second Nuclear Era', *Science*, 29 June 1984.

50 K. E. Stahlkopf, J. C. DeVine, and W. R. Sugnet, *US ALWR Programme Sets Out Utility Requirements for Future Plants* (Electric Power Research Institute, Palo Alto, CA, 1988).

51 C. F. McDonald, 'Nuclear Power – A Technology Vector in Carbon Dioxide Emission Reduction and Acid Rain Abatement', paper delivered to 10th International Conference SMiRT, Anaheim, CA, 14–18 Aug. 1989.

52 L. Hahn and B. Nockenburg, 'Aspekte des Exports und der Militaerischen Nutzbarkeit von HTR-Modulanlagen', *Auftrag der Gruenen im Bundestag* (Oeko Institut e.V., Freiburg, Federal Republic of Germany, May 1989).

53 'Outlook on Advanced Reactors,' *Nucleonics Week*, 30 Mar. 1989, quoted in Flavin, n. 1.

54 Ibid.

55 N. Rader *et al.*, *Power Surge: The Status and Near-Term Potential of Renewable Energy Technologies* (Public Citizen, Washington, DC, May, 1989).

56 *Wind Energy in Denmark: Research and Technological Development, 1990* (Ministry of Energy, Danish Energy Agency, Copenhagen, Denmark, 1990). Based on levelized cost of 0.334 DK/kWh, and an exchange rate of $1 = 6.273 DK.

57 See Keepin and Barrett, n. 44.

58 J. Ogden, R. H. Williams, and M. Fulmer, *Cogeneration Applications of Biomass Gasifier/Gas Turbine Technologies in the Cane Sugar and Alcohol Industries* (Center for Energy and Environmental Studies, Princeton University, Princeton, NJ, 1990).

59 See Rader *et al.*, n. 55.

60 R. L. San Martin, *Environmental Emissions from Energy Technology Systems: The Total Fuel Cycle* (US Department of Energy, Washington, DC, Apr. 1989).

61 Note that this is equivalent to baseload electricity generation.

62 *The Potential of Renewable Energy: An Interlaboratory White Paper* United States Department of Energy, SERI/TP-260-3674, DE 90000322, Washington, DC, Mar. 1990), Appendix G.

63 J. Ogden and R.H. Williams, *Solar Hydrogen: Moving Beyond Fossil Fuels* (World Resources Institute, Washington, DC, Oct. 1989).

64 Ibid., p.19.

65 See Rader *et al.*, n. 55.

66 B. Bodlund, E. Mills, T. Karlsson, and T. B. Johansson, 'The Challenge of Choices: Technology Options for the Swedish Electricity Sector', in Johansson *et al.*, (eds.), *Electricity* (Lund University Press, Lund, Sweden, 1989). Reprinted in this volume.

67 O. Hohmeyer, *Social Costs of Energy Consumption; External Effects of Electricity Generation in the Federal Republic of Germany* (Springer Verlag, New York, 1988).

68 Conversions from 1982 Deutschmarks to US dollars were done by Sandia National Laboratories in Albuquerque, NM, using a factor of 0.63, as reported in Section IV-1 of Rader *et al.*, n. 55.

69 P. Jones, 'Social Costs of Energy', *Atom* (1990), vol. 403, pp. 23–7.

70 E. Teller, address to American Association of Petroleum Geologists, quoted in *San Francisco Chronicle*, 7 June 1990.

71 Headline on advertisement for Earth Day, 22 Apr. 1990, appearing in US magazines and Sunday supplements, sponsored by United States Council for Energy Awareness, Washington, DC, 1990.

72 C. Hohenemser, 'The Accident at Chernobyl: Health and Environmental Consequences and the Implications for Risk Management', *Annual Review of Energy 13*, (Palo Alto, CA 1988), pp. 383–428.

73 Ibid. See also F. v. Hippel and T. B. Cochran, 'Chernobyl: Estimating Long Term Health Effects', *Bulletin of Atomic Scientists* (Aug./Sept. 1986), vol. 3, no. 1. (The heroic Soviet helicopter pilot who dropped sand and concrete to cap the radiation spewing from Chernobyl contracted leukaemia and died in July 1990 of complications from a bone marrow transplant in Seattle.)

74 C. Flavin, 'Reassessing Nuclear Power', in *State of the World 1987*, (W. W. Norton, New York, 1987).

75 M. Simons, 'Study in East Finds Unsafe Atom Plants', *International Herald Tribune*, 8 June 1990.

76 S. Islam and K. Lindgren, 'How Many Reactor Accidents Will There Be?', *Nature* (21 Aug. 1986).

77 *Managing the Nation's Commercial High-Level Radioactive Waste* (Office of Technology Assessment, Washington, DC, 1985).

78 L. J. Carter, 'Nuclear Imperatives and Public Trust: Dealing With Radioactive Waste', *Issues in Science and Technology* (Winter 1987).

79 E. W. Colglazier and R. B. Langum, 'Policy Conflicts in the Process for Siting Nuclear Waste Repositories', *Annual Review of Energy 13* (Palo Alto, CA, 1988), pp. 317–57.

80 'Nuclear Cleanup Costs Go Higher: 50 per cent over original estimate', *San Francisco Chronicle*, 4 July 1990.

81 L. Roberts, 'Atomic Bomb Doses Reassessed', *Science*, 18 Dec. 1987.

82 M. J. Gardner *et al.*, 'Results of Case-Control Study of Leukaemia and Lymphoma Among Young People Near Sellafield Nuclear Plant in West Cumbria' and 'Methods and Basic Data of Case-control Study of Leukaemia and Lymphoma among Young People Near Sellafield Nuclear Plant in West Cumbria', *British Medical Journal*, 17 Feb. 1990.

83 L. Roberts, 'British Radiation Study Throws Experts into Tizzy', *Science*, 6 Apr. 1990.

84 'BNF cover fallout', *The Times*, 10 Mar. 1990.

85 D. Albright and H. A. Feiveson, 'Plutonium recycling and the Problem of Nuclear Proliferation', *Annual Review of Energy 13* (Palo Alto, CA, 1988), pp. 239–65.

86 United States Department of Energy, n. 62, p. 8.

Chapter 14: The Challenge of Choices: Technology Options for the Swedish Electricity Sector Birgit Bodlund, Evan Mills, Tomas Karlsson, and Thomas Johansson

Reprint with only minor editorial changes of the concluding chapter in
T. B. Johansson, B. Bodlund, and R. H. Williams (eds.), *Electricity: Efficient End-Use and New Generation Technologies and Their Planning Implications*, (Lund University Press, 1989), pp. 883–947. The *Electricity* project was sponsored by Vattenfall (the Swedish State Power Board) and marshalled an international team including energy experts from Swedish industry, universities, the US Congress

Office of Technology Assessment, several US National Laboratories, General Electric, and Royal Dutch Shell.

1   Swedish State Power Board, *The Vattenfall three-year plan: 1989–1991* (Stockholm, 1988), in Swedish.

2   This is the Vattenfall extension of the current forecast interval for 1997 to the year 2010. The 145-TWh demand-level represents the centre of a 120–170 TWh/year range projected for the year 2010. The corresponding range of average growth-rates is –0.4 per cent/year to 1.2 per cent/year.

3   Government of Canada, *The changing atmosphere: implications for global security* (conference statement, Toronto, 27–30 June 1988).

4   Swedish Ministry of Finance, *Long-term economic planning report*, Swedish Government Official Report (SOU) (Stockholm, 1987), in Swedish.

5   Swedish State Power Board, *Scenarios for long-term planning* (Stockholm, 1988), in Swedish.

6   See *Vattenfall plan*, n. 1.

7   By 'commercially available' we mean technologies that are available in today's market-place.

8   Structural change plays a large role in the development of household-appliance electricity use between 1987 and 2010. For example, in single-family homes the saturation of combination refrigerator/freezers increases from 9 per cent to 40 per cent; the saturation of single electric stoves decreases from 84 per cent to 30 per cent with a shift to microwave/electric stove combinations – increasing from 14 per cent to 70 per cent; the use of electric clothes dryers grows from 18 per cent to 85 per cent; and 45 per cent of homes are expected to have two combination refrigerator/freezers in the year 2010 versus only 6 per cent of homes in 1987. The model also accounts for growth in electricity services such as increasing TV size and viewing time, refrigerator volumes, and so on.

9   This sector includes a wide variety of customers and they are grouped in the model into two categories: floor-area dependent (for example, retail stores, wholesale stores, banks, athletic facilities, insurance, and defence) and floor-area independent (for example street lighting, trains, agriculture, and construction companies).

10 See Swedish Ministry of Finance report, n. 4.

11 The PREDECO model and data-bases (Lars-Göran Carlsson, personal communication, 10 Oct. 1988) gives a somewhat higher figure for single-family homes, 2.4 TWh for 1986. Note also that electricity consumption in vacation homes has risen from an average of 2,718 kWh/year in 1972 to 4,281 kWh/year in 1986. These homes are not subject to the national thermal construction standards.

12 Personal communication, Gunnar Larsson, Vattenfall, 31 Oct. 1988.

13 B. Bodlund, E. Mills, T. Karlsson, and T. B. Johansson, *Technical support document for the challenge of choices: technology options for the Swedish electricity sector* (Lund University, 1989).

14 Determining the Frozen-Efficiency baselines for space-heating and for the service sector is not as straightforward as for other sectors. In developing the heating baseline, we assume that there are no efficiency improvements beyond 1987, conversions to electricity occur as shown in the Reference Scenario, new homes are constructed at today's average use per home, and internal heat-gains increase according to the Frozen-Efficiency baseline for household appliances. The baseline for the service sector is an extrapolation of the 1970–87 growth trend.

Although an attempt has been made to remove electric heating from the historical data series upon which this estimate is based, the absence of high-quality statistics leaves open the possibility that heating growth in the 1980s has biased the extrapolation.

15 This is one of six scenarios (Scenario 'F') developed at Vattenfall in the Spring of 1988. See Swedish State Power Board, n. 5.

16 Defined as the difference between the value of annual energy-cost savings and the levelized capital cost of the conversion. Typical winter-time furnace efficiencies of approximately 80 per cent are assumed.

17 B. L. Gardiner, M. A. Piette, and J. P. Harris, *Measured results of energy conservation retrofits in non-residential buildings: an update of the BECA-CR data base* (Proceedings of the 1984 ACEEE Summer Study on Energy Efficiency in Buildings; also as Lawrence Berkeley Laboratory Technical Report no. 17881, 1984). Including fuel and electricity, this study contains 311 buildings (schools, small offices, hospitals, large offices, other services). The retrofits include operations and maintenance, lighting, ventilation, envelope measures, water-heating, load management, and others. The economic data are available for a subset of 134 buildings with electricity-saving retrofits. See the reference for general information and results; additional electricity-specific data are from Kathy Greely and Mary Ann Piette, Lawrence Berkeley Laboratory, memorandum of 9 Nov. 1987.

18 E. Abel, 'Use of electricity in commercial buildings', in T. B. Johansson, B. Bodlund, and R. H. Williams (eds.), *Electricity* (Lund University Press, 1989).

19 M. A. Piette, L. W. Wall, and B. L. Gardiner, 'Measured performance', *Ashrae Journal* (1986), vol. 28, no. 1; E. Mills, J. P. Harris, and A. H. Rosenfeld, 'Developing demand-side energy resources in the United States: trends and policies', *Énergie Internationale* (1988–9), L'Institut D'Économie et de Politique de l'Énergie, Grenoble, France, in French. Available in English as Lawrence Berkeley Laboratory Technical Report no. 24920.

20 All base-year values for electric heating are 1987 consumption, normalized to average-year weather conditions (personal communication, Anders Sjögren, Vattenfall, 15 Jan. 1989).

21 A. Elmroth, 'Building design and electricity use in single-family houses', in Johansson *et al., Electricity*. According to Elmroth's chapter, of all homes heated with electric-resistance systems and constructed before 1982, only 25 per cent of the window area (6.57 million square metres) is triple-glazed. Roughly 1 per cent of the area is single-glazed windows and 1 per cent is quadruple-glazed. Even more remarkable, only 60 per cent of the window area installed between 1975 and 1981 was triple-glazed.

22 According to the Reference Scenario, the increased consumption for single-family homes is 1.7 TWh/year by 2010. Were all of these homes heated at the efficiency described in Elmroth's chapter (see n. 21) – 2,500 kWh/y for space-heating and 2,500 kWh/y for water-heating – the resultant demand growth would be 1.1 TWh.

23 C. G. Granqvist, 'Energy-efficient windows: options with present and forthcoming technology', Johansson *et al., Electricity*.

24 T. Berntsson, 'Heat pumps', in Johansson *et al., Electricity*.

25 S. Eketorp, 'Electrotechnologies and steelmaking', in Johansson *et al., Electricity*. S. O. Santen and J. Feinman, 'Pilot plant studies of the PLASMASCRAP process', *Iron & Steelmaker* (Aug. 1988), pp. 24–8.

26 H. Schaefer and M. Rudolf, 'New electrothermal processes', in Johansson *et al.*, *Electricity*.

27 See n. 25.

28 The curves represent today's hydro and fuel-based generation plus that from the nuclear plants remaining in each year of the period up to 2010, at which time nuclear generation will be zero. The height of the curves includes today's accepted reliability margin, using the rule of thumb that the maximum tolerable demand = 0.80 x hydro production potential + 0.90 x thermal production potential. (Environmental restrictions will require additional investments in the existing fuel-based power plants if they are to be used much more heavily than is the case today.)

29 Based on an oil-boiler efficiency of 80 per cent.

30 Local Government's Research Institute on Public Finance and Administration (Amtskommunernes og Kommunernes Forskningsinstitut, AKF), Danish research project: potentials for electricity conservation, 1988.

31 J. Petäjä and H. Hausen, *The possibilities for electricity saving and decentralized power generation during 1986–2020* (Helsinki University of Technology, Report 24, 1988), in Finnish.

32 The SERI Solar/Conservation Study Group, *A new prosperity: building a sustainable energy future* (Andover, Mass., Brickhouse, 1981); R. H. Williams, 'A low-energy future for the US', *Energy the International Journal* (1987), vol. 12, pp. 929–44.

33 F. L. Krause, A. H. Rosenfeld, M. D. Levine, J. Brown, D. Connell, P. du Pont, K. M. Greely, M. Meal, A. K. Meier, E. Mills, and B. Nordman, *Analysis of Michigan's demand-side electricity resources in the residential sector* (Lawrence Berkeley Laboratory Technical Report no. 23025, 1987).

34 B. D. Hunn, M. L. Baughman, S. C. Silver, A. H. Rosenfeld, and H. Akbari, *Technical potential for electrical energy conservation and peak demand reduction in Texas buildings* (Report to the Public Utility Commission of Texas, Center for Energy Studies, The University of Texas at Austin, Conservation and Solar Energy Program, 1986).

35 A. Usibelli, B. Gardiner, W. Luhrsen, and A. K. Meier, *A residential conservation data base for the Pacific Northwest* (Report to the Bonneville Power Administration, Lawrence Berkeley Laboratory Technical Report no. 17055, 1983). Perhaps most relevant to the Nordic situation, this study evaluated the electric demand-side potentials in a large hydropower-based region of the Pacific Northwestern United States where a large generating company sells power to many small distributors. This study determined that the base-case forecast of residential-sector demand by the year 2000 (7,728 average megawatts) could be reduced to 58 per cent of their forecast levels if all technically feasible conservation measures costing less than 15 cents/kWh were implemented. Of this total, 87 per cent could be realized at a cost of 4 cents/kWh.

36 A. K. Meier, J. Wright, and A. H. Rosenfeld, *Supplying energy through greater efficiency: the potential for conservation in California's residential sector* (Berkeley, University of California Press, 1983); H. S. Geller, A. de Almeida, B. Barkovich, C. Blumstein, D. Goldstein, A. K. Meier, P. Miller, O. de la Moriniere, A. H. Rosenfeld, and L. Schuck, *Residential conservation power plant study: phase 1 – technical potential* (prepared for the Residential Conservation Services Department, Pacific Gas and Electric Company, American Council for an Energy-Efficient Economy, 1986).

37 Marbek Resources Consultants, *Electricity conservation supply curves for Ontario* (Report prepared for the Ontario Ministry of Energy, Toronto, 1987);.
J. B. Robinson, 'Insurmountable opportunities? Canada's energy efficiency resources', *Energy the International Journal* (1987), vol. 12, no. 5, pp. 403–17.

38 The CCE is effectively a 'busbar' cost indicator for conservation technologies and can thus be directly compared with levelized cost (fixed + variable) of new electricity supply. To ensure compatibility, we account for the reinvestment costs if efficiency technologies must be replaced during the thirty-year economic lifetime of a reference power plant. (Note: the economic calculations in this chapter are based on 1987 US dollars. We use a 6-per-cent real discount rate to determine the choice of end-use strategies, except in the Reference Scenario where consumer-investment behaviour corresponds to a significantly higher discount rate.)

39 For a given pool of electricity consumers that make investments to increase end-use efficiency, there will be a range of costs and savings. Thus, one can envision a corresponding distribution of costs of conserved energy. From a societal perspective, over-investment in efficiency may occur if some participants in the right-hand tail of this distribution have CCEs higher than the cost of new energy supply. This risk is low when the average CCE is itself well below this 'break-even' cost and can be further minimized by careful definition of the 'target group'. Some analysts allow the more economic projects to 'carry' the less economic ones, but our methodology is to judge each investment on its own merits.

40 E. Mills, *Energy and the marketplace for residential appliances in Sweden* (Department of Environment and Energy Systems Studies, Lund University, 1988), manuscript in preparation. Scatter diagrams of retail price versus total annual electricity use also show little or no indication of an extra cost for higher efficiency. This is true even within narrow size-ranges (for example, among 200–250-litre models). We have observed the same result for residential clothes-washers and for stand-alone domestic water-heaters.

41 Gross-domestic-product statistics from Organization for Economic Co-operation and Development, OECD National Accounts, Main Aggregates (1987), vol. 1, pp. 62–3, to 1980. Data for 1981 to 1987 are from Swedish Central Statistics Bureau, *Statistical abstract of Sweden* (Stockholm, 1988), p. 230, in Swedish. For the 1987 to 2010 estimate, we use the standard 1.9-per-cent annual growth estimate.

42 Decoupling of electricity and GDP is occurring in some other industrialized countries: see A. H. Rosenfeld and J. G. Koomey, *Promoting efficiency investments in new buildings* (testimony before the Wisconsin Public Service Commission, Docket no. 05-EP-5: Hearings on Advance Plan 5, 1988), for an illustration of trends in the United States.

43 S. F. Baldwin, 'Energy-efficient electric motor drive systems', in Johansson *et al.*, *Electricity*.

44 A. Usibelli, S. Greenberg, M. Meal, A. Mitchell, R. Johnson, G. Sweitzer, F. Rubenstein, and D. Arasteh, *Commercial-sector conservation technologies* (Lawrence Berkeley Laboratory Technical Report no. 18543, 1985).

45 The maximum acceptable loss-of-load probability (LOLP) criterion in Sweden is 0.1 per cent (9 hours per year over the entire system) and the maximum risk of energy shortage criterion is 3.0 per cent (rationing will occur 3 years out of 100). Historically, LOLP has been very low in Sweden, thanks to the large share of hydro-power in the system. However, the thermal-power share has increased due to the nuclear programme and along with it the issues of reliability. The generating capacity, upon which reliability calculations are based, now permits a demand level of 145 TWh/year (including the Vattenfall convention of including 5 TWh of imports) based on these criteria. The reliability factors are commonly summarized using the rule-of-thumb that demand must not rise above the level, defined in H. Tsuchiya, *Electricity conservation in Japan*, Proceedings of the NATO Advanced Study Institute Meeting on Energy Efficiency in Buildings (Portugal, 1987).

46 For district heating provided with natural-gas fuel, we assume the current cost in Sweden of 2.7 cents/kWh. To this we add 0.35 cents/kWh to account for the transmission system cost (Vattenfall estimates, 85-per-cent boiler efficiency).

47 K. Pillai, 'Pressurized fluidized bed combustion', in Johannson *et al.*, *Electricity*.

48 E. D. Larson, P. Svenningsson, and I. Bjerle, 'Biomass gasification for gas turbine power generation', in Johannson *et al.*, *Electricity*.

49 A. Hildeman, G. Rutegard, and G. Tibblin, *The tree-section method: integrated production of forest energy and pulp feedstock* (Swedish University of Agricultural Science, Department of Forest-Industry-Market Studies, Report no. 19, Uppsala 1986), in Swedish; M. Parikka, *Economic analysis of energy forest plantations – a 'future-oriented' calculation* (Swedish University of Agricultural Science, Department of Forest-Industry-Market Studies, Uppsala, 1988), in Swedish.

50 R. H. Williams and E. D. Larson, 'Expanding roles for gas turbines in power generation', in Johannson *et al.*, *Electricity*.

51 Official Report of the Swedish Government (SOU), *Sites for wind power* (Stockholm, Allmänna Förlaget, 1988), in Swedish.

52 The estimated cost interval is 6.3–7.9 cents/kWh (personal communication, Göran Svensson, Vattenfall, 10 Feb. 1989).

53 L. Blomen, 'Fuel cells', and D. Carlson, 'Low-cost power from thin-film photovoltaics', in Johannson *et al.*, *Electricity*.

54 Swedish State Power Board, *Biofuels* (Report no. UM-1988/40, Project no. 93078, Stockholm, 1988) (in Swedish) and see Larson *et al.*, n. 48.

55 See n. 54.

56 T. Olsson, *Production results in Swedish energy forest plantations* (Swedish University of Agricultural Science, Department of Ecology and Environment, Energy Plantations Group, Uppsala, 1986), in Swedish; L. Christersson, *Intensively grown woody biomass production on sandy soil. Biomassa och Energi*, 1985 (in Swedish).

57 This corresponds to a productivity of 14.4 tons of dry matter per hectare per year: T. B. Johansson, P. Steen, E. Bogren, L. R. Eriksson, S. Karlsson, and P. Svenningsson, *Perspectives on energy* (Stockholm, Liber Press, 1985), in Swedish.

58 The hydro estimate includes approximately 2 TWh of additional output beyond the 1987 level. The remaining capacity in oil-condensing and gas-turbine units (approx. 25 TWh/year) is allocated to providing reliability reserves and is thus not included in these 'typical-year' calculations. Because we dedicate these plants to this purpose, the construction of additional excess capacity is unnecessary to fulfil the reliability criterion. We construct our supply scenarios assuming no net power imports in a typical year.

59 See Larson *et al.*, n. 48.

60 See Bodlund *et al.*, n. 13.

61 We have apportioned the weather-independent consumption for our scenarios evenly across the months, except for industrial use in July which we reduce to 67 per cent of the annual average, due to the month-long national holiday: Swedish State Power Board, *Market information from ME* (Stockholm,1988), p. 18, in Swedish.

62 It has not been possible to identify the costs for all of the efficiency measures in the scenarios. In the Efficiency Scenario, the supply curve includes costs for 66 out of the 83 TWh efficiency improvement beyond 1987. There is no reason to believe that the remaining TWh are more or less costly, but we assume that they will cost 50 per cent more per kWh. In the High-Efficiency Scenario, we assume that the unmonetized electricity services cost 100 per cent more per kWh. No estimate is made for the Advanced-Technology Scenario.

63 Other important greenhouse gases are methane, CFC-11, CFC-12, nitrous oxide, and trophospheric ozone. Carbon dioxide is thought to be responsible for about 50 per cent of the warming effect.

64 Swedish State Power Board. *Natural gas, health, environment* (Stockholm, 1984), p. 104, In Swedish; I. Stjernquist, L. Brinck, P. Schlyter, P. Svenningsson, and T. B. Johansson, *Environment and energy* (prepared for the National Environmental Protection Board, Report 3238,1986), in Swedish.

65 Swedish National Energy Administration and National Environmental Protection Board, *New sulphur restrictions from combustion sources* (Report 3412, 1987). The 1995 emissions guidelines for power-production facilities are: sulphur (0.05 g S/MJ fuel burned), NO_x (0.05–0.10 g NO_x/MJ, units over 300 MW_e), and 0.10–0.20 (g NO_x/MJ, units below 300 MWe), particulates (20 mg/MJ, annual average for coal-based systems).

66 We select a Plasmascrap process based on natural gas. Plasmascrap can also use 45 kg coal per ton of steel produced (see Santen and Feinman, n. 25). To put this prospective emissions-increase in perspective, if SSAB's use of coal (650 kg/ton) remains the same in 2010 and its production grows from 3 megatons/year to 3.6 Mtons/year, then coal use will be 2,340 kilotons annually. Given Vattenfall's assumed production trends, steel output from electric arc furnaces would grow from 1.6 Mton/year to 1.9 Mtons/year. The corresponding incremental coal requirement in 2010 is 86 kilotons (at 45 kg/ton).

67 In calculating Sweden's total CO_2 emissions, we include the energy-related uses of coal, oil, and gas from: International Energy Agency, *Energy balances of OECD countries: 1985/1986* (Paris, 1988).

68 International Institute for Environment and Development and the World Resources Institute, *World Resources 1987* (Basic Books, Inc., New York, 1988), pp. 248 and 335.

69 World Congress on Climate and Development, Draft *'Hamburg Manifesto'* (1988); and see Govt. of Canada statement, n 3.

70 H. C. Cheng and M. Steinberg, 'A study on the systematic control of CO_2 emissions from fossil-fueled power plants in the U.S.', *Environmental Progress* (1986), vol. 5, no. 4, pp. 245–55.

71 See Eketorp, n. 25.

72 H. Geller, 'Implementing electricity conservation programs: progress towards least-cost energy services among utilities in the U.S.', in Johansson *et al.*, *Electricity*.

73 R. H. Williams, 'Innovative approaches to marketing electric efficiency', in Johansson *et al.*, *Electricity*.

74 O. de la Moriniere, 'Energy service companies: the French experience', in Johansson *et al.*, *Electricity*.

75 H. Geller, J. P. Harris, M. Ledbetter, M. D. Levine, E. Mills, R. Mowris, and A. H. Rosenfeld, 'The importance of government-supported research and development in advancing energy efficiency in the United States buildings sector', in Johansson *et al.*, *Electricity*.

76 D. R. Bohi and M. B. Zimmerman, 'An update on econometric studies of energy demand behavior', *Annual Review of Energy* (1984), vol. 9, pp. 105–54.. For a discussion of electricity-price responsiveness in Sweden, see E. Mills, *The role of energy prices in shaping electricity end-use structure and demand in Sweden* (Lund University, Department of Environmental and Energy Systems Studies, Report to Vattenfall's Uppdrag 2000 project, 1988), manuscript in preparation.

77 H. Ruderman, M. D. Levine, and J. E. McMahon, 'The behaviour of the market for energy efficiency in residential appliances including heating and cooling equipment', *The Energy Journal* (1987), vol. 8, pp. 1101–24; see also Williams, n. 73.

78 Swedish State Power Board, Uppdrag 2000 – Electricity Conservation Project at Vattenfall, *Electricity conservation: a resource for both Vattenfall and its customers* (Stockholm, 1988).

79 Swedish Central Statistics Bureau, *Statistical abstract of Sweden, 1987* (1988), p. 149, in Swedish.

80 Imported uranium today costs $425 million/year, based on Vattenfall's estimate of 0.652 cents/kWh for uranium fuel in 1987 and 65 TWh of nuclear-based generation. Let us consider two simplified cases. At one extreme, the fossil-fuel imports required to generate 74 TWh$_e$/year (the difference between the Reference Scenario demand and projected hydroelectric production) would be $1,600 million at 0.86 cents/kWh (fuel) coal-import price and 40 per cent conversion efficiency in the power plant. Thus, an adverse impact on the balance of payments would result. At the other extreme, in a low-demand scenario with biomass fuel (but accounting for 15 TWh fuel-switching to imported oil at $20 per barrel), the cost of fossil fuels would be only $250 million. In addition, were district heating to be provided from biomass fuel, oil imports could be further reduced by approximately $950 million. We have not estimated the effects of new power-plant construction and conservation-related capital investment, but most of these things can be produced in Sweden. It is clear that efficiency and a domestic-based fuel-mix could have a significant positive impact on Sweden's balance of payments in the future.

81 J. Goldemberg, T. B. Johansson, A. K. N. Reddy, and R. H. Williams, *Energy for a sustainable world* (New Delhi, Wiley-Eastern Ltd., 1988).

Acknowledgements: We thank Vattenfall's Market Analysis Group, Gunnar Larsson (Head), Matti Malinen, Drasko Markovic, and Anders Sjögren for their assistance with demand modelling and for review comments. Useful discussions and review comments were also provided by Enno Abel, Harry Albinsson, Thore Berntsson, Lars Brinck, Birgitta Dangården, Sven Eketorp, Arne Elmroth, Lars Gertmar, Claes Göran Granqvist, Anders Hedenstedt, Lars Jacobsson, Jon Koomey, Eric Larson, Gunnar Leman, Måns Lönnroth,

Jørgen Nørgård, John Robinson, Peter Steen, Robert Williams, and Bo Wiman. One of us (TBJ) acknowledges the gracious support of the Swedish Energy Research Commission (Efn).

Chapter 15: Tropical Forests Norman Myers

1 *Tropical Forest Resources* (Food and Agriculture Organization, Rome, 1981); N. Myers, *Conversion of Tropical Moist Forests*, report to the National Academy of Sciences (National Research Council, Washington, DC, 1980); id., *The Primary Source: Tropical Forests and Our Future* (W. W. Norton, New York, and London, 1984); R. A. Houghton, R. D. Boone, J. M. Melillo, C. A. Palm, G. M. Woodwell, N. Myers, B. Moore, and D. L. Skole, 'Net Flux of Carbon Dioxide From Tropical Forests in 1980', *Nature* (1985), vol. 316, pp. 617–20; J.-P. Lanly, *Tropical Forest Resources* (Food and Agriculture Organization, Rome, 1982); J. M. Melillo, C. A. Palm, R. A. Houghton, G. M. Woodwell, and N. Myers, 'A Comparison of Recent Estimates of Disturbance in Tropical Forests', *Environmental Conservation* (1985), vol. 12, pp. 37–40; J. Molofsky, C. A. S. Hall, and N. Myers, *Comparison of Tropical Forest Surveys* (US Department of Energy, Washington, DC, 1986).

2 N. Myers, *Deforestation Rates in Tropical Forests and Their Climatic Implications* (Friends of the Earth, London, 1989). The original report, being six times longer than this chapter, contains much detail of deforestation assessments on a country-by-country basis, backed by 400 references. It also presents information on research methodologies and reliability of data among other background factors, plus an analysis of carbon emissions from deforestation, as well as a number of policy-appraisal and conservation recommendations. The original report lists some 400 papers and other publications dealing with deforestation, almost entirely confined to the literature of the 1980s and with emphasis on those published from 1985 onwards. Further, the survey entailed copious correspondence among other forms of communication; several bulk mailings, totalling more than 600 items, were despatched, plus numerous follow-up enquiries.

3 See Myers, n. 2.

4 W. Booth, 'Monitoring the Fate of the Forests from Space', *Science* (1989), vol. 243, pp. 1428–9; Y. J. Kaufman, C. J. Tucker, and I. Y. Fung, 'Remote Sensing of Biomass Burning in the Tropics', *Advances in Space Research* (1988), vol. 9, pp. 265–8; N. Myers, 'Tropical Deforestation and Remote Sensing', *Forest Ecology and Management* (1988), vol. 23, pp. 215–25; C. J. Tucker and P. J. Sellers, 'Satellite Remote Sensing of Primary Production', *International Journal of Remote Sensing* (1986), vol. 7, p. 1395.

5 Note that forested Amazonia is much smaller than Legal Amazonia's 5 million km^2. Note in addition that the term 'forest' as used here refers to moist forest in accord with the definition postulated earlier, hence it specifically excludes the cerrado forests, being dry woodlands, to the south of Amazonia. A few references used in this section embrace cerrado forests as well; insofar as they present important data on moist forests, they are included in this review, while allowing for the cerrado component. See R. P. da Cunha, *Deforestation Estimates Through Remote Sensing: The State of the Art in the Legal Amazonia* (Instituto Nacional Pesquisas Espaciais, São Jose dos Campos, São Paulo, 1989); P. M. Fearnside, 'Forest Management in Amazonia: The Need for New Criteria in Evaluating Economic Development Options', *Forest Ecology and Management* (1989), vol. 27,

pp. 61–79; id., 'Deforestation in Brazilian Amazonia', in G. M. Woodwell (ed.), *Biotic Impoverishment* (Cambridge University Press, New York), in press; *Avaliacao da Alteracao da Cobertura Florestal na Amazonia Legal Utilizando Sensoriamento Remoto Orbital* (Instituto de Pesquisas Espaciais, São Jose dos Campos, São Paulo, 1989).

6 For some recent appraisals of the situation, see references given above, n. 5; also H. P. Binswanger, *Brazilian Policies that Encourage Deforestation in the Amazon* (Environment Department Working Paper no. 16, The World Bank, Washington, DC, 1989); R. J. Buschbacher, C. Uhl, and E. A. S. Serrao, 'Largescale Development in Eastern Amazonia', in C. F. Jordan (ed.), *Amazonian Rainforests: Ecosystem Disturbance and Recovery* (Springer-Verlag, New York, 1987); A. D. Johns, 'Economic Development and Wildlife Conservation in Brazilian Amazonia', *Ambio* (1988), vol. 17, pp. 302–6; D. J. Mahar, 'Government Policies and Deforestation in Brazil's Amazon Region' (Environment Department Working Paper no. 7, The World Bank, Washington, DC, 1988); J.-P. Malingreau and C. J. Tucker, 'Large-Scale Deforestation in the Southern Amazon Basin of Brazil', *Ambio* (1988), vol. 17, pp. 49–55; C. A. Nobre and A. Setzer, 'Deforestation Rates in Brazilian Amazonia', paper presented at Tropical Forests and Climate Change Conference, Royal Meteorological Society, London, 19 May 1990 (Instituto de Pesquisas Espaciais, São Jose dos Campos, São Paulo, 1990); C. Peres, 'Conservation of Primates in Western Brazilian Amazonia: Progress Report to World Wildlife Fund-U.S.' (Washington, DC, 1987); A. W. Setzer and M. C. Pereira, 'Amazon Biomass Burnings in 1987 and their tropospheric emissions', *Ambio* (in press); A. W. Setzer, M. C. Pereira, A. C. Pereira Jnr., and S. A. O. Almeida, *Relatorio de Atividades do Projeto IBDF-INPE 'SEQE' – Ano 1987* (Instituto Nacional de Pesquisas Espaciais, São Jose dos Campos, São Paulo, Brazil, 1988); G. M. Woodwell, R. A. Houghton, T. A. Stone, R. F. Nelson, and W. Kovalick, 'Deforestation in the Tropics: New Measurements in the Amazon Basin Using Landsat and NOAA Advanced Very High Resolution Radiometer Imagery', *Journal of Geophysical Research* (1987), vol. 92, pp. 2157–63.

7 See Mahar, n. 6; Malingreau and Tucker, n.6; and Woodwell *et al.*, n. 6; also P. M. Fearnside, 'Spatial Concentration of Deforestation in the Brazilian Amazon', *Ambio* (1986), vol. 15, pp. 74–81; id. 'Deforestation and International Economic Development Projects in Brazilian Amazonia', *Conservation Biology* (1987), vol. 1, pp. 214–21, and 'An Ecological Analysis of Predominant Land Use in the Brazilian Amazon', *The Environmentalist* (1988), vol. 8, pp. 281–300; W. P. Groeneveld, 'Can Alternatives to Present Unsustainable Land-Use Mitigate Effects of Deforestation? The Case of Rondonia, Brazil', in *Proceedings of Symposium on Amazonia, Deforestation and Possible Effects* (46th International Congress of the Americanists, Amsterdam, 1989); R. B. Nato, 'Dispute About Destruction', *Nature* (1989), vol. 338, p. 531, and 'Burning Continues, Slightly Abated', *Nature* (1989), vol. 339, p. 569; T. A. Stone, I. F. Brown, and G. M. Woodwell, 'Estimates of Land Use Change in Central Rondonia, Brazil, by Remote Sensing', *Forest Ecology and Management* (in press).

8 See Mahar and Malingreau and Tucker, n. 6; also R. Nelson, N. Horning, and T. Stone, 'Determining the Rate of Forest Conversion in Mato Grosso, Brazil, Using Landsat MSS and AVHRR Data', *International Journal of Remote Sensing* (1987), vol. 8, pp. 1767–84; though for a much smaller figure, see Setzer *et al.*, n. 6.

9 See Malingreau and Tucker, n. 6; J.-P. Malingreau, personal communication, 1989; C. J. Tucker, personal communication, 1989.

10 See Setzer *et al.*, n. 6.

11 See. Fearnside, n. 5 (both refs.); J. P. Malingreau, personal communication, 1989; C. J. Tucker, personal communication, 1989.

12 Estimate based on the author's discussions with some twenty-plus scientists involved.

13 See *Tropical Forest Resources* and Myers, *Conversion of Tropical Moist Forests*, n. 1.

14 Ibid.

15 Ibid.

16 See Mahar, n. 6, and Peres, n. 6; also H. P. Binswanger, *Fiscal and Legal Incentives With Environmental Effects on the Brazilian Amazon* (The World Bank, Washington, DC, 1987).

17 For a lower estimate – sharply contested – of 251,000 km^2, see da Cunha, n. 5, and *Avaliacao da Alteracao da Cobertura Florestal*, n. 5.

18 Estimates based on the author's discussions with some twenty-plus scientists involved.

19 P. Furley, *Land Cover and Land Cover Change Between Boa Vista and Maraca Island 1978–1985* (University of Edinburgh, Edinburgh, 1989); P. Furley (ed.),*The Rain Forest Frontier: Settlement and Change in Brazilian Roraima* (Routledge, London), in press.

20 See Nobre and Setzer, n. 6.

21 See *Avaliacao da Alteracao da Cobertura Florestal*, n. 5.

22 Ibid.

23 See Peres, n. 6.

24 See Johns, n. 6.

25 P. M. Fearnside, 'The Charcoal of Carajas: A Threat to the Forests of Brazil's Eastern Amazon Region', *Ambio* (1989), vol. 18, pp. 141–3.

26 Ibid.

27 See Fearnside, n. 7.

28 See*Tropical Forest Resources* and Myers, 'Conversion of Tropical Moist Forests', n. 1; F. White, *The Vegetation of Africa* (UNESCO, Paris, 1983).

29 H. Schissel, 'Zaire Seeks Better Climate for Timber', *Financial Times*, 11 Oct. 1989.

30 Department of Land Affairs, Environment and Nature Conservation (Zaire), 'Institutional Study of the Forestry Sector' (Kinshasa, 1988).

31 Ibid; R. F. W. Barnes, 'Deforestation Trends in Tropical Africa', *African Journal of Ecology* in press; Department of Land Affairs, Environment and Nature Conservation (Zaire), 'Zaire Forest Policy Review' (Kinshasa, 1988); C. Doumenge, 'La Conservation des écosystèmes forestiers du Zaire' (International Union for Conservation of Nature and Natural Resources, Gland, Switzerland, 1990); J. Goodson, *Conservation and Management of Tropical Forests and Biological Diversity in Zaire* (US Agency for International Development, Kinshasa, 1988); K. Kendrick, 'Equatorial Africa', in D. G. Campbell and H. D. Hammond (eds.), *Floristic Inventory of Tropical Countries* (New York Botanical Garden, New York, 1989), pp. 203–16; J. Kenrick, 'Deforestation in Zaire: Interim Report' (Institute for Ecology and Action Anthropology, Münchengladbach, 1989); see also C. Boeckle

and H. Croze, 'Tropical Forest Extent, Changes, Wood Production, Exports and Imports' (United Nations Environment Programme, Nairobi, 1986); and *Zaire: Conservation of Biological Diversity* (World Conservation Monitoring Centre, Cambridge, 1988).

32 For a review, see Myers, *Conversion of Tropical Moist Forests*, n. 1.

33 R. Roberts, Director of Forestry Sector, Canadian International Development Agency, Ottawa, personal communication, 1989.

34 See Kendrick, n 31.

35 See references, n. 31; R. Roberts, personal communication, 1989.

36 See *Tropical Forest Resources*, n. 1.

37 See Goodson, n. 31; Barnes, n. 31.

38 R. Cribb, 'The Politics of Environmental Protection in Indonesia' (Centre of Southeast Asian Studies, Monash University, Melbourne, 1988); J. Davidson, 'Conservation Planning in Indonesia's Transmigration Programme: Case Studies from Kalimantan' (Ministry of Transmigration, Jakarta, 1987); C. MacAndrews and C. L. Sien, (eds.), *Too Rapid Rural Development: Perceptions and Perspectives from Southeast Asia* (Ohio University Press, Athens, Ohio, 1982); L. Murphy, *A Selected Annotated Bibliography on Natural Resources and the Environment of Indonesia, and a Guide to Additional Resources* (International Institute for Environment and Development, Washington, DC, 1987); N. Myers, *Report on Visit to Jakarta for Cabinet Discussions, 12–15 September 1988* (World-Wide Fund for Nature, Zeist, Netherlands, 1988); R. G. P. Petocz, *Conservation and Development in Irian Jaya: A Strategy for Rational Resource Utilization* (World Wildlife Fund, Bogor, Indonesia, 1987); A. C. Smiet, 'Forest Conversion and Its Impact on Watershed Management in Indonesia', in T. F. Rijnberg, (ed.), *Proceedings of Joint Seminar on Watershed Management and Research*, 10–17 Feb. 1990 (Bogor, Indonesia, Duta Rimba, Jakarta, 1990); D. Setyomo, *A Review of Issues Affecting the Sustainable Development of Indonesia's Forest Land* (Ministry of Forestry, Jakarta, Indonesia, 1985); J. Tarrant *et al.*, *Natural Resources and Environmental Management in Indonesia: An Overview* (US Agency for International Development, Jakarta, 1987); A. Whitten, 'Indonesia's Transmigration Programme and Its Role in the Loss of Tropical Rain Forests', *Conservation Biology* (1987), vol. 1, pp. 239–46; A. J. Whitten, H. Haeruman, H. S. Alikodra, and M. Thohari, *Transmigration and Environment in Indonesia* (Conservation Monitoring Centre, Cambridge, 1987); *Indonesia: The Outer Islands: Issues in the Sustainable Use of Land and Forest Resources* (The World Bank, Washington, DC, 1987).

39 For regional reviews, see regional reports under the Regional Physical Planning Programme for Transmigration (Land Resources Development Centre, Overseas Development Administration, London, 1987–9; see also T. M. B. Abell, 'The Application of Land Systems Mapping to the Management of Indonesian Forests', *Journal of World Forest Resource Management* (1988), vol. 3, pp. 111–27; see also *Forests, Land and Water: Issues in Sustainable Development* (The World Bank, Jakarta, 1988).

40 See World Bank, n. 39.

41 Ibid.

42 Ibid.

43 For details, see Myers, n. 38.

44 For details of individual countries, see Myers, n. 2.

45 See references, n. 13.

46 See Myers, n. 2.

47 Ibid.

48 For some illustrative examples, see J. Battjees, *A Survey of the Secondary Vegetation in the Surroundings of Araracuara, Amazonas, Colombia* (Hugo de Vries Laboratory, University of Amsterdam, Amsterdam, 1988), on Colombia; M. C. J. Cruz, I. Zosa-Feranil, and C. L. Goce, 'Population Pressure and Migration: Implications for Upland Development in the Philippines', *Journal of Philippine Development* (1988), vol. 15, pp. 15–46, on the Philippines; Myers, n. 38, on Indonesia; D. Schumann and W. L. Patridge, *Human Ecology of Tropical Land Settlement in Latin America* (Westview Press, Boulder, Colorado, 1989), on several countries of Latin America; D. Southgate, *How to Promote Tropical Deforestation: The Case of Ecuador* (Department of Agricultural Economics, Ohio State University, Colombus, Ohio, 1990), on Ecuador; and W. C. Thiesenhusen (ed.), *Searching for Agrarian Reform in Latin America* (Unwin Hyman, Boston, Mass., 1989), on several countries of Latin America.

49 J. O. Browder, 'Development Alternatives for Tropical Rain Forests', in H. J. Leonard, (ed.), *Environment and the Poor: Development Strategies for a Common Agenda* (Transaction Books, New Brunswick, 1989), pp. 111–33; see also C. Uhl, 'Factors Controlling Succession Following Slash-and-Burn Agriculture in Amazonia', *Journal of Ecology* (1987), vol. 75, pp. 377–407.

50 E. G. Egler, 'A Zona Bragantina do Estado do Para', *Revistal Brasileira de Geografia* (1961), vol. 23, pp. 527–55.

51 See Battjees, n. 48.

52 A. H. Gentry, 'Northwest South America (Colombia, Ecuador, and Peru)', in Campbell and Hammond (eds.) (n. 31), pp. 391–400.

53 M. J. Dourojeanni, *Si El Arbol de la Quina Hablara* (Fundacion Peruana para la Conservacion de la Naturaleza, Lima, 1988).

54 A. V. Revilla, J. A. Canonizado, and M. C. Gregorio, *Forest Resources Management Report* (Forest Resources Management Task Force, Resource Policy Group, Manila, Philippines, 1987).

55 P. Hirsch, 'Deforestation and Development in Thailand', *Singapore Journal of Tropical Geography* (1987), vol. 8, pp. 129–38.

56 S. C. Chin, 'Managing Malaysia's Forests for Sustained Production', *Wallaceana* (1989), vols. 55 and 56, pp. 1–11.

57 S. M. Saulei, Director of Department of Forests, Lae, Papua New Guinea, personal communication, 1989.

58 F. N. Hepper, 'West Africa', in Campbell and. Hammond (eds.) (n. 31), pp. 189–97.

59 A. Bertrand, 'Déforestation en zone de forêt en Côte d'Ivoire', *Bois et Forêts des Tropiques* (1983), vol. 202, pp. 3–17.

60 M. D. Jenkins, *Madagascar: An Environmental Profile* (Conservation Monitoring Centre, Cambridge, 1987).

61 F. S. P. Ng, 'Ecological Principles of Tropical Lowland Rain Forests Conservation', in S. L. Sutton, T. Whitmore, and A. C. Chadwick (eds.), *Tropical Rain Forests: Ecology and Management* (Blackwell Scientific Publications, Oxford, 1983), pp. 359–73.

62 P. M. Fearnside, 'Brazil's Amazon Forest and the Global Carbon Problem: Reply to Lugo and Brown', *Interciencia* (1986), vol. 11, pp. 58–64.

63 C. Uhl, 'Factors Controlling Succession Following Slash-and-Burn Agriculture in Amazonia', *Journal of Ecology* (1987), vol. 75, pp. 377–407.

64 P. M. Fearnside, 'Human-Use Systems and the Causes of Deforestation in the Brazilian Amazon', paper presented at UNU International Conference on Climatic, Biotic and Human Interactions in the Humid Tropics, São Jose dos Campos, São Paulo, Brazil, 25 Feb.–1 Mar. 1985; see also A. E. Lugo and S. Brown, 'Brazil's Amazon Forest and the Global Carbon Problem', *Interciencia* (1986), vol. 11, pp. 57–8; P. M. Fearnside's reply (n. 62); C. Uhl, R. Buschbacher, and E. A. S. Serrao, 'Abandoned Pastures in Eastern Amazonia, i: Patterns of Plant Succession', *Journal of Ecology* (1988), vol. 76, pp. 663–81.

65 'An Interim Report on the State of Forest Resources in the Developing Countries' (Food and Agriculture Organization, Rome, 1988).

66 See Myers, n. 2.

67 For an illuminating critique of Brazil's opening-up of Amazonia, and for cogent commentaries on development policies that unwittingly stimulate far greater deforestation than intended in other areas, for example the Philippines, Malaysia, Indonesia and West Africa, see R. Repetto and M. Gillis, *Public Policy and the Misuse of Forest Resources* (Cambridge University Press, Cambridge, 1988).

68 *Forestry Development in Repelita V* (Ministry of Forestry, Jakarta, 1989); see also Myers, n. 38.

69 N. Myers, 'The World's Forests and Human Populations: The Environmental Interface', in K. Davis and M. S. Bernstam (eds.), special Supplement to *Population and Development Review* (1990), vol. 16, pp. 1–15; T. K. Rudel, 'Population, Development and Tropical Deforestation: A Cross-National Study', *Rural Sociology* (1989), vol. 54, pp. 327–38; R. P. Shaw, 'Rapid Population Growth and Environmental Degradation: Ultimate Versus Proximate Factors', *Environmental Conservation* (1989), vol. 16, pp. 199–208.

70 Barbira-Scazzocchio, (ed.) *Land, People and Planning in Contemporary Amazonia* (Centre of Latin American Studies, Cambridge University, Cambridge, 1980); Cruz, Zosa-Feranil, and Goce, n. 48; G. W. Jones and H. V. Richter, *Population Mobility and Development: Southeast Asia and the Pacific* (Development Studies Centre, Canberra, 1981); M. Palo and J. Salmi (eds.), *Deforestation or Development in the Third World?* (Finnish Forest Research Institute, Helsinki, 1988); W. J. Peters and L. F. Neuenschwander, *Slash and Burn Farming in Third World Forests* (University of Idaho Press, Moscow, Idaho, 1988); R. J. Pryor (ed.), *Migration and Development in Southeast Asia* (Oxford University Press, Oxford, 1979); H. Ruthenberg, *Farming Systems in the Tropics* (Oxford University Press, Oxford, 1983); W. Schulte, *Report on Population Data in Slash-and-Burn Forestry Communities in Asia* (Food and Agriculture Organization, Rome, 1981); D. Schumann and W. L. Patridge, *Human Ecology of Tropical Land Settlement in Latin America* (Westview Press, Boulder, Colorado, 1989); R. Sinha, 'Landlessness: A Growing Problem' (Food and Agriculture Organization Economic and Social Development Series no. 28, Rome, 1984); W. C. Thiesenhusen (ed.) (n. 48); H. Uhlig (ed.), *Spontaneous and Planned Settlement in Southeast Asia* (Fischer Press, Hamburg, 1984).

71 See. Malingreau and Tucker, n. 6.

72 See Myers, n. 2.

73 E. Salati and C. A. Nobre, 'Possible Climatic Impacts of Tropical Deforestation', *Climatic Change* (in press).

74 S. H. Schneider, *Global Warming: Are We Entering the Greenhouse Century?*, (Sierra Club Books, San Francisco, California, 1989).

75 J. McCormick, *Acid Earth: The Global Threat of Acid Pollution* (Earthscan, London, 1989); H. Rodhe and R. Herrera, (eds.) *Acidification in Tropical Countries* (John Wiley and Sons, Chichester and New York, 1988).

76 D. Zhao and B. Sun, 'Air Pollution and Acid Rain in China', *Ambio* (1986), vol. 15, pp. 2–5.

77 This section is based on the chapter 'Emissions of Greenhouse Gases' in the Friends of the Earth report (see Myers, n. 2), prepared by Dr Richard A. Houghton of the Woods Hole Research Center, Massachusetts, USA.

78 See Myers, n. 2.

79 J. Evans, 'Plantation Forestry in the Tropics – Trends and Prospects', *International Tree Crops Journal* (1986), vol. 4, pp. 3–15; D. Pandey, 'Growth and Yield of Plantation Species in the Tropics' (Food and Agriculture Organization, Rome, 1983); B. J. Zobel, G. V. Wyk, and P. Stohl, *Growing Exotic Forests* (Wiley Inter-Science, New York, 1987); see also S. Brown, A. E. Lugo, and J. Chapman, 'Biomass of Tropical Tree Plantations and its Implications for the Global Carbon Budget', *Canadian Journal of Forestry Research* (1985), vol. 16, pp. 390–4.

80 L. G. Brandao, 'Short-Rotation Forestry for Energy and Industry', in H. Egneus and A. Ellegard (eds.), *Bioenergy '84* (Elsevier Applied Science Publishers, London, 1985), ii, pp. 77–85.

81 For some parallel calculations, see G. Marland, *The Prospect of Solving the CO_2 Problem Through Global Reforestation* (Carbon Dioxide Research Division, United States Department of Energy, Washington, DC, 1988); S. Postel and L. Heise, *Reforesting the Earth* (Worldwatch Paper no. 83, Worldwatch Institute, Washington, DC, 1988); and M. C. Trexler, P. E. Faeth, and J. M. Kramer, *Forestry as a Response to Global Warming: An Analysis of the Guatemala Agroforestry Carbon Sequestration Project* (World Resources Institute, Washington, DC, 1989).

82 N. Myers and T. Goreau, 'Tropical Forests and the Greenhouse Effect: A Management Response', *Climatic Change* (in press); R. A. Houghton and G. M. Woodwell, 'Global Climatic Change', *Scientific American* (1989), vol. 260, pp. 36–44.

83 S. Postel and L. Heise, *Reforesting the Earth* (Worldwatch Paper no. 83, Worldwatch Institute, Washington, DC, 1988).

Chapter 16: Agricultural Contributions to Global Warming Anne Ehrlich

The author wishes to thank the following people for reading and commenting on the manuscript: Paul Ehrlich, John Harte, Cheryl Holdren, John Holdren, Pamela Matson, and Peter Vitousek. In addition, several individuals were extremely generous in providing information, references, and source material for this endeavour: Peter Gleick, John Harte, Rafe Pomerance, Joel Swisher, Peter Vitousek, and Brooks Yaeger.

1 IPCC Working Group 3 (Response Strategies), Policymakers' Summary, first draft, 1 May 1990. The best available summary of greenhouse gases is R. Watson, *et al.*,

'Greenhouse Gases and Aerosols', in *The Scientific Assessment of Climate Change*, report to the Intergovernmental Panel on Climate Change (IPCC), Working Group 1, Section 1, Peer Reviewed Assessment for Working Group 1 Plenary (25 April) (World Meteorological Organization, Geneva, 1990); IPCC Working Group 3 (Response Strategies), Subgroup on Agriculture, Forestry, and Other Human Activities, draft report and draft executive summary (World Meteorological Organization, Geneva, 1990).

2 P. H. Gleick and C. Shirley, 'Greenhouse Gas Emissions from Agricultural Activities', report for the Office of Technology Assessment (unpublished but available from Pacific Institute, 1681 Shattuck Ave., Suite H, Berkeley, CA 94709), 3 Dec. 1988.

3 *1990 World Population Data Sheet* (Population Reference Bureau, Washington, DC, 1990).

4 P. R. Ehrlich and A. H. Ehrlich, *The Population Explosion* (Simon & Schuster, New York, 1990); S. H. Schneider, *Global Warming* (Sierra Club Books, San Francisco, 1989); P. R. Ehrlich and A. H. Ehrlich, 'How the rich can save the poor and themselves: lessons from the global warming', in *Global Warming and Climate Change: Perspectives from Developing Countries*, proceedings of Tata Energy Research Conference, New Delhi, February 1989 (in press).

5 P. Ciborowski, 'Sources, sinks, trends, and opportunities', in D. E. Abrahamson (ed.), *The Challenge of Global Warming* (Island Press, Washington, DC, 1989); M. A. K. Khalil and R. A. Rasmussen, 'Sources, sinks, and seasonal cycles of atmospheric methane', *Journal of Geophysical Research* (June 1983), vol. 88, pp. 5131–44.

6 K. Shine *et al.*, 'Radiative Forcing of Climate', Section 2, Peer Reviewed Assessment for Working Group 1 Plenary 27 Apr. 1990; Watson *et al.*, see n. 1; IPCC Working Group 3 Subgroup on Agriculture, etc. (n. 1), cited a figure of 20 per cent. Somewhat lower figures relative to CO_2 for methane have been proposed in two recent papers, based on methane's short residence-time in the atmosphere. A number of only 3.7 times the effectiveness is calculated by D. A. Lashof and D. R. Ajuha, 'Relative contributions of greenhouse-gas emissions to global warming', *Nature* (1990), vol. 344, pp. 529-31. A different calculation produces a value of 5 for methane's direct effects, and 10 when its indirect effects are included (i.e. when photochemical reactions produce CO_2, O_3 and stratospheric water vapour. H. Rodhe, 'A comparison of the contributions of various gases to the greenhouse effect', *Science* (1990), vol. 248, p. 1212).

7 R. J. Cicerone and R. S. Oremland, 'Biogeochemical aspects of atmospheric methane', *Global Biogeochemical Cycles* (1989); D. R. Blake and F. S. Rowland, 'Continued worldwide increase in tropospheric methane, 1978–1987', *Science* (1988), vol. 239, pp. 1,129–31.

8 J. Chappellaz, J. M. Barnola, D. Reynaud, Y. S. Korotkevitch, and C. Lorius, 'Ice-core record of atmospheric methane over the past 160,000 years', *Nature* (1990), vol. 345, pp. 127–31. This study showed a close tracking of atmospheric CH_4 with temperature changes during several glacial and interglacial events; the authors also noted that 'the natural cycle of methane could provide a positive feedback in any future global warming'.

9 Watson *et al.*, n. 1 estimate 40–48 Tg; other sources (Ciborowski, n. 5, Cicerone and Oremland, n. 7, D. R. Blake and F. S. Rowland, n. 7) have slightly higher estimates – about 60 Tg.

536 NOTES

10 S. Hameed and R. Cess, 'Impact of a global warming on biospheric sources of methane and its climatic consequences', *Tellus* (1983), vol. 35B, no. 1, p.7; R. Revelle, 'Methane hydrates in continental slope sediments and increasing atmospheric carbon dioxide', in: *Changing Climate* (Carbon Dioxide Assessment Committee, National Research Council, National Academy Press, Washington, DC, 1983); M. A. K. Khalil and R. A. Rasmussen, 'Causes of increasing atmospheric methane: depletion of hydroxyl radicals and the rise of emissions', *Atmospheric Environment* (1985), vol. 19, pp. 397–407.

11 See Watson *et al.*, n. 1; D. A. Lashof, and D. A. Tirpak, (eds.), *Policy Options for Stabilizing Global Climate*, draft report to Congress (Environmental Protection Agency, Washington, DC, 1989), vol. 1, chap. 2; Gleick and Shirley, n. 2.

12 M. Wahlen, N. Tanaka, R. Henry, B. Deck, J. Zeglen, J. S. Vogel, J. Southon, A. Shemesh, R. Fairbanks, and W. Broecker, 'Carbon-14 in methane sources and in atmospheric methane: the contribution from fossil carbon', *Science* (1989), vol. 245, pp. 286–90.

13 See Ciborowski, n. 5; Revelle, n. 10; J. Leggett, 'Critique of the policy makers' summary of the scientific assessment of climate change', report to IPCC from Working Group 1, 3rd draft, 2 May 1990; Greenpeace International submission for the Working Group 1 Final Plenary, 23–25 May 1990 (submitted 17 May), and references therein.

14 See Watson *et al.*, n. 1.

15 Ibid., and refs., n. 7.

16 Derived from Watson, *et al.*, n. 1; IPCC Working Group 3, Subgroup on Agriculture, etc. (n. 1), 1990, incorrectly reports the respective percentages as 15, 9, and 8 in its undated draft report.

17 See Gleick and Shirley, n. 2; Khalil and Rasmussen, n. 5; Lashof and Tirpak, n. 11.

18 As estimated by IPCC Working Group 1. Other sources produce similar ranges: see Gleick and Shirley, n. 2; Cicerone and Oremland, n. 7; Lashof and Tirpak, n. 11.

19 H. H. Neue and H. W. Scharpenseel, 'Gaseous products of decomposition of organic matter in submerged soils', International Rice Research Institute, *Organic Matter and Rice* (Los Banos, Phillipines, 1984), pp. 311–28,; A. Holzapfel-Pschorn and W. Seiler, 'Methane emission during a cultivation period from an Italian rice paddy', *Journal of Geophysical Research* (1986), vol. 92, pp. 4, 225–30; R. J. Cicerone and J. D. Shetter, 'Sources of atmospheric methane: measurements in rice paddies and a discussion', *Journal of Geophysical Research* (1981), vol. 86, pp. 7203–209, 1981; R. J. Cicerone, J. D. Shetter and C. C. Delwiche, 'Seasonal variation of methane flux from a California rice paddy', *Journal of Geophysical Research* (1983), vol. 88, pp. 11,022–4.

20 See Gleick and Shirley, n. 2; Cicerone *et al.*, n. 19; Lashof and Tirpak, n. 11.

21 P. J. Crutzen, I. Aselmann, and W. Seiler, 'Methane production by domestic animals, wild ruminants, other herbivorous fauna, and humans', Tellus (1986), vol. 38B, pp. 271–184. Good summaries can be found in Lashof and Tirpak, n. 11, and Gleick and Shirley, n. 2.

22 *1988 Food Production Yearbook* (Food and Agriculture Organization, Rome,1989).

23 See Watson *et al.*, n. 1; Lashof and Tirpak, n. 11; Crutzen *et al.*, n. 21.

24 *World Agricultural Production* (WAP 3-90, Foreign Agricultural Service, US Department of Agriculture, Washington, DC, Mar. 1990); L. R. Brown *et al.*, *State of the World 1990* (W. W. Norton, New York, 1990).

25 See Watson *et al.*, n. 1. Some other estimates of biomass burning are higher: see e.g., Cicerone and Oremland, n. 7, who estimate 50–100 Tg/yr.

26 See Ciborowski, n. 5; D. Blake, 'Methane, CFCs, and other greenhouse gases', in D. E. Abrahamson, *The Challenge of Global Warming* (Island Press, Washington, DC, 1989); Watson *et al.*, n. 1.

27 See Ciborowski, n. 5.

28 See Blake, n. 26.

29 See Watson *et al.*, n. 1.

30 T. A. Steudler, R. D. Bowden, J. M. Melillo, and J. D. Aber, 'Influence of nitrogen fertilization on methane uptake in forest soils', *Nature* (1989), vol. 341, p. 314.

31 M. Oppenheimer and R. H. Boyle, *Dead Heat* (Basic Books, New York, 1990); see also Watson *et al.*, n. 1, Gibrowski, n. 5, and Cicerone and Oremland, and Blake and Rowland, n. 7.

32 See Watson *et al.*, n. 1; IPCC Working Group 1, Policymakers' Summary, 2 May 1990.

33 IPCC Working Group 3, Subgroup on Agriculture, etc. (n. 1), estimates that emissions could be reduced by 10 to 30 per cent, but offers no documentation.

34 P. M. Vitousek (personal communication); see Gleick and Shirley, n. 2.

35 See n. 1, IPCC Working Group 3, Subgroup on Agriculture, etc., n. 1

36 K. L. Blaxter and J. L. Clapperton, 'Prediction of the amount of methane produced by ruminants', *British Journal of Nutrition* (1965), vol. 19, pp. 511–22. More recent work has revealed the lower emissions resulting from a high starch–cellulose ratio in cattle feed. (New South Wales Department of Agriculture, Beef Cattle Nutrition Unit, CSIRO, personal communication).

37 See *Food Production Yearbook*, n. 22.

38 See Gleick and Shirley, n. 22.

39 See *Food Production Yearbook*, n. 22.

40 World Resources Institute, *World Resources 1988–89* (Basic Books, New York, 1989), using World Bank estimates.

41 See Brown *et al.*, n. 24.

42 See Lashof and Tirpak, n. 11; Watson *et al.*, n. 1. Lashof and Ahuja (n. 6) calculate a value of 180 for N_2O.

43 See Shine *et al.*, n. 6.

44 See Ciborowski, n. 5.

45 See Watson *et al.*, n. 1; M. Keller, W. A. Kaplan, and S. C. Wofsy, 'Emissions of N_2O, CH_4, and CO_2 from tropical soils', *Journal of Geophysical Research* (1986), vol. 91, pp. 11,791–802, 1986; P. A. Matson and P. M. Vitousek, 'Cross-system comparisons of soil nitrogen transformations and nitrous oxide flux in tropical forest ecosystems', *Global Biogeochemical Cycles* (1987), vol. 1, pp. 163–70.

46 See Watson *et al.*, n. 1; P. A. Matson and P. M. Vitousek, personal communication.

47 M. B. McElroy and S. C. Wofsy, 'Tropical forests: interactions with the atmosphere', in G. T. Prance, (ed.), *Tropical Rain Forests and the World Atmosphere* (Westview, Boulder, Colorado, 1986), pp. 33–60.

48 F. Luizao, P. Matson, G. Livingston, R. Luizao, and P. Vitousek, 'Nitrous oxide flux following tropical land clearing', *Global Biogeochemical Cycles* (1989), vol. 3, no. 3, pp. 281–5.

49 T. J. Goreau and W. Z. de Mello, 'Tropical deforestation: some effects on atmospheric chemistry', Ambio (1988), vol. 17, no. 4, pp. 275–81.

50 N. Myers, *Deforestation Rates in Tropical Forests and their Climatic Implications* (Friends of the Earth, London, 1989); World Resources Institute,*World Resources, 1990–91* (Basic Books, New York, World Resources Institute, 1990).

51 For a clear description of the complexities of the nitrogen cycle, see P. R. Ehrlich, A. H. Ehrlich, and J. P. Holdren, *Ecoscience: Population, Resources, Environment* (Freeman, San Francisco, 1977), Chap. 3.

52 Based on this figure and estimates of NO emissions per kg of fertilizer, Lashof and Tirpak (see n. 11) estimate an annual production of 0.14 to 2.4 Tg N from that source.

53 Committee on the Role of Alternative Farming Methods in Modern Production Agriculture, *Alternative Agriculture*, Board on Agriculture, National Research Council (National Academy Press, Washington DC, 1989); L. D. King, 'Sustainable soil fertility practices', in C. A. Francis, C. B. Flora, and L. D. King (eds.), *Sustainable Agriculture in Temperate Zones* (John Wiley & Sons, New York, 1990); personal communication from P. M. Vitousek.

54 See also IPCC Working Group 3 (Response Strategies), 1990, n. 1.

55 Ibid.

56 See Ehrlich *et al.*, n. 51, Chap. 11.

57 See Francis *et al.*, n. 53.

58 See Gleick and Shirley, n. 2; G. A. Breitenbeck, A. M. Blackmer, and J. M. Bremner, 'Effects of different nitrogenous fertilizers on emissions of nitrous oxides from soils', *Geophysical Research Letters* (1980), vol. 7, no. 1, pp. 85–8; J. M. Bremner and A. M. Blackner, 'Nitrous oxide: emission from soils during nitrification of fertilizer nitrogen', *Science* (1978), vol. 199, pp. 295–6; F. Slemr and W. Seiler, 'Field measurements of NO and NO_2 emissions from fertilized and unfertilized soils', *Journal of Atmospheric Chemistry* (1984), vol. 2, pp. 1–24; I. Fung, E. Matthews, and J. Lerner, 'Trace gas emissions associated with agricultural activities', EPA Workshop on Agriculture and Climate Change, Washington DC, 29 Feb.–1 Mar. 1988.

59 Lost nitrogen from inefficient fertilizing often ends up in waterways where it contributes to eutrophication problems – overfertilization of freshwater bodies – leading to algal blooms that produce methane: see C. W. R. Spedding, J. M. Walsingham, and A. M. Hoxey, *Biological Efficiency in Agriculture* (Academic Press, London, New York, 1981), Chap. 4.

60 The following suggestions were taken mainly from Gleick and Shirley, n. 2, with additional suggestions from P. M. Vitousek and P. A. Matson in the form of a personal communication.

61 See Gleick and Shirley, n. 2.

62 See Committee on the Role of Alternative Farming, n. 53; Francis *et al.*, n. 53; J. P. Reganold, R. I. Papendick, and J. F. Parr, 'Sustainable agriculture', *Scientific American* (June 1990); P. H. Abelson, 'Opportunities in agricultural research', (editorial), *Science* (1990), vol. 248, p. 941.

63 See Committee on Alternative Farming Methods, n. 53.

64 See IPCC Working Group 3, Subgroup on Agriculture, etc., n. 1.

65 Population Reference Bureau, 1990. The PRB's demographic projections are done in-house, but rely heavily on statistics and projections of the United Nations, World Bank, and other official sources.

66 Taken from a Food and Agriculture Organization representative, but not specifically cited.

67 L. Brown, *The changing world food prospect: the nineties and beyond* (Worldwatch Paper 85, Worldwatch Institute, Washington DC, October 1989); Brown, *et al.*, as n. 24.

68 United Nations Environmental Programme, *Environmental Data Report* (Basil Blackwell, Oxford, 1987); World Resources Institute, n. 40.

69 See Brown, n. 67.

70 For a discussion of the reasons, see A. H. Ehrlich, 'Development and Agriculture', in P. R. Ehrlich and J. P. Holdren, (eds.), *The Cassandra Conference; Resources and the Human Predicament* (Texas A & M University Press, College Station, Texas, 1988).

71 G. C. Daily and P. R. Ehrlich, 'An exploratory model of the impact of rapid climate change on the world food situation' (Working Paper no. 0034, Morrison Institute for Population and Resource Studies, Stanford University, Stanford, California, 1990).

72 For a biologists' view of just how narrow the scope is, see P. M. Vitousek, P. R. Ehrlich, A. H. Ehrlich, and P. A. Matson, 'Human appropriation of the products of photosynthesis', *Bioscience* (June 1986), vol. 36, no. 6, pp. 368–73.

Chapter 17: Third World Countries in the Policy Response to Global Climate Change Kilaparti Ramakrishna

1 World Climate Conference: *Declaration and Supporting Documents* (World Meteorological Organisation, Geneva, 1979).

2 Statement by UNEP/WMO/ICSU Conference on the Assessment of the Role of Carbon Dioxide and of Other Greenhouse Gases in Climate Variations and Associated Impacts (Villach, Austria, Oct. 1985), in B. Bolin, B. R. Doos, J. Jager, and R. A. Warwick (eds.), *The Greenhouse Effect, Climatic Change, and Ecosystems* (SCOPE/ICSU/UNEP/WMO, John Wiley & Sons, New York, 1986).

3 The proceedings of Villach and Bellagio Workshops appeared in a special issue of *Climate Change* (1989), vol. 15, nos. 1–2; Michael Oppenheimer (guest editor), *Greenhouse Gas Emissions: Environmental Consequences and Policy Responses* (Kluwer Academic Publishers, 1989).

4 The findings and recommendations of the Bellagio Workshop appear in the report, J. Jager, *Developing Policies for Responding to Climatic Change* (WMO/UNEP, Apr. 1988).

5 *Proceedings of the World Conference on the Changing Atmosphere: Implications for Global Security*, 27–30 June 1988 (WMO, no. 710, 1989).

6 See United Nations General Assembly, *Resolutions and Decisions Adopted by the General Assembly During its Forty-Third Session* (UN/GA43/49/Add.1, United Nations, New York, 1989).

7 WMO/UNEP IPCC, *Report of the First Session of the WMO/UNEP IPCC* (WMO/UNEP TD-no. 267, Geneva, 9–11 Nov. 1988).

8 WMO/UNEP IPCC, *Report of the Second Session of the WMO/UNEP IPCC* (WMO/UNEP, Nairobi, 28–30 June 1989); G. M. Woodwell and K. Ramakrishna *Second Session of the IPCC, Nairobi, June 28–30, 1989: A Summary of Proceedings* (the Woods Hole Research Center, July 1989).

9 WMO/UNEP IPCC, *Report of the Third Session of the WMO/UNEP IPCC* (WMO/UNEP, Washington, DC, 5–7 February 1990).

10 For a discussion of this issue, see G. M. Woodwell and K. Ramakrishna, 'Guest Editorial – The Warming of the Earth: Perspectives and Solutions in the Third World', *Environmental Conservation* (1989), vol. 16, no. 4, pp. 289–91.

11 *A Proposal for Assisting Developing Countries to More Effectively Contribute to an Improved Understanding of the Physical Basis of Global Climate Change, Assessment of the Socio-Economic Impacts Resulting from Climate Change, and the Formulation of Suitable Response Strategies* (IPCC-II/Doc.6, 8 June 1989); *Involvement of Developing Countries in the Work of the IPCC* (IPCC-II/Rev.1, 28 June 1989).

12 *Preliminary Budget Estimate for the Support of the Participation of the Developing Countries in the Activities of IPCC* (IPCC-II/Doc.8, 29 June 1989).

13 *International Conference on Global Warming and Climatic Change: Perspectives from Developing Countries*, New Delhi, 21-3 Feb. 1989 (Tata Energy Research Institute, the Woods Hole Research Center, UNEP, and the World Resources Institute, Feb. 1989).

14 K. Ramakrishna, 'Interest Articulation by the Developing Countries in the International Environment Movement', *Revue de Droit Contemporain* (1984), issue 2, pp. 45–56.

15 M. Tolba, 'Remarks' at the Ministerial Conference on Ozone Layer Protection, held in London, Mar. 1989.

16 World Commission on Environment and Development, *Our Common Future* (Oxford University Press, Oxford, 1987).

17 G. Harlem Brundtland, 'Our Common Future: A Climate for Change', see n. 5.

18 'The Noordwijk Declaration on Climate Change', adopted at the Ministerial Conference on Atmospheric Pollution and Climatic Change, 6–7 Nov. 1989, the Netherlands.

19 This was accomplished by convening a series of seminars under the auspices of the United Nations Regional Commissions and the Economic and Social Office in Beirut, during Aug. and Sept. 1971. For a summary of these meetings, see 'Regional Seminars on Development and Environment', (UN Doc. A/Conf.48/10, Annex III, pp. 1–9).

20 B. Johnson, 'The United Nations Institutional Response to Stockholm: A Case Study in the International Politics of Institutional Change', *International Organization* (1972), vol. 26, pp. 255–301.

Chapter 18: Managing the Global House: Redefining Economics in a Greenhouse World Susan George

1 Adam Smith, *The Wealth of Nations*, as cited in the *Oxford English Dictionary* under '*economy*'. I am grateful to my Transnational Institute colleague D. Smith and have used part of the problematique he presents in 'Towards a Green Political Economy: Notes for the TNI Seminar of 4 June 1990' (Transnational Institute internal paper).

2 Report of Working Group 3, International Union of Geological Sciences, Workshop on Global Change, Interlaken, Switzerland, 1989 .

3 S. Pain, 'On the Edge of Disaster', *New Scientist*, 28 Apr. 1990.

4 Calculated from World Bank, *World Development Report*, Table 5.

5 C. Flavin, 'Slowing Global Warming', *State of the World 1990* (Worldwatch Institute, Washington, DC, 1990).

6 P. Buhle, (US) *Guardian*, 14 Sept. 1988; J. Weston, 'For an Ecological Politics of Hope', *Monthly Review* (Feb. 1990), vol. 41, no. 9, in which Buhle is quoted.

7 J. Vargha, 'Green Revolutions in East Europe', *Panoscope* (periodical of the Panos Institute), London, May 1990. This whole issue of *Panoscope* focuses on Central and Eastern Europe, giving succinct information on the extent of ecological destruction and the state of green movements in 1990; Z. A. Medvedev, 'The Environmental Destruction of the Soviet Union', *The Ecologist* (1990), vol. 20, no. 1.

8 E. Pudlis, 'Who will pay for the clean-up?', *Panoscope* (May 1990).

9 F. F. Clairmonte and J. H. Cavanagh, 'Transnational Corporations and services: the Final Frontier', *Trade and Development: An UNCTAD Review* (1984), no. 5; for an earlier study of the impact of TNCs see R. Barnet and R. Muller, *Global Reach: The Power of the Multinational Corporations* (Simon & Schuster, New York, 1974).

10 GATT, *Le Commerce International 1987–88* (Geneva, 1988), vol. ii, pp. 57–8.

11 For detailed evidence of reckless lending and borrowing and its consequences, see S. George, *A Fate Worse than Debt* (Penguin, Harmondsworth, 1988), Chap. 1 and *passim*.

12 World Bank, *Annual Report 1989* (Washington, DC, 1989), p. 11.

13 Ibid., Tables 4–10, p. 76.

14 See in particular G. Hancock, *Lords of Poverty* (whose subtitle 'The power, prestige and corruption of the international aid business' is instructive) (Macmillan, London, 1989); C. Payer, 'The World Bank: A Critical Analysis', *Monthly Review Press* (New York, 1982).

15 See World Bank, *Annual Report 1982* (under loans to 'Tranportation'), p. 113; Jose Lutzenberger (who became Brazil's Minister for the Environment in 1990), 'The World Bank's Polonoroeste Project', *The Ecologist* (1985), vol. 15, no. 1/2; see also Payer (n. 14 above), pp. 345–51, who provides a detailed account of the decision-making process inside the Bank. In the Polonoroeste case, an anthropologist's well-founded warnings that thirty different Indian communities already resident in the forests would be decimated by the project were systematically ignored.

16 See Hancock (n. 14), p. 131, citing, for Rondonia, Bruce Rich, Senior Attorney of the Environmental Defense Fund.

17 P. M. Fearnside, 'Deforestation in Brazilian Amazon: the Rates and Causes of Forest Destruction', *The Ecologist* (1989), vol. 19, no. 6, p. 216.

18 S. Hecht, 'The Sacred Cow in the Green Hell: Livestock and Forest Conversion in the Brazilian Amazon', *The Ecologist* (1989), vol. 19, no. 6.

19 S. George, *A Fate Worse than Debt* (Penguin, Harmondsworth, 1988), Chap. 10, 'Financing Ecocide', p. 157, citing an account in *The Economist* Development Report of Nov. 1984. This chapter deals with the connections between Third World debt and the environmental crisis.

20 On Transmigrasi, see Hancock, n. 14, and George, n. 19; also *The Ecologist* (1986), vol. 16, no. 2/3, containing several articles on the subject.

21 N. Guppy, 'Tropical Deforestation: A Global View', *Foreign Affairs* (Spring 1984), vol. 62, no. 4, pp. 942–3.

22 See Hancock, n. 14, citing Barber Conable's speech to the World Resources Institute, Washington, DC, 5 May 1987.

23 See World Bank Report (n. 12), p. 50.

24 Rainforest Action Network, *World Rainforest Report* (1990), vol. 6, no. 2, p. 6.

25 R. Monastersky, 'Biomass Burning Ignites Concern', *Science News*, 31 Mar. 1990; id. 'Amazon forest unlikely to rise from ashes', *Science News* (17 Mar. 1990).

26 C. H. Farnsworth, 'Conable's World Bank: Finding Fault and Praise', *New York Times*, 1 Feb. 1990, cited in J. Cavanagh, R. Broad, and W. Bello, 'Rekindling the Development Debate' (draft article, typescript).

27 FAO, World Bank, World Resources Institute, and United Nations Development Programme, *The Tropical Forestry Action Plan* (FAO, Rome, 1987).

28 Environmental Policy Institute, 'The Tropical Forestry Action Plan: A Critique', (mimeo, Washington, DC, 15 Oct. 1989).

29 J. N. Barnes, Memorandum to M. Pissaloux, French Treasury, 26 Oct. 1989.

30 N. Hildyard, 'Amazonia: The Future in the Balance', editorial, *The Ecologist* (1989), vol. 19, no. 6.

31 L. Lohmann, 'Commercial Tree Plantations in Thailand: Deforestation by Any Other Name', *The Ecologist* (1990), vol. 20, no. 1. This long and extremely well-documented article shows how local businessmen, trans-national corporations, Japanese 'development aid' and the international UN agencies are all co-operating to destroy the livelihoods of several million rural Thais, who are responding with political activism and sabotage of the plantations.

32 See EPI, n. 28.

33 Ibid.

34 René Dumont, 'L'Afrique Noire est-elle perdue?', *Le Monde Diplomatique*, May 1990.

35 See Lohmann, n. 30; Rainforest Action Network, '1990: The Year to "Ban Japan" from the Rainforest'; *World Rainforest Report* (1990), vol. 6, no. 2; E. Schreiber, 'Global Warning: Japan spends more yen in the two-thirds world', *Bulletin of the Debt Crisis Network*, Feb. 1990.

36 European Campaign on Debt and Development, 'Tropical forests shrink as debt payments rise' (fact sheet and graphics based on World Bank and Friends of the Earth data, undated, 1990).

37 Calculated from trade figures in GATT, *World Trade 1987–88* (Geneva, 1988), and population figures from World Bank, *World Development Report 1989*.

38 P. Bunyard, 'Guardians of the Amazon', *New Scientist*, 16 Dec. 1989, acknowledging Dr M. von Hildebrand, head of Indigenous Affairs in Colombia and a major instigator of the policy.

39 See Farnsworth, n. 26.

40 J. Gordon, 'The Foreign Policy Challenge', speech at ICCET Conference on 'Environmental Challenges: the Institutional Dimension' (mimeo, London, Oct. 1989).

Chapter 19: Global Warming: A Greenpeace View Jeremy Leggett

1 International agreements on acid rain include the European Community Large Combustion Plants Directive and the Geneva Convention on Long-Range Transboundary Air Pollution. But the limits set for sulphur dioxide and nitrogen oxides emissions by such agreements fall short of the 'critical loads' which scientists have decided are needed to avoid harm to the environment. A critical load is defined as the highest load that will not cause chemical changes leading to long-term, harmful effects on the most sensitive ecological systems.

2 J. Sweet and A. Tickle,'Memorandum on the energy market implications of flue gas desulphurisation and alternative means of reducing sulphur emissions', evidence laid before the House of Commons Select Committee on Energy (Greenpeace Atmosphere Campaign Report, Apr. 1990).

3 The idea that CFCs might lead to depletion of ozone in the stratosphere was first put forward on theoretical grounds. See M. Molina and F. Sherwood Rowland, 'Stratospheric sink for chlorofluoromethanes: chlorine atom-catalyzed destruction of ozone', *Nature*, 28 June 1974.

4 The discovery of the Antarctic ozone hole was made by British Antarctic Survey scientists in 1982. The results were not published until early in 1985. Because the results were so surprising they were checked for two years. See J. C. Farman *et al.*, 'Large losses of total ozone in Antarctica reveal seasonal ClO_x/NO_x interaction', *Nature*, 16 May 1985.

5 H. Steven and A. Lindley, *New Scientist*, 16 June 1990, p. 48.

6 J. S. Hoffman and M. J. Gibbs, *Future concentrations of stratospheric chlorine and bromine* (US Environmental Protection Agency, 1988).

7 *Fifty percent more: the failure of the Montreal Protocol* (Greenpeace International, June 1990).

8 Intergovernmental Panel on Climate Change, Report to IPCC from Working Group 1, *Scientific Assessment of Climate Change* (June 1990), chap. 2.

9 Ibid, chap. 1.

10 Dr John Houghton, chief executive of the UK Meteorological Office and chair of the IPCC's Working Group1, introducing the IPCC scientists' finished report at a press conference near Windsor, 25 May 1990.

11 See n. 8, chap. 2.

12 J. K. Leggett, *New Scientist*, 6 July 1990.

13 J. Goldemberg, T. B. Johansson, A. K. N. Reddy, and R. H. Williams, *Energy for a sustainable world* (John Wiley and sons, 1988.)

14 Ibid.

15 S. Boyle and D. Olivier, *The relationship between economic growth and energy use/CO_2 emissions: some comments on the analysis by Professor Y. Kaya for the Energy and Industry Sub-Group of IPCC Working Group 3* (Greenpeace International, 13 Nov. 1989.)

16 J. F. Bookout, 'Two centuries of fossil fuel energy', *Episodes* (Dec. 1989), vol. 12, pp. 257–62.

17 In the UK, for example, UK Energy Secretary John Wakeham announced in the House of Commons on 19 Feb. 1990 that the '89–'90 research-and-development budgets for renewables and energy efficiency would be £18 million and £8.9 million, respectively. The nuclear R&D budget – even after the rejection by City-of-London financiers of nuclear-power in the electricity-supply industry privatization – was £137 million. Similar priorities can be seen in the EC, and – during the Reagan-Bush years – in the USA, as is detailed in the introduction to the *Greenpeace Report*.

18 See, e.g., the history of Salter's Duck, a wave-energy machine which was suppressed in 1982 by nuclear-energy supporters in the UK Department of Energy, at a time when it had proved capable of supplying electricity to the UK grid at 5.5 pence per kilowatt-hour. See J. Jeffrey, 'The parting of the waves', *Guardian*, 16 Feb. 1990.

19 See IPCC, n. 8., Policymakers Summary, p. 26.

20 Professor S. Manabe, speaking at a press conference at the 1990 meeting of the American Association for the Advancement of Science, New Orleans, 20 Feb. 1990.

21 R. Sivard, *World Military and Social Expenditures*, (1989).

22 Opinion polls cited in the introduction to the *Greenpeace Report*.

23 J. Goldemberg, presentation to the 39th Pugwash Conference on Science and World Affairs, Cambridge, MA, USA, 23 July 1989.

24 Intergovernmental Panel on Climate Change, Report to IPCC from Working Group 3 *Response Strategies* (June 1990)

25 See, e.g., S. Boyle and J. Ardill, *The Greenhouse Effect: A practical Guide to the world's changing climate* (New English Library, 1989); P. M. Kelly and J. Gribbin, *Winds of Change* (Hodder and Stoughton, 1989); F. Pearce, *Turning Up the Heat* (Paladin, 1989).

26 See, e.g., Association for the Conservation of Energy/ Worldwide Fund for Nature, *Solving the Greenhouse dilemma: A strategy for the UK* (June 1989).

27 Ibid.

28 J. Reganold, R. I. Papendick, and J. F. Parr, 'Sustainable agriculture', *Scientific American* (June 1990), pp. 72–8.

29 See Bookout, n. 16.

Index

NOTE: References are to chapter numbers and to sections within chapters. Main chapter numbers are printed in bold type. Where a chapter number alone is given, the entire chapter is predominantly concerned with the subject; an asterisk denotes the inclusion of the subject in the introductory preamble of the chapter.

Int. = Introduction.